SO-BOL-465

WITHDRAWN

THE COMMUNIST WORLD

Marxist and Non-Marxist Views

THE COMMUNIST WORLD

Marxist and Non-Marxist Views

Edited by HARRY G. SHAFFER

THE UNIVERSITY OF KANSAS

APPLETON-CENTURY-CROFTS / NEW YORK

DIVISION OF MEREDITH PUBLISHING COMPANY

CARL A. RUDISILL LIBRARY
LENOIR RHYNE COLLEGE

309.1
Sh l c
60748
Feb. 1968

Copyright © 1967 by
MEREDITH PUBLISHING COMPANY

Pages 526-535 copyright © 1967 by Edward Boorstein
Pages 61-88 copyright © 1967 by Samuel Hendel

All rights reserved

This book, or parts thereof, must not be used or reproduced in any manner without written permission. For information address the publisher, Appleton-Century-Crofts, Division of Meredith Publishing Company, 440 Park Avenue South, New York, N.Y. 10016.

677-1

Library of Congress Card Number: 67-21993

PRINTED IN THE UNITED STATES OF AMERICA
E 79685

To my wife Julie and to our children
Bernie, Ronnie, Lennie, and Tanya.

PREFACE

At the turn of the century, the ideological disciples of Marx and Engels were few in number and communism was a mere dream in the minds of a handful of men. Today, the Communist World occupies roughly one-fourth of the land surface of the earth, encompasses one-third of the world's population, and embraces fourteen countries, from little Albania and Cuba to China and the U.S.S.R., the giants in the Communist Camp. (The term "Communist World," it should be pointed out, is not meant to imply that these fourteen countries have achieved "communism," but rather that they proclaim their intention of building a communist society along Marxist-Leninist lines. This issue is discussed at great length in Chapter 1.)

In spite of some shortcomings and setbacks, the socialist countries can boast of remarkable successes in industrialization and economic growth. In the mid-1960's they claim forty percent of the industrial output of the world; illiteracy, once widespread in most of them, has been practically eliminated; doctors, hospitals, and medicine, formerly in many areas limited to the well-to-do, are now available to all, usually free of charge; universities, theaters, and resorts, once reserved for the nobility and the *nouveaux riches*, have multiplied in number and have become seats of learning and places of entertainment and recreation for workers and peasants; and almost everywhere the living standards of the present generation are well above those of any preceding one. In science, art, and military preparedness one of the fourteen countries—the Soviet Union—has reached approximate parity with the United States, and most of the others have made great strides forward. Their progress, moreover, has been achieved in a relatively short period of time. Twelve of the fourteen countries, as this book goes to press, have not yet celebrated the twenty-fifth anniversaries of their "Revolution"; several not even their twentieth; and even the oldest, the Soviet Union, is less than half a century old! No wonder that this Communist World poses a serious challenge to the institutions, the way of life of the West; no wonder that the developing countries, in search of the shortest path from underdevelopment to affluence, look inquisitively towards this new order. Surely, anyone who wants to understand what is going on in the world today must endeavor to understand the economic, social, educational, cultural, and moral fabric of the Communist World.

The preceding lines may leave the reader with the impression that the Communist World is a homogeneous entity. This, certainly, is not the case. There is considerable diversity among the fourteen countries (and even within some of them), partly as a consequence of varied historical, ethnological, cultural, and political backgrounds, partly attributable to the stage of economic development attained at the time of entry into the Communist Camp, and the stage of economic development achieved since. In ideological orientation, political structure, economic policy, and approach to problems of international relations and coexistence, there is no longer the degree of unity which prevailed when the Soviet Union was the uncontested leader of the Communist World. All fourteen countries are following what they conceive of as the Marxist–Leninist path, but each according to its own interpretation. Some of these paths may be strikingly similar (Bulgaria, for instance, adheres faithfully to the Soviet model), but others, such as those of China and Yugoslavia, are worlds apart. Some of the similarities and differences will become apparent to the reader as he proceeds through this book, chapter by chapter, familiarizing himself with the fourteen countries of the Communist World.

The primary purpose of the first part is to introduce the reader to the general philosophy that underlies the Communist World, to point out to him some of the features that are common to all fourteen countries, and to make him aware of some aspects of the heterogeneity within the Communist Camp. Part I is followed by chapters dealing with each of the fourteen countries. The "East European members of the Soviet Commonwealth of Nations" are treated together, in one chapter, but separate chapters have been reserved for Yugoslavia and Albania, the two East European Communist countries to which this designation does not properly apply. North Korea and North Vietnam appear to show enough similarities to be combined in one chapter, but sufficient dissimilarities to warrant separate treatment within that chapter.

Western scholars who specialize in a particular aspect of communist systems study original source material, publications by Marxist scholars representing the respective countries' views, and critical Western interpretations and analyses. As in his first two books,* the editor has once again decided

---

* *The Soviet Economy: A Collection of Western and Soviet Views* and *The Soviet System in Theory and Practice: Selected Western and Soviet Views,* both Appleton-Century-Crofts, New York, 1963 and 1965, respectively; a revised edition of *The Soviet Economy* is scheduled for publication in 1968.

to introduce the reader to this method by presenting, in each chapter, confronting views by Marxist and non-Marxist authors. It is hoped that the reader will find this approach both profitable and challenging.

On the non-Marxist side, most of the contributions are original, written especially for this book, and among the contributors are some of the outstanding experts on the respective countries or regions in the Western World. While probably none of the contributions would stand unchallenged in its entirety among Western experts, most of these essays would surely be accepted in their essence by the majority of Western non-Marxists in the field.

On the Marxist side, most contributions reflect the interpretation of Marxism–Leninism as officially expressed in the country or region with which the chapter deals. (Only the Marxist views on East Europe and on Cuba, and the supplement to the Marxist view on Mongolia were written respectively by American Marxists Scott Nearing, Edward Boorstein, and British Marxist Ivor Montagu.) In the case of China, Albania, North Korea, and North Vietnam, all attempts to secure the cooperation of the countries' authorities, or even of Western scholars representing these countries' official views, failed. Hence, the Marxist view on each of these countries was put together from a number of articles, speeches, documents, etc., all published within the respective countries, dealing with such issues as the historical background, the political structure, the economic conditions, and the ideological orientation of each country. The scholars, leaders, and resident observers from whose pens the various subsections of each selection come are identified in the introduction to each chapter and in editor's footnotes.

The book is intended primarily for college students, but it is not assumed that the reader has any previous knowledge of Marxist-Leninist ideology, nor that he has had a college level course in any of the social sciences. Explanatory footnotes have been added throughout the book to identify individuals and places mentioned in the text, and to clarify terms with which the reader may not be familiar. Contributors in their presentation, and the editor in his selection of reprinted material, have paid particular attention to readability: the nonspecialist should find both contents and style stimulating and interesting.

Since this book deals with highly controversial matters, it may raise more questions than it answers. However, if it but makes the reader aware that there are not always simple, ready-made answers, if it but convinces him that in this field no answer—no matter how plausible it may sound—should be accepted without further investigation, if it but arouses his curiosity and whets his appetite for further knowledge and greater understanding, it will have served a valuable purpose. To assist the reader who wishes to pursue further his search for materials on the country or countries of his interest, "Further Reading Suggestions" (most of them prepared by the contributors) have been appended to the Marxist and the non-Marxist contributions to each chapter, and a selected list of relevant periodicals can be found in an Appendix at the end of the book.

I wish to express my sincere gratitude to Vladimir Bogachev, First Secretary of the Soviet Embassy in Washington, to Alexei S. Belokon, former Counsellor in the Embassy's Press Department, and to V. Komolov, Director of the Novosti Press Agency Publishing House in Moscow, for making the arrangements with Soviet scholars to contribute the Marxist view on the Soviet Union. I am grateful to Sreten Babic, former Deputy Director of the Yugoslav Information Center in New York, for assisting in a similar arrangement with Yugoslav scholars. I also wish to acknowledge gratefully the cooperation of scholars, both non-Marxist and Marxist, who read my introduction to Chapter 1 and offered valuable critical comments: Alfred G. Meyer, Professor of Political Science at the University of Michigan, Herbert Aptheker, Director of the American Institute for Marxist Studies, and British Marxist R. Palme Dutt. I am also indebted to Slobodan Stankovic of the Yugoslav Desk of Radio Free Europe, Munich, to Professor Milos Samardzija of the University of Belgrade, and to Fric Frankl, Director of the Yugoslav Information Center in New York for their constructive criticism of my contribution to the chapter on Yugoslavia. I also want to thank each of the authors who read my introduction to the chapter to which he contributed and offered valuable critical comments: Samuel Hendel (CCNY) on the U.S.S.R., Jan S. Prybyla (Pennsylvania State U.) on China, R. V. Burks (Wayne State U.) on East Europe, and Ivor Montagu on Mongolia. My sincere appreciation and gratitude go to all the contributors who wrote their articles especially for inclusion in this book, and to all the authors and publishers who gave their permission to reprint previously published materials. I want to thank Janet C. Fencyk, Janice Lee Graham, Phyllis Saindon, and William Lee Stringer for secretarial assistance in preparing the manuscript. Last, but certainly not least, I am profoundly grateful to my wife, Dr. Juliet P. Shaffer, who has given so liberally of her time and effort in editing my work.

H. G. S.

CONTENTS

PREFACE   vii

I *THE COMMUNIST WORLD: AN INTRODUCTION*

1. The Communist World: A Non-Marxist View   *13*
        Alfred G. Meyer
            Professor of Political Science
            University of Michigan
2. The Communist World: Marxist Views   *32*
        R. Palme Dutt
            Member, Executive Committee
            Communist Party of Great Britain
        Herbert Aptheker
            Director,
            American Institute for Marxist Studies
        A. Arzumanyan
            Director, Institute of World Economics
            Academy of Sciences of the U.S.S.R., and others

II *THE UNION OF SOVIET SOCIALIST REPUBLICS: THE GREAT EXPERIMENT*

3. The U.S.S.R.: A Non-Marxist View   *61*
        Samuel Hendel
            Professor of Political Science
            City College of the City University of New York
4. The New Society: A Soviet Marxist View on the U.S.S.R.   *90*
        T. Shakhnazarov, Y. Krasyin, and V. Sukhodeyev
            Soviet Social Scientists

III THE PEOPLE'S REPUBLIC OF CHINA: A GIANT AWAKENED

5. Red China in Motion: A Non-Marxist View   *151*
   Jan S. Prybyla
      Professor of Economics
      Pennsylvania State University
6. The New China: A Chinese Marxist View   *184*
      Soong Ching Ling (Mme. Sun Yat-sen)
         Vice Chairman, People's Republic of China
      Lien Kuan
         Deputy Secretary General, Standing Committee
         National People's Congress
      Lin Hai-Yun
         Vice Minister of Foreign Trade, and others

IV THE SOCIALIST FEDERAL REPUBLIC OF YUGOSLAVIA: A COUNTRY ON ITS OWN ROAD TO SOCIALISM

7. Yugoslavia's "Own Road to Socialism": A Non-Marxist View   *223*
      Harry G. Shaffer
         Associate Professor of Economics
         The University of Kansas
8. Yugoslavia: A Yugoslav Marxist View   *260*
      Milos Samardžija
         Professor of Political Economy
         University of Belgrade
      Radoslav Ratković
         Head, Department of Sociology
         Higher School of Political Science, Belgrade

V THE EAST EUROPEAN MEMBERS OF THE SOVIET COMMONWEALTH OF NATIONS:

THE PEOPLE'S REPUBLIC OF BULGARIA
THE SOCIALIST REPUBLIC OF
   CZECHOSLOVAKIA
THE GERMAN DEMOCRATIC REPUBLIC
THE HUNGARIAN PEOPLE'S REPUBLIC
THE POLISH PEOPLE'S REPUBLIC
THE SOCIALIST REPUBLIC OF RUMANIA

9. Eastern Europe Under Communism: A Non-Marxist View   *295*
      R. V. Burks
         Professor of History
         Wayne State University

10. The Socialist Transformation of East Europe: A Western
    Marxist View   *325*
        Scott Nearing
            Chairman, Social Science Institute
            Harborside, Maine
            With a supplement by
        V. Isupov, B. Lodygin, V. Terekhov, O. Bogomolov
            Soviet Economists

VI *THE PEOPLE'S REPUBLIC OF ALBANIA: CHINA'S*
    BEACHHEAD IN EUROPE

11. Albania: A Non-Marxist View   *371*
        Athanas Gegaj
            Editor of the Albanian-American paper DIELLI
            (The Sun), Boston
        Rexhep Krasniqi
12. The People's Republic of Albania: An Albanian Marxist View *382*
        Harilla Papajorgji
            Albanian Economist
        Peti Shamblli
            Former Albanian Minister of Agriculture
        Pipi Mitrojorgji
            Albania's Minister of Education and Culture
        Bilbil Klosi
            Former Minister of Justice
        Dr. Fejzi Hoxha
            Chief of Albania's Hospital Clinics, and others

VII *THE MONGOLIAN PEOPLE'S REPUBLIC: THE ASIAN*
    MEMBER OF THE SOVIET COMMONWEALTH OF NATIONS

13. The Asian Heartland: A Non-Marxist View on the Mongolian
    People's Republic   *405*
        Harrison E. Salisbury
            Assistant Managing Editor
            THE NEW YORK TIMES
14. From Feudalism to Socialism: A Mongolian Marxist View on
    the Mongolian People's Republic   *413*
        Yumzhagin Tsedenbal
            President, Council of Ministers
            Mongolian People's Republic and
            First Secretary, Central Committee
            Mongolian People's Revolutionary Party
            With a supplement by
        Ivor Montagu
            British Journalist, Author
            Expert on Mongolia

VIII *THE KOREAN PEOPLE'S DEMOCRATIC REPUBLIC AND*
      THE DEMOCRATIC REPUBLIC OF VIETNAM:
      BETWEEN MOSCOW AND PEKING?

15. North Korea Under the Hammer and Sickle: A Non-
    Marxist View   *433*
            Klaus H. Pringsheim
                Associate Professor of Political Science
                McMaster University
16. Socialist Korea: A Korean Marxist View   *451*
            Jang Woo Tai
                A Director of the KDR's Ministry of Common
                    Education
            Pak Yung Ryong
                Vice Chairman
                Kangsu County People's Committee
                South Pyungan Province
            Kim Suk Doo
                Assistant Manager
                Pyongyang Silk Mill, and others
17. Ho Chi Minh's Democratic Republic of Vietnam: A
    Non-Marxist View   *464*
            Klaus H. Pringsheim
                Associate Professor of Political Science
                McMaster University
18. Heroic Vietnam: A Vietnamese Marxist View   *477*
            Ho Chi Minh
                President, Democratice Republic of Vietnam and
                Chairman, Vietnamese Workers' (Lao Dong) Party
            Pham Van Dong
                Premier, North Vietnam
            Nguyen Con
                Chairman, State Planning Commission, and others

IX *THE REPUBLIC OF CUBA: COMMUNISM'S BEACHHEAD*
    IN THE WESTERN HEMISPHERE

19. Cuba: The Economic and Social Revoluiton: A Non-
    Marxist View   *503*
            Dudley Seers
                Director General, Economic Planning Staff
                Ministry of Overseas Development
                Her Majesty's Government
20. The Castro Regime in Cuba: A Non-Marxist View   *517*
            Ernst Halperin
                Institute of Inter-American Studies
                Miami University

Contents

21. The Cuban Revolution: An American Marxist View   526

     Edward Boorstein
     Economist, Author

APPENDIX: 537

     Index of Selected Periodicals on
     Communism and the Communist World

The Communist World:
An Introduction

I

Area
(in square miles)
13,577,689

Population
(mid-1967 estimate)
1,124,336,000

Country (arranged in order of size)	Area (in square miles *)	Population (mid-1967 estimate **)
The Union of Soviet Socialist Republics	8,649,538	238,792,000
The Chinese People's Republic	3,691,523	721,518,000
The Mongolian People's Republic	592,667	1,144,000
The Polish People's Republic	120,665	32,392,000
The Federal Socialist Republic of Yugoslavia	98,766	19,922,000
The Socialist Republic of Rumania	91,699	19,385,000
The Democratic Republic of Vietnam	61,294	20,341,000
The Socialist Republic of Czechoslovakia	49,371	14,355,000
The Korean People's Democratic Republic	46,540	12,894,000
The Republic of Cuba	44,218	7,912,000
The People's Republic of Bulgaria	42,730	8,366,000
The German Democratic Republic	41,659	15,085,000
The Hungarian People's Republic	35,919	10,242,000
The People's Republic of Albania	11,100	1,988,000
TOTAL	13,577,689	1,124,336,000

* All figures have been taken from the United Nations' *Statistical Yearbook,* New York: United Nations, 1966, where they are given in square kilometers. For conversion to square miles the definition of an inch as equal to 2.54 cm. was used, as provided for in a 1959 agreement among English speaking countries. The conversion ratio was carried to ten places, i.e., 1 km² = 0.3861021585 mi².

** Population estimates for mid-1967 have been computed (and rounded to the nearest thousand) from the mid-1964 population figures and the growth rates given in the above cited United Nations' *Statistical Yearbook.*

The truth of the Marxist-Leninist conception of history has been fully borne out in practice.

FUNDAMENTALS OF MARXISM-LENINISM
(SOVIET MANUAL)

The community of socialist countries is the most powerful force of social progress, the main bulwark of universal peace.

ALEXEI NIKOLAYEVICH KOSYGIN
CHAIRMAN, COUNCIL OF
MINISTERS (PREMIER), U.S.S.R.

The socialist camp is not merely a body of socialist states: it belongs to the working people of the world. To them it is the wave of the future.

SOONG CHING LING (MME. SUN YAT-SEN)
VICE CHAIRMAN, PEOPLE'S REPUBLIC OF CHINA

INTRODUCTION

WHENEVER A COUNTRY EMBARKS ON THE TURBULENT JOURNEY toward economic development, a price must be paid for industrialization: the people must postpone raising their living standards so that more may be available to future generations. No economic system, no political structure, can change this fact because only by *not* consuming all that is being produced can the necessary resources be diverted to provide the factories, the machines, the tools, the equipment which can assure a substantially greater productive capacity later on. During the nineteenth century, this price was paid by the people of Western Europe and of the United States. The poverty-stricken masses in France and Germany, the children who worked long hours in British coal mines, the Negro slaves in the American South, the immigrants and the farmers' daughters who labored from dawn to dusk in the textile centers of New England to eke out a meager existence—all these paid the price of industrialization.

To the masses of farm laborers and city workers, the price thus paid must have appeared not only unreasonably high, but also utterly unjust and unfair, since the burden of the payment was not shared by *all* the people of the countries involved. They did not all chip in together, laboring as brethren to build a better society for their children. Under the economic system of capitalism, which is based on the private ownership of the means of production, a small minority succeeded in accumulating most of the wealth their age had to command, while the vast majority had little to look forward to either for themselves or for their children.

It was in those days, when capitalism in Western Europe and in the United States showed its ugliest face to the masses of its own people, that Karl Marx (1818-1883) came onto the stage of human history with a message which, for better or for worse, was to change the face of the earth and the destiny of mankind. A student of the history of human societies, an economist, a philosopher, and a revolutionary, Marx avowed that the capitalist system, as all others that had preceded it, was transient in nature and that it was to be replaced by a higher stage of social and economic development in which "the dominion of labor is at long last to be established."[1] Most of Marx's writing—the result of many years of intensive study and research— was devoted to an attempt to present scientific evidence that the downfall of capitalism was inevitable.

Arguing that the structure of every human society depends fundamentally upon its economic foundation (primarily upon the ways in which goods are produced), and pointing out that all economic, political, and social systems of the past played their role in the development of mankind, but eventually were superseded by new and more advanced systems, Marx acknowledged the great contributions of the bourgeoisie[2] which "during its rule of scarce one hundred years (220 years by the end of the 1960's) has created more massive and more colossal productive forces than have all preceding generations together."[3] But whatever its achievements, the time must inevitably come when capitalism—as all systems of the past—will have outlived its usefulness. At its highest stage of economic development, as Marxists see it, production is already socialized in the sense that tens of thousands of workers together, collectively, as it were, produce goods under the supervision of hired managers. Thus, there is no longer any economic function for the private owner to perform; yet he still pockets a part of the proceeds that emanate from the labor of the workingmen.[4]

To really understand Marx's scientific inquiries into the forces which, as he sees it, must inevitably lead to the downfall of capitalism we would have to follow him on his laborious path through some 2,500 pages of his *Capital,* and through some of his other works. We would have to gain a thorough understanding of his philosophical approach of *dialectic materialism* that conceives of all change in the real world as the result of the clash of opposing forces; we would have to study his *labor theory of value,* from which he derives a *subsistence theory of wages* and a *surplus value concept* (complete with mathematical formulas and historic examples), whereby he attempts to prove that,

[1] Karl Marx and Friedrich Engels, *The Communist Manifesto* (1848).

[2] Marx defines the "bourgeoisie" as the class of capitalists who, during the epoch of capitalism, owns the means of production, employs wage labor, and constitutes the ruling class.

[3] Karl Marx and Friedrich Engels, *The Communist Manifesto* (1848).

[4] Since, in Marxian analysis, class is defined in terms of the relationship of individuals to the means of production, a hired manager is by definition a member of the working class.

under capitalism, forces over which no individual has any control restrict the income of workers to a subsistence minimum while automatically leaving rent, interest, and profits in the hands of the capitalist employer; we would have to delve into his explanations of the historic role of the *class struggle,* and his analysis of this struggle in modern society, where the ruling bourgeoisie is challenged by the exploited proletariat (described by Marx as the class of industrial workers who have only one "commodity" for sale—their own labor power, who must sell this labor power in order to live, and who can sell it only if a capitalist finds it profitable to use it); we would have to become familiar with his analysis of the ways in which the bourgeoisie gained control over modern industrialized economies (Marx's theories of *primitive accumulation* and of *accumulation by surplus value*); we would have to grasp his concept of *the state as an agency of oppression,* used by the ruling class to oppress all other classes—even in present day, democratic-capitalist societies where the oppressed are "allowed, once every few years, to decide which particular representatives of the oppressing class should be in parliament to represent and oppress them;" [5] we would have to discover how all his theories lead him to his predictions concerning *the declining rate of profit, the increasing misery of the proletariat and so forth.*

Even a cursory survey of Marx's analysis of capitalist society would go far beyond the scope of this introduction. Yet, before we direct our attention to the post-capitalist era, we ought to turn, if briefly, to a consideration of the culmination of forces which, according to Marx, must result in the breakdown of the capitalist economic and political system. Let us cast a glance, therefore, at Marx's prediction of the recurrence of depressions (a prediction which, so far, has been borne out by history), and of the results thereof.

As industrialization and technology advance, Marx argues, capitalists find it to their advantage to substitute machinery for labor, especially during the brief periods when competition among employers drives wages above the minimum. But while each capitalist must install such machinery in the "dog-eat-dog" world of capitalist competition, a reduction of purchasing power on the part of the workers (and thus a drop in sales and profits for capitalists as a group) is the inevitable accompaniment of the socially un-planned and uncoordinated technological modernization of industry. Thus, capitalists are inevitably plagued by recurrent periods of economic crises

[5] Lenin quoting Marx in V. I. Lenin, "State and Revolution," E. Burns, comp., *The Handbook of Marxism* (New York, Random House, 1935), p. 744. Marxists argue that the masses of workers do not *really* have a choice of voting for candidates outside the traditional "bourgeois" parties because, with all means of communication and in-formation in the hands of the ruling capitalists, the masses of workers are continually told —and believe—that only capitalism assures them freedom, justice, and dignity, and holds out to them the hope of future affluence. And, present day Marxists add, should the truth ever dawn on the masses of a capitalist country's exploited populace, and should they vote in a government representative of their own interests, the military are likely to take over, presumably to "restore order" or "prevent a communist takeover," but actually to assure the maintenance of the *status quo.*

during which countless small businessmen (members of what Marx called the "petite bourgeoisie") go into bankruptcy, swelling the ranks of the proletariat and of the "reserve army" of unemployed. Eventually, the very process of competition that underlies the structure of capitalist economy results in the elimination of competition and the establishment of giant monopolistic concerns which control an ever greater part of the economy. These large enterprises, unable to sell their products to their own impoverished masses, then look for markets abroad. But since capitalists from many countries vie for foreign markets, imperialist wars are the unavoidable consequence. (Lenin, more than Marx, dealt with monopoly capitalism, colonialism, imperialism, and "the territorial division of the world by the great capitalist powers." [6]) Inevitably, Marx concludes, capitalism, weakened by recurrent depressions and wars, and torn asunder by its inherent contradictions, will break down. At this point, the working class will rise, take over the means of production, carry on where the capitalists left off, and prepare the stage for the final phase of human development—a world of perfect communism.

Trained social scientists in the Western World, and economists particularly have shown special interest in Marx's scientific analysis of the forces which, in his interpretation, make the change of the existing order and its replacement by a "higher order" inevitable; and many Western scholars have submitted his analysis to careful, critical scrutiny. But although Marx himself was not a moral philosopher (the question was not whether capitalism was "good" or "bad," but whether objective forces in capitalist society would lead inevitably to its eventual downfall), the masses of people have always been especially attracted by the moral aspects of Marxist ideology.

Much of Western interpretation describes communism as utterly "immoral" and "bad," a system under which a small leadership clique deprives the people of every right and freedom, be it the economic right to go into business for themselves, the political right to choose their own representatives, or the cultural and social right to express freely their thoughts, read the books of their choice, and enjoy artistic freedom. Communists, on the other hand, conceive of their ideology as a truly moral one, aimed at establishing a brotherhood that will embrace all mankind, a family of equals, a society of abundance in which the exploitation of man by man will have been ended once and for all, as all strive together toward common goals. They see themselves not as nonentities who have lost their individuality (as anti-Marxists so often describe them), but as individuals with common aims working together toward the construction of a perfect world order in which the happiness of each finds its fulfillment in the happiness of all. And as to freedom, their final goal is, indeed, a society of perfect freedom where no police, jails, armies, or any organized form of coercion will be necessary to

[6] V. I. Lenin, "Imperialism: The Highest Stage of Capitalism," *Handbook of Marxism* (New York, Random House, 1935), p. 690.

exact obedience to social laws. A new man, educated and reared to work unselfishly in the interests of society in a world in which the welfare of each is based on the welfare of all, will voluntarily and happily contribute to the best of his ability. He will take from the common stores what he needs; and production will have developed to such a degree that freedom from want will be assured for *all* the inhabitants of the globe. This belief, nay, this firm conviction of sincere communists that they are building a new and better world finds expression in all of their writings. To many Westerners their proclamations may appear to be mere propaganda, but communists the world over attach deep meaning to such statements as the one below, taken from the 1961 *Programme of the Communist Party of the Soviet Union:*

Communism accomplishes the historic mission of delivering all men from social inequality, from every form of oppression and exploitation, from the horrors of war, and proclaims *Peace, Labour, Freedom, Equality, Fraternity* and *Happiness* for all peoples of the earth.

While Marxists strive towards the attainment of what they believe will be a perfect society, they scorn Utopians who describe their ideal world but fail to outline the steps necessary to transform the existing order into the desired one. Unrealistically, these Utopians show little understanding for the necessity of overcoming the opposition of powerful vested interests, and they are too confident that, given the proper environment, man would immediately become perfectly rational and perfectly good. Marxists have always considered as utterly absurd the belief that the abolition of capitalism in and by itself would usher in the golden age without further preparation of man and of the economy. Equally absurd, or perhaps naïve—if not outright dishonest—are all assertions that reforms within the framework of a capitalist society could change the age-old order in which, according to Marx's lifelong friend and collaborator Friedrich Engels (1820-1895), "The produce of the labor of those who do work gets unavoidably accumulated in the hands of those who do not work." [7] A few minor concessions granted grudgingly by the bourgeoisie to the exploited proletariat neither change the fundamental injustice of the capitalist order, nor solve the contradictions inherent in capitalist society. [8] And how could things ever be different as long as the

---

[7] Friedrich Engels, "The British Labor Movement," *Handbook of Marxism* (New York, Random House, 1935), p. 200.

[8] In much of the capitalist world, such as in Latin America, the conditions of large segments of the population have remained fundamentally unchanged for decades, if not centuries; and in some places they have worsened. On the other hand, in some of the industrially more advanced capitalist nations, and especially in the United States, the lot of workers in general appears to have improved considerably, but Negroes, coal miners, unskilled workers, older laborers, etc., will testify that the phenomenon is by no means universal. And whatever progress has been made, present-day Marxists charge, has been achieved by shifting the burden from American workers to the more exploited laborers in the underdeveloped countries who are paid little for supplying raw materials, are charged high prices for the few industrial goods they can afford to buy, and must work long and hard so that foreign investors may be able to extract a maximum of sur-

means of production are privately owned and goods are produced, not with an eye on the needs of the masses, but with both eyes on profit? After all, the production of what is most needed (let us say milk or clothing for the children of the poor) is not always very profitable! Hence, Marxists deny the possibility of an adequate solution within the framework of a private enterprise system. In the words of *The Communist Manifesto,* "With us it is not a matter of reforming private property,[9] but of abolishing it; not of hushing up the class antagonism, but of abolishing the classes; not of ameliorating the existing society, but of establishing a new one."

Since vested interests attempt to preserve the obsolete capitalist order at all costs, and since even a large part of the downtrodden—raised to believe that any system other than capitalism is tantamount to slavery—stands in the way of the necessary changes in the social order, a revolution is, in most instances, unavoidable.[10] But this revolution must not come before conditions are ripe. It has been compared with a birth: a new life suddenly bursts forth; if it comes at the proper stage of development, the newcomer will tend to be healthy and to embellish the earth, but the more premature the newborn, the less likely that it will survive.

Once the means of production and the operation of government have passed into the hands of the class of industrial workers (the proletariat) a period of hard preparatory work for the final stage of communism lies ahead. During this intermediate period, this phase of "socialism," this era of the "dictatorship of the proletariat," the last vestiges of capitalism must be eradicated, the economic foundation for a society of abundance for all must be laid, and new generations must be reared in the spirit of unselfishness, cooperation, and comradeship, for these must be men and women fit to live in a society of free and equal human beings, a society based on the principle: "From each according to his ability, to each according to his needs."

Such, very briefly, is the theoretical foundation laid by Karl Marx with the support and collaboration of Friedrich Engels.[11] V. I. Lenin

---

plus value. Moreover, for many workers in the advanced countries gains are but temporary, since the inevitably recurring depressions reduce to naught the advances of the preceding years.

[9] *Private* property, in Marxian terminology (to be distinguished from *personal* property) refers not to personal possession of consumers' goods but to the private ownership of the means of production.

[10] At the address delivered at a convention of the First International in Hague, in 1872, Marx stated that in the United States, in England, and perhaps even in Holland, the change could come about peaceably, but that this is by no means the case everywhere. *See,* for example, Harry W. Laidler, *A History of Socialist Thought* (New York, Crowell, 1927), p. 194.

[11] In his scientific work, concentrated on proving the inevitability of the downfall of capitalism, Marx made no attempt to draw up a detailed blueprint of the "intermediate stage" of socialism, let alone the "final stage" of communism. Most of the details regarding the post-capitalist stages of the "dictatorship of the proletariat" and of "perfect communism" were added later by his followers. While these latter have never agreed with one another on precisely what Marx meant, there would be little disagreement on the broad outlines presented in this introduction to Chapter I.

(born Vladimir Ilyich Ulianov, and sometimes wrongly called *Nikolai* Lenin, 1870-1924), head of Russia's Bolshevik (Communist) Party, leader of the October (1917) Revolution that brought the bolsheviks to power, and premier of the "first socialist state"—the Soviet Union—from 1918 until his death in 1924, further developed Marx's ideas. He elaborated on the "final stage of capitalism" by investigating the nature of what he called "finance capitalism," "monopoly capitalism," and "imperialism"; he substituted "all toilers" (including especially the peasantry) for the "proletariat" as the ones destined to take over the reins of government from the bourgeoisie; he predicted socialist revolutions not necessarily in the most advanced capitalist countries but in the "weakest links in the capitalist chain"; he converted the structural concept of the Communist Party from that of "Communists [who] do not form a separate party opposed to other working class parties" [12] to that of an organization of professional revolutionaries "who will devote to the revolution not only their spare evenings but the whole of their lives;" [13] he formulated the concept of "democratic centralism" whereby, during the intermediate phase of socialism, freedom of discussion would be combined with unity of action, and wide political participation of the masses with strict obedience to the leadership [14] and so forth.

It was, then, the red banner of *Marxism-Leninism* that was raised on that fateful day in late October, 1917,[15] over the Winter Palace in Petrograd (the seat of Russia's provisional government); it was this banner which, in the months thereafter, was carried victoriously over most of the territory which today constitutes the Union of Soviet Socialist Republics—one-sixth of the land area of the earth; it is this banner which now flies over one-third of the inhabitants of the globe, from Moscow to Peking, from Ulan Bator to Tirana, and from East Berlin to Havana.

While in this book each of the fourteen countries which today comprise the Communist World will be discussed in detail by Marxist and non-Marxist

[12] Marx and Engels, *The Communist Manifesto* (1848).

[13] "The Urgent Tasks of Our Movement" (December, 1900), *Selected Works,* Vol. II (New York, International Publishers, 1943), p. 14.

[14] The fundamental idea of "democratic centralism" is that proposals are subject to discussion and to constructive criticism; but plans, once adopted, must be carried out. This can, in a way, be compared with standard procedure by, let us say, large American automobile manufacturers: wide exchange of ideas in regard to next year's models is encouraged; but once a decision has been reached, and the expensive retooling job has started, the plan must be carried out, at penalty of great losses to the corporation. For greater detail on all aspects of Marxism-Leninism, as interpreted by the Soviets and with special reference to its application in the Soviet Union, *see Fundamentals of Marxism-Leninism,* second edition (Foreign Languages Publishing House, Moscow, 1963).

[15] October 25 on the pre-Revolution Russian calendar; November 7 according to the Western calendar which, soon after the Revolution, was adopted by the Soviets.

experts on the respective areas, this introductory chapter is devoted to an analysis of the Communist World as a whole and of the validity, applicability, and meaningfulness of the theory upon which it is founded.

The non-Marxist view in this chapter has been contributed by Alfred G. Meyer. Born and raised in Germany, Meyer came to the United States in 1939. A Harvard Ph.D. in Political Science, he has been the recipient of Rockefeller, Ford Foundation, and Guggenheim fellowships and was awarded the Distinguished Faculty Award at Michigan State University in 1963. He has published numerous articles, pamphlets, chapters in symposia, and five books, including *Marxism: The Unity of Theory and Practice, Leninism, Communism, The Soviet Political System,* and with Gustav Hilger, *The Incompatible Allies.* In his academic career, he has held positions as Research Fellow, Assistant to the Director, and Assistant Director of the Russian Research Center at Harvard University, and Director of the Research Program on the History of the CPSU (Communist Party of the Soviet Union) at Columbia University. He taught at the University of Washington and for a decade at Michigan State University. At present he is Professor of Political Science at the University of Michigan.

On the Marxist side, a variety of views expressed by outstanding Marxist-Leninists in the United States, England, and the Soviet Union have been put together in an attempt to give a representative picture. Among the contributors are Herbert Aptheker, R. Palme Dutt, and A. Arzumanyan.

Herbert Aptheker, a Columbia Ph.D. in history, has published some twenty books and has contributed numerous articles to magazines and to many of the learned journals in the U.S., primarily in the field of the history of the Negro in the United States (e.g., *American Negro Slave Revolts,* 1943; *A Documentary History of the Negro People in the U.S.,* 2 vols., 1951; *Nat Turner's Slave Revolt,* 1966), but also in such areas as the "era of McCarthyism," socialist and communist ideology, etc. Aptheker is past editor of *Political Affairs,* one of America's leading communist periodicals. He is literary executor of the late D.W.E.B. Du Bois, was a Guggenheim Fellow in 1946, holds an honorary doctorate from Martin-Luther University in the German Democratic Republic (East Germany), and at present he is Director of the American Institute for Marxist Studies. In November, 1966, he ran for Congress from a Brooklyn district on a non-party-affiliated platform of peace, democracy, and equality.

Rajani Palme Dutt, educated at Cambridge, Balliol College, and Oxford (from which he was expelled in 1917 for propagandizing Marxism), holds an honorary doctorate in history from Moscow University. A prolific writer, Dutt has published countless articles (including one on communism and one on The International in the 12th edition of the Encyclopedia Britannica), as well as books on subjects varying from fascism, socialism, and communism to India, the British Empire, world politics, and problems of contemporary history. Former editor of the *Workers' Daily* and the *Daily Worker,* Dutt has been editor of the *Labour Monthly* since 1921, and member of the Executive Committee of Britain's Communist Party since 1922. He is also Chairman of the International Department of the Party.

A. Arzumanyan, Soviet economist, has published numerous articles and books (e.g., *The New Stage in the General Crisis of Capitalism, Important Aspects of the World Economy, Modern Capitalism and the Class Struggle* [titles translated from the Russian]). Since 1962, Arzumanyan has been a full member of the Academy of Science of the U.S.S.R. At present he is Director of the Academy's Institute of World Economics.

The contributors to the Marxist part of this chapter are probably all more closely aligned with the Soviet interpretation of Marxism-Leninism than with any other. In a way, this is unfortunate, since pro-Chinese Marxists would probably not agree with *all* passages in this selection (such as, for instance, with British Marxist R. Palme Dutt's statement that "the necessary practical path of solution is the policy of peaceful coexistence to replace the policies of the cold war.") But since space limitations precluded separate detailed presentations, in this introductory chapter, of the views held by the various factions of the Communist World, the editor felt that little could be gained by including a few isolated charges and countercharges which have issued in recent years in the Sino-Soviet split. This chapter, therefore, emphasizes Marxist views which—both in regard to the theories of Marxism-Leninism, and to the past achievements and future prospects of the Communist World—would be acceptable to all factions.

The Communist World:
A Non-Marxist View

ALFRED G. MEYER *
PROFESSOR OF POLITICAL SCIENCE
UNIVERSITY OF MICHIGAN

As used in this chapter, the term "Communist World" shall designate those countries or states governed by parties or political movements describing themselves as communist or paying allegiance to an ideology they call Marxism-Leninism. It therefore includes the Soviet Union and all of Europe east of the Elbe, with the exception of Greece and Finland; and the People's Republics of China, Mongolia, Korea, and Viet Nam. Whether Cuba should be included is difficult to decide; many of the generalizations I will make about the communist world do not apply to that country. I shall try to survey the nature of these social systems by discussing their origins, official ideology, structure, functions, and possible trends of development. To do this, especially within restricted space, cannot but involve over-generalizations and a rather arbitrary selection of salient points. Hence it involves the author's subjective judgment. I have no remedy for this failing except to call it to the reader's attention.

ORIGINS

Contemporary communist societies, like all socio-political systems, have been born in revolutions. All revolutions, while not, perhaps, inevitable, can be explained, and must be explained, by reference to the inequities or inadequacies of the systems they destroyed or replaced. At the same time,

* This contribution has been written especially for this book.

we can distinguish between communist systems by the type of revolution through which they came into being: some of them arose out of revolutions which we might call spontaneous or genuine—uncontrolled and uncontrollable chaotic reactions by entire nations to the decay of previous systems—while in other cases the revolutions were, shall we say, contrived by agents outside the society; or at least their outcome was significantly skewed by military and diplomatic influences. Russia, China, and Cuba (if we are to include her) are examples of the former type; the latter generalization applies to most other communist countries; Yugoslavia is a special case not falling clearly into either category. Some writers might say the same about Czechoslovakia.

The more genuine communist revolutions have occurred in countries that might be characterized as underdeveloped, but disturbed by imperialism, i.e., by the encroachment of the West into their autochthonous culture. In short, these were countries outside of the mainstream of European or Western history, but with incipient industrialism and incipient capitalism. They had an intelligentsia, i.e., a small minority of people with a Western education, hence committed to modern science and modern social ideas, often in their most radical form. In addition, these societies had developed national consciousness, usually of considerable strength. Almost every one of the spontaneous communist revolutions was preceded by a major war, which overstrained the fabric of the social system. Finally, in every case, the communists came to power in countries already racked by revolutions which had, months or years before, removed the traditional political order.

The more contrived communist revolutions have taken place (or been made to take place) in what we might call semideveloped countries, nations which were on the margins of Europe not only geographically but also with regard to economic development, social structure, and political culture. Given a range of developmental stages which comprises East Germany and Czechoslovakia on the one hand, and Albania and Bulgaria on the other, this is obviously an overgeneralization. Before becoming part of the Communist World, these Eastern European countries, too, had been prepared for revolutions by years of war and foreign occupation, and by profound social changes due to war and occupation, including the decimation of former ruling classes and the nationalization of large sectors of their economies. Before the war, many of the countries also had been ruled by relatively exploitative, oppressive, inefficient, and corrupt regimes and in this fashion also been prepared for revolution. In referring to the revolutions placing these societies into the Communist World as contrived, I imply, first, that without diplomatic and military pressure other parties might have come to power, and, second, that even if Communist Parties had come to power unaided, their policies would have differed from those which diplomatic, military, and geographic pressures imposed on them for the initial years of their rule.

IDEOLOGY

Communist revolutions are led, and communist states are ruled, by parties committed to a doctrine or ideology they call Marxism-Leninism. Derived from the writings of Marx and Engels, this doctrine posits an egalitarian, self-governing, classless and stateless, collectivist, industrial social system called communism as the goal toward which all mankind is striving. The doctrine specifies that this goal can be reached only by a proletarian dictatorship which eliminates capitalist and imperialist rule, and class antagonism, as well as exploitation and waste; this proletarian dictatorship will establish socialism, which is defined as a political system based on the spontaneous consent of all and as a nationalized economy managed on the basis of a comprehensive production plan. In turn, socialism can succeed in its long-range goals, and indeed the working class can achieve any of its objectives, only if the Communist Party can attain and maintain sovereignty within the nation. For the Party, according to its own doctrines, is the repository of true consciousness, hence the only legitimate representative of the workers and of all mankind. The dictatorship of the Communist Party therefore is a benevolent, nay democratic, dictatorship, because it alone promotes the interests of the people.

Communist leaders, proclaiming the writings of Marx and Engels to be the key to all rational knowledge, have elaborated selected elements of Marx's method of inquiry into universally applicable philosophic dogmas and have sought, not entirely successfully, to make this dogma, which they call *dialectical materialism,* function as the binding guide in all fields of human inquiry. From the generalizations Marx and Engels made about man and society, past and present, the communist ideologists have distilled another doctrine, called *historical materialism,* which they proclaim to be the scientific summary of all human history. How much either dialectical or historical materialism [1] have in common with the ideas of Marx and Engels is a highly controversial and, perhaps, somewhat scholastic question.

Communist ideology furthermore includes an economic doctrine which seeks to explain the economics both of capitalism and imperialism, on the one hand, and of socialist construction, on the other. Like other elements of communist ideology, this too is supposedly derived from the ideas of Marx and Engels. Finally, it contains a body of political thought and practical guidelines, now called *scientific communism,* which deals, first, with the strategy and tactics of communist revolutions, and, second, with

[1] Perhaps the most convenient, comprehensive, and up-to-date introduction to these subdivisions of communist ideology is provided by the Soviet textbook on ideology, *Fundamentals of Marxism-Leninism* (Moscow, 1961) and subsequent editions. [EDITOR'S NOTE]

political problems of socialist or communist states. Until about a decade ago, this was called *scientific socialism*. Without indulging in overgeneralization one can say that in actual practice scientific socialism was little else than a didactic summary of experiences made by the Communist Party of the Soviet Union, both before and after coming to power, i.e., both as a contender for power and as the manager of an underdeveloped society. Hence, the imposition of scientific socialism on all communist parties as binding dogma implied the attempt to make them carbon copies of the Soviet party in structure, ideology and policies, and indeed to mold the entire societies of the Communist World in the image of the Soviet Union. Since, in fact, the social bases of the various communist regimes differed significantly from that of the U.S.S.R., this attempt, where it was successful, created serious difficulties for the communist regimes involved.

The precise relationship between the professed ideology and the policies actually pursued by a communist party is complex and uncertain; hence it is one of the most controversial themes in studying the Communist World. Opinions range from what one might call ideological determinism, i.e., the assumption that ideology functions as the chief impetus in the operations of communist systems, to Machiavellian hypotheses dismissing ideology as a mere public relations device used to justify any and all actions taken. No simple formula, however, can describe the actual relationship, which probably differs from one communist state to another, and, within each state, from one social group to another. The matter has been complicated further by the recent destruction of whatever ideological unity prevailed in the Communist World. This destruction was speeded by the death of Stalin; it has split the Communist World into hostile camps offering divergent and opposite views on every important element of the common ideological heritage, even though each camp claims to be the sole true disciples of Marx and Lenin; and, of course, they all employ the same vocabulary and profess to promote identical basic goals. Once one steps beyond these elements all communists still hold in common, it becomes impossible to derive a person's or a party's aims, attitudes, or likely behavior from the mere fact that he or it subscribes to Marxism-Leninism.

FORMAL STRUCTURE

Communist states have either referred to themselves as dictatorships of certain classes (workers, or workers and peasants) or democratic states expressing the will of all the people (People's Democracies or Democratic Republics). In using the designation of proletarian dictatorship, they sought to symbolize the destructive task they set themselves, namely, the abolishing of private property in the means of production and the ousting of former ruling classes. Designations of the latter type are to symbolize the socialist nature of the regimes, i.e., the claim that in the Communist World essential inequalities have been abolished together with private property; that even though classes still exist the struggle between them has yielded to collaboration and harmony; and that the interests of each individual truly coincide with the public interest, so that obedient and disciplined compliance with the will of the state is in every individual's self-interest.

Throughout the Communist World, official spokesmen stress the leading role of the Communist Party (whatever its official name) [2] in the state. The party describes itself as the actual fountainhead of all authority, the repository of all scientific knowledge, and the legitimate shaper of all behavior patterns, norms, and opinions. The state is a workers' state because it is governed by the party of the workers. It is a people's democracy because the party that has created it is the party of the entire people. This assumption that the Communist Party truly represents the interests of the people is the heart of the communist theory of state, the article of faith on which all other features of their self-image are based. Acceptance or rejection of this claim is one of the surest indicators of a person's attitude toward communist systems in general.

All states of the Communist World have written themselves constitutions describing the formal structure of their governments. According to these constitutions, sovereignty in these states lies with the people, who exercise it through representative assemblies elected on the basis of a universal, free, equal, and secret franchise. These national assemblies and their territorial and local counterparts are the sources of all law as well as of all administrative and judicial authority. Communist states are unitary states. Their spokesmen repudiate the division of powers or systems of checks and balances because, they argue, the government of the people, being good government, ought not to be weakened. Whether the representative institutions are called something like soviet or have more old-fashioned names, whether the government has federal or unitary form, this principle determines its basic structure.

Communist constitutions are further distinct by their open ambivalence to the rights of the citizens. On the one hand, they provide a wider range of citizens' rights than the liberal constitutions of the nineteenth century, and they seek to improve on those liberal constitutions by spelling out certain guarantees of these rights. On the other hand, they match rights with specifications of citizens' duties and they make it quite clear that in any conflict of individual interest with the interests of the state, the former

---

[2] In Poland, the party calls itself the Polish United Workers Party; in the German Democratic Republic, the Socialist Unity Party; in Yugoslavia, the Yugoslav League of Communists; and so forth in various other communist countries. [EDITOR'S NOTE]

must yield to the latter. The Communist World is firmly committed to collectivist and statist principles,[3] which are implied in the notion of socialism as they understand it.

In putting their political machinery to work, communist systems profess to apply the principle of democratic centralism. This term symbolized Lenin's attempt to combine the advantages of democratic debate with those of militant discipline and centralized bureaucratic management in conducting the affairs of Communist Parties and all their ancillary organizations. In practice, democratic centralism almost from the beginning stressed centralization and discipline at the expense of consultation, discussion, freedom, and other democratic practices; and although various social and ideological forces repeatedly challenge centralizing tendencies in the management of life, democratic centralism is still little more than a synonym for strict authoritarianism.

A THEORETICAL MODEL OF COMMUNISM

Many Western scholars have been tempted to summarize their perception of the communist world by describing its component societies as totalitarian. Totalitarianism is a word of comparatively recent coinage which is still in the process of being defined. In applying it to communist societies, the observers stress all or some of the following features:

Dictatorship. Whatever the formal arrangements, communist states have been ruled by individuals or small groups exercising supreme and absolute command over party and state. Despite the formal democratic arrangements, the political machines run by these men have not been obliged to conform to the expressed wishes of the public or to account for their actions. In this sense, communist government is irresponsible government. It justifies this relationship by a paternalistic rhetoric, according to which communist government exercises leadership for the purpose of educating the masses for self-government. Furthermore, communist leadership, in statist fashion, regards itself as the driving force of progress, the prime mover of modern history.

Terror. Communist regimes have not, as a rule, shown great hesitation to use extralegal methods of coercion, including mass violence, the threat of violence, and organized peer group pressure, for the sake of eliminating opposition, fortifying their authority, and compelling compliance of all citizens. Repeatedly, mass terror has been applied quite indiscriminately, so that for many people communist rule is synonymous with the police state and with bloody arbitrariness.

Indoctrination and organization. Communist Parties, subscribing to an all-embracing ideology, have made vigorous and persistent attempts to impose their own dogmas on all social and individual thought processes. They have tried to

---

[3] Statism denotes the belief that the interests of any individual are subordinate to the interests of the state, and that in case of a conflict between these interests, those of the individual must yield.

remake the entire personality of their citizens according to their preconceived pattern by means of a program of perpetual indoctrination and by insulating their citizens, through censorship and through the party monopoly over all means of communication from all extraneous influences. Monopolistic control by the party over all social organizations and associations further aids the homogenization of society, or the universal socialization of all citizens for a life conforming to the party's plans.

Socialism. Throughout the Communist World, the major means of production and distribution have become national property; and this economic establishment is managed by the government in accordance with national plans concerning resource allocation, output, and distribution.

Total mobilization. Citizenship in communist states is defined more as a set of duties than one of rights; and through a variety of means all communist regimes have made vigorous efforts to mobilize all citizens for active participation in public affairs, directed especially towards the achievement of a high level of output in areas of work deemed socially useful. Because the need for investment has been great and the economic basis from which the communist regimes had to start has as a rule been low, the Communist World has sought to extract a maximum of productive work in return for minimal rewards. The Communist World therefore has been characterized by an atmosphere of perpetual consumer austerity and by the work tempo of the sweatshop.

While the features listed above might be a fairly adequate summary of the totalitarian syndrome, the term, as used by contemporary social scientists, has a number of implications I would consider misleading; hence I should prefer to dispense with it altogether. Instead, it might be possible to gain an adequate understanding of communist political systems by comparing them with complex modern bureaucratic organizations anywhere. Precisely what type of bureaucracy furnishes the most convenient model for a given communist society may vary: for the Soviet Union, the business corporation comes to mind; but in the case of China the aptest comparison may be with an army.

Like modern bureaucracy, communist rule is an attempt to impose a rational managerial order over life by means of complex organization. Like bureaucracy, it has evolved certain basic principles of organization and management, the most noteworthy of which are the following:

The monocratic or hierarchic principle, according to which all authority flows downward through individual line commanders personally in charge of their particular organization, in a neat pyramidal pattern. A countervailing principle of collegial responsibility, which visualizes committees rather than administrative chiefs as the seats of responsibility, occasionally challenges the hierarchic tendencies of communist management, but has not as a rule prevailed over it.

Structural differentiation according to specialized functions. All complex administrative organizations engaged in a great diversity of tasks must allocate responsibilities and jurisdictions to specialized agencies and must perpetually strive for the most rational form of organization. The most rational organization would be one which can so distribute authority to subsidiary agencies that all operations become smooth and predictable routines, because all work is broken up into specialized functions. Rationality would also include that kind of authority distribution which gives maximal initiative and discretion to subsidiary agencies without depriving the administrative center of control. Finally, the most rational distribution of authority would be one which, in allocating jurisdictions, knows precisely whether to create territorial or functional subdivisions. Students of modern bureaucracy know that this complex notion of administrative rationality is an abstract ideal which cannot be realized in practice. For this reason, all complex managerial structures are perennially plagued by organizational problems and are perpetually seeking to solve them by reorganization. Precisely this preoccupation with organizational questions is a trait which communist political systems share with modern bureaucracies.

Recruitment according to merit. One might argue that this principle merely extends the notion of structural differentiation to the individual and that it seeks to create a social system in which every person is performing work which fully corresponds to his inclinations, talents, skills, and experience. By implication this means also that a person's other qualities, such as sex, age, religion, social origins, and the like, should have no influence on his work assignment and career. Only competence should count.

Although most bureaucracies, including communist systems, have been remarkably successful in instituting the merit system, all of them in actual fact, in recruiting their personnel, must consider not only competence, but also loyalty to the organization. Hence the merit principle is never fully operative. To be sure, competence and loyalty may be mutually reinforcing; but they are so only to a degree, for underneath the dispassionate rationality of a bureaucracy always is a political system based on social stratification and other distinctions and conflicts, which in all likelihood the bureaucratic machinery helps to perpetuate. In the Communist World, competence and loyalty considerations have often been in conflict with each other because of the regimes' revolutionary origins: people with greater skills and experience were likely to identify with the former ruling strata, while the most enthusiastic supporters of communism came predominantly from less educated classes. In the short run, communist systems have tried to solve the resulting problem of elite recruitment by strictly supervising the "bourgeois specialists" taken over into their public service. In the long run, they have sought to rear a new generation of citizens educated entirely under communist auspices, who can therefore be expected to combine their various skills and accomplishments with a commitment to the communist system.

Two implications follow from the urge of Communist Parties to perfect a system of elite recruitment based on competence. One is the need for a national network of educational institutions, the curricula of which are carefully adjusted to the entire society's requirements for trained personnel in various fields, with the party, of course, defining society's requirements. The other is the need for standardized procedures of checking and evaluating each individual's and each administrative agency's performance, so that rewards as well as assignments, promotions, demotions, transfers, and changes in jurisdiction, can be determined dispassionately, strictly on the basis of merit or past performance.

Rules and regulations. Bureaucratic management has as one of its aims to transform decision-making processes into routines based on the dispassionate application of established rules and procedures. In this sense, bureaucracy strives toward government by law rather than men. The goal is never reached, partly because no rules or regulations can foresee all problems that may come to the attention of the managers, and partly because the masters of the administrative machinery retain the freedom to change the rules or simply to disregard them. In the Communist World, the ruling parties have made ample use of this freedom and thereby subverted the state-according-to-law they claim to have created. Nonetheless, communist systems are also strongly committed to bureaucratic regularity, hence also to the wide use of law and legal processes as regulators of social life. The self-image they present often is couched in surprisingly legalistic form, which seems old-fashioned as well as naïve to Western social scientists.

Planning and accounting. Another bureaucratic practice, closely related to this legalism, is the commitment to planning and its various implications, including cost accounting and the keeping of records on every single action taken by administrative agencies. Communist systems, like the giant bureaucratic structures of the Western world, are managed with the help of vast floods of directives, memos, reports, receipts, and other paperwork.

Incidentally, this flow of communication must be controlled and channeled systematically to prevent an intolerable information glut. Hence communist systems, like all modern bureaucracies, are very much preoccupied with the maintenance of proper communication channels and also with secrecy.

Again, like complex organizations everywhere, the Communist World is plagued by the pathological features seemingly inevitable in the well-entrenched bureaucratic way of life. These features include the impossibility of finding the ideal organization, and the resultant instability of administrative structures; the seemingly inevitable conflicts between specialists and generalists, between staff officials and line commanders; the intense competition between individuals and between administrative agencies and empires, a phenomenon related to the equally inevitable formation of group interests and group loyalties within an allegedly monolithic command structure. The pathology of bureaucracy, and therefore, also of communism, includes overorganization and excessive regulation, the overrigid structuring of communication channels and authority relations, the chronic tendency to burden individuals as well as agencies with tasks that are mutually contradictory or so burdensome that they cannot possibly be accomplished, and the perversion of the collective endeavor because the actors involved are interested primarily in fulfilling the measurable performance standards by which their superiors judge them. As a reaction to these ills, communist states, like other bureaucracies, develop informal practices that break down established rules, authority relations, and communications channels. Such practices may range from selective enforcement of rules through collusion and evasion to actual corruption. The entire pathological syndrome of bureaucratic ills is compounded in the Communist World by the relative political backwardness and economic austerity of the countries involved.

Let me conclude this comparison of the Communist World with modern bureaucracy by pointing out that the personality types which Western scholars have found to be prevalent in complex organizations seem also to predominate in communist systems, and that in the various patterns of adjustment to the bureaucratic way of life we can, despite substantial differences in cultures and traditions, discover significant parallels between communist and Western organization men.

The totalitarian and the bureaucratic models of communism are complementary rather than mutually exclusive. They highlight different elements of the Communist World and may well be applied jointly. In using the former, we stress the novelty and uniqueness of communist rule as well as the terroristic, coercive, and manipulative methods of rule; in preferring the latter, we point to striking similarities it has with organizations familiar to all of us, and we imply that in criticizing the communist way of life we should not be blind to analogous failings in our own. The main reason, however, why I prefer the bureaucratic as against the totalitarian model of communism is that the latter, if at all adequate, probably applies to communist systems only for a limited initial period of their development, a period of growing pains, of system-building, a period devoted to the primitive accumulation of both the means of production and the authority to rule. In contrast, the bureaucratic model more likely applies to the presumably much longer period of settled existence within a well-established system.

Whatever model we may use, several features more readily associated with the democratic way of life rather than the totalitarian or bureaucratic have to be added. Among these I should mention the effort made by communist ruling parties either to educate the citizens for a certain measure of self-government or at least to draw them into active participation in public life. Citizenship in the Communist World is defined as active and constructive participation rather than mere obedience, even though the range and direction of activity are prescribed and limited by the party. A second feature is the egalitarian ethos which expresses itself foremost in the virtually universal opportunities for upward social mobility given to all citizens, and guaranteed by a system of free public education. Finally, communist states, within the restrictive limits of their economic potential, are, or try to be, welfare states. Although the Communist World is primarily interested in rapid industrialization and a strong national defense—pursuits which require heavy investment yielding no (or no immediate) return to the consumer—and although the level of economic development from which most communist states were forced to start is relatively low, the ruling parties at least try to put a floor under the general living standard through social security schemes, free medical care, and various other public services.

Despite the strong egalitarian ethos, however, communist societies have shown tendencies toward the development of new patterns of social stratification. In the attempt to mobilize all citizens for a maximal effort on behalf of the goals established by the party, the leaders of the Communist World have learned that they cannot rely solely on revolutionary enthusiasm, nor on mere terror, but must give their citizens tangible incentives to work. Methods of coercion and persuasion must be supplemented by rewards. Nor can these rewards be given indiscriminately, equally to all, but must instead be differentiated on the basis of the individual's performance, or his worth to the regime. In short, communist rulers, however reluctantly, have felt the need to establish systems of managed inequality in which material welfare, power, status, and honor are distributed unequally. Communist societies are therefore stratified just as Western societies are. In many of them, the status pyramid is steep. The competitive struggle of individuals to climb closer to the top appears no less fierce than in the so-called capitalist world.

Whether this structure of differentiated rewards or managed inequality has transformed communist societies into class societies is a matter of definition, which has remained controversial among both Marxists and non-Marxists. It may also be a scholastic question. Whatever terms we use—class, stratification, elite, status pyramid, or others—the unquestionable fact remains that the Communist World is economically and socially stratified and, politically, in the hands of a self-appointed and self-perpetuating elite, the Communist Parties. The power of these parties is so great that I propose to call them the sovereign of communist systems. Or, to return to the model of the business corporation, I should say that the communist parties in their relationship to their total political systems are analogous with the owners of the corporation and their elected representatives, i.e., with the stockholders and the board of directors. In their total dependence on such a sovereign body, communist societies might then be compared to old-fashioned American company towns.

FUNCTIONS

In asking about the functions of a social system, we seek to inquire into the achievements, accomplishments, results, and consequences of the system's operations. Thus in speculating about the functions of political systems in general, scholars might argue that they serve as mechanisms of societal self-regulation for the purpose of preventing anarchy, or that they are instruments by which a ruling class perpetuates its power; or one might advance a variety of other functions. Accomplishments and consequences, in turn, are difficult to separate from the intentions and purposes of the leading actors in a system. Hence a discussion of functions inevitably touches the aims a system sets itself.

The functions of communism have been defined in different and quite conflicting ways by Western observers. Some argue that the principal function of communism is to establish communism over the entire globe, to replace free enterprise, so called, with socialist planning, to eradicate religion, eliminate all individuality, do away with national sovereignty, and set up a Communist World state under one single dictatorship. In short, the entire Communist World is seen as a machinery geared to the fulfillment of an ideological goal, a goal which many of these observers reject as totally undesirable. Or else, even though the ideological goal is regarded as the primary determinant of all communist organization and action, the stress is laid on the struggle for power that supposedly is to implement this utopian quest. The conquest of individual countries by the party and the alleged plans to conquer the whole world then come to be viewed as the chief function of communism, and all its moves and policies fall into their proper places within the framework of this overriding goal. In such a goal, ideology and geopolitics reinforce each other.

Yet other Western interpreters of the communist world argue that ideological motivation is a negligible factor. Instead, they regard the communist world as the manifestation of a pure power urge, possibly reinforced by nationalism. Geopolitics, in this hypothesis, reinforces nothing else than a Machiavellian preoccupation with power.

While the interpretations mentioned so far concentrate on the alleged global aims of communism, other views focus on the domestic functions. Here, too, a widely prevalent Machiavellian interpretation pays attention primarily to power. It does so either by defining all communist politics as a function of the power struggle within the highest levels of communist parties, so that the entire system becomes an extension of personal competition between a handful of party leaders. Or, once this struggle has been decided and a supreme leader has established itself, the system becomes one vast machinery of self-protection surrounding the dictator. Many learned books thus describe communist government machineries as control mechanisms geared primarily to the task of keeping rival leaders as well as the masses at bay. This approach can be taken also if, instead of a single dictator, a ruling oligarchy is the focus of attention.

I take issue with most of these views, for a number of reasons. First, they seem too one-sided or one-dimensional to do justice to the actual complexity of communist systems. Second, they tend to be unhistorical in neglecting to account for changes in functions. This failing is particularly grievous with regard to revolutionary societies or, more general, social systems of very recent origin, which are still in the process of establishing themselves and which, therefore, are engaged in experiments, false starts, and strategic retreats of major proportions. Finally, I suspect that the views listed above pay excessive attention to the intentions—expressed or attributed —of the communist leaders, and too little attention therefore to changing environmental determinants. The intentions forced on the leaders by circumstances usually are more important in their effects than the intentions with which they have initially set out. Moreover, the unplanned, unwanted, and unforeseen effects of a system's operations are too easily neglected when we concentrate on ideological or psychological determinants. My own summary of the outstanding functions of communism would stress the following preoccupations and results.

The outstanding function of communism seems to me to be entrepreneurship. In other words, the chief aim and/or effect of communism has been and still is the promotion of rapid economic growth and, more specifically, industrialization. Communism therefore functions as a substitute for the capitalist entrepreneur, who is weak or nonexistent in most of the countries where communism has come to power. The style of communist entrepreneurship is the crash program, i.e., a really desperate attempt to industrialize very quickly against seemingly overwhelming obstacles, such as economic backwardness, the absence of trained cadres, and a firmly rooted peasant way of life.

Any society engaged in a program of industrialization must face up to certain adjustments imposed by such a transformation: it must find the material resources needed for ambitious investments that do not promise immediate returns; and if the national economy is not to go into debt to wealthier nations, the consumers must make sacrifices for the purpose of releasing the required resources. It must also expect thorough changes in the social structure, in authority patterns, and in life styles, with all the pains and strains that such restructuring engenders. If industrialization is to be accomplished as rapidly as possible, in a crash program, then the price in strains and sacrifices becomes very heavy; the pace of transformation becomes hectic; a certain degree of irrationality creeps into the process; and the entire effort can be sustained only if it is organized, managed, and enforced by a dictatorial command which will not shrink from the most drastic means of enforcing its will. The history of the Communist World in general confirms these generalizations.

Let me restate this by saying that communism functions as a program of primitive accumulation necessary for the establishment of an industrial empire. This program has unwanted and unplanned consequences strikingly similar to the growing pains of (capitalist) industrialization in the West: mass misery and harsh exploitation for the laboring class; sharp social differentiation; the political disenfranchisement of the masses, despite a prevalent democratic rhetoric; and a repressive, puritan moral atmosphere.

One essential requirement of industrial society is a generally literate people with a large supply of highly educated specialists in a host of technical and managerial fields. Because communism has established itself predominantly in societies deficient on both counts, one additional function of communism has been to create or expand educational institutions for the purpose of wiping out illiteracy and rearing an educated elite possessing the many skills required in industrial society. Finally, communism attempts a thorough restructuring of all the citizens' minds and personalities so as to eliminate all traces of traditional thought and behavior patterns associated with the peasant way of life. The aim of this restructuring is to adjust people to life and work in a modern industrial setting, to acquaint them with machines and the machine age, with cities, modern hygiene, and the assumptions of modern science. Communists refer to this transformation as the cultural revolution. One might summarize the aims and effects of this revolution by arguing that one of the chief functions of communism is the forced modernization of traditional or semitraditional societies. In saying this, one has to be aware that the concepts of "modern" or "modernization" as well as "traditional" are controversial; and the communist definition diverges from definitions advanced by contemporary Western writers. Some Western writers might even argue that the very notion of forced modernization is self-contradictory, because the use of force is a traditional rather than a modern method of rule. Many communists would undoubtedly reply that without applying force complete modernization cannot be achieved because powerful traditional elements such as religion, peasant culture, tribal allegiances, and the like, cannot be eradicated otherwise.

One other function of communism is easily overlooked, because it is so obvious. Let me call this function "system-building." It is required in all societies which are the products of revolutions. All revolutions, in turn, can be divided into at least three distinct phases. The first phase is that of system-destruction. The second one usually is an interregnum marked by various kinds of disorder, false starts, failures, and retreats. The third is that of system-building. In this phase a new social order is, in fact, created and establishes itself.

This act of creation, again, entails a number of processes which the revolutionary (or, better, post-revolutionary) leadership must promote and which include society-building, i.e., the creation of a new social structure, a new system of political institutions, and new organizational forms which become standard for the society's entire organized and associational life. This effort can succeed only if it is accompanied or preceded by the primitive accumulation of authority and legitimacy, meaning a process by which the communist party and the entire new authority pattern it seeks to create come to be accepted as legitimate by the citizens. Since Communist Parties have either come to power as unpopular minorities or have managed to make themselves unpopular by some of the policies they pursued after coming to power, their need for legitimacy was desperate; and their reliance on terror as well as their commitment to total and unceasing indoctrination are indications of this desperation. Finally, system-building entails the creation and institutionalization of social traditions and social myths, which not only take the form of systematic and articulate "official" doctrine, but must also be seen in doctrinal taboos, i.e., in unmentionable topics glossed over or left out of the official ideology.

COMMUNISM AT A CROSSROADS

In one part of the Communist World, the principal aims summarized above have been achieved—industrialization, the cultural revolution, and system-building. We must therefore assume that the system of government and management, the authority relations, traditions, and assumptions developed and institutionalized by communist systems of the past have become obsolete. At least the communist way of life that is familiar to students of Russia and Eastern Europe could be explained as a social system attuned to the problems of primitive accumulation of industrialism and authority. Stalinism, to use the convenient label, is the rough politics of the crash program. In Eastern Europe, especially in countries already well industrialized, it is explained primarily by the openly exploitative relationship of the U.S.S.R. toward these countries: Stalinist methods were imposed in order to reduce these countries to helpless dependencies of the Soviet Union. Communism in Eastern Europe thus was dysfunctional rather than functional to the internal needs and developments of the countries concerned.

Since the death of Stalin it has become apparent that the Soviet Union has crossed the threshold of industrialization. Her social structure by now has become similar to that of Western Europe and North America. Her system of institutions and organizations is no less complex, its many component structures are no less interrelated than comparative systems and structures in the West. Her population is generally literate and includes a broad stratum of people with higher education and long experience in wielding authority. The Eastern European countries, in turn, are in the process of gaining a fair amount of independence. Moreover, the leaders of their Communist Parties appear to have become aware of the drawbacks of Stalinism, of crash programs, and of the entire style of rule associated therewith, drawbacks which are especially acute in countries that had traditions of individualism, self-government, and intellectual independence. But even in the U.S.S.R., where these traditions have been weak, the party may find it impossible to go back to the unchecked authoritarianism and terrorism associated with Stalin's style of leadership, because in succeeding with his crash program, Stalin created a social order so heterogeneous and interdependent, a people so much in need of a system providing for compromise, accommodation, and for the give-and-take of opinions and interests, that mere command, control, and brutal enforcement are no longer sufficient. Instead, communism in the Soviet Union and Eastern Europe today faces the task of developing rational management processes for keeping together and improving comparatively modern industrial societies. One might argue that during the crash program phase of communism political considerations outweighed economic ones. Or, using somewhat old-fashioned terms, one might say that in that early phase the state assumed supremacy over society, if only because a new society had to be fashioned. Now that this task is largely accomplished, the relationship is beginning to reverse itself, as the political system reverts to a more superstructural role.

In the communist political system's adjusting to this new role, one can probably expect several trends to manifest themselves with greater and greater persistency. One of these is an increasing sophistication in managerial processes, including the greater use of decentralization, market mechanisms, computers, permissiveness, accommodation, and wider participation on the part of the rank-and-file citizens. Further, we can expect the Communist World to rely more on rewards than on punishment, more on socialization than on coercion, in mobilizing its citizens for such participation and for useful work. Communist societies are likely to become more and more heterogeneous in their occupational structure; hence we must look forward to more obvious manifestations of interest group formation, with the possible consequence that the function of political authority may change more and more from sovereign command to interest aggregation and mediation. Finally, one can assume that the Communist World of Europe will be able and willing to improve the material welfare of all its citizens at an increasing rate. If in the past the Communist World has been preoccupied with the supply side of economic growth, its western half will be increasingly able to devote some attention to questions of demand and distribution.

These trends are sometimes summarized in the word "liberalization." Their strength varies from one country to another, depending in part on differences in national traditions or differences in national culture. Hence, in time, we must expect greater and greater national differentiation within the Communist World, depending on the rate and direction of change within each country. The strength of liberalizing trends also varies from one period to another in each individual country; nor is it equal in all fields of endeavor. Hence liberalization, if that is what we ought to call it, does not proceed at an even pace. Moreover, even without the evidence we have about strong resistance to these trends within the Communist World, we would have had to assume that several strong interests within this world are opposed to these tendencies and regard them as a threat to the communist order itself. Indeed, divergent conceptions of what the communist way of life is or ought to be, what structures and procedures, what style of rule and behavior, are most expedient or appropriate for it, are today contending with each other more openly than before in the European half of the Communist World. The strength and persistence of liberalization tendencies will depend on the outcome of these conflicts.

One reason that the conflict between conservative, authoritarian, or paternalistic trends, on the one hand, and reformist, liberalizing, democratic, or humanitarian trends, on the other, has become more open is the disappearance of ideological and political unity within the Communist World. This disappearance, in effect, dates from the death of Stalin. Out of the disintegration of what had looked like a monolithic communist bloc, two principal types of communist societies are emerging at the present time; they might be characterized as follows: on the one extreme, there are modern industrial communist countries quite capable of sustaining a respectable rate of economic growth and a standard of living comparable to that prevailing in Western Europe. On the other extreme, there are communist countries in which industrialization and modernization have hardly begun. For the former, the main problem is system-maintenance and management, for the latter, system-building and accumulation. These divergent orientations lead to divergence also in organization, practices, outlook, foreign relations, and style of life. These differences show tendencies of becoming so fundamental that the commonly professed allegiance to Marxist-Leninist ideology will no longer serve as a common bond. Indeed, because it must now become a bone of contention, the ideological heritage which all branches of communism share may exacerbate the conflicts between them and hasten the schism. As a result, the Communist World may soon be split into a western and a nonwestern branch.

COMMUNISM IN PERSPECTIVE

In my attempt to give a summary description of the Communist World, I have emphasized two comparisons, that with complex modern organizations, especially business corporations, and that with developing nations in general. According to the present chapter, communism appears very much as a function of economic, political, and cultural underdevelopment. It could then be defined as the application of the corporate pattern of entrepreneurship and management to modernizing countries. Having said this, one ought, perhaps, to bring out the differences that distinguish the Communist World from both the corporation and other developing nations. The principal difference from the corporation is easily stated: in the communist society, corporate patterns of organization and rule have been extended to the total social life, so that one might define communism as the corporation "writ large."[4] The difference between communism and other developing nations is less easily stated, though one might venture a few general observations. One would be that, on the whole, the countries of the Communist World have started from a somewhat higher level of development. At the time of the revolution they had a somewhat more industrial economy than, let us say, Ghana or Indonesia at the time of their emancipation from colonial rule. They had a more numerous and influential intelligentsia; and one might add that contacts with the West had been of longer standing and more intimate, and Western influence more significant. Another difference lies in the fact that Communist Parties have come to power in countries which already had national consciousness, whereas the newly emancipated former colonies, as a rule, have to engage in nation-building simultaneously with other aspects of system-building and economic construction. There is, in addition, the obvious ideological difference: the Communist World confesses its adherence to Marxism-Leninism; other developing nations do not, even though in fact their leaders may think along similar lines and may indeed often use the vocabulary of Marx and Lenin, whether they are aware of it or not. The question, as to whether the ideological differences are essential or, perhaps, merely ideological is exceedingly intriguing, but cannot be answered here.[5] Some scholars might add to this that communist countries have shown themselves on balance more efficient in attaining their objectives than other developing nations. I am not sure whether there is sufficient evidence to prove or disprove this assertion; and even if it is correct, one might visualize that in the future some other developing societies might outstrip the Communist World in this regard.

FURTHER READING SUGGESTIONS

Bromke, Adam, ed., *The Communist States at the Crossroads*. New York: Praeger, 1965.

Brzezinski, Zbigniew K., *The Soviet Bloc*. Cambridge, Mass.: Harvard University Press, 1960.

Dallin, Alexander, *et al.*, eds., *Diversity in International Communism*. New York: Columbia University Press, 1963.

[4] The expression is borrowed from Plato, who wished to explain the organic unity of the Greek *polis* and therefore described it as analogous to an individual human being, though in a larger framework or on a higher plane—hence the individual writ large.

[5] It would require a chapter in itself. I have tried to answer some of the questions I raise here in my article, "The Functions of Ideology in the Soviet Political System, *Soviet Studies* (January, 1966).

Daniels, Robert V., *A Documentary History of Communism*. New York: Random House, 1960.

————, *The Nature of Communism*. New York: Random House, 1962.

Gyorgy, Andrew, *Issues of World Communism*. New York: Van Nostrand, 1966.

Meyer, Alfred G., *Communism*. New York: Random House, 1960.

Seton-Watson, Hugh, *From Lenin to Khrushchev*. New York: Praeger, 1960.

Skilling, H. Gordon, *The Governments of Communist East Europe*. New York: Crowell, 1966.

Swearer, Howard R., and Richard P. Longaker, *Contemporary Communism*. Belmont, Calif.: Wadsworth, 1963.

Ulam, Adam B., *The Unfinished Revolution*. New York: Random House, 1960.

2

The Communist World:

Marxist Views

HERBERT APTHEKER

DIRECTOR, AMERICAN INSTITUTE
FOR MARXIST STUDIES

R. PALME DUTT

MEMBER, EXECUTIVE COMMITTEE,
COMMUNIST PARTY OF GREAT BRITAIN

A. ARZUMANYAN

DIRECTOR, INSTITUTE OF WORLD
ECONOMICS, ACADEMY OF SCIENCES
OF THE U.S.S.R.

AND OTHERS *

I. THE NATURE OF OUR ERA [1]

We live in a world that is constantly changing and progressing. Historical development is growing in pace and scope. . . . The half a century since 1917 has seen important changes in all spheres of man's material and mental creativity. In these decades the turbulent scientific and technical revolution has provided mankind with unprecedented opportunities to gain mastery over the forces of nature.

* Aptheker's contribution to this chapter was written especially for this book. The selections from Dutt's writings have been excerpted from his *The Internationale* (London, Lawrence & Wishart, Ltd., 1964), Chapter IV, and are reprinted here by permission of the author and of the publishers. The passages by Arzumanyan have been excerpted from his "The Contemporary World-Wide Revolutionary Process," *The Marxist Quarterly* (Summer, 1965), entire issue, and are reprinted here by permission of the publisher. Since the various parts of the Marxist section of this chapter have been taken from different sources, footnote credit throughout the section will be given in each case, so that each passage can be readily identified as to author and original source of publication.

[1] By Soviet economist N. Kolikov, translated from his "The Main Forces in the World Revolutionary Process Today," *Mirovaya Ekonomika i Mazhdunarodnye Otnosheniya* (No. 3, 1966), and distributed in English translation by the Soviet Embassy in Washington.

But the greatest changes have been in the social setup of the world. All you have to do is compare the political maps of 1917 and 1966 to see that the world has become different in the past half century. Fifty years ago capitalism ruled unchallenged. A small group of colonial powers considered it their "natural" right to order the lives of hundreds of millions of "natives." Any attempt by people in the colonies and semicolonies to throw off the burden of imperialist rule was brutally suppressed.

Today, however, one-third of mankind has already broken with capitalism and embarked on building a new society. There now exists a world system of socialist countries. The overwhelming majority of the colonies and semi-colonies have achieved political independence and are now working for economic independence; some have taken the path of noncapitalist development. The working-class and democratic movements in the capitalist countries have grown in size and strength. The communist movement has become broader, has been tempered, and today is a genuinely world movement. This has led to a qualitative change in the alignment and balance of class forces in the world arena, to an immeasurable increase in the power and intensity of the revolutionary process and to a substantial modification of its conditions and forms. . . .

II. THE WORLD SCENE 100 YEARS AGO [2]

Let us recall what the world was like in 1864, when the International Working Men's Association was founded. . . . At that time the bourgeoisie as a class had not yet exhausted its progressive role. Capitalism was still on the ascendant. The capitalist form of private ownership facilitated relatively rapid creation of productive forces that were incomparably greater than those of all the preceding social formations combined. Capitalism initiated an industrial revolution in a number of European countries and the United States of America, substituted machines for manual labor, created a world market and tore down the fences between national economies.

But the bourgeois form of ownership was an historically limited accelerator of social development due to the inherent contradictions it created. While stimulating the development of some aspects of social life, capitalism retarded and paralyzed progress in other aspects. Extravagantly, it squandered the wealth accumulated by society as a whole. Having passed its period of *sturm und drang,*[3] capitalism was no longer able to serve as an instrument of social advancement and acted as a brake on progress. It gave birth to its class antagonist, the industrial proletariat, a class destined to create a new society free from exploitation. As soon as the working class emerged on the

[2] By A. Arzumanyan (*see* footnote, p. 32 above).
[3] Storm and stress. [EDITOR'S NOTE]

arena of history and discovered its own strength, the bourgeoisie shed its revolutionary features and concluded a reactionary pact against the proletariat with the remnants of the old society—the feudal landowners, militarists and clergy—its adversaries of yesterday.

III. CAPITALISM IS THE LAST EXPLOITING SYSTEM [4]

Having developed its productive forces to an enormous extent, capitalism became a tremendous obstacle to social progress. It alone is responsible for the fact that the twentieth century, a century of colossal growth of the productive forces and of great scientific progress, has not yet put an end to the poverty of hundreds of millions of people, has not provided an abundance of material and spiritual values for all men on earth. The growing conflict between productive forces and production relations imperatively demands that mankind should break the decayed capitalist shell, release the powerful productive forces created by man and use them for the good of society as a whole.

Whatever the specific character of the rise and development of capitalism in any country, that system has everywhere common features and objective laws. . . .

Under capitalism, the basic and decisive means of production belong to the numerically small class of capitalists and landowners, while the vast majority of the population consists of proletarians and semiproletarians, who own no means of production and are therefore compelled to sell their labour-power and by their labour create profits and riches for the ruling classes of society. The bourgeois state, whatever its form, is an instrument of the domination of labour by capital.

The development of large-scale capitalist production—production for profit . . .—leads to the elimination of small independent producers, makes them wholly dependent on capital. . . . The economic laws of its development necessarily give rise to a huge army of unemployed, which is constantly replenished by ruined peasants and urban petty bourgeoisie. . . .

Capitalism, by concentrating millions of workers in its factories, socialising the process of labour, imparts a social character to production; nevertheless, it is the capitalists who appropriate the fruits of labour. This

[4] From the *Programme of the Communist Party of the Soviet Union, Adopted by the 22nd Congress of the CPSU, October 31, 1961* (Foreign Languages Publishing House, Moscow, 1961).

fundamental contradiction of capitalism—the contradiction between the social character of production and the private-capitalist form of appropriation —manifests itself in production anarchy and in the fact that the purchasing power of society falls short of the expansion of production and leads periodically to destructive economic crises. Crises and periods of industrial stagnation, in turn, are still more ruinous to small producers, increase the dependence of wage-labour on capital and lead more rapidly to a relative, and sometimes an absolute, deterioration of the condition of the working class. . . .

The process of concentration and centralization of capital, while destroying free competition, led in the early twentieth century to the establishment of powerful capitalist monopoly associations—syndicates, cartels, and trusts— which acquired decisive importance in the economy, led to the merging of bank capital and immensely concentrated industrial capital, and to intensive export of capital. The trusts, which encompassed entire groups of capitalist powers, began the economic division of a world already divided territorially among the wealthiest countries. Capitalism had entered its final stage, the stage of monopoly capitalism, of imperialism.

The period of a more or less smooth spread of capitalism all over the globe gave way to spasmodic, cataclysmic development causing an un-precedented growth and aggravation of all the contradictions of capitalism —economic, political, class, and national. The imperialist powers' struggle for markets, for spheres of capital investment, for raw materials and labour, and for world domination became more intense than ever. In an epoch of the undivided rule of imperialism, that struggle necessarily led to devastating wars.

Imperialism is decaying and moribund capitalism; it is the eve of the socialist revolution. *The world capitalist system as a whole is ripe for the social revolution of the proletariat.*

The exceedingly high degree of development of world capitalism in general; the replacement of free competition by state-monopoly capitalism; the establishment, by banks as well as associations of capitalists, of machinery for the social regulation of production and the distribution of products; the growing cost of living and the oppression of the working class by the imperialist state, and the immensely increased difficulty of the economic and political struggle of the proletariat; and the horrors, hardships, and ruination brought about by imperialist war have all made inevitable the downfall of capitalism and the transition to a higher type of social economy.

The revolutionary break-up of imperialism does not take place all over the world simultaneously. The uneven character of the economic and political development of the capitalist countries under imperialism leads to revolutions occurring at different periods in different countries. . . .

IV. THE PATH OF MARX AND LENIN [5]

One hundred years have passed since the foundation of the International Working Men's Association or First International. If we look back to the original foundation of the Communist League, the first international organization of communists, in 1847, and its declaration of programme, the *Manifesto of the Communist Party,* drafted by Marx and Engels and published in 1848, a distance of only 117 years, or less than twelve decades, separates us from that starting point.

A long road has been travelled in this short space of time—a mere moment, in terms of years, in the life-span of human development. During these years, the handful of tiny groups gathered in one corner of one continent in the Communist League has extended . . . to the present-day international communist movement of some ninety communist parties spread all over the world. . . .

Communist Parties lead the fortunes of their peoples in the victorious socialist revolution over one-third of the earth. . . . Half a century ago imperialism dominated the entire world. Today imperialism has become the minority sector of the world.

This change continues to go forward at an accelerating pace. The shift in the economic balance of the world moves every decade further in favour of socialism. The extension of the Socialist World, of the peoples in one country after another moving forward to mastery of their countries and socialist reconstruction through the leadership of their Communist Parties and the guidance of the principles of Marxism-Leninism, does not stop at the magic number of fourteen countries. The conditions are ripening in a number of countries, where the Communist Parties are already the leading parties of their peoples. Similarly the number of newly independent countries sweeps forward, as well as the resistance to the attempts of imperialism to maintain its hold in one guise or another or undermine the independence of the peoples who have won liberation. The final end of colonialism draws in view.

There is no parallel in history, or in prehistory for that matter, for this advance. . . . But this advance itself is only the expression of the transformation of the world in our time, the economic, social, political, scientific and technological transformation of the world from the last stage of the old social orders of class society to the transition toward a classless society based on the common ownership of the means of production. . . .

Marxism is no religion, but the expression of a rational scientific approach to the mastery of the real world and the laws of development of

[5] From R. Palme Dutt's *The Internationale* (*see* footnote, p. 32, above).

Table 2-1. Political Map of the World in 1919 and the Beginning of 1964

| | 1919 | | | | Beginning of 1964 | | | |
| | Area | | Population | | Area | | Population | |
	in millions sq. km.	*in percent*	*in millions*	*in percent*	*in millions sq. km.*	*in percent*	*in millions*	*in percent*
I. The world	135.3	100	1,777	100	135.3	100	3,240	100
1. the socialist world	21.7	16	138	7.8	35.2	26	1,134	35
2. the rest of the world	113.6	84	1,639	92.2	100.1	74	2,106	65
II. The major imperialist powers (USA, Britain, Germany-FRG, France, Japan, Italy) and their colonies	60.3	44.6	855	48.1	14.3	10.6	524.8	16.2
III, Colonies, semicolonies, and dominions	104.5	77.2	1,230	69.2	9.3	6.9	45.8	., 1.4
IV. Former colonial and semicolonial countries that became sovereign after 1919 (excluding socialist countries)					76.3	56.4	1,380	42.6

SOURCE: This table has been reprinted here from A. Arzumanyan's article in the Summer, 1965 issue of *The Marxist Quarterly*, p. 7 (*see* footnote, p. 32 above). It compares the situation at the beginning of 1964 with that of 1919. Two years earlier, before the 1917 October Revolution in Russia, the "socialist world" was, of course, nonexistent. [EDITOR'S NOTE]

human society. Communism and the extension of the world socialist system is no empire (the present acute and open differences between leading socialist countries is sufficient evidence of that), but the expression of the advance of the peoples all over the world to throw off the shackles of class and national oppression and build a classless society based on the common ownership of the means of production, capable of realizing on earth the aim of human brotherhood. . . .

The world has indeed changed during this little over a century. And it has changed along the lines and general direction indicated by the teachings and practical leadership of Marx and Lenin, not in the sense of any automatic fulfilment of some rigid scheme along a predetermined groove predicted by a magic conjuror, but in the entirely rational sense of development along the lines indicated by a realistic and scientific social theory, whose correctness has been proved . . . by the event, by the outcome, by practice. And the development along these lines has shown at the same time abundantly more variety, complexity, emergence of new forms, or shifts in the tempo of the time schedule, sometimes slower and sometimes quicker, than could have been within any human capacity to predict.

The world has moved along the general lines indicated by Marx and Lenin, and in a direction entirely opposite to all the assumptions of their contemporaries, whether the nineteenth-century statesmen and theorists who saw in the spread of pre-monopoly free trade capitalism the ultimate eternal outcome of human progress, or their successors, the apostles of imperialism, who saw in the various empires they were building the sublime supreme aim and highest form of human social organization. Now that all their theories have vanished into the dustbin, their disillusioned successors have fallen into a mood of black pessimism, cynical denials of the—in their view—obsolete and exploded nineteenth-century illusions of progress, or surrender to fatalist cyclical theories of history and of the inevitable decline of civilizations.

Marx, already in 1848, in the mid-nineteenth century, at a time when all the foremost contemporary political leaders, economists, or social theorists of capitalism were seeing in liberal free trade capitalism the ultimate highest outcome of human progress and the supposed eternal and immutable laws of political economy; or when the utopian socialists had envisaged the dream of a social order based on justice through common ownership, but had no more idea how to attain it than to appeal to the crowned heads of Europe: Marx already at that time laid bare the transient character of capitalism as a historical stage, with a beginning and an end and its own laws of motion, the last stage of class society preparing the conditions for its replacement. Marx showed how capitalism was creating its own gravedigger in the industrial working class; and how the working class, with the development of organization and solidarity in the daily struggle against capitalism, and with the development of political understanding, would advance to leadership of all sections of the working people to end the class rule of the capitalists and establish its own political power, the dictatorship of the proletariat, in order to wrest out of the hands of the capitalists the means of production and establish socialism, the first stage of the advance to the future classless communist society.

At that time Marx and Engels still anticipated that this advance to the socialist revolution would follow rapidly in the further unfolding of the democratic revolutions then impending in Western and Central Europe, and especially in Germany. But as soon as the failure of the democratic revolution of 1848 had been demonstrated in Western and Central Europe by 1850, Marx from 1850 onwards corrected this anticipation as erroneous and transferred his focus of the future of the revolution to a world scale in the unfolding of the battle against world capitalism. "History has proved us, and all who thought like us, wrong," wrote Engels frankly half a century later (in his Preface to Marx's *Class Struggles in France,* March 6, 1895) referring to the expectation of the socialist revolution in Western Europe in the period of 1848, and emphasising that capitalism had still at that time "great capacity for expansion" beyond Western Europe.

Marx by 1850 (in a letter from London on January 31, 1850, published in the *Neue Rheinische Zeitung*) was already stressing the significance of the world development of capitalism as narrowing the role of Western Europe to second place, predicting the change of the centre of gravity of capitalism to American capitalism displacing the supremacy of British capitalism; and further predicting that the Western European capitalist countries would fall into "industrial, commercial and political dependence" on American capitalism, unless they entered on the path of the socialist revolution.

While maintaining his close association with the advance of the working-class movement in the European countries, Marx was giving increasing attention to extra-European development.

Marx in 1850 (in the same letter) was already demolishing the myth of the supposed inevitable eternal conservatism of China, and was anticipating the future victory of the Chinese Republic when he declared that Western reaction, seeking to find a final bastion of reaction in China, might find instead inscribed on the Great Wall of China: "REPUBLIC OF CHINA: LIBERTY! EQUALITY! FRATERNITY!"

By the later eighteen-seventies and early eighties, during the years before his death, . . . (Marx) reached the conclusion that Russia now represented the vanguard of the revolution:

This time the revolution will begin in the East, hitherto the unbroken bulwark and reserve army of counterrevolution.

Marx, letter to Sorge, September 27, 1877

Russia forms the vanguard of revolutionary action in Europe.

Marx and Engels, 1882 Preface to the Russian edition of the *Communist Manifesto*

Lenin in 1902 gave the same perspective as Marx . . . had done, of the coming victory of the revolution first in Russia, and of the consequent international significance and vanguard role of the Russian revolution for the whole international working-class movement:

History has now confronted us with an immediate task which is more revolutionary than all the immediate tasks which confront the proletariat of any other country. The fulfillment of this task, the destruction of the most powerful bulwark, not only of European, but also, it may be said, of Asiatic reaction, places the Russian proletariat in the vanguard of the international revolutionary proletariat.

Lenin, *What Is To Be Done?*, 1902

. . . World development has continued to move forward along the lines indicated by Marx and Lenin. The Socialist revolution conquered first in Russia, the weakest link of the imperialist chain and the base of the most advanced vanguard of the international revolutionary working class, as predicted by Marx in his concluding years. . . .

Lenin in 1915 predicted that the victory of socialism might first come in a single country ("the victory of socialism is possible first in several or even in one capitalist country, taken singly"), and that in that case "the victorious proletariat of that country" would "organize its own socialist production" and confront the capitalist world, "attracting to its cause the oppressed classes of other countries" (*The United States of Europe Slogan*, 1915). . . .

No more difficult testing ground of socialism could be found than the one in which it first was tested—the Soviet Union: [6] economically backward, to begin with, and this backwardness intensified by the devastation of the First World War; mass illiteracy, mass hunger, mass superstition; a ring of hostility about her—blockade and intervention her portion. And always, "the penalty of being first," in Thorstein Veblen's words,[7] and being first in the most difficult, most decisive and most precedent-shattering undertaking yet to befall Man.

And then, the supreme test of World War II: some twenty million killed; about thirty million wounded; half the homes destroyed; half the cattle slaughtered; schools, libraries, factories gutted; whole cities disemboweled. But victorious; and then, despite hostility once more, despite frightful human error and crimes—still, on the unbreakable foundations of socialist organization and will—rebuilding better than before and forging ahead, with one of the fastest rates of economic growth in the world, and already the second industrial power, with clear possibilities of becoming the first, perhaps before this century has run its course.

The prediction of Marxism-Leninism, voiced in 1934, that if capitalism were to unloose a second world war, the outcome would see, not only the "complete defeat of the aggressors," but the disappearance of the old regime in a number of capitalist countries, "revolution in a number of countries in Europe and Asia" and "the destruction of the bourgeois-landlord govern-

---

[6] This and the subsequent paragraph are by Herbert Aptheker; the rest of section IV, again, from R. Palme Dutt's *The Internationale* (*see* footnote, p. 32 above).

[7] Thorstein Bunde Veblen (1857-1929); American economist and critic of orthodox, classical economics; especially well known among noneconomists for this book *The Theory of the Leisure Class* (New York, Macmillan, 1912). [EDITOR'S NOTE]

ments in those countries," [8] was once again proved correct by the outcome in the sequel of 1945, with the development of the people's democracies in Europe and the extension of socialism from one country to a world socialist system.

The historic victory of the second greatest socialist revolution, following the Russian socialist revolution, took place . . . as Lenin had predicted,[9] in China, with the final victory of the Chinese People's Republic in 1949.

Even since the 1960 Statement of the eighty-one Communist and Workers' Parties, defining the new world situation, and describing the advance of international communism and the extending victories of socialist revolution and national-liberation revolutions, the process therein described has gone further forward. The heroic resistance of the Cuban people, supported by the socialist countries, to the repeated offensives of American imperialism has been accompanied by the accession of Cuba to join the ranks of the new socialist states, and the announcement in 1961 of the decision to build a unified party on the basis of Marxism-Leninism. The victory of Algerian national independence in 1962, after a seven years war of liberation against French imperialism, has been a further landmark in the extending series of advances of national independence in many countries during these recent years.

At the same time the working-class movement has advanced in strength in the Western imperialist countries, together with far-reaching changes in economic, social, and political conditions. . . .

V. THE TANGIBLE FEATURES OF THE COMMUNIST WORLD

Human history covers more than three million years. This is a gigantic river of time and on its banks working people of all epochs yearned fervently for happiness, for equality and fraternity, for life without exploitation, without social and national oppression; they dreamed of a social system which would ensure equitable relations between peoples and countries.

This has been written about in books; it has inspired poems and songs

[8] The statement was made by Stalin in his Political Report to the 17th Congress of the CPSU (Communist Party Soviet Union) in 1934, quoted in part in Dutt's *The Internationale,* pp. 286-87. [EDITOR'S NOTE]

[9] In his last article, "Better Fewer, But Better," published in March, 1923, Lenin predicted that the development of the revolution in the three most populous countries of the world—Russia, China, and India—would prove decisive for the victory of world socialism. This issue is discussed, and the passage from Lenin's article quoted, in Dutt's *The Internationale,* pp. 182-83. [EDITOR'S NOTE]

[10] Condensed from A. Tkachenko, *Community of Fraternal People* (Moscow, Novosti Press Agency, 1966). Distributed in English by Soviet Booklets, Soviet Embassy, London, England.

which have come down to us through the generations. And no matter whether it was the faraway land of Utopia born of the imagination of Thomas More, or the fairy-tale City of the Sun conceived by Tommaso Campanella, or the paradise in far-off America described by Robert Owen, or the wonderful "dreams" created by Nikolai Chernyshevsky, they all depicted the Golden Age, the happy society of the future: a society in which there is no slavery or dependence, no poverty or lawlessness, a society in which all material blessings and spiritual wealth belong to those who create them. But these were only dreams—mankind knew not how to realize them, how to achieve a happy life. . . . The path to the new, radiant world was blazed by those great thinkers and fighters: Marx, Engels, and Lenin. They were the first in world history to show the working people the way to the most equitable society on earth, the first to determine the revolutionary forces destined to destroy the old world and build the world of socialism and communism.

Marxist-Leninist teaching lighted the nation's way to the realization of cherished aspirations. At first dozens and hundreds of people, and then thousands and millions, inspired by the ideals of communism, advanced to storm the old world. The Paris Commune, the Great October Revolution, the socialist revolutions in a number of countries of Eastern Europe and Asia, the Cuban Revolution—those are the most important historic stages in the heroic struggle waged by the international working class for the new world.

And that new world is already triumphant. We see it in the gleaming lights of thousands and thousands of construction projects, in the new schools and colleges that belong to the millions, in the flights of the space-ships *Vostok* and *Voskhod,* in the peaceful aspirations of the socialist community which are manifested in the call to exclude war from the life of mankind, in the call for the peaceful coexistence of the two social systems.

The socialist camp has become the centre of attraction for all the progressive forces in the world. There is no spot in the world today where the mighty influence of the great community of socialist countries does not make itself felt. This is only natural. Socialism best demonstrates its immeasurable advantages over capitalism, its triumphant march through the world, in the language of facts and figures through the experience of people's governments and people's management of the economy, through the new type of relations between countries.

It is evident from a comparison of the present political map with that of 1917 that socialism is no longer being built on a solitary island in the midst of the capitalist sea but on a vast area stretching from Cuba in the West to the Bering Strait and the China Seas in the East. The socialist camp occupies more than one-fourth of the land surface of the globe, while its population of roughly 1,134 million is 35.5 percent of the world's population.

The population of the socialist countries is more than double that of the big imperialist powers. This means that imperialism has lost forever its dominion over the greater part of humanity. The nations have chosen the highroad along which to advance, and its name is socialism.

The socialist countries' rate of economic development is a barometer showing the irresistible, ever-increasing force of world socialism. The countries of socialism are truly advancing with seven-league strides. The average yearly increase in industrial production is almost three times greater than in the bourgeois world. Whereas in 1955 the socialist countries accounted for 27 percent of the world production of the basic industrial goods, their share rose to 38 percent in 1964.

In the socialist countries unemployment has disappeared forever. The very word "unemployed" has become an anachronism, the same as "mill owner," "land-owner," and "money-lender."

The contrast in the cultural development of the two worlds is also striking. In the Socialist World illiteracy has been wiped out. Over 300 million people in the socialist countries are pupils or students enrolled in schools, institutions of higher learning, technical and agronomical courses, and schools and courses for raising qualifications.

Is it not significant that in Mongolia—a country where formerly 95 percent of the population could not read or write, illiteracy has been completely eliminated? Is it not significant that Mongolia has more students per ten thousand of population than many capitalist countries, including Japan, Italy, West Germany, and Austria? The same can be said of People's Bulgaria. As regards the development of culture, education and the health services, she has left her capitalist neighbours, Turkey and Greece, far behind. In Bulgaria there are 95 students to every ten thousand of population, whereas in Greece there are only 29, and in Turkey 25. . . . It can be said that not only the Russians but the people of all the socialist countries are living a rich spiritual life. This is only to be expected: culture, science, and art in those countries are now for the masses.

The transition to socialism and communism is accompanied by a constant improvement in the health services, and a reduction of the working day and the working week. It goes together with concern for lightening the work of mothers in every way, for providing security for pensioners and for bringing up a healthy, optimistic younger generation.

The contrast between the Socialist and Capitalist Worlds is most striking in the distribution of the national income. In the socialist countries the national income belongs to the working people—it is the public income in the full sense of the word and is distributed in the interests of society as a whole. *In the Soviet Union three-fourths of the national income is spent for satisfying the people's material and spiritual needs,* while the remainder is allocated for accumulation, that is, for expanding socialist production, as well as for defence expenditures and for other national and public needs.

Karl Marx wrote: *"Communism is real happiness for all mankind."*

In the socialist countries this happiness is being forged today, and many of its features are already discernible. It is to be seen in the rapid upgrowth of the economy and culture in the U.S.S.R. and other fraternal countries. It is to be seen in vitalizing internationalism whose banner is carried high by over a thousand million builders of the new world.

Communism which was once only a dream has become the greatest force of our time.

VI. CONFLICT AND THE FUTURE [11]

But, say the critics, how is it possible to speak at the present time of the triumphant advance of communism during the past century and a third, when at this moment the international communist movement is rent by a fierce internal controversy and ideological dispute threatening its unity and endangering the unity of the system of socialist states?

Certainly it is true that at the moment a very serious controversy has developed. Its highly polemical public expression has given great pleasure to the enemies of communism, who have been busily speculating, as they have always loved to speculate, on a "crisis of communism" and the impending break-up of the movement. It is also true that this controversy has taken on a character in some respects more serious than the previous very intense controversies which have accompanied the development of the communist movement, inasmuch as the theoretical and tactical controversy has become to some extent entangled with particular questions raised affecting relations between socialist states. . . .

This serious and dangerous situation has not yet at the time of writing been resolved by the international communist movement. Matters may even grow worse during the phase immediately ahead, before they improve. The controversy is still fluid and in motion, so that any attempt to treat it here would be out-dated before it could appear.

The very varied theoretical and basic tactical questions raised in the controversy (include): peaceful coexistence; the assessment of imperialism; the attitude towards nuclear war; the relationship of national liberation to the world socialist revolution; peaceful and nonpeaceful forms of transition to socialism; revisionism and dogmatism, and the relative weight of either danger at a given moment; the appraisal of the Twentieth Congress of the Communist Party of the Soviet Union [12] and of the vanguard role of the Communist Party of the Soviet Union; and the relationship between com-

---

[11] Sections VI and VII are reprinted from Dutt's *The Internationale*.

[12] At the Twentieth Party Congress in 1956, the famous secret session in which Khrushchev denounced Stalin took place. [EDITOR'S NOTE]

munist parties, and correct forms of procedure in the event of differences arising between communist parties. . . .

All serious communists throughout the world have always had and have the deepest affection and respect for the Soviet people, for the Great October Socialist Revolution, the pioneer of the world socialist revolution, and for the Communist Party of the Soviet Union, "the universally recognized vanguard of the world communist movement" (in the words of the 1960 Statement, agreed on by all communist parties). All have also the deepest affection and respect for the Chinese people, for the glorious Chinese People's Revolution, the second greatest socialist revolution, and for the heroic Communist Party of China, which has led to victory and is now leading in the construction of socialism one quarter of mankind, whatever the concern and questioning at the moment arising from some disturbing recent manifestations and expressions. All serious communists are concerned to do everything in their power to assist in the resolution of differences affecting the relations of the parties of the two leading countries of socialism, as of all socialist countries and communist parties, and for the promotion and strengthening of cooperation and friendship of the Soviet Union, the Chinese People's Republic and all socialist states, and of all communist parties. . . .

Grave as is the present phase of intense controversy within the international communist movement, exceeding any previous precedent, and serious as are the further dangers to which it could give rise, if present trends are continued and extended, it is necessary to see also this situation with some sense of perspective, and in relation to the long record of history of the international communist movement. The advance of the international communist movement over the past century and a third from the tiny handful of pioneers to one-third of the world has been no smooth and easy road. The record has been full of storms and conflicts, often fierce and embittered, no placid theoretical debates of disinterested observers, but shot through with personal passions and unsparing denunciations, sometimes even reaching a tornado height, and threatening to wreck the ship. Yet through every such phase the international communist movement has emerged in the end the stronger and the more united to achieve new triumphs. . . .

Whatever the ordeals which may still have to be passed through—and the present dangerous situation, as has been already noted, may grow worse before it grows better—there is every ground, in terms of a longer historical judgement, for firm confidence in the future of the international communist movement and of international communism; in the deep underlying bonds of friendship and cooperation of all socialist states; in the unity of the international communist movement; in the future triumph of communism throughout the world. . . .

The differences affecting the socialist countries . . . do not arise from any objective inevitable differences of interests, but are temporary subjective differences in the interpretation of those interests or of the most fruitful immediate steps in their fulfillment, and are capable of being resolved because of the basic identity of interests of the socialist economic system directed to the maximum development of production, cooperation and interchange for the material and cultural advance of their peoples, and because of the basic community of aims of communists throughout the world.

VII. TOWARD THE GOAL OF COMMUNISM

Modern world conditions, with the accelerating speed of communications and the technique of large-scale production beating against the limitations of old state barriers, and with the destructive power of new weapons transforming the questions of major war or peace, have brought home to all the necessity of internationalism. On the other hand, the simultaneously intensified antagonisms of rival property interests, by no means softened or diminished with the advance of science and technology and the scale of productive and trading operations, but, on the contrary, tremendously sharpened with the advance to the present giant super-monopolies and state monopoly concentrations fighting one another with every weapon in their armoury block the path to the fulfillment of the international aims which modern economic and political conditions demand.

Under these conditions the League of Nations or United Nations, whatever the dreams of some of their founders may have been, become either distorted to the role of instruments in imperialist power conflicts or, at the best, a useful international forum (weakened so far by the unjust exclusion of China) for the expression of the opinion of the participating nations. . . .

What is the solution? Many nonsocialist observers, and also some professed socialists, speak of the sovereign "nation-state" as an out-dated anachronism, or demand the establishment of an "international police force" to maintain international "law and order." They fail to take into account that the international "law and order" which they assume as requiring to be upheld is in fact the "law and order" of imperialist property relations extending their grip over two-thirds of the world, and that the sharpest conflicts and wars which have arisen in modern conditions have arisen when the newly independent nations have sought to take over the assets of the imperialist monopolies (Suez, Iran, Indonesia, Cuba). Thus their "international police force" becomes under these conditions, not a plan for solving the problem of internationalism, but a plan to establish an international gendarme to protect the interests of imperialism.

What, then, is the solution? It is evident that the problem of internationalism, of replacing international conflicts and wars by international cooperation, cannot be treated as an abstract political problem. It cannot be separated from the social and economic conditions of the modern world which give rise to international conflicts.

In the short term, given the present parallel existence of imperialism and socialism in the world, together with the increasing number of newly independent nations which are seeking to move towards socialism, the necessary immediate practical path of solution is the policy of peaceful co-existence to replace the policies of the cold war: that is, the promotion of peaceful relations between the countries of socialism and capitalism; recognition of the right of every people to choose their own social system without external interference; no export of revolution and no export of counter-revolution; endeavours to end the arms race, ban nuclear weapons and work towards the aim of disarmament; steps to promote international trade and economic cooperation.

Such a short-term solution would provide the most favourable conditions for advancing to the only final long-term solution. For the final long-term solution requires the elimination of the rival property-owning interests which are the breeding ground of international conflict and war. So long as capitalism and imperialism exist, the economic ground exists for international conflict and war. Only when the majority of the peoples of the world have advanced to the basis of socialism, alongside the completion of national liberation in all countries, and the rivalries of private and class property ownership have been eliminated, will the conditions have been reached for the realization of the age-old dreams of internationalism, of lasting peace and cooperation of the peoples. The goal of communism, however difficult still the struggles in reaching it, represents the fulfillment of internationalism, of human brotherhood.

Marx prophesied, in the Address of the General Council of the First International on July 23, 1870, on the occasion of the Franco-German war:

A new society is springing up whose International role will be *Peace,* because its national ruler will be everywhere the same—*Labour!* The pioneer of that new society is the International Working Men's Association.

Marx, *The Civil War in France,* 1871

At the same time in that same immortal work Marx warned that the working class

to work out their own emancipation, and along with it that higher form to which present society is irresistibly bending by its own economic agencies, will have to pass through long struggles, through a series of historic processes transforming circumstances and men. They have no ideals to realise but to set free the elements of the new society with which the old collapsing bourgeois society itself is pregnant.

Already at the end of *The Communist Manifesto* Marx had declared that the downfall of capitalism and the future victory of the working class was "inevitable." When he said "inevitable" he by no means implied some fatalist theory of history, as if the life of human society were to be regarded as some mechanism pursuing a predetermined course independent of human will and action. The entire life-work of Marx, his ceaseless effort and devotion and expenditure without reserve of all his health and strength in the cause of the working class and communism, proved the opposite. His affirmation of "inevitability" was his affirmation of confidence in humanity, in the capacity of the working people to overcome the obstacles and find their way forward, through whatever errors and "long struggles" and "historic processes" on the way, to the only solution which could answer the problems posed by the breakdown of the old social order and "set free the elements of the new society."

Every step along this path of more than a century, from the handful of pioneers to the victory of the working class and communism over one-third of the world, has only been won by the conscious will, the organisation, the limitless devotion and sacrifices, and the heroism of millions and millions of human beings, inspired and guided by the teachings of Marx and Lenin, and united by comradeship in service to a common cause, the cause of the future of human brotherhood, of communism.

Thanks to the efforts of those who have gone before, the path now opens out more bright with promise than ever before. But the menace from the final explosions of the old dying social order is also more urgent than ever. The time for the transition from capitalism to socialism was already due in terms of material conditions, and of the ending of the progressive role of capitalism, when nineteenth century capitalism passed into monopoly capitalism ("moribund," "parasitic," "decaying" capitalism, as Lenin called it). Delay in the readiness of the subjective factor, represented by the working class movement in the leading imperialist countries, has already cost two world wars, the miseries of mass unemployment, fascism, and now the menace of nuclear war. All the new marvels of modern science in the twentieth century, the releasing of nuclear energy or the magic wand of the latest chemical discovery and techniques, should have belonged to the era of socialism, speeding the path to abundance for all. The fact that these new powers, appropriate only to socialism, should have come into the grip of the out-dated monsters of the monopoly capitalist jungle is producing in our time new horrors, abortions, and menaces on a scale never before known.

For this reason the absolute and unqualified confidence of communists in the future is not, and can never be, a blind, empty, facile optimism. The fulfilment of the great possibilities of our epoch depends on human consciousness and human effort. Therefore at the present time, to meet the needs of the present epoch, and to defeat the dangers which are obvious to all, the call sounds all the more urgently for renewed effort and activity in the cause of the working class and the peoples and of peace. The call sounds for the extension of political consciousness, inspired by the teachings of Marx and Lenin, among ever wider sections in all countries; to build up the unity and strength of the working class and democratic and national-liberation movement; to build up the unity and strength of the international communist movement; and along this path to speed the day when the divisions and conflicts of class society shall belong to the past, and *the Internationale shall be the human race.*[13]

VIII. IS MARXISM-LENINISM APPLICABLE TO MID-TWENTIETH-CENTURY AMERICA? [14]

Sometimes it is held to be perfectly clear that whatever may be true in other parts of the world, in the United States social development has reached the point where the Marxist-Leninist analysis is simply irrelevant. Hence, it is concluded, persistence in adherence to Marxism-Leninism for an American must reflect either extreme mental backwardness, perverseness, or allegiance to a hostile foreign power.

But *is* Marxism-Leninism irrelevant to modern America? I think not. The essential purpose of Marxism is the elimination of exploitation and oppression. In our era this means the elimination of monopoly capitalism, racism, colonialism, impoverishment, and war.

Were there no such conditions and relations there would be no revolutionary philosophy, no revolutionary movement, and no Marxism. Said Marx, in commenting on the ideas and organization of socialism, just after the Paris Commune had been drowned in blood: "The soil out of which it grows is modern society itself. It cannot be stamped out by any amount of carnage. To stamp it out the Government would have to stamp out the despotism of capital over labor—the conditions of its own parasitical existence."

Even here, in the United States—in Golden America, blessed with its continental size, its inexhaustible resources, its repeated invigoration by the coming of millions of people from the four corners of the earth decade after decade, its separation from the continual wars ravaging Europe, Asia and Africa (wars from which the U.S. grew richer), its parasitic relationship to the so-called underdeveloped peoples of the world (as in Latin America, peoples who are underdeveloped because they have been overexploited),

[13] "The Internationale" is the international anthem of the world communist movement. In one English language version the last line reads, "The International will be the human race." Another English version of the song reads, "The International Party shall be the human race." [EDITOR'S NOTE]

[14] Sections VIII and IX are by Herbert Aptheker (*see* footnote, p. 32, above); the last paragraph of section IX is from the translation of N. Kolikov's article (*see* footnote, p. 32, above).

even here and still today, the four historic crosses of mankind—impoverishment, illiteracy, inequality, and war—lie heavily upon its back:

Impoverishment? At least thirty-five to fifty million Americans—and according to the National Bureau of Economic Research, as many as seventy-seven million—today lie in this zone of hell, in the grip of poverty, in the ceaseless pursuit of sufficient food and raiment to provide nourishment and keep out the cold. Meanwhile, millions of workers who desire employment find themselves totally without work. And the impact of automation has just begun!

Illiteracy? Today, states the National Education Association, eleven million adult Americans are quite illiterate, and functional illiteracy afflicts perhaps twice as many; [15] there are, indeed, seventeen states today where over ten percent of the adult population can neither read nor write.

Inequality? For this, percentages are not necessary. When it comes to the poison of racism, anti-Semitism, and chauvinism our nation is "outstanding"; its supremacy in this regard is challenged only by the Republic of South Africa. No civilized human being can read the factual record as presented in the 2,000 pages of the 1961 and 1963 Reports of the U. S. Civil Rights Commission without wincing; and no American who loves his land and takes pride in the dream of this country can read those Reports without tears of shame and outrage.

And War? The militarization of our society, the pervading and perverting impact of war preparations and conduct upon our economy, the scandal of the Bay of Pigs,[16] and the atrocity of the interventions in the Dominican Republic and in Vietnam—complete with napalm bombs, phosphorus shells, chemical sprays, "beneficent" gases, and torture—these need only be mentioned. The escalated warfare, to be sure, has provided some relief from the unemployment discussed above, since many hundreds of thousands have now found temporary employment in the production of ever more "efficient" means of destruction, while other hundreds of thousands have been made to take these means of destruction across the oceans to kill and be killed on distant shores.

It is not a communist, but rather the most honored historian of the Western World who writes in a book recently published by the Oxford University Press:

[15] Functional illiteracy refers to those who have a record of school attendance (and figures on illiteracy in the U.S. are based on absence of such a record) but who can actually neither make sense out of the written or printed word, nor themselves write.

[16] The Bay of Pigs (Bahía de Cochinos) was the place in Cuba where, on April 15, 1961, an invasion force of 1,600 Cuban refugees landed in an attempt to overthrow the Castro regime. Trained in the United States and Central America, the troops were transported in old U.S. merchant ships and escorted most of the way by U.S. Navy destroyers. Prior to the invasion, American planes bombed three military air bases in Cuba. The invading forces were completely routed within four days; an estimated 400 of the invaders were dead or missing, practically all others surrendered. [EDITOR'S NOTE]

America is today the leader of a worldwide anti-revolutionary movement in defense of vested interests. She now stands for what Rome stood for. Rome consistently supported the rich against the poor in all foreign communities that fell under her sway; and, since the poor, so far, have always and everywhere been far more numerous than the rich, Rome's policy made for inequality, for injustice, and for the least happiness of the greatest number.

We have quoted the words of Sir Arnold Toynbee, from his *America and the World Revolution* (New York, Oxford University Press, 1962, pp. 92-93).

In the face of this kind of reality and these kinds of policies, *is* a basically radical critique of the United States as it is today outmoded? Is it irrelevant? This quite apart from its being labeled "un-American" or "subversive" or "seditious"—words which no American who knows the best traditions of his country, and has the barest inkling of its history, from the days of the Jeffersonians to those of the Abolitionists, from the days of that old rebel, George Washington, to those of that old jailbird, Eugene Victor Debs,[17] can hear as applied to himself without bristling and without contempt for the slanderers.

On the contrary: I think, in the face of this kind of reality, any effort to curb the fullest and most radical critique and analysis of our society is the most serious disservice to our country; if anything is un-American, it is "the black pall of fear" that hangs over intellectual life and discussion in our country as a result of over a decade of McCarthyism and McCarranism.

When socialism comes to the United States, it will come and can come only because the overwhelming majority of American people want it and want it so passionately that it can no longer be kept from them. In no other way can Socialism come to this land. This is a fundamental commitment and principle of the Communist Party of the United States. The charge that this Party is an agent of a foreign government is, therefore, a lie.

And as to the rest of the human race: The majority of mankind, still, as the Reports of the United Nations tell us, are chronically hungry, are quite illiterate, live under conditions of inequality and indignity and carry the fearful burden of paying for past wars and preparing for new ones. In our era, technical and productive developments and social organization have reached the point where none of these need be endured any longer. Knowledge of this momentous fact is out now; the peoples of the world know that they *can* end their suffering and that they *can* build a life of fruitfulness, creativity, fraternity, and peace. It is this knowledge—and not thermonuclear energy—which is the greatest force in the world today; and *this better life can no longer be denied them.*

[17] Eugene Victor Debs (1865-1926), American labor leader; five times presidential candidate on the Socialist Party ticket. Frequently imprisoned for his labor union and political activities, Debs, in 1920, polled close to one million votes, campaigning from a jail cell. [EDITOR'S NOTE]

IX. A FINAL WORD

The attractive power of Marxism-Leninism is shown not only in its political advances and in its material, cultural and social victories. The power is shown also in the fact that it is the outlook embraced by more people throughout the world than any other single outlook. This is true, not only for those countries where the socialist transformation is or has been in process. It is true elsewhere: consider the fact that nearly two million people belong to the Communist Party in Italy where one voter in four—some seven million in all—voted Communist in the last (1963) election; and hundreds of thousands are Party members in countries as distinct one from the other as is Japan from France.

Moreover, the power of this outlook is shown in the fact that it has attracted many of the greatest geniuses ever to live, from Dreiser to Du Bois, from Picasso to Aragon, from Siquieros to Neruda, from O'Casey to Brecht, from Nexo to Seghers, from Caudwell to Needham to Bernal. One need not agree with these people; but to declare them criminals is sheer madness.

The power is shown, too, in the homage paid its qualities by every scholar of distinction in the past fifty years—including those who for one reason or another have not found its views satisfactory. Not to go beyond the United States, those who have publicly acknowledged their great debt to Marxism and have spoken of its supremely penetrating nature include the greatest figures associated with American universities: John R. Commons, Franz Boas, E. R. A. Seligman, Thorstein Veblen, Charles A. Beard, Albion W. Small, and James Harvey Robinson.

Surely no American scholar of recent times was more revered than the late Carl Becker of Cornell University. In his final book, published posthumously, *Freedom and Responsibility in the American Way of Life* (New York, Knopf, 1945, p. 104), we find these words:

. . . the differences between Fascism and Communism in Germany and Russia are important. Communism rests upon a reasoned philosophy of history and politics that was propagated for fifty years before it was established in Russia. Fascism was scarcely more than an invention of Mussolini and Hitler to serve their personal ambitions, and it is supported by a philosophy, if you call it that, hastily devised after the event. Taking the two philosophies as standards for judging the two systems, the differences are radical. Communism is democratic—that is, the dictatorship is regarded as temporary, a necessary device for carrying through the revolution, to be replaced ultimately by a government of, by, and for the people. Fascism is anti-democratic—the dictatorship and the suppression of individual liberties are regarded as permanent. Communism is international—it preaches the brotherhood of man and the equality of nations; Fascism is anti-international—it denies the equality of nations as well as the equality of individuals, and preaches the supremacy of the nation or of the master race. Communism is pro-intellectual —it declares that social progress rests on knowledge and that knowledge can be attained only by the disinterested search for truth. Fascism is anti-intellectual— it regards science and the search for truth as of no importance except insofar as they can be used for the attainment of immediate practical ends.

Marxists view world development in an optimistic light. The world has changed essentially in the past half-century, and the main social trend of the changes leaves no doubt that a mode of production based on man's exploitation of man will soon be a thing of the past. The struggle of the world socialist system, of the revolutionary forces of the national liberation movement, and of the international working class against imperialism will inevitably lead to the triumph of socialism the world over.

FURTHER READING SUGGESTIONS

This list of "Further Reading Suggestions" was compiled by Herbert Aptheker.

Aragon, Louis, *A History of the USSR*. New York: McKay, 1964.

Budish, J. M., *Is Communism the Next Stage?* New York: International Publishers, 1965.

Burns, Emile, *An Introduction to Marxism*. New York: International Publishers, 1966.

Dimitroff, George, *The United Front: the Struggle Against Fascism and War*. New York: International Publishers, 1938.

Dobb, Maurice, *Soviet Economic Development Since 1917*. New York: International Publishers, 1948. Revised and enlarged edition, 1966.

Dutt, R. Palme, *The Internationale*. London: Lawrence & Wishart, Ltd., 1964.

Fundamentals of Marxism-Leninism: A Manual, second revised edition. Moscow: Foreign Languages Publishers, 1963.

Lewis, John, *The Life and Teaching of Karl Marx*. New York: International Publishers, 1965.

Programme of the Communist Party of the Soviet Union, adopted by the 22nd Congress, CPSU, October 31, 1961. New York: Cross-Currents Press, 1961.

Shakhnazov, G., *et al.*, *Man, Science and Society*. Moscow: Progress Publishers, 1965.

II

The Union of Soviet
Socialist Republics:
The Great Experiment

ARCTIC OCEAN

Moscow

SOVIET UNION

MONGOLIA

KOREA

IRAN

CHINA

Area
(in square miles)
8,649,538

Population
(mid-1967 estimate)
238,792,000

Almost half a century has passed since our homeland set out on the path of socialist development.

It was a difficult and unexplored path. Today, the Soviet Union is a mighty socialist power that is advancing together with other socialist countries toward our common great goal.

For all its victories our country is obliged to the wise guidance of the Leninist Party, its unshakable fidelity to Marxism-Leninism, its ability always to rely, as Vladimir Ilyich [Lenin] said, on a most wonderful force—the force of the workers and the peasants.

ALEXEI N. KOSYGIN
CHAIRMAN, COUNCIL OF MINISTERS
(PREMIER), U.S.S.R.

The U.S.S.R. has always stood, and will continue to stand for the peaceful co-existence of states with different social systems, on the basis of complete equality and non-interference, and at the same time, has always been and will go on being, an irreconcilable opponent of imperialist aggression and interference in the affairs of other countries and people.

LEONID BREZHNEV
GENERAL SECRETARY, CENTRAL COMMITTEE
COMMUNIST PARTY OF THE SOVIET UNION

INTRODUCTION

"TWO GENERATIONS AGO PEOPLE DEBATED THE QUESTION OF WHETHER a Socialist economy could possibly work. History removed the question from the agenda. The last generation changed the question to whether the Soviet economy could work at all efficiently. That question has also been answered. My discussion takes for granted that the Soviet economy is reasonably efficient. . . ." Thus testified Joseph S. Berliner before the Joint Economic Committee of the United States Congress in 1959.[1]

Indeed, whether one approves or disapproves of the Soviet system, it is no longer possible to deny that a society constructed along lines indicated by Marx, Engels, and Lenin can not only survive but can achieve considerable progress. Surely the Soviet Union, in her half a century of existence,

[1] Joseph S. Berliner, "Managerial Incentives and Decisionmaking: A Comparison of the United States and the Soviet Union," *Comparisons of the United States and Soviet Economies* (Washington: U.S. Government Printing Office, 1959), Part I, p. 356.

has proven it. The precise accomplishments and shortcomings of the
Soviet system and the hopes it holds or fails to hold for its people are
matters taken up by the contributors, Marxist and non-Marxist, to this
chapter. But there is no denying that in a relatively short period of time that
nation of formerly poor and largely illiterate peasants has become an economic and military power second only to that of the United States, and
that one third of the world's population has followed the general path originally charted by the "first socialist state." With another third of the world's
people as yet uncommitted but by no means uninfluenced by the Soviet
example, Khrushchev's challenge to the West, in the days when he was
Soviet premier, has not lost any of its significance:

Let us prove in practice whose system is better. This is our appeal to the statesmen of capitalist countries. Let us compete without war.

The non-Marxist view on the Soviet Union has been contributed by
Samuel Hendel. A Columbia University Ph.D., Hendel has published
widely not only on the Soviet Union but also on issues dealing with the
American political system. *Basic Issues of American Democracy,*[2] a book he
co-edited, is now in its fifth edition and has sold over a quarter of a million
copies. In the Soviet area, *The Soviet Crucible,* now in its third edition, is
probably his most widely known publication.[3] He has also co-edited (with
Randolph L. Braham) and contributed to a 1967 symposium volume, *The
U.S.S.R. After Fifty Years: Promise and Reality.*

Hendel has lectured on Soviet affairs throughout the United States.
The recipient of a Ford Faculty Fellowship and of a grant from the Inter-
University Committee on Travel Grants, he has visited the Soviet Union
three times, the last, in the summer of 1966. He has held Visiting Pro-
fessorships at Columbia University and at Claremont Graduate School.
At present, he is Chairman of the Academic Freedom Committee of the
American Civil Liberties Union, on the Council of the American Political
Science Association, and he holds the academic positions of Professor (former
chairman of the Department) of Political Science and Chairman of the
Russian Area Studies Graduate Program at the City College of the City
University of New York.

The Marxist view to this chapter has been especially written for publication herein by three young Soviet social scientists, Yuri Krasin, Vladimir
Sukhodeyev, and Georgi Shakhnazarov. The first two hold the degree of

[2] Hillman M. Bishop and Samuel Hendel, *Basic Issues of American Democracy*
(New York, Appleton-Century-Crofts, 1965).
[3] Samuel Hendel, *The Soviet Crucible* (New York, Van Nostrand, 1967).

candidate (the approximate Soviet equivalent of the American Ph.D.) from Leningrad State and Moscow State University respectively; the last is a graduate of Azerbaijan State University. The editor wishes to express his gratitude to the Soviet Embassy in Washington and to the Novosti Press Agency in Moscow for having made the arrangements for this contribution.

3

The U.S.S.R.:

A Non-Marxist View

SAMUEL HENDEL *

PROFESSOR OF POLITICAL SCIENCE AND
CHAIRMAN, RUSSIAN AREA STUDIES GRADUATE PROGRAM,
THE CITY COLLEGE OF THE CITY UNIVERSITY OF NEW YORK

In my view, the Union of Soviet Socialist Republics is a complex inter-penetration and amalgam of many forces which include Marxist ideology, the compulsions of the practical and expedient, the quest by Soviet leaders for personal and national power, the persistence and continuity of the old Russian conditions, traditions and mores, and the recalcitrance of the human condition. It is, in short, a unique historical phenomenon, at one and the same time, in significant respects, Marxist, non-Marxist and anti-Marxist— and, as such, it defies monistic interpretation and characterization. What is more, the Soviet system, in nearly fifty years of history, has to its credit some truly noteworthy accomplishments and successes and, at the same time has been responsible for some great failures and near disasters.

These statements are made not to create some artificial or mechanical balance but because they correspond to the reality which neither Soviet apologists, in some respects, nor many Western Soviet critics, in others, are prepared to recognize or accept. In support of these propositions, it will be useful to begin with a brief description of the historical background.

SETTING AND HISTORICAL BACKGROUND

The U.S.S.R. had an estimated population of 234 million on January 1, 1967. In 1959, according to the official census, its population was 208.8 million—

---

* This contribution has been written especially for this book, but it is also being published in substantially the same form in Samuel Hendel and Randolph L. Braham, eds., *The U.S.S.R. After Fifty Years* (New York, Knopf, 1967).

of whom 55 percent were women and 45 percent men. The disproportion is largely attributed to the massive loss of male lives during World War II.

The U.S.S.R. covers an area of over 8.5 million square miles, extending across one-sixth of the surface of the globe, and is more than twice the size of the second largest country, China. Its land which runs to some 800 miles north of the Arctic Circle stretches south to the borders of China, Afghanistan and Iran, and west from the Pacific Ocean to the Baltic and Black Seas. In general, the country lies so far north that Yalta, at the southern tip of the Crimea, is approximately the same latitude as southern Minnesota.

With much of its territory a vast plain lacking natural frontiers—its borders add up to a length of well over 30,000 miles—Russian history for centuries was an almost continuous series of wars of invasion and expansion. As consequences, as V. O. Klyuchevsky wrote, "The state swelled and the people grew thin"; and serfdom at a time when it was already being abolished in western Europe continued to develop in Russia, so that the country could be organized to meet the exigent demands of war and each village be held communally responsible for money and men.

The Russian Tsar was an autocrat of unlimited power long after a series of checks upon absolutism had developed in western Europe. No representative National Assembly met in Russia between the seventeenth and twentieth centuries. The Revolution of 1905 led to the promulgation of a Constitution and provision for a Duma, or elected National Assembly, which convened in 1906 but the Duma was reconstituted and made less representative soon after the revolutionary tide had ebbed. Even so, when it raised some serious and embarrassing questions, it was suddenly and arbitrarily dismissed.

The church and the nobility with rare exceptions were docile or willing instruments in the hands of the Tsar. No Tsar went to "Canossa" to kneel in the snow and beg forgiveness of a Russian pope. No Russian ruler yielded effective authority English monarchs were compelled to grant in Magna Carta, the Bill of Rights and Petition of Rights. The Renaissance, the Reformation, the English, French and American Revolutions, each in its own way affirming the dignity and worth of the individual with vast consequences for Western society, had little contemporary impact upon Russia. Illiteracy, superstition, monarchical cruelty or obtuseness in unparalleled degree characterized old Russia.

The Russian people, to be sure, had gained some experience in a form of self-government through the *mir,* or village commune, an institution of peculiarly Slavic origin, in existence from at least the sixteenth century. Operating through a village assembly and elected officials, the *mir* had considerable authority over the peasant household and was responsible for manpower, taxes, the uses, allotment and repartitioning of lands and the admission of new members.

Similarly *Zemstvos,* first established in 1864, served as elected district and provincial Councils, agencies of local self-government, with the obligation to keep roads and bridges in repair, look after primary education and sanitary affairs, and take measures against threat of famine. However, fearing that even such limited authority posed a threat to autocratic power, imperial officials in 1890 curtailed the role and activity of the *Zemstvos.*

Also constituting a challenge to autocracy and contributing to the enlightenment of the Russian people, were the amazing creative awakening and ferment in the nineteenth century which produced such great poets as Pushkin and Lermontov, such extraordinary novelists as Tolstoy, Dostoevsky, Turgenev, and Gogol, a host of remarkable musicians, artists, scientists, historians and, not least, a radical intelligentsia, many of whom contributed to and inspired—and some of whom lived to witness—the March and November revolutions of 1917.

Notwithstanding these moderating forces, in the twentieth century Russia was steeped in backwardness and autocracy; it was a semi-Asiatic and barbaric despotism (to use a favorite phrase of Lenin's) which proclaimed the monarch as an unlimited autocrat obedience to whom was ordained by God himself. The Russian people were in large measure lacking in literacy, understanding or appreciation of free elections, parliamentary institutions, and civil liberties. In 1917, as such "fortress of reaction," as Engels had called it, Russia certainly was infertile soil for the establishment of a political *democracy.* In this connection Harold J. Laski wisely wrote, "A people, as every profound revolution has gone to show, must grow into the use of political freedom. It cannot plunge into its full employment directly after a long immersion, amid manifold disasters, in a semi-barbaric and wholly reactionary despotism." Similarly in the early years of the twentieth century, as an overwhelmingly agricultural country without a highly developed industrial base and a mature and powerful proletariat, Russia was unripe for a *socialist* revolution. And for many years Lenin shared this view, believing as the Marxists generally did, that Russia would first have to go through a phase of further capitalist development producing "the gravediggers" of capitalism before it would be prepared for proletarian revolution and socialism.

However, the fundamental and historic backwardness and inequities of Russia's political, economic, and social structures and, more immediately, the privations of war, the inequalities of burdens, the incompetency and corruption of the imperial court, military inefficiency, and widespread agitation culminated in March, 1917, in the collapse of Tsardom. And, in the months that followed, the failure of the Provisional Government, an essentially broad coalition, to assuage the land hunger of the peasants and end a war, so stained with imperialist purposes and Russian blood, created the massive dissatisfaction and disaffection that made possible the Bolshevik seizure of power in November, 1917, and the establishment of a so-called dictatorship of the proletariat which made the transition toward the building of a socialist state.

THE SOVIET POLITICAL SYSTEM

According to Marx and Engels, the destruction of capitalism would bring about the dictatorship of the proletariat, that is, "the proletariat organized as the ruling class," and "establish democracy." This, explained Lenin, while involving suppression of the bourgeoisie would at the same time lead to "an immense expansion of democracy" for the proletariat, that is to say, "democracy for the vast majority of the people." All officials without exception would be subject to election and recall. And from the time of its taking power, the proletarian state, as an instrumentality of force in the hands of the vast majority directed against a small minority, would begin to wither away until, after a protracted period of time, there would exist only a stateless, classless society.

More specifically, the dictatorship of the proletariat, as Lenin, the Bolsheviks and Marxists generally conceived of it *before* the Bolshevik seizure of power in November, 1917, would have permitted all leftist parties to compete for the support of the masses. No Marxist then thought of the dictatorship of the proletariat as equivalent to the dictatorship of one party and certainly not of any one group within a party. It is true that Lenin, with specific regard to Russia, "amid the gloom of autocracy," opposed the use of broad principles of democracy in the organization of the Russian socialist party in the *preparation and making* of the revolution. But for many years he was convinced that Russia, as a backward, agricultural country, *after* the revolution, would be ready only for a bourgeois, capitalist phase of development and probably would be governed by a coalition of parties, representing the proletariat, peasantry and sections of the bourgeoisie. Lenin, for example, had rejected the Parvus-Trotsky formula which had called for a minority dictatorship of the proletariat in Russia.   While after April, 1917, he came closer to accepting this formula, the fact is that even the revolutionary seizure of power in November, 1917, was in the name of the Soviets in which several parties were represented.

Under Lenin, however, in the years that followed, the Bolsheviks suppressed all other working class and peasant as well as bourgeois parties and their press and, in addition, outlawed all organized "factions" within the Communist Party itself. Lenin, to be sure, had proposed or agreed to these measures in the face of war, civil war, intervention, and desperate economic circumstances. And while he lived, he and his ideas were openly criticized and attacked at Party congresses and conferences; on occasions, he was even outvoted.

In any event, whatever the explanation, the dictatorship of the proletariat became under Lenin the dictatorship of the Communist Party and at times of the Politburo, a small group of Party leaders, while under Stalin it degenerated from a dictatorship of a small group of Party leaders into as thoroughgoing a dictatorship of one man as modern history has offered. While circumstances and conditions may explain if they do not justify the concentration of power in Lenin's day, there is no similar explanation or justification for Stalin's dictatorship.

SOVIET SOCIALIST "DEMOCRACY"

In 1936, at the very apogee of Stalin's power, the present Soviet constitution was adopted and proclaimed by him to be "the only thoroughly democratic constitution in the world"; as one Soviet writer put it, "a million times more democratic than that of the most democratic bourgeois republic." The Soviet people, asserted Khrushchev, "are the freest of the free in the world," and this view continues to be echoed by Soviet leaders and writers to this day.

The whole question of Soviet "democracy" might perhaps be dismissed with the statement that these affirmations rest on a particular definition and that the U.S.S.R. is free to define democracy any way it pleases. But it is not a question of semantics. The concept of democracy corresponds to one of the deepest and noblest aspirations of mankind and has great attraction and appeal throughout the world. It is well to consider, therefore, whether the Russian claim can be supported by any meaningful, reasonable and consistent definition of democracy—non-Marxist or Marxist.

To begin with, no honest observer could seriously maintain that Soviet practice conforms to the criteria suggested in the West, for example, by Ernest Barker, one of Britain's leading political philosophers, who wrote that democracy

is not a solution, but a way of seeking solutions—not a form of State devoted to this or that particular end (whether of private enterprise or public management), but a form of State devoted, whatever its end may be, to the single means and method of determining that end. The core of democracy is choice, and not something chosen; choice among a number of ideas, and choice, too, of the scheme on which those ideas are eventually composed. . . .

And, to make those choices meaningful, as Professor Robert M. MacIver has insisted, it is a necessary condition of democracy that opposing doctrines remain free to express themselves, to seek converts, to form organizations, and so to compete for success before the bar of public opinion.

If these "Western" standards are not applied, what then *are* the bases upon which the claim of the Soviet regime to democracy is made to rest? Allegedly of particular importance are the guarantee (In Article 125) of the Soviet Constitution of freedom of speech, press, assembly, and street processions and demonstrations with the proviso that these rights are "ensured" by placing at the disposal of the working people printing presses and other material requisites for their exercise.

But the fact is that the very provision granting these rights imposes the limitation that they must be exercised "in conformity with the interests of the working people, and in order to strengthen the socialist system," judgments resting, of course, not with the proletariat or with the people themselves but with the Party or, more accurately, with the Party leaders.

Even before these constitutional guarantees of freedom of speech and related freedoms were adopted, *Pravda,* on June 2, 1936, warned that:

He who makes it his task to unsettle the socialist structure, to undermine socialist ownership . . . is an enemy of the people. He gets not a scrap of paper, he does not set foot over the threshold of the printing press, to realize his base designs. He gets no hall, no room, no cover to inject poison by word of mouth.

And, of course, the Party continues to exercise pervasive control over press, radio, television, and other media of information and influence within the U.S.S.R.

A second basis upon which the U.S.S.R. predicates its claim to democracy is the widespread participation of its people not only in formal state elections but in the running of factories, farms, and enterprises. Soviet writers have boasted that the turnout at the polls is much higher than in any other non-socialist country and that their representatives can "in all justice be called the elect of the people, because all the electors, with scarcely any exception, vote for them."

Now it must be conceded that on what Sir John Maynard years ago called "the lower planes of public affairs" there is a "kind of democracy which is altogether *sui generis*" in the sense that factories, farms, and enterprises are run under the continual criticism of workers who freely express opinions and make suggestions. What is more, workers' dwellings are managed by committees chosen by and responsible to them. And it is true that on occasion the Party invites widespread public discussion of policies under consideration. Recent cases in point were the national debates over a new family law and new model rules for collective farms. But to suppose that this enables the Soviet people to change its rulers without force or the violation of law is plainly untrue. Furthermore, there is a clear and vital distinction between general freedom of criticism and of choice and public discussion of policies selected, submitted, delimited and ultimately decided from above.

As for almost unanimous approval of the single slate of candidates offered to the Soviet voters, these "ritualistic exercises in unanimity," as they were called by a largely friendly observer of the Soviet scene, must inherently be viewed with suspicion. But, how is it possible, Soviet writer V. Denisov asks, "to force the people of a huge multi-national state to vote against their own will and interests, when there is universal and equal suffrage by secret ballot (whose existence none deny)?" "The question alone," he maintains, "demonstrates the absurdity of such allegations."

It may be asked in turn, how is it possible to explain that in the 1938 election to the republican Supreme Soviet, 99.8 percent of the Volga Germans went to the polls, of whom 99.7 percent voted for the official list of candidates, while three years later the entire population was accused of harboring "tens of thousands of deviationists and spies" and deported *en masse* for disloyalty? How explain, in general, that although in the course of World War II seven nationalities were deported *en masse* for disloyalty their votes in favor of the official list in the elections to the Supreme Soviet in 1937 were stated to have been well in excess of 90 percent?

Nor is the further argument of Soviet writers that "the genuine freedom of Soviet elections consists first and foremost in the fact that candidates are nominated by the workers themselves, from among themselves" any more persuasive. It is true that Article 141 of the Soviet Constitution vests the right to nominate candidates for all Soviets in "public organizations and societies of the working people: Communist Party organizations, trade unions, cooperatives, youth organizations and cultural societies." However, while in theory this makes possible a number of candidates, in all elections thus far held for the Supreme Soviet (including the one in 1966) the name of only one candidate has appeared on the ballot in each constituency. What is critical, therefore, is obviously the process of elimination of nominees. And this process designed to assure "dependable" candidates, it is clear, is carried on by and through the Communist Party which is declared by the Constitution (Article 126) to be "the leading core of all organizations of the working people, both public and state," and "the vanguard of the working class."

The leadership of the Communist Party, in turn, although theoretically constituted on the basis of free elections in ascending hierarchies, in fact represented at the height of Stalin's power a virtual dictatorship of one man, and in more recent times continues to reflect a marked concentration of power. With rare exceptions, since Lenin's death the leaders at the top of the hierarchy have been able to control and limit the discussion of policy at all lower levels and in all media, and determine or control the selection of personnel for all important positions. There is a vast difference, as Plekhanov once pointed out, between the dictatorship of the proletariat and of a group.

Another basis upon which the U.S.S.R. claim to democracy is advanced is that under the leadership of the Communist Party it has, in fundamental and far-reaching respects, served the interests and advanced the well-being of the Soviet peoples. By turning the means of production into the property of the people, by destroying exploitation, by eliminating poverty and unemployment, the Soviet peoples, it is maintained, have achieved *real* freedom. In this view, the existence of a democracy is determined, as G. F. Aleksandrov wrote, "by the substance of the policy pursued by the state, by whether this or that policy is carried out in the interests of the people, in the interests of its overwhelming majority, or in the interests of its minority."

It cannot be gainsaid that, under the domination of the Communist Party, the U.S.S.R. has made great advances in industrialization, in education, in cultural areas, and in the eradication of many forms of discrimination and inequality characteristic of the Tsarist period. Concomitantly, particularly in the process of rapid industrialization and collectivization, great hardships and burdens were imposed upon the Soviet people. But important as the benefits conferred and hardships imposed are for other purposes, they have little or no relevance to the existence or nonexistence of *political* democracy in the Soviet Union. The essence of democracy, in any meaningful sense, must surely lie in self-government rather than in service to the interests of the people (although it is of course probably true that in the long run self-government alone will provide good government). If democracy does not involve self-government then the term not only loses all connection with its historic connotations but may be reduced to a manifest absurdity to describe the most thoroughgoing dictatorship provided only that it is benevolent or enlightened (or, perhaps, only claims to be so). What is more, to deny or denigrate self-government as the essence of democracy, would be, as has been shown, to do violence not only to conceptions of capitalist democracy but to *Marxist* conceptions of socialist democracy as well.

But we are told that because of the "great concord" of the Soviet peoples and in the absence of hostile or antagonistic classes there is no need for Western indicia of self-government since "there are no grounds for the existence of several parties, and therefore for the existence of freedom of such parties in the U.S.S.R." "The Party and the people in our country are as one," said Khrushchev, "so why do the Soviet people need other parties? Or are they to be created especially for the people in capitalist countries who are not satisfied with the socialist system?" The Soviet people, Soviet writer D. Zemlyansky tells us, "are all united in a common purpose: the construction of a happy classless society, communism."

It is revealing, when a measure of opposition or dissent is permitted to find expression in the U.S.S.R., how quickly the notion of a "great concord" is dispelled. But even assuming the absence of antagonistic classes in the U.S.S.R. and a great concord on Marxist *ends,* is it really possible to argue in light of the known facts of Soviet history that at all times the Soviet people agreed on *means?* Were all "as one" on the tempo of industrialization, on "socialism in one country," on aid to World Revolution, on the Nazi-Soviet pact, on the dissolution of the Comintern, and on official attitudes toward religion, art, and literature? Did not (and do not) good socialists disagree among themselves about these and myriad other questions—especially in light of occasional sudden and drastic shifts of policy—without finding any legal means to express dissent, except on those occasions when invited from above? The answers to these questions are in part given by the *official* denunciation of the wanton purges of the 30's based, concededly, in good part on nothing more than honest disagreement with Stalin.

It remains to deal with the most recent conception of socialist democracy in the U.S.S.R. According to the New Program of the Communist party, adopted in October, 1961 (only the third formal program in the history of the Party), the U.S.S.R., which "arose as a state of the dictatorship of the proletariat has in the new, present stage turned into a state of the entire people, an agency expressing the interests and will of the people as a whole." This development, it is maintained, involves a comprehensive extension and perfection of socialist democracy, including active participation of all citizens in the administration of the state and management of the economy. And, it is contemplated, "As socialist democracy develops further, the agencies of state power will gradually be transformed into agencies of public self-government."

Parenthetically, in relation to the question of the continuity of Marxist theory in Soviet practice, it must be said that the whole conception of "a state of the entire people" is alien to Marxism and quite possibly anti-Marxist. In the Marxist view, the state arose with the rise of antagonistic classes and is *necessarily* an organ of domination and oppression of one class by another; the existence of the state, to cite a passage from Engels quoted approvingly by Lenin, "is tantamount to an acknowledgment that the given society has become entangled in an insoluble contradiction within itself, and it has broken into irreconcilable antagonisms, of which it is powerless to rid itself." With the disappearance of classes, Engels added, the State too will inevitably disappear. The integral connection between the existence of the state *and* antagonistic classes was proclaimed in the second program of the Communist Party, adopted in 1919, as follows:

In contrast to bourgeois democracy, which concealed the class character of the state, the Soviet authority openly acknowledges that every state must inevitably bear a class character until the division of society into classes has been abolished and all government disappears.

Now, it is officially maintained, as we have seen, that there are no longer hostile or antagonistic classes in the U.S.S.R. Why then the state? The Soviet Union has explained the failure of the state to wither away by the fact that it continues to live in a predominantly nonsocialist and to a marked extent hostile, world. However, whatever the objective necessity for the U.S.S.R., in the absence of class conflict, to maintain its panoply of state power, its continuance is clearly inconsistent with basic Marxist theory and assumptions.

In any event, it is abundantly manifest that "the state of the entire people" is not intended to interfere with the hegemony, power, and control of the Communist Party. The New Party Program, which proclaimed this stage, added that it "is characterized by a further *rise in the role and importance of the Communist Party* as the leading and guiding force of Soviet society." (Italics in original.) And that such role is not to be limited to criminal, parasitic, and pro-capitalistic elements is evidenced, to cite an important example, by continuing close control (despite some relaxation) over the press and the arts. Speaking to the 23rd Party Congress in 1966, Brezhnev went to special pains to assert that the Party is "unswervingly guided by the principle of party-mindedness in art, a class approach in the evaluation of everything that is done in the field of culture."

And it is clear that there is no intention to allow open, public presentation of opposing positions nor factional organization within the Party. Khrushchev, on his ouster in 1964, for example, was afforded no opportunity to reply to his denunciation in *Pravda* for "harebrained scheming, immature conclusions, hasty decisions, actions divorced from reality, bragging, phrasemongering, and commandism." Of course, this was no worse than the fate meted out by Khrushchev to the so-called Anti-Party group in 1957, which included Malenkov, Molotov, and Kaganovich, who were subjected to even worse vilification without opportunity to respond.

THE WIDENING SCOPE OF CONTROVERSY

On the other hand, since the death of Stalin in March, 1953, it cannot be doubted that there have been some highly significant changes in the U.S.S.R. which, while they do not amount to a thoroughgoing democratization of Soviet society, do represent a substantial liberalization and widening of the scope of permissible controversy and dissent. These changes are reflected in virtually every facet of Soviet life including the economy, law, science, literature and art. Proposals for reform of economic practices and procedures have been widely reported in the West so I shall cite only some other illustrations.

With respect to the Soviet legal system, for example, despite the reimposition of harsh criminal penalties in 1961 and 1962 for serious economic offenses, there has been a far-reaching and genuine liberalization of both substantive and procedural law including the elimination of the use of terror in legal guise, and of punishment by analogy, i.e., by reference to a law proscribing a similar act; curbs on the powers of the security police, the uses of confession testimony, and searches and seizure; and some extension of the right to counsel prior to trial.

In scientific discussions the president of the Soviet Academy of Sciences, M. V. Keldysh, has condemned "the monopoly position" of T. D. Lysenko and his followers who with Party support for a long time dominated Soviet genetic investigation and imposed their views with great damage to scientific inquiry. So also Soviet physicist Peter Kapitsa took to task some Soviet philosophers who "dogmatically applying the method of dialectics proved that the theory of relativity was without foundation" and rejected cybernetics as a "reactionary pseudo-science."

Expression of literary ferment, to refer to only a few dramatic illustrations, is to be found in the publication *within the U.S.S.R.* of: the memoirs of Ilya Ehrenburg, which revealed that although many had known of Stalin's abuses they had seen no alternative but to remain silent and live "with clenched teeth"; Alexander Solzhenitsyn's *One Day in the Life of Ivan Denisovich,* an understated and thus all the more powerful story of life in a Soviet concentration camp; Viktor Nekrasov's *On Both Sides of the Ocean* and *A Month in France,* unusually balanced accounts of his visits to Italy, the United States, and France; and, not least, the poetry of the outspoken and courageous anti-Stalinists typified by Yevgeny Yevtushenko's "Stalin's Heirs," with its appeal "To double, to triple the guard . . . so that Stalin may not rise, and with Stalin, the past. . . . Here I mean by the past the ignoring of the people's welfare, the calumnies, the arrests of the innocent."

It is true that in the years after Stalin's death there have been some swings of the pendulum involving greater restraint (as well as latitude), of which the Sinyavsky-Daniel trial is a case in point, and that the Party retains its hegemony and the legal basis with which to curb dissent. It is still a crime, according to Soviet law, to carry on "agitation or propaganda" with the object of undermining or weakening state power or to disseminate or even possess materials of such defamatory nature. But reinstitution of systematic and pervasive terror, to assure the virtually total outward conformity and uniformity that marked long periods of Communist Party rule, seems to me extremely unlikely for a variety of reasons.

The Soviet people know the massive, wanton, and often senseless cruelty which so poignantly affected so many of their lives, and are likely to resist its recurrence. What is more, they—and particularly the youth among them—have breathed some of the intoxicating air of greater freedom and developed expectations of greater benefits (material, cultural, and political) that they will not willingly forego. In an important sense, too, the leadership has staked its own future, against internal and external pressures, on its anti-Stalinist position. But apart from concern with self-preservation, no doubt many of the new leaders recoil from the reimposition of the rule of terror as a matter of principle and, in any event, as inexpedient if the creative energies and initiative of the Soviet people are to be fully released.

Then, too, while the Soviet leaders may be unimpressed with appeals for greater freedom from cold war and ideological opponents, they must concern themselves with the opinion of neutrals and, even more assuredly, with that of allied Communist parties. A striking illustration is the late Italian Communist leader Palmire Togliatti's call, published in September 1964 (in the U.S.S.R. as well as abroad), for "open debates on current problems" and for greater attention to overcoming the "restrictions and suppressions of democratic and personal freedom introduced by Stalin." Subsequently, in October, 1964, the summary dismissal of Khrushchev from all positions of party leadership evoked the comment from Togliatti's successor, Luigi Longo, that "The manner in which this change in the summit of the Soviet party and state occurred leaves us preoccupied and critical." Similar concern was expressed by Party leaders in France, Hungary, and Poland.

It is, I believe, true, too, that the leadership which came to power with the ouster of Khrushchev shares power *collectively* to an extent largely unparalleled in Soviet history. It is possible, of course, that in this instance, as in the past, collective leadership will prove only to have been a brief prelude to the emergence of a single peerless *vozhd;*[1] but it appears to me dubious that in the foreseeable and predictable future—barring a great catastrophe—any one man could arrogate to himself the plenitude of power of a Stalin or even of a Khrushchev. For one thing, each ouster, with its revelation of prior abuses, makes it more difficult to cloak a new leader with the necessary charisma and mantle of infallibility. For another, any attempt at organized and massive terror of the kind on which Stalin relied to curb all opposition, real, potential, and imagined, would undoubtedly meet with great resistance.

In all these circumstances, I conclude that while it is incorrect to suggest that political democracy in any thoroughgoing sense (Western or Marxist) exists in the U.S.S.R., a return to a prototype of Stalinist totalitarianism and terror seems to be excluded. What is more, at and near the top of the Party, governmental and other hierarchies, there has been some diffusion of power and responsibility; and, at lower levels, increased participation and activity by the Soviet people in public affairs. In general, as Professor Frederick C. Barghoorn has written, "there has recently been an encouraging revival of rational and empirical thinking in many fields," and there has developed "the rudiments of a free, critical public opinion" which, though shackled, is "almost unimaginable when measured by the Stalinist yardstick." The U.S.S.R. continues to retain and foster slogans and appeals toward a more far-reaching and more genuine socialist democracy. Hopefully, in the coming years, the Soviet people will imbue the slogans and appeals with greater substance and reality.

THE STRUCTURE AND CONTENT OF SOVIET INTRA-NATIONAL RELATIONS

One of the proudest boasts of the U.S.S.R. is that "it has solved the nationality problem—completely and finally." While this is unquestionably a gross exaggeration, the U.S.S.R. must be credited with great achievements in the educational, cultural, and economic development of its far-flung areas of mixed

[1] Leader. [EDITOR'S NOTE]

populations and national minorities—estimated as 194 distinguishable races, nationalities and tribes in the 1926 census and as 126 in the 1959 census— who speak some 125 different languages or dialects and adhere to 40 different religions.

It must be remembered that Tsarist governments, in good part, had attempted to deal with national minorities by a policy of repression and forcible Russification. The written use of non-Russian languages was discouraged and sometimes forbidden. Outlying areas were left undeveloped and largely treated as fit only for exploitation; their populations were frequently steeped in ignorance and superstition. Tsarist officials often thought it expedient to sow national hatred and discord among them and at times even to organize or condone pogroms against particular minorities.

Appraisal of contemporary Soviet policies and practices affecting national minorities, in my judgment, must proceed from a recognition of this background and from two standpoints, political and nonpolitical.

FEDERALISM AND POLITICAL EQUALITY

In formal structure, the U.S.S.R. is declared by its Constitution to be "a federal state, formed on the basis of a voluntary union of equal Soviet Socialist Republics," of which there are 15. The national legislature, the Supreme Soviet, "the highest organ of state power," is a bicameral body "with equal rights" for the two houses consisting of "The Soviet of the Union," to which delegates are elected throughout the U.S.S.R. purely on a population basis, and "The Soviet of Nationalities," with a specified number of deputies from each Union Republic, Autonomous Republic, Autonomous Region, and National Area.

Soviet writers, in maintaining that a genuine and advanced type of federalism prevails in the U.S.S.R., emphasize the coordinate legislative power of the Soviet of Nationalities and point out, as did A. Denisov and M. Kirichenko in *Soviet State Law* published in 1960, that the Soviet Republics enjoy "the right of nations to self-determination including the right to secession and the formation of independent states."

In reality, since the Communist Party, throughout the U.S.S.R., in both theory and practice, is a highly centralized body which, as early as its second Party congress in 1903, strongly repudiated the federal principle of organization (rejecting autonomy for any national group), and is the source of all important legislation, "federalism," in the sense of political independence or autonomy, has been from beginning to end a pretense. The fact is that repeatedly over the years national boundaries have been altered (e.g., the transfer of the Crimea from the Russian Soviet Federative Socialist Republic (R.S.F.S.R.) to the Ukraine in February 1954, and the absorption of the Karelo-Finnish Soviet Socialist Republic into the R.S.F.S.R. in July

1956), the division of powers modified, and whole populations uprooted, without resort to any "federal" procedure of decision-making.

As for the constitutional "right" of secession, it obviously has no meaning without the right of advocacy; and such advocacy has been considered a counter-revolutionary crime in the U.S.S.R. Many hundreds if not thousands of officials, teachers, and writers, at the very least have been expelled from the Party or lost their positions, and at worst have been imprisoned or executed on charges of bourgeois nationalism, a term of opprobrium automatically applicable to anyone seeking the separation of any nationality from the U.S.S.R.

On the other hand, however devoid of real content *political* federalism in fact is, it cannot and should not be denied that, in many important non-political respects, Soviet treatment of its national minorities has been far-sighted and forward-looking.

FEDERALISM AND SOCIAL EQUALITY

Article 123 of the Soviet Constitution provides that "Equality of rights of citizens of the U.S.S.R., irrespective of their nationality or race, in all spheres of economic, government, cultural, political, and other public activity, is an indefeasible law." It makes any restriction on such equality "as well as any advocacy of racial or national exclusiveness or hatred and contempt" punishable by law.

In support of these principles basic to Marxism and civilized society the Soviet Union, with an occasional glaring exception, has utilized its media of education and persuasion—schools, books, press, journals, radio, television, and mass organizations—to underscore the essential equality of all men and to undermine national and racial prejudice. Bigotry, to be sure, dies hard, and it would be fatuous to suppose that it no longer exists in the U.S.S.R.; but it cannot be denied that official policy vigorously combats it.

Additionally, apart from preaching equality, in practice, in certain basic areas of Soviet life, substantial equality of all peoples and races has been achieved. Literacy has been brought to all the nationalities of the U.S.S.R., including about 50 for whom a written language had first to be developed. Overall literacy was raised from 51 percent in 1926 (it was less than 30 percent at the end of the Tsarist period) to 98.5 percent in 1959 (when the last official census was taken). Particularly in the "backward" areas, the level of elementary, secondary, and higher education has been dramatically raised. For example, in the territory of the five Central Asian Republics, regarded as among the most backward under Tsarism, in 1914-15 there were only 136,000 pupils in the elementary and secondary schools or about one percent of the number of such pupils in the whole of Russia, but by 1955-56 these schools had an enrollment of 3.59 million, a 25-fold increase. This brought the total to about 13 percent of the whole, a figure corresponding to the area's proportionate population. And, whereas before the Revolution institutions of higher learning were virtually nonexistent in this area, by 1955 such institutions had an enrollment of 155 thousand students, or about 9 percent of the total for the U.S.S.R. In 1914 there were only 400 students in the elementary-secondary schools in the whole of Tadzhikistan; in September 1965 the number had reached 535,000. Similarly, while in the pre-Revolutionary period the territory of present-day Uzbekistan had not a single institution of higher education, 154,000 students were enrolled in such institutions in September, 1965.

In addition, the evidence shows that, generally speaking, other educational and cultural facilities, including theaters, sportstadia, clubs, libraries, newspapers, journals, radio and television stations, have been provided on the basis of equality or relative equality. Similarly, medical attention has been made widely available throughout the U.S.S.R.; so that, for example, in 1961 in Turkemia there were 17 doctors per 10,000 population; well in excess of the number found in many parts of the United States.

In the process of industrialization and overall economic development, it appears to be true, too, that there has been little or no significant discrimination in favor of the Great Russian area. On the contrary, it is fair to say that the allocation of investment for economic development had often involved (because of initial backwardness) disproportionate benefits to the outlying regions; so that Armenia, for example, once one of the least is now one of the most advanced economic areas in the U.S.S.R.

Now it is true that some imbalances favorable to the Russian Republic continue to exist. For example, in 1960 according to official Soviet figures there were 19 college-trained specialists for every 1000 inhabitants in the R.S.F.S.R. but only 9 per 100 among the Kazakh, Kirghiz and Turkmen people and only 8 among the Tadzhiks and Uzbeks. Similarly, official statistics reveal that in 1962 in the R.S.F.S.R. the output of electric power was over 2000 kilowatt hours per inhabitant but only 513 among the Tadzhiks, 555 among the Byelorussians, and 598 among the Turkmen.

These continuing imbalances, however, while they appear to suggest some favoritism for the Russian Republic, may be explainable in good part by the inherent difficulties involved in massive equalization programs, and by legitimate concern for economic efficiency and defense needs which do require some concentration of resources and efforts.

In sum, speaking generally, the conclusion is warranted that the U.S.S.R. has afforded its minorities a large measure of equality of treatment in education, economic opportunity, cultural and social benefits—always, to be sure, within the context of and limitations imposed by the Soviet formula, "national in form, socialist in content."

THE SPECIAL CASE OF THE JEWS

The Jews, like other officially recognized nationalities in the Soviet Union, for many years enjoyed cultural autonomy. In the 1930's and into the 1940's there were numerous Yiddish theaters, newspapers, and journals, several *thousand* writers, poets, and actors producing and performing in the Yiddish language, the largest network of Yiddish schools and the only Jewish institution of higher learning in the world. In predominantly Jewish areas even some local Soviets conducted their proceedings in Yiddish.

With the development of the campaign against "cosmopolitanism" in the late 1940's, virtually every distinctive institution and facility of Jewish cultural life was destroyed, and thousands of Jewish writers and actors were imprisoned (many of whom were subsequently executed). The campaign against the Jews culminated in the charge in January 1953 that a number of prominent Jewish doctors had been engaged in a plot to kill and had actually killed important Soviet leaders. (While some non-Jewish doctors were also named, emphasis was placed on the Jewish "conspirators.")

On the death of Stalin in March, 1953, the Jewish doctors' plot was promptly and officially exposed as a fabrication from beginning to end. Nonetheless, very little indeed has been done to restore Jewish cultural institutions. And this continues to be true despite the fact that according to the 1959 official Soviet census, 2,268,000 persons declared themselves to be Jews, of whom 472,000 named *Yiddish* as their native tongue—which in the context of nationality development in the U.S.S.R. means for many, particularly of the older generation, their *only* spoken and written language.

The failure to restore Jewish cultural facilities has been the subject of severe criticism by many leading communists throughout the world. To cite one example, in October, 1964, the editor of *Political Affairs,* the theoretical journal of the Communist Party of the United States, while denying that official anti-Semitism exists in the Soviet Union, nevertheless pointed out that "the restoration of Yiddish cultural institutions admittedly falls considerably short of what existed prior to 1948." Specifically, he noted that "the publication of books in Yiddish has so far been limited to a small number of volumes. There are no Yiddish newspapers other than the *Birobidjaner Shtern*.[2] Nor are there any Jewish newspapers in Russian or other languages. The state theater in Moscow, headed by Mikhoels, has not been restored. No schools or classes or even textbooks in the Yiddish language exist."

By way of contrast, it is noteworthy that the Volga Germans, removed *en masse* from the Soviet borderland in 1939, have nonetheless been accorded opportunities for a full cultural life in their native language. And

[2] This is a triweekly published in a very small edition and circulated locally in an area remote from the large centers of Jewish population.

consider that in 1963 alone Soviet presses produced 90 books for the Maris (1959 census population 504,000) and 117 for the Yakuts (population 236,000) in their own tongues. Parenthetically, Poland, another communist land, with no more than 25,000 Jews, has a daily newspaper published in Warsaw in Yiddish, a Yiddish theater, and a thriving Jewish cultural life.

In the face of these facts, it is clearly impossible to accept the official Soviet explanation (as many communists outside the Soviet Union have recognized and admitted) that the Jews have been linguistically and culturally assimilated and have no further need for separate institutions.

EGALITARIANISM IN GENERAL

A fundamental, theoretical "end" of Marxism is the realization of a thoroughly egalitarian society. It was Marx's view that in the socialist phase, the economic system would provide payment to its workers "proportioned to the labor they supply," and equality would consist "in the fact that measurement is made with an equal standard, labor." But true equality would be achieved only in the higher, communist phase, "after the productive forces have also increased with the all-round development of the individual, and all the springs of cooperative wealth flow more abundantly." Then would the standard prevail, "From each according to his ability, to each according to his needs."

In the aftermath of the Bolshevik revolution, and during the period of "war communism," equality to its uttermost limits was the order of the day. As David J. Dallin wrote, "Everything that stood in the way of equality was to be abolished, at once, completely: that was the spiritual crux of the November revolution and of the ideology of the early period of the Soviet regime." Workers' control of factories, division of the landlords' estates, equality in the distribution of food and housing, elimination of army ranks— all were instituted to destroy every vestige of the old inequality.

In this period wages too tended toward equality, and by 1921 workers of widely varying qualifications, skill, or performance received nearly equal wages. But this equality, extorted from an economy of want and scarcity (a base that made a travesty of Marx's vision[3]), had to be abandoned to restore the ravaged economy. Under the New Economic Policy (NEP), traders and small entrepreneurs were invited back and peasants given the right to sell their products in the free market. The inevitable effect was marked differentiation in income. With the ebbing of revolutionary élan

---

[3] In most of his writings, Marx foresaw the downfall of capitalism when it reached its highest stage of development. Before the subsequent dictatorship of the proletariat could be transformed into a perfectly communist society, according to Marx a much higher stage of economic development would have to be reached. [EDITOR'S NOTE]

and under conditions of poverty, higher earnings provided the strongest incentive to more productive and skilled work for the working class as well. NEP lasted until the introduction of the first Five-Year Plan in 1929 under which by June, 1931, Stalin was decrying "the consequences of wage equalization" which deprived unskilled workers of incentive to become skilled workers, and led to heavy turnover in labor. "In order to put an end to this evil," he said, "we must abolish wage equalization and discard the old wage scales."

In typical fashion, Stalin sought to make a virtue of what may well have been a necessity; and, what is more, carried the inequalities far beyond the needs, or even utility, of the case. Accordingly, in 1934, Stalin characterized the views of those who "think that Socialism calls for equalization, for levelling the requirements and the individual lives of the members of society" as "petty-bourgeois views of our leftist blockheads." With regard to their "one time" attempt to organize industry to provide equal compensation for skilled and unskilled workers, he added: "You know what harm these infantile equalitarian exercises of our 'left' blockheads caused our industry."

More inequality became the fashion and the cry. As a consequence, the piecework wage became the prevailing system and gross disparities developed between the earnings of the skilled and the unskilled so that as early as 1927 Soviet labor law provided for seventeen wage gradations, with the highest eight times as much as the lowest. (This was accompanied by Draconic measures of labor discipline.) And, in 1940, a decree was issued requiring payment of tuition fees for upper secondary and higher education.

In light of these developments, it was quite generally predicted in the West that egalitarianism had been permanently and irrevocably abandoned as a goal of Soviet policy. Typical was the statement of Arthur Koestler in 1942 that a survey of the trends in the U.S.S.R. "contradicts the alleged temporariness of these expedients and reveals a continuous and coherent movement in a direction opposed to fundamental principles of socialism."

But it is noteworthy that with post-war recovery and further progress in building a high industrial base, a number of measures were adopted to restore greater equality. These included currency devaluation (which had a particularly adverse effect on high income groups who had to yield their savings, that is to say their old currency, for new currency in decreasing ratio, and on black marketeers who, in addition, risked exposure), the ending of the tuition system (making education generally available to the talented, at all levels, without tuition fee), an increase in minimum wages and pensions, extension of the pension system to farm workers, special tax concessions for low income groups, and reduction in the use of the piecework system—all of which have been of special and substantial benefit to those at the bottom of the economic scale. Labor benefited, too, from a shorter work-week, and reform and liberalization of the labor code.

It must be said, too, with respect to the living standard of the Soviet people, particularly since Stalin's death in 1953, that there has been a fairly steady improvement. According to the Soviet claim (which is probably exaggerated and so must be discounted but cannot be dismissed), in the past decade, the real income of its working people increased substantially; by the beginning of 1966 about half of the population had moved into new homes or improved their housing; public fund expenditures encompassing costs of social insurance, pensions, stipends, vacation pay, education and medical services, sanitaria and rest home facilities, and child care in kindergartens and nurseries, etc., had increased from 15 million to about 41.5 million rubles (the ruble is officially valued at $1.11); and, whereas in 1939 about 16 million people had a higher or secondary school education, by 1964 there were more than 70 million, or four-and-a-half times as many. And according to Mark G. Field, an American specialist, in his *Soviet Socialized Medicine,* published in 1967, the U.S.S.R. has one of the highest, if not the highest, doctor-patient ratios in the world—about 50 percent higher than the corresponding ratio in the United States.

THE SOVIET ECONOMIC SYSTEM

At the outset, I pointed out that the U.S.S.R. is a unique historical phenomenon combining Marxist, non-Marxist and anti-Marxist elements. So far as its political system goes, as I have attempted to show, its power base and institutional structures bear little resemblance to Marxist and early Leninist conceptions.

I am persuaded, however, that the Soviet economic system, despite distortions which derive from its political structure and from what John Plamenatz has called the "premature" nature of a Marxist revolution in a backward country, is in a basic sense Marxist in conception and spirit. I regard this proposition as central to understanding, particularly in light of some recent notions in the West that the Soviet Union is abandoning socialism and substituting a "profit" system. I shall deal with it, therefore, before turning to a consideration of some recent Soviet economic developments and future prospects.

THE INFLUENCE OF MARXISM [4]

In the *Communist Manifesto,* Marx and Engels wrote that "the distinguishing feature of communism" is "the abolition of bourgeois property," a sys-

[4] For a fuller analysis of the influence of Marxist theory on Soviet practice, see this author's "The Soviet Union: The Search for Theory," in William G. Andrews, ed., *European Politics I: The Restless Search* (New York, Van Nostrand, 1966), pp. 216-240.

tem based on "class antagonism, or the exploitation of the many by the few," and added that "in this sense, the theory of the Communists may be summed up in a single sentence: Abolition of private property."

The Soviet constitution proclaims that "the economic foundation of the U.S.S.R. is the socialist system of economy and the socialist ownership of the instruments and means of production." It provides that "the economic life of the U.S.S.R. is determined by the state national-economic plan," and declares work to be "a duty and a matter of honor for every able-bodied citizen." While some provisions of the Soviet constitution are devoid of significance, and others more honored in the breach than the observance, these institutions are so fundamentally rooted in the beliefs of the people including the leaders that, for the foreseeable future, they are as unlikely to be abolished as is the basic system of private property in the United States.

Now it is true that the ultimate end Marx had in mind was the full and free development and integration of man in society—"to end human alienation by changing the world," as Robert Tucker cogently put it—and it would be difficult to maintain that this objective has been approximated, let alone achieved, in the U.S.S.R. The fact however cannot be gainsaid that from a *Marxist* point of view the basis for the development of unalienated man was made to rest on the abolition of private ownership, a centrally planned economy, and production for use instead of for profit—and insofar as the U.S.S.R. corresponds to this conception, as it surely does in substantial degree, it may be said in a real and meaningful sense to derive from Marxism.

It is also true that dictatorial controls in the U.S.S.R. mean that the Marxist scheme, particularly in its conception of socialist democracy, has not been realized. Undeniably, this lack of freedom, in turn, affects and limits the common ownership of property, but it does not negate it. Milovan Djilas,[5] for example, goes too far when he maintains that in effect the communist political bureaucracy owns the nationalized property because it "uses, enjoys, and disposes" of it. While their controls give the bureaucrats important and special benefits, so long as marked fluidity prevails and national property may not be inherited, the privileges of the party leaders, as Molotov, Malenkov, and Khrushchev discovered, fall far short of ownership.

Not only does the fundamental organization of the economy reflect the Marxist scheme, but the strength of ideology is shown by frequently stubborn adherence to doctrine at the expense of rationality and efficiency. For example, planners in the U.S.S.R., basing themselves on Marx's proposition that only labor creates value, for a long time considered themselves ideologically debarred from imposing an interest charge for the use of capital. If used, it would have served as a means of efficient allocation and

---

[5] Partisan leader during the war and former Vice-President of Yugoslavia who was expelled from the Party in 1954 and subsequently imprisoned for years for his sharp attacks on communist systems in power. (For greater detail, *see* footnote 94, p. 284.)

rationing of scarce capital. To be sure, the Russians succeeded in part in getting around this difficulty by using certain other devices but these were not entirely satisfactory substitutes.

So also, recent steps taken to provide for interest on capital, a system of plant and individual "profit" incentive, a new pricing system to more accurately reflect labor and material costs and to stimulate production of new items and improve quality, fines for delivery delays, and other techniques are designed to improve the planning system, not to replace it. In any event, ultimate intrusion of elements of rationality into the planned economy is akin to the fact that welfare state measures are permitted to alter our free enterprise system without destroying it. I, for one, see no reason to doubt the basic validity of Kosygin's statement with regard to the new economic techniques that "Our underlying principles are inviolate. There are no means of production in private hands. . . ."

Agriculture presents an even clearer and more dramatic example of the compulsion of theory. Now, it must first be said that there are many explanations for the failure of the U.S.S.R. to achieve the repeatedly promised high level of agricultural production. These include the infertility of much Soviet land, inadequate rainfall, lack of mechanization, storage, and transport facilities, and heavy dependence on the labor of women and children— but surely a primary factor is the basic inadequacy of the present system of collectivization itself. It is not only tied up in the peasant's mind with bitter memories of forced collectivization but simply does not give him sufficient incentive to produce abundantly.

This failure is pointed up by the vitality of the dwarf private farm sector. Although only 1.4 percent of the total agricultural land area and 3.3 percent of the total sown area in 1962, this sector contributes a heavily disproportionate share of the total output of many important foods such as fruit, vegetables, potatoes, meat, milk, and eggs. That year, according to official Soviet sources, the private sector accounted for about a third of gross agricultural output including 45 percent of total meat and milk production, 76 percent of eggs, 22 percent of wool, 70 percent of potatoes, 42 percent of vegetables and 66 percent of fruit. By contrast, the results achieved in the public agricultural sector are incredibly low.

Soviet leaders have frequently admitted the comparative inefficiency of Soviet agriculture. Characteristically, Khrushchev commented in 1956 that "Available data show that in our country considerably more labor is spent to produce a ton of milk or meat than in the United States," and in 1963, that Soviet agriculture tolerated uneconomic practices which would be "inconceivable to an American farmer." More recently, Brezhnev said that some Soviet collective farms have become virtually unmanageable.

Why then does the Soviet Union continue to adhere to the collective and state farm systems (with a preference for the latter as the more ideologically advanced)? Surely a primary consideration must be a deep and genuine commitment to Marxist theory. Socialized property, after all, was a basic Marxist goal, out of dedication to which the Soviet leaders became revolutionaries and languished in Tsarist prisons. And, whatever compromises may be dictated by practical exigencies today, it would not seem possible for any Soviet leader to dismantle or fundamentally alter the collectivist industrial and agricultural systems to restore private property and free enterprise.

RECENT ECONOMIC DEVELOPMENTS

Viewed historically, the rate of industrial development and overall economic growth of the U.S.S.R. has been quite phenomenal. In a relatively short span of nonwar years, the Soviet Union rose from relative backwardness and underdevelopment to become the second most powerful industrial nation in the world. At the same time it must be recognized that this spectacular record of growth was achieved in good part at the expense of the consumer whose preferences were not consulted, and upon whom heavy sacrifices were imposed. This is a long and complex story. I shall limit myself largely to recent economic developments and their implications.

It is undeniable that the past few years have seen a sharp decline in the Soviet Union's rate of economic growth. To understand what has happened, and why, the reader must bear with a few key statistics. According to official Soviet sources, in the basic area of industrial production, in which the U.S.S.R. consistently claimed growth by 10 to 20 percent in the late 1940's and the 1950's, the rate of increase reported was 9.1 percent in 1961, 9.7 percent in 1962, 8.5 percent in 1963, 7.1 percent in 1964 and precisely 8.6 percent in both 1965 and 1966. If we take account of other sectors of the Soviet economy, including agriculture, with its admittedly poor record in 1962 and 1963 and unimpressive record in 1965, and transmute the figures into terms of gross national product (GNP)—a concept used in the West to cover the sum of *all* goods and services produced—the official Soviet claim suggests an average overall rate for the period of about 5 percent.

This figure, however, has been substantially discounted by many Western economists. In 1964 experts in the United States in separate studies submitted to the Joint Economic Committee of Congress and the Central Intelligence Agency estimated the Soviet Union's economic growth for 1962 and 1963 at less than 2.5 percent. In October 1965 Gardner Ackley, chairman of the American Council of Economic Advisers, reported that a State Department study had shown that, in general, the growth rate of Soviet national output had fallen one-third during the past five years, from "a very impressive" $6\frac{1}{2}$ percent a year during the 1950's to an average of about 4.3 percent per year since 1960.

In any event, while there is a dispute among Western specialists as to the *extent* of the decline in the Soviet rate of growth—some question the low figures set in the cited reports—what is indisputable (and acknowledged by the U.S.S.R.) is that a sharp drop has in fact taken place. Why has this happened? The explanation is complex and it is possible to suggest here only in summary form some of the relevant factors. Furthermore, to judge their significance, it is necessary to distinguish between those difficulties which may be temporary and those which appear to be more deep-rooted and intractable.

A major element in the poor growth of the Soviet Union in recent years undoubtedly lies in the high priority given by the U.S.S.R. to its military and space programs which have preempted a large share of the highly trained men, machinery, and materials which might otherwise have been devoted to modernizing industry and agriculture. Another factor has been the failure of agriculture, accounting for almost a third of Soviet GNP, to keep pace with industry. Part of the explanation for this lies in the disastrous weather conditions in major farm areas in the U.S.S.R. in recent years. Beginning with 1959 the U.S.S.R. had only two good harvest years—1964 and 1966; and these were preceded by the extreme drought in 1963—the worst in three quarters of a century—while the 1965 harvest was a relatively poor one. As a consequence, the U.S.S.R. had to buy millions of tons of grain abroad and slaughter 40 percent of its national stock of pigs, the number of which declined from 70 million in 1962 to 52.8 million in 1964. In 1965, the Soviet Union admitted that "plans for procurement of meat, milk, eggs and wool" in 1964 "were not fulfilled." One Western specialist estimates that "the net agricultural product—a more meaningful measure than the gross product—showed in 1964 no more than a 5 percent increase over that of 1958, while the population grew 9.7 percent during the same period." The Soviet agricultural deficiency, in turn, concededly adversely affected the processed food industry and related branches of light industry.

Looking ahead, it is obvious that a continued favorable turn in the weather will bring substantial gains in agricultural output. It is also probable that improvement will result from implementation of the plans outlined by Party leaders in March, 1965, and subsequently. These provide for stable grain procurement and delivery prices, a substantial increase in prices to be paid by the state for planned agricultural purchases, a considerable increase in state investments in agriculture, strengthening of the authority of local agricultural specialists, and cancellation of the debts of many of the weak *kolkhozes*.[6] Nonetheless, a serious question remains as to whether the persistently poor performance of the agricultural segment—which employs about 40 percent of the Soviet labor force to produce the food and fiber to meet the needs of the Soviet people, while the 8 percent employed in agriculture in the United States oversupplies the American people—can be

---

[6] Collective farms. [EDITOR'S NOTE]

drastically improved within the framework of the present collective farm system.

Other factors retarding the growth rate of the Soviet economy are due to the shift in investment emphasis from heavy industry, raw materials, and power supply to agriculture, chemical technology, and service and consumer areas. These have already led and may continue to lead to a decline in the productivity (growth intensity) of investment. "It was easier," one analyst commented, "to build more and more steel mills and cement plants and hydroelectric dams than it is to build chemical plants and diversified consumer goods."

Another cardinal difficulty derives from the very nature of a centrally planned and directed economy which threatens to drown Soviet planners in a paper ocean. With the inherent complexity of planning the production of literally millions of items in their multiple interrelationship, the use of computers and other advanced instruments and techniques may be expected to mitigate, but not to eliminate, the difficulty.

Other defects of the Soviet system of planning—at least as heretofore practiced and applied—have been the failure to use adequate devices to set reasonable limits on the amount of capital enterprises will seek to employ, the inefficient dispersal of capital investments, the lack of a price system which properly measures the real cost of resources, the chronic understatement of production goals to improperly enhance enterprise profit and bonuses, and the pressure to meet set quotas at the expense of quality, diversity, and technical advances. It remains to be seen whether the proposals of some leading Soviet economists for a variety of techniques to improve Soviet economic performance, which were tested in some instances and are supposed to be gradually introduced, will be extensively adopted and, if so, prove practical within the framework of a centrally planned and governed economy.

To conclude our discussion at this point would be to give a partial and one-sided view of Soviet reality. Its centrally planned economy also has certain strengths and advantages. To begin with, it now seems to be firmly established that the Soviet institutional arrangements are such that its system is not subject to severe depressions or recessions. (It can no longer be argued, as it once was, that this would prove true only in the period of initial and rapid industrialization.) Related is the fact that, notwithstanding the inefficiency and waste involved in central planning and in the actual distribution and application of resources, the U.S.S.R. does employ the resources it has developed to full or nearly full capacity. It would be unthinkable, in short, for the U.S.S.R. to have the capacity to produce, let us say, 90 million metric tons of steel and in the presence of continuing social need produce only half that amount. Even in agriculture—where the Soviet failure in light of the input of effort has been egregious—a centrally planned economy makes possible extensive and systematic mechanization. It is true, too, that the nature of that system discourages expenditures for the production of socially useless, or even harmful, products and services. It must be said, finally, that while the rate of economic growth in general has slowed down in recent years in the U.S.S.R. as compared with the trend in the 1950's and the performance of countries like Japan and West Germany for a number of years in the post-war period, the Soviet Union continued throughout to make progress which, by generally prevailing international standards, is quite respectable.

THE NEW FIVE-YEAR PLAN

All of the factors just mentioned are pertinent to an evaluation of the prospects of the new Soviet Five-Year Plan, adopted by the 23rd CPSU Congress in 1966.

First, let us take a look at the Plan's promises and prognoses. It envisages increases in the five-year period 1966-1970 of approximately 40 percent in national income; 30 percent in real per capita income; 50 percent in industrial output; 25 percent in farm output (predicated in part on extraordinarily large capital investments; 30 percent in housing construction; and 40 percent in the sale of consumer goods of improved quality and variety including a rise in production of refrigerators from 1.7 to 5.5 million, of TV sets from 3.7 to 7.6 million, and of automobiles from 201,200 to 750,000.

In addition, the Plan anticipates institution of monthly guaranteed remuneration for collective farmers corresponding to the level of wages paid to state farm workers; a number of wage increases and a further narrowing of the disparity between high and low incomes generally; a rise in minimum old age pensions for workers and farmers; marked improvement in the population's diet and its increased access to fabrics, clothing, and knitted goods; a substantial increase in educational opportunities at all levels; and marked improvement of medical services including a 2,680,000 increase in hospital beds.

Several comments are in order. It is noteworthy that the new plan sets goals which are substantially below those projected by Nikita Khrushchev for 1970 at the 22nd Party Congress in 1961. Nor does the new plan assert that the Soviet economy will catch up with (let alone surpass) that of the United States by 1970—a claim repeatedly put forth by Khrushchev. Furthermore, if the goals of the new plan for 1966-1970 are contrasted with actual achievements in the preceding five years, it must be said that they appear fairly moderate. Specifically, the planned increase in national income of 40 percent, industrial production of 50 percent, and agricultural output (in comparison with *average* annual output in the preceding five years) of 25 percent compares with actual increases for 1961-1965 in these categories of

35 percent, 50 percent and 10 percent respectively. Finally, the fact is that the plan reveals more concern for consumer interests and desires than has characterized Soviet economic planning for several decades.

However, in light of continued emphasis on heavy industry and space expenditures, the deficiencies of collectivized agriculture, imbalances of the Soviet economy, chronic shortages, unfulfilled plans, and Soviet international obligations, it is not improbable that the U.S.S.R. will fail to meet *some* of its production goals in the time set. But it would be well to recognize that by Soviet standards the goals are fairly modest and realistic and hence would appear to be largely realizable.

The long-range implications of these varied considerations are difficult to project. There is every reason to believe that, notwithstanding its problems, the Soviet economy, barring war or major catastrophe, will continue to grow systematically and steadily and make substantial progress toward the realization of its economic and welfare goals. By contrast, there is no assurance of similar regular and consistent growth with respect to the American economy whose performance, viewed historically, has been much more erratic and cyclical. And this remains a problem although, in light of the knowledge and experience gained in the past several decades, a serious depression in the United States would seem to be excluded and our needs in important respects are quite different. For the U.S.S.R., for example, a substantial increase in agricultural production is vital; but we have no need to increase our already ample food supply for internal consumption. Also, as a society of relative scarcity, the Soviet Union must still concern itself greatly with quantity; we, on the other hand, can afford to concern ourselves more with quality (and, increasingly, it is hoped, will concern ourselves more with equality).

Finally, it is worth emphasizing that while economic factors are vital to any evaluation, particularly of a society in the stage of overcoming backwardness, as Karl Kautsky [7] pointed out, in the final analysis "it is not technical and economic innovations but the human aspects of a society that matter."

SOME CONCLUSIONS

The conclusions of this essay will not appeal to those who are attracted to tidy and simplistic explanations. In my opinion the Soviet record is a mixed one of successes and failures, of hopes realized and hopes shattered. And, specifically with respect to the continuing importance of Marxism, that record clearly demonstrates that certain of its doctrines, in the hands of the

[7] Karl Kautsky, outstanding leader and theoretical spokesman of the German Social Democratic (Socialist) movement in the late nineteenth and twentieth centuries.

Soviet leaders, have been attenuated, perverted, deferred, and, in some instances, discarded. Soviet "democracy," for example, bears no relation to its Marxist conception. And the failure of the Soviet state to wither away, in the face of the claim that the U.S.S.R. has already achieved socialism and a classless society, however justified or rationalized, is nonetheless in contradiction with Marxist theory.

On the other hand, it is demonstrable that some Marxist doctrines have to an important extent influenced and shaped decisions of the Soviet leaders. This has been true with respect to the fundamental nature of the economy grounded upon the principle of collective ownership and control. And, however tarnished the record in some respects, it seems to me undeniable that Marxist theory has had and continues to have a significant impact in underscoring the essential equality of all races and peoples. Finally, while the motivations for social welfare in the U.S.S.R. are varied and complex, I think it is reasonable to conclude that the egalitarianism suggested in Marx's vision of a socialist society—a vision in which the Soviet leaders, like the Soviet people, have been educated and reared—played an important part.

To say, as Irving Kristol has said, that "Marxism as an intellectual system and a *Weltanschauung*[8] is dead" and that what alone survives are "movements and governments which use the tatters of its ideology as a justification for autocratic rule" or to maintain, as W. W. Rostow has done, that Soviet leaders are concerned with the welfare of the Soviet people only or mainly as a reflex to their power goals is, in my judgement, to be guilty of oversimplification, as guilty as those in the U.S.S.R. who wrote in the New Party Program (1961) that a "bourgeois republic, however democratic" inevitably constitutes "a machine for the exploitation and suppression of the vast majority of the working people by a handful of capitalists."

In general, the demise of Marxist ideology, like Mark Twain's comment on the report of his death, has been greatly exaggerated; and there may be more than a little truth to Clark Kissinger's comment that "When they [the old left] proclaim the end of ideology, it's like an old man proclaiming the end of sex. Because he doesn't feel it anymore, he thinks it's disappeared."

Similarly, to conceive of Marxist ideology as a species of opium with which the Soviet leaders lull the people while taking care never to inhale themselves is, as R. N. Carew Hunt, has wisely said, "to attribute to them an ability to dissociate themselves from the logic of their system—an ability which it is unlikely they possess."

So, also, to maintain that because departures from Marxism have been far-reaching in some areas, Marxism cannot possibly have *any* continuing impact or significance, is to insist upon the absolute indivisibility of Marxist doctrine—a test we would be unable to apply to other doctrines. By so rigorous a standard, it would be impossible to explain the coexistence of democ-

[8] Ideology. [EDITOR'S NOTE]

racy and slavery in the United States for nearly 100 years, or the coexistence of Christianity (and other religions) and un-Christian-like tyranny for nearly two thousand years.

Even in the areas where distortion or perversion of Marxism has manifestly taken place, it is revealing to observe how "old truths" persist so that a measure of relaxation promptly brings people to the fore who seek to restore Marx's true meaning and purpose. Typical is that group of intellectuals in the U.S.S.R. today whose attitude is perhaps best (or at least most overtly) expressed by Yevtushenko who cautioned that "those who speak in the name of communism but in feality pervert its meaning are among its most dangerous enemies, perhaps even more dangerous than its enemies in the West," and by Boris Slutsky who wrote: "Time to bring the dreams to pass. Yes, with neither doubt nor hesitation—To get to work and bring the dreams to pass."

It is one thing, however, to recognize the continuing importance of the revolutionary dynamic; it is quite another to predict the future configuration of Soviet society or specifically to maintain that relaxation of the dictatorship in the U.S.S.R. cannot and will not be halted or aborted short of realization of a democratic socialist society truly in the image of Marx. Such a far-reaching projection belongs in the realm of prophecy which this writer, mindful of J. B. Bury's pungent comment that "it is the function of history to belie prophets," will not essay.

FURTHER READING SUGGESTIONS

Barghoorn, Frederick C., *Politics in the U.S.S.R.* Boston: Little, Brown, 1966.

Campbell, Robert W., *Soviet Economic Power.* New York: Houghton Mifflin, 2nd ed., 1966.

Daniels, Robert V., *The Nature of Communism.* New York: Random House, 1962.

Dmytryshyn, Basil, *U.S.S.R.: A Concise History.* New York: Scribner, 1965.

Fainsod, Merle, *How Russia Is Ruled.* Cambridge: Harvard University Press, 2nd ed., 1963.

Florinsky, Michael T., *Russia: A History and an Interpretation.* New York: Macmillan, 2 vols., 1955.

Meyer, Alfred G., *The Soviet Political System.* New York: Random House, 1965.

Nove, Alec, *The Soviet Economy.* New York: Praeger, 2nd ed., 1966.

Schapiro, Leonard, *The Communist Party of the Soviet Union,* New York: Random House, 1960.

Schwartz, Harry, *The Soviet Economy Since Stalin.* New York: Lippincott, 1965.

Wolfe, Bertram, *Three Who Made a Revolution.* New York: Dial Press, 1948.

4

The New Society: A Soviet Marxist View on the U.S.S.R.

T. SHAKHNAZAROV, Y. KRASYIN, and
V. SUKHODEYEV *

SOVIET SOCIAL SCIENTISTS

INTRODUCTION

People live in society; consequently their desire to grasp the meaning of social life is quite natural. Since times of yore man's inquisitive mind has striven to penetrate not only the innermost secrets of nature, but also the intricate mechanism of social relations. Why is it that some wield wealth and power while others suffer from poverty and lack of rights? What are the reasons for social inequality? Can the road to a society of fair play for all be found? What kind of road and society must they be? These and many other questions have faced people in the past, and continue to trouble them today.

For centuries the vast majority of mankind languished under the oppression of the exploiters. The slave owners, feudalists, capitalists, and colonialists did everything in their power to impose spiritual slavery in addition to economic slavery. Arguments designed to justify and legalize the system of social injustice were invented and propagated. The people were fed false myths about the supposed eternity and immutability of social orders in which a small group of the "elite" exploits the working people.

Whenever the working people rose in rebellion against the exploiters, it was, in the main, new exploiters who enjoyed the fruits of rare victories and not those who did the fighting. As before, the dreams of social justice and an ideal society remained mere dreams.

* This contribution has been written especially for this book.

It was only in the last century that an ideology evolved that gave the working people the key to a scientific explanation of social life and the course of the development of history. This ideology was destined to play a tremendous role both in scientific knowledge and in the revolutionary transformation of social relations.

It was the doctrine of Marx and Engels, ideologists and leaders of the working class. In the new historical conditions of our century it was creatively developed by Vladimir Ilyich Lenin; hence the name *Marxism-Leninism*.

THE PHILOSOPHICAL BASIS OF SCIENTIFIC COMMUNISM

Transformation of social relations and building a new society requires primarily a correct conception of the reality around us, its development, man's place in the world, and the meaning of his life and activities. Such a conception is provided by Marxist-Leninist philosophy—dialectical and historical materialism—the science of the more general laws on the development of nature, society, and consciousness.

The opponents of communism have tried and are trying to depict materialism as the rejection of ideals, spiritual values, and ethical principles. Actually, the essence of materialism consists of striving to understand the world as it actually is, without extraneous considerations, without the myths that are the product of human imagination distorting the picture of reality.

Society has its own objective laws of development independent of the will and mind of people. History is neither a conglomeration of accidents, nor the result of the arbitrariness of great personalities. It is an objective process which can be studied and understood. But in order to do so one must proceed not from the ideas and concepts that have taken hold of people, but from the material, economic conditions of their life.

In the long run we find the explanation for the behavior of large social groups or classes, and also political parties and leaders defending the interests of these classes, in the material conditions of the people's labor and life. Material conditions are also the basis of the whole complex system of social relations; they determine the character of the state laws, morals and other social institutions.

Basing itself on a dialectical-materialistic world outlook, the ideology of socialism and communism rejects utopian dreams which have no roots in life and turns to a study of life itself, of those material conditions which alone can be the basis for building a socialist and communist society. The ideology of socialism and communism has been transformed from a utopian theory into a science dealing with the laws of the rise and development of a new society.

THE ROAD TO SOCIALISM LIES THROUGH REVOLUTION

The road to socialism and communism is not as simple as it seemed to Socialist Utopians of the past. It is not enough to draw up a plan for a new society; it is also necessary to find in life the real force that can transform the entire system of existing relations and set up a new system. This force has to be considerable, since the ruling, exploiting classes use every available means to defend their power and wealth, wielding the entire might of state authority.

To overthrow the rule of the exploiters, break down their resistance, and bring about the radical transformation of the entire system of social relations, the working people must carry out a socialist revolution. But it will only be successful if they are united and organized, if they clearly see the aims facing them and consistently fight for them without vacillating.

Marx, Engels, and Lenin saw the working class as the leading force in the struggle for the victory of the socialist revolution and the construction of socialism and communism. The working class unites, becomes disciplined and organized by the very conditions of capitalist production. Life in all its complexities develops revolutionary traits: staunchness, courage, solidarity, the ability to defend the aims of the revolution firmly and to the end. The working class advances from its midst a class-conscious vanguard—the party —which, in accordance with scientific theory, formulates the program of struggle for socialism and organizes the actions of the working class and its allies. All this makes the working class the natural leader of the masses. It unites around itself the oppressed and dispossessed—first of all, the peasants and petty craftsmen who are scattered by the conditions of petty production and do not always clearly recognize their own interests as a social class and stratum.

The working masses accomplish the socialist revolution and take power into their own hands. At the beginning, right up to the time a socialist society is built, such power of necessity must be the dictatorship of the proletariat. This is quite comprehensible. The working class which has been the leader of the revolution quite naturally provides political, state leadership of society during the transitional period from capitalism to social-ism. After all, this class is consistently revolutionary; it sees more clearly the tasks of the struggle for socialism, and steadily defends the interests of the working people. The dictatorship of the proletariat is the instrument for the struggle against the enemies of the revolution, the instrument for the political education of the masses and the all-around development of socialist democracy, the instrument for the construction of a new society. As ex-perience shows, when socialism is built, the enemies of the revolution are vanquished once and for all, and the masses of people are able to run the state. Then, the dictatorship of the proletariat becomes unnecessary and is replaced by a state of the whole people.

In October, 1917, the ideas of scientific communism were corroborated by revolutionary practice in Russia. For the first time in history the working masses took power into their own hands.

Tremendous difficulties were shouldered by the working people. The construction of socialism began in a country which was surrounded on all sides by hostile capitalist states supporting the internal counterrevolution. The difficulties were aggravated by the fact that Russia was not a technically and economically highly developed country. Moreover, its economy was ruined by the war.

The working people had taken power into their hands. Now, a scientifically substantiated plan for building a new society was necessary. This plan was elaborated by V. I. Lenin.

LENIN'S PLAN FOR BUILDING SOCIALISM

Industrialization of the country, the collectivization of agriculture, and the cultural revolution—these are the three basic ideas in Lenin's plan for building socialism.

A mighty, heavy industry was necessary for ensuring the country's political and economic independence, a rapid growth in labor productivity and higher living standards. Without all that, socialism was inconceivable.

The collectivization of agriculture was intended to draw the broad masses of the peasantry into building the new society. The workers and peasants are true allies in the fight against exploitation. However, unlike the worker engaged in large-scale machine production, each peasant toiled on his separate plot of land. He couldn't do away with poverty and cultural backwardness all by himself. There was only one way to develop agriculture— the creation of a large-scale, socialist agricultural sector in which modern machines could be employed. But how could this be done without infringing on the interests of the peasants? Only by uniting the peasants into cooperatives that would be given the support and the help of the socialist state.

Finally, in building socialism there must be a cultural revolution, which provides the working people with access to culture and cultural pursuits.

GREAT SOCIAL EXPERIMENT

The October Revolution and the radical social transformations it brought about in Russia are frequently called a social experiment. This is to some extent correct, for the socialist revolution in Russia was the first practical test of the viability of Marxist-Leninist theory. Now it can be boldly stated that the great social experiment undertaken in 1917 has been successfully implemented. The socialist society has ceased being a model, an idea, a project; it has become a fact.

Of course, building a new society is not like putting up a structure according to precise blueprints. Though the builders of socialism did have a scientific plan, the enormity of the problem facing them made it necessary to seek solutions to unforeseen situations. The road to socialism demanded heroic efforts. There were the joys of victory and the bitterness of defeat, wise political decisions as well as miscalculations and mistakes.

But all this does not affect the significance of what has been accomplished. In place of backward tsarist Russia a mighty socialist power has emerged, a country which holds second place in the world for industrial output, the first to blaze the trail into outer space, the land which has become a bulwark of peace and a beacon of progress for all mankind. This is unquestionably the best proof of the advantages of socialism, the best argument in favor of the new social system.

The day is not far off when progressive humanity will mark the fiftieth anniversary of the October Revolution and formation of the Soviet Union. This event will unquestionably heighten the keen world-wide interest in the Soviet experience with all its ups and downs. The aim of this article is to tell in brief the story of Soviet socialist society, of the U.S.S.R.'s economic, social and political system, and of the tasks the Soviet people are accomplishing on the road to communism.

THE ECONOMIC SYSTEM OF SOCIALISM

The factories, mines, and other means of production in the U.S.S.R. belong to the people. No class is deprived of the means of production and there is no class of private owners. No one is in a privileged or, on the contrary, an inferior position in regard to ownership of the means of production. It is for this reason that public ownership of the means of production excludes the possibility of the exploitation of man. It is only when people cannot appropriate the fruit of other people's labor, that one's own labor becomes the only lawful source of subsistence.

The overwhelming bulk of the means of production and other material values in the U.S.S.R. are owned by the socialist state. All Soviet people use state property: the workers use the machines and machine tools in the process of production; scientists handle the equipment of institutes and laboratories; children use the school buildings, equipment in the workshops and apparatus in school labs. And it is the state factories and institutions that are in charge of state property.

The managers are given authority by the state to administer the factories and institutions, and the personnel has the right to check on what is done by their managers. That is why we have full grounds for saying that the staff runs the factory or institution.

The state may place public property at the disposal of citizens for their use through its organizations (after all, the factory, the institute and schools are state organizations) or directly. In this way state-owned apartment houses in cities and workers' settlements are put at the disposal of the people. However, under all circumstances, the state remains the owner of state property and decides what is to be done with it.

The main distinction between state and cooperative property is in the level of pooling of the means of production. State property makes the means of production public on a nation-wide scale, hence the property of the whole people. In the case of collective farm property the means of production are pooled for a separate farming enterprise, hence accessible to a specific group of people.

State Property (Belonging to All the People)	Cooperative (Group) Property
The land, its mineral wealth, waters, forests, industrial enterprises and their output, large state-organized agricultural enterprises (state farms) and their produce, repair and technical stations, banks, transportation, means of communication, municipal catering and service enterprises, and cultural establishments (hospitals, clinics, holiday homes, schools, institutes, stadiums, etc.), and the bulk of dwelling houses in cities and industrial areas.	The commonly owned enterprises of collective farms and cooperatives, with livestock, inventory, implements (tractors, combines, etc.), buildings connected with the economy of the cooperatives, clubs, etc. (The land occupied by the collective farms is turned over to them for free use in perpetuity.)

The distinctions between state enterprises [industrial or agricultural] and collective farms are bound up with the two different forms of socialist ownership: workers at state enterprises receive a straight cash wage; the labor of collective farmers is remunerated both in cash and kind depending on time worked;[1] state enterprises and collective farmers differ also in the form of management. The head of a state enterprise is appointed by the state and is ac-

[1] More specifically, different tasks carry different numbers of "workday units" which, upon completion of the task, are credited to the collective farmer's account. That part of the net earnings of the collective farm that is set aside for direct disbursement is then distributed among the collective farmers according to the number of workday units each has amassed. Hence, a collective farmer's income depends not only on time

countable to the state for the plant's activities.[2] The supreme body at the
collective farm is the general membership meeting, which elects a managing
board and its chairman. The collective farmers decide all questions pertaining to the organization and management of the farm on the basis of existing
laws (especially the Collective Farm Charter), they adopt plans in the
interests of both the farm itself and the state, vote on the report of the
managing board, decide how income is to be distributed, and so forth.

The socialist state gives the collective farms a great deal of assistance. It
supplies them with farm machinery, fertilizers, and high-grade seeds, organizes the training of management personnel and farm specialists, provides
veterinary control, helps popularize and adopt advanced methods, grants
credits to the collective farms, and buys their produce according to established practice.

PERSONAL PROPERTY

Besides public property there is also personal property under socialism. The
right to personal property in the U.S.S.R. is guaranteed and safeguarded by
law.

What kinds of personal property are there in the Soviet Union? Income and savings derived from work, an apartment, a dwelling house, a
summer cottage, a yacht, a car, a motor boat, a collection of paintings. In
the case of collective farm members, this also includes farm buildings and
cattle, and produce obtained from their individual holdings.

With regard to *personal* property it should be stressed that it radically
differs from capitalist *private* property. What is the distinction? Primarily
that personal property in a socialist society is based on personal labor and
cannot be used to make money at the expense of others. For instance, an
ordinary sewing machine can be used for different purposes. If the housewife
uses it to sew for her family, then this is a case of personal property. But
if she hires a worker to sew things for sale and pays her part of the earnings
derived, then this sewing machine becomes private property. Personal property is quite common in the U.S.S.R., while private property, such as the example we have just given, does not exist.

THE OBJECTIVE OF SOCIALIST PRODUCTION

What is the objective of socialist production? The answer is simple: to establish the conditions for a happy and free life, which means first of all ensuring

---

worked, but also upon the type of job or jobs performed and upon the income of the
collective farm. At the time this is being written (summer, 1966) a guaranteed minimum
wage is being introduced on Soviet collective farms. [EDITOR'S NOTE]

[2] The situation is almost identical in the case of state farms. State farms, so to
speak, are agricultural factories and as such state enterprises. [EDITOR'S NOTE]

a high living standard, creating an abundance of material and spiritual values. Such is the age-old dream of communism for which the socialist revolution was fought and a communist society is being built. Under socialism all production is directed toward improving the people's welfare.

The Soviet people's living standards are steadily rising. Food consumption is growing; the consumption of manufactured goods has increased sharply, especially clothes and shoes as well as other items of consumer use.

The Soviet Union has far outstripped the most developed capitalist countries in the number of apartments being built annually. During the 1960-65 period, houses totalling 393 million square meters of living space were built in cities, workers' settlements and at state farms, and over 2 million houses in collective farm villages. More than 10 million people moved into new apartments.

True, not everyone in the Soviet Union is well off. Although there has been great progress during Soviet times there are still certain difficulties. People cannot always afford to buy what they want. There is still a housing problem. The reason for all this is obvious: the Soviet people had to start to build a new life amidst economic backwardness and ruin—the legacy of tsarism. Tremendous damage was inflicted on the national economy by the war with Hitler Germany. The state is still forced to earmark large sums of money for defense purposes. True to their internationalist duty the Soviet people also render economic aid to the newly freed countries. Still, tremendous progress has been made. Working to the best of their ability, Soviet people improve their life day by day.

DISTRIBUTION OF MATERIAL VALUES[3]

Under socialism, every person receives material values produced by society in accordance with the quantity and quality of his labor.

In referring to the law of distribution according to labor, it must be borne in mind that only a part of the total product is distributed. Before considering the distribution of the products of labor among individual workers, it is necessary to make a number of deductions from the social product for public needs: to take care of depreciation of the means of production, expansion of production, funds for education, medical services, disability benefits, defense expenditures, costs of administration, etc. The remaining portion is then distributed amongst those engaged in socialist production.

Every worker of a socialist society has a stake in expanding production,

[3] "Material values," in this context, refers to material goods produced. The concept of "distribution of material values" is thus closely related to what in the West is called "real income," and refers to the number of goods that can be purchased with one's income. (For an important distinction between Soviet and U.S. national income analysis, *see* footnote 5, p. 99 below.) [EDITOR'S NOTE]

education, medical care, disability benefits, strengthening the country's defense, etc. Hence, production for social needs is as necessary for each member of society as production for the satisfaction of personal needs.

The principle of the distribution of material values in accordance with the quantity and quality of labor does away with the greatest injustice in an exploiters' society, where an insignificant minority appropriates the biggest share of the material values produced. Under socialism, money even in big amounts is no longer a means of wielding power, or an object of reverence. You cannot buy a factory to exploit the workers, nor a Deputy's mandate or a ministerial post in a socialist society. Only personal ability and labor for the good of society are measures of man's value under socialism.

Pay in accordance with one's labor permits the consistent implementation of the principle of material incentives. The better a person works, the more he gives society, the higher his remuneration. This stimulates people to work better and try to raise labor productivity.

Besides material incentives, moral, or to be more exact, ideological incentives for labor exist in a socialist society. Such incentives inspired people immediately after the October Revolution. The emancipation of labor engendered enthusiasm, the desire to build a new society as quickly as possible, and to create a better life for all. People were ready to deprive themselves for the sake of the great idea; they were moved by faith in a radiant future, by the desire to hasten that happy day by their deeds. The same hopes inspired hundreds of thousands of young men and women who took part in ploughing up virgin soil, in setting up new industrial bases in Siberia and the Far East.

The combination of material and moral incentives for labor is graphically manifested in socialist emulation. Socialist emulation is the competition between working people for the successful fulfillment and overfulfillment of plans, improvement in the quality of manufactured goods, lowering of production costs, economy in raw materials and fuel, greater labor discipline, improving skills, etc. Yet, the main principle of socialist emulation is passing on experience—having those who are doing well help the ones lagging behind, and by doing so help achieve a general rise in production.

HOW THE U.S.S.R.'S NATIONAL INCOME IS DISTRIBUTED

The real national income consists of means of production and consumer goods: raw and processed materials, machines, machine tools, grain, sugar, clothes, shoes, books, etc. Since there is commodity production [4] under socialism, besides a natural form, the national income is expressed in a monetary form.

---

[4] "Commodity production" refers to the production of goods which are offered for sale on the market. [EDITOR'S NOTE]

The national income is created by workers engaged in material production: industry, agriculture, construction, transportation, etc. Those in non-productive spheres—health promotion, public education, the arts, and the army—do not contribute to the national income.[5] Since their efforts are also beneficial and necessary for society, all expenses connected with the non-productive sphere are paid out of the national income.

How then is the national income distributed in the U.S.S.R.? The socialist state distributes the national income in a planned way, taking into account the harmonious development of society as a whole. Approximately one-quarter of the national income is spent on the expansion and improvement of production, the other three-quarters go for direct consumption.

About 90 percent of the entire consumption fund is distributed in the form of pay, in accordance with the quantity and quality of labor expended. The rest goes for the construction and maintenance of educational institutions, hospitals and clinics, dwelling houses and municipal enterprises, scientific and cultural establishments, etc.

In December, 1965, the U.S.S.R. Supreme Soviet approved the country's 1966 budget for the following amounts: revenues—105.4 billion rubles,[6] expenditures—105.3 billion; 43.8 billion was allocated for the development of the national economy; 40.3 billion, to be spent on science, education, health protection and physical culture, pensions, benefits, stipends—in other words, on social cultural needs; 13.4 billion for strengthening the country's defense and 1.1 billion for maintaining the state apparatus.

The U.S.S.R. must allocate the necessary funds for strengthening the country's defense potential as long as the threat of imperialist aggression exists. But most of the state funds are invested in the development of the national economy and culture, for improving the people's welfare.

PLANNING

Every enterprise in the U.S.S.R. is a unit of the national economy, and all of them are interconnected by thousands of ties. There is no private enterprise in a socialist society, everything belongs to one master—the people.

---

[5] Marxist-Leninist ideology refers to direct services (services the value of which is not included in a material good) as "nonproductive." Nonproductive (or unproductive) does not mean undesirable. It simply means that those in the direct service sector are not deemed to increase directly and immediately a nation's material wealth. As a society becomes more affluent, it finds it easier to afford larger nonproductive sectors, which will tend to improve the nation's health, level of culture, entertainment, etc. Contrary to U.S. practice, income derived from direct services is not counted as part of national income in Soviet national income analysis. [EDITOR'S NOTE]

[6] At the official exchange rate in the Soviet Union, one ruble equals $1.11. The term "billion," throughout this book, refers to the American usage, i.e., one billion equals one thousand million, and *not* to the British usage where one billion equals one million million. [EDITOR'S NOTE]

And where there is only one master, there is a common objective and single program of action—the plan.

The plan is a most effective force. Let us say a new chemical plant is under construction. While the buildings are going up, chemical engineering enterprises throughout the country are manufacturing the necessary equipment, oil refineries are instructed to provide the new plant with raw materials, railwaymen have the task of delivering the raw material to the plant on time and transporting the finished product to the consumer; chemical engineering institutes introduce special training for their last year students who are to become designers, engineers, and foremen at the plant; and future workers obtain the necessary skills and knowledge in general and vocational schools.

Precise calculations, coordinated work and unity of action are required everywhere and in everything. And all this is attained thanks to the plan —a state document outlining what has to be produced and who is to produce it, where the materials are to come from and where the output will go, how many people will be needed and what training will be required of them. The plan outlines the tasks necessary for boosting production, raising people's living standards, and developing culture. It determines the scope of domestic and foreign trade, and so on.

Planning the national economy is one of the most important advantages that socialism has over capitalism. For the first time in its history, society controls the conditions of production, providing conscious, planned direction, achieving thereby the utmost economy in social labor. Once and for all it does away with detrimental competition and the anarchy of production,[7] as well as economic crises. And it is primarily the public ownership of the means of production that enables the socialist economic system to plan the economy and consciously to organize production.

THE BIRTH OF A PLAN

The planning of the economy starts at the factories, mines, collective and state farms, and transport, construction, trade and other organizations. Wage and salary earners as well as farmers participate, both directly and through their public organizations, in the management of production. They submit their calculations and suggestions for the development and improvement of the work of the enterprises. These proposals usually have to do with boosting output, raising quality, mechanizing and automating labor processes, improving working conditions, making more rational use of raw materials,

---

[7] Anarchy of production, in Marxist-Leninist parlance, refers to the capitalist mode of production in which each producer makes his own output decisions without any knowledge regarding the output decisions of his competitors, i.e., without an overall plan. [EDITOR'S NOTE]

fuel, electric power, and equipment, organizing production more efficiently and profitably, and so forth.

After a joint discussion with the staff of a given enterprise and after thorough consideration, the management draws up the draft of a plan for the next period (according to the system adopted in the U.S.S.R., current plans are for 1 or 2 years, long-range plans, for 5 to 7 years, and prospective plans, for 15 to 20 years).

The plans proposed by the separate enterprises and organizations are checked, corrected, and generalized by the Ministries concerned, and made into a draft plan for territorial production councils which include firms, production administrations, and economic councils.[8] Simultaneously, health promotion, educational, scientific and cultural bodies, the trade unions, and different public organizations draw up draft plans for the non-productive sphere, proceeding from the need for growth in the corresponding fields. All this data is coordinated in a single plan for the development of the economic region.

Combined draft plans are then drawn up. There is a central planning body, the State Planning Commission, in every Union Republic. It is concerned with maintaining specialization and ensuring comprehensive utilization of the mineral and power resources, as well as manpower of its republic. As Lenin emphasized, the U.S.S.R. State Planning Commission carries out scientific planning of the entire national economy. It serves to ensure a centralized economic policy and a coordinated development of separate branches of the economy.

The draft plan is finally approved by the U.S.S.R. Council of Ministers and the session of the Supreme Soviet. Once adopted by the supreme governmental bodies, the plan acquires the force of law, obligatory for all.

Planning is an extremely involved science. Planning bodies have to coordinate thousands of pieces of information; they must simultaneously ensure technical progress and reveal beforehand the more promising trends in economic development. At the same time they must see to it that industrial enterprises are given the broadest possible opportunities for independent activity, to intensify the workers' initiative.

The economic organization of a socialist society offers great advantages. A comparison of rates of annual industrial growth for a relatively long period shows that they are approximately three times those of capitalist

[8] The territorial administrative subdivisions called regional economic councils were established in 1957. They were abolished by the Central Committee of the CPSU in September-October, 1965, and new ministries were set up. The so-called all-union ministries (such as the Ministry of Transport Construction) administer directly the enterprises subordinated to them; the so-called Union-Republic ministries (such as the Ministry of Agriculture) operate through counterpart ministries in the Republics. Hence, the action taken by the CC CPSU in the fall of 1965 amounted to a decrease of territorial economic controls and greater emphasis on functional controls (according to the branch of industry). [EDITOR'S NOTE]

CARL A. RUDISILL LIBRARY
LENOIR RHYNE COLLEGE

countries. The Soviet Union had outstripped all capitalist countries with the exception of the United States in total industrial output even before the war. But at that time its volume of industrial production was not much greater than England's. Now, however, it exceeds the combined industrial output of England, France, Italy, Canada, Japan, Belgium, and the Netherlands.

Accelerated rates of development are characteristic of socialist economy. From 1913 to 1964 Soviet industrial production increased more than 55-fold. Soviet industry is growing at a much faster pace than that of the United States—the most developed capitalist country. From 1918 to 1964 industry developed three times faster than in the United States. By now the U.S.S.R. exceeds the United States in, and holds the world record for, total production of iron ore, coal, coke, various products of the engineering industry, cement, woolen fabrics, butter, sugar, and some other foods. On the whole, in 1964 Soviet industrial output amounted to over 65 percent of that of the United States.

All this illustrates the advantages of the socialist economy over the capitalist. Socialism reveals boundless possibilities for rapid economic progress in the interests of the working people.

THE SOCIAL AND POLITICAL SYSTEM OF SOCIALISM

Soviet people are used to the socialist order of things and it seems to them that's how it has always been. But by comparing the Soviet system to what it was like in old Russia some fifty years ago, the basic transformations will become clear to all.

In the social sphere: the exploiting classes and the exploitation of man by man have been completely eradicated; Soviet society consists only of working people—workers, peasants and the intelligentsia; the inviolable friendship of the peoples of the U.S.S.R. is an accomplished fact.

In the political sphere—democracy for all: all Soviet citizens are able to participate in running the state and the economy; persuasion and education are increasingly becoming the means by which the state influences the individual.

In the cultural sphere: the cultural level of the people has risen immeasurably; the moral make-up of the working man, his outlook and ethical ideals have changed.

WORKING PEOPLE OF A SOCIALIST SOCIETY

By the beginning of 1966 the Soviet Union had a population of 232 million. Three-quarters of them (to be more exact—75.4 percent), including their families, are wage and salary earners, and a little less than a quarter (24.4 percent) are collective farmers.

The working class is mainly engaged in socialist industry, producing the means of production and the manufactured consumer goods. Workers are also employed on state farms. The working class supplies the farmers with the chief agricultural instruments and mineral fertilizers. Farm produce is processed in state factories. According to the estimates of Soviet economist Academician S. Strumilin, approximately one-half of all grain produced in the U.S.S.R. represents the labor of state farm workers. The leading place in production, a wealth of political experience, a high degree of discipline and selflessness all ensure the working class the leading role in society.

Socialism has brought about radical changes in the composition of the working class. Prior to the revolution, the light and food industries had the greatest number of workers. Today more workers are engaged in engineering, metal-processing, the iron and steel industry, and the chemical and petroleum industries.

Technical progress has resulted in more highly skilled industrial workers, and many new vocations. The cultural and general educational level of workers has risen. Before the revolution more than a third of the factory workers were completely illiterate. Now, about 44 percent of the workers have either a secondary or higher education, and in branches like the steel industry, the chemical industry, and the printing trades—more than half. The majority of workers attend evening schools, specialized secondary schools and higher educational institutions while working. The workers are beginning to approach technicians and engineers in the nature of their work and education.

Socialism has also changed the make-up of the peasantry. The collective-farm peasantry is approaching the working class in labor conditions and cultural level. They work on large socialist farms based on collective labor, up-to-date machinery, and the achievements of modern science. Completely new vocations have found their way to the villages: there are now combine and machine operators, electrical engineers and electricians, radio operators, etc. More than a quarter of the collective farmers have a seven-year, a complete secondary, or a higher education.

The intelligentsia has changed too. It is now a social group and not a special class, since it does not hold an independent status in social production. As a whole it consists of skilled specialists engaged in material production, science, technology and culture, health protection, and in state and public administration.

The intelligentsia is a rapidly growing group in Soviet society, and the percentage of engineering personnel and scientists is increasing fast. Whereas in 1926 there were 2.7 million intellectuals; by 1957 the figure had risen to 10 million; and by 1964 it surpassed the 24 million mark. The growth of the intelligentsia will continue, for it accords with the need for developing the national economy and culture.

NEW SOCIAL RELATIONS

What is the pattern of social relations in Soviet society? In a socialist society all people enjoy equal status in political and civic rights, and participation in social labor. Now let us see what happens in production—the decisive sphere of human activities. The workers, farmers, and intellectuals have equal opportunities for working for their socialist society, hence for themselves, and they have like interests in a flourishing national economy and culture. The status of people and their material welfare depend on personal labor, abilities, and knowledge; not on the class to which they belong. Equality prevails also in the political sphere: all Soviet citizens, irrespective of their class or stratum, enjoy the same rights in running the state. The fact that people belong to the working class, the peasantry or intelligentsia does not give them special privileges in the cultural sphere. Socialism has made education accessible to all citizens, and it has created favorable conditions for developing talents from among the people in all branches of science and technology, culture and art. Soviet socialist society is a society of working people enjoying equal rights. Social, political, and ideological unity of all the people has evolved in the socialist society.

Building socialism in the U.S.S.R. has also wrought other important changes in social relations. Under socialism there is no contradiction between mental and physical labor, or between city and countryside, since the social conditions whereby brainwork afforded the propertied classes special privileges and whereby the city could exploit the countryside have been swept away.

Can there be social equality in a society based on private enterprise? Many bourgeois ideologists assert that all people are equal before the law in a capitalist society, that in the so-called free world everybody has equal rights and an equal say in society. But is that really so? Why is it that to this very day half the population of the world over 15 years old is illiterate? Why is it that in South Africa the African is fined 300 pounds or sentenced to a prison term of up to three years if he sits down on a bench reserved "For Whites"? Why is it that in many capitalist countries a woman, doing the same work as a man, receives less pay? The answer to all these questions is quite simple. If the factories, the land, the banks, and the mines are owned by a small group of people, then it is precisely this group that benefits the most. And inequality in property engenders inequality in all other spheres: political, juridical, cultural, national, etc.

At the same time it would be incorrect to think that the distinctions between the working class and the peasantry under socialism have been completely obliterated in regard to social relations. Of course there are still some distinctions in a socialist society. It is one of the tasks of building a communist society in the U.S.S.R. to completely eradicate these distinctions.

A UNION OF EQUAL NATIONS

The first socialist state is the home of over a hundred peoples and national-ities—more than in any other country.

When the working class, led by the Communist Party, took power in its own hands, the working people, the majority in every nationality, were given the right to self-determination. The population of pre-revolutionary Russia suffered from two evils: class oppression and national oppression. That is why confidence between the peoples could only be built up by granting them the right to self-determination, by revoking all national and religious privileges and restrictions.

The Communist Party carried out the plan elaborated by Lenin for uniting the Soviet republics, on the basis of full equality and free will, in the Union of Soviet Socialist Republics.

Just what does equality of all nationalities, big and small, mean in the Soviet Union? People of all nationalities, men and women alike, receive equal pay for equal work in any part of the country. There is no discrimina-tion in political life. There are frequent cases in the Soviet Union when a city with a predominantly Russian population elects, say, an Uzbek as its Deputy to the Supreme Soviet, and Georgians might well vote for a Ukrainian nominee.

However, actual equality among the nationalities didn't come about at once, for the people were at greatly differing stages of social development. There were advanced nationalities, backward peoples and small ethnic groups. Thus, in most of the areas of Central Asia feudal relations prevailed. The tribal system existed in a number of areas in the Far North. In order to raise the backward peoples to the level of the advanced, it was necessary to ensure the accelerated development of their economy and culture. That is the policy the Party adopted.

Here are some eloquent figures showing the results of such a policy. Between 1913 and 1963 there was a 52-fold increase in the general growth of large-scale industrial output for the whole of the country, while in Kazakhstan there was a 78-fold increase and in Kirghizia industrial output increased 82 times. Today there are highly skilled specialists in all the na-tional areas.

Socialism enables the culture of previously backward peoples to thrive. About 50 peoples have created their own written language and developed their literature since the formation of the Soviet state. Schooling is conducted in 65 languages of the different nationalities; the Union Republics have their own Academies of Science, numerous research institutes, national theatres and cinema studios.

With the mutual fraternal aid of all the peoples, and first of all the great Russian people, many formerly backward peoples have made the transition from the Middle Ages to socialism within three to four decades and avoided capitalist development.

The fact that socialism has done away with national oppression and created the conditions for formerly backward peoples to flourish indicates the justice and humanity of the socialist system. Speaking of his impressions of Soviet Uzbekistan, Indian writer Pandit Sunderlal stated: "If Uzbekistan could become a highly developed country under the Soviet system—and it really did!—then the Soviet system is the best in the world."

THE SOVIET FEDERATION

The U.S.S.R. is a federative state. But to go no further in describing the Soviet state would be to ignore the most important feature: the nationalities of the country are united by common destinies and aims, consolidated into one working socialist family. The Soviet federation makes it possible to combine harmoniously the rights of every national Republic and Region with the interests of the entire country, the interests of all the people.

The national bodies of state power decide the more general problems concerning the development of the national economy and culture. Peoples of the U.S.S.R. all have Soviet citizenship. There is a national budget, a uniform monetary system, and armed forces for the whole country.

At the same time every Union Republic has its own Constitution, draws up its own plan for economic development and its own budget, runs the industrial enterprises within its jurisdiction, and is in charge of health promotion, social security, education, etc. Every Union Republic can enter into direct relationships with other countries, and exchange diplomatic representatives with them.

In several of the Union Republics there are numerous nationalities. Where a national group lives as a more or less compact body, the state structure assumes the form of an autonomous republic, autonomous region, or a national area. Within the borders of its territory the Autonomous Republic develops its economy and culture, has its own bodies of power, and its own Constitution.

The Soviet state has the task of ensuring the correct, harmonious coordination of general state interests with the interests of separate nationalities. This is accomplished through the two-chamber system of the U.S.S.R. Supreme Soviet (parliament). The two chambers differ from the two Houses of Parliament in many Western countries. The Supreme Soviet does not have an Upper and Lower House; both are absolutely equal and a bill is considered adopted when passed by both chambers. The difference between them is not in their rights but in their composition. The Soviet of the Union represents the general interests of all the working people of the

U.S.S.R., irrespective of nationality. That is why representation for all Republics is on the basis of population: one Deputy per 300,000 people. But since the Soviet Union includes Republics with populations that greatly differ in size, if there were only one chamber making up the U.S.S.R. Supreme Soviet the large Republics would actually have an advantage over the smaller. To avoid such a situation, another chamber has been set up—the Soviet of Nationalities, concerned with the specific interests of the various nationalities of the U.S.S.R. All Republics, irrespective of the size of their territory and population, have equal representation in this body. For instance, the Russian Federation which has a population of more than 124 million, and Estonia, with a population of just slightly more than 1 million, have the same number of Deputies in the Soviet of Nationalities. Thus, it is not only the proclamation but the actual realization of equality for all nations and nationalities of the Soviet Union that is the great achievement of our age.

The Soviet Union is a fraternal community of socialist nations and nationalities. The friendship of the peoples of the U.S.S.R., their mutual assistance and support is one of the main wellsprings of the might of Soviet society.

THE SOVIET SOCIALIST STATE

What are the main functions of the Soviet state? There are economic organizational functions. The state is the collective owner of the main means of production. It sees to the planned development of all the branches of the national economy, organizes the people's labor, and concerns itself with raising their standard of living.

The latter is closely tied in with the state's cultural and educational functions. The Soviet state directs public education, determines the activities of scientific establishments, operates the theatres, museums, cinema studios, publishing houses, etc.

And the socialist state is vitally concerned with the struggle for peace, the strengthening of cooperation with the countries of the socialist camp, the development of economic and cultural ties with all countries. As long as the threat of a military attack on the part of imperialism exists, the Soviet state must also see to defense to ensure the country's security.

The socialist state acts on behalf of the people, in the interests of the people. It is the instrument of people's rule.

SOVIETS OF WORKING PEOPLE'S DEPUTIES

All power in the U.S.S.R. is vested in the working people through their representative bodies—the Soviets of Working People's Deputies. The Soviets function everywhere: in the city, workers' settlements, in every region, territory, and republic. They are the basis of the Soviet state and the foundation of socialist democracy. They are the organs of genuine people's power. Why is this so? Firstly, the Soviet represent all sections of Soviet society: the workers, farmers and the intelligentsia. Secondly, the Soviets are both ruling and executive bodies: at their sessions and in committees the Deputies adopt decisions, and then they themselves, or through the executive committees of the Soviets, implement them. Thirdly, the Soviets have full power: they decide all fundamental political questions, are in charge of all public wealth, manage the economy, guide the development of culture. As local bodies of people's self-administration, they are combinations of both state and public organizations.

Full representation of the people's interests in the Soviets is ensured by a democratic election system. Elections in the U.S.S.R. are universal. This means that all citizens on reaching the age of 18, irrespective of social origin, nationality, race, sex, education, religion, domicile, property status or past activities, have the right to vote in the elections. The only exception is the insane.

There is equal and direct suffrage in the U.S.S.R. All citizens participate in the elections on an equal footing. Each person has one vote. The Deputies are elected directly to the local Soviets and the Supreme Soviet. Nobody can interfere with the free expression of the voter's will: elections in the U.S.S.R. are by secret ballot.

On reaching the age of 18, citizens can be elected to the local Soviets of Working People's Deputies, at the age of 21—to the Supreme Soviets of the Union and Autonomous Republics, and at 23—to the U.S.S.R. Supreme Soviet.

Communist Party members run for election along with non-Party people who belong to trade unions, cooperatives, the Young Communist League, and to cultural and other mass societies of the working people. The public at large also exercises control over the course of the election campaign. More than 20 million people—campaign managers, members of electoral committees and canvassers—take part in the organization of these campaigns.

Deputies to the Soviets are not professional politicians. The vast majority of them work in factories, collective farms, institutes, and scientific laboratories; in other words, they are inseparably bound up with the people. They regularly report to the Soviet and directly to their constituencies.

At each new election at least one-third of the membership of the Soviets is replaced. This not only improves the work of the Soviets themselves but also ensures the inflow of fresh forces, new hundreds of thousands and millions of working people going through the school of state administration.

THE U.S.S.R. SUPREME SOVIET

The U.S.S.R. Supreme Soviet is the Soviet Union's highest organ of state power. The U.S.S.R. Supreme Soviet, in which full power is vested, considers and decides the more general and important questions of the Soviet Union's domestic and foreign policy.

Deputies to the U.S.S.R. Supreme Soviet are envoys of the working class, peasantry, and the working intelligentsia. Out of 1,443 Soviet parliamentarians, 646 are workers and collective farmers directly engaged in production. Fifty-six nationalities and peoples are represented in the highest organ of state power. One-third of the total number of Deputies, 390 in all, are women; 209 Deputies are below 30; and 405 are in the 30-40 age bracket.

The U.S.S.R. Supreme Soviet meets regularly to settle important state matters. At a joint sitting of the First Session of every convocation the two chambers (the Soviet of the Union and the Soviet of Nationalities) elect a Presidium of the U.S.S.R. Supreme Soviet for conducting current work as collective president of the Soviet state. The Presidium of the U.S.S.R. Supreme Soviet consists of a Chairman, 15 Vice-Chairmen—one from each Union Republic, a Secretary, and other members of the Presidium. The Presidium is accountable and subject to the control of the Supreme Soviet and acts on behalf of the Supreme Soviet in the interim between sessions.

THE U.S.S.R. COUNCIL OF MINISTERS

The U.S.S.R. Council of Ministers—the highest executive and administrative body of power in the Soviet Union—is formed at the joint session of the Soviet of the Union and the Soviet of Nationalities of the U.S.S.R. Supreme Soviet. It includes the chairmen of the Republican Councils of Ministers by virtue of their office, since the Union Republics participate in deciding all national questions. The U.S.S.R. Council of Ministers is accountable only to the Supreme Soviet and, when it is not in session, to its Presidium.

The U.S.S.R. Council of Ministers guides the development of the economy and culture, issues orders and instructions on the basis of and in pursuance of the decrees and laws of the U.S.S.R., verifies their execution, and protects the interests of the state and the rights of citizens. It determines Soviet foreign policy and is responsible for the country's defense. On especially important matters, joint decisions are passed by the Communist Party Central Committee and the Council of Ministers. These decisions are binding on all administrative State and Party bodies. The U.S.S.R. Council of Ministers coordinates and directs the work of ministries and other institutions under its jurisdiction.

REPUBLICAN AND LOCAL BODIES OF
STATE POWER AND ADMINISTRATION

The Union Republics have parallel organs of state and government. The highest organ of power in the Union Republic is the Supreme Soviet. It adopts laws binding within the limits of the Republic, approves the budget of the Republic, etc. The Supreme Soviet of the Union Republic differs from the U.S.S.R. Supreme Soviet in that it has only one chamber. The republican Supreme Soviet elects its Presidium, whose functions are defined by the Republic's Constitution. The republican Council of Ministers is the highest executive and administrative body of the Republic.

The highest organ of state power in the Autonomous Republic is its Supreme Soviet. It elects the Presidium, appoints the Council of Ministers, and elects the Republic's Supreme Court.

Local Soviets play an important place in the system of organs of state power. Territorial, regional, autonomous region, area, district, city, and rural Soviets of Working People's Deputies are elected for a term of two years. The Soviets guide the work of enterprises, institutions, and organizations under their jurisdiction, draw up the local budget, guide the activities of subordinate administrative bodies, and ensure the maintenance of law and order, and the protection of the rights of citizens. An important task of the local Soviets is the improvement of public services. The local Soviets elect their executive committees. For everyday guidance of the economy and culture, the Soviets usually set up a planning commission and departments for different branches of economic and cultural development.

THE COURT AND THE PROCURATOR'S OFFICE

All state bodies are charged with responsibility for the strict observance of Soviet laws, the maintenance of law and order, and the safeguarding of the rights and interests of citizens. But it is the system of courts, headed by the U.S.S.R. Supreme Court and the Procurator's Office, which occupies itself exclusively with the supervision of the judicial activities of the U.S.S.R.

The chief link in the judicial system is the regional People's Court. There is one in every region and city. Judges of People's Courts are elected for five-year terms on the basis of universal, equal, and direct suffrage by secret ballot. Judges are accountable to their constituency and may be recalled. Together with the judges there are People's Assessors who take part in the work of the court, on a voluntary basis. They are elected at general meetings of working people by open vote for two-year terms. All civil and criminal cases are decided by the judges and People's Assessors jointly. Courts of the areas, autonomous republics, territories, regions, and Union Republics are elected by the respective Soviets for five-year terms. The members of the U.S.S.R. Supreme Court are elected for a term of five years by the U.S.S.R. Supreme Soviet.

Judges are independent and subject only to the law. Judicial proceedings are conducted in the language of the Union Republic, Autonomous Republic or Autonomous Region. Everyone concerned in a court case has the right to speak in his native tongue. Trials are ensured objectivity and (with the exception of very few cases stipulated by law) are conducted publicly. The accused has the right to defense.

Crime is combatted by the stern punishment of dangerous criminals and the application of social sanctions to first offenders who can mend their ways under the influence of the collective. The public now plays a much greater role in dealing with breaches of the law (Comrades' Courts, People's Patrols, etc.).[9]

The Procurator's Office is a special judicial body for supervising the strict observance of the law. It institutes proceedings and investigates criminal cases, gathers evidence against criminals and their accomplices, and exercises supervision over the legality of the actions of other investigative bodies. The court tries cases lodged by the procurator's office and the procurator appears in court in the capacity of state prosecutor. The Procurator's Office is responsible for a uniform interpretation of the law throughout the vast country. It is also the special duty of this office to protect the personal immunity of Soviet citizens. No person may be placed under arrest except by court order or the sanction of a procurator.

The Soviet Procurator's Office constitutes a single, strictly centralized system independent of local bodies of state power and administration. The Procurator's Office is headed by the Procurator-General of the U.S.S.R., who is appointed by the U.S.S.R. Supreme Soviet for a seven-year term. The Procurator-General appoints republican, territorial, and regional procurators. The area, district, and city procurators are appointed by the procurators of the Union Republics subject to approval by the Procurator-General of the Soviet Union. Each lower body is subordinate to the higher one which ensures the rapid, precise fulfillment of the tasks of each.

[9] In recent years, the Soviets have made increasing use of popular participation in the administration of justice. Such bodies as public-order squads and comrades' courts, set up at factories, offices, collective and state farms, etc., have strictly limited powers to deal with minor offenses. Thought of as educational rather than punitive agencies, they use persuasion and public condemnation in front of the "collective," exposure in satirical newspapers, leaflets, and photographic displays, etc. Such public bodies will also vouch for individuals who have gone astray but appear to repent sincerely. According to Soviet sources, there are indications that 99 percent of such individuals justify the trust placed in them. See N. Mironov, "Persuasion and Compulsion in Combatting Anti Social Acts," in Harry G. Shaffer, ed., *The Soviet System in Theory and Practice: Selected Western and Soviet Views* (New York, Appleton-Century-Crofts, 1965), p. 447. [EDITOR'S NOTE]

SOCIALIST LEGALITY

The Soviet system establishes guarantees for the strict observance of Soviet laws. Soviet laws express the will of all the people. They regulate economic and other social relations, maintain socialist order, define the rights and duties of citizens and officials, and protect public and personal property. The main objectives of socialist law are the establishment of strict and just public order and the education of the people towards increasing intolerance of antisocial acts. The whole system of socialist law is directed towards ensuring every Soviet man and woman the conditions for free development. This is directly manifested in the rights and duties of Soviet citizens.

UNITY OF RIGHTS AND DUTIES

The following are rights that Soviet people enjoy.

The right to labor. One of the basic social rights of the individual is the right to work. This right is guaranteed by the socialist economic system, which excludes crises and unemployment. Soviet people are ensured full freedom in the choice of any occupation or specialty, freedom to manifest their creative individuality providing it does not conflict with the interests of society and the nation.

The right to education. Soviet youngsters begin school at the age of seven and once they finish their primary education millions of them continue their studies at specialized secondary and higher educational institutions. The right to education is guaranteed. Education is free in the U.S.S.R. all the way from first grade through university and postgraduate school and, in addition, a considerable part of the student body receives state stipends and enjoys other privileges. No wonder the U.S.S.R. now has more college students than any other country! And besides tuition-free schools, there are also boarding schools where children are maintained at state expense.

When we say that Soviet citizens have the right to an education we mean that every person actually has a chance to study. Prior to the October Revolution almost four-fifths of the children lacked the opportunity to attend school. In old Russia when a worker or peasant could read and write he was considered "learned." But times have changed. Today eight-year schooling is compulsory in the U.S.S.R., while a full secondary and higher education is accessible to all. The state spends huge sums on secondary and college education and the payment of stipends.

There are many people in the world trying to find out why the Soviet Union has outstripped such countries as the United States in many spheres of education, science, and technology. After all, the U.S.S.R. now graduates annually three times as many engineers as the U.S.A. The reason for this is no secret. The answer lies in the socialist system and the state's concern for the development of science and public education.

Let us compare the status of students particularly in Moscow's Physico-Technical Institute and America's Massachusetts Institute of Technology. The Soviet student only pays for a place in the dormitory (no more than 17 rubles, approximately 19 dollars a year). He does not pay for tuition or study aids. Moreover, he receives a stipend, which amounts to 500-odd rubles (approximately 550 dollars) a year. But the position of the American student is quite different. He has to spend more than 1,500 dollars a year on tuition alone. Naturally, not many can afford it and few are lucky enough to get scholarships. And this is but one of the many obstacles that stand in the way of the American working people obtaining an education.

In the U.S.S.R. all citizens are free to enter a college, irrespective of their nationality, race, or property status. Moreover, thousands of young people from all continents attend Soviet higher schools. Young men and women from Africa, Asia, and Latin America, people of different nationalities and races receive a good education in the U.S.S.R. Striving to assist the developing countries the Soviet Government has opened the Patrice Lumumba Friendship University, where the youth from the newly freed countries are studying side by side with Soviet young folk. Thus the Soviet Government, which shows the utmost solicitude for its own young people, is doing everything possible to help the countries that have set about to achieve free, all-around development.

In the U.S.S.R. education has indeed assumed a national scope. More than 70 million people are studying. Correspondence courses and evening schools where workers, collective farmers, and office employees get a general, secondary specialized or college education are serving a real need. There are also hundreds of different courses and lecture series for improving the skills of people in production. And with every passing year the number of people receiving an education is growing. But it is not "all work and no play" for Soviet people. Aside from work and study there are ample opportunities and facilities for relaxation.

The right to rest and leisure. An important guarantee of the right of Soviet citizens to rest and leisure is an annual vacation with full pay to which all factory and office employees are entitled. These vacations range from two weeks to 24 workdays and more, depending on the nature of the work. For those working underground or at harmful occupations, an additional paid leave of 12 working days or more is tagged onto their vacations. Every year more than 12 million get treatment or just spend their vacations at sanatoriums and holiday homes. Many pay nothing at all for their accommodations, others just 25 percent of the cost.

The right to maintenance. Concern for the health of the Soviet people is an important aspect of state activity. Free medical services, a wide network of hospitals, clinics, maternity homes, and medical stations, as well as women's and children's consultation points are all part of a comprehensive health service. The extent of this service can be judged by the following figures: in 1913 there was a total of 208,000 hospital beds in all of Russia, by 1964 the number had mounted to 2,043,000. Moreover, the high cost of medical service and scarcity of doctors in tsarist Russia deprived a considerable section of the population of the possibility of obtaining medical attention. Thus, whereas in 1913 Russia had 1.5 doctors per 10,000 people, in 1963 the figure stood at 20.6, not counting dentists. One of the striking results is the sharp rise in the average life span of the population. In 1896-97 it was 32 years, whereas in 1960-61 it was 72 years. It could be said that in the Soviet Union man has acquired a second life.

Solicitude for the people is manifested in many ways aside from medical care. Soviet citizens have the Constitutional right to maintenance in old age, in case of sickness, or where there has been loss of the breadwinner. This is guaranteed by the system of automatic social insurance for wage and salary workers. They themselves do not contribute anything to the insurance fund; the state pays the full cost. But if any employee falls sick he doesn't have to worry: he is entitled to sick benefits of up to 90 percent of his pay, and in case of an industrial accident or occupational disease—100 percent.

Wage and salary earners are entitled to pensions—men on reaching 60 with a work record of 25 years, and women at the age of 55 who have worked for 20 years. People employed in difficult and hazardous occupations have certain privileges: the pension age for men is 50-55 (with 20-25 years seniority), and for women, 45-50 (with 15-20 years seniority). Besides state pensions are paid to invalids disabled at work, to war invalids, to families of military men who had been killed, and to those who have lost the breadwinner. The pension system has now been extended to include collective farmers. The number of homes for invalids and the aged, who are granted full maintenance by the state, is being increased.

The state spends tremendous sums every year on social insurance and social welfare. In 1966 14.6 billion rubles were allocated for social insurance. Altogether 40.3 billion rubles out of a total 1966 state budget of 105.4 billion rubles were earmarked for social and cultural needs.

The equality of Soviet citizens. The social rights of Soviet citizens are safeguarded by state and public bodies. Attempts to restrict the rights of citizens on account of their nationality or race are considered a crime punishable by law. Personal immunity of the individual is guaranteed.

Freedoms and duties of Soviet citizens. Besides social rights Soviet people enjoy broad political rights and freedoms: freedom of speech, freedom of the press, freedom of assembly and meetings, the right to hold street processions and demonstrations and the right to unite in mass organizations. Political freedoms are guaranteed by law and by material means: printing shops, stocks of paper, publishing houses and newspaper offices, radio, film and television are placed at the disposal of the working people and their organizations. In short, freedoms are guaranteed by the entire socialist system.

Of course, there have to be some restrictions on political freedoms. The Soviet Press, for instance, will never use its pages to advocate war, or moral depravity. Propaganda aimed at creating national discord and misanthropy is prohibited in the U.S.S.R. And this is quite natural: all this is harmful to the people, to socialism.

Along with equal rights, the people have also equal duties. What duties does society and the state place on Soviet citizens? It is quite understandable that those who work well are anxious to preserve the fruits of their labor. Hence, society makes it the duty of every citizen to safeguard and be conscientious about socialist property, the foundation of the people's well-being.

PUBLIC ORGANIZATIONS

The mass organizations in the Soviet Union are the trade unions, the Young Communist League, cooperatives, and scientific, technical, sport, and cultural societies. To all intents and purposes they embrace the entire adult population of the U.S.S.R.

It is impossible to compare the status of Soviet trade unions with trade unions in most other countries, where they have to defend the rights of the working people in bitter struggle against employers and the state. In the U.S.S.R., state interests and the interests of the trade unions and of all organizations of working people are one and the same. That is why the role of Soviet trade unions, their tasks and methods of work, are entirely different from those of trade unions in bourgeois society. In the Soviet Union the state more than cooperates with the trade unions: it creates all the conditions for increasing their participation in running the country. Always serving the interests of the people, the state is doing everything possible to better the working conditions and raise the living standards. The workers and farmers do not have to go on strike to better their lot.

The trade unions were the first of the public organizations to be given important functions formerly performed by state bodies. In 1933 the U.S.S.R. Central Trade Union Council took over the functions of the People's Commissariat (Ministry) of Labor of the U.S.S.R.

That same year the trade unions were granted the right to handle the funds allocated by the state for social insurance. At present the state social insurance budget, which is included in the U.S.S.R. State Budget, is drawn up by the Central Council of Trade Unions and administered by trade union bodies.

In addition, the trade unions:

Participate in planning the development of the national economy;

Issue instructions, rules and explanations on the application of the existing
labor laws;

Establish regulations and standards for labor protection and industrial hygiene;

Participate in drawing up regulations for internal labor organization at factories and offices;

Participate in setting piece rates, wages and salaries;

Supervise the fulfillment of housing construction plans, and participate in
the distribution of living quarters;

Supervise the observation of labor legislation;

Investigate and submit information about people guilty of violating labor
laws in order to institute disciplinary or criminal action against them,
and fine directors and managers guilty of violating labor laws.

At the present time the general, overall management of sanatoriums
and holiday homes has been placed under the General Council of Trade
Unions which, together with the state bodies of the U.S.S.R. and the Union
Republics, plans the extension of the network of sanatorium and health
resorts.

Without the consent of the factory or local trade union committee,
not a single wage or salary earner can be fired by the management. At the
same time the trade unions have the right to demand the removal of administrators who violate labor laws.

The trade unions make a tremendous contribution towards educating
the working people and raising their cultural level. They run more than
16,000 clubs, about 19,000 motion-picture theaters, 30,000 public libraries,
155,000 recreation rooms (specially equipped rooms in factories and offices
for holding cultural and educational activities), and thousands of sporting
and tourist accommodations. Every month more than 200 million people
use these cultural facilities.

This far from complete enumeration of trade union functions shows
what a valuable contribution Soviet trade unions make in matters of extreme importance to the working people and the country as a whole. By participating in the various aspects of trade union activities all wage and salary
earners obtain beneficial experience in management and self-government.

THE YOUTH LEAGUE

Most Soviet young people belong to the Leninist Young Communist League
(Komsomol). Its importance lies in the fact that it is not merely a youth
organization but a communist union of young people closely allied to the
Communist Party, working under its leadership as its militant aide. Young
people are the country's future, the future of communism. And while they
may lack the knowledge and experience of the older generation, their en-

thusiasm and desire to master knowledge and gain experience make up for it.

From 1918 to 1964 the Young Communist League educated 80 million people, which means that half the adult generation at one time were Young Communist League members.

The urge for creative endeavor is characteristic of the youth. New blast and open-hearth furnaces, the world's biggest electric stations, and factories are being erected by industrious young folk.

The Young Communist League is also an active assistant of the Party in the effort to promote agriculture. Members of the League manifest enterprise and initiative everywhere.

The total membership of the Young Communist League at the present time is more than 22 million but its influence is felt by all Soviet young folk. The Young Communist League has direct charge of the children's Communist organization—the Lenin Young Pioneers. The Party has entrusted the Komsomol with guiding the younger generation.

The Soviet youth, the Young Communist Leaguers in their thoughts and aspirations respect the Communist Party members for their principles, for the example they set. From them they learn to be true to ideals, to be courageous and selfless in the struggle for communism.

COOPERATIVE ORGANIZATIONS

Soviet collective farms are voluntary cooperative unions of peasants based on collective production and self-administration. The main means of production in the collective farms—farm structures, implements, draft animals, fodder, and seed—are common property. The land, which is nationalized, is granted to the collective farm for its free and perpetual use.

At their general membership meetings, members of the collective farms elect their board of management, the chairman of the board, and the auditing committee. They vote on the acceptance and expulsion of members, on the way their funds should be spent, on production quotas, on piece-rates, and on the obligatory minimum of labor each member must contribute. They decide on the size of individual holdings,[10] etc. On large farms a number of questions are decided at meetings of representatives, trustees, and at team meetings. There are also standing committees chosen by the general meeting. This makes it possible for all farm members to take part in discussions on collective farm life.

The collective farms have been given ample scope in planning farm production and cattle breeding. They themselves decide such matters as

[10] This refers to the small private plots, usually about half an acre in size, on which collective farm families (as well as families on state farms and often city workers' families) may raise farm products for their own use or for sale on the market. [EDITOR'S NOTE]

improving and extending the villages, or establishing nurseries and kindergartens, schools, hospitals, and libraries.

There is also a consumers' cooperative in the U.S.S.R. concerned with trade in the countryside. It organizes the sale of surplus farm stocks, and serves the rural population. It consists of over 43 million share holders. Another cooperative deals with housing construction to help improve living conditions.

There are many other public organizations made up of people with like occupations or hobbies (for instance, hunters' or anglers' societies). Some of them organize public scientific and cultural activities. These include the Society for the Dissemination of Political and Scientific Knowledge, societies of teachers, societies of medical workers, numerous scientific and technical societies, inventors' societies, unions of writers, journalists, composers, artists, film workers, architects, and other sections of the creative intelligentsia.

There are sports societies and societies for civilian defense. These include the Union of Sports Societies and Organizations, the Volunteer Society for the Army, Air Force and the Navy, the Red Cross and Red Crescent Society, societies to protect nature and greenery. There is a whole group of societies concerned with the struggle for peace, and the promotion of friendship with the peoples of other countries. These are the Soviet societies for friendship and cultural ties with foreign countries, the Soviet Peace Committee, the Women's Committee, the Soviet Youth Committee. All these and numerous other societies function on the basis of public self-administration. They influence millions of people.

THE COMMUNIST PARTY

The most important socio-political organization in a socialist society is the Communist Party—the militant, tested vanguard of the Soviet people. It unites on a voluntary basis the advanced and conscientious part of the working class, the collective-farm peasantry, and the intelligentsia. The Soviet Communist Party is the vanguard which headed the struggle of the working people for building a new, just society. It was founded by Vladimir Lenin who elaborated the principles of its structure, the norms for internal Party life and the methods of work.

Every great revolution brings to the fore its own heroes—civil and military leaders and organizers, such as Spartacus and Münzer, Marat and Robespierre. The October, 1917, Revolution also had its outstanding figures. Lenin's collaborators who became organizers and leaders of the first socialist state included people endowed with the most varied talents: wonderful organizers, gifted military leaders, and brilliant publicists. All of them had much in common: devotion to the Party's cause, personal courage, high principles, and resolute readiness to give of themselves. They all possessed in full measure the qualities which can be considered inseparable traits of each and every true communist: "Clean hands, a cool head and a fervent heart" (Dzerzhinsky).

But it was not just the Party leaders who possessed these qualities. They came to be expected of the hundreds of thousands of communists of all generations. During the Civil War and foreign intervention, at a time of struggle against hunger and ruin, in the grim years of World War Two, the communists were always to be found where it was hardest, and their motto became: "Communists in the forefront."

Here is the typical biography of a communist, and there are very many like him.

Kirill Orlovsky joined the Party at the age of 23. His entire life is a model of devotion and service to the Party and nation. In the early twenties Orlovsky fought against the White Poles. In 1936 he fought in Spain. When the Nazis attacked the Soviet Union in 1941 he fought as a partisan in the Byelorussian forests. There were years of struggle against the fascist troops and dozens of daring raids. One of the battles ended tragically for him: a serious wound, the amputation of one arm, a delicate operation on the other, and almost complete loss of hearing.

"My physical defects no longer permit me to remain a military man," Colonel Orlovsky wrote to his party organization. "But having been brought up by the Communist Party, there is no greater joy in life for me, no other aim, than to work for the good of my beloved Motherland. Now I am faced with the question: what else can I do for my country, for the Party?" In 1945 he left Moscow for the Byelorussian village of Myshkovichi that had been razed by the fascists, and he now heads the local collective farm, Rassvet (Dawn). Again tense work, study and sleepless nights. Now Rassvet is one of the country's best farms. Much of the credit for this belongs to Communist Orlovsky, Hero of the Soviet Union and Hero of Socialist Labor.[11]

The construction of socialism—this is the main result of the work of the Party—the Party which has gained the firm confidence and support of the nation. For Soviet people the Communist Party is the political organization not only of the working class, but also of the collective-farm peasantry, of the intelligentsia—of all sections of society.

WHY THERE IS ONLY ONE PARTY IN THE U.S.S.R.

In many countries people have the notion that democracy inevitably means a number of parties. Since there is only one party in the U.S.S.R., the Communist Party, we are frequently told by opponents of communism that

[11] The titles Hero of the Soviet Union and Hero of Socialist Labor are two of the highest honors attainable by Soviet citizens. [EDITOR'S NOTE]

there cannot be true democracy in our country. But it is incorrect to think that the extent of democracy is always and everywhere dependent on the existence of several parties.

It is quite natural that in the capitalist countries, where antagonistic classes exist, there are different political parties to defend the interests of the different classes. However, as we see it, this is no real guarantee of democracy. The level of democracy is by no means determined by the number of parties in a country, but by who actually holds the reins of power and determines the policy of the state.

Socialist democracy does not exclude the possibility of several parties. In Bulgaria, the German Democratic Republic and a number of other countries building socialism, there are other parties, besides the Communist Party which plays the leading role. As for the Soviet Union, the course of historical development was such that the Communist Party turned out to be the only party. In the course of the historic trials and tribulations the Soviet Union has experienced, the working people of the U.S.S.R. have become convinced that it is the Communist Party which consistently and staunchly defends their interests.

The Communist Party has 12.5 million members and candidate members. More than 70 percent of the communists are occupied in the various branches of material production, working directly in factories, construction and transport, and on collective and state farms. The Soviet Party is made up of members from all of the hundred-odd nationalities and peoples inhabiting the country.

METHODS AND FORMS OF PARTY LEADERSHIP

The Soviet Communist Party is the ruling party in the country. In what way and by what methods is Party leadership implemented? Above all, the Party elaborates the basic principles of Soviet domestic and foreign policy. In addition to the Party Programme, which outlines the general political course for a whole historical period, the Party congresses and plenary sessions of the Central Committee set concrete political tasks, including time limits and ways and means of accomplishing these tasks.

Among the Party's most important and engrossing tasks is the working out of directives for developing the country's industry and agriculture, and for determining general principles and methods of economic management. Questions of economic development are the main concern at Central Committee plenary sessions.

Another important method of Party leadership is its direct organizational activity. This is reflected in the fact that as the ruling party, the CPSU does a tremendous amount of work in selecting and training cadres. In recommending people for responsible posts, the party organizations take into account the opinions of the personnel at plants and institutions, the trade unions and other public organizations. Due consideration is also given to the business and political qualifications of people, their special knowledge, general cultural level, organizational abilities, honesty, and high moral principles.

The Communist Party guides communist construction through state and public organizations. It does not dominate these organizations and does not do their work. It determines the main tasks and the place of every organization in the mainstream of communist construction.

The political and organizational activities of the Party are inseparably connected with its ideological work (explaining the Party's policy and mobilizing people to carry it out), and with its concern for education and culture (promoting the development of science, literature, and all aspects of professional and amateur art activities on a mass scale).

The following general rule holds good for all methods of Party leadership: political, organizational and ideological activities are based on a study of modern science and the logic of social development, i.e., on the actual processes taking place in society.

PARTY STRUCTURE

The primary Party organizations [12] are the basis of the Party. They are formed at the places of work of Party members—factories, state farms and other enterprises, collective farms, units of the Soviet Army, offices, educational establishments, etc., wherever there are not less than three Party members. Communists who are not occupied in social production (pensioners, housewives) are organized in party organizations according to place of residence. Thus the production principle is observed in Party structure. Within large primary Party organizations there may also be Party units in departments of institutions, shops, sections, farm divisions, and teams.

The highest organ of the primary organization is the Party meeting, which is held at least once a month. Non-Party people are welcome to attend open party meetings.

A bureau or executive committee, headed by a secretary, is elected at a yearly meeting to conduct day-to-day activities. Important current matters are decided jointly by the secretary and other members of the party bureau.

What are the main activities of the primary organization? To work with people, to better their political and ethical education, to help them learn how to run state and public matters, to organize labor and improve living conditions.

People constantly turn to communists for advice and help on all

[12] In English, the primary Party organization or primary Party unit is frequently referred to as the Party cell. [EDITOR'S NOTE]

kinds of questions. Communists are concerned with every social problem: the reconstruction of shops, the state of affairs at the factory kindergarten, proposals for improvements, personal problems and injustice. They take an active interest in the housing question and the organization of facilities for the people to spend their leisure. And it is not just a matter of being interested. The management, the trade union committee, and the Young Communist League committee take up such questions on the proposal of the Party bureau or the entire primary organization. Once a decision is made it is up to the Party bureau to see it is carried out.

The primary Party organizations are represented in the Party organization of the district, city, area, region, and territory in which they are located. In this way the territorial principle of Party structure is observed.

What does the combination of the production and territorial principle mean to the Party? It ensures the self-reliance of every collective of Communists while simultaneously uniting them in one big organization. The production of material values is, after all, the most important matter. That is why the basic questions of social life are settled at plants, factories, farms, institutes, etc., where efforts to boost labor productivity result in raising living standards and culture. It is quite understandable that communist collectives working at enterprises and offices have an opportunity to influence directly the course of affairs.

Uniting Party organizations into district, city, and higher bodies permits comprehensive Party leadership in the different branches of the economy and culture.

THE PARTY'S HIGHEST BODIES

Party leadership is vested in collective bodies elected in a democratic way. The highest leading body of the Party organization is the general membership meeting (for the primary organization), the conference (for district, city, area, regional, and territorial organizations), and the Congress (for the Communist Parties of the Union Republics and of the Soviet Union as a whole). The bureau and committees elected at membership meetings, conferences, and Congresses are the executive organs to guide the current work of the respective organizations.

The supreme body of the Soviet Communist Party is, thus, its Congress. Every Party Congress is an important landmark in the life of the Party and the people. The Congress sums up what has been accomplished since the preceding congress and sets new tasks for the future. The Congress hears and approves the reports of the Central Committee, the Central Auditing Commission, and other central bodies; reviews, amends, and endorses the Programme and Rules of the Party; determines the Party line on questions of domestic and foreign policy; considers and decides the most important questions of communist construction; elects the Central Committee and the Central Auditing Commission.

Congresses are convened at least once every four years. Announcement of the convocation of a Party Congress and its agenda is made at least six weeks before the Congress in order to prepare for the session adequately. When very urgent matters have to be decided before the next regular Congress, an Extraordinary Congress can be convened.

In the interim between Congresses all Party activities are directed by the Party's Central Committee. The Central Committee is the heart and the brains of the Communist Party. It is the collective leader of the Party and people, the crux of ideological, political, and organizational leadership in building communism. The Central Committee consists of the most experienced communists who have a profound understanding of Party and economic affairs, people well versed in industry, agriculture, culture, science, and military affairs. The decisions of the Central Committee are binding on all Party organizations, and on each and every member of the Party. The Central Committee meets in plenary sessions at least twice a year. It elects a Politburo [13] to direct the work of the Central Committee between plenary sessions and a Secretariat to direct current work, chiefly the selection of cadres and the supervision of the fulfillment of Party instructions and decisions.

DEMOCRATIC CENTRALISM

The structure and activities of the Party are based on the principle of democratic centralism. What does this mean? First of all, it means the election of all leading Party organs from the lowest to the highest.

The principle of democratic centralism presumes periodical reports of Party bodies to their Party organizations and higher Party bodies. Democratic centralism also means strict Party discipline and the submission of the minority to the majority, with decisions of the higher organs being obligatory for all lower Party bodies.

Internal Party democracy is inconceivable without freedom of opinion, without free and businesslike discussion of all political questions. This is natural and necessary. Communists do not have the same theoretical background or the same political and social experiences. Each of them has his own approach to solving problems. Free exchange of opinion makes it possible to find the best solution. However, once a decision is made and adopted by majority vote, unity of action and strict discipline are obligatory.

[13] From 1952 to 1965 the Politburo was called the "Presidium." In the fall of 1965, the name "Politburo" was readopted. [EDITOR'S NOTE]

ELIGIBILITY FOR PARTY MEMBERSHIP

People join the Party because of ideological motives—a desire to unselfishly devote themselves to serving communist ideals. Who then is eligible for Party membership? Any citizen of the Soviet Union may become a member of the Communist Party, providing he agrees with the Party Programme and Rules. This is essential since the Communist Party is a party of like-minded people, and the Programme and Rules express the common ideological platform which unites all communists. But that is not all. One may accept the policy of the Party without belonging to the Communist Party. A member of the Communist Party is one who actively works to implement Party policy and fulfill his duties as laid down in the Rules.

The qualities of communists are manifested in full measure in the collective, wherefore according to the Rules, to be considered a communist one must be active in one of the Party organizations, carry out Party decisions, and be a member in good standing.

Every communist has the right to take an active part in the life of the Party. A Party member has the right to vote for representatives in and be elected to Party bodies. He takes part in the free and businesslike discussion on questions of policy and practical activities of the Party at Party meetings and in the Party press. A Party member has the right to criticize any communist, irrespective of the post he holds, and demand that he attend in person any Party meetings that discuss his activities or conduct. A communist can address any question, statement, or proposal to any Party body up to and including the Party's Central Committee and demand an answer on the substance of his address.

THE PARTY PROGRAMME

The Supreme objective of the Communist Party is to build a communist society. This aim and the means to attain it are outlined in the new Party Programme. Lenin attached special importance to the Party Programme. He said that without a programme the party was inconceivable as an integral political organism capable of maintaining its line under any circumstances. The programme of a Marxist party is based on scientific theory; it formulates the tasks which proceed from the needs of social development and it expresses the interests of the masses.

The first Party Programme was adopted at the Second Congress of the Russian Social-Democratic Labor Party in 1903. Lenin and the newspaper *Iskra*, which he had founded, spent a long time working out this programme. The programme set the party and the working class the task of fighting for the dictatorship of the proletariat which was realized as a result of the Great October Revolution and the establishment of Soviet power.

The second Party Programme was adopted by the Eighth Congress of the Russian Communist Party (Bolsheviks) in 1919. It was drawn up with Lenin's direct participation and guidance as chairman of the Programme Committee and discussed in the party organizations prior to the congress.

Lenin delivered the report on the Programme at the Eighth Party Congress. By that time it was the programme of the party that held power and led the world's first socialist state. It was the programme to build socialism in the country. Like the first programme, it was successfully carried out by the Party and the Soviet people. The tremendous changes that took place in the Soviet Union made it possible for the Party to draw up and adopt a new Programme. In October, 1961, the 22nd Party Congress adopted a new Programme, the third in the history of the Party, a scientifically substantiated plan for the construction of communism in the Soviet Union.

The Party Programme, based on Marxist-Leninist theory, benefited from the historic experience of our Party, and the experience of the international communist and working class movements. The Programme states clearly and precisely what the Party had already achieved, what it is struggling for, and the tasks it must accomplish in the near future.

The introduction to the Programme gives a general analysis of the more than one hundred year development of Marxism-Leninism, the victory of socialism in the Soviet Union and a number of other countries of Europe and Asia, and stresses that the supreme objective of the Party is to build a communist society on whose banner will be inscribed: "From each according to his ability, to each according to his needs."

The first part of the Programme deals with the special features of transition from capitalism to communism. It gives a brief description of capitalism as the last exploiting system, shows the historical inevitability of the transition from capitalism to socialism, and points out the historic mission of the working class and the Communist Party. It deals with the main object lessons in the history of the Communist Party and the Soviet people, and gives a brief analysis of Soviet experience. This section also outlines the urgent tasks concerning the development of the world socialist system, the international revolutionary working class movement, and the national liberation movement. It analyzes the reasons for the crisis of world capitalism, and of bourgeois and reformist ideology.

Part two, which is longer, explains communism and communist construction. "The CPSU regards communist construction in the Soviet Union as a component of the building of a communist society by the peoples of the entire world socialist system." Communism is represented in the Programme as the natural result of the development of human society, as the apex of mankind's entire economic, socio-political and cultural progress.

For Soviet people the Party Programme serves as a practical manual in the construction of a communist society. The Programme states: "The Communist Party of the Soviet Union, true to proletarian internationalism, always follows the militant slogan 'Workers of All Countries, Unite!' *The Party regards communist construction in the U.S.S.R. as the Soviet people's great international task,* in keeping with the interests of the world socialist system as a whole and with the interests of the international proletariat and all mankind."

The 23rd Party Congress held at the end of March and the beginning of April, 1966, set the basic tasks for the Soviet Union's development in the next five years (1966-1970). The main objective of the new five-year plan is to ensure considerable growth in industry as well as a high and steady rate of development in agriculture, and on this basis to attain a considerably higher standard of living and a fuller satisfaction of the Soviet people's material and cultural requirements. During the next five years industrial output will increase perhaps 50 percent and agricultural production 25 percent.[14] As a result, the working people's real incomes per capita will rise nearly 30 percent.

THE ROAD TO COMMUNISM

THE DEVELOPMENT OF SOCIALISM INTO COMMUNISM

In drawing up the plan for socialist construction Lenin wrote: "Striving for socialism we are convinced it will develop into communism."

THE DISTINCTIONS

Socialism is the initial phase, the first step in the construction of a communist society. It is quite natural that it differs from communism, the second stage of a communist society which grows out of the first just as any organism passes through various stages of maturity.

In principle there is a great deal in common between socialism and communism. They have one and the same economic basis: public ownership of the means of production—hence the absence of the kind of social classes engendered by the wage labor system. Socialism and communism have one and the same objective: to prevent the accumulation of huge per-

---

[14] The figure for anticipated percentage increase in agricultural production was not clear in the original manuscript. The figure of 25 percent was inserted by the editor. It has been taken from the Directives for the five-year plan adopted by the 23rd CPSU Party Congress, as published in *Pravda* (April 10, 1966). The Directives gave as one of the goals of the five-year plan "to increase the average annual output of agricultural products in the years 1966-1970 by 25 percent in comparison with the average annual output of these products in the preceding five-year period." [EDITOR'S NOTE]

sonal wealth derived from profit and to eliminate "production for the sake of production," replacing it by production to satisfy the multitude of man's needs. In other words, the objective is the ever greater satisfaction of the growing material and cultural demands of each and every member of society.

But there are, of course, essential differences between socialism and communism. First of all, there is the level of the productive forces: under socialism the scope and technology of production are still insufficient to introduce the communist principle of distribution according to needs. Under communism, production must attain a degree of mechanization and automation that will permit the creation of true abundance, and on this basis ensure the all-around development of the individual. Simultaneously the work week will be sharply reduced.

The distribution of the main bulk of consumer benefits under socialism, as has already been mentioned, directly depends on the labor contribution of every working man and woman—according to the quantity and quality of work. Here the principle of equal pay for equal labor irrespective of sex, nationality, or race, is observed. Quite naturally, higher wages are paid for higher skills, more productive or harder work and work under greater tension.

At the same time, even now in the U.S.S.R., one-quarter of all consumption expenditures are paid out of public funds at no cost to the individual (free health service, free or low-cost cultural services, housing, pensions, stipends, benefits to mothers of large families, social insurance, and so forth).

Under communism all material and cultural values will be distributed according to the principle: from each according to his ability to each according to his needs, in keeping with individual demands and tastes. Trade and money will become things of the past.

A certain amount of socio-economic and cultural inequality still exists under socialism. There are still classes: the working class and the peasantry, and also a special social stratum—the intelligentsia. However, there is no enmity, there are no antagonistic contradictions between them. The vast majority of the members of society are united by a common goal—they are striving to build a new society.

Under socialism there are still substantial distinctions between conditions of rural and urban life, and between those engaged in manual and those engaged in mental labor. And there are still the vestiges of inequality between men and women, especially since women are burdened with household chores.

Communism, however, presumes the full socio-economic and cultural equality of all members of society, i.e., the absence of any classes and social groups whatsoever. The substantial differences between the city and the countryside, and between physical and mental labor will be overcome. Communist society is a community of highly conscious and equal people, based on their joint labor and free self-administration.

In a socialist society the vestiges of the past—egotism, avarice, self-interest, the inability to take into account the interests of other people, the desire to live at the expense of others, etc.—still remain as characteristics of many people. These negative manifestations are frequently aggravated by insufficient earnings (primarily for unskilled workers), and unsatisfactory living conditions (especially in remote areas of the country). That is why, together with the steady rise in the living standards of the working people in the U.S.S.R., a great amount of day-to-day educational work is being done to enhance the consciousness of the masses, to overcome prejudices and vestiges of the past in people's minds.

In freeing all its members from concern about their daily bread, communist society creates unprecedented opportunities for the free and harmonious development of the individual. The reduction of the working day to a minimum will ensure plenty of leisure time to spend on favorite occupations and pastimes, on cultural growth, on acquiring knowledge, and on mastering new vocations.

The transition to the higher phase cannot take place at once, by some kind of revolution: it would be naïve to think that some day one will go to sleep under socialism and wake up in a communist society. This transition is a comparatively long process. Communism gradually evolves from socialism. Hence, there is no need to break up everything and begin to build communism anew: what is required is the development, improvement and, wherever necessary, transformation of the production basis and of the social relations of socialism.

The gradual and continuous development of socialism into communism does not mean that it takes place by itself. Not at all! The construction of communism requires the active, creative solution of problems facing society. Communism is being built by the conscious, directed activities of the working people of our country under the leadership of the Communist Party. What then are the chief tasks of Soviet people in the period of the transition from socialism to communism?

The production of material values is the basis of society. Hence, the main task in communist construction is to create the material and technical basis of communism. This is the chief but not the only task. Obviously it is necessary to mold communist social relations to achieve communism. This is the second task of building a communist society. And, since the ultimate goal of communist transformation is the all-around development of the individual, the third task is the education of the new man.

The interrelation of these main tasks in building communism is evident at first glance. In building new factories and increasing public wealth, the Soviet people are paving the way for the transition to the communist principle of labor and distribution, that is, the perfection of social relations. The development of social relations leads to a transformation in people's way of thinking, the inculcation of new ethical qualities. In turn, the formation of communist social relations and the education of the new man have a great influence on the development of productive forces.

THE MATERIAL AND TECHNICAL BASIS OF COMMUNISM

The material and technical basis of a society is that level in the development of production on which the given social system is based and from which it can fully develop. What are the chief elements of the material and technical basis of communism? These are:

The complete electrification of the country,
The comprehensive mechanization and automation of production,
The widespread use of chemistry in the national economy,
The organic fusion of science and production,
The national use of all the available resources,
A high cultural level and degree of technical skill of the working people, and
A high level of labor productivity.

The creation of the material and technical basis of communism is a highly complex matter. The Soviet people will have to overcome many difficulties and obstacles in achieving it. But the great aim gives rise to a great energy of the masses, and great achievements have already been scored in the construction of the material base of communism in the U.S.S.R.

TOWARD A CLASSLESS SOCIETY

It has already been stated that the main reason there are still class distinctions in the U.S.S.R. is that the labor of the workers is bound up with property belonging to all the people, and the labor of peasants with collective-farm property. These distinctions will disappear when one single communist ownership of the means of production takes the place of the two forms of socialist property. How will this come about?

Property belonging to all the people develops in the course of the construction of the material and technical basis of communism. It grows in volume: with every passing year thousands of new factories, schools and houses, motion picture theatres and clubs, clinics and stadiums begin to function, industrial facilities are modernized, and production capacity increased. At the same time, mass production on a large scale is introduced wherever economically feasible, and specialization and co-operation among enterprises becomes the order of the day; the distribution of productive forces is improved, and the management of the national economy is perfected.

Socialist property belonging to all the people directly develops into communist property. As for collective-farm property, it's a more difficult matter: it has to become increasingly the property of all the people. This requires the ever broader introduction of new machinery in farming, wide-scale application of scientific achievements in field work and cattle breeding, and better organization of labor—in other words, a sharp upsurge in the productive forces in agriculture. With the modernization of agriculture, collective and state farms will turn into real factories producing grain, meat, milk, and other products. The labor for such factories will be industrial labor requiring not only a higher culture but also a higher level of collectivist spirit among the workers. By then, what formerly had been collective farm property will have become the property of the whole people.

When this process is completed, the main distinction between classes will disappear. How will this manifest itself?

All production workers will be employed at industrial and agricultural enterprises belonging to all the people.

All will have approximately equal working conditions.

All will receive remuneration for their labor from the state and be able to use alike the benefits distributed through the public funds.

TOWARD COMMUNIST LABOR AND DISTRIBUTION

The realization of the principle of payment according to one's work is one of the greatest gains of socialism. It did away with the monstrous inequality in the distribution of material and spiritual values under capitalism.

But pay according to one's work does not signify full equality in living standards. People doing work that is more skilled earn more and, quite naturally, live better than those who are less skilled. Families, too, differ in size, which also leads to disparity in living standards. These vestiges of social inequality will disappear when society is in a position to fully implement the communist principle of labor and distribution: "From each according to his ability, to each according to his needs." What conditions are required to make this possible?

There must be an abundance of material and spiritual values. Productive forces must develop to ensure a productivity of labor sufficiently high to permit society generously to satisfy all the needs of its members. Since the demands of the people are growing all the time, this means that social wealth has to increase at a still faster pace. When it comes to the prime necessities of life—food, clothes, footwear, and housing—this is a comparatively simple matter. Scientists have estimated the amount of calories required by the human organism for normal vitality, the amount of protein, fats, carbohydrates, and vitamins needed; how many shoes, dresses, suits, and other clothing it is feasible to have in one's personal wardrobe; what space is required for a healthy and cultured life. Such indices are called rational standards. Knowing the size of the population and taking into account its growth, it is possible to determine how long it will take to fully satisfy a specific need.

Of course, human requirements change, the esthetic tastes of people develop, fashion engenders new styles in clothes, shoes, and furniture. But these changes are not so significant and, once the satisfaction of urgent needs is assured in keeping with rational standards, perfected production will be able to cater to diverse demands and the most discriminating tastes.

In addition, growing production, science, and technology give rise to completely new demands, which become as necessary as, say, the need to dress well. Thirty years ago there was no need to have a television set—now television is a necessity in every home, and radio engineering has the task of satisfying this demand in the next several years.

An abundance of material and spiritual values is the first but not the only condition for the transition to the communist principle of distribution: it is not simply a matter of distribution, this principle also holds good for labor. Where will the abundance come from, who will be able to satisfy the overgrowing demands if not the very same people, if not by their labor for the good of society as a whole? That is why another most important condition for implementing the communist principle of distribution is the readiness of all members of society to work to the best of their abilities, generously to contribute their knowledge and skill, talents and energy to society. In the course of building communism, labor itself turns into a prime necessity, just as natural and necessary as the air we breathe.

"Communist labor," Lenin wrote, ". . . is free labor for the good of society, labor done not to serve a definite term of conscription, not to receive the right to certain commodities, labor not according to established and legalized norms, but voluntary labor, labor outside of norms, labor given without counting on remuneration, without any conditions for remuneration, labor as a habit to work for the general good . . . labor as the requirement of a healthy organism." It turns out that both parts of the communist principle of labor and distribution are inseparably interconnected: without labor according to ability there cannot be satisfaction according to needs. Therefore both matters have to be resolved simultaneously: to create an abundance of material values and to inculcate a communist attitude to labor in members of society.

THE ECONOMIC, SOCIAL, AND CULTURAL DEVELOPMENT OF NATIONALITIES

Socialism has consolidated the numerous nationalities and peoples of the Soviet Union into one big family. And just like any healthy, harmonious family, it is growing and thriving: the economy and culture of the peoples are developing, and their bonds of kinship, their ties, are strengthening.

Under Soviet socialism there have been two simultaneous trends: the development of nationalities and their coming closer together, with one being very much a part of the other. Indeed, it is precisely the friendship of peoples and their mutual aid that has enabled formerly backward outlying regions of the Russian Empire to rise to the level of development of the country's central areas, and to achieve the chief task of Lenin's national policy—the genuine equality of nationalities. Now all national republics comprising the U.S.S.R. possess a highly developed industry and mechanized agriculture, as well as skilled specialists in all branches of the national economy and culture.

On the other hand, it is precisely the development of the nationalities and their equal status in the state that creates the need for ever closer co-operation between them. At the present time any major construction project requires the products of numerous plants from many Soviet Republics, and such gigantic undertakings as cultivating the virgin lands and setting up new industrial bases in the eastern parts of the country have only been possible with the joint efforts of all Soviet peoples.

The development of every nationality is of tremendous benefit to society as a whole, and it engenders profound mutual esteem and strengthens the friendship of the peoples. Due to the fact that the nationalities are coming ever closer together and mutually enriching each other, spiritual features deriving from the new type of social relations and embodying the best traditions of the peoples of the U.S.S.R. have taken shape.

National character is extraordinarily stable; it is formed under the influence of all the aspects of a nationality's life. Evidently no one will argue against the fact that definite national traits connected with, for instance, differences in temperament, are apparent among people of every nationality or groups of related nationalities. But this does not at all prevent the development of new, common features of the *Soviet man*. These include an economically rational attitude and outlook, selflessness in labor and confidence in success, magnanimity and generosity, straightforwardness, and adherence to high principles, and many other traits which have become common as a result of the influence of new, communist ethics.

In the process of building communism a culture is evolving that is common to all Soviet people, a prototype of culture that will be common to all mankind, the culture of communism. Thus, although Soviet writers, composers and artists manifest a great diversity of styles and forms, they use one single method of creative art—the method of socialist realism.

Modern architecture too serves as a characteristic example in this respect. The architects of every nationality in the U.S.S.R. quite naturally make use in their creative endeavors of the best qualities encountered in the practice of their particular national architecture. At the same time they strive to put up structures that correspond to the esthetic ideals of our age. They seek simpler and more expressive forms, and try to make the buildings more economical and convenient. The same goes for new materials: concrete, plastics, and glass. As a result there arises a new architectural style which embodies the best national traditions. This is not an eclectic combination of different styles and fashions, but precisely the synthesis of the general and national style of architecture.

When communism triumphs on a world scale, national distinctions will finally be obliterated, and a common language and culture reflecting the entire wealth of national cultures will prevail. But this process is exceptionally long, and it is impossible at present to venture even an approximate guess as to how long it may take to achieve.

EDUCATION OF THE NEW MAN

Communism has to be built with the "human material" that history has provided, but this material is not all the same—there is much that is good, and a lot that is bad. The trouble is that people are not melodrama characters, each in a mask indicating a specific trait—one a rascal, another a kind-hearted man, one the embodiment of evil, another endowed with all the virtues. In man's spiritual world the good and the evil frequently go side by side in the most inconceivable manner. And the only way to rear people is to recast their way of thinking, their attitude towards labor, society, the family—in other words, to cause a revolution in man's mind in the fullest sense of that word.

Can such a problem be solved?

"No!" assert bourgeois sociologists and moralists. "Man," they say, "is by nature immutable. For two thousand years he has been taught: do not kill, do not steal, do not deceive anyone; nevertheless, just as before, blood is being shed, theft flourishes in the world, and brother betrays brother. Of course, to some extent people may be adapted to the community, may be brought up within the framework of observing outward politeness, but never will it be possible to eradicate the beast in man, to get rid of his sins."

Marxists maintain this problem can be solved! The conditions of social life determine people's consciousness and this maxim is corroborated by the entire history of the human race. In the course of two or three millennia man's outer appearance has remained much the same, and if an ancient Roman were to suddenly appear in our midst dressed in a modern suit, he would not stand out in a crowd. But the contemporary spiritual world is immeasurably richer than the world of the ancients and even that of the last century.

As far as vice is concerned, here too bourgeois ideologists and moralists are mistaken. Human evils inevitably will die out when the social conditions that caused them no longer exist. Private property and the exploitation of man by man are the main evils.

Proletarian ethics bring out the best ethical qualities in man. Communists consider that man is not a slave of the elements, but the smith of his happiness and the master of nature; he is not a speck of dust in the whirlwind of social storms but the creator of history. He is capable of ridding himself of everything that is humiliating to his dignity, and he does so himself, with his own hands, by building a new world for himself.

Of course, the revolution in the human mind is the most difficult of all revolutions. But it will inevitably triumph in the society where the very conditions of life of the people are objectively conducive to changes in their psychology, to the triumph of new, communist ethics.

Soviet people are born into a world where everything is subordinated to the laws of comradeship, where there are no exploiters and exploited, where each and every able-bodied person is duty-bound to work. The force of collective labor makes its imprint on the entire way of thinking of Soviet people, and inculcates in them the best moral qualities.

The fact that the economic and political system of socialism is conducive to the formation of an all-around developed man does not at all mean that the revolution in people's minds takes place by itself, spontaneously. School, literature and art, the press, radio, television, and other means of influencing people's minds and hearts popularize the heroism of labor, the ideas of collectivism and humanism, and develop the traits worthy of a communist man.

The combination of objective factors with ideological influence is a reliable guarantee that society will be able to solve the immense task of educating the new man. However, to a great extent the time this will take also depends on the people themselves. It is difficult to implant good qualities in one who refuses to admit his shortcomings. There is nothing that hastens and facilitates the process of education so much as the sincere desire of people to become better, in other words, *self-education.*

The efforts to achieve communism inspire Soviet people to enhance their knowledge and labor skills, to aspire to ethical perfection. Of course, the builders of communism, the first who are to live under communism, are vitally interested in preparing themselves and their comrades for this.

But how is one to find the answers as to what kind of person one should be, and who is worthy of respect? Should the perfect communist perhaps be sought in some of our science fiction stories? These novels describe truly remarkable people in the full sense of the word; but why imitate fictional heroes when there are living ones? Communist features of social consciousness are expressed in the thoughts and actions of foremost Soviet people, in their attitude towards work, in their adherence to principle, honesty, and other high moral traits.

LOOKING AHEAD

In our time Soviet people have a realistic idea of a communist society. Of course, we cannot categorically predict all its details. The solution of many specific problems will be suggested by life itself, the practice of communist construction. But the most important, the most essential features of the future are clear.

Communism Proclaims:

Peace

For the first time in its much-suffering history, humanity will be able to breathe easily. No one and nothing will hamper its prosperity. There will be an end to the senseless expenditure of human energy for the creation of means of destruction. Thousands of factories in all countries now producing lethal weapons will go over to the manufacture of goods designed to satisfy people's needs. Instead of fighter planes and bombers they will produce fleet-winged passenger liners and powerful transport planes; space-ships will take the place of ballistic rockets; there will be tractors instead of tanks, and refrigerators and vacuum cleaners instead of guns and shells.

And what brilliant prospects will open up before science! Research establishments and scientists now working on new types of weapons and means of defense against them (involving more than two-thirds of all scientists) will switch over to the quest for new types of energy and materials, to designing machines for lightening the labor of man and making life more beautiful, to endeavors to eradicate disease and lengthen the span of man's life.

The word "war" will only be used in connection with such humane concepts as war against disease and senility, war against drought and bad harvests, war against natural calamities.

Mankind will be able to direct its efforts to the exploration of new worlds. Of course, this is by no means a matter of forcing our will on the possible inhabitants of other planets but a question of exploring outer space and spreading civilization.

Labor

Under communism, labor becomes the main content of social life and the essence of the life of every human being. Social efforts will lead to a tremendous development of productive forces ensuring an abundance of all products necessary for life. As Marx stated, under communism riches will flow in abundance.

The flow of wealth will increase at an ever greater pace thanks to the organic unity of science and production. Science has already become a great productive force, but the benefits we now enjoy are nothing compared to what is in store for us. Science is now on the threshold of solving a number of problems capable of bringing about a veritable revolution in the production of material goods, to say nothing of the promise for the future.

The most important of these tasks is unquestionably the problem of mastering controlled thermonuclear reactions, which will ensure a practically inexhaustible reserve of energy. It is not difficult to imagine the importance of discovering ways of directly influencing the growth of plants and living organisms; the impact of the ability to control the weather which will help put an end to drought; the significance of artificially preparing proteins, as well as many other substances which nature did not bother to make for us.

The extremely high productivity of social labor, attained through the development of science and technology and through raising the scientific, technical and cultural level of the working people, will form the basis for the upsurge of productive forces. When people talk about communist production they think of a system of automatic self-operating devices carrying out all the work, from drawing up blueprints to the output of ready products—and all man must do is control them.

Under communism, labor, as a source of prosperity and joy, will become a vital necessity for every member of society.

Equality

The implementation of the main principle of communism, "from each according to his ability, to each according to his needs," will mean that society will have established complete social equality.

Let us now examine to what extent the principle of meeting people's demands according to their needs corresponds to the idea of equality. As pointed out on page 99 above, under socialism some people still earn more and live better than others. The implementation of the communist principle of distribution will eliminate this distinction, will help overcome the injustice of Nature, which endows people with unequal abilities for labor and creative endeavors.

From a formal point of view one might consider the principle of communist distribution a violation of equality since it means satisfying everyone's needs fully, irrespective of the quantity and quality of his labor. Communism, however, establishes supreme justice, the true humane ideal of equality: let everyone contribute what he can to society, and society will generously take care of all reasonable demands.

Communist equality is also expressed in doing away with socio-economic and cultural distinctions between the city and the countryside.

The vestiges of inequality in the social status of women will likewise be done away with once and for all. The question here is primarily one of emancipating woman from burdensome domestic chores (preparing food, washing clothes, sewing, etc.), and making it easier to take care of children, especially very small ones.

Unified communist ownership of the means of production and the eradication of class distinctions will lead to the development of a *classless society*. This is the acme of equality, and talk of more than that has no meaning: people will always differ among themselves in abilities and tastes, and justice does not consist of trying to make them all alike, but of creating for each individual and all together the best conditions for life and creative work.

Freedom

There can be no equality without freedom because only free people can be equal, and only equals can be free.

The socialist revolution emancipates the working people from exploitation. All subsequent development of society is directed towards creating conditions under which *every man can freely develop and find application for his creative abilities in work*. The communist ideal of freedom consists in that.

The experience of socialist society has fully corroborated Lenin's words to the effect that the people are an inexhaustible spring of talents. Now it can be boldly stated that the well-spring has gushed forth to the surface. But the real flourishing of folk creativity is yet to come. Under communism the spring of talents turns into a mighty torrent, because the better our life and the higher the level of public education, the greater the opportunities for creative work in all aspects of human endeavor, enabling people to express their talents and abilities in a multitude of ways.

Under communism all monotonous work will be done through automation while man will have the task of creating and controlling the machines. Thus, any job will be of creative character. A broad educational and cultural background will enable people, aside from their interest in their main vocation, to develop and apply their other abilities. In other words, the man of the communist age is an all-around developed man, possessing spiritual wealth, moral purity, and physical perfection.

The span of man's life will sharply increase (some scientists believe it may be as much as 150, and some even 200 years), owing to particularly favorable material and spiritual conditions of existence, and successes in biology, medicine, and other sciences.

Society as a whole will also gain from the prolongation of human life. Man now devotes 10–20 years of his life to study and 25–40 years to work and creative endeavors. At the height of maturity, when experience and knowledge have already been acquired, man's strength begins to wane:

how many wonderful undertakings remain unrealized, what inexhaustible treasures of the human mind are lost because nature is so sparing in determining the span of human life! That is why it is easy to imagine what it would mean to social progress if centenarians were to find themselves in the prime of physical prowess.

On viewing the prospects of the all-around development of the individual even in the most cursory way, we begin to understand the grandeur of freedom asserted by communism. Under capitalism people dream of emancipation from poverty and exploitation, of coming into their own. Socialism has provided such freedom, and now Soviet people are building with their own hands a society in which freedom will find its highest expression in the unfolding of human personality.

An inseparable element of the free development of the individual is his participation in public self-government. High-minded, conscious discipline ensures the harmonious, precise work of all organizations administering the affairs of society.

The question of the moral concept of freedom is connected with this. There are people who feel that freedom is the right to do as they please without taking into consideration the established order, the interests of other people. But if everyone were to act arbitrarily, it would not be freedom, but anarchy.

No, freedom *in* society does not at all mean freedom *from* society: freedom of the individual does not mean arbitrariness. When personal interests and public interests merge in the minds of people, they can only conceive of freedom as the possibility of acting for the good of society. It is precisely this understanding of freedom, shared by socially conscious builders of communism, that will finally triumph in a communist society.

Fraternity

Where equality and freedom reign, there will inevitably be established the fraternity of all working people, of all peoples. We use the term "fraternity" to designate the truly humane relations without which it is impossible to conceive communism.

The more general expression for these relations is collectivism, cooperation, and mutual aid. Collectivism, as we know, expresses the substance of social relations under socialism; it cannot be otherwise because public ownership of the means of production inevitably engenders collectivist relations and collectivist consciousness. In the process of building communism, collectivism steadily develops, is enriched with new content, and assumes new forms.

Individuals cannot proceed towards communism alone, one by one; a communist society can be built only by joint efforts, and those in the lead must consider it their primary duty to help those who for some reason or other lag behind. This principle, so persistently advocated by the Communist Party, finds ardent response among the Soviet people. Advanced Soviet people and whole collectives do just that: they lend a helping hand to those who are lagging behind.

The collectivist consciousness of the Soviet people that is shaped by the Communist Party is strikingly embodied in the readiness of Soviet people to share their achievements with the people of the world socialist system and with the countries and peoples of Asia, Africa, and Latin America, seeking independent development. Soviet people—engineers and workers at the Bhilai steel and iron project in India, builders of the Aswan Dam in the United Arab Republic, railwaymen in Afghanistan, geologists in India, doctors in Ethiopia—always and everywhere embody the idea of collectivism, contributing their knowledge and efforts to further the progress and friendship of the peoples.

And when socialism and communism score the final victory everywhere on the planet, the most wonderful dreams and aspirations of all peoples will come true. National distinctions will gradually be obliterated, and only the names will remain as a reminder of the past. United in a single fraternal family, mankind will attain the peak of its power, and carry out the most daring plans for the conquest of nature.

Happiness

The creative labor of free and equal people—brethren in conditions of eternal peace—is not that the happiness which communism brings to the peoples?

It is difficult to find on earth two people who have the same answer for the question of what constitutes happiness. For one, happiness consists of being able to occupy himself with his beloved pursuits without diverting himself to the petty things in life. Another cannot conceive of happiness without active public life; the third will talk about being well off, enjoying tasty meals and good clothes. The fourth will certainly mention sports. Many will put love, family, and parental joys first. All of these joys and many others will become accessible to everyone in full measure. The communist man will be able to repeat Marx's meaningful words: "Nothing human is alien to me."

Of course, no one can issue guarantees for happiness. Human destinies evolve differently. Evidently no one will be able to do away with such causes of distress and conflicts as dissatisfaction with one's work, disappointment, jealousy, and rejected love. In short, writers will have plenty to write about: life will engender themes not only for vaudeville and comedies, but also for dramas and tragedies. Neither will the piercing weapon of satire grow rusty: as long as mankind marches ahead it laughingly shrugs off its shortcomings.

Mankind will always progress, and nothing is capable of giving people greater joy than knowing that they too are taking part in this movement, that they are in step with the times, fighting for the happy future of all mankind.

A WONDERFUL FUTURE FOR MANKIND

The wonderful future that awaits man is no figment of the imagination. The contours of the future are already being shaped in the countries of socialism, which embrace more than a third of humanity, and the vision of the future is already becoming apparent. But those who think that socialism and communism will come into being without a struggle, without overcoming difficulties, are greatly mistaken. All that has been achieved in the Soviet Union and the other socialist countries has been attained at the price of consistent struggle and persistent labor. Now, too, every new achievement in these countries is the result of the selfless activities of the working masses. Socialism has become a mighty force which draws into its orbit ever new countries. But socialism too has its difficulties and its contradictions. The new system cannot quickly rid itself of the legacy of the past, of the burden of old traditions and prejudices created by the thousands of years of exploitation. The difficult problems of establishing new, just principles in relations among people and among nations have to be decided gradually, step by step.

The modern age is extraordinarily complex and contradictory. Not a single era of the past has known such a heterogeneous, strange intertwining of diametrically opposed social forces and tendencies. The world of socialism and the world of capitalism, the working class and the bourgeoisie, the oppressed and the exploiters, freedom and slavery, national development and colonialism, peace and war, wealth and poverty, high labor productivity and economic underdevelopment of vast areas—all these exist and follow their own course on one and the same planet. It might seem at first as if there were no possibility of disentangling this intricate net of contradictions of the modern age. However, if the principal tendencies of historical development, beginning with October, 1917, are carefully analyzed, the main direction of human history in our times becomes clear. The paramount content of the modern era is the transition from capitalism to socialism.

From victory in one country, to its triumph in a great number of countries, to its transformation into the decisive force in the history of humanity—such is socialism's road of development. It is by no means fortuitous that hundreds of millions of people now believe in socialism, that the progressive forces of countries that have liberated themselves from colonialism see their morrow in socialism.

Capitalism's sphere of power is constantly narrowing. The peoples do not wish to cast their lot with a moribund system which has wrought so much ill and suffering. The colonial system of imperialism, for so long a means of ruthless exploitation for capitalist monopolies, has crashed and disintegrated. The general crisis of capitalism, which has pervaded its economy, politics and ideology, is steadily deepening.

One of imperialism's greatest threats to mankind is a world thermonuclear war. The entire history of capitalist society is filled with bloody wars of conquest. Especially devastating was World War II unleashed by fascist Germany. It destroyed 60 million human lives and an incalculable amount of material and spiritual values created by many generations. Even now, 20 years later, the deep wounds inflicted by World War II have not as yet been healed, but the imperialists are again brandishing arms.

That is why the task of all progressive forces of our times is the prevention of the outbreak of a world thermonuclear conflagration. Now, when socialism is becoming the decisive factor in world development, when the forces of peace and progress are superior to the forces of war and aggression, a world war can be prevented. The united strength of the socialist countries, the peace-loving independent states, and the peoples of all countries can bar the road to the imperialist warmongers.

Consistently fighting for peace, the Soviet Union conducts a policy of peaceful coexistence with states of different systems. In the modern age this is the only realistic policy that accords with the interests of all the peoples, the interests of the working masses, the interests of socialism. The policy of peaceful coexistence means the rejection of war as a means of settling arguments between states; it means noninterference in the internal affairs of other lands, respect for the sovereignty and national independence of all countries, and equality in relations among all nations, big and small alike.

Peaceful coexistence presumes an irreconcilable struggle against the aggressive policy of imperialism, which contradicts the elementary norms of international law. Experience shows that imperialism, American imperialism above all, has no intention of abandoning its policy of military adventures. This is illustrated by open U.S. aggression against the heroic people of Vietnam, a fact which arouses the wrath and indignation of mankind. It is clear that it is impossible passively to observe imperialist military provocations. The policy of appeasing an aggressor is alien to socialist foreign policy. The Soviet Union regards it as its international duty to render all possible assistance to a country which has become the victim of imperialist military attack.

How can imperialist military adventures be blocked before they develop into a world thermonuclear war? There is only one way—united action by all anti-imperialist forces in their struggle against imperialism. This is the only way to halt the imperialist acts of aggression and open the road to peace.

*   *   *

In this short article, we have briefly outlined the ideals and the aims of communists and have tried to show what has been achieved in the Soviet Union, where the people entrusted Lenin's party with the leadership of society half a century ago. Is there anything in these ideals, objectives, and affairs that is contrary to the interests of the working masses, the interests of the people? No; the activities of the Communist Party are dedicated to the interests of the people, to the struggle for the liberation of all oppressed and expropriated.

Anticommunism quite consciously, intentionally, is used by the imperialists as a sword to split the unity of the world liberation movement. The combination of forces in the world now is such that imperialism cannot withstand the mighty revolutionary wave, cannot impudently realize its plans of expansion. The only thing that could to some extent bolster the shaken positions of imperialism is a split of the revolutionary forces—and imperialist strategists are well aware of this. They are resorting to every trick in an attempt to sow mistrust towards communists, to villify their ideas and activities.

The unity of the socialist countries, the national liberation movements, the international working class—the unity of all the revolutionary forces—this is now the prime concern. Different sections of the world liberation movement have their own interests, their own approach to the solution of various problems. But all have one common enemy—imperialism. All of them are united by common, basic interests in the struggle for peace, national independence, and social progress. In our troubled age of severe struggle and grave trials, the unity of the revolutionary forces of all the progressive circles is the only hope for guaranteeing a radiant future for mankind.

FURTHER READING SUGGESTIONS

A catalogue of books, booklets, magazines, etc., in English, imported from the U.S.S.R., can be obtained from Cross World Books and Periodicals, Inc., 333 South Wacker Drive, Chicago 6, Ill.

Books:

Constitution (Fundamental Law) of the Union of Soviet Socialist Republics. Moscow: Foreign Languages Publishing House, 1962.

Fundamentals of Marxism-Leninism, second revised edition. Moscow: Foreign Languages Publishing House, 1963.

History of the Communist Party of the Soviet Union. Moscow: Foreign Languages Publishing House, 1960.

Outline History of the U.S.S.R. Moscow: Foreign Languages Publishing House, 1960.

Programme of the Communist Party of the Soviet Union. Moscow: Foreign Languages Publishing House, 1961.

BOOKLETS: *

Berkhin, Y., *This Is How Socialism Began.* . . .

Kelle, Valdislav, *Communism—the Real Embodiment of Humanism.*

Kharchev, A., *Marriage and Family Relations in the U.S.S.R.*

Laptin, Miknail, *Material and Moral Incentives Under Socialism.*

Leontiev, L., *Fundamentals of Marxist Political Economy.*

Semionov, Vadim, *Aim: A Classless Society.*

U.S.S.R.: Questions and Answers.

MAGAZINES AND JOURNALS:

The Current Digest of the Soviet Press.†

Problems of Economics.†

Soviet Law and Government.†

Soviet Life (formerly called *U.S.S.R.*).‡

Soviet News.§

---

* All booklets here recommended have been published recently by the Novosti Press Agency. These and numerous others can be obtained from Soviet Booklets, 3 Rosary Gardens, London, N.W. 7, England at an annual subscription rate of $1.50 for all booklets published in English during the year.

   † Translations from original Soviet Publications.

   ‡ This magazine is distributed by the Soviet Embassy in Washington under a reciprocal agreement whereby the United States Embassy in Moscow distributes a magazine called *Amerika* in the Soviet Union.

   § Published and distributed free of charge (on request) by the Soviet Embassy in London.

III

The People's Republic of China: A Giant Awakened

SOVIET UNION

MONGOLIA
Peking○

CHINA

INDIA

VIETNAM

KOREA

TAIWAN

Area
(in square miles)
3,691,523

Population
(mid-1967 estimate)
721,518,000

The Chinese revolution is a continuation of the Great October Revolution [in Russia]. . . .

Mao Tse-tung's thought has been the guide to the victory of the Chinese revolution. It has integrated the universal truth of Marxism-Leninism with the concrete practice of the Chinese Revolution. . . .

Ours is the epoch in which world capitalism and imperialism are heading for their doom and socialism and communism are marching to victory. . . .

LIN PIAO
VICE CHAIRMAN, CENTRAL COMMITTEE OF THE
COMMUNIST PARTY OF CHINA;
VICE CHAIRMAN AND MINISTER OF DEFENSE OF THE
PEOPLE'S REPUBLIC OF CHINA;
HEIR APPARENT TO MAO TSE-TUNG

No alliance in the world can defeat the principal bastion of socialism—the People's Republic of China—over which waves the proud and stainless banner of Marxism-Leninism.

ALBANIA NEWS AGENCY, MAY, 1966

On the basic issue in their dispute with the Soviet leaders the Chinese are right. History will prove them so. But attempts to force the pace of history may bring on disasters worse than the ones they are intended to avert.

LEO HUBERMAN AND PAUL SWEEZY
EDITORS, *Monthly Review* (AN AMERICAN
"INDEPENDENT SOCIALIST MAGAZINE")

INTRODUCTION

WHEN IN 1949 MAO TSE-TUNG'S VICTORIOUS TROOPS DROVE THE remnants of Chiang Kai-shek's armies from the Chinese mainland, world communism won its greatest victory since the October 1917 Revolution in Russia. China's entry into the socialist camp added a territory larger than that of the United States to the Communist World, a territory on which there lived approximately one-fourth of the world's population. But a poor population it was, hungry and illiterate; and the problems ahead were formidable, the hoped-for era of affluence at best far off. Yet, the Chinese have tackled their arduous tasks with courage and determination; and in spite of difficulties, of some serious errors of judgment, and of occasional setbacks the Chinese have made substantial progress toward realizing their goals.

The Soviet Union initially extended substantial aid and assistance to the newcomer. But the two giants did not long continue to see eye to eye, as they had at the outset. Before a dozen years had passed there was open disagreement on the estimation of Stalin's role and on the usefulness of Stalinist methods and tactics; on the question of the self-reliance of socialist countries (self-sufficiency versus economic specialization and mutual interdependence); on the approach towards underdeveloped countries; on the relationship with Yugoslavia and with the United States; and on numerous other problems.

Apart from such differences in views as there were, Chinese jealousy of Soviet living standards and envy of the Soviet leadership position in the world communist movement probably contributed to the schism which, in the 1960's, split wide open not only the socialist bloc of nations but also many of the communist parties in the noncommunist countries. As the 1960's progressed, the invectives hurled against each other by the Soviet Union and Communist China increased in intensity and bitterness, the two countries accusing each other of betraying Marxism-Leninism, splitting the international communist movement, refusing to give the necessary assistance to the North Vietnamese in their fight against the "American imperialists," etc. In the fall of 1966, the break had reached such proportions that the Soviet government ordered all Chinese students expelled from the U.S.S.R., asserting that the action was taken in retaliation for the ouster of Soviet students from Communist China.[1] In early 1967, the Sino-Soviet split reached new heights when mobs of Chinese harassed and threatened Soviet Embassy personnel in Peking for days on end, shouting of overthrowing the Soviet government and of making "short work" of Soviet political leaders. According to the Soviets, these actions were "without precedent in the history of diplomatic relations;" they warned the Chinese that "the restraint and patience of the Soviet people are not boundless," [2] and eventually recalled the families of Soviet Embassy personnel in Peking to the U.S.S.R.

All over China, in the meantime, a "cultural revolution" was in progress. Based on an orthodox Maoist interpretation of Marxism-Leninism—its faithful followers convinced that Mao could never err—the "cultural revolution" was directed at wiping out the last vestiges of the "old" system, from non-revolutionary street names to cosmetics in drug stores. (The Soviets report that the Chinese have even substituted "eyes left" for "eyes right" in military parades, and that the Red Guards want the traffic regulations changed so that henceforth a red light would signify "go.") China explains this "cultural revolution" as a necessary part of the struggle against "bourgeois" and "revisionist" elements inside the country and the Party. But other communist parties, inside and outside the socialist camp, see Mao's cultural revolution as "a deification of Mao Tse-tung, a suppression of creative thought, and an

[1] *Soviet News,* October 11, 1966, p. 11.
[2] *Pravda,* February 5, 1967.

effort to liquidate all opposition to the present dogmatic, fanatical anti-Soviet policy of the current leadership." [3]

At the time this book goes to press, China's cultural revolution has met bitter and bloody opposition from workers and peasants in several provinces. Even some units of the armed forces are reported to have joined the anti-Mao uprising, but it appears that, for the time being, the pro-Mao forces are likely to keep the upper hand. The long-run effect of the cultural revolution on China's internal economic and political system, and the longevity of the cultural revolution itself, cannot yet be assessed. Whatever the outcome, there is little doubt that China's regression to extreme orthodoxy has had a detrimental effect on her influence on the world communist movement.

The non-Marxist view on China has been contributed by Jan S. Prybyla. Born in Poland, Prybyla holds a Ph.D. degree in economics from the National University of Ireland, and a post-doctoral diploma in Higher European Studies from the University of Strasbourg, France. He has to his credit some eighty articles published in outstanding economics, Soviet area, and Chinese area journals on three continents. He is co-author of the recently published *World Tensions: Conflicts and Accommodation*,[4] and co-editor, together with the editor of this book, of a forthcoming book on Western, Soviet, and Chinese models for underdeveloped countries. At present, Prybyla is professor of economics at Pennsylvania State University, which named him Liberal Arts Scholar in the Spring of 1965.

The Marxist view on China has been put together from fifteen different, recently published articles, all of them representing the Chinese-Marxist position. Among the authors of these articles are Soong Ching Ling (Mme. Sun Yat-sen), Vice Chairman of the People's Republic of China and Chairman of the China Welfare Institute; Lien Kuan, Deputy Secretary General of the Standing Committee of the National People's Congress and one of the vice-presidents of the Chinese People's Institute of Foreign Affairs; and Lin Hai-Yun, Vice Minister of Foreign Trade in the People's Republic of China.

[3] Reported as an official statement by the Communist Parties of England, Spain, Czechoslovakia and Bulgaria in *Pravda* (Moscow, Sept. 17, 1966).

[4] Elton Atwater, Kent Foster, and Jan S. Prybyla, *World Tensions: Conflict and Accommodation* (New York, Appleton-Century-Crofts, 1967).

5

Red China in Motion:
A Non-Marxist View

JAN S. PRYBYLA *

PROFESSOR OF ECONOMICS,
PENNSYLVANIA STATE UNIVERSITY

The emergence of China since 1949 as a major force in international life is perhaps the single most significant event of contemporary history. Communist China is on the move internally as well as abroad, and the movement is that of an awakened giant impatient to catch up after centuries of restless slumber. It is an aggrieved, have-not power in search of change, disdainful of those who work to preserve the *status quo*. Its policies at home and abroad are flexible though couched in dogmatic terms, a mixture of truculence and elegance, rashness and prudence, aggressiveness and moderation. It undoubtedly holds an attraction not only for much of the international communist movement, but for some segments of the so-called uncommitted, underdeveloped, noncommunist world of Asia, Africa, and Latin America. It speaks over the heads of national governments directly to "the people," hosts representatives of dissident movements from the four corners of the world, and at the same time enters into formal treaties and commercial agreements with governments of any political hue it judges inoffensive. Its "five principles of peaceful coexistence" seem to be compatible with its avowed support for "national liberation" movements.[1] Internally,

---

* This contribution has been written especially for this book.

[1] The so-called "Five Principles of Peaceful Coexistence" were first hammered out in an agreement which China signed with India in April, 1954. The agreement acknowledged China's sovereignty over Tibet and contained provisions for trade between Tibet and India. In June of that year, Jawaharlal Nehru and Chou En-lai issued a joint communique in New Delhi in which they reiterated the Five Principles, or as they were often referred to, the *Panch Sheela*. The principles are general and platitudinous, but had strong appeal at the time to Asian neutralist sentiments. They cover: (1) mutual respect for each other's national territory, (2) nonaggression, (3) noninterference in

it has unleashed the power of its 700 million people in a round-the-clock effort to change the present and build a different future. Nothing could be more disastrous for the Western world than to ignore or even underestimate the implications of this great awakening. Such self-imposed blindness can only lead to a patchwork of hasty and ill-conceived policies which smack of the principle of the fire brigade. Resolving little, they may draw the world nearer to nuclear disaster.

"WE HAVE STOOD UP!"

In September, 1949, just before the formal assumption of power, Mao Tse-tung declared: "Our nation will never again be an insulted nation. We have stood up." In these words he voiced the strong nationalistic content of the Chinese Communist Party and echoed the feeling of many thinking Chinese.

Communism and nationalism are not mutually exclusive, especially not in underdeveloped countries where nationalism is spurred by deep-seated anticolonialist and anti-Western biases. One could, in fact, go so far as to say that in communism there is nationalism with a coercive economic program that is not merely drafted but enforced. The program is all the more appealing because it is radical, because it will have no truck with a humiliating past, and because it has proved successful in a number of well-documented instances. Nationalism seeks national self-respect, international prestige and power. None of these can be gained merely by writing passable poetry in a few country homes. In fact, none of these can be achieved at all without eliminating economic backwardness. Communism, whether in its Stalinist or Maoist versions, offers a handy guide to such development. It is totalitarianism exercised in the name of economics elevated to the rank of objective law. It uses the social metaphysics of Marx as an inspirational backdrop for relentless action charted by Lenin, Stalin, and Mao Tse-tung.

With the possible exception of Yugoslav socialism, Mao's communism is the product *par excellence* of its environment. Though dogmatic in its underlying faith and zeal, it is flexible, shifting, and pragmatic in its tactics. It was born in Kiangsi and the caves of Yenan of revulsion against

---

each other's internal affairs, (4) equality and mutual benefit, (5) peaceful coexistence. From June, 1954, to about mid-1957 the Five Principles became the major theme of communist China's diplomacy. They were embodied, with only minor modifications, in the Bandung Declaration of Asian and African powers (1955), and in nearly all treaties and agreements concluded by Asian countries in the years immediately following the Bandung Conference. (The text of the original Five Principles may be found in a *New China News Agency* release of April 29, 1954.)

Kuomintang[2] rule and impatience with the bungling of the Soviet-inspired Comintern. Distrust of the foreigner, capitalist and socialist alike, isolation, and a guerrilla mentality characterized it. Unlike communist movements elsewhere, it had, on coming to power, almost three decades of administrative experience and could, if it so wished, benefit from the contemplation of its own and other peoples' (for example the Soviets') errors. Its leadership had shown a remarkable stability and knack for survival over the years. Except in the psychology of its dialectical materialist faith, it was a thing apart.

The land it inherited by stubborn struggle was proud, poor, and backward in the arts of modern living. The nationalism which had convulsed it since Sun Yat-sen, had in the hands of the Kuomintang spent itself in aimless pursuits and a protracted war against the Japanese aggressor and the domestic foe. The collapse of the old China was not engineered in Washington or in Moscow: it followed from intolerable internal strains in which the communists themselves played a not inconsiderable part. China was a land ravaged, steeped in blood, and exhausted.

By the communists' own count, even as late as 1956, China had only some 100,000 "superior intellectuals," meaning doctors, scientists, professors, top technicians, and writers, and a further 3.8 million "ordinary intellectuals," presumably laboratory and higher grade skilled workers, in a population exceeding 650 million. As late as 1957, over 70 percent of the Chinese people (or some 450 million in all) could neither read nor write any of the 40,000 odd ideographs which make up China's two main languages. Comparisons with even such a relatively underdeveloped country as Tsarist Russia was in 1913 are most unfavorable to China as it was prior to 1949, the year of the communist takeover. In 1913 Russia produced over twenty-seven times as much petroleum as did China in 1943 and three-and-a-half times as much steel. On a *per capita* count the discrepancy is, of course, even more striking. At the beginning of collectivization (1929) the Soviets possessed 210,900 tractors; the Chinese 400 in 1949 and 19,300 in 1956 when collectivization had been completed. In 1913 the Russians had 73,000 kilometers[3] of railroads; the Chinese 21,740 in 1950, much of it single track and in poor repair. The geographic distribution of the railroad network was another problem: the lines clustered along the seacoast and went inland only so far as was needed to bring the products of the land out to the waiting ships. The lines were built neither to unite nor to develop the

[2] In Chinese, *kuo* means nation(alist); *min,* people('s); and *tang,* party. The Nationalist People's Party was founded in 1911 by Sun Yat-sen (1866-1925), China's famous political leader who organized the revolution against the Manchu dynasty which had ruled China for almost 300 years, and who was president of China from 1921 to 1922. Afterwards, the Kuomintang was controlled and led by Chiang Kai-shek. At the time of this writing, the Kuomintang government controls only Taiwan (Formosa) and some nearby islands. [EDITOR'S NOTE]

[3] One kilometer equals 3,280.8 feet or about five-eighths of a mile. [EDITOR'S NOTE]

country. A round-trip road journey from Lhasa in Tibet to the Chinese town of Chengtu took from four to six months. Domestic scheduled airlines were few and far between, and were manned mostly by foreign pilots. With more than 14,000 kilometers of coastline, 1,600 rivers, and some of the best natural harbors in Asia, China before 1950 had no shipbuilding industry, no merchant marine it could call its own, only a few meager and antiquated ship repair facilities, and a total of less than 75,000 kilometers of navigable inland waterways (150,000 in 1958). In 1936, the last year before the outbreak of the Sino-Japanese war, agricultural production accounted for about 65 percent of national income, while industry (including mining and construction) represented no more than 12 percent. Public administration, eroded by the corruption of public officials (itself a phenomenon of poverty, disorganization, low and irregular pay, and inflation), made up 4 percent of national income. At a rough guess, China's net domestic product in 1933 was in the neighborhood of 25 billion U.S. dollars. During the twelve years which preceded the collapse of the Kuomintang, commodity prices in China increased more than eight thousand million times.[4] Foreign capital controlled industry: in 1936 about 74 percent of total industrial capital was in foreign hands (over 82 percent in the case of pig iron production). Industrial workers represented in 1937 just 0.25 percent of the population. In that year the Soviet Union counted 35 "workers and employees" for every 100 of the population; the Chinese share was two, fifteen years later. In 1933 the per capita daily caloric intake derived from food crops was 1,940, while calorie intake from other sources was very small. If starvation were to be avoided, there could be no more crop failures. Yet droughts and floods and with them death and hunger had been regular features of Chinese life. Intestinal and lung diseases were endemic. Before 1949, the use of chemical fertilizers was practically unknown to Chinese agricultural practice; only one-sixth of the cultivated area was irrigated while about half of the country's farmland was thought to require irrigation. In China's main agricultural areas rainfall is concentrated in the summer and fall seasons and drought becomes the major threat to production and the most important cause of agricultural loss. A quarter or more of the cultivable area is subject to periodic floods caused in part by reckless deforestation and consequent erosion of the soil. The middle and lower reaches of the Yangtse, the Pearl River delta, and the Huai river basin in the provinces of Hopei, Honan, and Shantung are the hardest hit. Water control, therefore, should have been a first priority for any national government. Yet, in 1949 China had only 42,000 kilometers of do-it-yourself dikes and most of these had either been wantonly destroyed by the Japanese invader and the contestants in the

---

[4] According to Chou En-lai (*A Great Decade* [Peking, Foreign Languages Press, 1959] p. 2) in the twelve years from July, 1937, to May, 1949, the volume of currency issued by the Kuomintang government increased over 140 million times, while commodity prices rose over 8.5 billion times.

civil struggle, or else had been neglected and had fallen into disrepair. The annual net population increase of over 2 percent (or about fifteen million people) did not help matters. The implicit assumption appears to have been that the land lacked natural resources, although no one really had ever seriously bothered to find out. In 1949 there were in China fewer than 200 practising geologists.

These, in Leninist or any jargon for that matter, were the objective causes of the revolution and these are the causes of revolutions to come. Anyone looking around for an issue found plenty close at hand. With organized persistence and a dogged faith in the future, with an organizational theory tested in years of overwhelming odds, and with a program for change designed to expurgate the past, a man could move mountains of inertia. The Chinese Communist Revolution was a revolution by default.

There is a little Chinese socialist realist ditty, derisively quoted by the Russians, wise as they are these days in the ways of personality cults, which goes something like this:

> Dawn glows in the East, the sun is rising;
> Mao Tse-tung has appeared in China.
> He wants the people to be happy;
> He is the Savior of the people.

The lessons of saviors are often harsh, and the results of their saving not worth the candle. Let us see what China's new dynasty of saviors has so far accomplished and what the cost has been.

POLITICAL UNIFICATION AND THE ONE MIND

Among their major accomplishments the Chinese Communists can count the speedy unification under central control of almost the whole traditional Chinese empire, including such borderlands and regions as Manchuria, Inner Mongolia, Sinkiang, and Tibet inhabited by non-Han peoples.[5] The process of unification was substantially completed in 1952, although disaffection occasionally verging on open rebellion persisted for some years in Tibet and Sinkiang. Outside the border regions comprising about 40 million people and almost one half of China's territory, scattered and disorganized guerrilla activity was, for all practical purposes, brought to an end by 1952.

[5] All Chinese governments, including the Kuomintang, have claimed suzerainty over Tibet, but not all of them were always in a position to enforce their claims. No foreign power has ever recognized the independence of Tibet *de jure*. However, the Tibetans, among whom nationalist feeling and ethnic separatism run strong, have managed to maintain their independence for a long time, largely by default. Chinese governments of the Republican period were both too weak and too taken up with civil war to subjugate the Tibetans. Prior to the communist invasion of Tibet, the country had been free from Chinese control for about forty years.

The Tibetan uprising of 1959 was put down with calculated brutality, although most of the Khamba guerrillas who led the revolt were never caught, and they retreated to the mountains of southeast, northeast, and west Tibet and into the remote valleys of North Nepal. Trouble, too, erupted sporadically in Sinkiang, a nuisance which Peking ascribed to Soviet subversive agents, and Moscow to Peking's forced labor camps in the region. These, of course, are the quantifiable aspects of disaffection; what may be termed the "inner opposition" defies measurement, first because the dissenter in a totalitarian setting keeps his doubts and his reservations tightly locked up in the innermost recesses of his constantly assaulted self to the point where, literally, in his crowded loneliness he doubts his own doubts; and second, because those outsiders who are anxious to detect and weigh such hidden disaffection are denied access to the subject of their inquiry. That there is much latent opposition within China to the methods, if not always to the objectives of the communists is, to say the least, a fair assumption. That this opposition is effectively frustrated, repressed, and where possible nipped in the bud, is an apparent fact. "Poisonous weeds" are not allowed to stunt the growth of the "fragrant flowers of socialism."

The extent and strength of this opposition, which until 1965 could only be guessed at, was revealed during Mao's and Lin Piao's Great Proletarian Cultural Revolution, especially in the latter part of 1966 and early 1967. Resistance to putting Maoist thought and politics in charge of economics, technology, and schooling came from within the Party apparatus; and was identified with the persons and following of Liu Shao-chi, the Head of State, and Teng Hsiao-ping, the Party's General Secretary. Because the opposition was rooted in the Party, and to some extent apparently also in the army, it was hard to extirpate without disrupting the orderly process of government. The line taken by the Mao-Lin faction was that those who opposed the Cultural Revolution's political euphoria were "a handful of persons in authority who had taken the capitalist road," or "traitors, anti-Party, anti-socialist elements, devils with the spirits of snakes and the souls of oxen, bourgeois agents who plotted in coordination with international revisionism and imperialism to destroy socialism and bring back capitalism." The epithets were probably as erroneous as the mathematics. If in fact—and this is very unlikely—the opposition was limited to "a handful of persons in authority," it showed itself extremely agile and able to withstand the repeated massive onslaughts of Maoist forces, including the teen-age Red Guards recruited by the Mao-Lin faction to harass and demoralize all opponents. The strength of the opposition lay in its thesis that modernization was not exclusively a function of the political will, in its belief that material incentives for workers and peasants did not mean an abandonment of socialist principles, in its tactical agility which confused the Maoists, and above all, in its firm hold on the levers of authority at all levels of the political and economic machine. By mid-1967, in spite of the Maoist faction's claims to success, the God-like authority and alleged infallibility of China's "great leader and helmsman" had been profoundly shaken. To be a dissenter in China was still fearfully dangerous. But to doubt the charismatic power of Mao's thought no longer implied loneliness. It meant, in fact, that one was in excellent and rational company.

The "Common Program," a provisional constitution adopted by the Chinese on September 29, 1949, directed the government to "liberate all the territory of China, and accomplish the cause of unifying the country." Besides Taiwan, the Pescadores, and the offshore islands, which Peking regards as an integral part of China's national territory (in much the same way as the West Germans look upon East Germany and parts of present-day Poland), the Chinese Communists had at various times claimed Korea, the Ryukyu Islands (Okinawa), parts of Burma, Bhutan, Nepal, Annam (North Vietnam), parts of India, Outer Mongolia, Hong Kong, Macao, and large tracts of Soviet central Asia (about half a million square miles, according to the outraged Soviets). Not all of these claims are seriously pushed by Peking, but they are held in reserve as useful political irritants. At the height of the Sino-Soviet dispute (July 10, 1964), Mao Tse-tung told a group of visiting Japanese socialists that China wanted back from the U.S.S.R. territories in central Asia taken from China by the Tsar a century earlier. In a *Concise Geography of China* published in 1964 by Peking Foreign Languages Press, Hong Kong and Kowloon [6] are shown as part of Chinese territory, the Sino-Soviet frontier along the Amur, and the frontier with North Korea along the Yalu and Ussuri rivers are left undefined. China's borders in the South China Sea are brought down south as far as Sarawak, a cartographer's correction which includes in Chinese territory the Paracels to the annoyance, it may be presumed, of the Vietnamese, north and south of the seventeenth parallel. To what extent Soviet headaches in Outer Mongolia (the Soviets' last outpost in Asia) [7] are due to Chinese prodding, is not clear. What is plain, however, is that in 1964 scheduled flights by Communist China's national airways to Ulan Bator [8] were suspended, that in June 1964 the Mongolian government invited some 3,500 Chinese workers to leave the country, and that on September 10, 1964, *Pravda* under the heading "Shady Schemes of Chinese Leaders," accused Peking of "having long dreamed of turning the Mongolian People's Republic into an outpost of China under its rule." This amounted to putting the shoe on the other foot, when it is recalled that at Yalta Stalin made sure to extract from the Western powers (without consulting China) a solemn

[6] A peninsula opposite Hong Kong island, part of the British colony of Hong Kong. [EDITOR'S NOTE]

[7] Located between China and the U.S.S.R., the country's official name now is the Mongolian People's Republic. So far, the country has sided mostly with the Soviets in the Sino-Soviet dispute. [EDITOR'S NOTE]

[8] Capital of the Mongolian People's Republic. [EDITOR'S NOTE]

assurance that the *status quo* in Outer Mongolia be respected, and later struck a bargain with Chiang Kai-shek about Outer Mongolia's independence from China and the Soviets' rights in Manchuria, Dairen, and Port Arthur.

"To defend in order to attack, to retreat in order to advance, to take a flanking position in order to take a frontal position, and to zigzag in order to go straight—these are the inevitable phenomena in the process of development of any event or matter," Mao had said. After retreating and zigzagging for a while, the Chinese reasserted their rights in Sinkiang, Dairen, Port Arthur, and over the Eastern Railway, poked at Outer Mongolia with indifferent success, and took a flanking position in Hong Kong and Macao, their two major foreign exchange earners. With Burma, Nepal, Pakistan, and Afghanistan they made reasonable frontier bargains, which only went to show how obstinate and reactionary the Indians could get. By smiling their way through apprehensive Cambodia, they retreated to harrass obstinate South Vietnam and threaten Thailand. And all this with 500 million illiterates and a sheer "mass of flesh," as Khrushchev with his earthy peasant insight had once typed them!

In a land somewhat larger than the United States, inhabited by diverse peoples whose standards of literacy and knowledge of modern techniques had for centuries been as modest as their pride had been great, unification means more than the building of trunk railroads through the wilderness and the teaching of some 2,000 basic ideographic symbols (4,000 for town dwellers). In such a setting, unification demands nothing short of a cultural shock and a profound social upheaval. Within a relatively brief span of time, the Chinese Communists numbering some 17 million leaders and cadres and another 30 million members of youth and other auxiliary organizations, had managed to impose on the Chinese people forms of behavior that in their puritanical ardor and blinkered concentration on regimented work are seen by many as distinctly "un-Chinese." The power of the local warlords was broken by physically extinguishing or mentally "re-educating" the lords; the social and economic framework of the countryside was shaken to its foundations by the land reform of 1950-52 and the Soviet-patterned, relentless class warfare in the villages, during which at least 3 million (some put the number at 20 million) landowners were put to death in the midst of an Orwellian concerted jubilation of bystanders, or deported to Sinkiang and Inner Mongolia to brood over their obstinacy. Tens of thousands of Tibetan lamas, recalcitrant men, women, and children were driven into China along two newly built military highways dubbed by the *Peking Review* "Roads to Happiness." The Struggle against "incorrect" thought was organized and implemented with the same thoroughness as the fight against rats, flies, and other pests. Much more than the Soviets at the pitch of their Stalinist inhumanity of man to man, the Chinese Communists outdid themselves in feats of human engineering in which intimate *hsueh hsi* or study groups alternated with nation-wide "Three-Anti" and "Five-

Anti" campaigns.[9] Terror against those who opposed the Party and would not be reformed, repetitious persuasion, through forced labor if need be, for those who would rather stand in the wings. " 'You are not benevolent!' Quite so. We definitely do not apply a policy of benevolence to the reactionaries and the reactionary activities of the reactionary classes. . . . The people's state protects the people. Only when the people have such a state can they educate and remold themselves on a country-wide scale by democratic methods and, with everyone taking part . . . rid themselves of the bad habits and ideas acquired in the old society." So wrote Mao Tse-tung in an essay "On the People's Democratic Dictatorship" back in 1949. More than the Soviets in the heyday of Stalinist paranoia, the Chinese Party and State are interested in what people think and are resolved that they should think correctly, that is along Party lines. Tacit acceptance is not enough; there must be active involvement in strictly organized, ritualistic exercises even if this should conflict with productivity in the factory and on the farm. Permanent tension becomes the rule of life. Re-education, emulation, remolding campaigns follow one another in quick succession, and pervading it all is the method of analogy, the doctrine of equivalents, inherited from Stalin: you may not have committed a crime of thought or deed, but had you had the opportunity, you would have. Therefore, you are guilty. The one thing in which the Chinese have so far outstripped the capitalist West on both a gross and a per capita basis is the technique of thought control. The old and the new are harnessed to this task: the press and radio, the wayside billboard, the professional lecturer who endlessly repeats what the press and the radio and the wayside billboard have said a thousand times, the street block committee and the inquisitive neighbor, the fellow worker, and one's own children.

Like all the great organized faiths of the past, Chinese Leninist Maoism uses the carefully selected old to make the programmed new. The ancient village story teller is now a state employee "telling revolutionary stories in a big way," while story tellers "emulate one another to occupy the cultural front in the countryside." Scripts are supplied to the Party bards on such inspirational topics as the "Bridge of Happiness" ("the unprecedented happiness brought to the peasant masses by the people's communes through the construction of a bridge in the commune"), the "Hsin Family Dam"

---

[9] The "Three-Anti" was a concerted campaign against age-old corruption, waste, and bureaucratism (provincial regionalism included). The "Five-Anti" was a movement designed to eradicate the "Five Evils" of bribery, tax evasion, cheating on government contracts, theft of state property, and theft of economic information from government sources. Both were at their height in 1951-52, and were designed not only to achieve their stated purpose, but to undermine, frighten, and reduce to submissiveness the merchant and business class. A new "socialist education" campaign directed against intellectuals and rural cadres was launched in 1962, transforming itself into a nationwide revivalist session (the "Great Proletarian Cultural Revolution") in 1965. It calls on the intellectuals to "become one with the workers, peasants, and soldiers" and takes the People's Liberation Army as the model of socialist behavior and probity.

("depicting local peasants having flooded their own land to build a dam for the benefit of the whole locality"), "A Chicken" ("which elucidates the relationship between the State, the collective, and the individual"), and "The Sister and Her Brother" ("which advocates late marriages").[10] The traditional Lunar New Year continues to be recognized as an official holiday in the guise of the Spring Festival and under the slogan "change old habits and customs, and replace old with new." The usurious pawnshop trade which flourished in the days of old has been nationalized and now grants loans only on articles of personal clothing. Thus, short of going about naked, not much borrowing can be done. Family reunions are to be used for discussion on how to improve work methods, and instead of the traditional homage to the family, respect is to be paid to officially designated revolutionary families. Transportation to and entertainment at the locales of collective merry-making are provided by the ubiquitous State. After a shakeup, the People's Liberation Army (PLA) is being advanced as the model of discipline, hard work, perseverance, and Yenan community spirit [11] for others to copy. Villagers are urged not only to practice the "Five Good" virtues exemplified by the PLA, but to invite the "five-good veterans," old blades of the army, the Party, the soil, and the factory who can tell all they know about how bad the past had been and how good is the rebirth through "unity-criticism-unity." [12] Re-education of those who are not "outside the people" is to be as "a gentle breeze and fine drizzle," but with 2,000 calories

[10] *Kuang-ming Jih-pao* (Peking, March 18, 1964), p. 4. Available translation in: *Union Research Service* (Hong Kong, Vol. 35, No. 19, June 5, 1964), pp. 304-306. *See also* the discussion of this problem in *URS, ibid.,* pp. 303-319.

[11] Yenan, modern capital of northern Shensi province, located among towering hills, is a symbol of achievement to Communist China. It was in Yenan where, in October, 1936, 30,000 Red Army men and the Central Committee of the Chinese Communist Party under the leadership of Mao Tse-tung ended their "Long March." During the preceding twelve months, this "Long March" had brought them in an eight-thousand-mile semicircle from the Kiangsi base in southeast China where they had been unable to defeat Chiang Kai-shek's troops. Here, in Yenan, these men from the Central Red Army became the nucleus of the fighting force which during the following fourteen years was to capture all of mainland China. [EDITOR'S NOTE]

[12] The so-called "Five Good" emulation campaign, launched in 1963, was based on the experiences of the People's Liberation Army, but its relevance was extended to industry, agriculture, tax officials, savings agencies, retail stores, and Communist Party members. In PLA terminology, the "Five Good Fighters" are good in (1) political thinking (that is, thinking according to the guidelines laid down by Mao Tse-tung), (2) military skills, (3) the "Three-Eight Working Style," (4) fulfilling assigned tasks, and (5) physical training. Applied to rural commune members it means: (1) observing the laws and decrees of the government, (2) protecting the collective, (3) attending to labor, (4) uniting with, and (5) helping other commune members. In principle, various economic sectors may set their own "Five Good" objectives of struggle in accordance with their own special conditions. Regular study, for example, is sometimes included as a sixth good. *See* "Premier Chou En-lai Reports on the Work of the Government," *Peking Review* (January 1, 1965), pp. 6-20; "The Emulating, Learning, Overtaking, and Assisting Movement in Industrial Enterprises," *Union Research Service* (URS), Hong Kong, Vol. 34, No. 11 (February 7, 1964), pp. 169-186; Niu Huang, "China's Industries— New Stage in Labor Emulation," *China Reconstructs,* Peking (December, 1964), pp. 9-11; "Penetratively Launching the Emulation Drive for Five Good Tax Units and Tax Cadres," *Ta-kung Pao,* Peking (January 25, 1964), p. 2, in *URS,* Vol. 35, No. 4 (April

drawn daily through the courtesy of the Party-State, gentle breezes and fine drizzles can chill one to the bone. Workers' dormitories have been transformed into "battle positions" of class education. Chairman Mao's works have replaced *The Three Musketeers* and *The Story of Chi Kung.* "They had nothing to do during spare-time in the past," wrote the Peking *Chung-kuo Ch'ing-nien Pao* in March, 1964, "they are very happy now. They indulged themselves in eating and drinking in the past; they emulate one another to be more frugal today. . . . One only took care of oneself in the past; friendship is boundless today." And then, just before the lights go out, the bachelor denizens of workers' dormitories sing revolutionary songs; in the past "these young men were singing songs [but] they liked mostly unhealthy tunes." Now things are different. There is a choice between "Take Over the Rifle of Lei Feng," "Sing a Song to the Party," and "My Home Is the Collective Farm."[13] All this goes by the name of "socialist education" and "cultural revolution" that began in the last days of the "anti-rightists" and "rectification" campaigns of 1957 and has been revived in September, 1962 and 1965. It is addressed to urban and rural youth, children, veteran workers, peasants, soldiers, Party cadres, women, returned overseas Chinese, minority nationalities, nonveteran peasants and workers, students, and intellectuals. It relies mainly on moral pressure, but does not shirk from employing physical force and the dunce's cap—public confession method of breaking down a recalcitrant man. In addressing itself to the peasants, it sets up living examples, commends the eager and chastises the laggards, explains the reasons

---

14, 1964), pp. 53-57; "Recent Developments in Socialist Education," *URS,* Vol. 34, No. 1 (January 3, 1964), pp. 1-12; "Hong Kong Reports on Socialist Education Movement in Communist China," *URS,* Vol. 33, No. 9 (October 29, 1963).

The "Invite the Five Good Veterans" movement is an offshoot of the general Five Good campaign. Potential guests to a village Five Good unit are (1) veterans of the PLA, (2) veteran Party members, (3) veteran village cadres, (4) labor pace and quality setters, and (5) veteran poor peasants. *See* "Inviting Five Veterans to Tell Village Histories and Visiting the Elders to Fill in the Family Records," *Chung-kuo Ch'ing-nien Pao* (July 4, 1963), in *URS,* Vol. 34, No. 1 (January 3, 1964), p. 9. The "Three-Eight Working Style," mentioned above, refers to a concept written in Chinese in three phrases and eight additional characters. The "three" refers to the three mottoes: keep firmly to the correct political orientation, maintain an industrious and simple style of work, be flexible in strategy and tactics. The "eight" refers to the eight characters which mean unity, alertness, earnestness, and activity. *See* "Guarantees of New Victories for Socialism," *Peking Review* (January 8, 1965), p. 22; Jan S. Prybyla, "Communist China's Strategy of Economic Development, 1961-1966," *Asian Survey* (October, 1966), pp. 589-603.

[13] For a sample of modern Chinese literature *see The Young Coal Miner and Other Stories* (Peking, Foreign Languages Press, 1961), and the four-act play *Comrade, You've Taken the Wrong Path* (Peking, FLP, 1962). The revolutionary sing-along is held during the workers' statutory eight spare time hours. In between songs "they gather together to discuss problems in their study and work." For some samples of the kind of material used *see Songs from the Yumen Oilfields* (Peking FLP, 1957); *Songs of the Red Flag* (on the Great Leap Forward), *ibid.* (1961); *Unity Is Strength, ibid.* (1964), and "My Home is the Collective Farm," in *Songs of New China, ibid.* (1955). Regarding the "Learn from Lei Feng" movement see *URS,* Vol. 31, No. 24 (June 21, 1963), pp. 857-875.

in simple terms and often in barnyard language that even the village idiot can understand, and proceeds from the assumption that patient persuasion based on personal experience is the royal way to the soil tiller's heart. In propagandizing the soldier it recalls to mind "the class sufferings and national sufferings and . . . the crimes committed by the U.S.-Chiang gang." Treason, in army terms, is not just taking a junk to Taiwan: "To forget the past is to commit treason . . . to know nothing about exploitation is to know nothing about revolution," warned the *People's Daily* on July 26, 1963. Whole companies of demobilized soldiers are directed to outlying regions to set up new people's communes and bring under the plough vast, formerly barren areas. When you are through for the day with pushing the plough, weeding the fields, planting rice, and piling up earth with your bare hands on a new dyke, you engage in "subsidiary activities" like cloth-making, machine repairing, and attending meetings to tell of past sufferings, or arranging exhibitions of family histories, writing reports, and generally raising your ideological consciousness. "However," the Canton *Nan-fang Jih-pao* wrote on August 17, 1963, "there are still some comrades who fail to have an adequate understanding of this, saying that the education by recollection and comparison has been conducted many times since the liberation and that . . . recollection of the past which makes people weep is meaningless. Such a view is wrong."

The aim of socialist education and cultural remolding is to bring up a militant, tense, ascetic, and humorless *Homo Sinicus* who with complete ingenuousness accepts and approves everything that is decided on top, a man who, having rejected the paternalism of the lord of old, gives himself up totally and without question to the new paternalism of Mao.

The process of unification is thus not only, or even mainly, one of military control and effective central administration: it is first and foremost an effort to find sameness at a common class denominator through political education by pressure, fear, persuasion, and rote to the point of internalized assent.[14] Just as every well-organized church uses a widespread network of parish priests, so Marxist Leninism has a field organization of cadres whose main duty it is to see to it that the mass line elaborated by the Party bishops

---

[14] The common class denominator is the "proletariat," the have-nots of Marx's *Das Kapital,* the most politically progressive social stratum, according to Marx. Maoism insists that the class enemy is always there, like the evil spirits and the devil of the theologians. "Class struggle will exist for a long time in a socialist society," writes Tien Chu, "and the struggle to promote proletarian ideas and eliminate bourgeois ideas in the ideological and cultural fields will be protracted, complex, and have its ups and downs." (Tien Chu, "Fruits of the Cultural Revolution," *Peking Review,* [October 15, 1965], pp. 5-7.) Man's thinking must be remolded to conform with the invincible red banner of Mao Tse-tung's thought: "Once man's thinking has undergone changes, he is able to find all the answers. And only then can he create miracles." (Su Hsing, "The High Standard of Quality Stems from Thinking on a High Plane," Hung-chi [Red Flag], Peking, No. 1 [January 1, 1966], in *Survey of China Mainland Magazines* (SCMM), U.S. Consulate General, Hong Kong, No. 509 [January 31, 1966], pp. 29-32.)

is carried out to the letter. These cadres, or local agents of the Party, have had their troubles and moments of soul-searching, as the events of 1965-1967 have shown. When careful selection, indoctrination, and intensive training fail, as they do on occasion, the built-in weapons of mutual surveillance, denunciation, self-examination, public confession, and humble reform are brought to bear on the offender. Just as the Party's Mao faction maintains a state of constant tension within the nation as a whole, a tension not limited to the almost permanent overcommitment of resources, but embracing the inner-most recesses of the self, so inner-Party struggle and nonviolent purges are the lot of deviant Party cadres. "In the future we aim to conduct a rectifica-tion campaign every year or every other year," Mao Tse-tung was quoted as having said back in 1957, after he had cut down ninety-nine of the hun-dred flowers he had encouraged to blossom,[15] "a very short campaign, as one of the main methods of resolving various social contradictions in our coun-try during the whole period of transition."

Marxism-Leninism, especially in its Stalinist and Maoist adaptations, is not very pretty, but it does get the job done. Early capitalism, as a matter of historical record, was not a thing of beauty either. It did, however, give the Leninist socialists something to catch up with, and it outgrew its teen-age crudeness and cruelty. The material success and the human tragedy of Marxism are that all the coercive methods of early capitalism, which Marx decried, have been re-enacted many times over and improved upon by the successors of the prophet of human betterment. "Our comrades must under-stand," Mao Tse-tung wrote in Yenan, "that we do not study Marxism-Leninism because it is pleasing to the eye, or because it has some mystical value. . . . Marxism-Leninism has no beauty, nor has it any mystical value. It is only extremely useful." The usefulness of Marxist faith, the Marxist perspective, and the Leninist method for the attainment of na-tional aims are the underlying theme and distinguishing feature of Chinese communism. Lenin, Stalin, and Mao Tse-tung were men of action for whom the turgid works of Marx were a source of inspiration and a well from which ex post authority could readily be drawn. They used it in much the same way as Cromwell used the Bible.

The process of national unification has even been extended to the 15 million Chinese who reside overseas and who in some countries form a sizeable minority of the population (e.g., Malaysia, Indonesia, Thailand). Various methods have been employed to attract their loyalty and their ex-changeable currencies to Peking.[16]

[15] The shortlived policy of "letting a hundred flowers bloom and a hundred schools of thought contend" was first enunciated by Mao Tse-tung in January, 1956, when he declared it the Party's intention to invite frank and open criticism. [EDITOR'S NOTE]

[16] See "Overseas Chinese Investment in Communist China," URS, Vol. 35, No. 10 (May 5, 1964); A. Doak Barnett, Communist China and Asia (New York, Vintage Books, 1960), Chapter 8; Jan S. Prybyla, "Communist China's Foreign Exchange," Queen's Quarterly (Kingston, Ont., Winter, 1965), pp. 519-27.

CHILDREN AND THE MALTHUSIAN
COUNTERREVOLUTION

Since the communists came to power in China, over 200 million children have been born and another 200 million have reached maturity. "Children are the masters of the new society," is a principle enunciated as early as 1931 by a decree of the Central Executive Committee of the then Chinese Soviet Republic.[17] One of the observable phenomena on which practically all travellers in Communist China agree is the contrast between the neat, well-fed, and carefree look of children under six, and the obedient, serious, and melancholy decorum of children above that age. Although in their official pronouncements China's communist leaders adhere to the Marxist populationist theme and deplore the opposite view as not much better than bourgeois cannibalism, they are realistic enough to know that a net population increase of 2.2 percent a year demands from agriculture a much more formidable leap forward than that so far achieved. Marxist dialectics, moreover, is perfectly capable of reconciling a birth control policy with an essentially populationist tenor of the doctrine.[18]

The primary initial impact of public health measures on a developing society is to raise the rate of net population increase by reducing infant mortality. In spite of shortages of medical personnel, drugs, and equipment, Communist China has made important advances in the fields of sanitation, disease prevention and cure. Traditional Chinese medicine is used to fill the gaps left by insufficient numbers of doctors, nurses, and equipment. Even though the diet is Spartan, available food supplies are more evenly distributed than ever before, special care being given to the proper feeding

[17] The Chinese Soviet Republic was set up by Mao Tse-tung after the communist defeat at the hands of Chiang Kai-shek in 1927. The first Chinese Soviets were established in the mountain strongholds on the Hunan-Kiangsi border toward the end of 1927. In May, 1928, Mao Tse-tung's guerrilla bands in the area were joined by an army under Chu Teh and thenceforth the areas under communist control were gradually expanded. The new regime was based on peasant support and conducted guerrilla warfare in the countryside, avoiding urban concentrations. Land reform was the government's major platform. For his disregard for the "no workers, no communism" thesis, Mao Tse-tung was dismissed from the Politbureau of the Chinese Communist Party and from the Party Front Committee. He was not rehabilitated till the winter of 1928. *See* Edgar Snow, *Red Star Over China* (New York, Grove Press, 1961), Chapter 5, and C. P. Fitzgerald, *The Birth of Communist China* (Baltimore, Penguin, 1964), Chapter 3.

[18] Thomas Robert Malthus (1766-1834) advanced the theory that population will always tend to outrun the world's food supply. By his assertion that the populace always tends to have more children than it can support, Malthus absolved the wealthy from the age-old blame for the misery of the masses. [EDITOR'S NOTE] Marxism repudiates the Malthusian principle of population. However, actual Chinese population policy has, on occasion, adopted a frankly Malthusian remedy: "moral restraint" or postponement of marriage until the age of thirty for men, and twenty-five for women. [AUTHOR'S ADDITION TO EDITOR'S NOTE]

of children and expectant mothers. If present trends continue unabated, China's population will pass the billion mark by the mid-1970's.

From 1949 until 1957 China's fast-expanding population was viewed by the communists as a national asset. In 1953 the first population census using modern demographic techniques (as well as Soviet demographers and some 2 million Chinese census takers) was completed, revealing a mainland population of 582 million. From the time the census figures became known, the Party's attitude toward the problem began gradually to change in favor of demographic restraint. By 1957 a full-scale birth control campaign was under way and the merits of family planning were extolled next only to the planning of the national economy. Toward the end of the year this frenetic campaign was suddenly called off, although the Marriage Law of 1950 (which raised the minimum marriageable age to twenty for men and eighteen for women) and virtually free abortion and sterilization (first introduced in 1953) remained on the books. Discreet populationism reigned through the Great Leap Years (1958-1960).[19] Then, beginning in 1962, the official attitude shifted again in the direction of family planning. Along with Lei Feng, the youth of China were given another model on which to try their moral fibre: Wang Chuan Chuan, the reluctant bride who put off her marriage three times "for production and study." She had "correctly handled the relations between marriage, work, and study," said the Peking *Chung-kuo Fun-nu* (May 1, 1963), and as a result had achieved "very good results in the spare time engineering university." Since all good things come to those who wait, Wang Chuan Chuan "had gloriously attended the Shanghai Municipal Conference of Advanced Collectives and Advanced Workers in Industry and Other Fields."

It would seem that the massive birth control campaign of 1957 had found little response among the poor and the illiterate. If, in fact, that was the case, it would tend to shed doubt on other storming campaigns where the real effect is more difficult to measure and where dissimulation, though difficult, does not cry in the corner for all the village to hear.

THE STAGES OF ECONOMIC GROWTH

Any fair evaluation of Communist China's economic performance has first to negotiate the political and technical obstacle of insufficient, tilted, fragmentary, and highly selective statistics. The Chinese frankly admit that statistics are for them a weapon of the proletarian state. Privately they also acknowledge that, in spite of Soviet professional help, data-gathering and statistical techniques still present grave problems for the planners. In short,

---

[19] The attempted crash industrialization program known as "The Great Leap Forward" is discussed on pp. 173-176. [EDITOR'S NOTE]

Chinese published statistics suffer from official reluctance to broadcast the bad along with the good, from obsessive security consciousness, occasional blatant lying, insufficient information about methodology, and from distortion (due to incompetence or a desire to look revolutionary) at the local, fact-gathering level. To this day there is no such thing as a regularly issued statistical yearbook of mainland China. It is only fair to point out, however, that much progress has been made since 1949 in improving data collection and analysis, which is essential for any attempt to run efficiently a centrally planned economy. On the other hand, little if any advance is apparent in the manner in which statistics are released for public consumption. The one is mainly a technical, the other a political problem.

One thing must be made clear: China's communist leaders are determined to break out of the vicious circle of poverty and to develop rapidly the country's economic potential, although they disagree on how to do it and on when to let the benefits of industrialization seep down to the consumer level. It is a will backed by the full might of a tightly organized, centralized, restless yet forbearing totalitarian Party and State. Human misery and oppression are not new to the great mass of the Chinese people; they are, in fact, an endemic condition. Something like 50 million people had perished from disease, natural calamities, and the hand of man in the course of Chiang Kai-shek's tenure of power, and they died for nothing. No fate is worse than purposeless oppression and a life of suffering from which death is the only deliverance. Much of the strength of Chinese communism derives from the simple fact that there is no going back, no social model to be drawn upon from the past. Capitalism, packaged and exported by foreign investors, unwrapped and greedily used by a thoughtless clique of native warlords, is certainly not the solution for which even the most uncompromising noncommunist Chinese would lift the little finger of his left hand. "People's capitalism" of the American variety and the welfare state of Western Europe are for him incomprehensible delusions, not unlike full communism. He compares himself not with other people's present but with his own past. What the West exported to China in that past were the worst features of primitive capitalism and not the more humane, high consumption, and democratic product of the mid-twentieth century. In a sense, the West jettisoned abroad its discarded capitalistic forms, its prejudices, and outlived political conceptions. What was no longer good enough *in* England or France was still good *for* England and France when used in Asia and Africa. It is in this historical setting that the achievements and the costs of China's communist construction must be seen and understood. It is this, more than the brute nature of communist force, that can help explain the relative passivity of the Chinese peasant caught in the web of human engineering, forced-draft industrialization, the Great Leap, and the Cultural Revolution.

Communist China's economic race against time may be divided into five rather distinct phases: 1949-52, the period of reconstruction, seizure of power, and consolidation; 1953-57, the years of Stalinist construction, Sino-Soviet cooperation, and socialist transformation; 1958-60, the Great Leap Forward; 1961-65, the time for thought, a "one step back," or as the Chinese put it, a policy of "readjustment, consolidation, filling-out, and raising standards";[20] and 1966 to the present—the phase of internal struggle, "cultural remolding" along Maoist lines, and of bitter opposition from within the Party apparatus.

1949-52: RECONSTRUCTION

A great deal had to be done. It was done quickly and without mercy. During this period the force of arms and physical violence against real and imagined opponents of the new order were much in evidence.

China's most immediate and urgent problem was agriculture. As far as can be determined, and the figures are not too reliable, China at the time of the communist takeover cultivated only about 250 million acres of its 3.7 million square miles of territory.[21] Shortage of arable land combined with a fast-growing rural population; the absence of primogeniture rules in land division;[22] a desperate lack of agricultural capital; soil exhaustion, low productivity, and rural underemployment; a per head arable land holding of 0.45 acres; and technical ignorance of a most deep-rooted and pernicious kind, confronted the new regime with a problem of gigantic proportions. On the institutional side, the process of communist land reform in China followed rather closely the pattern established in other communist countries. The first step consisted in the distribution of land to the peasants under the Agrarian Reform Law of June 1950. As in other communist countries, the reform was meant to achieve not only the redistribution of land but, above all, the political transformation of the countryside through the elimination of the existing social structure. "Class struggle" was unleashed against landlords and rich peasants by egging on the poor and treating the middle peasants as temporary allies. An elaborate Maoist theory of class structure in the countryside was embodied in State decree to serve as a guide to action. According to official Chinese sources, the reform resulted in the distribution of land to 300 million peasants, or some 0.33 acres per

[20] *See* Fang Cheng, "An Economic Policy That Wins: A Survey of the Policy of Readjustment, Consolidation, Filling Out, and Raising Standards," *Peking Review* (March 13, 1964), pp. 6-9.

[21] One square mile equals 640 acres. [EDITOR'S NOTE]

[22] Especially prevalent during the feudal era, "primogeniture" was the legal right of the eldest son to inherit all of his father's estate. The primary purpose of this rule was the prevention of the gradual decomposition of the family estate which was the main source of the power of the ruling class—the landed aristocracy. [EDITOR'S NOTE]

Economically, primogeniture prevented the subdivision of land holdings into non-viable units. It is not enough to distribute land among the landless and so correct a social wrong. Land holdings must be economically viable, profitable, efficient within the existing technical and social framework. [AUTHOR'S ADDITION TO EDITOR'S NOTE]

head. Since millions of Party workers, soldiers, members of communist mass organizations and their families were also granted plots of land, the final per capita holdings were probably below this figure, especially in the populous coastal areas. To collectivize is first to demonstrate that private ownership will not work, and a sure way of making it not work is to parcel out nonviable land holdings to millions of capital deficient peasants. Having uprooted the class enemy by destroying his economic base, his social standing (recall the humiliating public trials and abject confessions of the once mighty), and often his person, the Party had opened the way to collectivization. Apart from being able to walk up and down their tiny strips of land, the peasants were no better off than before. Sales and consolidation of holdings soon began to appear, and with them speculation in grain and land values and class differentiation. All this, the Party said, only went to show how creeping capitalism could be and how necessary it was to use other, more "correct" ways of dealing with it. Before the period was out, experiments began with mutual aid teams involving the joint use of draught animals, farm implements, and labor during the sowing and harvesting seasons or, in some cases, all year round. By the end of 1952, over 40 percent of peasant households, or nearly 45.5 million households, were members of 8.3 million such teams.[23] Elementary agricultural producer cooperatives accounted at that time for only a very small proportion of the total number of peasant households. Agricultural investment in this early period, while not lavish, was quite substantial. Both the State-contributed and the self-generated parts of this investment were disbursed mainly in support of irrigation and water conservation projects, most of which involved repairs of and improvements to already existing facilities. Apart from frequent demonstrations designed to familiarize the peasants with modern agricultural machinery, investment in mechanized farm equipment was negligible. This trend, incidentally, continued through the First Five-Year Plan (1953-57) so that by the end of 1957 China had only 24,000 tractors.

Total fixed investment rose steadily, even if not as sharply as in later years. The share of investment in gross national product was also rising. The evidence on this score is conflicting, but a rate of about 10 percent of G.N.P. in 1952 seems to be a fairly reasonable estimate. By 1952 it was asserted that the output of 33 major industrial products had exceeded the prewar peak levels by 26 percent: 16 percent in capital goods, and 32 percent in consumer goods (mostly cotton textiles). Technical innovation and the introduction of new products were put off until later except for a very few items in the machine industries. The stress was on rehabilitation of the existing capacity, especially in the industrial regions of Manchuria where in years past the Russians had been busy carting off everything within sight.

[23] *Ten Great Years* (Peking, Foreign Languages Press, 1960), p. 34.

Inflation was stemmed through the application of stringent fiscal and monetary measures (including, on the institutional side, control over the banking system) accompanied by political anti-speculation campaigns. By 1952 about 50 percent of the modern industrial sector (which accounted for about 60 percent of the gross output value of modern industry) had been nationalized. As in some of the Eastern European countries, private enterprise was at this stage used to help the State in the work of reconstruction and, additionally, in supplying goods needed to pursue China's Korean adventure. As early as 1950, however, measures were taken to supervise the activities of the private sector. These turned into a campaign of harassment from January to April, 1952, under the slogan of combatting the "Five Evils." When the campaign was over, private enterprise in industry and trade had been reduced to virtual impotence, while the number of State stores had risen five-fold compared with 1950. By the end of 1952 the State controlled over 60 percent of the wholesale trade, more than a third of the retail, and 93 percent of foreign trade.[24]

The people's Liberation Army and the millions of land reform and "Five-Anti" victims undergoing thought reform were harnessed to the Herculean task of rebuilding railroad lines, bridges, tunnels, and drainage ditches. New trunk lines built during this period included the Lanchow-Paotow railroad totalling some 900 kilometers and the Chengtu-Chunking railway connecting Szechwan Province with the Yangtse river port of Chunking. Work was also started on the Szechwan-Tibet military highway and the Chinghai Province-Tibet road. The combined length of these two roads was 4,400 kilometers, and their construction represented a feat of human endurance and engineering. Ship salvage operations were pressed forward, and new harbor facilities began to be built. Even before the launching of the First Five-Year Plan (1953-57), Chinese shipyards were turning out vessels of 10,000 dead weight tons.

[24] Even though nominally still in control of a substantial portion of total wholesale and retail turnover, private enterprise was, by 1952, hemmed in by numerous regulations, taxes, fines, investigations, and so on. The state, it should be recalled, was by then in command of banking and other "commanding heights" of the economy. After 1952, the private sector was further restricted by the expansion of "state capitalism," i.e., the introduction of joint state-private enterprises in which the management, planning, and personnel policies were determined by the state. The process of restricting private wholesale and retail trade is described in the following terms by Kuan Ta-tung in *The Socialist Transformation of Capitalist Industry and Commerce in China* (Peking, Foreign Languages Press, 1960), p. 44: "After the founding of the People's Republic restrictions were placed upon capitalist industry and commerce. These included the scope of their production and business, purchasing, marketing and prices, taxation and profits, and the working conditions for the workers. Naturally these restrictions clashed with the narrow class interests of the national capitalists, some of whom continually opposed or violated them. . . . The policies of use and restriction were for the purpose of carrying out the socialist transformation of private enterprises." *See also* Hsueh Mu-chiao, Su Haing, Lin Tse-li, *The Socialist Transformation of the National Economy in China* (Peking, Foreign Languages Press, 1960).

It was during this period that the groundwork for Sino-Soviet economic cooperation was laid and the seeds of future disputes were sown. On February 14, 1950, the Soviet Union and China concluded a Treaty of Friendship, Cooperation, and Mutual Assistance which, among other things, provided for a Soviet loan of $300 million at one percent interest, the amount payable to China in five yearly installments.[25] Khrushchev was later to refer to some "unequal elements" in Sino-Soviet relations dating from that time. These certainly included the joint Sino-Soviet companies in shipbuilding, petroleum (Sinkiang), civil aviation, and a number of other key sectors, as well as provisions relating to the status of Port Arthur, Dairen, and the Changchun railway.

1953-57: STALINIST CONSTRUCTION AND SOCIALIZATION

Preliminary work on China's First Five-Year Plan began in 1951. The plan, officially inaugurated in 1953 but not published until 1955, embodied the policy tenets outlined in a 1952 statement entitled "The General Line of the State for the Period of Transition to Socialism." Industrialization and socialization were the basic guidelines. Industrialization was to stress heavy industry in which the bulk of technological innovation was to be concentrated. Investment resources for this purpose were to be obtained overwhelmingly from domestic sources with foreign (mainly Soviet) loans being used to introduce modern prototypes of plants and machinery and advanced technical know-how. Socialization of industry, commerce, and agriculture was to be gradual with emphasis being put on such intermediate forms of ownership as joint stock companies with State participation, mutual aid teams, and elementary cooperatives. Originally it was planned to bring no more than 20 percent of all peasant households into agricultural producers' cooperatives of the advanced type by 1957. In the course of the Plan, industry was scheduled to receive 61.8 percent of resources allocated to investments, and agriculture 6.2 percent. Transportation—mainly railroads and inland shipping—was to get 17 percent.[26] The Plan was Stalinist in concep-

[25] The loan was to be repaid in 10 yearly installments of $30 million each from 1954 through 1963. See Jan S. Prybyla, "Sino-Soviet Economics," *The Quarterly Review* (London, July, 1965), pp. 283-292; and "Unsettled Issues in the Sino-Soviet Dispute," *The Virginia Quarterly Review* (Autumn, 1965), pp. 510-524.

[26] As may be expected from the state of China's statistics, there is considerable disagreement among Western analysts about China's economic performance. The figures used here are based on Alexander Eckstein's "The Strategy of Economic Development in Communist China," *The American Economic Review,* Papers and Proceedings (May, 1961), pp. 508-517. For other computations see William W. Hollister, "Capital Formation in Communist China," in Choh-ming Li, ed., *Industrial Development in Communist China* (New York, Praeger, 1964), pp. 39-53; Cheng Chu-yuan, *Communist China's Economy 1949-1962* (Seton Hall University Press, 1963); and Richard T. Gill, *Economic Development: Past and Present* (New York, Prentice-Hall, 1963), Chapter 6.

tion and even more so in execution.[27] There were, of course, some local adaptations. Because of China's high annual rate of population growth the problem of mechanizing agriculture was not as pressing as it had been in the Soviet Union during a comparable period of development. Soviet-type rates of expansion of industrial output could conceivably have been obtained with a slower rate of urbanization by simply absorbing the urban unemployed and raising the labor participation ratio.

Although the basic guidelines of the Plan were retained throughout, actual performance revealed wide departures from the original blueprint. In the end, industry's share of total gross investment came to only 56 percent (of which heavy industry absorbed 49 percent), agriculture's share was raised to 8.2 percent, and that of transportation to 18.7 percent.

Agricultural investment took on "traditional" rather than "modern" or "innovating" forms. Much work continued to be done on irrigation and water conservation projects, and a resolute (and effective) anti-pest campaign was launched. Simple new tools and improvements on existing implements were introduced and propagandized, and efforts were made to introduce double cropping and high yielding strains. Innovation and modernization were largely restricted to heavy industry. In this task Soviet assistance in the form of machinery and technical advice was crucial, but scanty when matched against Soviet capabilities. In addition to the 1950 loan of $300 million, the Soviet Union in 1954 extended an additional credit of $130 million to China. Other loans were given to help the Chinese conduct their Korean intervention—but no grants. In this period the Russians trained 13,600 Chinese students in the U.S.S.R., and sent to China a total of 10,800 technicians and scientists for various terms of duty, as well as more than 24,000 complete sets of scientific and technical blueprints.[28] Most Soviet aid, however, took on a tit-for-tat trade form: what the Chinese received, they had to pay for in cash or on a short-term deferred payment basis. No wonder that even though the food situation in China throughout the period left much to be desired, the Chinese continued to export to the U.S.S.R. and to the Soviet bloc a sizeable portion of their basic food commodities. The total value of Soviet exports to China from 1950 through 1957 was $4.9 billion, most of it capital goods. In 1957, complete plants accounted for 77 percent of the value of China's machinery and equipment imports from the U.S.S.R.

A specifically Stalinist feature of the Plan's execution was the sudden

[27] On the components of a Stalinist strategy of economic development *see* Jan S. Prybyla, "The Economic Problems of Soviet Russia in Transition," *The Indian Journal of Economics* (October, 1964), pp. 135-151. *See also* Donald S. Zagoria, "Some Comparisons Between the Russian and Chinese Models," in A. Doak Barnett, ed., *Communist Strategies in Asia: A Comparative Analysis of Governments and Parties* (New York, Praeger, 1963), Chapter 1.

[28] M. Kuranin, "14th Anniversary of Soviet-Chinese Treaty," *Pravda* (February 14, 1965), p. 5. *See also* Mikhail A. Klochko, *Soviet Scientist in Red China* (New York, Praeger, 1964).

stepping up of socialization in general and of agricultural collectivization in particular in 1956-57. The unbalanced pattern of growth subsumed in the Plan (the economics of walking on one foot) produced strains and bottlenecks in the economy which came to a head in 1955. Apart from the resurgence of class differentiation in the countryside, marketable farm output was not keeping pace with population growth and threatened to undermine industrial expansion. In spite of the "anti" campaigns and the liquidation of former class enemies, economic control over millions of peasant-owners was incomplete; in short, the capital needed to execute the ambitious plans for industrial expansion was not forthcoming from the only source which could provide it. In July, 1955, Mao Tse-tung gave the green light to accelerated collectivization. In October of the same year the Party's Central Committee issued the necessary directives. By June of the following year, 91.9 percent of China's peasant households had been collectivized with a minimum of fuss. By the end of 1956 everyone was in. As of that date, private industry had ceased to exist and private commerce accounted for only 4 percent of the total value of retail sales. "Transition to Socialism" could henceforth become the "Construction of Socialism."

The difference in investment rates between industry and agriculture was reflected in average annual rates of growth in factory and farm output. These were officially given as 16.5 and 4.5 percent respectively, but considerable doubt attaches to both figures, especially the agricultural. It seems reasonably certain, however, that in spite of serious natural disasters in 1953-54, 1956, and 1957, grain output did rise significantly (from about 164 million metric tons in 1952 to 195 million metric tons in 1957), and that wholesale starvation was avoided. At the end of the Plan period (1957) the Chinese claimed that steel output was 5.35 million tons compared with 1.35 million tons in 1952, pig iron 5.94 million tons compared with 1.93 million tons five years earlier, electric power 19.3 billion kwh (7.26 billion kwh in 1952), coal 130 million tons (65.53 in 1952), crude oil 1.46 million tons (436,000 tons in 1952), and chemical fertilizer 631,000 tons (181,000 tons in 1952).[29] In 1957 China for the first time produced its own trucks, power generators, locomotives, and small arms (assault rifles, carbines, machineguns, grenade launchers, 81 mm mortals, etc.). First steps were being taken to establish an aircraft industry, synthetic rubber plants, tractor factories, various branches of the chemical industry, and a Soviet-made atomic reactor. A breakthrough was made in oil exploration in 1955 with the discovery of the rich Karamai fields in Sinkiang. That year, work began on a large refining complex in Lanchow, parts of which went on stream in 1958. From 1953 through 1957 about 5,000 kilometers of new railroad lines were built, most of them reaching into the interior of the country. A noticeable shift

[29] The First Five-Year Plan for Development of the National Economy of the People's Republic of China (Peking, FLP, 1956), and "Communique of the Fulfillment of the First Five-Year Plan," Peking Review (April 21, 1959).

took place in the location of key industries, a shift away from the coastal areas into hitherto underdeveloped regions of central and northwestern China. Production of consumer goods lagged behind the expansion of the capital goods sector and many key consumer items continued, from 1953 on, to be strictly and severely rationed. Thus, for example, output of cotton cloth rose from 3.8 billion meters in 1952 to only 5 billion meters in 1957. Peking, in fact, made no bones about it: in its interpretation of first things first, consumer welfare came chronologically last. According to official figures, the annual average increase per capita of consumer goods during the period of the Plan was only $1.69. This, however, it should be added, was better than the Chinese had seen for decades.

Western estimates point to an annual average rate of growth in net domestic product during this time (in constant 1952 prices) of about 6 percent.[30] This is probably a minimum figure, and higher estimates of 7 and 8 percent cannot be discounted. Whatever one thinks of the methods used to achieve this performance, the result is impressive—almost double the rate of growth achieved by India during a corresponding period.

1958-1960: THE GREAT LEAP FORWARD

Then, suddenly, all relative caution was thrown to the winds. In September 1956 the Party's Eighth National Congress approved a proposal for a Second Five-Year Plan (1958-62) the essence of which was to transform China into an industrialized country with heavy industry leading the way. The original proposal was merely a stepped-up version of the First Plan with industry scheduled to receive about 60 percent of investible resources and agriculture about 10 percent. Greater stress was to be put on chemical fertilizers and the introduction of advanced type agricultural implements.

Actually, as things turned out, China never had a Second Five-Year Plan. In 1957 it became clear to the leaders that the Stalinist recipe for economic development was not suitable to Chinese conditions. In spite of official claims regarding the growth of agricultural output from 1952 to 1957, farm output probably just about kept pace with population increase, pressure on the available land mounted, and an imbalance between installed capacity and raw materials supply was rapidly developing, seriously impairing further industrial expansion. At the same time political and ideological relations with China's major capital goods supplier, the U.S.S.R., were deteriorating to the point where future relief from that quarter became

[30] E.g., Ta-Chung Liu and Kung-Chia Yeh, "Preliminary Estimate of the National Income of the Chinese Mainland, 1952-59," *The American Economic Review, loc. cit.,* p. 494. *Cf.,* Wilfred Malenbaum, "India and China, Contrasts in Development Performance" *ibid.* (June, 1959), pp. 284-309; Sidney Klein, "Recent Economic Experience in India and Communist China: Another Interpretation," *ibid.* (May, 1965), pp. 31-39.

doubtful.[31] It became increasingly plain to the Chinese leaders that in years to come the country would have to rely mainly on its own efforts to reach the goals which it had set for itself.

A new strategy of economic development began to appear in the winter of 1957 and the spring of the following year. Known as the "General Line of Going All Out and Aiming High to Achieve Greater, Quicker, Better, and More Economical Results in Building Socialism," or the Great Leap Forward, it was essentially a political drive in which economic rationality, prudence, and calculation played a minimal role. The crux of the Great Leap was general mobilization of underemployed rural labor, a drive unprecedented in the history of humanity to put to work every hour of the day hundreds of millions of bare hands. This strategy, if indeed it may be called that, required new tools of development which even the Soviets regarded with incredulity. The key tool was the "People's Commune" a form of agricultural organization once tried but rejected by the Soviets. Within a few months China's 752,000 collective farms were transformed into some 26,500 communes encompassing practically all peasant households. As against an average number of 158 households in a collective, the number was 5,000 in a commune.[32]

The objectives of the People's Communes may be summed up as follows. First, they were a labor and rural capital mobilization device. The labor and capital were mobilized not only for strictly agricultural tasks but, most important, for (a) labor intensive investment projects such as irrigation, water conservation, and afforestation, and (b) small scale industry such as cloth weaving, the manufacture of simple tools, repair of machinery, and the making of a wide range of industrial products, of which the smelting of pig iron was the most widely publicized though by no means the most significant. The mobilization was made possible by vesting in the communes many of the functions formerly exercised on the local or *hsiang* (township) level by government offices. The communes thus administered within their region such diverse activities as marketing, commerce, education, public health, labor, public security, communications, small-scale industry, and, of course, agriculture. The commune ran scientific research institutes, spare time schools, and so on. Labor was organized in production brigades (encompassing the original collectives), and in smaller production teams, but the commune was the production and accounting unit. In short, the commune was something more than the Soviet-type *kolkhoz* (collective farm)

[31] Jan S. Prybyla, "The Economics of the Sino-Soviet Dispute," *Bulletin of the Institute for the Study of the USSR* (December, 1963), pp. 17-24; W. Griffin, *The Sino-Soviet Rift* (Cambridge, Mass., M.I.T. Press, 1964).

[32] The number of 26,500 communes was officially given during the Great Leap. In October, 1963, China's Minister of Agriculture, Liao Lu-yen, writing in the Cuban periodical *Cuba Socialista*, put the number of communes in 1958 at 74,000. See Liao Lu-yen, "Collectivization of Agriculture in China," *Peking Review* (November 1, 1963), pp. 7-14. The national average was 1,620 households per commune in 1966.

or *sovkhoz* (state farm).[33] It was an economic, social, political, and cultural arm of the state in the countryside. Second, the People's Communes were rationing devices. Whereas under the collective system the peasant household was the unit of income distribution, in the commune at least half the income was distributed in the form of ration tickets redeemable at the commune mess halls and tailoring establishments. The other half was paid in monthly wages determined according to economic and political criteria among which ideological consciousness, as revealed by the individual's attitude toward the commune's labor tasks, played an important role. Ideologically, the Chinese proclaimed the communes an advanced form of socialist organization enabling China to reach full communism in a fraction of the time it took the Soviets to get within sight of that state of perfection. As such the communes became an additional source of irritation in a dispute which could well have done without it. There is a technological footnote to all this. It has usually been referred to by the Chinese as the method of "walking on two legs," and applies to technological dualism. Under the commune system, large-scale, modern, capital-intensive sectors of the economy (e.g., steel mills, large hydroelectric power projects, huge dams, trunk railroads, and so forth) taken care of by the State, coexisted with small-scale, labor-intensive, and largely "traditional" sectors financed from local resources.

Travellers in China at the time of the Great Leap bear witness to a land in convulsion: every day some 90 million peasants smelted iron in homemade backyard furnaces (most of it brittle and unusable), 60 million women tended to communal kitchens, laundries, and commune nurseries, and 90 million peasants collected human and animal manure. After a hard day's work in the fields, 77 million Chinese moved tons of earth to build irrigation works, and another 100 million exerted themselves in deep ploughing.[34]

Their efforts were matched only by those of the statisticians. From Peking incredible claims of production successes poured out throughout the year 1958. Steel output, having hit the 11 million ton mark, was soon to reach 35 million tons, they claimed, and in one year grain production had risen from 195 million metric tons to 375 million tons (not even counting the soya beans). But soon, to errors of human judgment were to be added the calamities of nature, first in 1959, then in 1960 and 1961. The fantastic claims and actual gains of 1958 were wiped out. If the unusable portion of the steel output is subtracted, steel production in 1958 was not 11 million tons, but 5, slightly below, that is, the 1957 level; the production of grain was not 375 million metric tons, but a revised official 250 million, and in actuality probably less than the 1957 figure of 195 million metric tons. And so it went all along the line. That the Great Leap Forward had involved a considerable

---

[33] For a discussion of Soviet collective and state farms, *see* pp. 95-96 above. [EDITOR'S NOTE]

[34] Nicolas Spulber, "Contrasting Economic Patterns: Chinese and Soviet Development Strategies," *Soviet Studies* (July, 1963), pp. 1-16.

amount of waste motion cannot be denied. Nor can it be questioned that by 1960 the Chinese leadership was confronted with an even more serious problem than that which had faced it three years earlier, for the only real Great Leap was in the number of mouths to feed: about forty million. However, the calamity of the Leap can be, and has, in fact, been exaggerated in the West. On a long-term view it was not a total failure. It was an impetuous and imprudent thing, to be sure; cruel and ugly, yes, but not utterly useless. In a country which regards men first and foremost as producers, such monumental errors can be taken in stride.

What then were the more lasting features of this frenzy? For one thing, dislike it as we may, it was an educational process, a barracks-type education in unthinking discipline and an army-like approach to the economic battle line. It familiarized millions of backward peasants with industrial techniques at great immediate cost, but at an equally great potential benefit. It liberated China from excessive reliance on the Soviet developmental model which, whatever its strengths, was not suitable to a populous Asian land. It taught the leadership a lesson in economics which, until 1965 at least, they appear to have taken to heart. It achieved a strategically and economically significant dispersion of industry and an increase in the number of home-made scientists and technicians. In short, the Great Leap showed the virtues and the limitations of self-reliance. By 1962 China's meager army of scientific and technical personnel had almost doubled; important inroads had been made on illiteracy; and the number of types of steel, rolled steel, and nonferrous metals had increased by 200 percent, and those of machine tools by 150 percent. Quality continued to be a problem, but in an underdeveloped land such things tend to come last. Contrary to oft-repeated assertions in the West, the commune system of socio–economic organization was not jettisoned, merely made more rational. But the fever was spent.

1961-65: READJUSTMENT

The harvest of 1960 was worse than the most pessimistic forecast. Reports of malnutrition and the pillaging of rice stores began to filter out of China. There was also evidence that in the grip of revolutionary ardor, machinery had been misused and left unrepaired, planning had become all but impossible, and the nation was no longer responsive to frenzied appeals for more and more work. In fact, it is remarkable that in Communist China's eighteen years' history, long range economic planning has been absent except for the 1953-57 period. In November of that year the official organ of the Chinese Communist Party, *Hung Chi*, discovered a new objective law: the simultaneous development of industry and agriculture, according to which all things were equal but agriculture was more equal than others. In January

1961 this "law" was embodied in policy, and since that time agriculture has come to be the favored sector. It took the Soviets forty years to come around to the view that unbalanced growth must sooner or later be corrected; the Chinese grasped it in twelve, but then seemed to have lost hold of it again.

Broadly, the new strategy of development which emerged after 1960 may be summed up in the following points. 1. The growth of the national economy must be based on agriculture. As Chou En-lai repeatedly put it, "The plan for national economic development should be arranged in the order of priority of agriculture, light industry, and heavy industry." [35] The scale of industrial development should correspond to the volume of the marketable grain and the industrial raw materials furnished by agriculture. All departments and trades should henceforth orientate themselves to serve agriculture and the countryside. 2. As a result, the primary function of heavy industry is to provide agriculture with increasing amounts of machinery, chemical fertilizer, insecticides, fuel, electric power, irrigation equipment, and building materials, and at the same time supply increasing amounts of raw materials to the light industries. Industry thus becomes the "leading factor" and agriculture the "foundation" of China's economic development. 3. Greater attention must be paid to the quality of the produce both of agriculture and industry. This is essential in view of China's overseas trade commitments and in order to reduce waste motion at home. 4. Self-reliance while still the "foundation stone of the cause of revolution and construction," must not be interpreted narrowly. There is such a thing as the advantage of backwardness which means simply that by importing the results of foreign expertise and the accumulated knowledge and invention of economically advanced countries, China can spare herself much costly tinkering and, above all, much time. Self-reliance does not imply cutting yourself off from the rest of the world. A country which aspires to great power status must try to seek out friends and influence people abroad. In fact, Communist China had in 1965 trade and economic relations with 125 countries, with some of which it had no formal diplomatic contacts (e.g., South Africa, Portugal, and West Germany).[36] Also, between December 1960 and the end of 1964, the Chinese had bought 21.5 million metric tons of grain from such "intermediate zone imperialists" as Canada, France, and Australia. Since then, grain imports have been stabilized at about 5 million tons per year. 5. Great emphasis was put on technical and managerial expertise and on the training of large numbers of technical and scientific

[35] Chou En-lai, "Report on the Work of the Government to First Session, Third National People's Congress," *Peking Review* (January 1, 1965), p. 10.

[36] See Jan Prybyla, "Communist China's Economic Relations with the U.S.S.R. and Western Europe," *Business Review,* Boston University (Spring, 1964), pp. 3-14; "Communist China's Economic Relations with Africa 1960-1964," *Asian Survey* (November, 1964), pp. 1135-1143; Li Hai-yun, "China's Growing Foreign Trade," *Peking Review* (January 22, 1965), pp. 519-527; Jan S. Prybyla, "Pragmatic Marxism Peking Style," *Challenge* (November, December, 1966), pp. 12-14, 42.

personnel, including agronomists. For example, there are at present 29 agricultural colleges in China, 12 specialized research institutes under the Chinese Academy of Agricultural Sciences, and 28 provincial agricultural research institutes. Specialized research is supplemented by mass- and spare-time research on hundreds of thousands of experimental farms. The thirst for knowledge is perhaps the single most striking phenomenon in present-day China. And the thirst is being assuaged and frustrated all at once. The experts are constantly being reminded not to lose sight of ideological work: "Politics is the commander, the very soul of our work," headlined the Party's *Jen-min Jih-pao* in announcing the launching of the Third Five-Year Plan on January 1, 1966. "Politics takes first place relative to science and technology."

The commune system has not been formally dismantled. It has, however, undergone far-reaching reforms in the direction of economic rationality. Management functions have been vested in the production teams, and those were the units which also supervised the distribution of income. Commune members have been not only allowed but encouraged to cultivate private plots the proceeds from which they were until 1966 permitted to keep or sell on the free market.

Since 1962, harvests have been relatively good and the food situation has gradually improved. In 1964, industrial output was said to have risen 15 percent over the previous year. A Third Five-Year Plan, beginning in 1966, was announced in December, 1964, and appeared to be continuing the policy of economic restraint inaugurated at the close of the Great Leap, with, however, a gradual shift of emphasis toward heavy industry.

1966-67: THE GREAT PROLETARIAN CULTURAL REVOLUTION

In the autumn of 1965, the proponents of the leaps-and-bounds theory of economic development, using Mao's name and prestige, stepped up their attack on the relatively pragmatic policies that had been in force since the collapse of the Great Leap. The Great Proletarian Cultural Revolution, as this offensive came to be known, unleashed millions of youngsters (organized into "Red Guard" detachments) against all who within the Party apparatus or outside it were suspected of opposing the thoughts and policies of Mao and his closest lieutenants. As the turmoil unfolded, after the Central Committee meeting of September, 1965, it became apparent that the Chinese Communist Party was going through a most severe crisis. The mounting wave of harassment and denunciations, the humiliation of many top Party executives, the purges and virulent attacks on "freaks, monsters, and devils" who had allegedly insinuated themselves into positions of authority—all this presented a picture of near madness unparalleled even by the excesses of the

Great Leap. By the end of 1966, the Head of State Liu Shao-chi, whose book *How To Be a Good Communist* was once prescribed as compulsory reading, had been declared an outcast, a traitor deserving of the death penalty, and a corrupt man openly disavowed by his children. The book came in for some severe criticism in April 1967 when it was described as "a poisonous weed" and mere "deceitful talk." Linked with Liu was the Party's General Secretary Teng Hsiao-ping. Other victims included Peng Chen, Mayor of Peking and First Secretary of the city's Party Committee, Lu Ting-yi, Alternate Member of the Politbureau and Head of the Central Committee's Propaganda Department as well as Minister of Culture, and Lo Jui-ching, Minister of Public Security and Chief of Staff of the People's Liberation Army since 1959. Early in 1966, the Chairman of the Chinese Academy of Sciences and of the All-China Federation of Literary and Art Circles, seventy-four-year-old Kuo Mo-jo, was made to confess publicly his alleged trespasses against Mao Tse-tung's thinking. "All the works I have written," he was reported as saying, "should be burned." The editorial boards of a number of newspapers and magazines were purged. Included were the boards of the Party's theoretical organ *Hung Chi (Red Flag)* and *Jen-min Jih-pao (People's Daily)*.

All schools were shut down for a year on the pretext that curricula had to be revised in a more revolutionary spirit. Millions of youngsters were encouraged to roam the countryside and go to Peking, Shanghai, and other cities to "exchange revolutionary experience." A few years earlier many of these same youngsters had been told to go just the other way, into the countryside to strengthen the production front on the farms. Some marched on foot in imitation of the Long March, but most, apparently, preferred to take the train, particularly since a red armband was equivalent to a ticket.

As has been shown before, the Great Proletarian Cultural Revolution did not just happen overnight. It had been building up for years under the cover of the Socialist Education Campaign and of the various drives for cadre rectification. The events of 1966 and 1967 were merely the culmination of a drawn-out process. The historical perspective needed to evaluate this phenomenon is still lacking, but some general remarks on the motives and early results of this highly uncultural event may be ventured.

The reasons for Mao-Lin's new Great Leap into uproar and confusion were probably the following:

1. Factional struggle for succession to Mao Tse-tung's position of leadership.

2. Fear that the younger generation, which has not known at first hand what revolutionary struggle was really like, might grow up to be overcomplacent, self-centered, morally fat and flabby—and thus "revisionist" or even "capitalist."

3. The belief that seizure of political power and economic modernization are part of the same process of permanent revolution in which pure and

"correct" political will, asceticism, barrack-like discipline, and an unquestioning obedience to the revolutionary principles expounded by the leader, are the keys to success.

Of these three basic motivations, the last is the most important in the long run. The quarrel raging below the surface of the Cultural Revolution is not so much concerned with who exactly will succeed Mao, as with which general conception of "building socialism" is ultimately to prevail. If it means anything, the construction of socialism in China implies economic and technical modernization of which the acquisition of other than political know-how is a most important component. Economic development, another name for modernization, does involve the constant replacement of the old by the new, but after a certain point it is unheroic drudgery. It means not only hard work, but a minimum of rational calculation in distributing the burden of labor; it calls (as even Stalin had found out) for a careful rationing out of the fruits of toil so that those who labor for socialism may feel in their daily life that the effort has been worthwhile. Moral incentives are all very well, but they are not enough. That is something that many of China's aging leaders are apparently reluctant to admit. In one of their polemical statements the Soviets once lectured the Chinese on the economic essence of the construction of socialism. "The CPC [Communist Party of China] leaders hint that, since our party has made its aim a better life for the people, Soviet society is being "bourgeoisified," is "degenerating." According to their logic, if people wear bast sandals and eat thin soup from a common bowl— that is communism, and if a working man lives well and wants to live better still tomorrow—that is very nearly the restoration of capitalism."[37] At the time, this description of Chinese attitudes seemed tongue-in-cheek, but subsequent events have shown that *some* CPC leaders did, in fact, see economic advance in that light. Those leaders banded together in 1965-66 to form the Mao-Lin-Chen Po-ta faction, a shifting collection of men whose ideas had not evolved very markedly since the guerrilla days of Kiangsi and Yenan. It is they who refuse to come to terms with China's modest but tangible material achievements, fearing the very things for which they had once stood. They deny man's basic desire for a better life now, because they believe

[37] Open Letter of the Central Committee of the Communist Party of the Soviet Union to All Party Organizations, to All Communists of the Soviet Union (July 14, 1963), *Pravda* (July 14, 1963). The text will also be found in: *The Polemic on the General Line of the International Communist Movement* (Peking, Foreign Languages Press, 1965). The relevant quotation is on p. 560 of the latter source. Two important documents dealing with the Cultural Revolution are the "Decision of the Central Committee of the Chinese Communist Party Concerning the Great Proletarian Cultural Revolution" (Adopted on August 8, 1966), *Survey of China Mainland Press* (August 16, 1966), No. 3761, and the "Communiqué of the Eleventh Plenary Session of the Eighth Central Committee of the Communist Party of China," (Adopted on August 12, 1966), *Survey of China Mainland Press* (August 17, 1966), No. 3762. Both Documents are reprinted and analyzed in A Doak Barnett, *China After Mao* (Princeton, N.J., Princeton University Press, 1967).

that higher living standards breed revisionist ideas, and revisionist ideas lead straight back to capitalism. They are fearful of the Marxist vision's coming home to roost in their lifetime.

This guerrilla approach to economic development is sharply contested by other leaders, especially those in charge of the day-to-day conduct of the economy. They, too, admit that economic development is a combination of pioneering spirit and science, but tend to see the precise equilibrium differently from the Maoists. Too much pioneering is bad, they argue, if it interferes with growing rice.

The Cultural Revolution in its first year had apparently failed to disrupt the economic process as much as might have been expected from all the turmoil that went on. This was due in large measure to the fact that the young cultural rebels were kept to the streets and occupied in writing wall posters, and that on occasion they were chased out of farms and factories by workers who had better things to do than listen to teen-age sermons, or to put up with youthful arrogance. But strikes, delays, congestion on the railroads, armed clashes, and local uprisings (including army dissention in Sinkiang) have been reported. Early in 1967, Chinese exports to Hong Kong and Japan fell sharply, trade negotiations were postponed, foreign vessels were tied up in Shanghai, and urgent pleas were launched from Peking for everyone, especially the army, to get down to the business of spring cultivation. There is, in China, only a narrow margin between food supplies and population growth. The danger of famine has not been completely banished. There is, therefore, little time for revivalist distractions.

The opponents of Mao's "politics in command" could point to some quiet but impressive achievements in the period 1961-65. Steel production which, as we have seen, was about 5 million tons in 1960, had probably been doubled by 1965. According to Western estimates China's gross national product, which the Great Leapers had succeeded in pushing down from 108 billion yuan in 1958 to some 92 billion yuan in 1961, was back at the 1958 level in 1965, the year the Cultural Revolution was launched. These achievements, and many others, risked to be nullified if the cultural rebels got their way. By 1967 it was fairly clear that Maoism lacked a program, that it was poor in analytical content, in short, that it had little to offer to China's quest for modernization. Its days may well be numbered.

THE PROSPECTS

China's economic and political crusade is just beginning. Its course in future years cannot be predicted, if only because of the profound role which individual leaders play in the history of communist states. China's leadership centers around the idolized figure of Mao Tse-tung, a man in his seventies whose disappearance could prove to be a most significant event in the country's long socialist march. His Yenan philosophy,[38] as that of his immediate collaborators, may prove one day to be the major contradiction in a land educated on a daily fare of industrial gadgets. But the economic, scientific, and technical spadework done in years of hardship has more durability. Whatever the exact content of Communist China's future policies, it is a nation that has once and for all stood up and which others can underestimate only at grave peril to themselves.

FURTHER READING SUGGESTIONS

Barnett, A. Doak, *China After Mao*. Princeton: Princeton University Press, 1967.

————, *China on the Eve of Communist Takeover*. New York: Praeger, 1963.

Birch, Cyril, ed., *Chinese Communist Literature*. New York: Praeger, 1963.

Boyd, R. G., *Communist China's Foreign Policy*. New York: Praeger, 1962.

Chandra-Sekhar, Sripate, *Red China: An Asian View*. New York: Praeger, 1961.

Cheng, Chu-Yuan, *Communist China's Economy 1949-1962*. Orange, N.J.: Seton Hall University Press, 1963.

China as Photographed by Henri Cartier-Bresson. New York: Bantam, 1964.

Cowan, C. D., *The Economic Development of China and Japan: Studies in Economic History and Political Economy*. New York: Praeger, 1964.

Doolin, D. J., and R. C. North, *The Chinese People's Republic*. Stanford, Calif.: Hoover Institute, 1966.

Eckstein, Alexander, *Communist China's Economic Growth and Foreign Trade: Implications for U.S. Policy*. New York: McGraw-Hill, 1966.

Li, Choh-Ming, ed., *Industrial Development in Communist China*. New York: Praeger, 1964.

Mende, Tibor, *China and Her Shadow*. New York: Coward-McCann, 1962.

Myrdal, Jan, *Report from a Chinese Village*. New York: Pantheon, 1965.

[38] The "Yenan philosophy" is an ascetic view of life reflecting the guerrilla circumstances in which it evolved. It emphasizes plain living, self-denial, hard work, an almost military discipline, and strict adherence to the political teachings of Mao Tse-tung. It is suspicious of the expert who puts expertise before ideology, and professionalism before politics. *See* Benjamin Schwartz, "Modernization and the Maoist Vision," *The China Quarterly*, London (January-March, 1965), pp. 3-19. For a clear statement of the self-reliance component of this philosophy *see* Lu Hsun, "On China's Guideline of Self-Reliance in Socialist Construction," *Ching-chi Yen-chiu* [Economic Research] Peking (July 20, 1965), in: *Survey of China Mainland Magazines*, U.S. Consulate General, Hong Kong, No. 488 (1965), p. 12.

Schram, Stuart R., *The Political Thought of Mao Tse-tung*. New York: Praeger, 1963.

Shabad, Theodore, *China's Changing Map: A Political and Economic Geography of the Chinese People's Republic*. New York: Praeger, 1956.

Wu, Yuan-li, *The Economy of Communist China: An Introduction*. New York: Praeger, 1965.

Yu, Frederick T. C., *Mass Persuasion in Communist China*. New York: Praeger, 1964.

6

The New China:

A Chinese Marxist View

SOONG CHING LING
(MME. SUN YAT-SEN)

VICE CHAIRMAN
OF THE PEOPLE'S REPUBLIC OF CHINA

LIEN KUAN

DEPUTY SECRETARY GENERAL, STANDING COMMITTEE
NATIONAL PEOPLE'S CONGRESS

LIN HAI-YUN

VICE MINISTER OF FOREIGN TRADE

AND OTHERS *

I. SIXTEEN YEARS OF LIBERATION [1]

Sixteen years have passed since Chairman Mao Tse-tung announced to the world that the Chinese people had broken their chains, stood up and taken their destiny into their own hands. The significance of that event has grown with the years.

The old China has become the new China. Gone is the poor and backward country, racked with disease, famine, and flood. In its place is a China vibrantly alive as it bests nature and takes firm strides toward prosperity. Our people are scaling the heights of education, science, and culture. Epidemics have been wiped out, and health work has made tremendous advances. Famine can no longer stalk our land, for ours is a collective society and we are organized against it.

* Since the various parts of the Chinese Marxist section of this chapter have been taken from different sources, footnote credit throughout this section will be given in each case, so that each passage can be readily identified as to original source of publication and, where available, as to author.

[1] Excerpts from Soong Ching Ling (Mme. Sun Yat-sen, Vice Chairman of the People's Republic of China), "Sixteen Years of Liberation," *China Reconstructs* (January, 1966).

Gone is the chaotic semblance of a state, riddled with corruption, the slave of imperialism, and the oppressor of the people. It has been overthrown by the armed struggle of the masses led by the great Chinese Communist Party and Chairman Mao Tse-tung, and we have erected in its place the People's Republic of China. This is a proletarian dictatorship which has united our country as never before and brought together our nationalities in fraternal solidarity. All those entrusted with the affairs of state are democratically elected and directly accountable to their constituents. China is no longer a slave to anyone, but rises among the nations fully independent.

No longer can anyone use the insulting phrase "sick man of Asia" in reference to our country. China is brimming with health and vigour, a great power, yet one that is resolute in defending principle and punctilious in respecting other countries, big or small, a never-wavering champion of the right of all nations to their sovereignty, sparing no effort in support of all peoples in their struggles for social and economic progress.

Sixteen years is not a long period of time. Yet during it, China has climbed out of the depths to high pinnacles. . . .

II. SOCIALIST SOCIETY AND THE DICTATORSHIP OF THE PROLETARIAT [2]

The theories of the proletarian revolution and the dictatorship of the proletariat are the quintessence of Marxism-Leninism. The questions of whether revolution should be upheld or opposed and whether the dictatorship of the proletariat should be upheld or opposed have always been the focus of struggle between Marxism-Leninism and all brands of revisionism and are now the focus of struggle between Marxist-Leninists the world over and the revisionist Khrushchov clique.

At the 22nd Congress of the C.P.S.U. (Oct., 1961) the revisionist Khrushchov clique developed their revisionism into a complete system not only by rounding off their antirevolutionary theories of "peaceful coexistence," "peaceful competition" and "peaceful transition" but also by declaring that the dictatorship of the proletariat is no longer necessary in the Soviet Union and advancing the absurd theories of the "state of the whole people" and the "party of the entire people."

The Programme put forward by the revisionist Khrushchov clique at the 22nd Congress of the C.P.S.U. is a programme of phoney communism, a revisionist programme against proletarian revolution and for the abolition of the dictatorship of the proletariat and the proletarian party. . . .

[2] Condensed from "On Khrushchov's Phoney Communism and Its Historical Lessons for the World," by the Editorial Departments of "Renmin Ribao" and "Hongqi," *Peking Review* (July 17, 1964).

What is the correct conception of socialist society? Do classes and class struggle exist throughout the stage of socialism? Should the dictatorship of the proletariat be maintained and the socialist revolution be carried through to the end? Or should the dictatorship of the proletariat be abolished so as to pave the way for capitalist restoration? These questions must be answered correctly according to the basic theory of Marxism-Leninism and the historical experience of the dictatorship of the proletariat.

The replacement of capitalist society by socialist society is a great leap in the historical development of human society. Socialist society covers the important historical period of transition from class to classless society. It is by going through socialist society that mankind will enter communist society.

The socialist system is incomparably superior to the capitalist system. In socialist society, the dictatorship of the proletariat replaces bourgeois dictatorship and the public ownership of the means of production replaces private ownership. The proletariat, from being an oppressed and exploited class, turns into the ruling class and a fundamental change takes place in the social position of the working people. Exercising dictatorship over a few exploiters only, the state of the dictatorship of the proletariat practises the broadest democracy among the masses of the working people, a democracy which is impossible in capitalist society. The nationalization of industry and collectivization of agriculture open wide vistas for the vigorous development of the social productive forces, ensuring a rate of growth incomparably greater than that in any older society.

However, one cannot but see that socialist society is a society born out of capitalist society and is only the first phase of communist society. It is not yet a fully mature communist society in the economic and other fields. It is inevitably stamped with the birth marks of capitalist society.

In socialist society, the differences between workers and peasants, between town and country, and between manual and mental labourers still remain, bourgeois rights are not yet completely abolished, it is not possible "at once to eliminate the other injustice, which consists in the distribution of articles of consumption 'according to the amount of labour performed' (and not according to needs),"[3] and therefore differences in wealth still exist. The disappearance of these differences, phenomena, and bourgeois rights can only be gradual and long drawn-out.

Marxism-Leninism and the practice of the Soviet Union, China and other socialist countries all teach us that socialist society covers a very, very long historical stage. Throughout this stage, the class struggle between the bourgeoisie and the proletariat goes on and the question of "who will win" between the roads of capitalism and socialism remains, as does the danger of the restoration of capitalism. . . .

As long as imperialism exists, the proletariat in the socialist countries

[3] Lenin, "The State and Revolution," *Selected Works* (Moscow, Foreign Languages Publishing House, 1952), Vol. 2, Part 1, p. 296.

will have to struggle both against the bourgeoisie at home and against international imperialism. Imperialism will seize every opportunity and try to undertake armed intervention against the socialist countries or to bring about their peaceful disintegration. It will do its utmost to destroy the socialist countries or to make them degenerate into capitalist countries. The international class struggle will inevitably find its reflection within the socialist countries. Lenin said:

The transition from capitalism to Communism represents an entire historical epoch. Until this epoch has terminated, the exploiters inevitably cherish the hope of restoration, and this *hope* is converted into attempts at restoration. . . .[4]

Comrade Mao Tse-tung, examining the objective laws of socialist society from the viewpoint of materialist dialectics, points out that to ensure the success of socialist construction and to prevent the restoration of capitalism, it is necessary to carry the socialist revolution through to the end on the political, economic, ideological and cultural fronts. The complete victory of socialism cannot be brought about in one or two generations; to resolve this question thoroughly requires five or ten generations or even longer. . . .

Judging from the actual situation today, the tasks of the dictatorship of the proletariat are still far from accomplished in any of the socialist countries. Therefore, it is necessary for all the socialist countries to uphold the dictatorship of the proletariat. In these circumstances, the abolition of the dictatorship of the proletariat by the revisionist Khrushchov clique is nothing but the betrayal of socialism and communism. . . .

III. CHINA'S POLITICAL SYSTEM [5]

China is a people's democratic dictatorship led by the working class and based on the alliance of workers and peasants. The masters of the state are the people, to whom all power belongs. The organs through which the people exercise their power are the National People's Congress and the congresses at provincial, county and *hsiang* (or township) [6] levels. All are elected on the basis of universal suffrage. Deputies to the people's congresses at the basic level are elected by direct vote. Those to all higher congresses are successively elected by the deputies at lower levels.

[4] Lenin, "The Proletarian Revolution and the Renegade Kautsky," *Selected Works* (Moscow, Foreign Languages Publishing House, 1952), Vol. 2, Part 2, p. 81.

[5] The first two paragraphs of this part have been excerpted from Lien Kuan (Deputy Secretary General of the Standing Committee of the National People's Congress), "Further Consolidation of the People's Democratic Dictatorship," *China Reconstructs* (March, 1965); the rest of this part has been condensed from Wang Min, "New China's Electoral System," *Peking Review* (January 8, 1965).

[6] The *hsiang*, composed of several villages, is an administrative unit below the county level.

The nature of the people's democratic dictatorship is shown in the Electoral Law.[7] The right to vote and to stand for election is guaranteed to all workers, peasants and other sections of the masses, providing the widest democracy. The Constitution specifies that all Chinese citizens who have reached the age of eighteen have the right to vote and stand for election no matter what their nationality, race, sex, occupation, social origin, religious belief, education, property status or length of residence. But dictatorship is exercised over reactionary classes and elements. According to the Electoral Law, therefore, no person of landlord class whose status has not yet been changed by law, no counter-revolutionaries or others who have been deprived of political rights according to law, have the right to vote or be elected. This is absolutely necessary for the full protection of the democratic rights of the people. . . .

The Electoral Law also prescribes that the number of deputies to the people's congresses at all levels and their election are based on a fixed proportion of the population with due allowances for various regions and units. The ratio of deputies to population differs between the cities and the countryside. For instance, the number of people represented by each Deputy in the Third National People's Congress varies as follows: one Deputy for every 400,000 persons in the provinces and autonomous regions; and one Deputy for every 50,000 persons in the cities directly under the central authority, in industrial cities with more than 300,000 population, and in industrial cities, industrial and mining districts and forestry districts with less than 300,000 population but with more than 200,000 industrial workers and their family.

China is a country with a vast rural population. Its cities are the political, economic and cultural centres where the working class live and industrial enterprises are found. The provision that the number of person represented by each Deputy varies between city and rural area reflects the leading role played by the working class in the state. . . . But those provinces and autonomous regions which have extremely small populations are each allowed to elect no less than ten Deputies to the National People's Congress, so that they can have an adequate number of Deputies in the Congress. . . .

As stipulated by the Electoral Law, candidates for election as deputies to the people's congresses at all levels are nominated by electoral districts or electoral units. The Chinese Communist Party, the democratic parties, the people's organizations and voters, or representatives who do not belong to any of these parties or organizations, may all put forward, jointly or separately, their lists of candidates for electoral districts or units. For instance, before the draft lists of candidates are made public in the elections at the basic level, there have been repeated exchanges of views and full discus-

---

[7] The Electoral Law of the People's Republic of China was promulgated in 1953. [EDITOR'S NOTE]

sion among all parties, organizations and representative persons concerned. These lists are then fully discussed by the voters. The formal lists of candidates for Deputies are decided in accordance with the opinions expressed by the majority of voters. Then comes the election. The voter may vote in accordance with the list of candidates, or vote for any other person or persons he prefers. This not only ensures the integration of leadership and the masses and brings together the opinion of the masses, but makes it possible for the voters to elect, fully in accordance with their own will, the persons they consider suitable. . . .

The electoral units and constituents, in accordance with legal procedure, may at any time recall their elected Deputies. Hence, no People's Deputy can go against the people's will. . . .

To ensure voters the free exercise of their inviolable electoral rights, the Electoral Law provides for all election expenses to be paid from the national treasury. This is an important measure to give both the voters and candidates a material safeguard, so that they may in practice enjoy their right of free elections. The state makes all the newspapers, broadcasting stations and places for holding meetings available to the voters, so that they can make use of these facilities to conduct electoral propaganda and activities. . . .

The democratic and socialist electoral system in China is a fruit of the victory that the people of all nationalities, under the leadership of the Chinese Communist Party and Comrade Mao Tse-tung, gained after arduous and protracted revolutionary struggle. . . .

IV. AGRICULTURE [8]

IMPORTANT TASK

China's peasants have long dreamt of solving the problems of food and clothing by ensuring stable, high yields. But the old society with its feudal system of landlord exploitation stifled the peasants' enthusiasm for production and obstructed the growth of the productive forces. Undernourished and inadequately clad, the peasants with their small individual plots were powerless against natural calamities. Under such conditions, it was impossible to realize their aspirations.

After liberation, nationwide land reform was carried out and the peasants became masters of the land they tilled. They grew rapidly in political understanding and their initiative and enthusiasm in production soared. In 1953, Chinese agriculture took the path of collective farming. Five years

[8] This part has been condensed from two articles, i.e., from Chen Hsueh-nung "To Get Stable, High Yields," *Peking Review* (June 4, 1965), and from Hu Chi, "How Industry Helps Agriculture," *Peking Review* (December 11, 1964).

later, with the birth of the rural people's communes, the peasants' collectives became larger and of a more developed socialist character. With more manpower, greater financial and material resources and stronger leadership than the co-op farms, it became possible to plan production and construction on a large scale. This opened the way for faster and greater developments in agricultural production. . . .

Chinese agriculture is entering a new stage of development. The farmers of China have been inspired by successive years of increased yields, and enlightened and encouraged by the growing number of farms that have achieved stable, high yields. Nevertheless, harvests in the main still depend too much on the current weather and the level of farm production as a whole is still relatively low. . . .

EFFECTIVE WAY TO EXPAND FARM OUTPUT

There are only two ways to expand agricultural production—either by bringing more land under crops or by raising yields.

Of China's surface area, only 11 percent is now cultivated. Large areas of the remainder can be turned into cropland, and since liberation the government and people have put considerable effort into reclaiming it. Tens of millions of *mu* of new land have been brought under the plough and in coming years more wasteland will be opened up in a planned way. But for some time to come, the stress in China's agricultural development will not be on reclaiming wasteland but mainly on creating stable, high-yield farms and by raising yields.

This method gives more immediate and bigger benefits and needs less capital outlay. . . .

MODERNIZING AGRICULTURE

One of the goals of the Chinese people in building socialism is the modernizing of agriculture. . . .

Farm modernization means mechanization, electrification, extensive irrigation and widespread use of chemical fertilizers and other farm chemicals. But the transition from traditional hand tools to full-scale mechanization of the nation's farms will be a long process. It must be done step by step, passing through the intermediate stage of semimechanization.

MORE CAPITAL GOODS SUPPLIED

In recent years, and especially since 1962 when the general policy for developing the national economy was formally announced, industry has provided agriculture with increasing amounts of capital goods. As a result, aggregate capacity of mechanized rural pumping stations in 1963 was 30 times the 1957 figure; the number of tractors grew by 360 percent; rural electric power consumption increased by 1,600 percent; the supply of chemical fertilizer, 160 percent. . . .

Such effective industrial aid has greatly changed farming conditions. Today (December, 1964), 90 percent of China's 2,000 counties have power-driven irrigation equipment watering an area six times the 1957 figure. More than 70 percent of the counties are served by 1,500 farm machinery stations run either by the state or the people's communes which have more than 100,000 tractors (in terms of 15 h.p. units); this is more than five times the 1957 figure. In recent years the farm machine-building industry has developed more than 100 successful types of semi-mechanized farm implements. More than 30 million such implements are being used in ploughing, irrigation, plant protection, harvesting, threshing, transport, livestock breeding, and processing farm products. There has been a steady increase in the quantity of chemical fertilizer and insecticides used on the nation's farms. The amount of power consumed in the rural areas relative to the national total has also grown. . . .

A nationwide repair network is being set up to support the increasingly widespread use of farm machines. In addition, skilled workers and technicians go to the countryside to coach or run classes to train farm machine operators and maintenance men. Industrial departments also arrange demonstrations of their machines, fertilizers, and insecticides for the peasants and help them master the skills needed for efficient use.

PAST ACCOMPLISHMENTS AND PROSPECTS FOR THE FUTURE

Backed by the collective economy of their people's communes and increasing aid from industry, China's peasants are today in a better position than ever before to cope with natural calamities. At the same time, as a result of recent efforts, an increasingly large area of farmland is able to give high and stable yields.

China's experience shows that by aiding agriculture, industry not only accelerates agricultural growth but also speeds up its own development and that of the national economy as a whole. We have every reason to be confident that, guided by the general line for building socialism, by implementing the general policy of developing the national economy with agriculture as the foundation and industry as the leading factor and integrating the modernization of industry with that of agriculture, we shall succeed in raising the overall level of China's national economy and building up an independent, comprehensive and modern national economic system at a relatively rapid pace.

V. INDUSTRY AND LABOR [9]

TREMENDOUS GROWTH

Old China's basic industries were extremely backward due to the reactionary rule of imperialism, feudalism, and bureaucrat-capitalism. There were no more than a few mining and metallurgical enterprises, and what engineering works existed could only handle repairs and assemble imported parts. Most of them were controlled by the imperialists and comprador-capitalists.

New China launched its First Five-Year Plan in 1953 after three years of rehabilitation. In that five-year period, China built and renovated a number of enterprises which formed the backbone of the basic industries.

During the first three years of the Second Five-Year Plan, i.e., 1958-60, under the guidance of the general line for building socialism, the basic industries forged ahead rapidly both in scale of production and in technical levels. From 1961 onward they were developed in accordance with the policy of readjustment, consolidation, filling out, and raising standards.[10] As a result of all these efforts, China today has a fairly comprehensive and powerful system of modern basic industries.

OWNERSHIP BY THE WHOLE PEOPLE MUST BE PRESERVED

China's state-owned industrial enterprises are socialist in nature, being economic organizations owned by the whole people and forming an organic part of the national economy. Whether they are enterprises under the management of the central authorities or are run by local authorities, they all belong to the socialist state and are productive units in the economic sector owned by the whole people, i.e., the state sector. At the same time, these enterprises operate independently and keep their own independent business accounts.

What then are the chief manifestations of ownership by the whole people in a socialist, state-owned industrial enterprise?

Firstly, its means of production—machinery, equipment, buildings, raw and other materials, land and mines, etc.—are all owned by the state. . . .

---

[9] This part has been condensed from four articles, i.e., Chien Kuang-chun, "A System of Modern Basic Industries Develops," *Peking Review* (January 29, 1965); Ma Wen-kuei, "China's State-Owned Industrial Enterprises—Their Nature and Tasks," *Peking Review* (June 26, 1964); Ma Wen-kuei, "Industrial Management in China," *Peking Review* (February 26, 1965); and "China's Trade Unions" (no author given), *Peking Review* (April 30, 1965).

[10] This refers to the downward readjustments after the period of the "Great Leap Forward." [EDITOR'S NOTE]

Secondly, it carries on production under the unified leadership of the state and according to its unified plan. . . .

Thirdly, its products belong to the state. It must market its products strictly in accordance with the allocation plans and prices fixed by the state; and it must not dispose of the products it manufactures without authorization.

Fourthly, it must pay taxes to the state according to regulations; besides laying aside according to state regulations a small portion as a bonus, it must hand in the larger part of its profits to the state as part of state revenues to meet overall state expenditures.

Fifthly, the wage scale and grading system for its workers and staff members are fixed by the state on the basis of the socialist principle of "from each according to his ability and to each according to his work." . . .

In any department, locality or enterprise, production must be organized strictly in accordance with the state's unified policy, plan, regulations, and systems of work. Otherwise, ownership by the whole people will be weakened or impaired, and there may arise the danger of its being changed into ownership by a department, by a locality or a single unit; there would thus be the danger of a socialist economy degenerating into a capitalist economy. Lenin rightly said: "Any move, direct or indirect, to legalize the ownership of their respective production by workers in a particular factory or of a particular trade, or to legalize their right to weaken or obstruct the carrying out of the order of the state power is the greatest distortion of the fundamental principle of Soviet power and a complete abandonment of socialism." [11] . . .

RELATIVE INDEPENDENCE OF STATE-OWNED ENTERPRISES

But does this mean that such an enterprise does not have a certain degree of independence? Of course not. As we said before, in China a state-owned industrial enterprise is a unit in the economic sector owned by the whole people which operates independently and keeps its own business accounts. It, therefore, maintains a certain degree of independence under the centralized leadership and unified planning of the state. This independence is manifested mainly in the following ways:

Firstly, such an enterprise has the right to use the fixed and circulating capital put at its disposal by the state; it engages in production according to the state plan and keeps its independent business accounts.

Secondly, it has the power to sign economic contracts with other enterprises and the obligation to fulfill them strictly.

Thirdly, it has the right to arrange credits and loans with the state bank and open its own account in a bank for financial transactions.

[11] Lenin, "On the Democratic System and the Socialist Nature of Soviet Power" [1918], published in *Pravda* (April 22, 1957).

Fourthly, once the enterprise's plan is finally approved, and it finds it has surplus capacity it may, subject to the approval of the higher administrative body in charge, accept local orders or orders from other establishments within that capacity. . . .

Fifthly, it may, in accordance with state regulations, exchange what excess raw and other materials and fuel it has saved up with other establishments and enterprises in order to increase the production of the goods. It must not, however, exchange such materials for consumer goods.

Sixthly, it has the right to make use of the bonus given it by the state to improve the working and living conditions of its workers and staff members.

It must be pointed out that the independent running of an enterprise is conditioned at all times by the fact that it must subject itself to the centralized leadership of the state and the state's unified plan. . . .

As experience in our country shows, in order to handle correctly the relations between the state and such an enterprise, the former must prescribe for the latter what to produce and determine the scale of production, set the amount of its fixed and circulating capital, decide the size of its labour force and its organizational form, fix consumption norms for the principal raw and other materials, fuel, power, and tools, find sources of supply for it, and define its relations of coordination with other enterprises so that the given enterprise does not have to worry about all these things and can devote itself to production.

At the same time, the responsibilities of an enterprise to the state must be well defined. As required by the state, it must undertake to fulfil the state plan specifying the variety, quality and quantity of its output; not to overspend the total wages fund set by the state; to produce at planned cost and do its best to lower costs; to hand over profits to the state according to plan; and see to it that its principal equipment lasts out the prescribed time. When an enterprise has fulfilled its responsibilities to the state, it is entitled to deduct as its bonus fund a prescribed portion of the profits due to be handed over to the state. The amount so deducted depends on how well it fulfils its tasks. If an enterprise fails to fulfil its tasks and its responsibilities to the state, it will get no bonus.

Under the socialist system, the production plan which the state lays down for every enterprise reflects the social demand for goods which production in that enterprise is to meet. Thus, so far as an individual enterprise is concerned, whether or not it has fulfilled its task can best be judged by whether or not it has fulfilled the plan laid down by the state.

The fundamental task of a socialist industrial enterprise, however, is not merely to fulfill satisfactorily the production plan laid down by the state; it must also satisfactorily fulfil the quota of profit set by the state. A socialist enterprise does not rule out profit-making. On the contrary, under centralized leadership and unified state planning, it must, by working hard and practising economy, give earnest attention to profit-making, and strive to fulfill and overfulfill the task of making profits for the state as it is entrusted to do by the state so as to help expand socialist accumulation.

Profits from enterprises are an important source for the accumulation of funds for socialist construction. The success or failure of an enterprise to make a profit and fulfill the quota of profit set by the state directly affects the state's financial revenue and has a bearing on the scale and tempo of expanded socialist reproduction. At the same time, profits from enterprises are also a source from which the various common needs of society are supplied. For instance, the need to pay wages to workers and staff members in non-productive service departments, payments for the state's administrative and national defence expenditure, appropriations for necessary reserves and various public welfare funds—all these are necessary expenses if socialist construction and social life are to be carried on normally. As far as an enterprise is concerned, profit is also an important indication of labour productivity and managerial ability. . . .

Of course, production in a socialist industrial enterprise must not be regulated spontaneously by profit. To regard profit-making as the sole task of an enterprise, to encourage and leave it free to seek profit by all means possible and without adhering to the state plan and considering social needs —these are incompatible with the nature of a socialist industrial enterprise.

INDUSTRIAL MANAGEMENT

Democratic centralism is fundamental in the administration both of our state and of our socialist state-owned industrial enterprises. . . .

In leading socialist construction in China, our Party has developed a whole system of management which integrates a high degree of centralization with a high degree of democracy. Practice has proved that its correct implementation helps bring about in our industrial enterprises a vigorous and lively political atmosphere in which there is both centralism and democracy, discipline and freedom, unity of will and personal ease of mind. . . .

The following are among the major features of this system of management: the director assumes full responsibility under the collective leadership of the Communist Party committee; a conference of staff and workers' representatives; cadres participate in labour and workers participate in management; and close cooperation among leading cadres, technical personnel, and workers.

1. The director assuming full responsibility under the collective leadership of the Party committee is a fundamental feature of the system of management in our state-owned industrial enterprises. The essence of this is the proper integration of collective leadership and personal responsibility with the leadership of the Party as the core. . . .

2. In state-owned industrial enterprises, the staff and workers' representatives conference is an important form through which the staff and workers all participate in management. The conference may hear and discuss the director's report on the work of the enterprise, examine and discuss production, financial, technological and wage plans as well as major measures to realize them, check regularly on the implementation of these plans and put forward proposals. It may examine and discuss the use of the enterprise's bonus, welfare, medical, labour protection and trade union funds as well as other funds allotted for the livelihood and welfare of the staff and workers. On condition that the directives and orders issued by higher authorities are not violated, the conference may adopt resolutions on the expenditure of the above funds and change the administrative or other departments concerned to carry them out. It may criticize any of the leaders of the enterprise and, when necessary, make proposals to the higher administrative authorities for punishing or dismissing those leaders who seriously neglect their duties and behave badly. Should there be disagreement with the decisions of the higher administrative authorities, the conference may put forward its own proposals, but if the higher authorities insist on the original decisions after due study, it must carry them through accordingly. . . .

3. Another important means of correctly implementing the mass line in the management of industrial enterprises is that of cadres participating in physical labour and workers participating in management. . . .

As regards the significance of cadres' participation in labour, the Central Committee of the Chinese Communist Party has pointed out: "When leading cadres take part in productive labour and become one with the masses, this helps in the timely discovery and practical solution of problems, helps improve the style of leadership and consequently makes it easier to avoid and overcome many errors of bureaucracy, sectarianism and subjectivism, and helps to change the attitude of despising physical labour which exists in society. . . . The Central Committee holds that provided they are fit for physical work, not only cadres working at county, district and *hsiang* levels, but also the main leading personnel of Party committees at various levels above the county and the leading Party cadres who are working in government organs and people's organizations, including the members of the Party's Central Committee, must devote some time every year to doing some physical labour."[12] . . .

The participation of workers in management embodies the Party's principles of running enterprises well by relying on the working class. This takes various forms. In addition to the above-mentioned staff and workers' representatives conference, workers take part in the management of the routine work of the production groups. . . . In this way, the workers'

[12] Directive of the Central Committee of the Chinese Communist Party Concerning Participation in Physical Labour by Leading Functionaries at All Levels (May 10, 1957).

role as masters in their own house can be brought into fuller play. . . .

4. The close cooperation among leading cadres, technical personnel and workers of industrial enterprises to study and solve problems of production technique and management is a practical application of the Party's mass line in the period of socialist construction. This method not only stimulates the initiative of the broad masses but also brings into play the initiative of the technical staff—those who are technically better qualified as well as those who are not so highly qualified. . . .

CHINA'S TRADE UNIONS: NATURE AND TASKS UNDER SOCIALISM

China's trade unions are mass organizations of the working class led by the Communist Party. They are the Party's assistant in mass work and a link through which the Party keeps in touch with the masses, a social pillar of the people's democratic state power, and a school of communism for the workers. . . .

Political and ideological work. Trade union work in China is work dealing with man. Priority is given to political and ideological work. Workers and their families are educated in socialism and especially in the class struggle. The purpose is to acquaint them with the situation in the class struggle, both at home and abroad, and the Party's principles and policies continuously raise their level of class consciousness and in this way bring their initiative and creativeness into play to fulfill the tasks in production and construction assigned to them by the state. . . .

Work to help boost production. All trade union work is designed to help enhance the workers' political consciousness and boost production. The trade unions undertake to organize enterprises and workers to take part in the movement to "compare, learn, catch up and help" so as to enable more enterprises and workers to achieve the goal of "five goods." For enterprises, this means good political work, fulfilment of production plans, efficient management, good living arrangements for workers, and a good working style of cadres. For individual workers it means a high level of political consciousness, competent fulfilment of tasks, strict observance of labour discipline, persistence in studies, and unity and mutual help with others. . . .

Welfare work. The trade unions work constantly to improve the material and cultural lives of the workers and to educate them correctly to link their immediate interests with the long-term interests of the working class, and to combine their personal interests properly with those of the collective.

The administration of the labour insurance fund is entrusted to the trade unions by the state. China's workers today enjoy the benefits of a very comprehensive system of labour insurance with all the expenses borne by the managements. The system gives wide assistance in relation to childbirth, old age, sickness, injury, disablement and death. Workers who may have financial difficulties are helped out with grants from trade union funds.

There are more than 2,800 sanatoria, rest homes and overnight sanatoria with a total of 90,000 beds run by the trade unions, factories, mines and other enterprises.

The trade unions assist the managements in running collective welfare establishments such as workers' housing estates, canteens, medical and health centres, public baths, nurseries and kindergartens. This is done by organizing the workers to take part in the democratic management of these undertakings.

Educational work. In cooperation with the managements and other departments concerned, the trade unions organize workers' spare-time education to extend general knowledge and raise technical levels. In many large and medium-sized enterprises, a comprehensive spare-time educational system has been established, ranging from literacy classes to spare-time study at the university level.

The trade unions help to organize workers' recreational activities as a means to educate them in socialism and enrich their cultural life.

International activities. True to the spirit of proletarian internationalism, China's trade unions actively support the revolutionary struggles of workers in other countries and strive to strengthen workers' unity throughout the world. Together with workers the world over and progressive mankind, China's trade unions wage struggles against imperialism headed by the United States, and for world peace, national liberation, people's democracy and socialism.

STRUCTURE AND ORGANIZATIONAL PRINCIPLES
OF CHINA'S TRADE UNIONS

China's trade unions are organized on both an industrial and regional basis. This means that all members of the same enterprise, government office, or educational institution, irrespective of their specific jobs, are organized in the same primary trade union. These primary organizations at places of work are the foundation of China's trade unions. Today, there are 160,000 of them. . . .

Industrial unions are organized on national and provincial levels. There are today 16 national trade union committees. . . .

There are also provincial, autonomous regional, municipal and county trade union councils not organized on an industrial, but on a regional basis. These give unified leadership to all trade union organizations in their respective areas, including the local industrial unions at the same level. . . .

Both local trade union councils and national industrial unions are led by the A.C.F.T.U.[13] which is the national leading body of China's trade union movement. Trade union organizations at all levels are led by the Communist Party committee at the same level. . . .

The basic organizational principle of China's trade unions is democratic centralism—centralism based on democracy and democracy under centralized guidance. Its main content is:

1. The leading bodies of the trade unions at all levels are democratically elected.

2. The leading bodies of the trade unions at all levels observe the principle of integrating collective leadership with personal responsibility. All matters of importance are discussed and decided upon collectively.

3. The trade unions at all levels carry on their work in accordance with the Constitution of the Trade Unions and decisions of trade union organizations. They submit reports on their work at regular intervals to the membership and give heed to criticisms and opinions voiced by members or lower organizations.

4. Every member must carry out trade union decisions. The minority abides by the decisions of the majority, and the lower trade union organizations abide by the decisions of the higher bodies. . . .

VI. NEW CHINA'S PRICE POLICY [14]

The old China went to its end in a state of economic chaos. It left a legacy of currency inflation and sky-rocketing prices. One of the most pressing economic problems in the early days of the People's Republic was to end that chaos and pave the way for sound economic development.

The runaway inflation grew steadily more serious in the last dozen years of reactionary Kuomintang rule. At first prices rose several hundred percent a year; then they soared several hundred percent each month; and finally they were shooting up, doubling, trebling and more nearly every week. Prices sky-rocketed 8,500,000 million-fold in the 12 years from 1937 to May 1949, when the Kuomintang government finally collapsed. . . .

This was one of the main economic difficulties confronting New China at its birth. The imperialists and reactionaries at home and abroad were confident that this seemingly insurmountable difficulty would bring the young People's Republic to its knees. They prophesied that although China had won the War of Liberation, it would fail to overcome the financial and economic difficulties. To make the situation worse, the U.S. imperialists and their vassals imposed a "blockade" and "embargo" on New China. But

[13] All-China Federation of Trade Unions. [EDITOR'S NOTE]
[14] Condensed from Yang Po, "New China's Price Policy," *Peking Review* (November 20, 1964).

events took an entirely contrary course to what they expected. Their hopes were utterly dashed. Under the wise leadership of the Chinese Communist Party and Comrade Mao Tse-tung, the People's Republic halted the currency inflation and stopped the rise in prices by March, 1950, within six months. Since then prices have been kept stable and irrational price relations left over from history have been readjusted step by step in a planned way.

HOW PRICE WAS HALTED

How was New China able to stop the chaos of soaring prices so swiftly? The following were the chief measures taken:

1. Confiscation of bureaucrat capital and transformation of the enterprises it owned into socialist state concerns. Direct state control of the production and distribution of important means of production.

2. Establishment and development of state commerce to control commodities of major importance to the people's livelihood, to regulate market supply and demand, and ensure the supply of necessities.

3. Establishment and development of the state bank to control the financial market and regulate the volume of currency in circulation.

4. Checking up on and increasing financial revenue and economizing on expenditures to maintain a balanced state budget.

5. Strict administration of the market; control of private banks and money houses, prohibition of buying and selling of gold, silver and foreign currency, and measures to combat commercial speculation.

6. Centralization of control over the nation's finances and economy to end the decentralized control which prevailed in the past. . . .

As the six measures mentioned above were adopted promptly and began to take effect state revenue and expenditures were balanced, speculative capital was defeated and prices were swiftly stabilized. If the national wholesale price index in March, 1950, is taken as 100, then it dropped to 85.4 by December of the same year. . . .

READJUSTING IRRATIONAL PRICE RELATIONS

It should be noted that prices were stabilized in 1950 on the basis of price relations formed in the old China and in consequence there were many irrationalities. The main irrationality was that prices of agricultural products were unduly low, and prices of heavy industrial products unduly high. It was, therefore, necessary to tackle these irrationalities in price relations after the price level had been stabilized. . . .

After prices were stabilized throughout the country the People's Government readjusted the irrational price relations stage by stage and in groups in a planned way. In the 12 years between 1951 and 1963 prices paid by the state for agricultural products were raised an average of 57.4 percent and for grain by 61.4 percent whereas, over the same period, retail prices of industrial goods sold by the state in the rural areas went up on an average by only 13.7 percent. During that period, apart from a few agricultural products which sold at slightly higher prices, retail prices of the great majority of commodities in the cities, including grain, cotton piece-goods, coal and vegetables, remained stable in the main. Between March, 1950 and 1963, retail prices in Peking, Shanghai, Tientsin, Shenyang, Wuhan, Canton, Chungking, and Sian rose an average of only 11 percent while wages of workers and staff rose by a much bigger margin. Under these conditions the livelihood of the mass of workers and staff improved. Since 1952, with the establishment and rapid growth of our own heavy industry, prices of most heavy industrial products have tended to decline gradually.

FORMULATING A CORRECT PRICE POLICY

In a capitalist country, the law of value regulates prices spontaneously according to the values of commodities and supply and demand; through price fluctuations, it regulates spontaneously the production, circulation, and consumption of commodities. . . .

In a socialist country, production, circulation and consumption of commodities are arranged through the state plan in accordance with the needs of the state and the people and the proportions that objectively exist in the national economic development. Commodity prices are fixed by the state. . . .

How then do we fix prices and formulate a correct price policy in accordance with the requirements of the law of planned and proportionate development [15] of the national economy and the law of value?

1. *When fixing the price of a commodity, we see to it that it corresponds roughly to the value of that commodity, that is, the amount of socially necessary labour embodied in that commodity.* . . .

2. *We take account of supply and demand.* In drawing up the economic plan and fixing prices for various commodities, the state carefully considers the supply and demand situation on a nationwide scale and over a fairly long period of time. . . . A socialist country must fix the price of a commodity on the basis of its value. But when necessary, the state may raise or lower the purchasing price of a certain product to an appropriate extent to influence the amount produced and procured; it may also raise or lower the price of a certain consumer item to an appropriate extent to influence the amount sold. . . .

3. *We take account of the livelihood of workers, staff and peasants as well as the accumulation of capital for the state.* Prices in a socialist country

---

[15] The "law of planned and proportionate development" refers to the necessity of developing all sectors of the economy simultaneously in such a manner that no sector be held back by bottlenecks caused by inadequate supplies emanating from another sector. [EDITOR'S NOTE]

are an important level for distributing and redistributing national income. Commodity prices should be fixed in such a way as to help stabilize and improve the livelihood of workers, staff, and the peasants and at the same time ensure appropriate accumulations for the state. . . . A socialist state may improve the life of workers and staff either by raising wages or by reducing prices. In China the method generally adopted is to raise wages gradually as production and labour productivity increase while keeping prices stable. . . .

By fixing prices of industrial and agricultural products roughly in accordance with their values and gradually closing the price "scissors" between industrial and farm products, which was left over from history, so that farm products are exchanged for industrial products according to the principle of equivalent exchange, most satisfactory results have been achieved in encouraging the peasants' enthusiasm for collective production, in developing agricultural production and improving the peasants' livelihood. . . .

State accumulation comes mainly from taxes and profits turned over to the state by state enterprises; only a small part comes from the agricultural tax. In fixing commodity prices, therefore, we strive to ensure that the state industrial and commercial enterprises concerned will be able to pay taxes and make reasonable profits. In addition, we fix the prices of a few items which are not necessities, such as tobacco and wines, at levels higher than their values so as to limit their consumption and increase state accumulation.

4. *In formulating our price policy, we also see to it that it helps to consolidate and develop the socialist economy, curb speculative activities and promote the socialist transformation of capitalist industry and commerce.* . . .

Our state price policy played a significant role in the socialist transformation of China's capitalist industry and commerce. Our practice was to have the state control the ex factory prices [16] of all industrial goods offered by private manufacturing plants and so restrict and regulate in a planned way the amount of profit going to private industry. The state also undertook to determine rationally regional and seasonal differences in the prices of various commodities as well as the differences between wholesale and retail prices in order to restrict and regulate in a planned way the profit made by private commerce. By these means, the leading position of the socialist sector in the market was consolidated and market prices were unaffected or less affected by the free competition of capitalist industry and commerce. Speculative activities of all kinds were curbed, and industrial and commercial capitalists were thus brought to accept socialist transformation voluntarily. . . .

MAINTAINING MARKET AND PRICE STABILITY

The basic reason for the stability of our market and prices over the years is that China is a socialist country. The socialist state can, through the regula-

[16] F.o.b. (free on board) prices; prices at the place of manufacture, not including transportation charges. [EDITOR'S NOTE]

tory effect of state plans, maintain a balance between supply and demand with regard to all the various products and between commodity supplies and the purchasing power of society. In this way, it ensures price stability. But it is not possible for our economic plans always to conform fully to actual economic developments. This is especially so in regard to agricultural production, which is still to a considerable extent dependent on natural conditions. Thus, a certain degree of disequilibrium is unavoidable. In view of this, apart from holding a certain amount of goods in constant reserve, we make timely readjustments in state plans according to changing circumstances, trying to maintain the balance of the plans as far as possible and thus help stabilize the market and prices.

There are two kinds of disequilibrium: disequilibrium between supply and demand in a certain number of commodities and disequilibrium between commodity supplies and social purchasing power. Both can cause unstable prices. The latter form of disequilibrium, especially, may cause an overall fluctuation of prices.

Disequilibrium between supply and demand in a certain number of commodities may occur frequently. When supplies of certain *essential* consumer goods fail to meet demand, we never try to restore the balance by raising prices. Instead, while stepping up production of these goods, we adopt the method of rationing in order to guarantee their proper distribution. This method enables us not only to maintain a relative balance between supply and demand but also to stabilize prices and satisfy the basic needs of the people. Of course, in the case of shortages in the supply of certain *secondary* consumer goods it is neither necessary nor possible for us to adopt this method of rationing. What we do is to readjust production plans to increase the output of such goods and at the same time appropriately readjust their prices so as to restore the balance quickly between supply and demand. It should be noted that where there is a balance between total commodity supply and the total purchasing power of society, a short supply of certain commodities is invariably linked with over supply of certain other commodities. Hence, the consequent readjustment of prices necessarily involves the raising of the prices of certain commodities and the lowering of prices of certain other commodities, so that the general price level is, in the main, kept intact.

In a socialist country, there is an urgent desire to speed up economic construction and improve the people's living standards. On the other hand, however, state plans cannot always tally with actual economic developments, especially when there are crop failures caused by natural calamities. As a consequence, purchasing power in a socialist society may sometimes outstrip commodity supplies and this may result in strain on the market over a certain period. When such a situation arises, what we do is, on the one hand, readjust production and capital construction plans to ensure an increase in the output of agriculture and light industry, and on the other hand, appropriately restrain the growth of social purchasing power so as to keep it in proper proportion to the increase in the supply of consumer goods. This enables us to stabilize the market and prices and rapidly restore a balance between the supply of commodities and purchasing power.

During the years 1959-61, China was stricken by serious natural calamities, and as a result of this and other things, the output of agriculture and those light industries using farm products as raw materials declined and fell out of line with our then swiftly expanding heavy industry and rapidly increasing purchasing power. This led to shortages in the supply of certain commodities. In tackling this situation, we introduced the policy of "readjustment, consolidation, filling out and raising standards." This policy mainly comprised:

1. concentrating our efforts on reinforcing the agricultural front in order to restore and develop farm production as quickly as possible;

2. appropriately curtailing those branches of industrial production and capital construction which it was necessary to curtail and developing those which needed to be developed and readjusting relations between the various branches of industry;

3. increasing the variety of industrial products, raising their quality and economizing on the consumption of materials.

At the same time, we strengthened our planned control of the market and prices, and in order to satisfy the basic needs of the people temporarily adopted the method of rationing in the distribution of certain staple consumer goods which were in short supply. Thanks to these efforts, stability of the market and of price as well as stability in the life of the people were assured, a swift restoration and development of agriculture and industry as well as a rapid increase in the supply of commodities on the market were achieved, and the imbalance between commodity supply and purchasing power was quickly replaced by a new balance.

Now, our national economy has made an overall turn for the better, and a new upsurge of industrial and agricultural production is shaping up and developing. . . .

VII. SOCIALIST COMMERCE IN CHINA [17]

GROWTH OF SOCIALIST COMMERCE

Immediately after the founding of the People's Republic of China, the bourgeoisie still possessed considerable economic strength. Capitalist speculators, taking advantage of the then unstable financial and economic situation, engaged in frantic speculation, hoarded commodities and manipulated market prices in pursuit of exorbitant profits. A sharp struggle against these profiteers was swiftly launched. Early in 1950, the Central People's Government introduced a unified control of economic and financial work through-

[17] Condensed from Yao Kuan, "Socialist Commerce in China," *Peking Review* (February 21, 1964).

out the country, concentrated all economic strength in the hands of the state, took deflationary measures and stabilized commodity prices, thereby putting an end to the market chaos which prevailed in old China over a dozen years as a result of soaring inflation. In the struggle to stabilize prices it dealt a deadly blow to capitalist speculators.

With the stabilization of prices, the Government, in an effort to speed up restoration of the national economy, carried out a readjustment of private industry and commerce. It used and restricted private enterprises by supplying them with raw materials, purchasing their products and placing orders with them to process and manufacture goods. Private industry was thus placed under the leadership of the state-owned economy and its production gradually brought within the state plan's orbit. . . .

Meanwhile, supply and marketing co-operatives were set up throughout the countryside. . . .

Towards the end of 1952, the Chinese Communist Party set forth the task of carrying out the socialist transformation of agriculture, handicrafts and capitalist industry and commerce throughout the country step by step. . . .

Beginning in autumn 1953, the Government adopted the policy of planned purchase and supply of grain. Planned purchase and supply of edible oils and cotton were instituted later. Most of the former private retail dealers in these goods became retail distributors or commission agents for state trading organs. More and more private dealers in other lines of trade soon followed suit and they, too, became retail distributors or commission agents for the state companies.

In 1954, energetic steps were taken to bring capitalist enterprises under joint state-private operation to speed up the tempo of the socialist transformation of capitalist industry and commerce. Early in 1956, an upsurge in socialist transformation of capitalist industry and commerce took place in the wake of the high tide of agricultural cooperation that occurred in the winter of 1955. By the end of the year, private industry and commerce, in the main, had come under joint state-private operation, and most small workshops and stores had been turned into cooperative concerns.

Socialist commerce has been the most efficient and most economical commerce known in China's history. Compared with the early post-liberation period, the total volume of the nation's retail sales has multiplied, while the number of personnel working in the commercial establishments has decreased instead of increasing, and costs in commodity circulation have been reduced. . . .

SERVING THE PEOPLE'S LIVELIHOOD

The aim of developing production under socialism is to satisfy the growing needs of the people. This is realized through exchange and distribution.

Socialist commerce therefore operates in the service of the people, and is fundamentally different from profit-seeking, capitalist commerce.

During the past 14 years, the Chinese Communist Party and People's Government have made great efforts to satisfy the basic needs of the urban and rural population and improve their livelihood on the basis of increased production. This was so even in the periods when our country met with temporary difficulties in socialist transformation and socialist construction. For instance, in 1959-61, when market supplies were seriously affected by three successive years of natural calamities, great effort was still exerted to ensure the basic needs of the people and to stabilize prices of staples.

Before liberation even one year, let alone three consecutive years, of natural calamities would have brought widespread starvation in the affected areas. Peasants would have been made homeless and forced to sell their children; many would have died of hunger. The striking contrast with the past fully testifies to the advantages of our socialist system.

Now, our national economy has begun to show an all-round turn for the better, and the supply of commodities is growing steadily and the market is becoming increasingly buoyant. Apart from daily necessities, an ever richer variety of goods is available to meet the many and various needs of the people.

UNIFIED SOCIALIST DOMESTIC MARKET

China's domestic market today has three channels of commodity circulation: state trade, cooperative trade and trade in rural local markets. These three channels, each playing its specific role in circulation and distribution, combine to form a unified socialist domestic market.

State trade based on socialist ownership by the whole people is the mainstay and leading factor in our commerce. The state trading organs control and distribute the bulk of commodities at home and handle all our foreign trade. . . .

Cooperative trade based on collective ownership is another form of socialist commerce. It serves as an able assistant to state trade, and will operate in our country throughout the historical period when our agriculture and handicrafts remain collectively owned. . . .

Trade in rural local markets is a necessary supplement to state and cooperative trade. So long as our agriculture is still based on collective ownership and so long as our people's commune members still retain their tiny garden plots and engage in family side-occupations, this kind of trade is an essential channel through which the peasants exchange their produce and each makes up what the other lacks. . . .

Rural local market exchanges are conducted between producers who sell their own produce and consumers who buy for their own use. Prices are negotiated by buyers and sellers.

Trade in rural local markets has a dual character: on the one hand, it stimulates farming and rural sideline production and enlivens the rural economy; on the other hand, it can disturb the planned market and make for speculative opportunities. The state must therefore exercise its leadership over such markets by economic and administrative measures—organizing supply and marketing cooperatives to go in for buying and selling in these markets to help stabilize prices; setting a limit on the scope of operation of such markets; requiring all traders and pedlars to register with the Government; prohibiting all speculative activities on the market and levying taxes in accordance with regulations. Such trade therefore is entirely different from trade in the capitalist market. . . .

VIII. CHINA'S FOREIGN TRADE [18]

China's foreign trade relations have developed extensively during the past few years. . . . At present (January, 1965) our country has trade relations with 125 countries and regions. Forty countries have signed intergovernmental trade agreements with us. The volume of our import and export trade has increased in varying degrees with quite a number of these countries and regions. We have consistently based our foreign trade relations on the principle of equality and mutual benefit and this has been recognized and welcomed by the people of all countries. . . .

TRADE WITH SOCIALIST COUNTRIES

In our trade relations with the countries of the socialist camp, we have consistently upheld the spirit of proletarian internationalism combined with patriotism. In accordance with the principle of active cooperation, equality, mutual benefit, and concrete possibilities we carry on trade with the socialist countries in a planned way according to the needs and capabilities of ourselves and our trading partners in order to promote a common upsurge in the economies of all the socialist countries on a basis of self-reliance. . . .

CHINA'S ASIAN-AFRICAN TRADE

China is now trading with more than 60 countries and regions in Asia and Africa. The volume of import and export trade between China and these countries and regions has been increasing each year. The total volume in 1963 was more than three times what it was in 1950, and now accounts for an important share of China's foreign trade. . . .

[18] Condensed from Lin Hai-yun (Vice-Minister of Foreign Trade), "China's Growing Foreign Trade," *Peking Review* (January 22, 1965).

CHINA'S LATIN AMERICAN TRADE

The development of China's trade with the Latin American countries has been relatively rapid over the past few years. There were only five countries in Latin America which traded with us directly in 1952; now we trade with more than 20 countries and regions. The volume of this trade has increased markedly. . . . As industrial and commercial circles there are calling ever more forcefully for more trade with China, the U.S. imperialists are increasing their efforts to make trouble and wreck our relations with these countries; but our concerted efforts will certainly succeed in surmounting all artificial barriers and outside interference to clear a way for the extensive development of our trade relations with the Latin American countries.

TRADE WITH WESTERN COUNTRIES

We have also been actively developing our trade with Western countries. . . . More and more governments and manufacturers and firms in the Western world wish to expand their trade relations with us and this is especially so in circumstances where the struggle for domination and the counter-struggle against domination becomes sharper than ever between the United States and other Western countries, and competition is becoming ever more intense in the capitalist world market. . . .

The U.S. imperialists are going to great lengths in their efforts to obstruct and sabotage such trade, but just as their "blockade" and "embargo" and other policies of trade discrimination against China went bankrupt, so their new conspiracies are meeting and are bound to meet ignominious defeat.

PROSPECTS FOR THE FUTURE

The great achievements in the development of our foreign trade eloquently prove that we have friends all over the world. U.S. "blockade" and "embargo" and all its attempts and underhand schemes to isolate and "contain" China have failed ingloriously. The demand of the people all over the world to develop friendship and economic and trade relations with China is like a mighty torrent which cannot be held back by any reactionary force. We are confident that in the wake of the continuing victories in our socialist construction and the steady expansion of our foreign relations, our trade relations with countries throughout the world will continue to be consolidated and grow and expand on the basis of equality and mutual benefit.

IX. ART, LITERATURE, EDUCATION, AND MEDICAL SERVICES [19]

China is in the midst of a deep-going socialist revolution on the cultural front. The historical experience of the proletarian dictatorship tells us that after the seizure of state power the proletariat must carry the socialist revolution forward to victory not only on the economic front but also on the political and ideological fronts, otherwise the danger exists of abandoning the socialist revolution halfway and forfeiting all its previous achievements. Cultural work is an integral part of work on the ideological front. . . .

In a socialist society classes and class struggle still exist and the struggle between the socialist road and the capitalist road continues. Bourgeois ideology still exerts considerable influence in the cultural, educational, artistic, and academic spheres. It is therefore necessary to develop the new, socialist culture of the proletariat and wage a protracted, blow-for-blow struggle against bourgeois ideology and culture and all other reactionary ideologies and cultures in order to eliminate their influence step by step and carry the socialist revolution on the ideological and cultural fronts through to the end.

VIGOROUS REVOLUTIONARY SITUATION

A vigorous revolutionary situation now prevails on the cultural front as on other fronts in China. Great endeavours are being made in our cultural, educational, public health, and scientific research work, to implement the policy of serving the politics of the proletariat, serving the workers, peasants and soldiers and serving the socialist economic base. Large numbers of intellectuals have taken part in the socialist education movement in the cities and in the countryside and been steeled and tested in the class struggle. The great, socialist cultural revolution is already yielding most fruitful results.

In the field of art and literature, the National Festival of Peking Operas on Contemporary Revolutionary Themes held in June last year has given a powerful impetus to the revolutionization of the various types of local operas and of modern drama, music and dancing. Plays and operas on contemporary revolutionary themes are now taking the stage and the heroic images of workers, peasants, and soldiers have replaced those of the emperors, kings, generals, ministers, scholars, and beauties of old. The epic in song and dance *The East Is Red,* the Peking Opera *Red Signal Lantern,* and the

[19] Condensed from Tien Chu, "Fruits of the Cultural Revolution," *Peking Review* (October 15, 1965).

ballet *Red Detachment of Women* are all outstanding achievements in their respective fields. The masses of workers in art and culture have group by group taken part in the socialist education movement and joined the cultural work teams going to the countryside. They have set some fine examples and gained a certain experience in serving the peasants. In the performing arts a lively repertoire of short plays and operas penetratingly depicting life in the countryside has been created. . . .

NEW EDUCATIONAL DEVELOPMENT

In education, our full-time schools are making great efforts to further the elimination of the influence of bourgeois educational ideas so as to implement the policy of putting education at the service of proletarian politics and integrating it with productive labour. An important new development in our educational revolution today is the establishment of the work-and-study and farm-work-and-study system. This has given rise to a new type of school in which education is closely linked with physical labour. These schools have already trained large numbers of people. Reports from many parts of the country show that such schools are well liked by the workers and former poor and lower-middle peasants. . . .

From a long-term point of view, this new type of school system points to the future direction of socialist and communist education. It will create conditions for the gradual elimination of differences between mental and manual labour. Viewed in the light of the historical experience of the proletarian dictatorship, it is a fundamental measure for bringing up a new generation of revolutionaries who can do both mental and physical labour and are both "red and expert," and for preventing any restoration of capitalism.

MEDICINE AND PUBLIC HEALTH

In medicine and public health in the past 16 years, we have come a long way under the leadership of the Chinese Communist Party. Many of our achievements in medical science rank amongst the most advanced in the world. . . .

Our medical and public health workers have come to realize fully that, since more than 80 percent of the Chinese people are peasants, the socialist policy of serving the workers, peasants and soldiers would be just idle talk if the peasants' needs in this field were not effectively met. Public health authorities in every part of the country are therefore taking radical measures to make medical and public health work available in the countryside. Across the land, medical people are going down to the countryside to see to the needs of the peasants. Tens of thousands of public health workers, many of them nationally known doctors and specialists, have left the big cities to tour the rural areas and mountain regions. Effective steps are being taken throughout the country to train rural public health workers and set up or improve public health organizations at the grassroots. Departments in charge of the production and supply of medicinal products are studying the needs of the peasants with a view to turning out better products at lower prices. Prices of drugs are being reduced. A list of the first batch of medicines at these lowered prices has recently been made public. . . .

Our achievements on the cultural and educational fronts are not only in the large-scale popularization of culture and education. We have also achieved considerable successes in reaching advanced world levels in science. We have exploded two atomic bombs. We have won a succession of new victories in our efforts to reach world levels in sports. We have also achieved outstanding successes in other spheres of culture. All this reflects the lofty ambition and energetic spirit of the Chinese people who, holding high the red banner of Mao Tse-tung's thought, have the daring to scale the scientific and cultural heights of the world.

The victories already won have been tremendous. But these are only beginnings. The road ahead of us is long. . . .

X. THE ROLE OF THE PEOPLE'S MILITIA [20]

Over a century ago, Marx and Engels already stressed the significance and role of arming the people. Engels predicted that after the proletariat and other revolutionary people had taken political power into their own hands, then under the new social system, "every member of society who is fit for war can be taught, along with his other activities, to master the use of weapons, as much as is needed, not for taking part in parades, but for defending the country." . . .[21]

Later, Lenin also raised the slogan of "arming the whole people." He said: "So long as there are oppressed and exploited people in the world—we must strive, not for disarmament, but for the universal arming of the people. It alone will fully safeguard liberty." . . .[22]

Comrade Mao Tse-tung's complete set of theories on turning all the people into soldiers, advanced while leading the Chinese people's revolutionary struggles, is an important development of Marxist-Leninist thinking on arming the people. Guided by Comrade Mao Tse-tung's great mili-

[20] Condensed from Liu Yun-cheng, "The Role of People's Militia," *Peking Review* (February 5, 1965).
[21] Marx-Engels, "Elberfeld Speeches," Feb. 8, 1845, *Works*, Russ. ed. (State Publishing House of Political Literature, Moscow, 1955), Vol. II, p. 539.
[22] Lenin, "The Army and the Revolution," *Selected Works*, Eng. ed. (International Publishers, New York), Vol. III, p. 339.

tary thinking on people's war, our Party not only built up an extremely proletarianized and extremely militant people's army—the People's Liberation Army—but also mobilized, organized and armed the masses to form a powerful people's militia force. . . .

A MEASURE OF STRATEGIC SIGNIFICANCE

The system of turning all the people into soldiers played an inestimable role during the protracted revolutionary wars. It also has been a basic measure for consolidating national defence and the dictatorship of the proletariat, and an important guarantee for defeating armed imperialist aggression and preventing a capitalist restoration during the new period of the socialist revolution and socialist construction. . . .

Since the victory of the Chinese people's revolutionary war, the liberated Chinese people have been determined to build their motherland with their own hands into a powerful socialist country with a modern agriculture, industry, national defence, and science and technology. But, U.S. imperialism, part of whose nature is to slaughter others, is not reconciled to its failures in China and other parts of the world, and it is still frantically making war preparations and pursuing an aggressive policy. It seizes by force our territory of Taiwan and incites its flunkey, the Chiang Kai-shek gang, to harass and attack the Chinese mainland. U.S. imperialism establishes many military bases surrounding China, organizes aggressive military blocs, and carries out a military encirclement and economic blockade against China. It launched military aggression and intervention in Korea and the Indo-China region, both China's close neighbours. In spite of repeated warnings from the Chinese people, it continues to intrude into our territorial air and waters and engages in frenzied military provocations. The danger of imperialism launching an aggressive war poses a serious threat to us.

From Comrade Mao Tse-tung we have been taught: "At a time when the imperialists are bullying us in such a manner, we have to deal with them seriously. True, we have a powerful regular army, but we still need to organize the people's militia on a great scale. Against a powerful regular army and a nationwide militia, the imperialists would find it difficult to move a single inch in our country in the event of invasion." Guided by the correct policy of the Party's Central Committee and Comrade Mao Tse-tung, the organization of the people's militia has developed on an unprecedented scale, expanding swiftly from a force of tens of millions to a powerful army of hundreds of millions. Militia units are not only found throughout the rural areas, but are universally organized in urban factories, mines, enterprises, government offices and schools. In addition to hundreds of millions of peasants, tens of millions of industrial workers, staff members and revolutionary intellectuals have also joined the ranks of the people's militia. Having a fairly high cultural level in general, they are in a better position to learn how to master and use various kinds of modern weapons and equipment. This can provide powerful reserves for the various technical arms of a modern army, thereby making the building of a militia serve to build a modern army. As the people's militia becomes stronger and stronger, its weapons and equipment have also been greatly improved. . . .

The militia masses regard the defence of their socialist motherland and peace in Asia and the world as their sacred duty. . . .

MORAL ATOM BOMB

In frantically carrying out its policies of aggression and war, U.S. imperialism often tries to intimidate the people of all countries by brandishing nuclear weapons, and she vainly attempts to blackmail them into submission. The modern revisionists are also shamelessly serving imperialism. The more the imperialists try to intimidate us, the more the modern revisionists slander us, the more we must seriously implement Comrade Mao Tse-tung's concept of a people's war, closely rely on and arm the masses and turn all the people into soldiers. Only in this way can we deal with imperialism which brandishes nuclear weapons.

Comrade Mao Tse-tung hit the nail on the head when he pointed out: "The atom bomb is a paper tiger which the U.S. reactionaries use to scare people. It looks terrible, but in fact it isn't. Of course, the atom bomb is a weapon of mass slaughter, but the outcome of a war is decided by the people, not by one or two new types of weapon." [23]

Our country has successfully conducted its first nuclear test. This is a tremendous encouragement to the revolutionary people of all countries engaged in struggle, and a big contribution towards safeguarding world peace. However, we are developing nuclear weapons not because we believe them all-powerful, and want to use them. On the contrary, we are developing nuclear weapons to break the nuclear monopoly, to oppose nuclear blackmail, and to do away with such weapons. In the past we considered the atom bomb to be a paper tiger; we still do today. We have always believed that the outcome of war is decided by man, not by weapons of any kind. The destiny of China is decided by the people of China; the destiny of the world is decided by the peoples of the world, not by nuclear weapons.

We know that nuclear weapons and guided missiles are powerful weapons and we are determined to go forward in science and technology, spare no effort to scale the peaks in these matters and catch up with and surpass the most advanced imperialist countries in modern science and technology. On the other hand, it is more important for us to know that no matter how

[23] "Talk With the American Correspondent Anna Louise Strong," *Selected Works of Mao Tse-tung,* Eng. ed. (Peking, Foreign Languages Press, 1961), Vol. IV, p. 100.

powerful the new types of weapons, they can never alter the truth that the army and the people are the foundation of victory. The atom bomb is very powerful, but the moral atom bomb is thousands of times more powerful. This moral bomb is the just stand of our opposition to aggressive wars, a common hatred for the enemy, and the heroic, stubborn fighting spirit of hundreds of millions of people. Reliance on the masses of the people is our greatest advantage, while antagonism to the masses is the enemy's fatal weakness. The material atom bomb is something we have already mastered, while the moral atom bomb is a thing which the enemy can never obtain. . . .

XI. THE GREAT PROLETARIAN CULTURAL REVOLUTION [24]

An upsurge is occurring in the great proletarian cultural revolution in socialist China whose population accounts for one-quarter of the world's total.

For the last few months, in response to the militant call of the Central Committee of the Chinese Communist Party and Chairman Mao hundreds of millions of workers, peasants and soldiers, and vast numbers of revolutionary cadres and intellectuals, all armed with Mao Tse-tung's thought, have been sweeping away a horde of monsters that have entrenched themselves in ideological and cultural positions. With the tremendous and impetuous force of a raging storm, they have smashed the shackles imposed on their minds by the exploiting classes for so long in the past, routing the bourgeois "specialists," "scholars," "authorities" and "venerable masters" and sweeping every bit of their prestige into the dust.

Chairman Mao has taught us that class struggle does not cease in China after the socialist transformation of the system of ownership has in the main been completed. "The class struggle between the proletariat and the bourgeoisie . . . will continue to be long and tortuous and at times will even become very acute. The proletariat seeks to transform the world according to its own world outlook, and so does the bourgeoisie. In this respect, the question of which will win out, socialism or capitalism, is still not really settled." The class struggle in the ideological field between the proletariat and the bourgeoisie has been very acute right through the 16 years since China's liberation. The current great socialist cultural revolution is precisely a continuation and development of this struggle. The struggle is inevitable. The ideology of the proletariat and the ideology of all the exploiting classes are diametrically opposed to each other and cannot coexist in peace. The proletarian revolution is a revolution to abolish all exploiting classes and all systems of exploitation; it is a most thoroughgoing revolution

[24] Condensed from "Sweep Away All Monsters," *Renmin Ribao* editorial, *China Pictorial* (August, 1966), pp. 6-7.

to bring about the gradual elimination of the differences between workers and peasants, between town and country, and between mental and manual labourers. This cannot but meet with the most stubborn resistance from the exploiting classes. . . .

The proletarian cultural revolution is aimed not only at demolishing all the old ideology and culture and all the old customs and habits, which, fostered by the exploiting classes, have poisoned the minds of the people for thousands of years, but also at creating and fostering among the masses an entirely new ideology and culture and entirely new customs and habits— those of the proletariat. This great task of transforming customs and habits is without any precedent in human history. As for all the heritage, customs and habits of the feudal and bourgeois classes, the proletarian world outlook must be used to subject them to thoroughgoing criticism. It takes time to clear away the evil habits of the old society from among the people. Nevertheless, our experience since liberation proves that the transformation of customs and habits can be accelerated if the masses are fully mobilized, the mass line is implemented and the transformation is made into a genuine mass movement.

As the bourgeois cultural revolution served only a small number of people, i.e., the new exploiting class, only a small number of people could participate in it. The proletarian cultural revolution, however, serves the broad masses of the working people and is in the interests of the working people who constitute the overwhelming majority of the population. It is therefore able to attract and unite the broad masses to take part in it. . . .

The stormy cultural revolution now under way in our country has thrown the imperialists, the modern revisionists, and the reactionaries of all countries into confusion and panic. . . . Dear Sirs, your wishful thinking invariably runs counter to the march of history. The triumphant progress of this great and unparalleled cultural revolution of the proletariat is already sounding the death knell not only of the remnant capitalist forces on Chinese soil, but of imperialism, modern revisionism and all reaction. Your days are numbered.

Illuminated by the great Mao Tse-tung's thought, let us carry the proletarian cultural revolution through to the end. Its victory will certainly further strengthen the dictatorship of the proletariat in our country, guarantee the completion of the socialist revolution on all fronts, and ensure our successful transition from socialism to triumphant communism!

IV

The Socialist Federal
    Republic of Yugoslavia:
A Country on Its "Own
        Road to Socialism"

Area
(in square miles)
98,766

Population
(mid-1967 estimate)
19,922,000

To negate the market would be as useless as to negate the Plan. We want to create an optimal balance between decentralized planning and the market mechanism. We have no dogmatic prejudices, none whatever . . .

KIRD GLIGOROV
YUGOSLAVIA'S SECRETARY OF FINANCE

In its foreign policy, the Yugoslav government is guided, as are those of many other countries, by the principle of peaceful co-existence and non-alignment.

MARK NIKEZIC
YUGOSLAVIA'S SECRETARY FOR FOREIGN AFFAIRS

Nothing that has been created should be so sacred to us that it cannot be transcended and superseded by something still freer, more progressive, and more human.

PROGRAM OF THE LEAGUE OF
YUGOSLAVIA COMMUNISTS

INTRODUCTION

WHEN, BEFORE THE END OF THE 1940's, YUGOSLAVIA DARED TO disobey the orders of Stalin, she became the first country to shatter the monolithic command structure of the Communist World. Ever since, Yugoslavia has remained the most unorthodox among the group of nations which presumably are building new societies along Marxist-Leninist lines. In the economic sphere, the establishment of workers' councils, the powers bestowed upon them, the utilization of the tools of a market economy, and the extent of economic freedom granted to individuals has not only preceded the beginnings of such developments in other communist countries but has gone much farther than any of them are expected to go in the foreseeable future. In the political arena, contests between two or more candidates for votes in public elections, rotation in office both in government and Party positions, a diminution of political influence over economic decisions (brought on in part by a decrease in the share of enterprise incomes going to the political communities) are unique among communist nations, and the present trend to reduce the leadership function of the Communist Party to a new role limited to ideological guidance would be unthinkable in any of the others.

In her international relations, Yugoslavia also stands alone in the communist camp with her openly declared policy of nonalignment, her stress not merely on peaceful coexistence but on permanent peaceful cooperation with noncommunist nations, and the extent of her willingness to "do business" with the West. Likewise, in regard to her ideological orientation, Yugoslavia is unequalled in the communist world in her nondogmatic approach to Marxism, contending openly for all to hear that Marx cannot be expected to have provided more than a general guide to action, and that each communist country must be free to seek its own road to socialism in the general direction indicated by Marx, Engels, and Lenin (although the last is but rarely mentioned in Yugoslav ideological discussions). Moreover, Yugoslavia has now declared that an acceptance of Marxist ideology is not required for membership in the Socialist Alliance of the Working People of Yugoslavia (the popular mass organization, not to be confused with the Party which goes by the official name of the League of Communists of Yugoslavia). As regards the Party itself, Yugoslavia, alone among communist countries, now denies its permanency, asserting that it (just like the state) must and will in time wither away.

In social, cultural, and other areas, the same unorthodox style and the same lack of constraint prevail. While the "thaw" has melted more economic, political, and ideological ice in Yugoslavia than in any of the other communist countries, "liberal" Yugoslavs—from Marshal Tito to the new brand of economists and planners who are spearheading the economic reform movement—would be the first to agree that the road ahead is still long and promises to be arduous. But the struggle against the "conservatives" who have paid lip service to all progressive reforms (but who have fairly effectively retarded their implementation) has progressed unabatedly, and the complete victory of the liberal forces appears very likely.

While many of the less developed countries in Asia and Africa observe with interest Yugoslavia's journey along her "own road to socialism," the Yugoslav example has already had considerable influence (especially in the economic and planning spheres) upon most of the communist countries of Eastern Europe. The introduction of an interest rate in Hungary, the "new economic model" in Czechoslovakia, the far-reaching economic reforms in East Germany and Poland, all bear traces of that influence. But, fearful that the full implementation of Yugoslav ideas could threaten the very foundations of socialism, no communist country has gone nearly as far as Yugoslavia in discarding orthodox ideology or introducing practical economic and political reforms. In a sense, then, the Yugoslav experiment still remains what the Organization for Economic Cooperation and Development has referred to as "the only experiment of its kind in the world." [1]

The non-Marxist view on Yugoslavia has been contributed by Harry G. Shaffer. A New York University Ph.D. in economics, Shaffer has pub-

[1] "Socialist Federal Republic of Yugoslavia," *Economic Survey by the OECD* (Paris, July, 1963), p. 3.

lished widely in professional journals, mostly on the economies of the Soviet Union and the communist countries of Eastern Europe. Articles of his have appeared not only in English, but also in French, Spanish, Italian, German, and Hungarian. Shaffer is also editor of *The Soviet Economy: A Collection of Western and Soviet Views,* of *The Soviet System in Theory and Practice: Selected Western and Soviet Views,* and of this book, all published by Appleton-Century-Crofts, New York, 1963, 1965, and 1967 respectively. At present, Shaffer is Associate Professor of Economics at the University of Kansas.

The Marxist view on Yugoslavia has been written especially for inclusion herein by two Yugoslav professors, Dr. Milos Samardžija and Dr. Radoslav Ratković.

Samardzija has published numerous articles on Marxist economic theory and on price theory and policy in Yugoslav journals, and he is the author of a new (1965-66) textbook on *The Economic System of Yugoslavia*. During the academic year 1966/67, Samardžija was visiting Professor at Western Michigan University. At present, he holds the position of Professor of Political Economy on the Law Faculty of the University of Belgrade.

Ratković has published articles on Marxist ideology, on politics, sociology, and the social sciences in general, and on various aspects of the Yugoslav system. He is the author of *Society and Class* (1952), *Views on the Problems of Contemporary Society* (1961), and *The Political Theory of Austrian Marxism* (1965), all published in Belgrade. At present, he is Professor of Sociology and Head of the Department of Sociology at the Higher School of Political Science in Belgrade.

Professor Samardžija wrote the first section and Professor Ratković the last section of the Marxist view on Yugoslavia.

The editor wishes to express his gratitude to the Yugoslav Information Center, New York, for having made the arrangement for this contribution by Yugoslav social scientists.

7

Yugoslavia's "Own Road to Socialism": A Non-Marxist View

HARRY G. SHAFFER *

ASSOCIATE PROFESSOR OF ECONOMICS
THE UNIVERSITY OF KANSAS

During the days of World War II, Yugoslavia's Communist Party attained the leadership of the resistance movement. After the war, the Party, headed by Marshal Josip Broz Tito, established a "people's democracy" and proceeded to nationalize the means of production. [Tito, as of mid-1967, is President of Yugoslavia and President of the League of Communists of Yugoslavia (LCY).] The Constitution of 1946 provided for the immediate nationalization only of mines, sources of power, transportation facilities, and such other means of production as had already been turned over to common ownership before or during the war, but it laid the foundation for "expropriating the expropriators," and it declared social ownership the basis for the future socio-economic system that was to be erected.

During the rest of the 1940's the state, through the socialization of basic industries, attained virtually monopoly power. (The only backsliding occurred in agriculture, when, beginning in 1948, those farms for which collectivization either had not been economically rational or was not supported by a majority vote of the participating members were returned to individual private ownership. Over 80 percent of all arable land in Yugoslavia is still privately owned.) The state managed most sectors of the nation's economy by means of ministries and directorates. All aspects of production, including quantity of output, assortment of goods, prices of inputs and outputs, wages, investments, etc., were regulated from the center via the national Plan; and

* Shaffer's contribution is a thoroughly revised, expanded, and updated version of one of his articles which was published in German under the title "Jugoslawien's eigener Weg zum Sozialismus," in *Osteuropa* (April, 1966), pp. 227-245. Parts of the original article, in English translation, are used here by permission of the publisher.

individual economic enterprises were but economic organs of the state, owned by society at large and operated by the government. The state bore all economic risks, carried all losses, and was entitled to receive and to reallocate all profits. Enterprise directors were merely state functionaries, carrying out orders from above.

Although Yugoslavia today spearheads the reform in Eastern Europe, her break with Stalin in 1948 can thus not be interpreted as a rebellion against a strongly centralized dictatorship but rather as an expression of the independent spirit of Yugoslavia's leadership and as an unwillingness to submit to the dictates of Moscow. Economic decentralization and political and cultural liberalization had at that time not yet begun to penetrate the country's ideological orientation or economic, social, and political structure.[1] Even today, official Yugoslav sources assert that during the later 1940's strict discipline was necessary to facilitate full concentration on the reconstruction and industrialization of a war-torn nation.

In June, 1948 an adamant Stalin had a recalcitrant Yugoslavia expelled from the Cominform,[2] thus bringing on the first split in the communist camp. Between May and July, 1949, the East European members of Cominform cancelled all trade agreements with Yugoslavia and together with the Soviet Union began an economic blockade against her. But, contrary to Stalin's expectations, Yugoslavia's solidly entrenched pro-Tito group was not dislodged from power.

Isolated from the Soviet Bloc countries, Yugoslavia was now forced to seek trading partners in the west. With Tito's active encouragement, voices which proclaimed a new, a *Yugoslav,* road to socialism now gained preponderance: the socialist structure was to be built from the bottom up on the foundation of workers' self-management in production (instead of being imposed from above by the coercion of an all-powerful Party-government apparatus).

A December, 1949 government directive providing for the election of workers' councils as advisory bodies to factory management was but a

[1] The Workers' Commissioners Act of 1945 had provided for workers' commissioners who were to represent the workers' interests before state authorities and before their own managers—but who also were to use their influence with the workers to prompt them to increase output (*Official Gazette,* No. 54, 1945); and the State Economic Enterprises Act of 1946 had given trade unions the power to make recommendations to management for the improvement of working conditions—and, incidentally, for measures to increase workers' productivity (*Official Gazette,* No. 62, 1946). But these laws could hardly be termed "decentralization" or "liberalization" measures, and they did not even foreshadow the course of coming events.

[2] Communist Information Bureau. Established in October, 1947, by the Communist Parties of Bulgaria, Czechoslovakia, France, Hungary, Italy, Poland, Rumania, the Soviet Union, and Yugoslavia for the declared purpose of exchanging information and coordinating activities; dissolved in 1956. Stalin was in virtually absolute control over the Cominform until his death in 1953.

preview of coming events.[3] June 26, 1950, is the day Yugoslavs refer to as the beginning of a new period in the development of their economic, social, and political system,[4] the day on which Yugoslavia set out on her "own road to socialism." On that day the "Basic Law on the Management of Enterprises by the Working Collective" was passed, a law that gave legal backing to experiments in workers' self-government which were already being carried on at the time. Section 1 of the act laid down the basic principles of workers' self-government:

Manufacturing, mining, communications, transport, trading, agricultural, forestry, municipal and other public undertakings shall, as the property of the whole nation, be administered in the name of the community by their work collectives as part of the said economic plan and on the basis of the rights and duties established by law.

The collectives shall carry out their administration through the workers' councils and boards of management of their undertakings . . .[5]

For the first three or four years under the new law, as the government and the Party were "feeling their way," legal provisions and the State economic Plans laid down so many "do's" and "dont's" to the bodies of workers' management that "their normative role was considerably restricted." [6] But as time went on, new regulations became more general, State economic Plans less specific, and ever more powers to make economic decisions were transferred from the central Party and government authorities to the workers' councils. Out of this gradual transfer of power evolved Yugoslavia's unique economic system. Intended to combine the economic advantages of a market economy with the social ownership of the means of production, it incorporates features of modern Western capitalism and of contemporary Eastern communism, while differing in significant aspects from both. Like a boat swaying on rough seas, Yugoslavia's economic system seems to be rocking back and forth between East and West without taking a definite turn in either direction. Although its captains have frequently deemed it expedient to change speed or to alter course slightly, they have never failed to turn back the bow unto the precharted course in the direction of a freer, but not an unplanned society. It is little wonder that the moderates, both East and

[3] The first workers' council was elected on December 29, 1949 at a cement factory in Solin, Dalmatia (*Nedeljne Informativne Novine* [NIN], December 27, 1964); within the following six months such workers' councils with advisory capacity only, were set up on an experimental basis in several hundred Yugoslav enterprises. (Harry Schleicher, *Das System der betrieblichen Verwaltung in Jugoslawien* [Duncker-Humbolt, Berlin, 1961], p. 31.)

[4] *See*, for example, "Workers' Management," *Yugoslav Survey* (April, 1960), pp. 10-11.

[5] Cited in *Workers' Management in Yugoslavia* (International Labour Office, Geneva, 1962), p. 1.

[6] "Normative Role of Workers' Management Bodies," *Yugoslav Survey* (October-December, 1961), p. 942.

West, have become reconciled to the Yugoslav experiment, which they condone but of which they do not necessarily approve. The more orthodox and more dogmatic elements, on the other hand, are less willing to compromise; to them Yugoslavia is but a wolf in sheep's clothing, either a totalitarian, communist dictatorship basically not different from any of the other Soviet Bloc dictatorships, or—to those at the other end of the political spectrum—an agent of American imperialism which has betrayed the cause of Marxism-Leninism.

A BRIEF INTRODUCTION TO RECENT LIBERALIZATION MEASURES

In recent years, Yugoslavia's Communist Party and Government have taken significant strides towards allowing freer interplay of market forces, strengthening workers' self-management, and reducing administrative interference.

The legal framework for the liberalization measures which, in Yugoslavia, are frequently referred to as "the Economic Reform," or simply "the Reform," was provided by the new 1963 Constitution, adopted after wide public discussion. Official Party and Government approval of "the Reform" soon followed. The Eighth Party Congress which met in December, 1964, clearly restated the issues involved and gave official Party backing to the reforms, and the July, 1965 session of the Yugoslav Parliament (the Federal Assembly) adopted them.

It was soon discovered that although the reforms were on the books, they would not automatically be put into practice. Therefore, the Third Party Central Committee Plenum, meeting in the spring of 1966, pushed for full-fledged implementation and the Party Central Committee Meeting on July 1, 1966, took effective steps to eliminate much of the influence of the "conservatives" in the Yugoslav Communist Party and Government.

Various aspects of these recent developments will be discussed in the appropriate sections below.

SOCIAL OWNERSHIP OF THE MEANS OF PRODUCTION AND THE STRUCTURE OF WORKERS' SELF-MANAGEMENT

"Under our economic system, both private capitalist control and centralized state direction of the economy is being brought to an end. The enterprise is the nucleus of the system we are in the process of building. . . . The workers don't want their destiny decided by any one man, nor by any group of men, capitalist or socialist. They want to be masters of their own destiny." Thus was the fundamental principle underlying the Yugoslav economic system explained to this author by Mr. Danilo Knezevic, editor-in-chief of Yugoslavia's labor union weekly *Rad*.[7]

At present, most productive property outside of agriculture is owned in Yugoslavia by "society at large," but each individual enterprise has been turned over to its workers to be managed by them. Both of these concepts— the social ownership of the means of production and workers' self-management—are still lacking theoretical and legal precision, and their actual meaning and practical significance are but gradually emerging. Yugoslavs stress that social ownership does not mean state ownership, and to the extent to which the state has given up not only control over the means of production but even the right to receive and to dispose of the return to socially owned property, they are correct. The workers, on the other hand, who have been granted increasing administrative powers over their enterprises, do not own these enterprises either; not only are they under legal restrictions as to the utilization of the "socially owned" property administered by them, death, retirement, discharge from their position, or voluntary change of job immediately extinguishes whatever rights a worker has in regard to the means of production at his enterprise's disposition. Thus, really no one "owns" Yugoslavia's means of production, and this is rather clearly stated in the 1963 Yugoslav Constitution:

Since no one has the right of ownership over socially owned means of production, no one—neither the social-political community, nor the working organization, nor the individual working man himself—may, on the basis of any claim to property ownership, appropriate the product of socially organized labor, nor dispose of such product, nor determine arbitrarily the terms of its distribution.[8]

Workers' self-management (or self-government, as it is often called) is the cornerstone of Yugoslavia's economic system. But while the Constitution guarantees workers the right "to manage the working organization directly or through organs of management elected by themselves,"[9] the Yugoslavs find it necessary to stress that workers' management must be carried out "in accordance with laws and other government prescriptions,"[10] and that

[7] The interview took place in Mr. Knezevic's office in Belgrade on June 23 and June 24, 1964.

[8] Translated by the author from *Die Verfassung der Sozialistischen Föderativen Republik Jugoslawien* (Belgrade, 1963), p. 6. Although the official English translation of *The Constitution of the Socialist Federal Republic of Yugoslavia* (Belgrade, 1963) is quite satisfactory in most other parts, this paragraph (p. 6) is both confusing and inaccurate. It contains, for instance, the absurd statement that no one may "manage . . . socially owned means of production and work. . . ."

Another recent Yugoslav publication explained the social "ownership" of the means of production in Yugoslavia as follows: "The State, which up to then [June 26, 1950] had been possessor of the ownership right lost this right but the collective did not gain it; the right was extinguished." (Max Sunderl, "Eine revolutionäre Wende in der Wirtschaftslenkung," *Zwei Jahrzehnte sozialistisches Jugoslawien* [Medjunarodna Politika, Belgrade, 1964], p. 42.)

[9] *The Constitution, op. cit.*, p. 13.

[10] "Normative Role," *op. cit.*, p. 939.

the working collective is "under obligation to . . . fulfill its legal duties towards the community." [11]

In actual practice, workers' self-management operates through periodic elections of the enterprises' workers' councils.[12] Varying in size from 15 to 120 members (the exact number determined by the enterprise's by-laws according to its size and structure) the workers' council is, so to speak, the legislative arm of workers' self-government in charge of determining "the over-all activities of the undertaking and its general policy; all fundamental decisions concerning the undertaking lie within its terms of reference." [13] The board of management of an enterprise is the permanent executive branch of workers' self-government. Elected by the workers' council, its membership fixed by each enterprise within the legal limits of 3 and 11 members,[14] it is charged with managing the enterprise according to the dictates of the workers' council with due consideration to the obligations imposed upon it by law and by its own enterprise's by-laws. The enterprise director, selected by a committee on which both the workers' council and the public authorities and occupational organizations (trade unions, enterprise associations, etc.) are represented, is the primary executive agent of workers' self-government. Formerly a state-appointed official in charge of the fulfillment of the tasks assigned to the enterprise by the national plan, the director's functions today are supposed to be connected primarily with the supervision of the technical aspects of production; but since he also bears the responsibility for the legality of the operation of the socially owned enterprise, his is the dual role of an economic chief executive (on the local level) accountable both to his workers and to society. There is the additional ambiguity in the director's role that, as the company's highest employee, he "independently settles current problems," yet must do so "in conformity with decisions" of the organs of workers' self-government.[15]

MATERIAL INCENTIVES AND DISTRIBUTION OF INCOME

The primary *economic* motivation for the gradual transfer of economic decision-making power from the center to the local producing units was the anticipated increase in productive efficiency resulting from giving workers

[11] "Workers' Management," *op. cit.*, p. 11.

[12] In small undertakings of fewer than thirty workers the entire labor force—called "the collective" in Yugoslav terminology—constitutes the workers' council.

[13] *Workers' Management in Yugoslavia, op. cit.*, p. 74. Roughly 75 percent of the total membership of workers' councils in Yugoslavia consists of production workers.

[14] In very small enterprises of fewer than seven workers, all of them sit on the enterprises' board of management.

[15] Hoffman, George W., and Fred Warner Neal, *Yugoslavia and the New Communism* (New York, Twentieth Century Fund, 1962), p. 242.

a greater interest in their own performance and in the performance of their enterprises. It did not take Yugoslavia's leaders long to realize that to create such personal interest, an increased voice in decisions relating to production was insufficient: the worker (and the manager) had to be given a personal, direct stake in his own and his enterprise's accomplishments.

During the early years of Yugoslavia's existence as a "communist" country, the "stake" consisted primarily of bonuses paid in addition to regular wages for the fulfillment and the overfulfillment of the output plan. As an incentive system, the payment of rewards or bonuses for the fulfillment of the quantitative output plan has serious weaknesses. The self-interest of workers and managers operating under such a system would, for instance, dictate that they conceal their enterprise's productive power as best they can in order to be assigned a more easily attainable target; that they try to obtain as much as possible in machinery, tools, and equipment from the planning authorities, irrespective of present production requirements and of the needs of other producing units (they have nothing to lose since they do not pay for it); that they produce as much as possible, even if it be at the expense of quality or assortment (since quantity of output is the measuring rod, a large output of unsalable goods which merely fill warehouses will yield bonuses, while a smaller output of goods which meet customers' demand may not), etc. In other words, such an incentive system fails to make the interest of the direct producers coincide with the interests of society at large or the intentions of the planners. The payment of additional bonuses for increasing labor productivity, for improving quality, for introducing new products, etc., has proven both cumbersome and ineffective. (Even the best central planners would find it difficult to decide on a quality bonus scale for, let us say, 165 dress manufacturers, producing dresses out of 12 different raw materials, in 19 different sizes, 65 different styles, and 749 different color and pattern combinations.) But if workers' and managers' incomes depended upon their enterprises' *profits* (as well as their personal contribution in the productive process) they would no longer wish to hide their plants' productive capacity, accumulate more capital goods than they need (since profits would be computed as a percentage of total capital), produce unsaleable goods, etc.! "Profit" appears to be the magic word designating the one achievement indicator that encompasses all others. The conviction that profitability is ideally suited for the measurement of an enterprise's performance and that workers' and managers' participation in profits is a type of incentive superior to any other used thus far in centrally planned economies is at the very heart of the major reform movements in communist countries, from "Libermanism" in the Soviet Union to the "New Economic Model" in Czechoslovakia.

In Yugoslavia a type of profit sharing was introduced in 1954 by granting supplementary pay over and above regular, government-decreed wage scales to workers in profitable enterprises. (Under this system the workers' share in profits earned during the year [1954] amounted to 4.8 percent. The federal government took 50 percent, the districts [16] 28.7 percent, and the rest went into various enterprise and social funds.) [17]

In 1961 new economic reforms placed increasing power over the distribution of the net income of enterprises in the hands of the individual workers' councils. As a result, under the new system of distribution, enterprises pay out of their total receipts all their production expenditures, make their "contributions" to society (in the form of taxes, interest, etc.), and determine how to allocate whatever is left between investments (to increase future earning capacity), collective expenditures (erection of recreation centers, nurseries, etc., in addition to those provided by the community), and direct monetary distribution among workers. More specifically, enterprises must defray out of their total receipts all their production expenses other than wages, must set aside a prescribed depreciation allowance, must pay their capital and sales taxes, and must make their contributions for a social welfare fund, a business fund (for working capital), and a reserve fund. Out of the remaining "gross income," as the Yugoslavs call it, contributions for social security, communal budgets, and housing are deducted. The remainder, left after these compulsory obligations have been taken care of, constitute the enterprise's "net income." It is this net income which workers can allocate as they see fit for the purpose enumerated above.

The new system of distribution, Yugoslavs proclaim, spells an end to formal wages altogether. Since each worker's income is supposedly no longer a predetermined wage but a share of the enterprise's income, the system is theoretically no longer a wage system but a system under which money is earned and distributed by "an association of free producers united in work who manage the socialized means of production entrusted them." [18] In actual practice, however, workers are paid a kind of wages in the form of advances against future income, and a minimum income is guaranteed, at least for a specified period, even if the enterprises should be losing money. Moreover, since a worker, especially in a larger enterprise, must feel that he is too minute a particle in the organization to influence the total output to any appreciable degree, there has been an increasing tendency to subdivide enterprises into "economic units," or, in other words, self-sufficient depart-

16 The Yugoslav Constitution recognizes four fundamental levels of political jurisdiction, called "social-political communities:" The *commune* ("being the basic social-political community"), the *district* ("to discharge affairs of common concern to two or more communes"), the *republic* (there are six such Republics in Yugoslavia: Serbia, Croatia, Slovenia, Macedonia, Montenegro, and Bosnia-Herzegovina), and the *Federation*. (*The Constitution, op. cit.*, chapter V, pp. 41-51.)

17 Rudolf Bicanic, "Interaction of Microeconomic Decisions in Yugoslavia, 1954-1957," in Gregory Grossman, ed., *Value and Plan* (Berkeley and Los Angeles, University of California Press, 1960), pp. 353-354.

18 Grujic Persida, *Distribution of Total Receipt, of Enterprises and Personal Earnings of Workers* (Belgrade, November, 1960), p. 15.

ments to provide more effective incentives.[19] In the many enterprises where the decentralization of economic decision-making has been carried down to the level of "economic units," it is the unit's rather than the enterprise's net income which provides the pie from which slices are distributed to each worker according to his individual performance, measured on the basis of such factors as output, saving of materials, responsibility of position, difficulty of tasks, working conditions, etc. In order to make this system of distribution according to work all-encompassing, the Yugoslavs have even embarked on the difficult task of starting to pay white-collar workers according to their productivity.[20]

It had been hoped that the workers would distribute the enterprises' incomes wisely, setting aside sufficient sums to replace and expand productive capacity so as not to kill the goose that lays the golden eggs. Experience, however, soon indicated that workers in many enterprises voted themselves increases in take-home pay higher than warranted by increases in productivity, thereby depleting enterprise funds. As a consequence, resolutions and regulations had to be passed in late 1961 and early 1962 which were tantamount to a recentralization of supervision over income distribution.[21] Since then, workers throughout the country have gradually been made to understand the need for continued capital investment, and regulations have been relaxed. However, the problem of correlating nongovernment investment with the investment needs of society as seen by the planners remains one of the but partially solved problems of the Yugoslav economy.

In recent years, discussions and resolutions concerned with the distribution of earnings have concentrated on the following problems: (1) direct versus indirect earnings, (2) the share of national income to be left at the disposal of the enterprise, and (3) the incomes and living standards of Yugoslav workers in general.

Since early 1964, demands for increasing direct, personal earnings (cash) at the expense of indirect social earnings (such as income distributed in the form of collectively owned recreational facilities or infirmaries) have

---

[19] "An economic unit," Mr. Danilo Knezevic explained to this author in the above-mentioned personal interview (*see* footnote 7 above) "is one technologically complete unit which produces a product that can have a price, so that the value of the contribution of each economic unit can be measured. The point is that each unit must be a viable unit, capable of managing its own affairs (including the hiring and firing of its own workers, investments for its own needs, etc.), capable of fulfilling all its obligations to society, which in turn will be able to impose its taxes directly or indirectly upon the economic units. The relationship between economic units will be based on the sale of the products from one economic unit to another."

Economic units can vary in size anywhere from 10 up to 300 workers. (*Borba*, December 8, 1963.)

[20] See, for instance, David Binder, "Yugoslavia Revises Pay of the Office Workers," *New York Times* (February 23, 1964).

[21] *See*, for example, *Review* (Belgrade, January, 1962), p. 4, and (June, 1962), p. 4.

gained momentum. It now has become apparent that these demands are being backed by most Yugoslav economists, labor union leaders, Party functionaries, government officials, and by the public as a whole. By mid-1966 Tito himself defended this emphasis on direct income as Marxist in conception:

I regard income, personal income, as the motive power for a more rapid increase and modernization of the economy, the development of the country, and further progress generally. That is also the way Marxist theory views the question. Marx, for example, analyzes very well the capitalist system and explains that profit contributed greatly to its rapid development. . . . We do not negate this in the first phase of Socialism. The question is merely how the profit is distributed and to whom.[22]

Regarding the enterprises' share in national income, the general trend of Yugoslav thought was well characterized by the admonition of the December, 1964 Party Congress that "changes in the distribution of national income in favor of enterprises are indispensable for the further development of self-government."[23] Actually, the share of national income left at the disposal of enterprises was enhanced several times between 1963 and 1966 by a number of reductions in the tax burden of economic enterprises, by the abolition of the General Investment Fund to which all enterprises had been obligated to contribute, and by an outright increase in the share of net income retained by the enterprises. (Before the "Reform" the "social community" took an average of 60 percent of enterprises' net income; by early 1966 it took only 40 percent, leaving the rest to be used at the discretion of the enterprises for wages, bonuses, investments, etc.) [24]

The voices demanding higher income for Yugoslav workers have been growing ever louder during recent years. Realizing that not the number of dinars but the goods and services workers can buy with their income represents "real" income, the demands for higher earnings and living standards have frequently been coupled with demands for increased production of consumer goods, if need be at the expense of investment outlays. These demands were fully supported by Tito who stated emphatically:

It is not true that they [our workers and experts] must still tighten their belts on the grounds that great sums of money are needed for investments and accumulation. If the worker is unable to consume various products, to buy what he needs, he will not be a good producer. . . . Better living conditions and a higher standard of living will make possible an ever more vigorous economic development.[25]

[22] *Yugoslav Facts and Views* (July 27, 1966).

[23] *Tanjug* (December 12, 1964).

[24] *Komunist* (March 26, 1964); *Borba* (April 20, 1964); Slobodan Stankovic, "Radical Economic Changes Outlined for Yugoslavia," *Research Departments Radio Free Europe* (Yugoslavia, June 22, 1965); Rudolf Bicanic, "Economics of Socialism in a Developed Country," *Foreign Affairs* (July, 1966), pp. 637-638.

[25] Tito, quoted in *Borba* (April 21, 1964).

Efforts to increase the proportion of direct personal earnings, to augment the enterprises' share in national income, and to raise workers' living standards are now all parts of official Party policy in Yugoslavia.

CENTRAL PLANNING VERSUS ECONOMIC DECENTRALIZATION

The regulations laid down from the center have become ever more general during the past few years, but the local political unit, the labor union, and, of course, the local unit of the Communist Party do still exert a considerable degree of influence over enterprise decisions. Yet, it cannot be gainsaid that enterprises have a great deal of independence in planning quantitative output, assortment of goods to be produced, investments, profit participation scales that go with the various jobs, and even prices at which to sell their products (a point to be taken up in greater detail a little later in the paper). But is this approach consistent with Marxist-Leninist ideology? Has not the derogatory term "anarchy of production" been used to describe decentralization of economic planning under capitalism? Was it not central planning which, in communist ideology, was supposed to cure the ills of economic depressions, instability, and unemployment?

Indeed, the "orthodox" interpretation of Marxism-Leninism still maintains that most of the economic decisions in a "socialist society, on its road towards communism," ought to be made at the center. The Yugoslavs, and other East European communist countries who have been following in their footsteps, on the other hand, have come to believe that especially in increasingly complex, industrializing economies there is something to be said for leaving market forces—in other words, the forces of supply and demand —relatively free to exert their influence. Mijalko Todorovic, Yugoslav economist and since the beginning of the Party reorganization in 1966, Secretary of the eleven-man Executive Committee of the CC LCY,[26] expressed the currently predominant Yugoslav view on central planning as follows:

. . . something that the plan, the center of society, the top, the leadership (at various levels) cannot do *alone* without the market, is infallibly to direct the trend of development, the composition of production, constantly and in detail,

[26] Central Committee of the League of Communists of Yugoslavia. By resolution of the Fifth Plenary Meeting of the CC LCY on October 4, 1966, the reorganization of the LCY was started; in mid-1967 (as this book goes to press), it has not yet been completed. Todorovic is President of the Commission for the Reorganization of the League. Prior to October, 1966 he also held the government position of President of the Federal Chamber in the Yugoslav Parliament, i.e., in the Federal Assembly. He no longer can hold this position because the Party Reorganization (aimed at diminishing the decision-making power of the Party) provides that in the future members of the Executive Committee of the CC LCY will not be able to hold government positions. (For more details, *see Yugoslav Facts and Views*, November 7, 1966.)

toward the actual relationships, wishes, interests, wants, etc., of individuals, of the parts and of the whole. The central plan cannot *perceive* the details nor can it effectively influence realization.[27]

The author of the lines above does not, however, advocate a return to a capitalist society where "price is the regulator of the entire process of production." He points out that the plan and planning is "the over-all regulator of the entire process of production" in Yugoslavia, but warns that unless planning "rests on the democratic will, on the desires and wishes of the individual, the parts, and the whole," it merely imposes the wishes of the planners upon the populace and is contrary to the well-being of the people: "The attitude that people, the individual, and the community, do not need what they want and what they think they need but what the planners think they need reflects the conflict between bureaucratic, centralized planning and life's demands, and violation of the latter by the former." [28]

In actual practice, then, Yugoslavia is striving for as much decentralization of economic planning as is compatible with her type of socialism. Yugoslavia's "own road" does entail a central plan but, as one Yugoslav source explains it, "the function of the over-all plan is reduced to setting the basic proportions in production and distribution." [29] In other words, although there is a basic overall plan, as many details as possible are left to individual enterprises to decide. However, should the central planners at any time consider it advisable to intervene, they have the authority, under the Constitution, to suspend the decision-making power of local economic units and to impose their dictates upon them.[30] In this sense, the power to make economic decisions at the local level is still a privilege rather than a constitutionally guaranteed right, and in this respect also the Yugoslav economic system attempts to follow a middle-of-the-road course between the automatically functioning system of "perfect capitalism" (where consumer sovereignty, business competition, and the profit motive exert their powerful influences via a freely determined market price) and the traditional Soviet system of central planning (with its corollaries of physical allocation of inputs and incentive bonuses for plan fulfillment and overfulfillment).

THE PRICE SYSTEM

Progressive Yugoslav economists have long been outspoken in their opinion that market prices, permitted to fluctuate freely, can perform important

---

[27] Mijalko Todorovic, "Some Questions of Our Economic System," *Socialist Thought and Practice* (January, 1963), p. 41.

[28] *Ibid.*, pp. 23, 24, and 43.

[29] "Workers' Management," *op. cit.*, p. 16.

[30] *The Constitution, op. cit.*, esp. Introductory Part, Section III, pp. 6, 7; Article 121, p. 47; and Article 124, pp. 48-49.

economic functions. "The market," wrote one of them (Todorovic) in 1963, "and the corresponding form of economic price, is a *sensitive seismograph* which registers each oscillation around the balancing point between supply and demand. It [the market] is, through a price of this sort, also a *mechanism which automatically* guides new productive forces and accumulation in the right direction."[31] And another, the head of the Institute of International Politics and Economics at Belgrade, explains that through oscillating prices, consumer preferences are registered, and he asserts that to "leave it to the consumer, for whom the production is meant, to assess the value and quality of products by freely showing his preferences . . . is the basic requirement in the humanization of the economic process."[32] However, no matter what the advantages of an economic system based on freely oscillating, market-determined prices might be, they could, and probably often would, register user preferences that are at variance with what the planners consider to be in the best interest of society. (Producers of refrigerators, for instance, might in light of consumer demand bid up the price of relatively scarce steel which the planners might wish to allocate for the production of machines or tractors.) Thus, in regard to price formation also, Yugoslavia is faced with the problem of fitting the economic advantages of a free market into the overall plan of a socialist economy.

"Our free market is a conditional term" said Edward Kardelj, member of the 35-man Presidium of the CC LCY and President of the Federal Assembly. "One must understand that the free formation of prices under our conditions means forming them on the basis of supply and demand within the general proportions of the plan. . . . Of course this does not mean that we should renounce the fixing of prices when important interests of the community are at stake."[33] "Our price system is one of *free prices under social control*," explained the editor-in-chief of Yugoslavia's labor union weekly RAD to this author.[34] And one Yugoslav commentator gave clear evidence of the difficult dualistic position of Yugoslavia by writing in one and the same paragraph: "The free market and the free formation of prices is one of the principles of the [Yugoslav] economic system. . . . It would, of course, be illusory to believe that in any socialist market economy society can renounce its right to interfere in economic and market movements."[35]

Actually, in Yugoslavia today, some prices are set or strictly limited by government decree. Thus, for example, rents are controlled, ceiling prices are placed on some consumer goods in short supply (such as salt), and the

[31] Mijalko Todorovic, *op. cit.*, p. 41.

[32] Janez Stanovnik, "Planning Through the Market," *Foreign Affairs* (January, 1962), p. 254.

[33] *Borba* (March 21, 1961).

[34] Interview with Danilo Knezevic, *op. cit.*

[35] Nikola Pilipovic, "Market and Development Plan in Yugoslavia," *Review of International Affairs* (December 20, 1963), p. 17.

prices of some commodities (especially industrial inputs such as steel or fuels) are centrally determined. At the other extreme there are some prices which are completely uncontrolled, such as the prices at which some individual craftsmen, in business for themselves, sell their wares to their customers. The prices of most industrial goods are "supervised" prices, which means that they are enterprise-determined but the central authorities reserve the right to refuse permission to increase them. In fact, for reasons discussed below, the Yugoslav government deemed it necessary in March, 1965, to declare a temporary "freeze" on most prices.

Eventually, Yugoslavia's goal is a market system, where prices are permitted to fluctuate relatively freely. "The present system of administrative regulation of prices is not suitable for our social and economic relations," proclaimed the Party Central Committee in March, 1966, asking for a "gradual transition to freer market relations."[36] But at that Central Committee Plenum, Tito warned of "disastrous consequences" if prices were to be generally freed, emphasized that the prices of "critical goods and materials" must remain frozen, but advocated that prices of other goods "should be left to form freely," concluding that "frozen prices must be abolished where possible, but firm control must be retained where necessary."[37]

Tito's preoccupation with continued price controls is understandable, for Yugoslavia has, in recent years, experienced such persistent inflationary pressures that in September, 1964 Yugoslavia's National Assembly resolved that "the organs of price control should take energetic and efficient measures to check the unjustified increase of prices."[38] Yugoslavia's economy achieved exceptionally high rates of economic growth, averaging (according to Yugoslav sources) nine percent annually during the decade from 1956 to 1966; but, primarily due to overexpansion of the investment sector, purchasing power greatly exceeded the production costs of goods actually offered for sale with the resulting, inevitable, pressure on prices, rise in the cost of living, and increasing deficit in the balance of payments.[39]

Continuously rising prices would necessarily have had increasingly adverse effects on exports and on the tourist trade, if foreign exchange rates had been maintained. It, therefore, came as no surprise when in late July, 1965 the Yugoslav Parliament established a new parity of the national currency, the dinar, amounting to 0.710937 milligrams of pure gold, which equals a rate of 1,250 dinars per U.S. dollar as compared with the previous

---

[36] "Resolution of the Third Plenum of the Central Committee of the League of Communists of Yugoslavia on Further Implementation of the Economic Reforms, held in Belgrade on February 25, 26, and March 11, 1966," *Yugoslav Facts and Views* (no date), mailed out by the Yugoslav Information Center, New York, in March, 1966, p. 4.

[37] *Yugoslav Facts and Views* (April 6, 1966), p. 5.

[38] *Borba* (September 16, 1964). Radio Zagreb announced on December 15, 1964, that, according to the Yugoslav Bureau of Statistics, the cost of living in November, 1964, was 11 percent higher than in November, 1963.

[39] *Yugoslav News Bulletin* (April 26, 1966).

exchange rate of 750 to 1.[40] Since January 1, 1966, a new dinar, equal in value to one hundred of the old dinars has been put into circulation. (Hence, 12.5 new dinars equal one U.S. dollar.)

Under the impact of inflationary pressures and the devaluation of the dinar, an overall price increase of 24 percent as compared with the 1964 average was decreed in mid-1965; to compensate for this price increase, enterprises, on recommendation of the National Assembly, began to raise workers' and office employees' earnings accordingly, and pensions and other welfare benefits were increased 23 percent by government decree.[41] In January, 1966, in order to compensate savers for the decrease in the value of their savings, the National Bank, on the basis of a Federal law, declared a special interest payment of 23 percent on all savings deposits. On the other hand, to prevent consumers from paying with new, devalued dinars for goods bought at old-dinar prices on credit "in the period immediately preceding the (mid-1965) reform" it was decided to levy an extra 25 percent interest on such consumer credits.[42]

To curb inflation, Tito recommended in January, 1966, that (in addition to the maintenance of price freezes) some capital projects as well as certain deliveries from abroad contracted in connection with such projects be postponed; [43] by May the legal maximum time for repayment of consumer loans was reduced from two and a half to two years, and some consumers' goods such as clothing and footwear were taken off the list of goods that could be purchased on installment.[44]

Thus, the Yugoslav price system, as is the case with other aspects of the Yugoslav economy, steers its way uneasily between a market economy and a centralized economic system. It was surely an oversimplification to say, as some Yugoslav writers did a few years back, that basically each firm sets its own prices, guided only by market conditions, and that government powers to influence selling prices "are utilized only in exceptional cases." [45] But it

[40] *Yugoslav News Bulletin* (July 26, 1965), p. 4. Actually, as of July 1, 1964, authorized Yugoslav banks and exchange offices, by decree of the Yugoslav Executive Council, had started purchasing foreign exchange from tourists and from residents who had acquired it in noncommercial transactions, at a premium of $33\frac{1}{3}$ percent, i.e., 1,000 dinars per dollar (*Borba* [June 27, and July 2, 1965]). And in June, 1965, Yugoslavia's Secretary of Finance, Kiro Gligorov, had revealed that to import raw materials, the government had had to "subsidize" exchange rates for some time, paying an average of 1,055 dinars per dollar (*Politika* [June 11, 1965]).

[41] *Yugoslavia News Bulletin* (July 26, 1965), p. 1. It should be pointed out that these increases were less, percentagewise, than the devaluation. With one dollar, for instance, the purchaser of dinars could obtain $66\frac{2}{3}$ percent more dinars (1,250 instead of 750) than before. When the new 12.5 per dollar dinar was issued, all prices, wages, etc., were of course simply divided by one hundred.

[42] *International Financial News Survey* (February 11, 1966), p. 45.

[43] *Yugoslav News Bulletin* (February 2, 1966).

[44] *Yugoslav News Bulletin* (May 19, 1966), p. 3. Most consumer credit in Yugoslavia is used for the purchase of durables.

[45] Zoltan Biro, *Die Rechtslage der Wirtschaftsunternehmen in Jugoslawien* (Belgrade, June, 1960), p. 10.

would be overstating the case in the opposite direction were one to assert that the market has no influence on price formation in Yugoslavia. Even the rather stringent price controls of late 1965 and early 1966 lacked effectiveness because, as Mijalko Todorovic phrased it, "in practice, through various forms, such as for instance a decline in quality, actually higher prices are formed than those which are thought to be under control." [46] Moreover, according to official Yugoslav sources, prices continued to rise after the introduction of the mid-1965 reform at the rate of one or two percent per month although the prices of 90 percent of all items were "frozen." [47] As of mid-1967, there are indications that a progressive unfreezing of many of the prices instituted in July, 1965, may not be too far off.

INVESTMENT AND BANKING

Before the introduction of decentralization reforms in 1952-53, investment projects were mostly centrally designated and financed on the basis of grants from the proper budgetary sources on approval by the planning authorities. There were either no interest charges, or at most a one percent charge to cover overhead expenses; and "loans" did not have to be repaid. While non-economic investments (such as hospitals, schools, or roads) are still financed out of budgets without provisions for interest or reimbursement, Yugoslavia, in 1953, became the first communist nation to introduce full-fledged interest charges on economic investment credits and to demand that economic enterprises repay loans,[48] thus bringing about increasing requirements that borrowing enterprises meet the tests of economic criteria. Yet, the central authorities continued to exert considerable influence on the general direction of investment credits not only via the national plan but also by prescribing, for instance, a low 2 percent interest rate for loans to agricultural collectives, newspaper publishers, and film producers, while maintaining a minimum 5 percent rate for most other enterprises,[49] and 7 percent for private producers. (The prescribed upper limit on interest rates was 12 percent.)

The decentralization measures of the 1950's thus placed few investment decisions in the hands of enterprises. But in 1964 opposition began to mount against the entire policy under which the lion's share of enterprise earnings was appropriated by one or another level of government which then returned it to the economy to be utilized according to its own plans, and not at the enterprises' discretion. Particularly denounced were so called "political

---

[46] *Radio Zagreb* (March 30, 1966).

[47] *Vjensik u srijedu* (Zagreb, April 13, 1966).

[48] Ljubo Sirc, "State Control and Competition in Yugoslavia," in Margaret Miller and others, *Communist Economy Under Change* (London, Institute of Economic Affairs, 1963), pp. 149-152 *passim.*

[49] Harry Schleicher, *op. cit.,* p. 89.

investments," i.e., investments undertaken for such noneconomic reasons as regional prestige. In April, 1964, Tito himself severely condemned excessive centralization of investment decisions, calling "not normal" a situation whereby, in 1963, "of a total of 1,500 billion dinars of investments . . . economic organizations as bodies which earn money should have only 30 percent at their disposal. . . ." And Tito proclaimed it "the duty of us who are at the highest level to put things right." [50] To "put things right" steps were undertaken, as discussed above, which included the abolition of the General Investment Fund and a great increase in the part of net earnings to be retained by the economic enterprises. Other investment funds of the Federation, the Constituent Republics, and the Communes have been cut back (since a smaller portion of enterprise income has been going to the various levels of government)—an achievement which, in the late summer of 1966, was acclaimed by Yugoslavia's Secretary of Finance, Kiro Glivorov, as a "decisive step toward extending the economic foundations of self-government and . . . cutting the roots of statism." [51] Another step aimed at "putting things right" was the enactment of new banking legislation, to be discussed below.

In the area of banking, the most significant trend has been the proliferation of local banking institutions. The pre-1952 era was a period of transition from capitalist to socialist banking. From 1952 to 1955, one single bank with its 463 branches carried on banking operations throughout Yugoslavia. During the latter half of the 1950's three other specialized federal banks were established (The Investment Bank, the Agricultural Bank, and the Bank for Foreign Trade), and banking was decentralized, primarily by the establishment of hundreds of communal banks. In 1961 the communal banks became the basic credit institutions maintaining direct business contact with all economic and noneconomic entities in their territories. The National Bank, on the other hand, withdrew from direct business contacts with local organizations, and became primarily a central banking institution.[52] Since, however, the communal banks were dependent upon credit extended to them by the National Bank, the latter was able to exert considerable influence over the policies of the former. Banking decentralization, to the extent to which it took place, was primarily on a regional basis, with the local *political* units gaining in influence.

Under new banking legislation, enacted in the spring of 1965, authorization was granted for the establishment of investment banks (mainly to

[50] *Politika* (April 21, 1964).
[51] *Yugoslav News Bulletin* (August 18, 1966), p. 3.
[52] Unless otherwise indicated, the information on investment and banking contained in the preceding three paragraphs has been extracted from Milos Vuckovic, "The Recent Development of the Money and Banking System of Yugoslavia," *The Journal of Political Economy* (August, 1963), pp. 363-377, and from George Macesich, *Yugoslavia: The Theory and Practice of Development Planning* (Charlottesville, Virginia, 1964), Chapters 8 and 10.

provide investment credits for fixed assets and permanent working capital), commercial banks (primarily to provide short-term credit to economic enterprises and long-term credits for housing and other community needs, and, secondarily, to assist in the long term financing of fixed assets) and savings banks (primarily for consumer credits).[53]

Under the new "Law on Banks and Credits" banks are independent commercial institutions and can be set up by 25 or more founders, consisting of economic units and socio-political communities. (A savings bank could be founded by a single socio-political unit.) The funds which these banks will have authority to lend out will come primarily from the deposits by economic units and socio-political communities, and control will apparently be in the hands of the depositors, with voting power proportionate to the size of deposits. At this stage of development, however, the political units have considerably more funds at their disposal than the economic enterprises. Since the declared purpose of the proposed banking reform is to free investment decisions from political control, a provision has been incorporated into the law, limiting a single organization to ten percent of the total votes controlling bank policies. As time goes on, economic enterprises, no longer required to make such substantial "contributions" to political units as previously, are expected to increase their deposits and gain a preponderant voice in the management of the banks. Although this would presumably place the large enterprises in a more favorable position, a stipulation which entitles enterprises to place their funds in any bank of their choice adds an additional feature of a decentralized, competitive banking system, preventing, as it were, banks from taking any depositor for granted.

The intent of the banking reform was well stated during the period of preliminary discussions by *Borba*: ". . . instead of the political forums, the producers [would] become the dominant power which, free of administrative measures and planning at will, [would] exert a healthy influence on the whole of our economic policy."[54] Yet, there was never any doubt that the bill in its final form would contain some measures which would assure that control over investments by the center is not completely surrendered. "The central bank does not intend to become a retired old lady of Belgrade's version of Threadneedle Street," said the London *Economist*,[55] and a recent Yugoslav publication defines the primary purpose of a bank in socialist Yugoslavia as follows: "The basic task of a bank is to satisfy the needs of organizations and to enable them to realize their plans *so long as these do not run counter to the interest of our society*"[56] (which, in turn, is presumably de-

---

[53] For a detailed discussion of Yugoslavia's new banking legislation, *see* H. Trend, "Modernizing Yugoslavia's Banking System," *Research Departments of Radio Free Europe, Bloc* (June 21, 1965).

[54] *Borba* (October 31, 1964).

[55] *The Economist* (December 31, 1964).

[56] *Privedni Vjesnik* (November 19, 1964). Italics mine.

cided by the general, national plan). Indeed, the Yugoslav regime has now established a more versatile central bank, the National Bank of Yugoslavia,[57] responsible only to the Federal Assembly and the Federal Executive Council, and charged with supervising the nation's credit policy in order to assure stable development, liquidity in foreign payments, and control over commercial bank policy. To this end the central bank was given broad powers, including such monetary controls as the right to change reserve requirements of commercial banks on their demand deposits and the right to grant or not to grant short-term credit to banks. Apart from such "quantitative" monetary controls, the National Bank was also given the "qualitative" control to lay down general criteria for credit worthiness of applicants, thereby enabling the central bank to influence the flow of investment funds by altering criteria for various branches of the economy. Finally, upon Yugoslavia's National Bank was also bestowed the exclusive right to issue money and it was charged with the supervision of all financial activities with foreign countries[58] and with the duties of a fiscal agent for the federal government, i.e., the collection and the disbursement of funds.

By the creation of independent commercial banks, by weaning the commercial banking system from local political control, by converting the Yugoslav Investment Bank in January, 1966, into an autonomous bank to be managed by its major depositors, thus freeing it from central control,[59] and by establishing a central bank which can exert influence on credit extension and on the economy, but primarily by indirect monetary policy, Yugoslavia has scored another first among East European countries in the direction of a diminished centralization of economic power and decision-making.

FOREIGN TRADE

To Yugoslavia, foreign trade is of great importance since, in the words of the new Secretary of the Party Central Committee's Executive Committee, "We are such a small producing community that in no case can we provide a full assortment and quantity of goods if we do not integrate much more decisively into the world market."[60] Thus, although her exports total already

---

[57] "Law on the National Bank of Yugoslavia," *Official Gazette of the SFRY,* No. 12 (1965).

[58] For a recent curtailment of the National Bank's powers in regard to transactions involving foreign exchange, *see* p. 242 below.

[59] Entitled to take part in the management of the bank are enterprises depositing 3,750,000 new dinars (12.5 dinars per U.S. dollar) for at least three years, or 3,125,000 new dinars for periods exceeding five years. The Bank was founded by the Federation, the banks of all six Republics and of two provinces, and by a number of leading enterprises and trade associations. (*Yugoslav News Bulletin* [February 2, 1966], p. 4.)

[60] Remarks by Mijalko Todorovic, reported in *Borba* (March 31, 1966).

approximately 12 percent of her national output,[61] Yugoslavia's aim is to increase her foreign trade.[62]

Until 1966, foreign trade, and especially the disposition of foreign currency earned in foreign trade transactions, was in Yugoslavia—as it still is in all other communist countries—under rather strict control from the center, so that Yugoslavs were not free to convert their dinars into foreign currencies at will. But here too, liberalization measures have been introduced. In the early spring of 1966, the Party Central Committee stated unequivocally that the development and stabilization of the economy should lead, "as soon as possible" to the convertibility of the dinar, and once convertibility has been achieved, foreign exchange "should in its entirety belong to the economic organization" which earned it, to be retained in a foreign exchange account, or sold to any commercial bank or to the National Bank at the discretion of that economic organization.[63] Mjlako Todorovic defined such convertibility as meaning "that every person who possesses a dinar has the right to go to the National Bank at any moment and convert that dinar into any convertible currency or, if he wishes, into gold" (note that not even American citizens in their country are allowed to own blocks of refined gold without a license from the Treasury Department, and are greatly restricted in their right to hold gold in monetary form), and he pointed out that Yugoslavs would then be able to buy goods wherever they were cheapest and, on the other hand, would strive to sell goods anywhere on the globe, wherever they would bring the best price, so that "rational world division of labor would be effected by the action and decisions of every individual economic corporation, and every individual enterprise would be based on sound economic considerations."[64] In the summer of 1966, the Yugoslav Parliament (Federal Assembly) adopted a series of laws aimed at the gradual implementation of such a new foreign exchange system, effective as of January 1, 1967. Under the new system, the number of dollars at the free disposition of Yugoslav enterprises, for instance, was tripled for 1967 as compared with 1966 (240 versus 88 million dollars),[65] foreign exchange quotas for specific types of goods, including some consumers' goods, were greatly liberalized,[66] and the National Bank lost its function of custodian

[61] *Yugoslav News Bulletin* (April 26, 1966), p. 5.

[62] Yugoslavia's foreign trade is highly concentrated, with Europe accounting regularly for about 70 percent of total exports and imports, West Europe being as important to her in this respect as the communist countries of East Europe. Yugoslavia's development from a predominantly agricultural to a rapidly industrializing nation shows up in the changing pattern of her exports. At the beginning of 1950, agricultural products and raw materials accounted for 50 percent of her exports; by 1966, 70 percent of her exports consisted of industrial products. *Ibid.*, pp. 4 and 5.

[63] *Borba* (March 13, 1966).

[64] *Politika* (April 30 and May 1 and 2), single issue.

[65] The details were published in *Borba* (June 17, 1966), prior to official passage of the law, once it had been approved by the Federal and the Economic Chambers of the Federal Assembly.

[66] *Tanjug* dispatch (July 14, 1966).

of foreign currencies since enterprises can now leave them with any of the large number of newly established commercial banks. In September, 1966 it was announced that in 1967 almost half of Yugoslavia's usual imports would be exempt from any restrictions, and that as of January 1 of that year, Yugoslav enterprises have the right to arrange independently for foreign credit for their requirements.[67] Thus, although the Yugoslavs are still hampered by "current hard currency difficulties," even usually fairly critical Western observers agree that "the increase in the freedom of enterprises to engage in foreign trade activities is in keeping with the recent and forthcoming changes in the Yugoslav system of economic management which are designed to loosen the hold of the remnants of the old bureaucratic and 'etatistic' system." [68]

REMNANTS OF CAPITALISM?

Collective ownership and operation of the means of production is the alpha and omega of socialist ideology. Yet, there are areas in Yugoslav economic life where private ownership and operation of productive capacity has either not been abolished or has been reintroduced.[69] Yugoslav peasant families have the legal right to own and operate for their own profit farms up to 25 acres in size (and in some special cases even larger ones), and although collective ownership of farm machinery, collective marketing of crops, etc., is quite usual, the fact remains that upward of 85 percent of Yugsolavia's farmland is in private hands.[70] (Tito pointed out in mid-1966 that the movement of many young people to the cities has made it difficult for many of their aging parents to continue cultivating their own land. But even in these cases, the private farmers have the opportunity to either sell or rent their land to collectives or state farms—a practice quite unthinkable in other communist countries.)[71] Private craftsmen in business for themselves have continued to operate their small shops since precommunist days; one out of

[67] *Tanjug* (September 22 and 26, 1966).

[68] Harry Trend (Economic Consultant, Radio Free Europe/Munich), "The New Yugoslav Foreign Trade System," *Research Departments of Radio Free Europe, Yugoslavia: Trade* (July 18, 1966).

[69] Seventy-five percent of Yugoslavia's total output is at present produced by its socialist sector, according to Lothar Schultz, "Der sowjetische Begriff des Revisionismus und das Jugoslawische Verfassungsrecht," *Recht in Ost und West* (January 15, 1964), p. 6. The official Soviet paper *Pravda* gives a figure of 76 percent of total social product and 75 percent of national income accounted for by Yugoslavia's public sector in 1961 (*Pravda,* February 10, 1963, p. 2).

[70] It is generally held in the West that about 85 to 90 percent of Yugoslavia's farmland is still privately owned (Lothar Schultz, *op. cit.,* p. 6, for instance gives the figure as 88 percent) and official Yugoslav statements confirm this estimate; 87 percent, for example, was the figure given on February 6, 1966, over Radio Zagreb by Dr. Kreshimir Pazhura, Chief of the Economic Department of the Agricultural Institute in Zagreb.

[71] *Yugoslav Facts and News* (July 27, 1966), p. 4.

every four trucks in Yugoslavia is privately owned, yielding the owner an estimated average income of $4,000 annually, and Slovenia now permits individuals to own up to three trucks;[72] since 1964 Yugoslav homeowners have been encouraged by liberal tax provisions and low-interest state loans to rent rooms to tourists, to establish wine cellars and snack bars for tourists in their private homes along the Adriatic coast, and to open small restaurants or rent state-owned ones to operate for private profit, and under a new "Basic Law on Domestic Trade" which became effective on March 1, 1967, some individuals are allowed to operate such facilities as mobile bookstalls, flower shops, and waste-collecting enterprises; and marketing agencies may lease small shops to private individuals to be operated independently by them.[73] Moreover, agreements for the production of Fiat and Citroen cars in Yugoslavia were reached with the foreign manufacturers in 1964, and the opening of a Volkswagen factory is tentatively scheduled for late 1968.[74] Lottery tickets are sold in Belgrade on street corners, in stores, and by peddlers in restaurants; and tips (considered by many Marxist ideologists a disgraceful remnant of the master-servant relationship prevailing during the presocialist era) are accepted by hotel and restaurant employees throughout the country.[75]

Marxist-Leninists explain that during the "capitalist era of history" it is inevitable that the private owners of the means of production hire workers and that part of the product produced by the latter is appropriated by the former in the form of rent, interest, or profit. This, to Marxist-Leninists, is the very essence of the capitalist mode of production. But once the capitalist order has been overthrown and the workers, under the leadership of the Communist Party, have taken over the means of production as well as the apparatus of government, the "exploitation of man by man" must be ended once and for all. Attempts of private individuals to continue "to extract surplus value out of the labor of others" have therefore been considered an extremely severe violation of socialist morality in countries of the "socialist camp," from Moscow to Peking. Yet, even on this aspect of a market economy, we find the Yugoslavs hedging and compromising, apparently for the sake of greater efficiency and increased output.

The new Constitution appears somewhat contradictory on the issue. Article 22 states:

No one shall employ the work of others to gain income. Subject to the restrictions

---

[72] *Borba* (February 15, 1964).

[73] *Borba* (May 16 and 21, 1964). *Vjesnik* (Zagreb, September 24, 1964). Harry Trend, "Yugoslavia's Domestic Trade Statute Becomes Law," *Research Department, Radio Free Europe, Yugoslavia: Domestic Trade,* March 1, 1967.

[74] *Tanjug* (March 11, 1967).

[75] The last two points are reported here from personal observation during a recent trip to Yugoslavia.

and conditions determined by law, the work of other persons may be employed in agricultural production, the handicraft trades and in other services or similar activities carried on by citizens with their own means of work.[76]

In actual practice, Yugoslavs who not merely own but also themselves operate their own businesses are now permitted, in some instances, to hire a very small number of employees.[77] Moreover, many Yugoslav firms have recently made serious attempts to enlist American capital in their plans for industrial expansion.[78] Although Yugoslav law does not permit foreigners to share in the "ownership" of Yugoslav industry, there is apparently nothing that prohibits participation in profits, or even governmental guarantees of foreign loans. In any case, such American business firms and investors as the Howard Johnson motel chain, the Pepsi-Cola Company, a "group of Texas oilmen," and even a "group of gambling casino operators from Las Vegas, Nevada," were reportedly willing, as early as the spring of 1965, to extend credit to the tune of tens of millions of dollars for the expansion of Yugoslavia's tourist trade;[79] as of the summer of 1966, Pepsi-Cola is being sold in Yugoslavia under a ten-year agreement which stipulates that the concentrate of the drink be furnished by the New York Pepsi-Cola plant while bottles, caps, and selling operations will be taken care of by the Yugoslavs,[80] and in September, 1966, the Yugoslav travel agency "PUTNIK" appeared to be completing negotiations with an American company for the construction of two large hotels on the Adriatic Coast.[81] Important as these concessions to private production may be, they are, however, still a far cry from a free enterprise system.

[76] *The Constitution, etc., op. cit.,* p. 13.

[77] In the spring of 1965, Slovenia, for instance, put into practice a private catering law which permits the employment of up to three workers besides members of the operating family. *Delo* (Ljuljana, April 1, 1965). Under the March 1, 1967 "Basic Law on Domestic Trade," private individuals who have leased small shops from marketing agencies may employ up to three persons. (Harry Trend, "Yugoslav Domestic . . ." etc., *op. cit.*)

[78] *International Commerce* (December 7, 1964). This U.S. Department of Commerce publication lists 33 offers by Yugoslav firms to "collaborate" with U.S. firms. Here is one example, an offer made by Interexport, Belgrade, as published in the above-mentioned magazine:

Manufacturing enterprise is interested in joint venture with U.S. firm for processing and marketing textile products. The firm would like to obtain shipments of raw cotton from a U.S. firm, process this cotton into finished fabrics and cooperate with the U.S. firm in marketing these products in third markets.

Other offers involve the production and marketing of a wide variety of products, including petroleum and petrochemical products, household appliances, leather products, cigarettes, steel rolls, cement, fiberglass boats and trailers, and many others.

[79] *Vjesnik* (Zagreb, March 14, 1965).

[80] *Politika* (December 27, 1965, and April 27, 1966).

[81] *Yugoslav News Bulletin* (September 13, 1966), p. 81.

FREEDOM, DEMOCRACY, AND THE DIMINISHING INFLUENCE OF THE CONSERVATIVES

It was probably inevitable that economic decentralization and liberalization with its emphasis on personal interest would be reflected in a certain degree of ideological, political, and cultural liberalization. Thus, economic reform in Yugoslavia found itself expressed also in a "humanization" of the system as a whole. "Socialism," proclaims the Program of the League of Communists of Yugoslavia, "cannot subordinate the personal happiness of the individual to any 'higher aims,' since the highest aim of socialism is the personal happiness of man." [82] Edvard Kardelj expressed the same view when he said: "We have . . . striven to make man . . . the essence of our entire system." [83]

"If you compare Yugoslavia with the United States, you could not call it a 'free' land," commented an official at the U.S. consulate in Zagreb to this author. "But," he continued, "Yugoslavia is far ahead of the other East European countries." Indeed, there is evidence in Yugoslavia of a degree of freedom that Westerners do not usually associate with life in a communist country. This author has found most Western papers including the *New York Times,* the *London Times,* and the West German *Die Zeit* prominently featured in hotel lobbies and at newsstands in major Yugoslav cities; he has seen a multitude of British, American, French, and West German films advertised in Belgrade motion picture theaters; he has listened to jazz, boogie-woogie, French chansonettes, and a theme from "Exodus" over Yugoslav radio stations or resounding from Wurlitzer juke boxes in Yugoslav restaurants; he has had an opportunity to observe young Yugoslav boys and girls dancing the most modern ballroom dances; and he has attended an exhibition that included the most abstract conglomeration of "pop" art paintings and sculptures he has ever come across.

Yugoslav workers are free to change jobs, many Yugoslav students study, and about 300,000 Yugoslav workers work in Western countries [84] (in West Germany alone there were more than fifty thousand in 1964),[85] and while

[82] Quoted in *Komunist* (August 8, 1963).

[83] *Review of International Affairs* (April 20, 1963), p. 20.

[84] *Borba* (January 1, 1966) reported "more than 200,000" in Western Europe, *Politika* (January 30, 1966), 250,000 "abroad"; *U.S. News and World Report* (June 20, 1966), 250,000 in "capitalist countries"; Radio Free Europe "about 300,000" in the West by early 1967 (*Research Departments, Radio Free Europe, Yugoslavia: Labor, Economics, Foreign Relations,* February 13, 1967); and Yugoslav sources foresaw the possibility of the figure reaching 400,000 by the end of 1967. (*Yugoslav Trade Union,* Belgrade, February, 1967, cited in *ibid.*)

[85] *Der Spiegel* (October 7, 1964) gave a figure of 53,057 Yugoslav workers employed in West Germany.

permits for such stays abroad are required, there are no mine fields, barbed wire fences, or "walls" to be noted along Yugoslav frontiers. Workers' strikes in socialist countries were recently defended in a Yugoslav newspaper article as a justifiable struggle waged by workers to protect their constitutional rights against violation by individuals or groups.[86] In an agreement unprecedented in the Communist World, diplomatic relations were resumed between Yugoslavia and the Vatican, and extensive rights and freedoms for religious communities in general and for the Catholic Church in particular were spelled out as the official stand of the Yugoslav government.[87] Yugoslavia's labor unions dared to reject the 1965 Economic Plan after it had been approved by the Party Congress,[88] and it actually became necessary to draft twelve different versions of the 1965 Plan.[89] In the selection of candidates to be presented to the Yugoslav electorate on election day, the Communist Party still plays a significant role, but according to amendments to the new, 1964, Electoral Law more than one candidate will henceforth be permitted to compete publicly for votes in nationwide elections,[90] and in April, 1965, two candidates on the average—and in elections two years later, four—competed for each of the more than 22,000 vacant seats in Yugoslavia's communal, city, provincial, Republican, and Federal assemblies.[91] In a 1965 article, a Zagreb professor spelled out clearly what Yugoslav intellectuals have been implying for some time, i.e., that even Marx himself is not above criticism.[92] And ever more statements have been forthcoming recently by top officials in the Party and the Government to the effect that the Party itself must relinquish its commanding position in Yugoslavia, must henceforth assume merely an educational role, and will in time "wither away" as Marx had predicted the state would.[93]

[86] *Vjesnik u srijedu* (Zagreb, June 8, 1966).

[87] "Protocol on the Talks Between Representatives of the Government of the Socialist Federal Republic of Yugoslavia and Representatives of the Holy See, Signed in Belgrade, June 25, 1966," *Yugoslav Facts and Views*, (no date), mailed out by the Yugoslav Information Center in New York in August, 1966.

[88] *Politika* (December 18, 1964).

[89] The twelfth version was finally adopted by the Yugoslav National Assembly after "the most extensive discussion ever on any of Yugoslavia's economic plans," according to Nicola Mincev, Director General of Yugoslavia's Federal Institute for Economic Planning (*Vjesnik* [January 26, 1965]).

[90] For a detailed discussion of present election procedures in Yugoslavia and of changes expected to result from the recent amendments to the Electoral Law, see Slobodan Stankovic, "Liberalization of Yugoslav Election Law," *Radio Free Europe, Research, Communist Area, Yugoslavia* (November 25, 1964).

[91] Slobodan Stankovic, "The Second Phase of Yugoslav Elections Closed," *Research Departments, Radio Free Europe, Yugoslavia* (April 5, 1965); *UPI* (April 9, 1967).

[92] Professor Danco Grlic wrote: "A faithful adherence to whatever has once been proclaimed true is nothing but a substitute for practical impotence. . . . This is the reason why it is absurd to insist, in Marx's name, persistently and in detail, on everything that Marx ever and on any occasion said or wrote." *Praxis, Zagreb,* No. 1, International edition [for January, February, and March, 1965], p. 52).

[93] Mijalko Todorovic, for instance, declared that the Party executive bodies must be deprived "from top to bottom, of state functions," and that the Party in Yugoslavia

Thus, the Yugoslavs seem to have come to accept one of the fundamental philosophies of Milovan Djilas [94] who wrote more than a decade ago: "There is and can be no other solution than more democracy, more free discussion, more free elections to social, State, and economic organs." [95]

The trends in the direction of enhanced economic decentralization and political and cultural liberalization have continued over the years with but brief, occasional setbacks. [96] The VIII Party Congress that met in late 1964

---

should "play only a leading ideological role," (*Politika* [holiday issue dated April 30, May 1, 1966]); Edvard Kardelj, advocated for Yugoslavia neither a one-party nor a multi-party system, but what he called a "non-party system" (reported in *Welt am Sonntag* [Hamburg, July 10, 1966]), a proposal made previously in official Yugoslav publications (*see*, for example, Alesandar Petkovic, "The Socialist Alliance—a Form of Self-Management," Socialist Thought and Practice [January/March, 1965], p. 88).

[94] Milovan Djilas, from 1941 to 1955 a member of Tito's innermost circle, held such high positions as Chairman of Yugoslavia's Communist Party, Vice President of the Republic, and President of the National Assembly, Yugoslavia's Parliament. Fearless in his criticism of what he thought wrong, he was sentenced to prison four times, first in 1954 for interviews granted to the *New York Times* and the *London Times* in which he demanded more freedom of discussion; the second time in 1956 for an article published in the U.S. weekly *The New Leader,* in which he praised the Hungarian revolution; again in 1957 for his book *The New Class,* his most famous criticism of the Communist system, written in jail and published abroad; and the last time in 1962 for another book entitled *Conversations with Stalin.* In that last case he was accused of having disclosed confidential data he had learned as a member of an official Yugoslav delegation, of having embellished and distorted the data, and of having thereby aggravated the cold war and discredited the Yugoslav socialist system. With over four years of his last eight year and eight month sentence still to go, Djilas was released from prison on December 31, 1966.

[95] *Borba* (December 20, 1953).

[96] A recent example of such a setback, illustrating the difficulty of eradicating completely the thought-control patterns of the past, is the case of Mihajlo Mihajlov lecturer at the Zadar Philosophical Faculty, who published a critical travelogue on the Soviet Union, entitled "Moscow, Summer, 1964," in the January and February, 1965, issues of the Belgrade literary monthly *Delo.* Mihajlov was widely attacked, even by President Tito in person, and his published defense that he considered Yugoslavia "the most democratic" of the socialist countries, and that he felt "greater respect toward the Soviet people than toward the Soviet regime" (letter to the editor, published in *Nin* [Belgrade, February 28, 1965], and cited in the *New York Times* [March 12, 1965]) did not help matters. Mihajlov was arrested (*Komunist* [Belgrade, March 4, 1965]), indicted for "having belittled and scorned the Soviet Union" (*Borba* [Belgrade, March 27, 1965]), suspended from his job (*Narodni list,* Zadar, No. 702 [March 13, 1965]), and sentenced on April 30, 1965, to ten months imprisonment (Slobodan Stankovic, "Intellectual Uproar in Yugoslavia," *Research Departments of Radio Free Europe, Yugoslavia* [June 1, 1965]). On appeal, the Supreme Court of Yugoslavia reversed the verdict of the lower court (itself a remarkable step, under the circumstances), but gave him a five-month suspended sentence for having published a banned article. When Mihajlov published a new series of articles, this time abroad, attacking the Yugoslav system, he was rearrested and, on September 23, 1966, sentenced to nine months imprisonment (plus three months of his previous suspended sentence) by the Zadar District Court (*Yugoslav News Bulletin* [September 24, 1966], p. 7). In April, 1967, Mihajlov was sentenced to another four and a half years for having spread hostile propaganda in three 1966 articles, and for having misrepresented political and social conditions in Yugoslavia, with the intention of bringing about an unconstitutional change of government. (*AP,* April 17 and April 19, 1967.)

pushed Yugoslav society further along the same path, drawing attention to the "need to ensure a freer influence of the market, adopting the position that enterprises should be more independent in disposing of investment funds," declaring itself in favor of "full freedom of scientific and artistic creativity," stressing that the "democratic battle of opinion is indispensable for the development of socialist relations," demanding the "consistent implementation of the principle of rotation and restriction of re-election" in public office, etc.[97] Such was the atmosphere at that the Congress that the correspondent of Radio Free Europe commented that to many delegations from other Communist countries "it must have been heady stuff, especially the complete freedom of expression, freedom of complaint and criticism, without fear of discipline."[98]

Although the liberals were not in uncontested control at the Congress,[99] there seemed to be strong indications that the conservative elements were incapable of stemming the trend towards liberalization in the economic sphere of Yugoslav life, nor the tide of political and cultural liberalization that appears to be accompanying it. This view was strengthened when truly liberal reforms (discussed elsewhere in this paper) were adopted by the Central Committee Plenum in the summer of 1965. But although all present paid at least lip service to the resolutions of the Plenum, it soon became apparent that the conservatives still had enough power to put substantial stumbling blocks in the way of implementation of the reforms.

At the Party Central Committee meeting on July 1, 1966, the showdown came. In his opening address, Tito attacked the "factional group" that had stood in the way of implementation of the Party line on economic and social reforms. He placed the blame primarily upon the state security service and upon the "conservative resistance of some officials." Singled out as the leader of the conservative faction (and long recognized as such by many Western observers)[100] was a man who, until then, had been Tito's heir apparent—Aleksandar Rankovic, Vice President of the State, Secretary of the Party Central Committee, and (together with Svetislav Stafanovic) head of the State Security Service. Although Rankovic was permitted to defend himself, he was in short order shorn of all his Party

[97] *Tanjug* (December 13, 1964), reporting on the final resolutions of the VIII Yugoslav Party Congress.

[98] *RFE Special* by telex/Mahoney (December 13, 1964).

[99] Rejected, for instance, was the proposal that the self-government system be made a leading principle in Party life; in other words, the proposal that Party units at lower levels (such as the district or the Republic levels) be given a great degree of independence in regard to policy formation. As early as two months before the VIII Congress met, opponents referred to this proposal as "but one more attempt to introduce 'through the back door' the multiparty system" (*Vjesnik u srijedu* [Zagreb, September 16, 1964]).

[100] Slobodan Stankovic of Radio Free Europe/Munich, for instance, wrote in January, 1966, that Rankovic "for many years has been known as the top conservative leader in the Yugoslav Party" ("Yugoslavia's Theory and Practice at the Turn of the Year," *Research Departments, Radio Free Europe, Yugoslavia: Internal Affairs* [January 19, 1966]).

and government posts [101] and at the Fifth Plenum of the LCY in early October, 1966, he was expelled from the Party.[102] Although soon thereafter, the demand for Rankovic's expulsion from the Party was backed also by the Central Committee of the small Yugoslav Constituent Republic of Montenegro,[103] the Party has not taken such action as of the end of October, 1966.

Informed Western observers, as well as most Yugoslavs, have heralded Rankovic's ouster from Party and government offices as "definitely a move leading to greater liberalization and democratization both in the Party and state." [104]

HOW SOCIALISTIC IS YUGOSLAVIA'S "OWN ROAD TO SOCIALISM"?

The Yugoslav position. The extent to which Yugoslavia's system is socialist or, more precisely, Marxist-Leninist in nature is one of the major points of dispute among Communists of various ideological shadings. Each group (pro-Soviet, pro-Chinese, Trotzkyist, or otherwise) appears convinced that it alone has found the "correct" interpretation of Marxism-Leninism and knows the "correct" path for reaching the proclaimed goal (a classless society of abundance for all); usually each group is also able to back up its contentions with quotations from the writings of Marx, Engels, and Lenin. The Yugoslavs, however, insist that the problem is not one of "correctly" interpreting Marxism-Leninism. Since socialism, they proclaim, "never appears anywhere in its 'pure' form," each country needs to find its own road contingent on its own specific conditions.[105] Yugoslavia wants all to know that she has found her "independent road, a road not traced after a foreign model," a road which, however, "does not appeal to those who are still slaves of dogma, and whose conception of proper socialism is restricted to their own narrow borders." [106]

The Chinese view. The Chinese Communists assert that workers' self-

---

[101] *Yugoslav Facts and Views* (July 14, 1966), contains the minutes of the Central Committee session, including Tito's address, Rankovic's defense statements, and the final resolutions which included the acceptance of Rankovic's resignation from Party posts, the expulsion of Stefanovic from his Party post, and a recommendation that Rankovic resign from the Vice-Presidency also.

[102] *Tanjug,* October 4, 1966.

[103] *Yugoslav News Bulletin* (September 24, 1966).

[104] Slobodan Stankovic, "Yugoslavia Before and After the Purge of Aleksandar Rankovic—Part I," *Research Departments, Radio Free Europe/Yugoslavia, Internal Affairs* (July 7, 1966).

[105] Edvard Kardelj, *Socialism and War* (Belgrade, Publishing House Jugoslavija, no date—probably 1961), pp. 202-203.

[106] "Two Decades of Socialist Yugoslavia," *Review of International Affairs* (December 5, 1963), p. 2.

management in and of itself is anti-socialist in nature [107] and that in Yugoslavia, moreover, there is no real workers' self-management but rather workers' exploitation by the Tito group, "the running dogs of U.S. imperialism." [108]

The Chinese, presumably the most dogmatic followers of Marxist-Leninist ideology, warn that the development of society from capitalism, via the "dictatorship of the proletariat," to communism is by no means a certainty. On the contrary, lest care be taken, a backward sliding towards capitalism is quite possible. In the case of Yugoslavia, they charge, the "Tito clique" has betrayed the cause of international communism and has actually restored capitalism. The restoration of capitalism in Yugoslavia manifests itself, according to Chinese interpretation, in many aspects of the Yugoslav economy, such as "the abandonment of unified economic planning by the state, . . . the use of profit as the primary incentive in the operation of enterprises, . . . the policy of encouraging capitalist free competition, . . . the use of credit and the banks as important levers to promote capitalist free competition," etc.[109] China also charges Yugoslavia with encouraging private enterprise in the cities ("There are 115,000 privately owned craft establishments in Yugoslavia. . . . The Tito clique admits that . . . some . . . employ 'five to six hundred workers,' " [110]) and with "expropriation of poor peasants and promotion of capitalist farms . . . in the sphere of agriculture." [111] Even worse, Yugoslavia has become a "dependency of U.S. imperialism, . . . a market for imperialist dumping, . . . an outlet for imperialist investment, . . . a base from which imperialism extracts raw materials, . . ." and the dictatorship of the proletariat has degenerated into "the dictatorship of the bourgeoisie." [112]

And for the Soviets the Chinese have this warning:

Out of our warm love for the great Soviet Union and the great C.P.S.U. [Communist Party of the Soviet Union], we would like sincerely to appeal to the leaders of the C.P.S.U.: Comrades and friends! Do not follow the Yugoslav road. Turn back at once or it will be too late! [113]

[107] They quote Lenin to prove their point:

Any direct or indirect legalization of the possession of their own production by the workers of individual factories or individual professions or of their right to weaken or impede the decrees of the state power is the greatest distortion of the basic principles of Soviet power and the complete renunciation of socialism (quoted from V. I. Lenin's *On the Democracy and Socialist Character of the Soviet Power,* in "Is Yugoslavia a Socialist Country?" translated in *Peking Review* [September 27, 1963], p. 19. The *Peking Review,* published in Peking, consists of translations from the two major Chinese papers, the *People's Daily* and the *Red Flag*).

[108] "What the New Yugoslav Constitution Means," *Peking Review* (May 17, 1963), p. 12.

[109] "Is Yugoslavia, etc.," *op. cit.,* p. 19.

[110] *Ibid.,* p. 16; the source given for the statement is one that dates back more than a decade, i.e., M. Todorovic, "The Struggle on Two Fronts," *Nasha Stvarnost* (March, 1954).

[111] *Ibid.,* p. 18.

[112] *Ibid.,* pp. 20-21.

[113] *Peking Review* (September 27, 1963), p. 27.

The Soviet view. The 1948 split between the Soviet Union and Yugoslavia was by no means healed by Stalin's death or by Khrushchev's de-Stalinization policies. In an off-the-cuff speech in Prague on November 11, 1957, Khrushchev (more lenient than Stalin, to be sure, but still showing mild hostility) addressed himself to the Yugoslavs: "You like your workers' councils," he said, "so keep them, and do not interfere with us, with our organizational forms. We shall not criticize you, and you do not poke your noses into our business." [114] After a new, rather liberal, Party Program had been adopted by the VII Yugoslav Party Congress in April, 1958, the Soviets renewed their vituperative attacks on the Yugoslav system and its leaders. The new Party Program was termed a "flood of antiscientific, non-Marxist reasoning" [115] and at the XXI Soviet Party Congress early in 1959 Khrushchev condemned the "Yugoslav revisionists" for "denying the necessity of international class solidarity and . . . leaving the position of the working class." [116] The following year, a statement adopted unanimously by the Moscow conference of 81 Communist and Workers' parties called the program of the League of Communists of Yugoslavia "anti-Leninist revisionist," accused the Yugoslav leadership of "betraying Marxism-Leninism" and charged that "the Yugoslav revisionists carry on subversive work against the socialist camp and the world Communist movement." [117] As late as April, 1961, the international Communist journal *Problems of Peace and Socialism* (published in Prague and representative of the Soviet Party position) contained such defamatory statements as:

The voices from Belgrade sound in unison with the chorus of bourgeois Erinyes, [furies] cursing the international Communist movement.

The leaders of the Yugoslav League of Communists . . . have fallen as low as it is possible to fall—they have descended to outright anti-Communism and slander.[118]

In a less harsh-sounding but hardly more conciliatory mood, the Program of the Communist Party of the Soviet Union, adopted by the XXII Soviet Party Congress on October 31, 1961, granted that Yugoslavia "took the socialist path," but charged that "the Yugoslav leaders by their revisionist policy contraposed Yugoslavia to the socialist camp and the international Communist movement, thus threatening the loss of the revolutionary gains of the Yugoslav people." [119]

[114] Quoted in "Khrushchev on Yugoslav Workers' Councils," *Radio Free Europe/Munich, Non-Target Area Analysis Department, Background Information Yugoslavia* (August 22, 1963), p. 3.
[115] *Komunist* (April, 1958).
[116] *Radio Moscow* (January 28, 1959).
[117] Cited in "What the New Yugoslav Constitution Means," *op. cit.*, p. 13.
[118] A. M. Martz, "Whither the Logic of Revisionism Leads," *Problems of Peace and Socialism* (April, 1961), pp. 85 and 88.
[119] *Programme of the Communist Party of the Soviet Union* (Moscow, Foreign Languages Publishing House, 1961), p. 20.

By 1962, undoubtedly under the influence of the Sino-Soviet split, the Soviet position had begun to change. At the November, 1962, Soviet Party Central Committee Plenum, Khrushchev talked about the need to "extend and deepen the democratic principles of the management of enterprises," and recommended enterprise production committees, elected by the workers, as advisory bodies [120]—a step in the direction of, but still a far cry from, the Yugoslav workers' councils. By early 1963, the Soviets were placing the "major share of the blame" for the deterioration of the relations between Yugoslavia's Communist Party on the one hand and the international communist movement (including the Communist Party of the Soviet Union) on the other upon the shoulders of Stalin, declaring nevertheless that "measures recently taken by the leadership of the League of Communists of Yugoslavia in the areas of Party life, economics and domestic and foreign policy have corrected much that the international Communist movement considered erroneous and harmful to the cause of building socialism in Yugoslavia." [121] In the late summer of 1963, Khrushchev visited Yugoslavia. He observed Yugoslav workers' councils in action and, while expressing fears that they "did not guarantee that the 'unity of leadership' was sufficient" he still hailed them as "progressive and modern." [122]

The new leaders of the Soviet Union, in power after Khrushchev's "voluntary resignation," appear to be following in his footsteps, accepting Yugoslavia as a member of the socialist camp, without extolling (nor actually rebuffing) the "Yugoslav road to socialism" as an example to be followed by other socialist countries. If anything, the friendship between Yugoslavia and the Soviet Union has become stronger since Kosygin and Brezhnev came to power. But Yugoslavia's declared intention to reduce the functions of the Party and to restrict them increasingly to the sphere of ideology has met with criticism in the U.S.S.R. A February, 1967, article in *Pravda* called such a step "completely inadmissible and harmful to the cause of socialism." [123]

An "independent socialist view." The attitude of Communist Parties in the noncommunist countries *vis-à-vis* Yugoslavia depends upon their particular ideological orientation. For instance Indonesia's Communists, loyal disciples of Mao that they were, were no less fierce in their condemnation of the "Tito clique" than the Chinese, while Italy's Communist Party looks by no means unfavorably upon the "Yugoslav road to socialism." As to unaffiliated Marxists, it is a safe bet that the overwhelming majority (surely of those residing in the West) are rather sympathetic towards Yugoslavia's system of "creative Marxism." A notable and interesting example of a minority view is that held by the well-known Western Marxists Paul M.

[120] "Khrushchev on Yugoslav Workers Councils," *op. cit.,* pp. 1 and 2.
[121] *Pravda* (February 10, 1964).
[122] *London Times* (August 22, 1963).
[123] *Pravda* (February 20, 1967).

Sweezy and Leo Huberman, co-editors of the "independent social maga-zine" *Monthly Review,* published in New York. Although in a fairly re-cent issue of the *Monthly Review* they have taken the position that the Chinese Communists are right "on the basic issues in their dispute with the Soviet leaders," [124] they are as disapprobatory of the Chinese views on Yugoslavia as they are fearful of socialism in that country. They grant that Yugoslavia "is still a socialist country," but see Yugoslav socialism as "de-generating" in "certain important and even decisive respects." They charge that the Chinese endeavor to prove that capitalism has been restored in Yugo-slavia is "both unconvincing and un-Marxist—a disappointing performance from beginning to end," [125] but they do not deny that the process of transi-tion from capitalism to socialism can be reversed (in this respect "our analysis supports the Chinese view"). At the conclusion of their detailed argumen-tation, the editors of the *Monthly Review* have these words of caution for the Yugoslavs: "Beware of the market; it is capitalism's secret weapon! Com-prehensive planning is the heart and core of genuine socialism!" [126]

What do non-Marxists say? To most non-Marxists the ideological "cor-rectness" or "incorrectness" of the "Yugoslav road" (measured by Marxist-Leninist standards) is of relatively little concern. They do not dig through the voluminous writings of the "founding fathers" to find passages which "prove" or "disprove" the ideological purity of the Yugoslav approach. In-stead, they look at the system as it is, analyze its various aspects, pass judg-ment on its accomplishments and shortcomings, and attempts to predict its future development without great concentration on the somewhat semantic question of whether Yugoslavia's reformist measures are "revisionism" or "creative Marxism." When, however, Western non-Marxist observers do touch upon the problem, they frequently tend to agree with the "dog-matists" in the communist camp, referring to the Yugoslav system as a deviation from, if not a complete negation of, Marxism. Non-Marxists have commented that the Yugoslavs "are surprisingly unhampered by Marxist ideology," [127] that "of all the communist nations, Yugoslavia has strayed fastest and farthest from the well-beaten path of orthodox Marxism," [128]

---

[124] *Monthly Review* (October, 1963), p. 304.

[125] "Peaceful Transition from Socialism to Capitalism?" *Monthly Review* (March, 1964), pp. 577, 578. The article, although unsigned, is the editorial lead article of the issue.

[126] *Ibid.,* p. 588. It should be pointed out that the editors of *Monthly Review* do not maintain that production for profit or market relations could be dispensed with immedi-ately or even in the near future in a socialist society. But they *are* arguing that "produc-tion for profit must be systematically discouraged and rapidly reduced to the smallest possible compass, and that market relations must be strictly supervised and controlled lest, like a metastasizing cancer, they get out of hand and fatally undermine the health of the socialist body politic" (*Loc. cit.*).

[127] John Fischer, "Yugoslavia's Flirtation with Free Enterprise," Part II, *op. cit.,* p. 12.

[128] Yarick Blumenfeld, "Report on Yugoslavia," *Newsweek* (December 28, 1964).

and that the Yugoslav system "can no longer properly be called Marxist."[129] While the three Western authors quoted above could perhaps quote chapter and verse to prove their point of view, so undoubtedly could such liberal-minded Yugoslav theoreticians as Jovan Rajcevic, who alleges that Yugoslav Communists are certainly Marxists, who "have accepted Marxism not as a dogma, but rather as a guide for action."[130] In any case, there can be no doubt that the Yugoslavs have been giving, and are apparently continuing to give, a new, more pragmatic and infinitely more liberal interpretation to Marxism-Leninism than has been given hitherto in any other communist country.

A prevalent image of Yugoslav communism in the minds of many Western observers is reflected in such comments as the one made recently by Slobodan Stankovic who heads the Yugoslav desk at Radio Free Europe/Munich:

While other Communist regimes gave the people they rule military parades at which the most modern weapons were displayed as a May 1st (1966) gift, Tito's gift to the Yugoslavs for the May Day celebration was to start selling Pepsi Cola produced in Yugoslavia under American license.[131]

SUMMARY AND CONCLUSION

Yugoslavia's "own road to socialism" represents an attempt to combine aspects of capitalism, socialism, and communism into a unique system in which the economic advantages of a limited market economy are to be realized without altogether surrendering national planning or the social ownership of the means of production, and in which the desirable features inherent in political and cultural freedom are to be built into a new interpretation of Marxism-Leninism without entirely relinquishing "democratic centralism" and the one-party system. There is little doubt that in economic, political, and cultural liberalization, Yugoslavia is years ahead of any of the other communist countries, but the apparent evolution towards an economically decentralized and politically and culturally open society is still circumscribed by the system of the past from which the new order is emanating. Thus ever increasing powers over the production of goods and the distribution of income have been bestowed upon the local producing units (which, presumably, are primarily motivated by the forces of a relatively free market), but the central planners prescribe the general direction of the economy, and they have retained sufficient power to prevent local decisions

[129] Ernst Halperin, *op. cit.*, p. 50.
[130] *Komunist* (August 8, 1963).
[131] Slobodan Stankovic, "Sofia Loren vs. Karl Marx: Pepsi-Cola vs. Slivovitz," *Research Departments, Radio Free Europe/Yugoslavia: Economics* (May 12, 1966).

from deviating too much from the overall plan; the July 1965 reforms went further than any previous ones in legislating economic liberalization, but even a communist commentator could not fail to observe that whatever successes the Yugoslav economy could show during the year following the passage of the sweeping reforms were "achieved within a system of temporary measures of a generally administrative nature (price ceilings, strictly controlled foreign trade and allotment of foreign currencies, etc.) and thus were not the result of the employment of the new economic instruments and conditions;"[132] recent banking legislation has greatly diminished central supervision over investment funds, but Tito stated in early 1967 that he did not know of a single bank that has completely adapted itself to the intentions of the Economic Reform."[133] Rotation in office is now provided for in Yugoslav elections from workers' councils to the highest bodies in the governmental and Party hierarchy, but President Tito was re-elected at the VIII Party Congress in December, 1964 by the unanimous vote of all 1,432 delegates as Secretary General of the Yugoslav League of Communists, a position he has held for more than a quarter of a century; and when the position of Secretary General of the LCY was abolished in October, 1966, Tito was elected—again unanimously—to the newly created position of President of the LCY; under a new law, two or more candidates are able to compete for elective offices, and did so for the first time effectively in the spring of 1965, but it is understood that no anti-Marxist candidates will be running; Djilas was freed after several years in prison, but Mihajlov was sentenced and imprisoned;[134] finally, to give one more example, free discussion has been encouraged and the new Party Statutes adopted at the VIII Party Congress give every Party member the right to criticize not only any other Party member but even any Party leader and functionary—but the first open criticism of Tito tolerated in the spirit of true freedom of speech has yet to come.

In order to eliminate the contradictions between central planning and the dictates of the market, it is necessary, Yugoslavs maintain, that the tasks of planning be clearly defined and that the instruments be determined "through which society will consciously influence the market and prevent the market mechanism from impeding the implementation of the economic plans." The "market" is used as a guide primarily because Yugoslavs appear to have become convinced that at least at this stage of economic development the "material interest of the producers in achieving the best possible effect on the market tends to assure the optimum utilization of the productive capacities." To assure the fulfillment of the national plan, Yugoslavs now believe, does not require the abolition of the market but, rather, "the conscious regulation of the market within the limits of market laws,

---

[132] Alojz Volf, "The Yugoslav Reform—Successes and Problems," *Predvoj* (Czechoslovakia, July 7, 1966).

[133] *Yugoslav Facts and Views* (January 17, 1967), p. 11.

[134] *See* footnote 96, p. 248 above.

namely the regulation of supply and demand *primarily by economic instruments."* [135] Rather than to dictate the details of production from the center, the Yugoslav government—to achieve the objectives of the National Plan— has thus begun to guide a freer (although by no means free) market via monetary and fiscal policies many of which are similar in nature to those utilized in modern Western capitalist nations.

The Yugoslavs are the first to admit that their system is as yet "neither perfect nor complete." [136] At times they blame some of its shortcomings on such undeniable deficiencies as the still existing shortage of trained managerial personnel; [137] but, over the less and less vociferous objections of the remaining dyed-in-the-wool dogmatists, the Yugoslavs appear to be seeking their solutions in greater liberalization, economic and political, and to be charging remaining shortcomings primarily to the slowness of progress in this direction. "The current system, despite all advantages and results achieved in it, seems as if it had been stopped half way, suffering from the state-oriented forms of economy," charged economic theoretician Jovan Rajcevic in a 1964 article in *Komunist;* [138] "the granting of freedom in 'little spoonfuls'" warned Vladimir Bakaric, Secretary of the League of Communists of Croatia, "does not make possible a proper solution;" [139] Tito, in his opening speech to the VIII Party Congress on December 7, 1964, insisted that the "negative phenomena" in Yugoslavia would disappear if the basic principles of the Yugoslav Party Program adopted at the VII Party Congress in 1958 (a program which was termed "out-and-out revisionist" by other Communist Parties, including the Communist Party of the Soviet Union) would only be properly implemented; [140] in 1965 the Party Central Committee came out more strongly than ever before in favor of a "radical reduction of direct state intervention," [141] and the mid-1966 purge of leading conservatives is evidence that Tito and his liberal followers "have finally come to realize that it is impossible to have liberal measures implemented while dogmatic leaders continue to command the Party apparatus." [142]

The Yugoslavs have begun—pragmatically and realistically—to superimpose some of the institutions and policies hitherto associated with a market economy and with a democratic form of government upon the eco-

[135] Leon Gerskovic, *Social and Economic Systems in Yugoslavia* (Belgrade, Publishing House Jugoslavija, no date, probably 1962), pp. 48-50. Italics mine.

[136] See, for instance, Jovan Djordjevic, "Basic Characteristics of the New Constitution of the Socialist Federal Republic of Yugoslavia," *Two Decades of Socialist Yugoslavia* (Belgrade, 1964), p. 38.

[137] *See,* for example, *Borba* (September 16, 1964).

[138] (May 7, 1964.)

[139] *Ekonomska Politika* (October 10, 1964).

[140] Slobodan Stankovic, "Tito Speech at the Eighth Party Congress in Belgrade," *Radio Free Europe, Research, Communist Area, Yugoslavia* (December 7, 1964).

[141] *Borba* (June 18, 1965); *Politika* (June 18, 1965).

[142] Slobodan Stankovic, "After the First Session of the Third Plenum of the Yugoslav Central Committee," *Research Departments, Radio Free Europe, Yugoslavia: Party Economics* (February 28, 1966).

nomic foundation of a primarily socialist economy and upon the political structure of a one-party system. Reforms along these lines are likely, in the opinion of this author, to enhance economic efficiency and eventually to lead to a better and happier life for Yugoslavia's inhabitants, but the initial steps have not yet solved all the problems which remain as a legacy of economic underdevelopment and a command-economy past. These initial steps, as a matter of fact, have necessarily added some problems of their own (such as, for instance, the previously discussed difficulties connected with letting inexperienced workers decide how much of their enterprise's income should be reinvested). Thus, the Yugoslavs have not—or at least not yet— "succeeded in blending the principles of free enterprise and collective ownership," as one observer asserted they had as far back as 1958.[143] On the other hand, the overwhelming majority of qualified Western observers who, in one way or another, maintain that the present trends are irreversible [144] are undoubtedly correct, although this author would want to qualify their statements by adding barring unforeseen circumstances, such as a major war or a series of major, natural catastrophes. How rapidly and how completely the present programs and resolutions will be implemented; how many new ones along present lines will be introduced, adopted, and put into effect in the foreseeable future; and how far the changes in the direction of present trends will eventually go seems impossible to predict. In any case, Yugoslavia's system represents, in the words of the authors of one of the most comprehensive studies on Yugoslavia's workers' councils, "a new alloy whose durability only the future can show but whose originality and interest can hardly be denied, even today." [145]

[143] Elis Hastad, "Types of Nationalized Industry," Paper delivered at the International Political Science Association (Rome, September 17, 1958). Quoted in George W. Hoffman and Fred Warner Neal, *op. cit.*, p. 240.

[144] For example: "The economic and social structure which has evolved in the past decade is now so thoroughly committed on all sides to further decentralization of economic decision making, that the trend may well be irreversible," wrote Albert Waterson (*Planning in Yugoslavia, Organization and Implementation*, The Johns Hopkins Press, Baltimore, 1962, p. 91); "In any case, the present trend of events cannot be stopped," commented Slobodan Stankovic ("Yugoslav Plenum Adapts Party to Workers' Self-Management System," *Radio Free Europe/Munich, Non-Target Communist Area Analysis Department, Background Information, Yugoslavia* [March 17, 1964], p. 71); "The genie is out; nobody, including Tito, could now stuff it back into a Soviet bottle" concluded John Fischer ("Yugoslavia's Flirtation with Free Enterprise," Part II, *op. cit.*, p. 15).

[145] *Workers' Management in Yugoslavia, op. cit.*, p. 39.

FURTHER READING SUGGESTIONS

Bicanic, Rudolf, "Economics of Socialism in a Developed Country," *Foreign Affairs* (July, 1966).

Fisher, Jack, *Yugoslavia—A Multinational State*. San Francisco: Chandler Publishing Co., 1966.

Fleming, J. Marcus, and Victor R. Sertic, "The Yugoslav Economic System," *International Monetary Fund, Staff Papers* (July, 1962), pp. 202-225.

Friedmann, Wolfgang, "Freedom and Planning in Yugoslavia's Economic System," *Slavic Review* (December, 1966), pp. 630-640.

Hoffman, George W., and Fred Warner Neal, *Yugoslavia and the New Communism*. New York: Twentieth Century Fund, 1962.

Macesich, George, *Yugoslavia: The Theory and Practice of Development Planning*. Charlottesville, Va.: The University of Virginia Press, 1964.

Pejovich, Svetozar, *The Market-Planned Economy of Yugoslavia*. Minneapolis: University of Minnesota Press, 1965.

Tornquist, David, *Look East, Look West: The Socialist Adventure in Yugoslavia*. New York: Macmillan, 1966.

Workers' Management in Yugoslavia. Geneva: International Labour Office, 1962.

8

Yugoslavia: A Yugoslav
Marxist View

MILOS SAMARDŽIJA

PROFESSOR OF POLITICAL ECONOMY
UNIVERSITY OF BELGRADE

RADOSLAV RATKOVIĆ *

HEAD, DEPARTMENT OF SOCIOLOGY
HIGHER SCHOOL OF POLITICAL SCIENCE, BELGRADE

TERRITORY AND NATURAL RESOURCES

There are very few European countries with such large geographic, cultural, and economic differences as Yugoslavia. In terms of size, its area of 255,000 square kilometers (somewhat less than 100,000 square miles) places Yugoslavia among middle-sized countries. It is located in Southeastern Europe and occupies mainly the northwestern part of the Balkan peninsula.

Yugoslavia extends along the shores of the Adriatic. It is narrow and small, and has elements of oceanic and subtropical climate and vegetation. Almost two-thirds of the entire territory is surrounded by a mountain range with a continental climate and with modest possibilities for the development of agricultural production. The economically most developed parts of the territory are in the north and northeast. Geographically, this region consists predominantly of the southern parts of the Panonian lowlands which are crossed by the Danube, the Sava, the Drava, and the Tisa rivers. On this territory, the land is used almost to a maximum. About 90 percent of the total area is productive land. Approximately 60 percent (about 15 mil-

* This contribution has been written especially for this book.

lion hectares) is devoted to agriculture, and around 30 percent is forested. Agricultural lands are extensively farmed, since almost 50 percent of these lands are pastures and grazing lands. About 8 million hectares (1 hectare = 2.5 acres) are plowlands. The possibilities for their expansion are very small. What is more, due to powerful erosive forces which threaten about half of these 8 million hectares, one of the basic aims of agricultural policy is the preservation of the existing plowland area. Today three-fourths of these lands are used for grains. Compared to the structure inherited in 1945, this represents a significant change in the direction of intensification of agricultural production.

With respect to energy sources, Yugoslavia is unusually rich in waterpower. According to generally accepted estimates, its full exploitation would lead to a yearly production of about 66 billion kilowatt-hours. As of now, one-eighth of this capacity is used; the yearly production of hydroelectric energy is about 8 billion kilowatt-hours. In addition to waterpower, Yugoslavia has large quantities of coal, but of low caloric content—90 percent of its coal reserves are composed of lignite. These reserves represent a significant source of thermoelectric energy. The importance of electric energy is increased by the fact that Yugoslavia's natural reserves of oil and high calorie coal are very small. In 1965, Yugoslavia's yearly production of petroleum rose to its maximum of somewhat more than 2 million tons, whereas the production of hard coal has for years stagnated at 1.2 million tons.

Among the mineral resources, nonferrous metals must be singled out. Copper, aluminum, zinc, and lead are available in such large quantities that in terms of this economic branch, Yugoslavia is one of the wealthiest countries in Europe. On the other hand, the possibilities for the development of ferrous metallurgy are very small. With 1.1 million tons of iron ore and 1.8 million tons of steel, Yugoslavia's domestic production still fails to meet national needs. The balance sheets of iron ore reserves show, however, that ferrous metallurgy can be developed so as to cover national needs. There is a wealth of natural resources in the branch of nonmetals; these reserves make possible, in particular, a developed industrial production of cement and sintermagnesite.

POPULATION

Almost twenty million people live in Yugoslavia today [mid-1967], averaging 77 inhabitants per square kilometer (about 200 per square mile). The growth rate of the Yugoslav population is one of the highest in Europe. Even though this rate was unusually low in 1965, it was still 1.2 percent. The main sources of the demographic increase are the economically underdeveloped regions of Yugoslavia, which have natural rates of increase of about 3 percent. Such a high rate of natural increase, coupled with almost insignificant emigration, leads to quick growth of the population. In the postwar period, population increased by about 4 million inhabitants. (In 1947 there were 15.7 million inhabitants; in 1965, 19.5 million.)

The economic development of the country has led to quick changes in the economic composition of the population. In 1939, 75 percent of the population derived their livelihood from agriculture. After the war the percentage fell rapidly. According to the 1961 Census, the agricultural population made up 50 percent of the total population in that census year, and it is even less than that today. There was actually an absolute decrease in agricultural population, numbering 10.6 million in 1948 and 9.3 million in 1961. These changes show that between 1947 and 1965 a profound demographic revolution took place, since the number of urban inhabitants doubled, or in absolute terms rose by over 5 million people. Such an accelerated increase of urban population was possible because of an effective policy of accelerated economic development which was manifested in a large increase of the labor force in nonagricultural branches, particularly in the socialist sector.[1] Immediately after liberation, in 1945, the number of workers employed in the socialist sector was 417,000; this number has since increased by over 3 million, and today it is over 3.7 million. A particularly rapid increase in employment has taken place in industrial production, which today involves more than 1.4 million workers.

This expansion of employment had to be accompanied by quick changes in the educational system. Mass illiteracy was a leftover from the past. In 1953, 25 percent of the population was still illiterate. The expansion of free schooling has decreased the illiteracy among the younger generation (between 10 and 20) to about 5 percent. The result of this system of elementary schooling is that 95 percent of the children between the ages of 7 and 11 receive basic schooling. In the age groups between 11 and 15, this figure is 50 percent. About 30 percent of the adolescents between 15 and 19 receive secondary schooling. In terms of the present labor force, the share of unskilled and semiskilled workers is 55 percent.

Ethnically, the majority of Yugoslavs (about 90 percent) belong to five Southern Slav nationalities, namely Serbs (42.2 percent), Croats (23.1 percent), Slovenes (8.6 percent), Macedonians (5.6 percent), and Montenegrins (2.8 percent), and to ethnically undetermined groups of Moslem Jugoslavs (5.2 percent). Among the national minorities (about 10 percent of the population) the most numerous are Albanians (4.9 percent) and Hungarians (2.7 percent).

---

[1] The socialist sector consists of economic enterprises which are not privately owned. [EDITOR'S NOTE]

HISTORICAL SURVEY

The geographic environment to a large extent conditioned the peculiar historical development of certain Southern-Slav peoples who settled on the Balkan peninsula in the seventh century. Because of the powerful influence exerted by the Byzantine Empire throughout the Middle Ages, these peoples lived without any real possibilities for creating a unified political community.[2] Practically all Yugoslav peoples entered the modern era as politically dependent communities. They lived within the confines of the Turkish Empire (in the eastern and southern regions) and within the Austro–Hungarian political federation (in the northern and western regions). Except for Serbia and Montenegro, they did not have independent communities even in the nineteenth century. Through the development of bourgeois society and the idea of nationalism in the nineteenth centuries, both of which had powerful influences on European nations, a movement for political independence came into being among the Southern Slavs as well. The movement for political and cultural unification developed in particular among those Southern Slavs who lived within the confines of the Austro–Hungarian monarchy.

The disintegration of the Turkish Empire and the Austro–Hungarian Monarchy led, right after the first world war, to the creation of a unified state of Southern Slavs (at the end of 1918). Though formally unified, the new nation contained all of the inherited heterogeneities; cultural, national, religious, and social. From the moment of liberation these led to resistance against a centralized and unified state apparatus in which the Serbian bourgeoisie played the dominant role. The entire period to the outbreak of the Second World War was full of national and social conflicts and antagonisms that made impossible the political stabilization of the new state, which in fact was under a dictatorship from 1929 to 1941. The only factor which really stood for integration of the Yugoslav community—an integration which would be organized on the basis of cultural and national autonomy, a federal government and the construction of nonexploitative social relations—was the Communist Party of Yugoslavia (CPY), outlawed as a political party as early as 1920.

The critical years after the outbreak of the Second World War led, after brief military resistance in April, 1941, to the complete collapse of the Yugoslav political and national community. Under conditions of occupation, political and social disorder, pogroms, and fascist terror, the Communist Party of Yugoslavia began a national liberation struggle (in July, 1941)

[2] The word "community," in this article, is frequently used in the sense of a political entity, sometimes referring to the local, sometimes to the Republic (State), sometimes to the national level. *See also* "the political system," p. 279, below. [EDITOR'S NOTE]

shortly after the Royal Army capitulated. The entire period until 1945 was a period of gradual and continuing strengthening of the liberation struggle and the social influence of the Communist Party of Yugoslavia. The political body representing the revolutionary and the liberation forces, the Yugoslav Anti-fascist Council for National Liberation, was founded at the end of 1942. At its second session, on November 29, 1943, in Jajce, on the liberated territory,[3] this body's resolutions established the basis for the organization of the new Yugoslavia. It was then decided that, due to its national heterogeneity, the new state had to be based on federal principles. With respect to the social organization of the new community, principles characteristic of socialist societies were already dominant by that period. These principles were legally formulated in the first socialist constitution of Yugoslavia, adopted on January 31, 1946.

In the first years after the liberation of the country, Yugoslav society was organized under the powerful ideological influence of the Soviet Union. However, the specific historical features of Yugoslav society required new solutions and new forms, and not a simple transplantation of Soviet solutions. Thus the question of the specificity of Yugoslavia's road to socialism, and especially the question of Yugoslavia's economic and political independence, led to disagreement with the Soviet party and government which was definitively manifested in the Cominform Resolution of 1948, in which Yugoslav communists were labelled renegades and their party was expelled from the Cominform. Political and economic pressure followed the break. Thus from 1948 until 1953, Yugoslavia was subjected to a blockade by the members of the Warsaw Pact.

In spite of its difficult situation Yugoslavia held out, because its social revolution had been indigenous and because through it were created mass political organizations, a new powerful army, a new state apparatus, and, in particular, firm bonds between the population and the political leadership headed by Marshal Tito. In June, 1950, the system of workers' management was introduced, and the constitutional law of 1953 created new economic and social organizations consistent with the principles of workers' management. After the 1955 visit of N. S. Khrushchev, relations with the U.S.S.R. were normalized. This normalization was based on principles of national and political independence and noninterference in internal problems, as well as on specific ways and methods for constructing socialism.

All these internal and international changes were given their corresponding theoretical expression in the spring of 1958 at the VII Congress of the Yugoslav League of Communists. The League's new program was adopted at the Congress. This program represents a further step in the construction of socialist relations in Yugoslavia. The ratification of the new Yugoslav Constitution in the spring of 1963 may be viewed as the closing of the first

---

[3] Territory under partisan (Yugoslav resistance forces) control. [EDITOR'S NOTE]

stage of the construction of a socialist society in Yugoslavia, a society based on self-management. The implementation of the constitution's principles is the basic problem of the present stage in the construction of the Yugoslav socialist community.

BASIC PRINCIPLES IN THE ORGANIZATION OF ECONOMIC LIFE

As regards the institutional aspect of the Yugoslav economy, it must be stressed that until 1950 it had the basic features of "state socialism." In concrete terms this meant (1) the elimination of private forms of owner- ship and management by means of nationalization of all sectors except agriculture and handicrafts, (2) the creation of state socialist property in the nationalized economic sectors and the organization of a state apparatus for the management of the economy, (3) planned management of the economy with expressed centralistic, statist market plans not based on the operation of market forces, (4) an organization of the distribution of the social product which conformed to the centralistic and statist organization of economic management, and (5) the introduction of cooperative forms of organization within the nonnationalized economic sectors.

A series of legal acts, in addition to the 1946 Constitution, institu- tionalized these principles into the legal system of the country. With respect to nationalization it should be pointed out that it was largely carried out through measures of confiscation of war gains, since a large number of enterprise owners had actively cooperated with the fascist occupiers. With the nationalization laws of 1946 and 1948, all economic branches except agriculture and handicrafts were nationalized. Capitalist forms of manage- ment were eliminated from agriculture by the Agrarian Reform of 1945, which limited peasant holdings to a maximum of 30 hectares, and non- agricultural holdings to 3 hectares. In 1953, the maximum agrarian peasant holding was reduced to 10 hectares. In the period after the war, co-operatives similar to Soviet kolkhozes were organized in agriculture, but the entire project was abandoned in 1953, and agricultural cooperation as well as the relationship of peasants to socialist institutions in general was based on new principles and given new forms (general agricultural co-operatives and so- cialist cooperation between co-operatives and private peasants).

The organized state management of the economy led to the creation of a powerful bureaucratic apparatus which continued to gain strength until 1950. The causes for this have to be sought in the level of economic development, in the relationships of social forces, in the historic, cultural and other backgrounds inherited at the time of the outbreak of the revolu- tion, and also in the international position of the new socialist community after the victorious revolution.

A socialist revolution concerns itself first of all with the problem of gaining political power. The political victory of socialist forces manifested itself in the construction of a socialist state organization which had all the important characteristics of state organizations in general: centralism, political coercion against the overthrown class enemy, bureaucratism. In the first moments after the victory of the revolution this type of organization was indispensable for the creation of social conditions necessary for the construction of socialist relations. In later periods the strengthening of the social power, influence and organization of the producer[4] has led to processes in which the political (state) forms have begun to disappear and the self-managing organizations of working people have grown stronger. However, this type of social development has not been general for all socialist societies. This is in fact characteristic of the Yugoslav road to socialism.

In 1950, a new stage in the construction of the Yugoslav economic system began. That year was the beginning of the construction of the institutional structure which is often referred to in the literature as the Yugoslav road to socialism. In June of that year a law on the management of economic enterprises by the workers was passed. Thus began a new organization of management in enterprises as well as a reorganization of the state apparatus. The goal was to weaken the state's influence on economic life (the theory of the withering away of the state under socialism) and to develop self-management in the economy (the theory of the producer and worker as the basic social force for socialist construction). The implementation of the law led to changes in the methods and forms of managing the economy. During the period until 1951, the central state plan was the basic instrument for organizing the economy. When the tasks of the first years of the five-year plan of 1947 to 1951 were realized, the material basis for the development of economic and social organizations of self-managing producers was laid, and the process whereby the enterprise could grow out of a state organization and into a self-managed organization was initiated.

The nationalized production stocks were transferred to the management of workers' collectives, and the socialist principle of "giving the factories to the workers" was realized in practice. The enterprise became the basic economic organization in which the function of management was taken over by the workers themselves, who execute their control through elected bodies, namely workers' councils and managing boards. The independence of the workers in the organization of their enterprises is evidenced by their right and their competence to make decisions regarding production, distribution, and the use of investment funds. Material goods are no longer assigned to enterprises according to allocation plans determined by the state apparatus. Under the new system based on self-management, the enterprises make their own independent decisions regarding the purchases of

---

[4] "Producer," in this context, means worker. [EDITOR'S NOTE]

inputs and the disposal of their productive outputs. Out of the income realized from the sale of their products, the enterprises set aside one part, through the distribution of their funds, which will enable them to operate independently, to develop the initiative of the working collective, to stimulate individual producers to increase the productivity of labor and thus to increase the quantity of goods produced and to extend the material basis of their self-management.[5]

The autonomous workers' organizations which are managed directly by the workers themselves or indirectly through their representative organs (workers' councils) are integrated through various ties.

First of all, economic ties express themselves through a complex of relations characteristic of market economies. Hence, the system of nonmarket planning has been abandoned and processes have made their appearance in which new forms of social planning are sought under conditions where socialist commodity production exists and develops.[6]

A second type of bond is based on technological and functional relations, vertical as well as horizontal, through which the enterprises are related to each other in various forms of associations, combinations, and integrated concerns. This type of integration process is particularly intensive in the contemporary Yugoslav economy. In this type of integration, it is crucial that the bonds be based on democratic, and not on hierarchic types of interrelations, that is to say, integration must be carried on for economic motives rather than being imposed by administrative decisions.

Finally, the third type of bond is the relationship between economic organizations and the political organizations of the community. The basic form of this political and territorial interrelation is the commune ("opstina"), which in its content and its methods represents a democratic form of local self-management. That's why the communal system together with workers' self-management is treated as one of the basic characteristics of the institutional structure of the Yugoslav economic system. The commune is a form of political power, but it is also a form of self-managed organization. This is manifest not only in the present content and work methods of the commune, but also in the organizational structure: the communal parliament has two houses—the commune council as the classical political body and the council of workers' communities as a form of social self-management of working people. Forms of integration based on these principles of "social self-management" (to differentiate it from self-management in workers' collectives[7]) also cover higher levels of political and territorial organization

---

[5] This refers to the parts of enterprise income set aside for investments and for incentive payments. [EDITOR'S NOTE]

[6] This refers to the Yugoslav economic model in which market forces are used extensively within the framework of a socialist economy. [EDITOR'S NOTE]

[7] This refers to the entire labor force of an economic unit, such as an enterprise. [EDITOR'S NOTE]

of the Yugoslav federation, namely the levels of the autonomous region, the socialist republic and the entire federation.[8]

In short, instead of building a hierarchically organized society, Yugoslavia is building and developing a wide association of working people in which, through democratic forms of interaction, the cardinal and central position of the producer, i.e., the worker, is becoming increasingly dominant.

CHARACTERISTICS OF THE SOCIAL ORGANIZATION OF LABOR

Special forms of social organization of labor correspond to the new institutional structure of Yugoslavia's socialist society. First of all, in the working organization the worker increasingly becomes the organizer of the production process; he is transformed into a self-manager. In this is manifested the real content of the social process which socialist theory knows as the process of liberation of labor, or more precisely as the process through which the worker's position as a hired laborer is eliminated.

The autonomy of the basic economic units, the enterprises, is the social basis on which market relations in Yugoslavia develop. For a long time socialist theory treated commodity[9] economy as the opposite of socialist economy. It was held that commodity production was characteristic of the capitalist economy and that the elimination of capitalist economic relations would automatically lead to the elimination of market relations. This concept was given its practical application in the policy of "war communism."[10] The concept had to be abandoned because the development of the economy and of economic relations showed that the negative attitude toward commodity production had a utopian character. In spite of inadequate theoretical analysis and explanation, commodity production has in practice been increasingly affirmed in the economic life of organized socialist communities. However, this process went through a series of stages which were imbued with the conviction that commodity production was nonsocialist or even antisocialist in nature, and that macro-economic organization of the economy through planning was needed.

---

[8] For a more detailed explanation of the political system *see* pp. 276-282 below. [EDITOR'S NOTE]

[9] The term "commodity" in Marxian analysis refers to an article which has utility, and which is produced by human labor for sale on the market. [EDITOR'S NOTE]

[10] During the era of "war communism," which lasted in the Soviet Union until 1921, steps were undertaken towards the discontinuation of market relationships. Those steps included the free distribution of some necessities, and attempts to abolish money altogether. While the final stage of communism is to be devoid of market relationships, attempts to terminate them before the economic and social conditions for communism have been provided are today considered premature in both Soviet and Yugoslav interpretations of Marxism-Leninism. [EDITOR'S NOTE]

Central planning of the economy was the basis for the social organization of labor during the era of state, i.e., administrative, socialism. It was characterized above all by the existence of a single center of decision making (monocentric planning) related to the political organization of society (statist planning) and by a negative attitude toward commodity production (resulting in product planning with a nonmarket character of the plan). It was held that as socialism became more developed, these characteristics of the planned economy would become even more pronounced. But the historical development of socialist economy has shown that even in countries where state socialist organization was the basis of the economic system, this type of planned economy is no longer adequate. Changes in the planning systems of many socialist countries confirm this evaluation.

The new institutional framework of the Yugoslav economy is based on self-management and on commodity production, and could not be harmonized with the planned economy of the period prior to 1950. It was essential to set up a new system of planning, but this could not be accomplished all at once.

The new planning system could not be statist, but had to be based on self-management and it had to start with the enterprise as the basic self-managing unit. This means that the plans of the work organizations (enterprises) are the basic plans while the social plans (federal, republican, communal) are synthetic plans, which merely coordinate and do not issue independent directives. To be consistent with the principle of self-management, planning could not be centralistic and monocentric. It had to start from the fact that there exists a net composed of a large number of independent units of economic activity. And finally, planning had to assume the commodity character of economic relations between the working organizations and thus had to be based, not on the contradiction between plan and market, but on socialist commodity economy as a planned economy. In the institutional changes which characterize the contemporary stage of development of the Yugoslav economic system, the construction of this type of planned economy is one of the basic problems whose solutions is being sought.

FORMS OF APPROPRIATION [11] AND DISTRIBUTION OF MATERIAL GOODS

In a socialist economic system it is characteristic that society appropriates the means of production. This does not mean only the negation of private ownership, of hired labor relations and of the exploitation of workers; it also means social management of the means of production. The content of social

[11] By "appropriation" is meant the acquisition of ownership and the taking of possession. [EDITOR'S NOTE]

management of the means of production is manifested in the historical development of socialist countries, especially Yugoslavia, in different ways. In the administrative socialism which lasted in Yugoslavia until 1950, the socialized means of production were managed by the state apparatus. The state determined the conditions for the replacement of material stocks, the compensation of the labor force, and the size and allocation of accumulation consistent with the goals of economic development defined by the general state plan. Thus the state apparatus acted as an owner, and the social ownership of the means of production was actually state ownership.

In the Yugoslav socialist economy with self-managed forms of organization, the management of socialized means of production and the appropriation of produced goods are given a new social content. Here it was unambiguously demonstrated that the state, even the socialist state, cannot be the holder of *social* property. If the context is social property, then the holder is society, but not as an amorphous mass. Society is the holder in the sense that it is an organized community in which every producer and association of producers manages means of production and appropriates a portion of the produced goods according to the role and function which it has in the working organization of the community. Labor, or more precisely participation in the labor process, is the basis for the management of means of production and for participation in the distribution of goods. Workers, working collectives (enterprises), economic associations, communes, socialist republics, the federation—all participate in the organization of the economy's activities and on the basis of their role and their contribution, they take part in the appropriation of produced goods. That's why there is no owner in the classical sense of the word.

The development of the self-management rights of producers and working collectives with respect to the management of means of production was given meaning and the appropriation of goods was realized in Yugoslavia through constant changes and improvements in the system of distribution. The basic trend which was manifested through these changes consisted of a constant expansion of the rights of the enterprise to make independent decisions regarding an increasing portion of its output. This led to the decentralization of funds and to the creation of new forms for their social mobilization through the construction of a credit system. Whereas in 1950 the dominant portion of the funds was allocated by administrative means, and investment funds were centralized in the hands of the Federation to the extent of more than 90 percent, in 1964 about one-third of the investment funds were in the hands of the enterprises, and most of the rest (over 50 percent) were distributed by means of credit through the banking system.

The most important elements in the functional aspect of distribution are the following: first, the total mass of produced goods is distributed in the commodity economy by means of commodity and money flows. Through the sale of its products the enterprise realizes a revenue which depends on the quantity of goods which is sold and on the price of the goods. Since the formation of prices and price policy have a special significance in distribution, Yugoslav economists call the distribution of revenue among enterprises "primary distribution." Secondly, once the revenue is in the hands of the enterprise, it is no longer distributed by means of the market to its basic destination. What takes place now is actually distribution in the narrower sense. This type of distribution is often called "secondary distribution."

The revenue realized is the basis for secondary distribution, which is carried out within the context of the enterprise as the basic economic unit. This distribution has two phases: the phase before the determination

Table 8-1. Basic Structure of Revenue Distribution

I. *Total Revenue*
   Minus: material expenditures
           amortization
           interest on working stocks
   Equals:
II. *Enterprise Income*
    1. Gross personal incomes
       a. Net personal incomes
       b. Contributions from personal income
    2. Enterprise funds
       a. Working funds
       b. Social consumption funds
       c. Reserve funds

of enterprise income, and the phase of distributing the income. With the decentralization of decision-making regarding the use of revenue and with the transfer of an increasing quantity of funds to the enterprise, the central institutional factor in the distribution of revenue becomes the enterprise, in other words, the working collective. Today, enterprises have complete autonomy in decisions on the use of funds for material expenditures and amortization. Interest on the working stock (a kind of capital tax) is actually a contribution to centralized investment funds. Changes which are being prepared in the system of distribution will also change the forms of capital formation. When material expenditures, amortization and contributions to the community are subtracted from total revenue, what remains is the income of the enterprise. This is distributed according to enterprise rules between personal incomes and funds. The determination of the proportion which goes to each of these two entities depends completely on the enterprise, namely on the workers' council which formulates the rules for the distribution of enterprise income and also for the distribution of personal income among the individual workers.

The part which goes to personal income is stated in terms of *gross personal income*; in other words, it includes proportional contributions to funds indispensable for covering the needs of social consumption: contributions for social insurance, for apartment construction, for the budget of the local community, and a contribution for education which is just being introduced in order to create separate funds for the financing of schools and educational institutions. The needs of social consumption are also partly covered by taxes and by contributions of citizens. The fiscal significance of the various types of taxes on the incomes of individuals is relatively small. The most significant tax in fiscal terms is the sales tax which, through changes that took place in 1965, has become a tax on retail prices which is paid directly by consumers.

Through the entire period during which the present Yugoslav system of distribution has taken shape, issues connected with the distribution of investment funds have been the most complex. The difficulties have concerned the sources of these funds as well as the holders who have used the funds and made decisions as to their use. In the earlier period, as a result of the inherited administrative management system, the dominant part of the funds came out of centralized funds, with allocation determined by the state apparatus. The process of decentralization and the removal of investment funds from state management were definitively formulated in the resolutions of the 8th Congress of the Yugoslav League of Communists, held in December, 1964. In principle, decision-making in regard to the use of investment funds was completely transferred to self-managed bodies. These changes were accompanied by a corresponding reorganization of the credit system, based on principles of self-management. The enterprises themselves have become the founders of the bank. The basic function of the bank is to mobilize the enterprises' investment funds and to make these funds available to enterprises and other self-managed units through investment credits in accordance with the aims of economic development and in particular of investment policy.

The part of the income which the enterprise keeps in its own funds goes mainly to the working capital or serves for the creation of investment stock or for payments on loans. A smaller part is put aside for the welfare fund and for the enterprise's reserves.

ECONOMIC DEVELOPMENT

With an income of about 135 dollars per capita and a yearly growth rate of national income of about 1.5 percent, pre-World War II Yugoslavia was

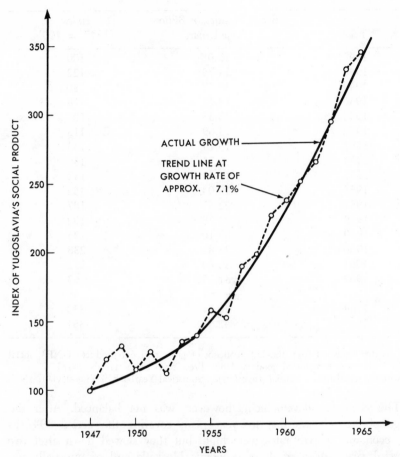

Figure 8-1. Graph of Growth of Yugoslavia's Social Products.

among the world's economically undeveloped countries. The slow rate of growth prevented an escape from backwardness in the foreseeable future.

After the war significant changes took place in this respect. (See Table 8-2 and Figure 8-1.) The policy of economic development with an emphasis on industrialization was accompanied by corresponding institutional changes which sped up and stimulated development and led to an average yearly growth rate of national income of 8 to 9 percent, if the strenuously harsh period before 1953 is excluded. This economic development amounted to a substantial increase of per capita national income, which reached a level of about 500 dollars in 1965. In a relatively short period, Yugoslavia's economic successes led her into the group of semideveloped countries.

Table 8-2. Growth of Yugoslavia's Social Product *
(In Constant—1960—Prices)

Year	Social Product in Billion New Dinars	Index (1947 = 100)
1947	12.08	100
1948	14.74	122
1949	15.77	130
1950	14.72	118
1951	15.38	127
1952	13.69	113
1953	16.14	133
1954	16.74	138
1955	19.09	158
1956	18.04	152
1957	22.57	187
1958	23.28	198
1959	27.10	225
1960	28.82	238
1961	30.44	251
1962	31.75	263
1963	35.61	295
1964	40.21	333
1965	42.5	351

* As distinguished from the U.S. concept of gross national product (GNP), social product includes only material goods and not direct services. [EDITOR'S NOTE]
SOURCE: *Statisticki godisnjak Jugoslavije* (Statistical Yearbook of Yugoslavia): 1966.

The economic development, however, was not balanced. After the passage of Yugoslavia's first five-year plan, covering the period 1947 to 1951, economic growth rates were high, but they slowed down after two successful years. As a result of economic blockade and of unusually unfavorable conditions for agricultural production in 1950 and 1952, total production fell. After 1953 there was again a period of quick development, and the 8 to 9 percent rate of growth mentioned above actually characterizes this period. This development was especially intensive at the beginning of the second five-year plan, covering the period 1957 to 1961, the basic goals of which were fulfilled in four years. The new five-year plan for 1961 to 1965 presupposed the tempo achieved in the earlier period, was not adequately balanced, and had to be abandoned in 1962.

After a period of adaptation, and especially after the changes of August, 1965, known as the "economic reform" conditions were created for the passage of a new five-year plan of economic development for 1966 to 1970, with a planned growth rate of between 7.5 and 8.5 percent a year.

As was pointed out earlier, the economic development of Yugoslavia was based on a policy of intense industrialization. This was manifested in the high rate of increase of industrial output, from an index of 79 in 1946 to 747 in 1965, with 1939 equal to 100. This growth of industrial production changed the structure of the social product in terms of its component branches and led to a dominant place for industrial production:

Table 8-3. Yugoslavia's Social Product
(in Billion New Dinars, 1960 Prices)

Year	Total	Industry percent		Agriculture percent	
1953	16.14	5.29	33	5.50	35
1963	35.61	16.73	47	7.39	21

In terms of some important indicators, industrial production showed the following development patterns:

Table 8-4.

		1939	1946	1965
Electric energy	(mil. kwh)	1173	1150	15,523
Coal—total	(mil. tons)	7032	6652	29,980
Petroleum	(1000 tons)	1.1	28.8	2063.1
Iron ore	(1000 tons)	101	84	1115
Steel	(1000 tons)	235	202	1769
Cement	(1000 tons)	844	698	3102

During the entire period there was a tendency toward constant strengthening of the socialist sector of the economy. Examined for the same period, this development process is shown by the following changes in the structure of the Yugoslav economy:

Table 8-5.

Social Product in Billion New Dinars	1953 Percent		1963 Percent		Index, 1953 = 100
Socialist sector	10.19	63	28.45	80	278.1
Private sector	5.95	37	7.16	20	120.3

The rapid development of industry, and particularly of light industry, has recently led to disproportions caused by lags in the resources, energy, and equipment sectors. This brought about an increase of imports which in

1964 led to a high deficit in the balance of trade.[12] Thus, in 1965, measures to stabilize the economy were undertaken. These measures are part of the economic reform and they have initiated a process which in the coming five years should lead to proportionate and balanced development, to the removal of bottlenecks and to increased activation of unused capacities. These measures should also enable Yugoslavia to participate more intensively in the international division of labor.[13] Due to these measures Yugoslavia's growth rate slowed down in 1965, but that year the balance of trade improved and the balance of payments [14] was in equilibrium for the first time during a long period.

THE POLITICAL SYSTEM OF YUGOSLAVIA

Yugoslavia's political system differs in a number of aspects from those of the western countries as well as from those of other socialist countries. It is distinct from the first because of the different social and economic structure on which it is founded, that is, society's ownership of the means of production. It differs from the political systems of the other socialist countries because of the position and role of the state in society which has a number of implications in social relations, the economy, political life, and culture.

WORKER-MANAGEMENT AND THE POLITICAL SYSTEM

The present-day political structure of Yugoslavia is the result of an evolution dating from 1950 when it took on a clearly defined direction. That was the year in which workers' councils were established in enterprises, thus making it possible for all the members of working collectives to participate in the management of the enterprise and in the distribution of income according to the work performed. Since then, development has been directed in its entirety towards the reinforcement of such relations in production and towards the extension of the principles of worker-management and their application to other areas of social life and activity (education, science, culture, social and health services, and public administration). The political system has changed in response to the relationships evolving from worker-

[12] A country's balance of trade is the relationship between the country's imports and exports of material goods during a given period. [EDITOR'S NOTE]

[13] Division of labor = specialization; international division of labor = division of labor among countries (implying the subsequent exchange of the commodities in the production of which each specializes). [EDITOR'S NOTE]

[14] A country's (international) balance of payments is a statement, presented in double bookkeeping (debit-credit) form, of all the transactions of that country with all other countries during a given period. The balance of payments includes exports, imports, capital flows, gold flows, tourist expenditures, immigrant remittances, etc. [EDITOR'S NOTE]

management. As the competence of the organs created by the members of working collectives has grown (workers' councils and such) the functions of state organs have diminished. The functions fulfilled by the state have been progressively transferred to the organs of worker-management and self-government.

The shrinking of the state's sphere of activity has been paralleled by a process of decentralization (the transfer of authority from higher to lower organs) and democratization (the creation of such conditions as to bring the most effective and direct influence of the people into the mechanisms of decision-making). As a result, the role of the communes has been growing, as they are the seat of decision-making most directly affecting the life of the people and their organizations and associations on any given territory.

Worker-management in production and its extension to other areas have made it possible for the people to have an increasingly direct say about the working conditions in the organizations where they are employed and from which they derive their income; decentralization and the democratization of the political system have created the conditions for their participation, either directly or through their elected representatives, in decision-making at every level of the political structure. In this way, a democratic society is taking form in which the people have not only the classic rights of citizens of a democracy in relation to political power but rights as well in the determination of production and of the distribution of income. Thus, a mutual interaction and fusion of political and economic democracy is manifesting itself.

The 1963 Constitution was adopted to give a legal framework and sanction to the results of the development of worker-management and decentralization, and to the transformations which had taken place in the political system.

THE CONSTITUTION

The Yugoslav Constitution is divided into two fundamental sections. The first defines and elaborates the social, economic, and political system. The basic relationships and institutions of the social system are legally defined and set down as applying to the whole country, thus ensuring a unified social system. Provisions are included on relationships among people in production and in the distribution of income, on property, on the freedoms, rights and obligations of the people as individuals and citizens, and on the forms of organization and functions of the various levels of government (the Commune, the District, the Socialist Republic, and the Federation). The second part of the Constitution relates to the organization of the Federation [i.e., the highest level of government]. Since Yugoslavia is a federal republic, the Federal Constitution establishes the jurisdiction of the organs of govern-

ment of the Federation, their structure and function, leaving it to each of
the constituent republics, Serbia, Croatia, Slovenia, Bosnia-Hercegovina,
Macedonia, and Montenegro, to draw up its own constitution for its republican government.

The social and economic system. The norms spelled out for the social
and economic system are of particular importance to the Yugoslav social
system as they give legal sanction to the basic relationships on which the
entire structure of society is founded.

Article 6 of the Constitution defines these relationships as follows:

The basis of the social and economic system of Yugoslavia rests on the right
of the freely associated working people to work with the socially-owned means
of production, and on self-management by the working people in production
and in the distribution of the social product in working organizations and the
community.

The working organization may therefore be defined as the institutionalized organizational form within which people, freely associated to
work, themselves manage the affairs of the organization and the distribution
of the income earned.

To guarantee that relations within working organizations will always
be those corresponding to free and equal people, the Constitution sets down
in detail the meaning of worker-management. The following rights and
obligations of the members of the working organization are among those
specified: the management of the working organization directly or through
the organs of management they themselves have elected; the organization
of production and other activities and the adoption of production and
development plans; decisions on the buying and selling of merchandise
and services and other business affairs; decisions on the utilization of all the
organization's assets; the distribution of the income realized; decisions on
working relations (employment, working day, safety measures, technical
training); participation in all decisions relating to the merging of their
working organization with other organizations or to the separation of their
unit or units to form a separate organization. Every act which in any way
represents a violation of these rights is proclaimed unconstitutional.

The prerequisite for the existence of such relationships among people
who are, at one and the same time, both producers and managers is the
elimination of every form of monopolistic ownership which could be used
as the basis to derive special rights to justify the appropriation or disposition
of the products of work. To meet this requirement, the Constitution
proclaims the means of production (the instruments of work and the natural
resources of the country) the property of society and precludes the right of
ownership as a basis for appropriating production or determining the conditions for its distribution, and it stresses the validity of these provisions as far
as the state or any other organizations or individuals are concerned. At the

same time, the Constitution establishes unequivocally that "only work and the results of work may determine the material and social position of the individual."

Therefore, social ownership as defined by the Yugoslav Constitution cannot be treated as ownership in the usual sense of the word as it does not guarantee monopolistic rights of any kind to any concrete entities whatsoever, be they private owners or the state. It must be dealt with as a completely new category which sets up work as the one and only basis for appropriation.

The Constitution leaves intact the already well-established private ownership of whatever serves a personal use or satisfies personal or family needs (including family dwellings and the like).[15] The derivation of income on the basis of personal labor of people self-employed in agriculture, the trades and other service activities is also guaranteed. In all these areas, the limited use of supplementary labor is permitted.

The political system. Worker-management in working organizations finds its logical extension in self-government in the communes, republics, and the Federation, referred to in Yugoslavia as the social-political communities. In some republics, districts are established as well as communes,[16] and in Serbia there are two autonomous provinces also treated as social-political communities.

In the social-political communities, self-government and political power are intimately bound up with each other, since the organs of self-government and state organs have fused into one, with the elements of self-government becoming stronger and the functions of state power diminishing.

The functions of government and the administration of social affairs are carried out by the representative bodies of the social-political communities, the assemblies. The commune is the basic social-political community; the more encompassing communities—the districts, provinces, republics and Federation—may take on only those functions assigned to them by the Constitution.

The elements of self-government in the social-political communities and the direct influence of the people on their operation are strongly reinforced by the composition of the assemblies, the electoral system, and the limitations placed on re-election to all the more important political, executive, and administrative positions.

All assemblies are made up of two types of houses: one in which the

[15] In other words, the right to private ownership of non-productive private property (consumers' goods) remains unchallenged. This holds *generally* true in all communist countries, although land, private dwellings, and the like may be communally or socially owned, and thus exempted from strictly private ownership, in some places. [EDITOR'S NOTE]

[16] The Yugoslav constitution provides that districts may be founded below the republic level "to discharge affairs of common concern to two or more communes" (Article 105). [EDITOR'S NOTE]

representatives of all the people of any given territory sit, and the second of representatives of the working people elected in the organizations or institutions in which they are employed. Through the deputies in this second type of house, known as the representatives of the working community, all producers from the different areas of social life (the economy, education and culture, health and social affairs, etc.) participate in decision-making on all questions pertaining to the domain of their activities and interests. At the republican level and for the Federation, the second house is organized on the basis of several chambers (economic, cultural and educational, social affairs and health, organizational and political). Generally, the two houses of commune assemblies are made up of only one chamber each. The Chamber of the Working Community seats representatives from all spheres of social activity while the Communal Chamber is elected by all the people living in the commune.

The electoral system is the logical counterpart of the assembly structure described. The members of the Communal Chamber are elected by all the voters, whether producers or not, and the members of the Chamber of the Working Community are elected by voters qualified to do so. The deputies to the district and republican assemblies as well as the Federal Assembly are delegated. This means that the commune assemblies elect representatives to the district and republican assemblies and to the Federal Assembly. The representatives elected in the communal assemblies to sit in the republican and Federal Assembly must be confirmed through a referendum by all the voters. If any given delegate fails to receive a majority, the commune assembly must elect a new delegate and his election must once again be submitted to confirmation by the voters in a referendum.

To ensure the democratic functioning of the system, the limitations placed on re-election and re-appointment to important positions are of utmost importance. The aim is to preclude any possibility of monopolization of political functions by a limited number of persons and the usurpation of power by the bureaucracy. Thus, the conditions have been created for ever larger numbers of persons to participate in the administration of social and state affairs. According to law, nobody may hold the same elective, executive, or administrative function for a period exceeding four years. For some positions, conditions are defined to permit exceptions and allow election or appointment for one more electoral period, but such exceptions require the existence of special circumstances and involve special procedures so that their occurrence in practice is extremely limited.

The organization of the Federation. The Federal Assembly is the highest organ of government of the Federation. It decides on all constitutional changes, adopts federal laws, economic plans, and the Yugoslav budget. It determines basic internal policy and foreign policy, elects the President and Vice-President of the Republic, the President and members of the Federal Executive Council, the President and judges of the Constitutional and

Supreme Courts of Yugoslavia, state secretaries and other senior officials. It supervises the work of top-level executive and administrative organs, decides on frontier changes and matters relating to war and peace and ratifies the more important international agreements and treaties.

The Assembly is composed of the Federal Chamber representing all the citizens of Yugoslavia and of four Chambers of working communities representing the working people by different areas of social activity (the Economic Chamber, the Cultural and Educational Chamber, the Social Affairs and Health Chamber, and the Organizational and Political Chamber).

Each chamber has 120 seats with the exception of the Federal Chamber which has 70 additional seats to which each republic delegates ten deputies and each of the autonomous provinces, five. These additional deputies to the Federal Chamber are elected in the republican assemblies and together constitute a separate chamber, the Chamber of Nationalities, which is charged with the special role of safeguarding the equality of the nationalities and which must be convened if changes to the Constitution are under consideration or in cases where the rights of nationalities or the republics are in question.

The area of jurisdiction of each of the chambers is clearly defined. Some questions are the exclusive competence of the Federal Chamber (foreign affairs, national defense, state security, and the like), whereas other questions are decided in the Federal Chamber in joint session with one or another of the other chambers (for example, economic questions with the Economic Chamber, educational questions with the Cultural and Educational Chamber, etc.).

The President of the Republic is elected at a joint session of all the Assembly Chambers for a four-year term and may be re-elected only once to another consecutive term. The President of the Republic represents Yugoslavia within the country and abroad and is the supreme commander of the armed forces. He signs into law federal legislation, names ambassadors, receives the credentials of foreign ambassadors, awards decorations, has the power to proclaim a state of war if the Assembly is not able to meet, etc. The President of the Republic proposes to the Assembly one of its members for the Presidency of the Federal Executive Council and is empowered to convene the Federal Executive Council and place specific questions on the agenda.

The Federal Executive Council is the organ of the Federal Assembly which is entrusted with its political-executive function. This organ has functions similar to those of a cabinet with the difference that its members, in contrast to ministers, are not necessarily the heads of specific governmental departments. It is composed of a President and a specified number of members elected in the Assembly from among its ranks. The Federal Executive Council makes proposals to the Assembly on domestic and foreign policy, and is charged with the implementation of policies adopted by the

Federal Assembly, the execution of federal legislation and of the economic plan, and the collection of revenues and disbursement of funds provided for in the budget. The Federal Executive Council supervises the work of the federal administrative organs, proposes legislation, decrees the manner of and spells out the instructions for the implementation of federal laws, etc.

The Federal Administration is composed of state secretariats, federal secretariats, and other organs (councils, commissions). State secretariats have been established to deal with affairs that are *exclusively* within the jurisdiction of the federal government (foreign affairs and national defense, for instance) whereas the federal secretariats deal with other affairs of the Federation. Senior officials in the administration are elected and replaced by the Assembly.

Courts in Yugoslavia are independent and function in keeping with the Constitution and laws. Decisions handed down by one court can be changed only by a court of a higher instance. There are courts at the level of the communes, districts and republics, and at the federal level—the Supreme Court of Yugoslavia. Judges are elected to their posts by the assemblies at the level in question. Special courts take care of cases arising in the economy, and the Army has its own tribunals.

Constitutional courts existing at the level of the republics and the federation are charged with guarding constitutionality and protecting the rights guaranteed by the constitutions. The Federal Constitutional Court consists of a President and ten judges elected by the Federal Assembly for a period of eight years.

IDEOLOGY

Those ideological viewpoints which have an immediate practical significance will be dealt with in brief here. Reference is made to a number of theoretical concepts related to current and fundamental social problems. These concepts present Yugoslavia's position in regard to ways of solving the respective problems.

The concept of the contemporary epoch. The Programme of the League of Communists of Yugoslavia assesses the present epoch as a period of transition from capitalism to socialism, involving the process of the disappearance of capitalism and the emergence of socialism, a process which reflects a variety of forms and evolves in extremely diverse ways and at various tempos in different places. Despite the variety of forms in which it manifests itself, however, this process is fundamentally the same and moves in the same general direction, its parts merging into one single world-wide process, the process of the emergence of socialism. "The capitalist mode of production," says the Programme of the LCY,[17] "and the capitalist social system are in their terminal stage. Mankind, with all its economic and other social relationships, is entering the period of transformation to socialism in various ways. Socialism is increasingly becoming a matter of practice in all nations, an integral world process and a world system."

This generalized assessment of the present epoch is based on an analysis of a multitude of major phenomena and developmental tendencies in the structure of society, characteristic of the past few decades. These manifestations may be grouped into three great areas of historical events.

First, there are the radical changes in the capitalist structure of society wrought by revolutionary means, by forcible deposition and expropriation of the bourgeoisie, a process launched by the Russian Revolution. Such means of social transformation have been used primarily in countries where internal contradictions, both economic and social, reached such a degree that they could be resolved only by changing the government by force.

Second, there are the profound and significant structural changes in the economy and in social relationships taking place in the industrially advanced capitalist countries, changes revolving above all around the new socio-economic role of the state. Although no sudden changes in the character of power and property relations has taken place in these countries, social forms which restrict and alter the capitalist socio-economic system in a specific way have evolved under pressure from the contradictions inherent in it which have made it absolutely impossible for society to continue expanding production in the old way. These processes, inaugurated by the world depression of 1929-32, have been developing at an accelerated pace since then, delving deeper and spreading wider, and receiving new impulse from the measures implemented during World War II and afterwards.

Third, there is the crisis and collapse of the colonial system and the appearance of new independent states which are not following the classic capitalist road of development since capitalist forms and methods cannot offer them the possibility of pulling themselves out of the quagmire of material and social backwardness.

The movement from capitalism to socialism is not and cannot be a uniform process proceeding along a straight and narrow path. It advances at different speeds depending on the specific conditions and the relationships among social forces. Socialism progresses by coming to grips with the forces endeavoring to preserve capitalism's remaining positions and the forces striving to establish and conserve the specifically transitional forms engendered by the highly intensified role of the state. All these elements considerably complicate social developments which reflect a broad range of forms and the simultaneous existence of the old and the new in virtually

---

[17] League of Communists of Yugoslavia. [EDITOR'S NOTE]

all contemporary social systems. From these emerge internal and international antagonisms which convulse contemporary society; unless they are surmounted, the trend toward socialism may be retarded in large measure. Should they cause an explosion in international relations, all the achievements of civilization may be placed in jeopardy.

In view of the fact that the trend toward socialism is determined by the effects of an aggregate of economic and social factors which are operative in all contemporary societies, there are no grounds for considering the process of the emergence of socialism as being closeted within definite state boundaries, or for identifying socialism with a specific military-political bloc (the so-called socialist camp). Yugoslavia, convinced that such views are erroneous, is a non-aligned country.

As the factors in society which represent the motive force of socialism combine in various ways and develop differently in different countries, the roads toward socialism and the forms in which socialist society takes shape need not be the same everywhere. This is the basis for the demand that socialist movements and socialist countries maintain full independence and equality.

Similar assessments provide the background for the Yugoslav concept of peaceful and active coexistence which does not mean passive coexistence between blocs but rather universal cooperation among all states and nations. In the Yugoslav view, coexistence does not consist of the maintenance of the political and social status quo but rather of growing democracy in international relations. As far as the Yugoslavs are concerned, coexistence is not a temporary tactic but a policy of enduring value which corresponds to the interests of progress.

The concept of socialism. The Programme of the League of Communists of Yugoslavia gives the following definition of socialism:

Socialism is a social system based on socialization of the means of production, in which social production is managed by the associated workers directly engaged in production, in which distribution of income is based on the principle of "to each according to his work" and in which, under the leadership of the working class—which is also changing as a class—all social relationships are gradually being rid of class antagonisms and of elements of exploitation of man by man.

The important thing about this definition is that it places the accent not on just any kind of socialization of the means of production, but on the kind in which the associated workers directly engaged in production manage production and distribute income in accordance with the work done. It is only such relationships in production that can provide a basis for the development of socialist society and the opportunity to eliminate exploitation, class divisions, and antagonisms. Only under these conditions can society transcend the wage labor relationship and alienation of the product from its producer, thereby bringing about the emancipation of labor. After self-government has been achieved at the very base of society, it can then spread to other spheres of the life of society and become a general form for its overall organization.

The theory of the role of the state under socialism. This is an important issue that has caused major differences of opinion in recent socialist thought and practice. Thousands upon thousands of pages have been written on the subject in Yugoslavia over the past decade. This brief survey permits the presentation of only a few fundamental theses.

One of the essential goals of socialist forces is to win state power and to utilize it for the purpose of establishing socialist relationships. However, any state apparatus, socialist included, contains the immanent tendency to become increasingly independent and to tear itself loose from the control of those who set it up. Those who hold government posts, the class of functionaries, the bureaucracy, become the protagonists of this tendency for the state to become an independent force. They strive to strengthen the state apparatus and to make it play a growing role in the life of society. They try to interject the state into all spheres of the life of society—economy, social organizations and associations, culture. In order to give these practices a theoretical foundation, the ideologists of bureaucracy set up theories about the identity of the socialist state and socialist society and on that basis demand the complete subordination of all individuals and collective bodies to the "higher interests" which are allegedly represented by the state.

Such bureaucratic-statist tendencies become a serious threat to socialist society, obstruct its development and can, if they continue to develop, lead to a specific type of restoration of exploitation. Should that happen, the goals of socialism could not be achieved: the producers would remain wage laborers in the hire of the state which has concentrated in its hands all economic, political, and ideological power.

The socialist forces must therefore treat the state as a "necessary evil." "Necessary," because state power is an instrument for defending the system, guiding social development and regulating social relations; "evil," because it constantly engenders the tendency to establish a bureaucratic and statist monopoly. If these tendencies are to be nipped, means of democratic control and forms of social self-government must be developed that will gradually take state functions upon themselves. Expansion of the sphere of self-government will therefore narrow down the sphere of state coercion. Taking the place of the state which is withering away will be the free associations of workers directly engaged in production; in this manner a coherent social system will be formed.

The theory of the motive forces of social development under socialism. According to bureaucratic-statist concepts, the socialist state is the motive force, the organizer and the guide of social development. The point of departure here is the thesis that socialist society must surmount the working of blind forces which must be replaced by conscious and planned management of the life of society. The state, proclaimed the personification of social consciousness, utilizes science (in actual fact the views of groups of experts and planners who have their own ideas as to what the needs and goals of society are) for the elaboration of plans providing guidelines for all economic and social development.

In the opinion of Yugoslav theorists, there is no need to guess at society's requirements, nor is there any need for anyone to do this in the name of society. It is simply considered better for social requirements and interests to manifest themselves freely and through democratic procedure, to interact, and to be corrected and coordinated in the proceess. If this is to be achieved, the organization of the production process and the social system in general must rest on certain specific propositions. Each individual who is part of any kind of cell which does any part of the labor of society must be in a position to bring influence to bear on his own material and social position, to be an active factor in the satisfaction of his own requirements and interests, to be able to manifest them freely and to fight for their assertion. It is further indispensable for these production cells—regardless of whether they are concerned with material production, services, education, or scientific research—to be able to express their common interest and to satisfy their needs. However, as society is not a collection of individuals or basic communities which exist contiguously but a complicated system of relationships, the application of this principle of free manifestation of requirements and interests and the struggle to assert them can but lead to tension and contradictions. Socialist society is not therefore a society free of conflict, although its conflicts do not have a class character and can be reconciled. Differing requirements and interests—material, social, ethical, and cultural—and the contradictions that arise on that basis, represent the dynamic motive force behind social development. Society should not consequently be organized in a manner that frustrates their manifestation; rather it should provide a suitable mechanism for coordinating diverse interests and surmounting contradictions in a democratic manner.

Fundamental trends in political life. The central problem in sociopolitical life in Yugoslavia is the consolidation, advancement, and development of self-government. As self-government is extended, it eats away at what is left of bureaucratic forms and privileges and naturally provokes the resistance of all those who find it in their interests to retain these privileges. The assertion of self-government is dependent upon the surmounting of such resistance. Socially and politically, a struggle is being waged over self-government, and it is upon this question that forces in Yugoslavia confront each other.

Apart from these processes through which the forces of self-government confront the forces of conservatism and bureaucracy, there is another group of processes through which the complex problems connected with the development of self-government and with the methods by which it functions are solved. As they take decision-making with regard to society's affairs into their own hands, the organs of self-government find themselves facing a number of issues on which individual, group, regional, and other interests clash. The central problem in self-government where decision-making is highly decentralized is how to ensure that the decisions adopted in numerous organizations and at various levels respect special interests while at the same time taking into consideration the interests of society as a whole and the prosperity of the entire community. It is for this reason that in the political process of self-government social consciousness and awareness of the goals and values of socialism play an exceptionally important role. The widespread acceptance of these goals and values by millions of citizens who make the decisions ensures that their individual decisions will contain elements reflecting the common requirements and interests of society. This makes it possible to achieve unity and integration in society through awareness of common requirements and roads of development rather than by coercion. Socio-political organizations have a special role to play, so as to enable society to integrate and develop toward the achievement of increasingly democratic and humane relations. Two of these are of particular importance: the Socialist Alliance of the Working People of Yugoslavia and the League of Communists of Yugoslavia.

The Socialist Alliance is an extremely broad-based organization comprising some eight million members which gives all citizens an opportunity to participate in political life, in the discussion of socio-political issues, in the analysis of the functioning of organs of government and administration, and in the presentation of proposals. It is a highly significant part of the electoral process for it is in the Alliance that the citizens discuss their candidates and nominate them for election to the assemblies. As the citizens put forward divergent views on social problems and give their support to different measures, common will is formed in the confrontation of their opinions, ideas are integrated, and alternatives on specific problems crystallized.

It is not necessary for members of the Socialist Alliance to accept Marxist ideology nor do their religious or any other kinds of similar convictions present any problem. The Socialist Alliance developed from the pre-war People's Front which followed the initiative of the Communist Party and fought against the dictatorship of the time, and from the broad-based Liberation Front which offered resistance to the fascist invaders during World War II. Today, it is a specifically Yugoslav organization which cannot be identified either with a one-party or a multi-party system. In a self-governed society based on direct democracy, it simultaneously exercises the functions of a social and a political organism. An instrument of direct action by the citizens, it is similarly a form of political organization of those same citizens.

The Yugoslav Communists had a prominent role in forming the

Socialist Alliance, but there is no tendency on their part to consider it an organization subjected to their command.

As the organizer of the National Liberation War and the Revolution, of the resistance to Stalinist hegemony, and of the development of a democratic, socialist society, the League of Communists of Yugoslavia has won a position of exceptional prestige among the people. People who adopt Marxist ideology and are willing and able to strive consistently for the consolidation and development of socialism can become members. The position and role of the League of Communists has changed with the advancement of the system of self-government. It has not set itself up as a ruling party which dominates social affairs via top positions in the government and administration but rather as an organization whose members are active in the Socialist Alliance, the Trade Union Federation, and other bodies, and in representative and similar organs, where they strive for the adoption of measures which are in line with socialist development. The League of Communists has no wish to influence socio-political processes as a ruling factor in society but rather as an ideological and political factor which wields influence by dint of its prestige in society, and by the force of conviction, persuasion and argument. It is not a power above society, but a force within it, constantly impelling it forward. "Nothing that has been created," reads the last sentence in the Programme of the League of Communists of Yugoslavia, "is so sacred that it cannot be transcended or give way to something that is even more progressive, more humane, freer!"

FURTHER READING SUGGESTIONS

YUGOSLAV:

New Constitution of the Socialist Federal Republic of Yugoslavia. Belgrade, 1963.

Programme of the League of Communists of Yugoslavia. Belgrade, 1958.

Socialist Thought and Practice, principal quarterly review published in English (The Yugoslav Information Centre, Belgrade).

Yugoslav Survey, monthly review. (The Yugoslavia Publishing House, Belgrade).

FOREIGN:

Hoffman, George W., and Fred W. Neal, Yugoslavia and the New Communism. Twentieth Century Fund: New York, 1962.

International Labor Office, Workers Management in Yugoslavia. Geneva, 1962.

V

The East European
Members of the Soviet
Commonwealth of Nations:

The People's Republic of Bulgaria
The Socialist Republic of Czechoslovakia
The German Democratic Republic
The Hungarian People's Republic
The Polish People's Republic
The Socialist Republic of Rumania

	Area (in square miles)	Population (mid-1967 estimate)
Bulgaria	42,730	8,366,000
Czechoslovakia	49,371	14,355,000
The German D.Rep.	41,659	15,085,000
Hungary	35,919	10,242,000
Poland	120,665	32,392,000
Rumania	91,699	19,385,000

Europe today is not what it was before the war. In the east and in the center of the so-called Old World there emerged a new, a socialist Europe in which half of all Europeans live. Their deeds and their struggle are a credit to our ancient continent.

LEONID I. BREZHNEV
GENERAL SECRETARY, CENTRAL COMMITTEE
COMMUNIST PARTY OF THE SOVIET UNION

INTRODUCTION

IN THE EARLY 1940's, PRACTICALLY ALL THE LANDS WHICH TODAY ARE occupied by the communist countries of Eastern Europe were under Nazi control; the rest (such as Albania) were in the hands of Mussolini's Italian fascists.[1] By 1945, the Soviet armies had driven the would-be world conquerors back into the very heart of Germany where the Soviets met up with allied forces who had launched their invasion of the European continent from the West (France) and the South (Italy); the "invincible" armies of the master race were shattered; Hitler was dead; and the German Reich that was to have lasted for at least a thousand years had collapsed. But for most of Eastern Europe the years in between had been years of death, destruction, and suffering beyond description.

With the utter collapse of the occupational and puppet governments, at the end of the war, much of Eastern Europe was a political vacuum. What a conglomerate of countries it was—politically, economically, culturally, and otherwise! There was what today is East Germany, then a part of Hitler's Reich; Hungary, Rumania,[2] and Bulgaria which had succumbed to false promises, threats, and military pressures and had joined the "new order" of the master race; Czechoslovakia, betrayed by the Western powers at Munich and taken over by the Nazis before World War II began; and there were Poland, Yugoslavia, and Albania, all of which offered courageous but futile resistance to the vastly superior Nazi war machinery, paying a high price—under German bombs and before German execution squads—for their resistance.[3]

[1] For a few months, starting in late 1940, the Greeks drove the Italians back and occupied about two-fifths of Albania, only to lose it again when intervening German troops forced the Greeks out; and the eastern part of Poland was occupied by Soviet troops from September, 1939, the beginning of the Second World War, to June, 1941, when Hitler's armies launched their gigantic attack against the Soviet Union.

[2] Romania is frequently spelled "Roumania" or "Rumania." The last spelling is the most widely used in Europe (and is used by this author); the Rumanians themselves prefer "Romania."

[3] Poland had been singled out to be vacated of members of that "inferior race" and to be resettled by "Aryans." Poland's intelligentsia was deliberately exterminated, and millions of Poles were transported to Germany to die in slave labor camps, in gas ovens, or as guinea pigs in concentration camp areas set aside for "scientific" medical experiments.

Some of them had known little democracy before the outbreak of World War II, but Czechoslovakia could boast of what was one of the most democratic governments in all of Europe; some of them such as Bulgaria, were agricultural, economically backward regions, while others such as East Germany and Czechoslovakia had reached a high level of industrial development. And the popular feeling towards the "liberators" who marched under the hammer and sickle varied greatly, affected by many influences among which wartime experiences were certainly of considerable importance. In Yugoslavia, for instance, where the people had suffered terrible losses under Nazi occupation, Tito with his record as a resistance leader was welcomed as a national hero; but in East Germany, where the Soviet troops had humbled the master race and were beginning to enforce the collection of war damage reparations, the feeling toward the victors was not so favorable.

Only two countries, the Soviet Union and Mongolia, had embarked upon the journey toward communism before the outbreak of World War II. After that great conflagration, the above-mentioned countries of Eastern Europe followed, some immediately on the heels of the retreating enemy troops, some within the ensuing months and years—all before the end of the 1940's. From the outset, the Kremlin—and Stalin in the Kremlin—was acknowledged as the undisputed leader of the communist camp. Yugoslavia was the first to break its allegiance to the Moscow-decreed Party line, and to seek its own independent road to communism. Albania, long after Stalin's death, left the Soviet Commonwealth of Nations, aligning herself with Mao Tse-tung's China at the very first signs of the Sino-Soviet split. (Yugoslavia and Albania are treated separately in this book, in Parts IV and VI respectively. In this chapter, attention is focused on the other six, the East European members of the Soviet Commonwealth of Nations.)

In the days of Stalin, then, the tightly knit unity of the communist world under the leadership of the Kremlin was marred only by the defection of Yugoslavia. But the violent demonstrations in East Germany in 1953, the uprisings in Hugary in 1956, and the almost simultaneous unrest in Poland loosened the grip of the Soviet leadership over the other communist countries, years before China took about two-thirds of the inhabitants of the communist world out of the Soviet fold. Although the six European members of the Soviet Commonwealth of Nations are still allied with the Soviet Union, they are certainly not "satellites." The degree of loyalty and obedience to the Soviet Party line varies from country to country: Bulgaria, for instance, shows little desire to deviate; Rumania is probably the most recalcitrant and independent of the group.

The internal economic structure of the six nations also shows great dissimilarities, from the private ownership of close to ninety percent of all land in Poland, to the almost complete collectivization of land in most other areas, and from the introduction of measures of extensive economic decentralization under Czechoslovakia's "new economic model" to Rumania's reluctance to participate in the economic reform movement that has its impact on all the others.

The monolithic unity of the communist world thus exists no longer, not even within the six East European members of the Soviet Commonwealth of Nations. One must not, however, assume that each of the six goes its own way, unaffected by the rest. Whatever their differences may be, they are all trying to build their societies along Marxist-Leninist lines; and the Soviet Party and government, although no longer able to exert the control over the bloc countries it once did, still carries considerable weight.

The non-Marxist view on Eastern Europe has been contributed by R. V. Burks. A Chicago University Ph.D., Burks has held a Social Science Research Council Fellowship, and a Fulbright Fellowship in Greece. From 1961 to 1965, he was Policy Director of Radio Free Europe, Munich, and he is presently Professor of History at Wayne State University. Burks has published extensively on Communist Eastern Europe. His principal work, *The Dynamics of Communism in Eastern Europe,* was published by Princeton University in 1961, and again in paperback in 1966.

The Marxist view on Eastern Europe was written by Scott Nearing, and a supplement to it by four Soviet economists. A University of Pennsylvania Ph.D., Nearing has taught at the University of Pennsylvania and at Toledo University, Toledo, Ohio. He has published more than fifty books and booklets (several together with his wife, Helen K. Nearing) with such titles as *Man's Search for the Good Life, War or Peace, The Soviet Union as a World Power, Democracy Is Not Enough, Socialists Around the World, United World, USA Today,* and *The Conscience of a Radical,* consistently taking a Marxist position. He has been a regular editorial contributor to the *Monthly Review,* an American periodical which classifies itself as "an independent socialist magazine." At present, Nearing is Chairman of the Social Science Institute at Harborside, Maine.

The supplement has been appended to Nearing's contribution primarily to acquaint the reader with recent developments (Nearing's book was published in 1962). Its authors are V. Isupov, B. Lodygin, V. Terekhov, and O. Bogomolov—all Soviet economists.

9

Eastern Europe Under
Communism: A Non-Marxist
View

R. V. Burks *

PROFESSOR OF HISTORY
WAYNE STATE UNIVERSITY

In evaluating communist rule of Eastern Europe, any Western observer should begin by pointing out that communism was brought to this part of the world by the Soviet armies, or as the consequence of guerrilla war. In no case did a communist regime come to power in Eastern Europe as the consequence of a free election. Only three free elections were held in the whole area. In West Berlin the communists got 5 percent of the vote cast in 1949. In Hungary, they got 17 percent in 1945. And in Czechoslovakia they got 38 percent in 1946. It is doubtful whether they could reach even these figures today, in the event free elections were possible.

In fact, the communist leaders accepted the risks of free election in Hungary and in Czechoslovakia because they believed their party could make an impressive showing, and that this would have its impact on the West, whose diplomatists were attempting to insist on free elections generally. In Hungary, the number one communist, Matyas Rakosi, apparently assured the Soviet commanders that the Communist Party, together with its Socialist ally, could achieve a majority. Actually, the two parties together only got 34 percent of the total vote. In Czechoslovakia, the communist leaders seem to have believed, after having won 38 percent on their own in 1946, that they could win a clear majority in the general election scheduled for June, 1948. Public opinion polls taken by the communist-controlled Ministry of Education in the fall of 1947, however, revealed that the com-

* This contribution has been written especially for this book.

munist vote had fallen, not risen. This change in public opinion was a contributing factor in the communist decision to seize supreme power by means of a *Putsch*,[1] in February, 1948. In short, even in that East European country in which public opinion was most favorable to the communists, the party could not come to power by peaceful means, even when it made a deliberate effort to do so. It should also be kept in mind that in the case of the free elections in Hungary and Czechoslovakia, the communists reassured themselves against failure by insisting (naturally with the backing of their Soviet sponsors) that the ensuing government be formed on the basis of a coalition in which they were to receive a certain number of key ministries, regardless of the electoral outcome.

Even so, Hungary and Czechoslovakia were exceptions. In general, the communists did not hesitate to use force. In two East European countries, in Yugoslavia and Albania, the communists emerged as the victors of a bloody civil war. They fought their way to power in the years 1941-45 by organizing guerrilla armies and leading them in combat, against both the local opposition and the German and Italian occupying forces. Each of these regimes thus had a *Hausmacht*[2] of its own; they were not dependent on the presence of Soviet troops for their seizure of power. In fact, Soviet troops never at any time entered Albania and their presence in Yugoslavia was a late event and, at Yugoslav Communist request, of brief duration. It was, interestingly enough, these two partisan regimes which first defied Moscow, the Yugoslav in 1948, and the Albanian in 1961, and subsequently followed independent policies of their own. This is not to say, however, that either the Yugoslav or the Albanian Communist Party could have won a majority in a free election. On the contrary, in all probability, they could not have done so.

Elsewhere in Eastern Europe communism was imposed by simple fiat. In the case of Poland, a government-in-exile known as the Lublin Committee was formed under Soviet auspices and then brought to Poland in the Soviet baggage train. In the case of Bulgaria, a Soviet declaration of war late in 1944 was followed by Soviet military occupation and the seizure of power by the communist-controlled Fatherland Front. In Romania, the communist-controlled Groza government came into being (March, 1945) as a consequence of a Soviet ultimatum to the Romanian king. The regime and state known as the German Democratic Republic was created, in 1949, on that part of Germany occupied by Soviet troops, by the unilateral action of the Soviet authorities. Since in none of these cases did the communists risk anything like a free election; and since in Hungary and Czechoslovakia,

---

[1] A sudden, forcible overthrow, actual or attempted, of government; a *coup d'état*. [EDITOR'S NOTE]

[2] Domestic fighting machine. [EDITOR'S NOTE]

where they grossly overestimated their popular strength, they did risk such elections, it is a reasonable conclusion that the results of free elections would have been catastrophic from the communist point-of-view. There is other indirect evidence that the communists had the support of only a small minority of the peoples they came to rule, but the electoral argument appears to us decisive.

THE WEST AND THE COMMUNIST SEIZURES OF POWER

The attitude of the West toward the emergence of communist regimes in Eastern Europe was one of increasing doubt, suspicion, and concern. The West believed as a matter of moral principle that the peoples of Eastern Europe had a right to governments of their own choosing. This was why Western diplomacy, as at Yalta, asked for the Soviet signature to a document calling for free elections in this area. In addition to the moral issue there was the practical fact that the imposition of an alien rule was bound, sooner or later, to lead to serious trouble. But the West was in no position to insist. The Soviets had borne the brunt of the land fighting against the Nazis, at the cost of terrible losses, and in the course of operations had occupied most of Eastern Europe. The Soviets for their part were determined that Eastern Europe should not for a third time become a glacis for a German assault upon Russia, and they felt entitled to take appropriate measures.

The West recognized this entitlement. Eastern Europe was not a vital Western interest, despite all the affinities of culture and ties of blood. Neither the resources of Eastern Europe, nor its location, were such that if it fell under the control of an unfriendly state the world balance of power would shift dangerously against the West. Furthermore, the peoples of the West were weary of war and hoped somehow to continue the alliance with the Soviet Union into and beyond the peace settlement as the power basis of a peaceful world. So, while the concern in the West grew as the communization of Eastern Europe proceeded, the governments of the West subordinated that concern to these larger interests.

The West maintained this attitude of tolerance, albeit with mounting discomfort, until the *coup d'état* of February, 1948, in Prague. This event came as a shock and can fairly be said to have produced such a reaction in Europe and America as to mark the commencement of the "cold" war. For the first time, influential people in the West came to believe that cooperation with the Soviet Union was impossible, that communism constituted a dangerous threat to world peace which must be faced, and that resistance to the further spread of this brand of totalitarianism must be organized at once.

The *coup d'état* in Prague produced this traumatic effect for a number of reasons. For one thing, Czechoslovakia had been the only East European state to produce a viable democracy in the interwar period. Most other East European states had begun with parliamentary governments in 1919 and had ended with native, right-wing dictatorships by 1938. Therefore, it was presumed in the West that the loss of democratic government was felt by the Czechs and Slovaks as a real deprivation. Furthermore, the Czechs (if not the Slovaks) were genuinely pro-Soviet, in the sense that they believed that, for the future, the security of their small country could be guaranteed only by close cooperation with the Soviet power in matters of foreign policy. The February *coup d'état,* therefore, was viewed in the West as going beyond the requirements of Soviet security and as depriving a weak and friendly population of a precious possession. It was an aggressive act of such a character as to suggest that, for at least the next several years, no compromise with Soviet communism was possible. Actually, the Prague *coup* was one of a series of aggressive acts. It had been preceded by the outbreak of guerrilla war in Greece and by a crisis over Trieste, and it was to be followed by the blockade of West Berlin, a guerrilla war in Malaya, and the invasion of South Korea.

THE STALINIZATION OF EASTERN EUROPE

What happened to Eastern Europe after the communist seizure of power may be described as "Stalinization," that is, the importation into the area of the institutions and policies characteristic of the Stalinist brand of communist totalitarianism. There were, of course, variations from country to country; there were also significant differences of timing; and some features of public life remained peculiar to Eastern Europe. An example of the latter is the formal retention by all the regimes of Eastern Europe of the multiparty system in symbolic form, perhaps as a concession to public sentiment, both in Eastern Europe and in the West. But in everything important, each country of Eastern Europe became a small version of Stalinist Russia.

This meant, in the first instance, the creation of a single-party state. Other parties continued a formal existence, as has just been indicated, and the regimes were referred to as Peoples Democracies, rather than as dictatorships of the proletariat. The local Soviets of Worker Deputies were known more simply as National Committees while the Supreme Soviets retained the traditional names of the national parliaments, *Sobranje* in Bulgaria, *Sejm* in Poland, and so on. But if the form was different, the content was that of the dictatorship of the proletariat; all authority was vested in the Communist Party (though the Party itself frequently carried another name, e.g., Romanian Workers' Party).[3]

In strict imitation of their Soviet mentor, the principal policy of the new regimes was that of forced industrialization. This applied as well to countries already heavily industrialized, such as Czechoslovakia or East Germany, as to highly agrarian states like Bulgaria or Albania. Regardless of the situation or needs of a particular country, it was the development of heavy industry which was emphasized, at the expense of factories producing consumers' goods. Czechoslovakia, which had developed extensive ceramic, textile and shoe industries, the products of which were largely exported to the West in exchange for such items as machinery, was forced to reorient its economy around the production of machine tools and tractors, which it could only sell to its eastern neighbors.

Most of the regimes concentrated great energy on the construction of a major iron and steel complex, which was to serve as a local Donetz basin or Pittsburgh. In Czechoslovakia there was the East Slovak Iron and Steel Works, near Kosice; in East Germany *die schwarze Pumpe* near Leuneberg; in Poland Nowa Huta not far from Cracow; in Hungary Stalinvaros, south of Budapest. These projects required enormous investment, and many of them are today far from completion. Western sceptics questioned whether countries whose population ranged from 8 million, as in the case of Bulgaria, to 29 million, as in the case of Poland, were justified in undertaking the construction of such huge complexes, especially since they would be heavily dependent upon the importation of large quantities of iron ore, coal, oil, and other raw materials from the Soviet Union itself.

The policy of forced industrialization was accompanied by the forcible collectivization of agriculture. This, too, was according to the Soviet practice, which found the capital for industrialization by forcing down the already minimal living standards of the peasant masses, and which created a large reserve of cheap, unskilled labor for the new factories by simultaneously pushing millions of peasants from the land into the cities. The device which permitted the Soviet leaders to accomplish both the depression of rural living standards and a mass exodus to the cities was the collective farm, of which the Belorussian peasants say that it is the nearest thing to hell on earth, since it neither permits the peasant to live, nor to die. There was a secondary motive for collectivization, namely, the need to assure an urban-based minority regime of political control over a hostile, heavily populated countryside.

But Eastern Europe is not Soviet Russia, and 1949, when forcible col-

---

[3] Needless to say, the party, which ruled in the name of the proletariat, was by no means made up exclusively or, in some cases, even largely of representatives of this downtrodden class. In the southern part of our area peasant elements played an important role, especially prior to the seizure of power, and throughout cadres of middle class origin held key positions. Despite their widely trumpeted proletarian claim, the parties in fact represented all social classes.

lectivization was begun by the new regimes, was not 1931,[4] either. In an already industrialized country, such as Czechoslovakia, there were other sources of investment capital than agriculture. Furthermore, both Poland and Yugoslavia have since learned how to maintain substantial rates of industrial growth with, respectively, non-collectivized and decollectivized agriculture. Nor have these two regimes to date lost control of the countryside. Nevertheless, the East European regimes collectivized, at the usual high cost in human suffering and with the usual depressing effects on per hectare production (as opposed to production per person engaged in agriculture).

The third feature of the Stalinist policy imposed on the East European satellites was the systematic use of terror. Forced industrialization, together with forcible collectivization, signifies a depression of living standards, longer hours of work in exchange for less purchasing power. One device familiar to Stalinist-style industrialization is the system of norms. This is a variant of the piecework system in which the worker receives, let us say, ten cents for each die stamped up to fifty, and thirty cents for each die over fifty, when a first class machinist in an eight-hour day can produce at most forty-five dies. In order to keep the worker producing under such a system it is necessary to threaten him with police measures, just as it is fear of the police that keeps the collective farmer producing grain and selling the bulk of it to the state at less than cost. To maintain this threat against the mass of the population requires an extensive and powerful secret police, a system of party-controlled courts, and a set of labor camps. In short, Stalinist industrialization has as an essential ingredient the systematic use of terror as an instrument of rule.

Terror reigns, however, not only among the masses; it governs the ruling party, the army officers, the corps of industrial managers, and the state bureaucracy as well. The masses cannot in the long run be driven unless the classes are also driven. In this situation it is the police, and not the party, which holds the whip. An illustration of how the system affects elite groups is provided by the great purges of so-called Titoists. When Yugoslavia was expelled from the Cominform, in June, 1948, Stalin initiated in each of the East European regimes remaining under his control a preventive purge of those leaders who might one day be capable of engineering a national deviation on the order of the Yugoslavs. Stalin also had in mind making use of the purgees as popular scapegoats for the mounting grievances of the populations. Since anti-Semitism is endemic in many of the countries of Eastern Europe, this led to the purging of many Jewish communists. In Hungary, there was the purge of Laszlo Rajk and his associates; in Poland the purge of Ladislav Gomulka and company; in Czechoslovakia the purge of Rudolph Slansky, Vlado Clementis and many others; in Bulgaria the purge of Traicho Kostov, and so on.

Another feature of the terror was the hermetic isolation of the popu-

[4] In 1931 the campaign for the forcible collectivization of agriculture reached its height in the Soviet Union.

lations of Eastern Europe from contact with the West (and indeed from contact with each other). This was symbolized by the barbed-wire entanglements, the mine fields and the sentry towers which came to characterize the frontier between communist Eastern Europe and the West. The communists said that such measures were necessary to keep Fascists and reactionaries from penetrating the lands of socialism and engaging in sabotage and subversion. But everyone knew that the communists lied, and that the real reason for the "iron curtain," as Winston Churchill called it, was the need to preserve discipline inside these countries by (1) preventing the bolder fellows from escaping to the West, (2) keeping the population in ignorance of the true state of affairs in the West, and (3) preserving an internal facade of workers' joy and unanimity (a subtle kind of cruelty).

The falsity of the communist claims was most clearly demonstrated in East Germany where, owing to the existence of a free West Berlin, it was impossible for the regime to cut off all nonofficial communication with the West. Between 1949 and 1961, when the Berlin Wall was erected by the communists, some 2.5 million East Germans fled, increasingly through West Berlin, to the West. Their motives were largely economic—poor pay, long hours, atrocious working conditions, nothing to buy in the shops— though many also came because they feared arrest by the secret police. As a consequence of this exodus, Eastern Germany was one of the few countries in the world whose population was declining, from 19 million in 1949, to 17½ million in 1961. The exodus made difficult the consolidation of the East German regime and was a major source of concern to the men in the Kremlin. It was perhaps fortunate for the peace of the world that the refugees were Germans and not, say, Hungarians or Poles, since the West felt that the Germans themselves were largely responsible for the mess in which they found themselves. Nonetheless, the evident sufferings of the East Germans did gradually effect a modification of Western attitudes on the German issue.

But the iron curtain was not only intended to prevent physical movement across frontiers, the escape of the most discontented to the West, or the entrance of tourists. It was also designed to impede the flow of ideas. Western publications were cut off, except those of the Communist Parties in the West, and Western radio broadcasts were jammed, both those of the state radios (BBC, VOA, RDF,[5] etc.) and those of Radio Free Europe, which was set up by the Americans in Munich as a kind of substitute free press for the captive peoples. Western movies were not shown, and Western plays not staged except for those which appeared to condemn the West. Cultural delegations were exchanged infrequently, and trade was restricted to the minimum necessary for the purchase of key items of equipment, though the West itself contributed to the constriction of trade by placing an embargo on exports considered of military significance.

[5] British Broadcasting Corporation, Voice of America, Radio Diffusion Française.

Under the Stalinist doctrine of socialist realism, moreover, the writers and artists of Eastern Europe had to pretend that the communists were creating a new and higher, or socialist, civilization; that most everything written or created in the West was decadent and corrupt; and that anyone who found praise for anything Western was a capitalist today. The communists developed a system of precensorship by the authors themselves which proved much more effective than the system of post-censorship employed by the more traditional tyrannies. One effect of this policy of isolation, aside from impoverishing the literature and the art of the peoples of Eastern Europe, was to antiquate the machine park of the East European countries. In Czechoslovakia, formerly one of the most advanced industrial countries of Europe, the average textile machine is today some forty years of age. It cannot be replaced by trade with Soviet Russia, because Soviet Russia in most cases doesn't manufacture the most advanced equipment, or at least not sufficient quantities of it, and because Czechoslovakia now does not earn enough currency in the West to be able to import it from that direction either.

Almost everyone now agrees that the period of Stalinist communism was an unhappy time for the peoples of Eastern Europe. Probably a majority of the East European communists would agree with this statement, though they would argue that the "achievements" of Socialism attained under Stalin far outweigh the costs, such as the "retardation" of living standards. Most Westerners, on the other hand, while not denying the existence of Socialist achievements, would feel that the costs were exorbitant.

ACHIEVEMENTS OF STALINISM

Before counting up the costs, let us take a look at the credit side of the ledger. The single most important accomplishment was that of rapid industrial growth. Measured as a percentage of Gross National Product, this ranged in the period 1948-1953 from six percent, in the case of countries already industrially developed, such as Czechoslovakia and East Germany, to twelve percent in the case of overwhelmingly rural countries like Romania and Yugoslavia. The growth rate of France in the same period was roughly five percent annually, that of Britain two, that of the United States three. On the other hand, the growth rate of noncommunist but industrial Japan in the same period was on the order of seven percent. Everyone, on both sides of the East-West line recognizes industrialization (a high rate of industrial growth) as a very important plus. In this twentieth-century world, countries which remain agrarian and raw-material-producing are generally a source of trouble to themselves and to every other country too. China is a good example of such a troublesome country; the Congo another; Peru still a third.

Secondly, there is the achievement of the government ownership of factories, mines, and transportation systems. This may not be regarded as a significant advance, or even an achievement at all, by most Westerners. But in Eastern Europe, where so many factories and mines had in the past been owned or managed by foreign nationals, and where the small size of national economies tended to give large private firms an undue influence in government, this is regarded as an achievement and therefore fair-minded Westerners must so regard it. It is generally believed by Western specialists on Eastern Europe that, when and if the day of liberation from communism comes, public ownership of the major instruments of production and transport will be favored by the large majority in each country. This statement is not meant to include agriculture, or the retail trade, or the service industries generally, but only the large-scale manufacturing and extractive industries.

Thirdly, there is the achievement which in the West is called social security, but in Eastern Europe under communism is especially sweeping and extensive: old age pensions, paid annual vacations for factory workers, free health insurance, low rents in state-owned housing, and the like. It is undoubtedly true that some of the regimes are already finding their obligations under this system onerous and are beginning to redefine their commitments. Both Warsaw and Belgrade have of late taken measures to introduce something approximating economic rents in public housing. But the system as such is probably too firmly established to be seriously modified by any future government, whatever its ideological character. Few Westerners would deny that an extensive system of social security, so long as it does not dull motivation or come at the cost of political liberty, is, in and of itself, a good thing, an achievement, whether of communist socialism or liberal democracy.

All this is true. But some other things are also true. For one thing, there is no necessary correlation between communism, on the one hand, and social security or government ownership of industry on the other. Government ownership and operation of major industry is not unknown in the West, and most Western governments have already gone far in the regulation of industry and seem likely to go further. Social security systems exist in most important Western states, even in that arch-capitalist power, the United States, although they may not be as extensive or as comprehensive as social security under communism. In short, the claim of communism to socialist achievement reduces itself to the claim of communism to industrialization.

Rapid industrialization of backward rural areas (and we must be frank to admit that much of Eastern Europe is backward and rural) is no mean accomplishment. On the contrary, as already suggested, it is one of the two or three most necessary achievements of our time. But again, we must point out that other than communist countries have undergone rapid industrialization. The United States in the period immediately following the American Civil War is one case in point; Germany after unification in 1871 is another; contemporary Japan another. In recent years the rate of growth of GNP in noncommunist Japan has been substantially higher than that of the communist-ruled Soviet Union. In fact, industrialization had begun in many East European countries at least a generation before the communists came to power; as we have already pointed out, the Czech provinces of Bohemia and Moravia were in 1948 among the most highly industrialized provinces in Europe. It seems reasonable to believe that any kind of government would have promoted industrialization in Eastern Europe, along with reconstruction, after 1945, because it would have been in its interest to have done so.

The real achievement, then, is not the mere fact of industrialization, important as this is. The real question is the rate, kind, and cost of industrialization. To justify the communists, in any moral sense, it would be necessary to show (1) that under their rule industrialization proceeded at a much higher rate than would probably have been the case under any other government (2) that under their rule the kind of industrialization undertaken was that which most closely corresponded to the interests of the peoples concerned, and (3) that under their rule the cost in political and social, as well as economic, terms was reasonable and not exorbitant.

On the question of rate, we may have to give the communists the benefit of the doubt. For one thing, rate is in part a function of the base from which the measurement is taken. Countries which are partly industrialized almost inevitably proceed at a slower *rate* than countries which are just beginning, even though the absolute increase per capita may be much greater in the case of the partly industrialized countries. Even under communism, the more industrialized countries of Eastern Europe, such as Czechoslovakia, have much lower rates of growth than the more rural countries, like Romania. Again, rate of growth is to a considerable extent dependent upon the absolute quantity of investment and, in a country in which the government is forcing industrialization, the absolute quantity of investment is in part a function of the extent to which the government is willing to depress, or capable of depressing, living standards. In this area a ruthless, totalitarian government has a built-in advantage. It would be a fair assumption, therefore, that on the average, the totalitarian communists would produce higher rates of growth than, say, democratic regimes, which would of necessity have to take public opinion more into account.

THE COSTS OF STALINISM

On the second point, the kind of industrialization, the communists fare badly. In theory, the communists lay stress on heavy industry because its construction is prerequisite to the development of a consumer goods' industry and thus to the raising of the living standard of the workers. In economic history, however, the relationship was the other way around. In the first country to be industrialized, Great Britain, the textile industry was the leader in mechanization and factorization, iron, steel, and coal production being pulled along afterward. In Soviet industrialization the immediate motive, at least, for placing emphasis on heavy industry, was military. In view of the rising Nazi threat after 1933 and considering what happened to Russia in World War I, this motivation is entirely understandable, when applied to the Soviet economy. But there is a question of whether the great iron and steel complexes of the Stalinist period in Eastern Europe—the Nowa Hutas and the Stalinvaros—are not in fact white elephants, standing as symbols of squandered resources and wasted effort.

Certainly the Soviet government under Khrushchev seemed to reverse Stalin and take this view, since it urged industrial specialization in accordance with the availability of natural resources, as opposed to industrialization across-the-board. The immediate reason for the quarrel between Bucharest and Moscow which broke out into the open in April, 1964, was the fact that Moscow was opposing the construction of a huge iron and steel complex at Galati. (The Romanian was the last of the regimes to get such a project underway.)

Additional proof of the incorrect character of Stalinist industrialization is to be found in the current effort of most regimes to shift their economies from a command to a semimarket basis, to a basis, in short, in which each enterprise will be expected to show a measure of profitability, or close down. It is already clear that economic reform of this kind will involve the shutting down of many regime-built factories, the conversion of many others to different products, significant temporary unemployment, and the transfer of large bodies of workers to other places of employment. These reforms are being undertaken by the communists themselves, in order to get their national economies functioning properly, and are thus a communist admission that, to some considerable extent, Stalinist industrialization built the wrong kind of factories.

Aside from having built many of the wrong factories, Stalinist industrialization introduced into the economies of Eastern Europe certain characteristic distortions. One of these is what might be called overinvestment-underinvestment. There was overinvestment in the sense that too high a proportion of the national income was committed to investment in new plant, and in the long run this produced in many countries a situation curiously like that of economic depression in capitalist countries. There was a sharp decline in the rate of economic growth, severe shortages of some essential consumers' goods (meat in Czechoslovakia, for example, or beer), and widespread unemployment, even though this fact was not acknowledged by the regimes. At the same time there was underinvestment, in the sense that an insufficient proportion of total investment was sunk into the extractive industries, energy sources and transportation, into what the economists call the infrastructure of the economy. Thus the railways were constantly overworked, in terms of both equipment and manpower, frequently without necessary replacements or basic maintenance being undertaken. In East Germany, incredibly enough, the age of the average steam locomotive around 1957 was something like fifty years. Accident rates were high and schedules difficult to maintain. Even more important was the failure to put enough money into the construction of electric power plants, the provision of water to major urban centers, the construction of adequate housing for workers, and the development of mines. As far as infrastructure was concerned, the communists were borrowing from the future or, to put it another way, they were living off the national capital. Sooner or later, and it turned out to be sooner, the nation was going to have to foot the bill for a major overhaul and reconstruction of the economic infrastructure.

Another characteristic distortion was excessive dependence upon Soviet raw materials. The textile industry of Poland, for illustration, worked almost entirely on cotton imported from Soviet Central Asia, the Polish iron and steel industry almost entirely on ore brought a thousand kilometers from Krivoi Rog in the eastern Ukraine, while such oil as was consumed by the Polish transportation system was almost entirely imported via the Friendship Pipe Line from the Caucasus. It was not only that such shipments were sometimes wasteful—Polish economists ruefully calculated that one-half the ore was slag—nor was it so much the fact that the U.S.S.R. had a tendency to charge more for such raw materials than prices on the world market would justify. It was above all the extensive political dependence which such reliance brought with it that was open to criticism. The Soviet Union could at any moment arbitrarily shut down Poland's textile industry, put out Poland's blast furnaces, and cripple Poland's transportation system.

Furthermore, all the regimes paid for industrialization with a stagnant agriculture. Broadly speaking, they got the same agricultural output for a much lower expenditure of manpower, the same meager expenditure of fertilizer and somewhat higher inputs of machinery. Outputs per man-hour had increased, per hectare production remained the same, and market deliveries went up. The regimes must be given credit for consolidating the scattered strips, inherited from medieval times, of which East European farms had previously consisted. But in exchange the regimes saw themselves becoming increasingly dependent upon imported foodstuffs, which the Soviet Union was more and more unable to provide, their agricultural populations overaged and weighted on the female side, and their vegetables and dairy production heavily dependent upon the ideologically obnoxious private plot.

In the post-Stalinist period the Hungarian communists began to experiment with various devices for interesting the peasant in increased (per hectare) output. One such device, the most widespread of all, was known as the Nadudvar incentive system, from the village in northeastern Hungary where it originated. In the Nadudvar system the huge collective fields, when these are devoted to row crops, are broken up after the planting into individual farms, and each farm is assigned to a peasant family. This family assumes complete responsibility for cultivation and for harvesting. The crop is shared, one-third to the peasant family and two-thirds to the state, though *trudoden* [6] payments do continue. Such share-cropping represents a substantial improvement in the economic position of the peasant families involved. Under the collective system, the peasant is only a residual claimant. He gets what is left after taxes have been paid, obligatory deliveries made, and some returns set aside for capital investment and operating expenditures. The collective peasant must pay for bad weather and pay for it alone. Under Stalin this system sometimes spelled outright starvation. But under Nadudvar the peasant gets a third, regardless of whether the crop is good or bad.

It is a significant moral comment on collectivized agriculture that sharecropping means an improvement in the status of the farmer, but here we are interested in what it reveals about the problem of motivation under Stalinist communism. Under Stalinism there is too little relation between effort and reward; the situation is worst in agriculture, where the population of *kolkhozniki* or collective farmers are little better than slaves. In industry, however, with the reintroduction of the piece-work system under the guise of "scientific norms," its use of prisons to combat absenteeism, and its standard shortages of consumers' goods, the situation is not much better.

But it is not the economic costs, high as these are, that condemn Stalinist industrialization in Western minds. It is rather the political costs which seem exorbitant, even if the right industries were being developed. The individual must surrender his civic rights. He no longer has a choice of parties at election time. He no longer has access to vital information affecting public issues. The courts will not protect him from the police. His property is confiscated without adequate compensation, whether it be a huge factory, a miniscule farm, or an urban dwelling. There is, as previously pointed out, little relationship between effort and reward, though the effort must be made in any case. To sum up, there occurs under Stalinism a general degradation of the human individual who is treated as both irresponsible and moronic by a party which sets itself up as the unique repository of truth, the only judge of morality and the sole arbiter of human destiny.

There are also heavy social costs which can be best evaluated if the far-reaching claims of the communists are placed side by side with the current realities of socialist society. For example, the communists claim to emancipate woman. But in reality they create a situation in which the average city-dwelling woman must attempt both to bring up a family *and* to earn her

[6] *Trudoden* payments are payments according to "work-day units." For detailed explanation, *see* footnote, p. 95 above. [EDITOR'S NOTE]

living as a factory or office worker. One result is a sharp increase in social disorganization among youth, what the communists refer to as "hooliganism." Children grow up without proper parental care or supervision. There are supposed to be state nurseries and state crèches,[7] but somehow there are never enough of these by far, even assuming for the moment that they constituted a satisfactory substitute. Another result is that women are constantly overworked, which is injurious to their health, not to speak of their appearance. Since they are tied to home-making in any case, they can undertake training or assume responsibility only with difficulty; consequently much of what they do in the factory or office has a menial and repetitive character. In these circumstances, women are not enthusiastic about having families. This is all the more the case since the state, in its haste to industrialize, has greatly neglected housing construction. In urban eastern Europe the rule is approximately one family to a room, with kitchen and living room and dining room serving also as family dwellings. Newly married couples often have to move in with one or the other set of parents. The consequence has been a decline in the birth rate and an astonishing increase in the number of abortions. In both Hungary and Czechoslovakia, for example, the number of abortions each year is now approximately as great as the number of live births.

Perhaps the sharpest commentary on the non-economic costs of Stalinism is provided by the attitude of youth toward the brave new world which the communists claim to be building. Despite education in communist-controlled school systems, despite extensive propagandizing in compulsory communist youth organizations, youth throughout Eastern Europe is negative, cynical, and materialistic. It is an accurate generalization to say that youth born under communism does not believe in it. Communist-educated youth firmly believes that the situation of youth in the West is much better than its own. Communist-indoctrinated youth has defied the regimes on the issue of Western music, such as jazz, which the regimes sought to prohibit as sign and symbol of the West and its way of life. Eastern youth and Western radio—Luxembourg and Free Europe in particular—combined to deal the regimes a stunning defeat on this issue; the regimes themselves had to get into the popular music business in order to influence their own younger generations. It is also probably true that communist-educated youth does not believe in Western democracy any more than it believes in Eastern communism. It has rather been taught by the harsh circumstances of its upbringing to believe in material comfort, professional education, and political adaptability.

With the advantage of hindsight, it is easy to see that the Stalinist industrialization of Eastern Europe was as much a reflection of Soviet state interests as anything else. The construction of heavy industry at a feverish

[7] Public nurseries where working mothers can leave their children during the day. [EDITOR'S NOTE]

pace provided Moscow with additional military strength in its struggle with the West. It is noteworthy that East European Stalinism became most extreme, its industrial goals the most exaggerated and its use of terror the most widespread, after the beginning of the Korean War. Eastern Europe was becoming in fact a processor of Soviet raw materials. The iron ore of Krivoi Rog was to be converted into steel at Kosice, the cotton of the Kuban made into cloth at Lodz, and so on. In the meantime, Eastern Europe would become inextricably and unalterably dependent upon the Soviet Union in an economic sense. It would virtually cease to trade with the West, and it would live from trade with the Soviet Union and the Soviet Bloc.

While the East European peoples were ruled in name by their respective Communist Parties, the vital decisions which affected their national interests and their national future were in fact taken in Moscow. These decisions were then transmitted down to bodies of Soviet "advisers" stationed in the Satellite countries. There were economic advisers with the national planning bodies and sometimes even in the factories; there were special advisers with the national security police. These Soviet advisers were the real rulers of the countries. It was, apparently, the Soviet police advisers in Prague who staged the arrest, interrogation and public trial of Slansky [8] and his fellows. In Poland, militarily the most significant of all the satellites, the command of the army was confided to Marshal Constantin Rokosovsky, an ethnic Pole who, born in Russia, had made a career first with the tsarist, then with the Soviet armed forces. Such facts make it much clearer why a Czechoslovakia, already highly industrialized, undertook to shift her existing industrial capacity from the production of consumers' goods to the manufacture of machinery, and why further growth was concentrated in the field of heavy industry with the raw materials imported largely from the U.S.S.R.

There has been much complaint that the reparations imposed by the Soviet Union upon such former Axis allies as Romania were excessive, that in the formation of joint Soviet-Hungarian or Soviet-Bulgarian companies the local government provided all the capital, or that the prices charged for Soviet raw materials were above world-market levels while the prices paid for Satellite finished goods were below. There was considerable truth in these charges. But they constituted only a secondary bill of particulars. The real indictment of Soviet policy in Eastern Europe is more serious and more far-reaching. It is that the Soviet Union, after forcing upon these populations governments which in their vast majority they did not want, proceeded to govern in the interests, not of the governed, but of Soviet power. The Soviet motto was a simple one: what is good for the Soviet Union is good for Eastern Europe!

[8] R. Slansky had been Secretary General of the Communist Party of Czechoslovakia and leader of the extremist faction. Since he and his fellow defendants were mainly of Jewish origin, the trial, which took place in 1952, had anti-Semitic overtones.

THE OVERTHROW OF STALINISM
AND THE RISE OF REVISIONISM

The Stalinist system in Eastern Europe was a failure, a costly failure, and a cruel one. This is not along the judgment of Westerners, experts and propagandists alike. It was also the view of the communists themselves, as demonstrated by the fact that, shortly after the death of the great dictator, they began to abandon the system he had created and ended up by denouncing it as a perversion of true socialism. As a symbol of their new approach, the leaders in the Kremlin caused the body of Stalin to be removed from the tomb, outside the Kremlin wall, which it had shared with the body of Lenin.

The attempt to relax the rigid controls which Stalin had imposed and to replace them with a more tolerable system proved a precarious and even a dangerous task. This was in itself additional proof, if any were needed, that the peoples of Eastern Europe had suffered grievously under Stalinism and were violently opposed to it. In May, 1953, the population of the Bohemian city of Plzen [9] rioted tumultuously in protest against currency reform measures which confiscated most of their savings. For a few hours the situation was out of control with the rioters in command of city hall, where they hoisted the U.S. flag and demanded major reforms. In June, 1953, a body of building workers in East Berlin went on strike in protest against new increases in the work norms. The workers also formulated certain demands. The news of the strike, together with a listing of the demands, was broadcast throughout East Germany by the American transmitter RIAS, situated in West Berlin. As a consequence there were strikes and protest marches throughout the country the following day. It was eminently clear that the vast bulk of the urban population, even groups which had been especially privileged, were opposed to the regime and wished for free elections. The movement was so widespread and so swift that Moscow at once set in motion parts of the twenty-two Soviet divisions stationed in East Germany to put an end to the demonstrations and restore order. But it was clear to all concerned that, except for the presence of these divisions, the East German Communist regime would have disappeared virtually overnight.

Three years later, in late October and early November, 1956, a rising of even more serious proportions took place in Hungary. In contrast with its East German predecessor, the Hungarian rising was preceded by a period of revolutionary ferment, particularly among party intellectuals. This ferment concerned itself primarily with two subjects—the restrictions of socialist realism, the party doctrine which turned all writers into witting

---

[9] Pilsen, in the German form. [EDITOR'S NOTE]

propagandists for the regime, and the fact that the Hungarian Stalinists who had been most directly responsible for the mass use of terror were still in power although their doctrine and their policy had been officially denounced. The ferment was greatly increased by the fact that the Hungarian leadership was split, the Stalinists retaining control of the party while revisionist elements dominated the government bureaucracy, and by the further fact that the peasants were permitted—for the first time in Bloc history—to leave the collective farms in great numbers and return to private agriculture.

The Hungarian uprising was a more serious affair than its East German forerunner on several counts. For one thing the communist government itself went out of control, announcing that Hungary was withdrawing from the Warsaw Pact and would shortly hold free elections. For another, the Hungarian Communist Party virtually dissolved during the uprising, the bulk of its members joining the resistance or going into hiding. For still another, the Soviet Union had to move in additional divisions to cope with the disturbance, and the fighting went on for several days, even though the resistance elements were badly out-armed and for the most part organized on the spot. The street mobs lynched members of the secret police whenever these could be identified. Again, it was clear to all concerned that without the intervention of the Soviet armed forces the Hungarian Communist regime would simply have disappeared. In free elections the Communist Party could, in all probability, have not received more than five or ten percent of the vote. This was the Hungarian verdict on Stalinism and all its works.

At almost exactly the same time there were comparable disturbances in Poland though, very fortunately, no mass shedding of blood. The Polish Communist Party, in an act of open rebellion, restored to the key position of first secretary an old-time communist who had been first deposed and then imprisoned under Stalin on charges of national deviation. The Soviet leadership ordered Soviet divisions stationed in East Germany and in the Soviet Union to move at once to the Polish frontier, while Soviet divisions stationed within Poland moved on Warsaw. The Soviet leaders then flew to Warsaw in a body with the intention of enforcing their will. They found upon arrival that they were virtually prisoners of the Polish security police and that they were faced with an ultimatum: return the Soviet divisions to their original positions at once and accept the new first secretary or face a general Polish uprising. This would have been a far more serious affair than even the Hungarian rebellion. The Polish Communists pretty largely controlled the Polish army and would probably have thrown it into action. In Hungary, the regime army for the greater part remained in its barracks, unwilling to take a stand either for or against the revolution. There were, furthermore, some thirty million Poles and only ten million Hungarians. Given the strategic location of Poland, widespread disturbances in that country might have spread into East Germany.

The baffled Soviet leaders, after assuring themselves that the restored Polish leadership had no intention of abandoning communism by calling for free elections, surrendered to the Polish ultimatum with as much grace as they could muster and left the country. It was understood on all sides, furthermore, that the Polish leaders would abandon certain key features of the Stalinist system, such as the systematic use of terror, the employment of force in the collectivization of agriculture (which, in Poland, still in 1956, in contrast with the situation in Czechoslovakia, for instance, remained overwhelmingly in private hands), and the stationing in Poland of Soviet advisers to work with the army, the security police, and the planning apparatus.

The risings of 1953 and 1956 were not only a condemnation of Stalinism; they also contributed to the emergence of a new kind of communism in Eastern Europe. For want of a better term we may call the new communism revisionist. The flash risings taught the communist rulers many things, among them that Stalinism had imposed an intolerable burden on the peoples of Eastern Europe, that there were distinct limits to the sacrifices which might be exacted by minority communist regimes from anticommunist majorities, and that steps would have to be taken to secure a minimum degree of positive cooperation from the populations. At the same time the East Europeans had learned a vital lesson, too. This was that the West would not risk war with the Soviet Union in order to free them from communist tyranny even in the event they rose in arms. They would have to live with communism for the indefinite future. They would therefore have to make some accommodation. There was thus laid the basis for a kind of silent bargaining between regimes and peoples, in which the regimes offered concessions in exchange for a minimum of positive cooperation. This bargaining process was one basis of revisionist communism.

There was another, however, and that was the emergence in Moscow of N. S. Khrushchev as Stalin's successor, but on a program of anti-Stalinism. Khrushchev and those who supported him agreed that Stalinism had to go, that it was no longer in the interests either of the World Revolution or of the Soviet state, and that a substitute system had to be worked out. Khrushchev, whose principal support in the struggle for succession had come from the party apparatus, the hard core of full-time party officials, was the principal formulator and advocate of the new system. The fact that the system was going to be radically changed was first announced by Khrushchev in a secret speech to the XX Congress of the Communist Party of the Soviet Union. This congress took place in February, 1956, and knowledge of the secret speech was one factor promoting the ferment which led to the upheavals in Poland and in Hungary in October of the same year. In this speech Khrushchev denounced Stalin as a bloody tyrant who had suffered from paranoia.

THE NEW SYSTEM: REVISIONIST COMMUNISM

Khrushchevian or revisionist communism was based on three principles. The first and most important of these is the renunciation of terror as an instrument of government. Stalin had ruled the party and the government through the security police. Under Khrushchev the police were downgraded and deprived of much of their authority and responsibility. Arbitrary arrests by and large came to an end. Defendants in criminal trials were given some opportunity to defend themselves and with time the innocence of the defendant even became the standard presumption. At the same time the dominant position in the regime was taken over by the party apparatus, in line with the practice of Lenin's day.

Secondly, revisionist communism meant the continuation of Socialist construction by the use of material incentives. To put it in plainer language, industrialization was to continue at a forced pace, but instead of driving the population to work by the use of terror, the regime would introduce a reasonable relationship between effort and reward. The population would be trusted, its patriotism appealed to, and its efforts compensated with higher living standards. The relationship between regime and population would become positive, one of mutual confidence and cooperation. In the long run, this would necessarily mean a shift in industrial priorities. Greater emphasis would have to be given light or consumer industry in order to satisfy the justified expectations of the population.

Thirdly, Khrushchev intended to put each of the ruling parties on its own. The Soviet advisers were withdrawn from the Peoples Democracies in Eastern Europe; Soviet party officials of long standing were appointed ambassadors to the satellite capitals; and there were regular conferences between Soviet and satellite party leaders for the coordination of policy. No longer were the day-to-day decisions made for each satellite party in Moscow and then transmitted to the resident Soviet advisers for communication to the local authorities. Each party was now in charge of its own internal affairs so long as it did not tamper with the fundamentals of the system. No longer was it necessary shamelessly to imitate everything Moscow did, nor to praise Moscow's actions without stint. As to foreign policy, more specifically as to policy toward the Western arch-enemy, Khrushchev assumed that, among brotherly parties, only a minimum of coordination would be necessary; in this area the leadership of the father party in Moscow would, he believed, be accepted by the son parties on the periphery without question.

What Khrushchev attempted to create was a humane totalitarianism. There was still the one-party system dedicated to rapid industrialization of the East and the ultimate destruction of institutional arrangements peculiar to the West. The security police, though now subordinated to the party and limited in their activity, were still in being. There were still censorship, propaganda campaigns, and socialist realism. Now, however, the populations were no longer to be badgered and terrorized into cooperation with the fluenced by the example of Yugoslavia, the one independent communist aims was to be secured by a system of material rewards supplemented by the traditional "brain-washing." Goulash communism, Khrushchev called it.

In formulating his new version of totalitarian communism, especially as it applied to the East European regimes, Khrushchev was probably influenced by the example of Yugoslavia, the one independent Communist state in Eastern Europe. An early sign of the direction in which he was moving was his reversal of Stalin's policy of excommunication of the Yugoslav heretics and his attempt to reach a reconciliation with them (May, 1955). (It is interesting to note in this connection that one of the key issues leading to a breach in the Cominform in 1948 was Belgrade's refusal of Soviet advisers for the Yugoslav security police.) In seeking reconciliation with the Yugoslavs, Khrushchev made their variant regime, or at least certain features of it, politically available in Eastern Europe.

Among other things, the Yugoslavs had worked out a curious compromise between the principle of central planning and the imperatives of market economics. This compromise, or at least certain aspects of it, no doubt appeared to offer to Khrushchev a way out of the gross inefficiencies which Stalin's central administration of the economy had brought with it. At the same time, in attempting a reconciliation, Khrushchev may have thought that he could persuade the Yugoslav Communists to rejoin what Khrushchev increasingly referred to as the "socialist commonwealth," since there were no more "advisers," and each ruling party enjoyed autonomy in its domestic affairs.

There can be little doubt but that goulash communism was for the sorely-tried peoples of Eastern Europe a major improvement and even a hopeful step in the right direction. Revisionism did not reconcile these peoples to communism or Soviet hegemony, but it did bring about a significant improvement in their daily lives. In addition, it gave them room for political maneuver and some bargaining power. The reaction of the West was a slow and qualified approval. Any improvement in living conditions was a prime *desideratum*, a contribution to the reduction of international tension. Opportunities to expand the influence of the West through increased trade, tourism, and cultural exchange were gradually seized upon. The slow and uncoordinated reaction of the West to the spread of revisionism was the replacement of the policy of containment with the policy of building bridges or, as it is sometimes called, the policy of peaceful engagement.

The acceptance of the West was thus provisional. It was the acceptance of an alleviation which was also an opportunity, not the acceptance of the *status quo*. There were, in fact, increasing signs that revisionism was a *provisorium* and that it would undergo evolution, perhaps even organic change, in an historically short period of time.

BREAKDOWN OF COMMUNIST DISCIPLINE

In a very few years it became apparent that the principle of the more or less automatic coordination of Bloc foreign policy would not work. Khrushchev undertook to visit Belgrade in 1955 and to denounce Stalin in 1956. By 1958 he was involved in a quarrel with the Chinese Communists so serious that it was probably even then irreparable. There were many reasons for this quarrel. For one thing, the Soviets were fearful that Chinese risk-taking might end by involving the U.S.S.R. in a nuclear war and thus destroy all or most of what the Bolsheviks had built up at such great sacrifice over two generations.

But probably the prime cause of the quarrel was the refusal of the Soviets to give all-out aid for the industrialization of China. Apparently the Chinese even expected the Soviets to accept lower living standards in order to industrialize China. At any rate, they could not understand why Soviet assistance went to Egypt, a country which imprisoned communists, or to India, China's chief competitor for the role of leading Asian power. The Chinese view was quite simply that the industrialization of their giant country in a generation or two would make of China a third superpower, alongside the U.S. and the U.S.S.R., and thus shift the balance of power sharply in favor of the Socialist camp and prepare the way for the final destruction of capitalism.

The Soviets, however, were evidently not so sure that the rapid industrialization of China was a good thing. They gave substantial aid, equipment for more than two hundred essential industrial complexes with the specialists to set them up and get them running; but they were not prepared to abandon, or even cut back, their aid to nonsocialist developing countries, much less reduce their own living standards. A Chinese superpower, communist or otherwise, could constitute a major threat to the U.S.S.R. Soviet fears seemed justified when the disappointed Chinese first expelled the Soviet experts and refused further aid, then denounced and damned their mentors, subsequently set about systematically to snatch from them the leading position in the world movement, and finally, in July, 1964, laid public claim to vast stretches of Soviet territory.

The national interests of Communist China and Soviet Russia were in direct conflict and the communist ideology, instead of making it easier to reconcile or compromise these differences, rather made them more difficult by escalating every difference to the level of ideological principle. What made it worse from the communist point-of-view was that the quarrel with the

Chinese rapidly became a schism in which both Moscow and Peking attempted to rally as many of the world parties, both those in power and those out, around their respective banners. This situation led to the defection of Albania from the Soviet to the Chinese camp. The fact that China was able to develop within Europe a satellite of its own was in itself a severe blow to Soviet prestige.

Significantly enough, the Albanian defection was intimately related to Khrushchev's effort to achieve a reconciliation with the Yugoslav Communists. At the time of the breach in the Cominform back in 1948, Albania had been in every sense of the word a Yugoslav satellite just as Poland, say, was a Soviet dependency. Actually, Belgrade had planned to incorporate Albania as a sixth Yugoslav republic; extensive groundwork for such incorporation had been laid. But the Albanians did not wish to be absorbed by Yugoslavia any more than the Yugoslavs desired to be dominated by the Soviets; Albania seized upon the breach in the Cominform to break off all relations with Yugoslavia and move into the Soviet orbit. Khrushchev's attempted rapprochement with Tito thus aroused the fears of Tirana, which anticipated being sold down the Yugoslav river by Khrushchev. Furthermore, the fears of Tirana were magnified by the fact that since 1948 Yugoslavia had gone revisionist in a rather startling way, whereas Khrushchev himself appeared intrigued by this heresy. The Albanian leaders feared revisionism and its effect upon their regime as they feared the plague. They clung to Stalin and all his works and sang his praises to the whole communist world. And they switched in 1961 a second time to another orbit, this time to the Chinese. The Soviet Bloc, startled and mortified by this strange development, cut off economic assistance and cast the doughty Albanians into outer ideological darkness. The contrast between the revisionist U.S.S.R. on the one hand, and Stalinist, or at least extremist, China, on the other, was now clearer than ever.

But more important than the growing ideological diversity was the fact that Soviet control over Eastern Europe had been undermined. As a totalitarian faith, by definition one in possession of absolute truth, communism could not brook two centers, two papacies, so to speak. In totalitarianism two centers are the same as no center because they will automatically come into conflict. Where there is no agreement about doctrine, the bonds of discipline, which reflect that doctrine, loosen and decay. It was not long before another party, this time the Romanian, attempted to take advantage of the new situation; by threatening to imitate Albania and change orbits, it managed to adopt a position of neutrality in the Sino-Soviet quarrel and in April, 1964, to declare its independence of Moscow. There are, said the Romanian Central Committee Declaration of April 22, 1964, in the world communist movement no father parties and no son parties; no party with a right to determine true doctrine for other parties; no party with a right to impose or depose leaderships on other parties; and no party with a right to abolish or dissolve other parties (a reference to the Soviet action of 1938 disbanding the Polish Communist Party). There was instead only the world family of fully equal and sovereign parties, each with the right to determine true doctrine, appoint its own leadership, and "build socialism" in accordance with the special circumstances prevailing in its own country.

The Romanian action was a pleasant, if somewhat unbelievable, surprise to the West. But it was no surprise to communist insiders, who were fully aware of severe disagreements which had arisen between Moscow and Bucharest. As in the Chinese case, it was again primarily a question of industrialization. The Soviet comrades desired Romania, which had not yet begun to industrialize in a major way, to specialize in petrochemicals, synthetic fertilizers, and food processing. The Soviet position was that the Romanians should develop those branches of industry for which the raw materials were present in the Romanian homeland. This would profit the Bloc as a whole as well as Romania herself, who could import complex machinery and iron and steel products from the members of the Bloc (the U.S.S.R., East Germany, and Czechoslovakia) who already possessed such facilities.

The Romanians objected strenuously. They wished to industrialize their country across-the-board. In particular, they wished to build an iron and steel industry even though, as the Soviets pointed out, Romania would have to import the raw materials for such an industry from abroad, perhaps from Krivoi Rog in the eastern Ukraine. The Romanians argued that to specialize prior to all-round industrialization, as the Soviets suggested, would be to make permanent their status as an agrarian and (by definition) backward country. Modern nations, whether great or small, had steel industries, in the Romanian view. When the Soviets refused all aid for a Romanian iron and steel industry, the Romanians cut back on their trade with the U.S.S.R. and used the difference to import the necessary equipment and technicians from Western Europe. As usual in such basic quarrels, one step led to another; the final act was the Romanian declaration of independence on April 22, 1964.

The Khrushchev policy of autonomy for ruling parties thus fostered defection and rebellion. Parties in power, once the Stalinist clamps were removed, tended to follow the national interests of the countries they ruled. Where these conflicted with those of the Soviet Union, serious trouble ensued. Stalin had lost Yugoslavia by insisting on his clamps, but Khrushchev with his policies of autonomy had lost China, and together with China, North Korea, and North Vietnam, not to mention Albania and Romania. Khrushchev's successors, it appears, came close to losing Bulgaria, too. At least in March, 1965, the Bulgarian security police broke up a conspiracy based on army units and led by former partisans. This conspiracy from all accounts aimed not at the overthrow of the regime but at independence from Soviet tutelage. It seemed likely that as time went on the other Communist Parties of Eastern Europe would seek and gain greater independence from the Muscovite center.

DECLINE OF CENTRAL PLANNING

As far as internal revisionism is concerned, that is, the general notion of persuading the population to give their positive cooperation to the totalitarian regimes, it is perhaps too early yet to speak of success or failure. At present writing one thing seems probable. Most of the regimes in Eastern Europe will have to abandon central planning in the sense of central management in order to make the system of material incentives work. In the long run it will prove impossible to work out a reasonably close correlation between effort and reward without bringing prices reasonably close to actual costs. This in turn signifies some considerable movement toward the free enterprise system, a synthesis of market and planned economy more or less along the lines which the Yugoslavs have been working out.

All the East European regimes except the Romanian and the Albanian are moving toward some synthesis of market and plan. In every case there is internal opposition to such reform from both the state bureaucracy and the party apparatus. It is not clear how far the bureaucracy and, what is much more important, the apparatus will succeed in denaturing or even derailing the proposed reforms and how far the requirements of economics and the need of the regime for popular cooperation will make reform inevitable. A number of factors favor the reformers. For one thing, the economies of Eastern Europe with the exception of the Romanian and the East German regimes find themselves in serious difficulties. The rates of economic growth are much below those required either by the political needs of the regimes or by the necessities of an incentive policy. To take the worst case as an example, Czechoslovakia in 1963 had a negative rate of economic growth—not a low rate, but no rate. It is precisely in Czechoslovakia that one of the most extensive and thorough-going reforms has been worked out, proposed, and, at least formally, adopted.

For another thing, it is probably now impossible for the regimes to return to the systematic use of political terror as a means of getting popular cooperation. Only in the event of some major disaster, such as war, would it be possible to rely heavily on the police power to keep the economy running. Even the Communist Parties themselves, with their tragic experience of purges and how easily they get out of control, would probably not otherwise tolerate a return to terror. In short, there is in present circumstances nothing to do but resort to greater use of material incentives.

Finally, the U.S.S.R. itself is no longer in a position to subsidize or bail out a regime in economic difficulties. The Soviets themselves are confronted with the same problem of material incentives and economic reform; they may have overextended themselves with their aid program for the developing countries; and the available evidence suggests that they themselves are encouraging the regimes to build up their markets in the West. Many of the regimes are faced with a problem of low labor productivity which can in present circumstances only be resolved by the import of high grade machinery from the West. The Soviets either do not make sufficient quantities of the machines required or do not manufacture them at all. In order to increase imports from the West, however, the regimes will have to augment their exports to this area. But this in turn involves producing exports which can compete in the European, that is, in the world market. As a general rule, none of the regimes can produce manufactured goods which will sell in the West unless they be sold at a loss, as is the case, for example, with Czechoslovak exports of Skoda automobiles. In order to compete in the West the regimes must greatly increase the efficiency of their economies; this means far-reaching economic reform.

In order to understand more precisely what is at stake, let us look briefly at the proposed Czechoslovak economic reform since it is one of the most radical of all those adopted so far. In the first place there is to be an end to central management. Factories will no longer report to the ministries in Prague nor will their capital funds be allocated to them by the state budget free of charge. Instead, factories producing related goods will be placed under the management of managerial concerns analogous to the trusts or cartels of the West. They will have to borrow their working capital from a set of banks which will be established and provided with funds by the state. The banks will loan money to the cartels and the factories on commercial principles. That is, the bank will make no loan unless there is a very good prospect that the loan will be repaid on schedule plus interest. The reform—and this is an indication of its radical character—calls for the introduction of interest rates, long denounced by Marxist-Leninists as a wicked capitalist device for the exploitation of the workers. The factories themselves will be expected to run on a profit and loss basis. Managers will be appointed and removed because of their ability or inability to produce a profit and not because of their political loyalty or their years of service to the party. The role of Party officials within the factory will be reduced; they will no longer be allowed to sap the workers' energies by calling interminable political meetings. Factories which remain in the red will be shut down even if this involves temporary unemplyoment. Factories which export to the West will be permitted to keep a substantial portion of their hard currency earnings instead of surrendering them entirely to a state office.

Above all there will be, according to the Czechoslovak proposal, price reform. Obviously the measures described above would have little value without price reform. Profit would have little meaning if the prices of transportation or machine tools were kept below cost by means of state subsidies. The Czechoslovak reforms envision in the beginning three types of prices. Some prices, such as those of basic raw materials, will continue to be fixed by central authority, though even in this case that authority is supposed to take actual costs into account. A second kind of price will be allowed to vary between fixed limits. A third will be subject only to the play of market forces. But this triple classification of prices is assumed by the reformers to constitute only a transition. Ultimately all prices, or virtually all prices, will be determined primarily by the play of market forces.

The reader may well ask what will be left of socialism if such a reform is actually carried out. The same question is put by the communist *aparatchiki* themselves as they fight vigorously against the reform. Under the Czechoslovak proposal central planning would remain only as a government office which could outline desirable areas and rates of economic growth but would have only indirect power to influence these areas and rates through the manipulation of interest rates, taxes, and the like. These are the controls which the governments of the West employ. Central planning, as both Stalin and Khrushchev had understood it, that is to say, as central management, would be dismantled. More important still, the role of the party apparatus in directing the economic life of the country would be greatly reduced. Cartels and factories would be run by a new managerial class selected on the basis of competence. This managerial class would in fact enjoy certain autonomy; as a class, they would have power in their own right. For a party whose mission had been the industrialization of a country by political means, this would be a morale-shaking blow.

Nonetheless, much of socialism would remain even after the reform. All industry would continue to be owned by the state even if operated by the managers. Trade unions would not be free to bargain or to strike. Agriculture would remain collectivized, a last stronghold of the embattled party apparatchik. Government would remain a dictatorship. Elections would continue fraudulent. The development of semimarket economies in Eastern Europe, however, from a Western point of view would constitute a major step in the right direction. It would at the same time signify a major failure of Khrushchevian revisionism in the sense that it would demonstrate that goulash communism, if possible at all, was only possible at heavy cost to the power and prestige of the ruling Communist Party.

Thinking back on it, the current economic crisis of communism in Eastern Europe appears to have been inevitable. How could the communist leaders have ever believed that capital could be treated as a free good without an interest charge when common sense would have suggested that capital can be accumulated only as the consequence of deferred spending? The very capital which they beat out of the backs of the collectivized peasantry? Or how could the communist leaders have been so naïve as to believe that they could run a complex economy efficiently without charging rent for the use of land or using profit as an indicator of enterprise efficiency?

There are two answers to these questions. One is that in an underdeveloped country, a country virtually without industry, it is relatively easy to industrialize by political fiat. An open pit mine, so to speak, can be dug by gangs of prisoners. Thus the inadequacy of Marxist economic theory did not particularly hamper the communists until they had developed a fairly complex industrial system or, as in the case of Czechoslovakia and East Germany, had taken over a country that was already industrialized. The second reason for the failure of communist industrial management is much simpler. Marxism-Leninism as an economic doctrine was essentially a creation of the nineteenth century. In the twentieth it was badly out of date. It was as if surgeons in 1967 should attempt to operate for cancer with the techniques of 1867, the year of publication of *Das Kapital*; the patient would almost surely die.

THE QUESTION OF POSITIVE COOPERATION

What we have been saying is that Stalinism in Eastern Europe was by 1953 an egregious failure, such that the communists themselves abandoned it and probably would not attempt to return to it except in the event of war. We also have been saying that Khrushchev revisionism, at least from the viewpoint of the communists themselves, had gotten off to a very bad start. Khrushchev himself was forced to preside over the beginnings of the dissolution of communism as a world system while the effort to develop a goulash communism is apparently leading to economic reforms which will make an end of central planning as both Stalin and Khrushchev understood it. The question remains whether even the development of semimarket economies will suffice to win for the communists the positive cooperation of the populations of Eastern Europe. Will material incentives, assuming a much closer correlation between effort and reward is achieved as a consequence of economic reform, suffice? Will Poles, Czechs, Hungarians, and the like settle for a slow but continued improvement in their living standards? Will they exchange political liberty for goulash? Especially when they see the French, the Italians, the Belgians, in short their brother nations of Western Europe, enjoying not only much higher living standards but also the personal freedoms of democratic government as well?

There are already, even before the question of economic reform has been settled, signs that goulash communism will not be enough. One is the proposal by an Hungarian communist (Otto Bihari) for revivifying the Hungarian parliament.[10] Bihari proposes that, instead of a single national list at election time, all members of which are automatically returned, Hungary go back to her traditional practice of single-member constituencies. In each constituency at least three candidates, all communists, of course, would run against each other; two would have to lose. Furthermore, parliament should

[10] "A kepviseleti demokracia" ("Democracy of representation"), *Tarsadalmi Szemle* (Budapest, August-September, 1965), pp. 42-55.

meet regularly and for long periods, according to Bihari, instead of twice a year for periods of two or three days. Parliament should debate national issues and deputies should make frequent use of interpellation. What is more, according to this proposal, the government should issue no decree without having first sought and obtained the advice and approval of the appropriate parliamentary committee. On crucial issues there might be held from time to time referenda, so that the population as a whole could express its views.

For a communist author and a communist periodical, at least in Eastern Europe, this is a fairly startling proposal, significant by the very fact that it could be made. Characteristically enough, the Yugoslavs have so far given broadest consideration to the revivification of parliamentary life. Their national parliament has already become a public forum for the discussion of major legislation. (In two or three instances the parliament has even rejected a government proposal!) Among intellectuals generally, and especially in university circles, there has appeared an ultra-revisionism, which takes pleasure in asserting publicly that the party cannot be the sole authority in matters of truth, and which hints broadly that the achievement of true socialism may not be possible without a restoration of the multi-party system. In March and April of 1965, the Yugoslavs held what for a communist country was a most unusual election. In accordance with existing electoral law, local voters' meetings played a major role in the selection of candidates for three levels of legislature—the communal or local, the republican, and the national. But contrary to previous practice, according to which there were to be no more candidates nominated than seats available, in the March-April 1965 elections there turned out to be twice as many candidates for the communal assemblies than there were seats, 40 percent more at the republican level and 15 percent at the national. Thus the voters were not only encouraged to influence the selection of candidates, but they were also on election day given some choice among candidates. It is true that all the candidates were communists; nonetheless ability to choose even among communist candidates is an important change. The other regimes, or most of them, are now imitating the Yugoslav experiment with market forces. In view of the problem of motivation which they face may they not also in due course undertake to breathe some life into their moribund parliamentary systems, perhaps along Yugoslav lines? And would not this reduce once again the role of the party, so essential to the Khrushchevian system?

EVALUATION OF THE REVISIONIST SOLUTION

If we take the whole range of revisionist development into consideration we see at once that revisionist communism, as far at least as Eastern Europe is concerned, is only a compromise between the demands of Soviet Russia and the desires of the peoples themselves. There is not the slightest doubt in anybody's mind as to the outcome of free elections in this area: the Communist Party would go down to irretrievable defeat. Revisionist communism emerged because Stalinism proved such an abysmal failure. The question now before Europe and the world is whether even revisionist communism can succeed in Eastern Europe. If the system is reformed sufficiently to make it work, that is to say, so reformed as to secure the positive cooperation of the peoples, will it not become a communist system in name only? And will not the Communist Parties, backed by Soviet Russia, therefore, end up by stopping further reform and settling for an inefficient yet communist tyranny? In short, even under revisionism the situation in Eastern Europe is an unstable one, and future developments will undoubtedly contain many surprises, as well for the West as for the Soviet Union.

The basic problem continues to be the fact that Eastern Europe remains an area of vital interest to the U.S.S.R. This interest is less vital than it was twenty years ago because the development of nuclear weapons makes the to and fro of land campaigns across Eastern Europe much less likely and important as a military way of settling the East-West conflict. In fact the area has even lost in importance in Soviet eyes as an early warning system, since with the development of long range missiles it is less likely that manned bombers will be used in attack on the U.S.S.R. Still, the Soviets have a vital interest, just as the U.S. continues to have a vital interest in Cuba, Mexico, and the Caribbean area.

The basic problem is, however, not only the Soviet interest in Eastern Europe; it is much more the insistence of the Soviet leaders on interpreting these interests through the filter of communist ideology. It is the association of Russia with the world communist movement which makes of revisionism at present the only practical alternative to Stalinism. If the state interests of the U.S.S.R. were all that was involved, it would be possible to work out for most of the East European countries a solution comparable to that of Finland or of Austria. There is reason to believe that such a solution would be eminently satisfactory to the East European peoples. The real obstacle to such solution is the fact that the formal abandonment of communism by any people which had once enjoyed its "benefits" would be a body blow to world communism and to communist regimes everywhere. Communism lives and grows in good part on the myth that it is morally and culturally superior to the way of life of the West. This is its great attraction in the developing countries, that it will bring modern industry in a hurry while simultaneously rejecting the imperialist West. To be sure, we can discern the beginnings of a process of disassociation between the Soviet Union and communism. This is in part the meaning of the schism between Moscow and Peking; Moscow is no longer willing to run such great risks as she once was in order to advance the communist cause. There is of course an intimate connection between this process of disassociation and the emergence of revisionism. Perhaps it is in this continuing connection that the hope of Eastern Europe lies.

FURTHER READING SUGGESTIONS

Burks, R. V., "Eastern Europe" in Cyril E. Black and Thomas P. Thornton eds., *Communism and Revolution. The Strategic Uses of Political Violence.* Princeton: Princeton University Press paperback, 1965, pp. 77-116.

————, "The Thaw and the Future of Eastern Europe," *Encounter* (London, August, 1964), pp. 24-32.

————, "Yugoslavia: Has Tito Gone Bourgeois?", *East Europe* (New York, August, 1965), pp. 2-14.

Griffith, William E., *The Sino-Soviet Rift.* London: G. Allen, 1964.

————, ed., *Communism in Europe. Continuity, Change and the Sino-Soviet Dispute.* Cambridge: The MIT Press, 1964.

Gross, George, "Rumania: The Fruits of Autonomy," *Problems of Communism* (Washington, D. C., January-February, 1966), pp. 16-27.

Grossman, Gregory, *Value and Plan: Economic Calculation and Organization in Eastern Europe.* Berkeley: University of California Press, 1960.

Montias, John Michael, "Background and Origins of the Rumanian Dispute with Comecon," *Soviet Studies,* XII (Glasgow, 1964), pp. 125-151.

Shaffer, Harry G., "Czechoslovakia's New Economic Model," *Problems of Communism* (September-October, 1965), pp. 31-40.

Skendi, Stavro, "Albania and the Sino-Soviet Conflict," *Foreign Affairs* (New York, April, 1962), pp. 471-478.

Zinner, Paul, *Communist Strategy and Tactics in Czechoslovakia 1918-48.* New York: Praeger, 1963.

————, *Revolution in Hungary.* New York: Columbia University Press, 1962.

10

The Socialist Transformation of East Europe: A Western Marxist View

SCOTT NEARING *

CHAIRMAN, SOCIAL SCIENCE INSTITUTE,
HARBORSIDE, MAINE

WITH A SUPPLEMENT BY

V. ISUPOV, B. LODYGIN, V. TEREKHOV, and O. BOGOMOLOV †

SOVIET ECONOMISTS

ONSET OF A SOCIAL REVOLUTION

East Europe, politically, has had a long record of conquest, subordination, dependence, and exploitation. For thousands of years the territory was over-run by migrants from Asia and northern Europe. Its rich plains, its fertile

* Except for a small passage added by Scott Nearing especially for publication here, his contribution has been condensed from his *Socialism in Practice: Transformation in East Europe* (New York, New Century Publishers, 1962), and is reprinted by permission of the author and the publisher.

† The main part of the supplement has been excerpted from V. Isupov, B. Lodygin, and V. Terekhov, "Economic Development of the CMEA (Council for Mutual Economic Assistance) Countries at the Present Stage," *World Marxist Review* (January, 1966), pp. 40-47, and is reprinted here by permission of the publisher. The subsection on "A Word on Recent Economic Reforms" has been taken from O. Bogomolov, "Management Reforms and Economic Cooperation Between Socialist Countries," *Voprosy Ekonomiki* No. 2 (1966), which appeared in English Translation in *The Daily Review: Translations from the Soviet Press* (April 5, 1966).

The supplement, under the subheading "Recent Economic Developments in the East European Member Countries of the Soviet Commonwealth of Nations: *A Supplement*," starts on p. 353.

valleys and its strategic location on the Mediterranean waterfront, astride the east-west trade routes between Europe and Asia and the north-south Africa-Europe traffic, made East European territory the logical seat of empire or the logical prize of empire builders. It was infiltrated, invaded and colonized by the Greeks; conquered and incorporated into the Roman Empire and, with the rise of Islam, much of the area was brought under Turkish domination.

After centuries of exposure to the benefits, lures and destructive conflicts of Western civilization, East Europe in 1900 was the seat of the loosely aggregated, unassimilated, jostling principalities and monarchies which constituted the Habsburg Empire.

The War of 1914-18 harried and disorganized East Europe. At the end of the war a number of the nationalist groups composing Austro–Hungary established independent governments. The states which emerged from the dismemberment of the Austro–Hungarian Empire were either republics (after the French and United States models) or limited monarchies.

Invaded and occupied by the Nazis between 1939 and 1945 and heavily damaged in the course of that general war, East Europe was liberated by the Soviet armies in 1945. Since that date Albania, Bulgaria, Czechoslovakia, the German Democratic Republic, Hungary, Poland, Rumania, and Yugoslavia have cleared up war wreckage, organized socialist republics, and begun building socialism.

Economically, East Europe made its living by farming, forestry, mineral production, transportation, trade, and commerce. The surplus grain which it produced during the present century had been going to West Europe in exchange for Western manufactures and services. Tiny peasant holdings barely large enough to provide a subsistence for their proprietors existed side by side with large estates, a few of which were farmed with machinery.

Eastern Europe was largely preindustrial in 1900. Its economy was built on primitive agriculture. Its power structure in the countryside rested on landlords, clerics and the military. The agricultural masses lived at or near the subsistence level. Wages and living standards in industry and transport were held down by the low countryside standards. Underemployment, poverty and backwardness limited the lives of a great majority of East Europe's population. . . .

The countryside was divided into four parts: widespread land holdings and sumptuous palaces and mansions of the landed aristocracy; the lavish establishments of the clergy; the comfortable quarters of the bourgeoisie in the towns; and the generally inadequate, unhealthy, cramped housing of the peasantry, who made up the majority of East Europe's population. Millions were employed on the great lay and clerical estates which occupied much of the best land in East Europe. Some peasants owned the land they worked; most worked for a mere pittance.

Aside from its dependence on the West European market (which was flooded with cheap grain and meat from Australia, Canada, and Argentina),

East Europe suffered from four curses: the shocking poverty of its country-side; widespread illiteracy; the underemployment of a temperate zone agrarian economy which lacked industrial part-time jobs; and scourges such as malaria and tuberculosis, unrelieved by adequate health services.

Class lines were sharply drawn. On one side were wealth, privilege and unearned income; on the other, poverty, underemployment, illiteracy and ill health. Palaces and cathedrals were surrounded by hovels and slums. Among the privileged were the nobility, the gentry, the clergy, the managers of commerce and industry, government officials, the military, and a host of small proprietors. In the cities were the badly housed underpaid wage workers. In the countryside were millions of wretchedly housed exploited tenants, peasants, and farm laborers. . . .

Most present-day revolutions have been associated with war losses and war suffering, which goad otherwise inert popular masses into action. War had exactly this effect on the peoples of East Europe. . . . War damage, military occupation and years of fighting from 1910 to 1945 tore in pieces the traditional culture pattern of East Europe. Millions lost their lives. Millions who survived lost their homes and their property. Their faith in the monarchy, in the church, in the stability and security of a competitive, acquisitive way of life was undermined or destroyed.

East European peoples were fed up with war, which they blamed on the ruling oligarchies. Peoples disillusioned and cast adrift by the two wars, and the decade of economic disruption that began in 1929, were prepared for alternatives. The rapid build-up of the Soviet Union from weakness in 1917 to a position of top-ranking importance among the world powers in 1945 was clear evidence that the socialists had found an answer to the problems besetting East Europe. The liberation of East Europe by the Soviet armies in 1944-45 tipped the balance in favor of socialism. Monarchy, the church and private enterprise were associated in the public mind of East Europe with disruption, disorganization, destruction, death. After centuries of oppression, exploitation, poverty and backwardness the people of East Europe rose in revolt against their oppressors and exploiters. . . .

Builders of socialism in East Europe were confronted at the outset of their endeavors by several vital technical problems, such as (1) a survey and effective utilization of local natural resources, particularly the sources of energy; (2) planning a socialist economy adapted to the needs and immediate possibilities of East Europe; (3) reorganizing rural economy and society, opening mines, establishing or modernizing industrial plants; (4) rebuilding old cities and founding new ones; (5) improving railway, road and water transportation; (6) speeding communication; (7) maintaining a workable balance between city and countryside; (8) providing the necessaries, the amenities and some of the comforts of a good life for the entire population; (9) safeguarding and improving health; (10) expanding and revolutionizing education; (11) providing attractive and satisfying recreation facilities for young and old; (12) developing helpful and harmonious relations with neighbor socialist countries; (13) dealing with the misrepresentations, lies, slanders, threats, interventions, and invasions from hostile fascist neighbors who were advised, financed, and armed by the surviving centers of imperialist reaction and counterrevolution.

These and additional urgent tasks would tax the available facilities and trained personnel in the most advanced communities. In East Europe the capital equipment needed to meet these demands did not exist. It had to be improvised or built at the same time that the services were being made available. Furthermore, the personnel to carry out such a far-reaching program had to be found and specially trained while the program was under way.

Despite its magnitude and diversity such a program is an essential feature of every successful social revolution. The program must meet a deeply felt public demand and inspire public confidence. It cannot fail. It cannot even hesitate. When mistakes are made they must be recognized, publicized, and corrected. Where one device proves inadequate, another must be substituted.

In the case of East Europe, recovery from war losses, the transformation of the economic and political institutions and an increase in domestic well-being depended upon fulfilling plans and making good on promises. The future of socialism hung in the balance. Socialism's enemies in the West were hoping, planning, and plotting to undermine and if possible to destroy East European socialism, root and branch.

A social revolution cannot be finished all at once. Like any process, it moves from phase to phase and stage to stage as old ideas and practices are replaced by new ones. Ever since 1917, East Europe has been preparing to discard the old and replace it by new economic, political and social forms. Changes have been particularly rapid since the war's end in 1945, and the tempo of this transformation continues without apparent diminution in its intensity.

CHANGES IN PROPERTY RELATIONS

Under any social system those who own and control the means of production exercise authority. This authority rests upon the possibility of giving or withholding the livelihood upon which their fellows depend for physical existence. . . .

East Europe's land, particularly the most productive land, had long been accumulated in large states. In the centers of commerce, industry and mining, business property had been similarly concentrated, often in the hands of foreign investors. Land and business properties were owned, sometimes personally, sometimes in family estates, sometimes by business corporations, sometimes by institutions (of which religious organizations were the most prominent), sometimes by the state.

As concentration of property-ownership increased, it became ever more difficult for young persons to strike out for themselves and more necessary for them to take jobs owned by someone else, whether on the land or in a business enterprise, and thus contribute to the job-owner a sizeable share of their product.

The masses, revolting against exploitation, wanted to stop paying profits to the job-owners and to retain the products of their own labor. In an agrarian society like that in East Europe, these goals and purposes put land reform at the top of the list of immediate demands, because it was the land from which people lived, and land ownership that provided the chief basis of unearned income.

At the time of the French Revolution, the recipient of even a small share in a large estate could provide a subsistence for himself and his family; but the land division in East Europe took place during a period of agricultural mechanization, which presents a basically different problem. Neither the farmer nor the local craftsman can build the combines, corn harvesters or cotton pickers needed in mechanized agriculture. Nor can they make the tractors which provide the motive power for heavy farm machines. In mechanized agriculture, the largest investment is not in land or buildings, but in mechanical equipment. . . .

Socialism, involving mining, manufacturing, and commercial towns and cities, depends on farmers for foods and fibers. Only on the basis of agricultural mechanization can sufficient surplus be produced on the farm to meet the demands of industries and urban centers. Mechanized agriculture, operated efficiently on large tracts of land, may be carried on by state farms or by collectives whose membership generally runs to several hundred member workers. On no other basis could a socialist economy be successful.

Socialist construction in East Europe began with the conversion of large land holdings and large business enterprises from private property into public property. Forests and mineral deposits generally became state property. Large country houses, castles and palaces which had been owned by business magnates, aristocrats, and royalty became public property and were used as rest homes, sanitariums, recreation centers, museums, art galleries, or for other public purposes. Outstanding examples of architecture were opened to the public.

Industries, commercial establishments, and other enterprises employing more than a minimum number of persons were also declared public property. Government ownership and operation of the social means of production included land and natural resources, mining, state farms and experiment stations, manufacturing, transportation, banking, insurance, and foreign trade. In each case the decision to convert private property into public property was made by asking "Does this enterprise, in private hands, permit the owner to exploit workers and live on unearned income?" If the enterprise permitted exploitation, it became public property. In some cases private owners were compensated when their property was taken. Property of enemy aliens and of citizens who had collaborated with the Nazis was confiscated without compensation. . . .

From many points of view, the crucial sector of East European economy is not the public sector but the social sector. The social sector of East Europe's economy consists of cooperatives and collective enterprises. Under this heading are included cooperative stores, owned and operated by membership organizations. A second function of these cooperatives is to buy products from the farmers and resell them to state purchasing agencies. In this respect the cooperative is a jobbing agency functioning between the farmer and the public sector of the economy.

Agricultural collectivization has taken various forms in East Europe. There is the collective farm in which the land and equipment belong to the enterprise. Labor power is organized by an elected chairman or brigade leader. The work norms are agreed upon by the collective (or by a brigade in the collective) and the proceeds of the enterprise are divided between the state deliveries in kind or taxes, the costs of operation, investment needs, and income of members. Member-income is generally paid in proportion to work norms completed. It may be paid in produce or in cash. In the early stages of collective farming member income was paid in produce after the harvest. Today member income is generally paid in cash throughout the year.

Most collective farms depend upon their own labor power, but at critical periods, such as harvesting grain, potatoes or fruit, they hire some hourly or day labor if they can get it. In the off-season, on the other hand, especially where winter is severe and prolonged, collective farms often make arrangements with local industries under which the farm guarantees the factory a certain number of workers during the slack season on the farm. At the moment, in East Europe, owing to the heavy demands of industrialization, labor is scarce. Under such conditions an industry is glad to turn to a responsible source of experienced labor power.

The private sector also occupies an important place in East Europe's economy. Consumer soft goods such as food, clothing and sports equipment are privately owned. So are consumer capital goods, from houses, autos, refrigerators, radio, and television sets, to tools and other equipment for the personal use of the owner or of the household.

Dwelling space is generally in short supply as a result of war damage, population increase and the substitution of modernized dwelling units for antiquated apartments, hovels, and shacks. The amount of dwelling space occupied per individual is therefore limited by law.

Dwellings equipped with modern conveniences are being built all over East Europe by municipal, state and national governments, and rented for amounts that range from 5 to 8 or 9 percent of the renter's income. In every one of the East European countries blocks of new attractive apartments are either already finished and lived in or being constructed.

Warsaw, to give but one example, was about forty percent destroyed in 1939. By 1944, the Ghetto and other sections of the city were razed to the ground, and only 20 to 25 percent of the city was left standing. This was part of the pattern of planned and systematic destruction perpetrated by the Nazis. The planned and systematic rebuilding of Warsaw followed, and after the vast clearing up operation of the ruins and rubble, the heart of the city, the Altstadt, was reconstructed at great expense and with artistic exactitude in complete duplication of the lovely old original buildings. New apartments and homes (as well as office buildings) were put up for 1,200,000 people. Thirty-three thousand to thirty-five thousand rooms are being built per year. By 1965, the new city had more inhabitants than before the war, and with an average of two persons per room.

Industrial enterprises such as mines and factories have also gone in for dwelling construction. So have trade unions and state and collective farms. Besides these dwelling construction operations, initiated by public and collective enterprises, government agencies, industrial enterprises, trade unions, and collective farms will lend money (usually at 2 percent interest) to an individual or a family wishing to buy or rent land and build a one- or two-family house. On many collective farms there are building brigades composed of building trade craftsmen which will help the prospective home owner to erect his house, or do the entire job on contract. The homebuilder may, if he wishes, do all the work himself. City planners frequently set aside city areas for private single-family house construction.

Homes built by or for the owners or bought by them are private property. They may be occupied, sold, given, or bequeathed, as the owners see fit. They may also be rented under certain restrictions. A city home owner may build a house in the country, at the seashore or lake front, or in the mountains for his own use during weekends or vacations. Such houses also may be disposed of as the owner decides, but rent must not become the chief source of the house owner's income.

Beside this very large domestic sector of the private economy, there are the farms owned and operated by individual farmers. Such farms aggregate millions of private enterprises operated as family farms, reaching a maximum in Poland, where they comprise 87 percent of the 3,600,000 farms in the country. . . .

Individual land plots on collective farms are another considerable part of the private sector. Individual plots of about one acre (43,560 square feet) of cultivable land per household usually adjoin the separate, single house in which the member and his family live. The plot may be cultivated individually or collectively. The produce belongs to the household on whose plot it was raised, and may be used or sold.

A large sector of the private economy consists of stores, shops and workshops operated by a proprietor and members of his family. Scores of thousands of such establishments are still functioning in East Europe. They are, of course, in competition with public and collective merchandising establishments. They are at a minimum in Bulgaria and Rumania and at a maximum in Yugoslavia, Czechoslovakia, Hungary, and Poland. . . .

Property changes in East Europe have modified the class structure of East European society. The expropriation of large-scale privately owned land and its resources and large-scale privately owned capital goods have destroyed or greatly weakened the economic foundations upon which both feudalism and capitalism were built and maintained. At the same time, many of the property forms which constituted the private sectors in feudal and especially capitalist economy have been preserved. Expansion of the public sector and the social sector of East European economy has created a situation in which the balance of political and social control has been tipped away from the private and toward the public and social sectors.

ECONOMIC AND SOCIAL PLANNING

Change from an economy dominated by the private sector to an economy dominated by the public-social sector has been accompanied in East Europe by a parallel change from an economy and society dominated by competition (and therefore generally planless) to an economy and society based upon cooperation-coordination (and therefore, of necessity, upon planning). . . .

Reasoned planning already had a history in East European public works such as seawalls, dikes, harbors, cities, water control, and irrigation, the construction of defenses and the organization of professional military forces. At the turn of the century East Europe was revamping its postal systems, developing highways and taking planned steps toward industrialization. There were plans for the maintenance of public order, public housing, public education, and public health, and plans for social security.

There was an even closer, more timely, and elaborate example of planning with which East Europe was familiar, at least by hearsay and report. Most East European leaders had been to the Soviet Union as students or visitors and had observed and studied social planning in action there. The efficacy of Soviet general economic and social planning of public affairs was being convincingly demonstrated by spectacular Soviet achievements. For more than two decades the Soviet Union, near neighbor to East Europe, had been experimenting with economic and social plans on a continent-wide scale. As these much publicized plans were fulfilled and surpassed, the Soviet Union had pushed forward with great rapidity from relative backwardness into a top-ranking position among the great powers.

Planning was an established social principle with many distinguished achievements to its credit. What could be more reasonable than to replace the competition and conflict that had brought East Europe to the verge of disaster with a rationally planned economy and society? This was the conclusion reached by the peoples of eight East European countries and written into the constitutions which were adopted after 1945. . . .

BALANCING EAST EUROPEAN ECONOMIES

East European economies, under feudalism-capitalism, were adjusted to hand and animal agriculture on small subsistence farms. They enriched landlords, officials, and businessmen, and impoverished small farmers, agricultural laborers, and industrial workers; they benefited West Europe to the disadvantage of East Europe. The result was comfort and luxury for a privileged minority, poverty and backwardness for masses of the exploited.

Three-quarters of East Europeans depended on agriculture for a livelihood. Big estates produced grain and meat for export to West Europe. Farm laborers, tenant farmers, and small farm owners could barely grub a living from the land. If there was a surplus of grain or farm animals, it went to the town or city market. The chief purpose of agriculture was subsistence. The entire farm household (men, women, children) gave all its available labor power in exchange for a meager living. At seed-time and harvest, human and animal power were fully employed and often overworked. For the balance (and the majority) of the year, farm productive capacity was underemployed or unemployed.

Prices for East European farm products, particularly for grain and meat, were fixed in the world market, in competition with Australia, Canada, Argentina. In these grain-meat producing areas, machinery and modern techniques were extensively employed. East European hand and animal energy were pitted against agricultural machinery, to the woeful disadvantage of East Europe.

East Europe's exports of hand-produced grain and meat paid dearly for imported manufactures and capital from West Europe. The economic relations between East and West were typically imperial-colonial. Dominant Western manufacturers, transporters, and financiers called the tune to which dependent Eastern land workers danced.

East Europe itself was divided. The best things went to the rich and powerful minority living mainly in towns and cities; the land-working majority had the leavings. The consequence of these relationships for the vast majority of East Europeans was unemployment, poverty, backwardness, dependence. It was these discriminations, inequalities, and injustices that sparked and motivated the social revolution that is still sweeping East Europe today. For a century this social revolution had germinated in East

Europe. Since 1945 it has had the public support which enabled it to carry through its program for raising the economic, social, and cultural level of the heretofore oppressed and exploited majority.

First among the steps taken to balance East European economy was an increase in the public-social sector sufficient to give it a dominating position in the total economy. The second step was a makeshift arrangement to establish or enlarge industries that could provide the most immediately needed consumer goods—clothing, household appliances, food processing, and preserving equipment, together with tools and implements required to mechanize farming, construct buildings, and carry on other pressing public activities. Immediately after the war's end in 1945, farmers could deliver food to the cities only if their basic requirements of city-produced or imported equipment were met. The same urgency held for building and for the consumer's survival necessaries.

Side by side with this crash program for provisioning towns and cities with food and the countryside with a minimum of manufactured equipment, East Europeans turned their attention to three imperatives for attaining economic independence: (1) to supplement human and animal energy with the natural energies available in wood, coal, oil, gas, and water power; (2) to achieve the fullest possible utilization of science and technology in order to convert natural resources into goods and services that provide the basic necessities of life, thus ending poverty and economic insecurity; and (3) to develop and make available the skills, experience, and capital equipment necessary to plan and direct such a program and carry it to a successful conclusion.

In the earlier stage of the industrialization of East Europe, assistance from the Soviet Union in the form of materials, machine equipment, technical skills, and capital was indispensable to the success of the program. In the eyes of most East Europeans, this stage came to an end in the early or middle 1950's. Once this critical point was passed, and basic necessities could be supplied to the productive apparatus on one hand and the consuming public on the other, the East European economies were able to establish a scale of priorities, adopt a formula for economic balance and advance at an agreed annual rate toward an economic equilibrium that guaranteed stability, security and continuous measured improvement. . . .

The facts concerning East Europe's economy are fully verified and irrefutable. History records that half a century ago East Europe was saddled with a backward, unbalanced economy that provided comforts and luxuries for the few and bare subsistence for the many, an economy in which East Europeans were forced to buy expensive manufactures from the West with foods and raw materials produced largely by human and animal energy in the East. This relationship strengthened the Western bourgeois economy while perpetuating poverty, underemployment, ignorance, and a high degree of preventable ill health in the East.

Today the situation has been radically altered in five most essential respects:

I. East Europeans are provided with the necessaries of life—food, clothing, and a minimum of shelter. They are even better provided with networks of health services, educational services, and agencies for rest, recreation, and entertainment that aim to meet the needs of city, town, and country-side. Unemployment and underemployment have given way to labor shortage. From year to year the supply of comforts and conveniences, generally available, is increasing. Experience thus far justifies the con-clusion that the new economy is relatively stable. Certainly it is progres-sive—advancing dependably year by year.

II. The new economy is more just than the old one. It is based not on the exploitation of the many by the few, but upon the sharing of the good things of life by the entire population, with special advantages for children and young people.

III. Individual new enterprises by the hundreds, well-equipped farms, mines, factories, transportation agencies, schools, health centers, com-munity centers, concert halls, and sport facilities, are springing up everywhere. Particularly noteworthy is the construction of modern housing units equipped with all of the facilities required to make family life in every neighborhood comfortable, convenient and pleasant.

IV. These advances are being made on a priority scale that operates not on the "first come, first served" principle of capitalism but on the "greatest need of the greatest number, first served" principle of socialism.

V. East Europe is rapidly developing a modern, increasingly automated, industrial economy planned to utilize distant as well as local resources and to provide local populations with an adequate and stable flow of goods and services. The new units of this economy will stand com-parison with similar enterprises in other parts of Europe; the proof of this parity is the steadily mounting export of East European manufac-tures to the world market in competition with the long established, more experienced enterprises of the West.

The most spectacular aspect of these advances is the fact that most of them have been made during the past twenty years, many are the product of the past decade and, above all, that they are continuing to unfold at a con-stantly accelerated tempo with the enthusiastic support of the vast majority of the East European population.

Peasants who thought that individual farming was superior to planned cooperative farming changed slowly and reluctantly, but came gradually to realize the greater benefits and general advantages of collective work and group ownership. Before the war, industry developed faster than agriculture; machines were expensive and man power was cheap. When technical equipment became more readily available in the new socialist society, agriculture forged ahead. The benefits of land reform, mechanization, fertilizers and intensive farming greatly increased the average yields of crops. There are larger fields to cultivate, there is cooperative handling of farm jobs and marketing. There are uniform prices, which make for greater possibility of getting necessary machines, easier bank credit for financing, unlimited opportunity for young people to go to agricultural schools, and easy access to advisory technicians and agriculturists, many of whom live right on the farms.

During 1965 and 1966,[1] four significant economic changes were taking place in East European countries. *First,* the economies were less centralized and more localized both geographically and in specific industries and plants, with a widened range for local initiative in planning, designing, and adjusting to local market conditions. *Second,* the economies were being reoriented from emphasis on productivity to an emphasis on consumer choice. *Third,* each of the East European economies was laying greater emphasis on national needs and on national independence from international planning and direction. This trend toward national economic self-determination was perhaps most noticeable in Yugoslavia and Rumania. *Fourth,* East European socialist governments were making contracts with business concerns in West European countries to set up production enterprises in East Europe and carry on productive operations under joint enterprise agreements such as joint enterprise agreements between "good" local capitalists and socialist governments. In summary (to quote a Reuters dispatch in the *New York Times* of May 30, 1966) East European socialist countries are trying "to raise living standards, increase industrial competition, reduce bureaucracy and promote trade with the West," that is, to co-exist. . . .

Thirty years ago, the East European countries were dependencies of the big European empires. In that brief period, East Europe has been able to stabilize its economies, greatly increase production and raise the living standards of its people to the highest level in their history. Production and consumption are in reasonable balance. Amounts paid out in wages and salaries are matched by goods and services awaiting purchasers. Exports pay for imports. Investment funds come in the main out of income, as borrowing from abroad has tapered off. Several countries, notably Rumania, Hungary and Czechoslovakia, have begun selling exports on long-term credits—a form of lending. East European countries are taking part in equipping and supplying the less developed peoples of Asia, Africa, and the Americas with goods and services needed to put them in a position to mechanize and modernize at their own tempo and in their own right. . . .

Compared with the tortured economic experiences of Argentina, Brazil, Mexico and other Latin American countries which have been trying vainly

---

[1] This paragraph was added by Dr. Nearing in the summer of 1966, especially for inclusion in this book. [EDITOR'S NOTE]

to win their economic independence and stabilize their economies under the capitalist system of private enterprise, the East European experience with socialist construction during the past decade is little short of miraculous.

SOCIALIST POLITICAL PATTERNS

Paralleling the revolution in East European economies is the transformation of East Europe's political structure. Only a few years ago East European governments were almost all monarchies. Close to the surface of power politics in the capital cities, the familiar trinity of landlord, priest, and military or police official sat around the tables where top-level decisions were made, or hovered in the background taking notes and waiting their turn. Business class forces were pushing in, demanding a voice and vote. In the countryside, where most East Europeans lived, the feudal trinity dictated and luxuriated in the midst of a pre-machine agriculture carried on by bitterly exploited farm laborers, some share tenants and a number of petty landholders operating farms too small to yield more than a bare subsistence.

Today this political structure has been replaced by states organized on the principle of democratic centralism and popular fronts designed to include every element in the community except the forces of counter-revolution. . . .

East Europe won its independence of the Austro-Hungarian Empire in 1919 and ended an era of feudal domination. Between 1943 and 1945 East Europe expelled the Nazi invaders and brought its fascist era to an end. Feudalism and bourgeois-fascism, with their succession of destructive wars, left East Europe physically wrecked, socially disorganized, economically impoverished and disrupted, and politically fragmented.

One way, and only one, offered East Europe an avenue of escape from post-war chaos. This way was marked plainly by three notable experiences. *First,* the Soviet armies ended Nazi domination in all of East Europe, aided, notably in Yugoslavia, by the working people's anti-Nazi guerrilla forces. *Second,* while West Europe had drifted, and Central Europe had turned to fascism, the Soviet Union had rolled up an impressive record of achievement in the building of socialism. *Third,* the Soviet Union, which had stood out for three decades as the only socialist country, was willing and eager to provide East Europe with the financial and technical assistance needed to speed up socialist construction. . . .

There are eight republics in South East Europe which presently call themselves socialist and are committed to the task of establishing a peaceful collective society. All eight of these republics have turned their backs on bourgeois society—its principles, foundations, purposes, institutions, and activities. All eight are enthusiastically developing toward a peaceful transition from feudalism-capitalism to socialism.

This is not to say that the eight East European republics have followed identical paths. Rather, it is the same background of historical facts that has led the peoples of all eight East European countries to attempt the transition from capitalism by peaceful, orderly, legal, constitutional steps. The experience of Czechoslovakia is typical of a trend observable throughout all of East Europe. The trend moves from monarchy to bourgeois republic, from bourgeois republic to fascist dictatorship (developed domestically or imposed by foreign military occupation), from fascist dictatorship to popular revulsion, revolt, and determination to build socialism, and from the determination to build socialism to the planned construction of a society under a strongly centralized, popularly supported democratic government, led by the Communist Party or its equivalent under another name.

Political patterns, presently emerging in East Europe, have their likenesses and differences. Taken as a whole, they represent a clearly marked trend which differs as much from West European bourgeois society as bourgeois society differs from its feudal predecessor.

Bourgeois Europe's declared purpose was the removal of feudal restrictions and the institution of a legal system which would enable business enterprise to make its own rules and to follow its own interests, wherever they led. This program was carried out under two slogans: *laissez-faire* (freedom of decision and action) and *caveat emptor* (let the buyer beware). Under this program, not only was greed institutionalized but greedy individuals were given unbridled opportunity and encouragement to accumulate wealth and concentrate power. To get rich quickly became the first and the last and the whole duty of man.

East European socialist countries have incorporated into their constitutions, and are teaching the rising generation, that the competitive struggle for wealth and power, reaching its fullest expression in general and total mechanized war, is both criminal and suicidal. The declared purpose of East Europe is the replacement of *laissez-faire* individualism by a clear recognition that carefully planned and effectively administered collective action is the first requisite for survival and well-being in the power age. Hence, in socialist East Europe this collectivism is regarded as the foundation for real freedom. . . .

Throughout East Europe the national parliament or assembly, elected by popular vote and generally sitting in one chamber, is the supreme organ of state power. In Czechoslovakia, "the National Assembly shall be the supreme organ of state power." The Bulgarian Constitution is similarly worded. In Rumania, the supreme organ of State authority is the Great National Assembly, which enacted and amends the Constitution, elects the President of the Republic and the Supreme Court. It is the supreme domestic authority and determines and controls foreign relations.

Authority, concentrated in the legislative branch of the national government, is limited in three ways. First, by the local authority exercised by constituent republics, autonomous national regions, districts, cities, towns, and villages, each of which is under the direction of an elected government. Second, by the organization of nonstate agencies such as trade unions and youth groups. Third, by the allocation of authority to volunteer groups, such as neighborhood volunteer police.

East Europe's political pattern is not a finished product. On the contrary, it is being modified, changed, developed constantly. Each newly adopted constitution contains new ideas and new wordings. The central purpose—an end to exploitation and the establishment of socialism—is universally accepted. The means of achieving the purpose vary from country to country and from stage to stage in the process of transition.

PRESSURE POWER GROUPS, OLD AND NEW

East Europe is working out new patterns of property relations and political institutions to replace those of a previous epoch. It is striving to provide its 115,000,000 people with the peace, independence, stability, security and opportunity they are demanding. Side by side with this development, there has been a radical transformation in the hierarchy or apparatus of power and in its day-to-day operations.

Every social revolution is a milestone in social history. Such an upheaval intensifies the competitive struggle between social groups. If the revolution succeeds, established pressure groups are removed, replaced or downgraded in the power hierarchy, while opposition groups push toward the power summit. When the established social groups win out in the struggle against the revolutionary forces, they put down the revolution and maintain their positions in the power hierarchy.

East Europe, in the present half century, is passing through a successful social revolution. During the competitive struggle for political power, the established power pressure groups of the pre-1914 period have been largely replaced by groups which occupied positions of minor importance at the beginning of the social revolution.

Established pressure groups in East Europe at the beginning of the present revolution were headed economically by landowners in the countryside, and by landowners and businessmen in the cities. Politically they were headed by the monarch who was titular leader of a power apparatus which included the state and its armed forces, the church with its propaganda apparatus, and in later years the rapidly growing business interests in cities and towns. Ideologically the church and the monarchical state were supreme. The industrial revolution pushed business groups toward the power summit at the same time that it eroded the foundations of the landlords and the monarchy. . . .

In present-day East Europe half a dozen pressure power groups play leading roles and constitute the Establishment which holds the society together, animates it, gives it plan and purpose. They are the Communist Party, the National or Patriotic Fronts, the trade unions, the government apparatus, the armed forces, the Academy of Sciences.

Communist Parties, organized in each of the East European socialist republics, assume responsibility for providing ideological, political, economic, and social leadership. Communist Party members in the East European countries are a relatively small minority of the total population. But they are selected people—competent, trained, tested, disciplined members who are ready at all times to subordinate personal interests to the interests of the Party and the people. Party members believe in the theories of Marxism-Leninism. Their lives are dedicated to putting these socialist theories into practice. They are in theoretical agreement concerning the measures necessary to transform a feudalist-capitalist society into a socialist society, and it is their responsibility to see the transformation carried to a successful conclusion.

Popular, Patriotic, or National Fronts have been established in a number of East European socialist republics. They aim to include and to represent all organizations, national, regional, local. They are the political expression of national, regional and social unity. They supervise the transition to socialism and assume responsibility for seeing that socialist construction is carried on efficiently, speedily, honestly.

East Europeans do not speak of the armed forces as independent of the state. In theory they are part and parcel of the state apparatus. In peacetime the armed services, particularly the officers and career men who make up their inner core, develop a solidarity and an individuality that necessitate independent classification.

The state apparatus is in a like case. Theoretically public officials are paid by the State to serve the people. In practice public officials in capitalist states develop solidarity, coherence, and an urge to maintain themselves and their associates in office, with policies, personnel, and loyalties that make them a recognizable unit in the Establishment. In the East European countries government workers are closely connected to the working people whose views and interests they at all times seek to express.

Academies of Sciences, representing the interests and members of all scientific societies and activities, are playing an increasingly vital role in the life of socialist countries. They are independently organized and take an important part in formulating and implementing public policy.

Though trade unions are classified as one of the private associations, we are inclined to include them in the pressure power Establishment of socialist countries because of their activities in making and carrying out public policy. In the West, trade unions (at least in theory) carry on an economic cold war with their employers, and are therefore in opposition to the Establishment. In East Europe they are an important part of the Establishment's working apparatus. . . .

It is significant and instructive to compare the pressure power groups in old and in new East Europe.

Table 10-1.

The Establishment of Old East Europe	The Establishment of New East Europe
The Court	The Communist Party
Landlords	The Popular or National Fronts
Churchmen	The trade unions
The State bureaucracy	The government apparatus
Businessmen	The armed forces
The armed forces	The Academy of Sciences

Three top pressure power groups of the old Establishment, the Court, the landlords and the businessmen, have disappeared from East European public life. The church has ceased to be a major pressure power group. Even in Poland, where it is relatively strong, it no longer arbitrates but engages in rear-guard actions. The armed forces, which played such a prominent role in the old Establishment, are subordinated to civilian authority in the new. Only the State bureaucracy, greatly increased in size and drastically modified in structure, content, and purpose, remains a factor in making and implementing public policy. The new Establishment consists largely of forces that did not exist before 1910, such as the Communist Party, Popular or National Fronts, the technological intelligentsia and the Academy of Sciences, or of groups like the trade unions and professional organizations, which were of small consequence before 1910 or were in active opposition to the Establishment.

East Europe's feudal-capitalist order was a loose alliance between the monarchy, landlords, churchmen, and the armed forces, with the new-rich businessmen pushing their way into the Establishment. East Europe's socialist Establishment is something of a monolith, strongly organized, planned, coordinated, with sharply defined long-range and immediate objectives. Some of the most drastic and dramatic consequences of the East European revolution are to be seen in the exchange of the old pressure groups for a coordinated authority with constituent parts fitted together in a tightly knit working organization.

THE REVOLUTION IN EDUCATION

Nowhere in present-day East European life is the social revolution more omnipresent than in the field of education. Under East Europe's old social system, education was closely related to privilege. It was generally church-dominated; it prepared students (chiefly male) for the learned professions; it was costly. Today in East Europe general education is available to all on equal terms. Schooling is free and is open to all comers who are prepared to concentrate on the work and meet the scholastic requirements. It is under state instead of church control. It provides technical and scientific training for every citizen who wishes to specialize in any field of legitimate human endeavor. It would be difficult to find a more complete right-about-face during a dozen or a score of years in the outlooks and activities of any important social institution. . . .

On the question of broadening educational opportunity, East European public opinion was unanimous. Practical details had to be worked out. If every East European child was to have a place in school and more elementary school graduates were to continue through the four years of high school and perhaps on into professional or technical courses at the university level, two needs had to be met—the need for buildings and equipment and the need for teachers and administrators. During the post-war years, along with the high priority for industrialization, housing and consumer goods, educational needs have been kept in the forefront of official and public attention. The result has been an extensive program of new construction and remodeling and a successful campaign to attract high quality men and women into the educational field.

East Europe's schools lay emphasis on the basic means of learning and of communication—the three R's. Besides the three R's two foreign languages are required. One, Russian, is generally compulsory throughout East Europe. The second language may be English, French, or German. Language study is begun early in the elementary grades and continues in high schools. Along with mathematics, science, technology, and sociology, they also stress peace and friendship among the nations.

There are new trade schools and apprentice schools for workers (many of them maintained in production establishments), technical schools for training technicians, engineering colleges for training engineers, institutes, and universities for training scientists and the teachers of teachers. In addition to the schools for children and young people, there are special courses and schools for adults

Twenty years ago illiteracy was rampant, especially in the East European countryside. In the new generation every person has the rudiments and everyone is exposed to the elaborations of modern education. The yearning to know, understand and participate extends across the entire community. Classes and courses, newspapers, magazines and books, movies, radio, television, theatres, concert halls, museums, libraries and reading rooms, excursions, expeditions, exhibitions, lectures, clubs and specialized circles are organized to meet the demands of a large population eager to take their places in a modernized East Europe. In Rumania, for instance, there are now 2 national libraries, 35 university libraries, 5,034 special (documentary) libraries, 5,762 school libraries, and 14,406 public libraries.

Education at all levels has been free since about 1960. Tuition fees in schools have been abolished. School authorities assume the costs of student maintenance where parents are unable to do so. To an increasing extent school books and school supplies are also provided free of charge. Education from the bottom to the top is given to those who have the interest and ability to take advantage of the opportunities for learning and culture. . . .

For East Europe, not long emerged from a feudal-capitalist background, the new education represents a revolutionary about face. East European education as it has developed during the past dozen years, and as it is still developing, is designed by socialists as one of the chief agencies preparing today's boys and girls for effective, enthusiastic participation in building socialism and taking the step from socialism to communism at the earliest appropriate moment.

HEALTH AND SOCIAL SECURITY FOR ALL

East Europe, forty years ago, was relatively poor in health facilities. Those which existed catered to the well-to-do. Even at that level they were often inadequately staffed. Aside from private charity and public outdoor relief, the poor shifted for themselves as best they could. Furthermore, health facilities (doctors, dentists, nurses, hospitals, and clinics) were located chiefly in the cities and towns. The larger and richer the population center, the better the health facilities. Villages and remote areas, where needs were often the greatest, had few means for handling sickness or accidents or for dealing with malaria, tuberculosis, and other scourges.

Present-day East Europe presents a totally different picture as far as health facilities and social agencies are concerned. Throughout East Europe no profits are made on sickness, any more than profits are made on education. Ignorance is dealt with by educators; ill health by medical personnel. Wherever there are people, free health and social agencies are available. . . .

Some idea of the growth of health services in East Europe can be gained by a comparison of available hospital beds. In Czechoslovakia the number of hospital beds doubled from 1940 to 1960. Poland had 69,361 hospital beds in 1938 and 154,131 in 1958. Rumania had 33,763 hospital beds in 1938;

69,221 in 1950 and 133,850 in 1960. Such a network of health facilities involved an extensive building program, which is still under way in villages, towns, and cities.

East European health authorities have paid particular attention to the plagues that used to sweep Europe, undermining health and causing countless untimely deaths. Typhus and smallpox are now rare. Malaria has been virtually eliminated. In Bulgaria, for instance, where malaria had been a serious threat in various sections it has ceased to exist, and the death-rate from tuberculosis declined from 14.8 per 10,000 of the population in 1944 to 1.9 per 10,000 in 1959. Their general death rate dropped from 13.4 per 1,000 population in 1939 to 7.9 per 1,000 in 1958.

Another measure of the advances made by public health services is the life expectancy of the population. Life expectancy in Bulgaria during the twenty years from 1940 to 1960 increased by 13 years for men and by 16 years for women (reaching 64 years for men and 68 years for women). Life expectancy at birth for Hungarian women was 51 years in 1930, 58 years in 1940 and 69 years in 1958. The parallel figures for men were 48 years, 55 years and 65 years. Similar improvements have been made in other countries.

Human beings living under the conditions of present-day civilization often suffer from ill health. Within the limitations imposed by available personnel and facilities, East Europe has made immense and successful efforts during the post-war years to set up agencies which deal with ill health in the same way that fire departments deal with fires.

In each modern community there is a fire-fighting apparatus, under the direction of an organized group of fire-fighters. In villages the personnel is voluntary. In towns and cities it is professional. When a fire is reported or discovered, the fire-fighters go to the scene of the fire as soon as possible and try to put it out before it has gained headway. Health authorities in East Europe deal with ill health in the same way. They get to the victim of ill health as soon as possible and use the available means to eliminate disease and restore health. Some of the personnel is voluntary, but most of it is professional.

Fire-fighting agencies are not satisfied to put out fires. One of their chief tasks is to deal with the causes that result in fires, and by removing the cause to see to it that the smallest possible number of fires occur. Hence their Fire Prevention Weeks and their campaigns to clean out rubbish in cellars, storehouses, and attics.

While all available means are used to treat the sick effectively and to restore their health speedily, East European public authorities are approaching the problem of ill health chiefly from the prevention point of view. The list of health-preserving, disease-preventing measures is long and varied. First place belongs to housing. Slums in cities and towns are notorious breeders of disease. East Europe is replacing its slums by building entire areas of modern housing, designed to provide sunshine, fresh air, and adequate sanitary facilities, plus order, beauty, and the social services (including health agencies) essential for present-day city dwellers.

Second on the list of disease prevention is rest, relaxation, recreation. East European constitutions guarantee the right to rest. Rest and leisure are made effective by a limited work day, by paid summer holidays, by the establishment of rest homes and vacation centers in the country, by the sea or lakeside or in the mountains, and by the organization of agencies which provide transportation plus many hotels, guest houses and other facilities. In this field the work of the Ministry of Health is supplemented by the Ministry of Sport, which is responsible for sports fields, sports centers, sports clubs, sports contests, all designed to improve health by exposing citizens to sunshine, fresh air, health-giving bodies of water and other opportunities for contact with nature.

Ministries of Culture and Ministries of Education supplement the work of other agencies with their provisions for fruitful leisure activities. Ministries of Culture are responsible for theatre, music, literature and the fine arts. Ministries of Education offer programs that include classes, courses, and excursions to points of historic or cultural interest.

Municipal authorities provide playgrounds, squares, parks. State and national authorities develop parks and recreation centers in forests, mountains, on waterfronts. Trade unions maintain weekend and vacation spots for their members. Production enterprises build gymnasiums, concert halls, swimming pools, establish social centers, rest homes, club facilities, and maintain libraries. East European authorities see to it that all city children have an opportunity during the summer vacation to spend a minimum of three weeks in summer camps and holiday resorts.

Two periods of helplessness are normal aspects of human life. One is infancy, the other is old age. East Europe takes special pride in its arrangements for handling both of these problems. Constitutional provisions, laws and a network of agencies have been set up to provide pre-natal care for expectant mothers and periods of rest before and after child-birth. Working women are released from their jobs with full pay for a total of six to eight weeks of maternity leave before and after babies are born. Maternity homes are maintained in cities, towns, and villages. In large institutions, provisions for mother and child are an essential part of the establishment. Like all health services, the care of mother and children is free.

Similar provisions are made for older people. Retirement ages are in the late fifties or the sixties—earlier by a few years for women than for men. Then pensions begin. After retirement, as well as before, health care is free to all citizens.

Before the beginning of socialist construction, health agencies were largely private, and available only to the well-to-do. Today they are one of the guaranteed services, free to all citizens. Especially noteworthy are those activities and agencies which look to the preservation of health rather than the treatment of disease. Considerable advances in the provisions for curing disease and establishing health have been made in little more than a decade. They are one of the outstanding contributions of East Europe's socialist revolution to the enhancement of human well-being.

THE CULTURAL REVOLUTION IN EAST EUROPE

East Europe's old society had a culture and a cultured class. It also had a class culture, jealously guarded by the privileged few who enjoyed its prerogatives. The privileged in the old society had wealth, prestige, power. They could read and write. They could enjoy music and the arts. They had leisure which enabled them to travel and study. They skimmed the cream from life. They could live the lives of ladies and gentlemen while consuming the products and services created by their working class "inferiors." They could hand on these privileges to their descendants. They held a jealously guarded class monopoly of the good things of life.

In East European cities like Budapest, Bucharest, and Belgrade, culture was the privilege of the few. These centers of wealth and authority had opera houses, theatres, concert halls, but seats were priced so steeply as to make opera, theatre, and concerts luxuries for the well-to-do.

In the East European countryside, where most people lived, the peasants and workers had no access to culture. Professional entertainment, even libraries, were not for them. The workers on the land and in work-shops were considered inferior beings and not up to the level of the elite. They worked with their hands and could not appreciate the finer things of life.

Cultural opportunities in the countryside, as in the cities, were reserved for the landed aristocrats, the high clergy and officials, who met one another at soirees, balls, and parties in country homes and spent a large part of their time in idleness on their country estates. It required no special talent to be a country squire in the days of oxcarts and mud roads. The cultured elite in the old society feasted and danced from sunset to sunrise and hibernated from sunrise to sunset.

This monopoly of leisure and cultural opportunities was safeguarded by the myth that enjoyment and improvement were the privileges of ladies and gentlemen. Parasitism was proclaimed a virtue—work a badge of inferiority. This absurd fallacy was accepted among privileged Europeans for centuries.

The new society which developed with the Industrial Revolution swept away this social pattern. It demanded and rewarded other and sturdier qualities. Work became a virtue; idleness a vice. . . .

In West Europe, these changes from the old to the new society began in the 12th century and continued for seven hundred years; but large areas of East Europe entered the 20th century with the theoretical and many of the institutional patterns of the old feudal world more or less intact. In extreme instances remnants of feudal society persisted in parts of East Europe (and particularly in its countryside) until after the war's end in 1945. During the next decade, modernizing forces picked up these backward East European areas and hurled them into the mid-20th century. . . .

The special interests and exceptional abilities necessary to plan, organize and administer a socialist society are being sought in every nook and cranny of the socialist world. The new leadership is coming from that neglected source, the "lower classes" of the old society; from an almost equally long-neglected reservoir of human capacity, the women; from among the hand workers and craftsmen in the rapidly growing centers of industry and commerce; from the vast reserve of little-used capacity in the countryside. This search for talent has diverted the genius of creative artists from the construction and decoration of palaces, cathedrals, and pleasure parks for the leisured, privileged classes to the wide range of construction and organization necessary to operate and improve the complex apparatus of a socialist community. It has also called writers, artists, and musicians to the serious task of arousing and inspiring their followers and devotees from corroding indifference, apathy, and cynicism to the urgent tasks of raising the cultural levels of the new society.

Instead of waiting for talent and genius to turn up and seek to assert itself in the face of public indifference, the conservatism of conformity, and the heavy odds of social disapproval that innovators in the old society so frequently encountered, the socialist builders of East Europe are ransacking countryside, town, and city in their search for special human interests and abilities. When such are discovered or even suspected, they are encouraged and given all the facilities and opportunities needed for their expression and training.

East Europe's old society limited and monopolized creators, performers, and audience. Under their stringent rules and regulations the best things of life were reserved for the few who were favored by birth or by status. East Europe's new society is spreading the feast of inspiration, enlightenment, enjoyment and opportunity before the whole people and inviting those who will to help themselves to the extent of their capacity—as audience, as performers, as composers and as the onrushing stream of youth, energy, ambition, and enthusiasm.

Success in arousing and mobilizing public interest begins with a place in which interest can center and out of which it may develop. In East European villages, this is a community building, with an auditorium, a stage, chairs or benches, library and reading room, motion picture apparatus, committee rooms, warmth, light, a kitchen and restaurant facilities, and a prominently displayed list of activities. In towns and cities, the community center becomes a civic center that includes universities, museums, libraries, reading rooms, movie houses, theatres, concert halls, opera houses, conservatories of music, exhibition halls, books, and music stores.

Such community and civic centers are not built in a day, but when plans were made to reconstruct war-torn East Europe, a high priority was given to facilities for developing popular culture. As villages have been improved, towns modernized and cities rebuilt, up-to-the-minute housing for cultural activities has had a prominent place in the program.

These provisions for housing and developing popular culture have included special classes, courses, and special schools for music, art, drama, dance, literature, and special organizations of musicians, actors, writers, and other professionals in the culture field. Professional writers, composers, artists, and performers are recognized, honored, have ample opportunity to exercise their professions, and live comfortably. . . .

For the first time in the recent history of East Europe, provisions are being made to end poverty, improve health, reduce physical hardship and provide the necessaries of life for all. These steps, together with economic stability, social security, leisure, and incentive, will offer universal cultural opportunity, not merely in the present, but for future generations.

Socialist society is not content to have individuals, households, villagers, town and city dwellers merely surviving, and adding to their comforts and eventually to their luxuries. It demands highly qualified, experienced individuals and citizens capable of functioning in and contributing to broadly based community enterprises that can guarantee successive generations the conditions necessary for effective collective endeavor—broadly based, rounded education; social guarantees against adversity, and the possibilities of rewarding leisure and cultural opportunity.

BALANCE SHEET OF TWENTY YEARS

Any report on the development of socialism in East Europe risks the danger of premature judgment. The entire period of East European socialist construction covers, at the maximum, twenty years. In some of the countries, notably East Germany, Poland, and Hungary, it was not until after the middle 1950's that sufficient stability was established to permit sustained efforts in building socialism. In none of the East European socialist countries does the period of planned stabilized socialist construction extend for more than a decade. Many of the most impressive advances have been made since 1957-58.

Twenty years is only a moment in the long sweep of modern history, a period too short to warrant generalizations on a development so vast and varied as the present social revolution. Yet, into the past twenty years of

East Europe's transformation a series of spectacular events has been packed that mark the end of an old epoch and the beginning of a new one. . . .

The immediate purpose of the revolutions in East Europe is better living conditions and better living for more people. Its larger purpose is a planned reorganization of a social pattern (Western civilization) which made important contributions to the welfare of humanity during its early phases, but which in its decline and disintegration has become a barrier to further social advance and must be supplanted and finally replaced by a social pattern better equipped to take advantage of the scientific and technological advances made during the past half century. . . .

In building a new society, the socialist countries of East Europe are developing a number of principles which compose an operational formula based on humanitarian rather than utilitarian assumptions:

1. Wherever possible, human need determines social action. This principle governs the distribution of scarce housing space, the allocation of stipends to students, the regulation of prices, the distribution of income.

2. Group necessity takes precedence over individual need because group necessity is broader and more crucial. Hence the first question is "What do we need?" rather than "What do I need?"

3. Social equality is paramount, notably equality in status and in opportunity. All over East Europe everyone talks to anyone, from prime minister to department chief. This results from the common touch that comes with the thrill of successfully concluded group projects in the planning and execution of which all have had a measurable share. Hence the frequent references to "our" steel mill, "our" university; "our" five-year plan.

4. Social stability and especially economic stability is giving the entire population the sense of assured well-being enjoyed by Western middle classes from 1880 or 1890 to 1914.

5. Policy decisions grow from the grass roots. The important role of trade unions and cooperatives with their millions of members, the emphasis on neighborhood responsibility for neighborhood law and order, and the widespread acceptance of "social work" (activities carried on not "for me and mine" but "for us and ours") have brought multitudes into positions involving shared social responsibility.

6. A new privileged class is emerging in East Europe—the youth. The privileges extend to all children, irrespective of color, race or economic status. As one East European put the matter: "We are building a form of society in which we expect that each member of the community will have the goods and services which meet the individual needs. This process takes time and doing. Meanwhile we propose that as soon as possible, and that means right now in the case of many goods and services in some communities, this formula should be put into operation at least for the children. If there is not enough as yet for adults to have abundance, the children will have their full share of what there is."

East Europe's social pattern, differing so widely from that generally accepted in the West, has another significant quality. It is neither finished nor final; it is still fluid, still "in the works." Social experiments, and their attendant successes and failures, have tested out new assumptions and generalizations and resulted in a widespread self-confidence that comes with the unity of theory and practice.

The new social pattern which is emerging in East Europe is designed to avoid war and other forms of waste, as a matter of tactics, while a new and creative strategy leads to the production of abundance and a wide open door of opportunity to enjoy the advantages which abundance brings.

This program has general support in East Europe. Only a small declining minority wishes for a return to the old order—with something approaching feudalism in the countryside and with capitalism as the dominant social force in the towns and cities. There are East Europeans, especially those trained and habituated to the old society, who do not yet understand what is happening there. Their number is diminishing. The purposes and principles of socialist construction are more and more widely understood and accepted.

Widespread support for socialist construction in East Europe does not mean irrational and unthinking backing for anything and everything that administrative authority may propose or initiate. Social criticism is as much a part of the new life as self-criticism. "We can do that job. We have proved our competence by fulfilling our obligations. Now let's ask ourselves: What mistakes have we made that should be avoided in the future? How can our equipment and our techniques be improved?" The idea of change and the need for change is accepted throughout East Europe. Indeed, it is one of their first principles.

Without question, socialist construction is transforming East Europe. . . . Today a growing majority realizes that socialism is the wave of the future.

A QUESTION MARK

East Europe, turned socialist, presents the sympathetic observer with many questions. The first and most frequent question is: *Are the East European countries satellites?*

Webster's political definition of "satellite" is: "A small state that is economically dependent on, and hence adjusts its policies to, a larger more powerful state." Under this definition, in the years immediately following 1945 most East European nations could only from a formal standpoint be termed "satellites" of the Soviet Union. They were no more dependent economically than Britain, France, and Italy during the same period were dependent upon Washington's billions of Marshall Plan aid, while the North Atlantic Treaty

Organization (also Washington-sponsored) gave political protection to countries so exhausted by war that they were unable to stand on their own feet. The East European countries looked to and received from the Soviet Union genuinely *brotherly* assistance free of political or financial conditions, in sharp contrast to the dependence which exists in Latin America, Turkey, Spain, South Vietnam, and other countries which are in the imperialist orbit of the U.S.A.

During the past fifteen years, the economic dependence of East Europe on the Soviet Union and of West Europe on the United States have decreased markedly, though political ties have continued in both East and West. Parts of East Europe are, by treaty and agreement, still occupied by Soviet armed forces. At the same time, every important country of West Europe (including Britain, France, Germany, and Italy), together with the sea and air approaches to the European continent, is still occupied by the armed forces of the United States.

Both East and West Europe enjoy a large measure of "home rule" in their domestic affairs. Their parliaments, municipal councils, national, regional, and local executives and courts follow their customary practices and routines. They are legally sovereign states; but in matters involving foreign policy—particularly issues of war and peace—Moscow is looked to as a leader among equals in East Europe, while Washington has a commanding voice in the West. East Europe is part of the eastern or socialist bloc. West Europe is part of the capitalist bloc. . . .

THE SOCIALIST ROAD AHEAD

The breadth, depth and breath-taking tempo of the social revolution running at full tide in the East European countries seem to justify certain conclusions concerning the course that the revolution is following and its probable effects on other parts of the world, including the Western Hemisphere.

First conclusion. East Europe is passing through its own particular phase of a planetwide social revolution. The onset of this world revolution was so gradual in its earlier aspects that it escaped the notice of all except the most perceptive. Its growth was slow. The locale of its development was spotted across the planet. The climax of the revolution, extending over the past half century, constitutes one of the most fateful episodes of human history.

Second conclusion. People in East Europe have accepted the implications of the current social revolution with a determination and an enthusiasm far greater than that with which the people of West Europe generally (and of the United States in particular) have rejected the revolution. Perhaps it would be more accurate to say the East Europeans have embraced rather than accepted the revolution. Most East Europeans now take the revolution as a matter of course. It is their way of life and they intend to make a success of it.

Third conclusion. Industrial and agricultural workers in East Europe are living on a higher level of economic adequacy, stability and security than they have known during the life of the oldest inhabitant. The same thing could probably be said of the small farm owners. These results are the immediate outcome of a generally supported program designed (1) to repair war damage as speedily as possible; (2) to build industry as rapidly as resources and income permit, and (3) to expand the social services to the point at which the necessaries and decencies are available to all citizens. The fulfillment of this program has ended unemployment, created an unprecedented demand for trained, skilled, experienced personnel, and presented an entire generation of young people with wide-open opportunities to improve their qualifications and do their bit toward promoting the general advance of East Europe's economic and cultural life.

Fourth conclusion. Purposes have been clear from the beginning, but the obstacles and obstructions in the path of East European socialist construction have been so formidable that even today it often seems necessary to take one step backward before the time is ripe for two steps forward. This has been particularly true of the economic problems associated with agricultural production and the political and ideological issues raised in those many parts of East Europe where the Roman Catholic Church has been the traditional policy maker.

Fifth conclusion. Socialism in East Europe is today a going concern; not, as the West thinks, because it has been forced upon the people by outside influences, but because socialism was the only logical way out of the critical situation in which East Europeans found themselves in 1945. Harrying war experience and the cold war threat of another general military conflict—in which atomic and nuclear weapons would be used extensively—have put the building of socialism at the top of the East European priority list.

Stepped-up training of large numbers of scientists, engineers and technicians has developed a rapidly growing body of competent and responsible citizens with a stake in the new social order and a solid belief in the promises of better things to come. This new group is becoming a determining factor in shaping policy and in building socialism. Most members of the group are young. They have had enough experience and scored enough successes to give them confidence. Their own futures are closely tied with the outcome of socialist construction.

Sixth conclusion. East Europe's experience is blazing a trail that should prove highly attractive to small nations and peoples seeking independence and self-determination. East European experience suggests that, as socialism develops, peoples suffering the rigors of capitalist overlordship can win independence and self-determination by building socialism, joining the socialist bloc and avoiding the anguishing generations of tutelage suffered by colonial and dependent peoples.

Seventh conclusion. The socialist road which East Europeans are traveling has its advantages, benefits, gains and its glorious vistas. At the same time it is fraught with difficulties and dangers. One observer in East Europe recently made this general comment on social revolutions: "It is easy to seize political authority and hold it for a longer or shorter period. It is less easy to change the political institutions and practices to which people have become accustomed. It is difficult to alter property relations, particularly where property is held by large numbers of individuals, and households are using their property for their own advantage. Most difficult of all is the task of changing long-established social customs and the physical, emotional and mental habits of individual human beings. It is in this fourth field that social revolutionaries face their greatest obstacles and their most stubborn oppositions." . . .

The socialist revolution of the 20th century demands for its fulfillment not only new knowledge, skills and techniques but mature human beings capable of reorientation and adaptation, and youth ready and eager to acquire the new knowledge, learn the new skills, practice the new techniques and shoulder responsibility for the complex enterprise called modern living. . . .

The fulfillment of the tasks ahead requires a cultural revolution, an end to the narrow limitations of class and caste, and an endeavor to provide maximum opportunities for all in a socialist society which is the complete opposite of the class culture of old East Europe. It marks the advent of an era of scientific endeavor to discover and utilize the full possibilities of humanity, of nature and of society, and to inspire this new society to build a living place worthy of the vast and infinitely varied human potential.

RECENT ECONOMIC DEVELOPMENTS IN THE EAST EUROPEAN MEMBER COUNTRIES OF THE SOVIET COMMONWEALTH OF NATIONS: *A SUPPLEMENT* [1]

In recent years economic development in the European socialist countries has entered a new stage. In most countries the structural renovation of the economy, associated with the revolutionary changes in production relations and with the abolition of the economic backwardness inherited by some of them from capitalism, has either been completed or is nearing completion. The comprehensive building of socialism and communism is now underway.

Because of this the qualitative side of the economic development acquires growing importance as the paramount task of socialist construction. Attainment of a level of labor productivity higher than that under capitalism necessitates accelerated technological progress and modernization based on the achievements of the scientific and technological revolution now taking place in the world.

[1] By V. Isupov, B. Lodygin, V. Terekhov, and O. Bogomolov (*see* footnote, p. 325).

In the past ten years the production capacity in the European socialist countries has increased two- to three-fold while industrial output is roughly nine times that of prewar.

So far economic growth in most socialist countries has been characterized by exceptionally high rates due mainly to extensive development. Now, however, the scientific and technological revolution confronts all the socialist countries with the task of intensive development. Growth of output is now being determined by raising labor productivity, by more effective utilization of production facilities, and by rational management.

The modification of the conditions in which the productive forces of socialism are developing and the corresponding structural changes effected in the economy have resulted in some of the countries in a temporary slowing down in rates of growth, in reduced returns per unit of investment, in the emergence of disproportions between the rapid expansion of industry and the slower pace of agriculture, and between manufacturing and extracting industries. Many raw materials and fuel are still in short supply. A disproportion between output of the means of production and consumer-goods output still persists in some of them. These difficulties were caused in no small measure by the unfavorable weather conditions of past years which adversely affected agriculture and, consequently, supplies of agricultural raw materials.

But the basic reasons for the slowing down should be sought in the methods and forms of organization and management which took shape at the time of laying the foundations of socialism and during the socialist reconstruction of the economy and which in the past provided a powerful stimulus to economic growth; these forms and methods no longer answer to the needs of the present stage of development of the productive forces. The system of planning and management built solely on directives from the top and regulating practically every detail of the functioning of the enterprises simply cannot cope with the expanded economic organism. . . .

The study of the difficulties, the search for scientifically grounded ways of overcoming them and of tapping all the reserves have been in the center of attention of the Party and governmental bodies in the socialist countries. All creative endeavor is now directed towards solving these problems.

In Bulgaria, Hungary, the GDR, Czechoslovakia, Poland, and the Soviet Union steps have been taken to improve the systems of economic management. The Ninth Congress of the Rumanian Communist Party held in July 1965 pointed to the need for further improving the organization and management of the national economy.

A WORD ON RECENT ECONOMIC REFORMS

What is envisaged is not partial changes or improvements in this or that sphere of economic life, but a comprehensive economic management reform.

It goes without saying, that in carrying through the reform each socialist country proceeds from its own concrete conditions. Even some of the common features of the reform cannot but assume diverse forms in the different countries. This is only natural; the socialist countries, being at different levels of economic development, are faced with various specific problems arising out of the concrete conditions under which they are building socialism. Hence, the different tempos of the reforms (which were initiated earlier in some countries than in others), their different depths and breadths, although their underlying principles are the same. A marked feature of the reform is the varying degree of independence granted to the enterprises and trusts, as well as the varying degree to which the commodity-money instruments and the law of value are used in planned management. Nor is it difficult to note the differences in the systems of workers' remuneration depending on the results of the work of the enterprise as a whole, in the methods of economic incentives to introduce new technologies, raise the quality of output, secure efficient use of fixed assets, etc. . . .

From the Party documents recently published in Czechoslovakia, Hungary, and Bulgaria it appears that the very concept of economic planning there is changing in many respects. Economic planning is no longer identified with the most detailed regulation of the economy from above. While in the past the plan was conceived as a directive or obligatory prescription, today it is regarded as an instrument of politico-economic guidance increasingly exercising an economic, rather than administrative, influence on production. The plan is obligatory only in the sense that the general line of long-term development is obligatory, but not every figure and every index contained in it. . . .

An important factor of the reorganization of economic management in the European socialist countries is the consistent practice of cost-accounting and elimination of the various artificial curbs. A characteristic feature of all countries seeking to improve their planning methods is wider use of the commodity-money levers—prices, profit, taxes, and credit.

A discussion on the place commodity-money relations hold in the socialist economy has been conducted in the socialist countries over the past ten years. The great majority of those participating in the discussion rejected the view that commodity relations are incompatible with socialism and should be regarded only as an inevitable evil that must be limited and banished by all possible means. The view has gained the upper hand which recognises the existence of commodity relations, the law of value, and the market in the socialist economy, and demands that they should be used in the best possible way in the interests of planned development.

The new measures are already beginning to produce positive results and are clearing the way to industrial and technological progress. After a certain decline in 1963, rates of growth rose again in 1964 and 1965.

ACHIEVEMENTS IN ACTUAL FIGURES

GROWTH OF INDUSTRIAL OUTPUT

Ever since the formation of the Council for Mutual Economic Aid industrial output of its members has risen at a growing pace, as can be seen from the following table:

Table 10-2. Dynamics of Industrial Output [2] (1950 = 100)

Years	Total Growth	Annual Growth Rate
1951	118	17.9
1952	134	13.8
1953	151	12.5
1954	168	11.1
1955	187	11.7
1956	205	9.6
1957	226	10.0
1958	250	10.5
1959	278	11.3
1960	306	10.1
1961	334	9.2
1962	364	9.0
1963	389	6.8
1964	418	7.5
Average for 1951-1964		10.8

[2] By way of comparison it should be noted that in these years the mean annual rate of industrial growth in the Common Market countries was 7.3 percent.

(Besides the six countries covered in this chapter, the growth figures in the table above (and the "total" figures in some of the tables below) include the Soviet Union and the Mongolian People's Republic. [EDITOR'S NOTE])

The rate of growth was not quite the same in all the countries. This is not surprising because the trend is towards an evening up of the general level. The one-time economically backward countries have demonstrated the fastest rates of industrial growth:

Table 10-3. Growth of Industrial Output (1950 = 100)

	1960	1964	Average Annual Rate of Growth for 1951-1964
Bulgaria	397	603	13.7
Hungary	267	367	9.7
GDR	292	367	9.7
Poland	338	465	11.6
Rumania	340	574	13.3
Czechoslovakia	276	330	8.9

The principal factor in the rapid growth is the steady rise in labor productivity. The latter acquires a particular significance today, now that the reserves of extensive development in most of the socialist countries no longer suffice to ensure fast rates of growth:

Table 10-4. Growth of Labor Productivity in Industry
(1950 = 100)

	1960	1963	1964	Average Annual Rate of Growth in 1951-1964
Bulgaria	190	229	246	6.6
Hungary	148	171	180	4.3
Poland	227	253	269	7.3
Rumania	237	291	320	8.7
Czechoslovakia	200	216	224	5.9

It should be pointed out that in some of the socialist countries the rate of growth tended to slacken somewhat in recent years, especially in 1963. However, the lag, a temporary one, was rapidly made good, as evidenced by a comparison of indices of industrial growth for 1963 with those for 1964 and the first six months of 1965:

Table 10-5. Rate of Growth of Industrial Output in
1963, 1964, and First Six Months of 1965

	1963	1964	First Six Months of 1965
Bulgaria	10	11.1	12.8
Hungary	6	9	6
GDR	4.3	6.7	6.7
Poland	5	9.3	10.7
Rumania	12.2	14.1	14
Czechoslovakia	−0.6	4.1	8.7

The focal factor in the development of modern economy is the fuel industry, particularly electric power. Between 1960 and 1964 industrial output
rose by 36 percent, while electric power generation rose by about 50 percent:

Table 10-6.   Electric Power Generation (1,000 Million Kilowatt-hours)

	1950	*1960*	*1963*	*1964*	*1964 in* $^0/_0{}^0/_0$ *of* *1950*
Total	135	406	555	616	455
Including:					
Bulgaria	0.8	4.7	7.2	8.7	1088
Hungary	3.0	7.6	9.7	10.6	353
GDR	19.5	40.3	47.5	51.0	262
Poland	9.4	29.3	37.0	40.6	432
Rumania	2.1	7.7	11.7	13.9	662
Czechoslovakia	9.3	24.4	29.9	32.0	344

Effectiveness of social production in the member-countries and their rates
of growth are in many respects determined by the expansion of the chemical
industry and machine building:

Table 10-7.   Comparative Dynamics of Output of Industry
as a Whole, Machine Building and Chemical Industry
(1964 Increase Compared with 1950)

	Industry *as a Whole*	*Machine* *Building*	*Chemical* *Industry*
Bulgaria	6 times	14 times	15 times
Hungary	3.7 "	5.2 "	9.8 "
GDR	3.7 "	4.8 "	3.9 "
Poland	4.7 "	12.8 "	8.3 "
Rumania	5.8 "	13 "	17 "
Czechoslovakia	3.3 "	5.6 "	6.3 "

Non-ferrous metallurgy is basic to machine building and capital construction. With the advance of the chemical industry and the improved technology of metalworking, the share of metal in industrial output tends to decrease. Hence the growth rate in the iron and steel industry lags somewhat
compared with industry as a whole, particularly machine building. Nevertheless, metal will long remain the principal construction material. Hence attention to metallurgy generally, and to the non-ferrous metal industry in particular, is not diminishing, all the more so since in some of the countries metal
is still in short supply.

Table 10-8.   Steel Smelting (Million Tons)

	1950	1960	1963	1964	1964 in %/% of 1950
Total	35.8	86.5	105.5	112.2	313
Including:					
Bulgaria	0.01	0.3	0.5	0.5	—
Hungary	1.0	1.9	2.4	2.4	240
GDR	1.3	3.8	4.1	4.3	339
Poland	2.5	6.7	8.0	8.6	341
Rumania	0.6	1.8	2.7	3.0	547
Czechoslovakia	3.1	6.8	7.6	8.4	268

Accelerated development of heavy industry in recent years has prepared the way for accelerated growth of consumer-goods production. . . .

The growth rates and volume of production for a variety of consumer goods can be seen from the following figures:

Table 10-9.   Manufacture of Cotton Fabrics (Million Square Miles)

	1950	1960	1963	1964	1964 in %/% of 1950
Bulgaria	71	186	217	231	325
Hungary	177	239	283	304	172
GDR	154	345	357	347	224
Poland	397	605	639	704	177
Rumania	148	248	301	302	204
Czechoslovakia	355	453	473	468	132

Table 10-10.   Output of Durables[3] (Thousand Units)

	1950	1960	1963	1964	Increase in 1964 Compared with 1950
Refrigerators	14	860	1,622	2,065	147 times
Washing machines	4	1,997	3,622	4,232	1,058 "
TV sets	12	2,717	4,001	4,550	379 "
Cars	96	275	338	347	3.6 "

[3] Includes U.S.S.R. [EDITOR'S NOTE]

The figures show not only rapid growth rates in light industry but also the deep-going structural changes in consumer-goods output in favor of more "expensive" durables.

AGRICULTURE

Special attention has been paid to agriculture in recent years. . . . Agricultural output is rising in all the countries:

Table 10-11. Dynamics of Agricultural Output (in %%% of 1950)

	1955	1960	1963	1964	Average Annual Rate of Growth Between 1951 and 1964
Bulgaria	137	181	186	208	5.4
Hungary	117	120	130	134	2.1
GDR	140	159	151	158	3.3
Poland	105	126	133	134	2.1
Rumania	162	170	170	181	4.3
Czechoslovakia	108	120	119	122	1.4

Table 10-12. Tractor Park in Agriculture (Thousand Units)

	1950	1964	Increase
Bulgaria	6.6	38.9	5.9 times
Hungary	13.4	60.6	4.5 "
GDR	36.4	119.5	3.3 "
Poland	28.4	106.7	3.8 "
Rumania	13.7	75.4	5.5 "

The rise in agricultural output has been achieved thanks to mechanization and application of chemicals.

It should be noted, however, that even the rapid growth of mechanization and chemicalization achieved in recent years no longer meets the needs of agriculture. Hence steps are being taken to increase further the production of agricultural machines and implements, and especially of mineral fertilizers. The member-countries have scored definite successes in grain production:

Table 10-13.   Grain Output (Million Tons)

	1950	1960	1963	1964	1964 in %% of 1950
Bulgaria	3.2	4.9	4.5	5.2	164
Hungary	5.5	6.9	6.5	6.9	125
GDR	5.6	6.4	5.5	6.2	110
Poland	12.0	14.8	15.1	14.0	117
Rumania	5.1	9.8	10.4	11.1	216
Czechoslovakia	4.7	5.7	5.6	5.3	111

In most countries output of other crops has increased considerably in recent years, with potatoes and sugar-beet playing the most significant part.

In those countries where the output of grain and other crops has risen, this has been directly due to higher per-hectare yields:

Table 10-14.   Yields of Cereals, Potatoes and Sugar Beet
(Tons per Hectare)

	Cereals		Potatoes		Sugar-beet	
	1950	1964	1950	1964	1950	1964
Bulgaria	1.03	2.07	4.9	10.5	8.5	27.0
Hungary	1.43	2.06	4.8	7.9	14.6	26.8
GDR	2.03	2.64	18.1	17.3	27.3	26.2
Poland	1.25	1.59	13.8	16.9	22.2	28.3
Rumania	0.74	1.66	7.0	8.5	8.8	19.3
Czechoslovakia	1.70	2.05	12.4	15.6	28.5	29.0

In most countries animal husbandry made relatively good progress. In some, however, the lag in fodder crops resulted in a slow rate in livestock breeding, especially in the increase of the head of cattle:

Table 10-15.   Head of Cattle and Pigs (Million Head)

	Cattle			Pigs		
	1950	1964	1964 in %% of 1950	1950	1964	1964 in %% of 1950
Bulgaria	1.9	1.6	83	0.8	2.6	319
Hungary	2.0	1.9	96	4.8	7.0	147
GDR	3.6	4.7	130	5.7	8.8	154
Poland	7.2	9.9	138	9.4	12.9	138
Rumania	4.5	4.8	106	2.2	6.0	273
Czechoslovakia	4.3	4.4	103	3.8	6.1	161

The problem of agriculture, still acute in most of the socialist countries, became particularly grave in recent years, due mainly to unfavorable weather conditions and to insufficient utilization of incentives. As is clear from the foregoing tables, the grain harvest in a number of the countries was unstable, which also adversely affected animal husbandry. Shortage of grain had to be compensated by purchase on the capitalist market.

To remedy this state of affairs and to accelerate growth, urgent measures are being taken, such as considerably bigger investments in agriculture, increased output of farm machines and improving their quality, much greater output of fertilizers and herbicides, strict cost accounting, abolition of the rigid centralized regimentation, better purchasing prices for farm produce, and more incentives.

CAPITAL CONSTRUCTION

Capital construction—the basis of extended socialist reproduction—is proceeding at a rapid pace . . . :

Table 10-16. Investments in the Economy (in National Currencies)

	1950	1960	1964	1964 in $\%\%$ of 1950
Bulgaria (ml. leva)	300	1,192	1,659	523
Hungary (ml. forints)	23,700	42,900	52,000	220
GDR (ml. marks)	3,600	15,600	18,200	511
Poland (ml. zloty)	38,600	100,000	129,100	334
Rumania (ml. lei)	5,700	24,400	41,000	719
Czechoslovakia (ml. Kor.)	14,800	43,700	45,400	306

Priority development for the more modern branches of industry is regarded as one of the most important means of raising the effectiveness of social production:

Table 10-17.   Share of Investments in the Power, Machine-Building and
    Chemical Industries in the Overall Industrial Investments in
        Some Member-Countries in 1964 (in %%%)

	Power	Machine-Bld.	Chemical Ind.
Bulgaria	16.3	12.1	5.7
Hungary	12.5	13.6	15.2
Poland	12.1	15.2	12.3
Rumania	14.7	6.5	15.1

PUBLIC WELFARE AND CULTURAL STANDARDS

The aim of production under socialism is to satisfy the constantly growing needs of all members of society. This, in the final analysis, is the objective of the entire economic policy of the socialist countries and the purpose of the recent measures taken to improve the systems of planning and management.

The growth of the national income is the basis of the rising well-being of the people:

Table 10-18.   National Income Growth (1950 = 100)

	1960	1963	1964	Average Annual Rate of Growth in 1951-1964
Bulgaria	282	332	354	9.5
Hungary	187	219	228	6.1
GDR	249	263	274	7.4
Poland	208	245	261	7.1
Rumania	268	338	377	9.9
Czechoslovakia	207	219	221	5.8

Table 10-19.   Real Wages and Salaries in Some Member Countries
                    (1950 = 100)

	1960	1963	1964
Hungary	154	164	168
GDR (1960 = 100)	100	106	109
Poland (1960 = 100)	100	106	109
Rumania	185	209	213
Czechoslovakia	136	139	142

Growth of real income has its corollary in increased retail trade.

Table 10-20. Dynamics of Retail State and Cooperative Trade
(in Fixed Prices, 1950 = 100)

	1960	1963	1964
Bulgaria	338	420	445
Hungary	310	360	390
GDR (1955 = 100)	150	157	162
Poland	255	310	320
Rumania	290	412	444
Czechoslovakia (1955 = 100)	128	139	143

However, the index of real wages and retail trade does not give a full idea of the growing well-being. A large and ever greater part of the needs of the working people is met, not by wages, but by public consumption funds. Year by year the socialist countries are increasing their outlays on housing, public health, social insurance, on education, the arts, recreation and public amenities:

Table 10-21. Number of Flats Built (Thousand Units)

				1964 in $^0/_0{}^0/_0$ of	
	1950	1960	1963	1964	1950
Bulgaria	—	49.8	43.9	47.2	—
Hungary	35.1	58.1	52.7	53.4	152
GDR	31.0	80.5	76.0	76.6	247
Poland	68.3	144.4	146.3	164	240
Rumania	49.3	133.9	122.3	123.9	251
Czechoslovakia	38.2	73.8	82.2	77.3	202

The education system in the socialist countries rests on a thoroughly democratic basis. For scale of education and number of students, the member-countries are among the most advanced in the world:

Table 10-22. Enrollment in General and Higher Schools
(Thousand Persons)

	General Schools		Higher Schools	
	1950/51	1964/65	1950/51	1964/65
Bulgaria	970	1,274	31	82
Hungary	1,282	1,659	33	92
GDR	2,514	2,396	32	112
Poland	3,610	5,864	125	231
Rumania	1,838	3,321	53	123
Czechoslovakia	1,736	2,356	45	145

The number of doctors per 10,000 persons increased between 1950 and 1964 as follows: [4]

Table 10-23.

	1950	*1964*
Bulgaria	7	16
GDR	7.4	10.6
Poland	4.6	15.6
Rumania	9.5	14.4
Czechoslovakia	9.2	18.0

* * *

The economies of these socialist countries is, as we have seen, developing rapidly, overcoming the temporary difficulties. But the facts also show that the economic competition with capitalism calls for an even more strenuous effort on the part of the working people of the socialist countries. Today as before the latter are ahead of the capitalist world for rates of growth. As a result the share of the socialist countries in world industrial output is steadily rising. Before the war it amounted to some 10 percent, in 1955 it rose to 27 percent, and currently it is in the vicinity of 40 percent.

The further consolidation of the economic strength of the Socialist World system is the internationalist duty of the socialist countries before the international working-class movement.

No small part in this is played by the measures to improve management and planning carried out in a number of the countries, the Soviet Union included. This is a manifestation of the genuine concern of the Communist Parties of the socialist countries for the vital interests of world socialism, for consolidating its positions in the sharp class struggle with the Capitalist World.

FURTHER READING SUGGESTIONS

Aptheker, Herbert, *The Truth About Hungary*. New York: Mainstream, 1957.
Cary, William, *Bulgaria Today*. New York: Exposition Press, 1965.
Hoffman, George W., and Fred Warner Neal, *Yugoslavia and the New Communism*. New York: Twentieth Century Fund, 1962.

[4] To compare: The United States, in 1964, had about 15 doctors per 10,000 population.

Kertesz, Stephen D., ed., *East Central Europe and the World*. University of
Notre Dame Press, 1962.

League of Communists of Yugoslavia, *Yugoslavia's Way*. New York: All
Nations Press, 1958.

Liber, B., *The New Rumania*. New York: Rational Living, 1958.

Macartney, C. A., and A. W. Palmer, *Independent Eastern Europe*. London:
Macmillan, 1962.

Sharp, Samuel L., *New Constitutions in the Soviet Sphere*. Washington,
D.C.: Foundation for Foreign Affairs, 1950.

Each of the East European socialist countries publishes current documents
and factual data in English.

VI

The People's Republic of Albania: China's Beachhead in Europe

YUGOSLAVIA

ADRIATIC SEA

ITALY

o Tirane
ALBANIA

GREECE

Area
(in square miles)
11,100

Population
(mid-1967 estimate)
1,988,000

*All power in the People's Republic of Albania belongs
to the working people of town and countryside. . . .*

CONSTITUTION OF THE PEOPLE'S REPUBLIC OF ALBANIA

*The exploiting classes and the exploitation of man by
man has remained in our country only as a memory of
the bitter past. . . . New Albania is uncontestable proof
of the incomparable superiority of the socialist order
over every oppressive and exploiting order.*

ENVER HOXHA
FIRST SECRETARY, CENTRAL COMMITTEE OF THE
ALBANIAN PARTY OF LABOR

INTRODUCTION

LITTLE ALBANIA, SMALLEST IN AREA AMONG THE COUNTRIES OF THE
Communist World and second smallest in population, is like a thorn
in the flesh of East European communism. Once a loyal follower of
Tito's Yugoslavia, Albania sided with the Soviet Union in the Stalin-Tito
split, reportedly fearful that Yugoslavia intended to incorporate Albania
within its borders. Perhaps these fears were reawakened upon the first indications of the pending rapprochement between the Soviet Union and Yugoslavia. Since, at that time, Communist China launched her first attacks on
the Soviet leadership under the disguise of condemning Tito's "revisionism,"
Albania began to turn towards China. An apparently Soviet-backed plot to
unseat Albanian Party leader Enver Hoxha gave the *coup de grâce* to Soviet-
Albanian relations. At the international conference of 81 Communist Parties
in Moscow in the fall of 1960, Hoxha delivered a violent denunciation of
the Kremlin leadership and placed his little country squarely on the Chinese
side in the rapidly developing Sino-Soviet split. In the early 1960's Albania
became the official mouthpiece of China, levying charges and accusations,
which the Chinese were not yet ready to verbalize, against the U.S.S.R.'s
"revisionist" leadership. When in 1961 Moscow decided to withhold all
support from Albania, Peking was ready to assume the role of benefactor.
Ever since, the little country's economy has leaned heavily upon Chinese aid.
In June, 1966, an economic communiqué issued by the Communist Parties
of China and Albania announced that for the period 1966-1970 Peking has
promised Tirana "credits, technical aid, and delivery of complete factory
installations as well as other machinery and construction materials"; and
according to the Albanian Party organ *Zeri i Popullit* (July 28, 1966) the
volume of this economic aid is to be substantially greater than in the preceding five-year period.

Albania is today the only country, not merely in Europe but in the entire world, to follow without reservation the Maoist line of Chinese communism.

The non-Marxist view on Albania was written by two Albanian émigré scholars, Drs. Athanas Gegaj and Rexhep Krasniqi. As the only non-Marxist view in this book contributed by natives of the country involved, and prepared and published under the auspices of organizations committed to the "liberation" of the respective areas from communist control, this contribution represents a particularly strong anticommunist, and especially anti-Albanian-Communist, view.

Co-authors Gegaj and Krasniqi hold Ph.D. degrees respectively from the University of Louvain in Belgium and from the University of Vienna. Formerly Professor of Literature and History in Albania, Gegaj is at present editor of *Dielli* (the Sun), an Albanian-American paper published in Boston, Mass. Krasniqi, formerly Professor of History and Geography in Albania, is at present President of the Free Albania Committee in New York, a regular member of the Assembly of Captive European Nations (ACEN).

The Marxist view on Albania has been put together from eight different books, booklets, and articles, all of them published in Albania's capital, Tirana. Among the authors are Harilla Papajorgji, Albanian Economist; Peti Shambeli, former Albanian Minister of Agriculture; Pipi Mitrojorgji, Deputy Minister of Education and Culture; Bilbil Klosi, Albanian Minister of Justice; and Dr. Fejzi Hoxha, Chief of Albania's Hospital Clinics.

11

Albania: A Non-Marxist View

ATHANAS GEGAJ and REXHEP KRASNIQI *

The present-day state of Albania was created in 1920, just after World
War I. After centuries of isolation and a chaotic national history, Albania
had to begin from scratch. The new state had to set up a system of communications. Roads and bridges, which would link various parts of the
country and join towns to villages, were essential. New government and
municipal buildings, schools, hospitals, military installations, and hotels had
to be built. The growth of the new state required the construction of new
plants and factories. But commercial life within the country and with the
outside world quickly developed. . . .

At the time Albania achieved independence, her inherited economy
consisted of a primitive type of farming and livestock raising. As a country
of peasants, she had no important industrial establishments, and modern
technical methods of agriculture were unknown. These facts explain to some
extent the present backwardness of the country both in agriculture and industry, especially in comparison with the rest of southeastern Europe. Modernization proceeded slowly up to the communist take-over, when an obses-
sion for industrialization at all costs resulted in the regrettable neglect of
agriculture and livestock, the principal natural resources of the country. . . .

THE COMMUNIST TAKE-OVER

Soon after Albania's occupation by fascist Italy,[1] the Albanian people rose
up against this foreign domination in a struggle which eventually grew into

---

* This contribution has been condensed from Athanas Gegaj's and Rexhep Krasniqi's *Albania,* a little booklet prepared by the Free Albania Committee and published in
1964 in New York by the Assembly of Captive European Nations. It is here reprinted
by permission of the authors and the publisher.

[1] Mussolini's fascist Italy occupied Albania from 1939 to 1943; Hitler's Nazi Germany from 1943 to 1944. [EDITOR'S NOTE]

an organized national armed resistance. The Albanian communists, however, launched their resistance movement only after Germany attacked the U.S.S.R.

While almost all political parties and groups were united against the Italian fascists, who clearly intended to turn Albania into a mere colony, some leaders of the nationalist parties displayed reluctance to fight the German invaders, who had promised the integration of Albania within her own ethnical borders. Profiting from this situation the Communist Party managed, in the name of "national liberation," to outmaneuver its opponents, the genuine nationalist movement.

The Albanian Communist Party and its "National Liberation Movement" was in fact organized by Yugoslav Communist agents, and was politically and ideologically directed by Marshal Tito of Yugoslavia. When the German Army withdrew from the country, it became master of Albania. A provisional government headed by Enver Hoxha, the Party's first secretary, installed itself in Tirana, the Albanian capital, as "the government of liberated Albania."

The transition to communism in Albania began in the earliest days of the new regime. By the end of November, 1944, the Party had consolidated its position in the country. Many of the opposing leaders of the nationalist forces fled to the West. Others were brought before "People's Courts," where they were charged with war crimes, fascism, or simply as enemies of the people. . . . Within a decade some 15,000 people were executed or murdered without trial, many perishing in forced labor camps, while another estimated 15,000 were thrown into prisons and labor camps for various "political" offenses. . . .

Elections for the Constituent Assembly were held in December, 1945. Although provisions were ostensibly made for the casting of "opposition" ballots, in compliance with a stipulation by the victorious powers of World War II, the police-organized terror of the Party made any opposition impossible.

The Democratic Front, a new communist agency replacing the former National Liberation Front, won a sweeping election "victory" for its single list of candidates. In January, 1946, the Constituent Assembly abolished the monarchy and proclaimed Albania a "People's Republic." In March, the new Constitution was promulgated. . . . On this occasion Riza Dani, a noncommunist leader of the National Liberation Movement and deputy of Shkodër, refused to accept the antiparliamentary nature of the Constitution's promulgation. Accused of treason, he was executed after the usual mock trial. The same fate was meted out to another group of deputies who had objected to the narrow, Soviet-oriented nature of the regime, and who had urged that relations be opened with the West. Some 16 deputies of the first legislature were thus liquidated in one way or another.

A SERIES OF TESTS

The present communist leaders of Albania have during the past decades claimed to have emerged "victorious" through a series of inner tests which have, in fact, seriously endangered their rule. The people's opposition to the regime was perhaps best demonstrated by the fact that Albanian nationalist guerrilla forces continued their long and bloody resistance in the mountainous regions of the country. Two revolts, that of the Kelmendi region in January, 1945, and that of the Postripa in Northern Albania, were particularly grave threats to the regime. The guerrilla forces continued their resistance despite the lack of any aid from the Free World, yet finally, after eight years of merciless and ceaseless pursuit, the regime was able to eliminate all organized armed resistance in 1952.

The dependence of the Albanian Communist Party on its Yugoslav sister Party during the "liberation" war became in time more and more marked. Albania was in reality a Yugoslav-ruled country, and plans for the merger of Albania as the seventh Federal Republic of Yugoslavia were under way. It was to be foreseen that the new Federal Yugoslav Republic would include in its administration the Albanian-populated regions of Kossova and Metohija, which Albania has always claimed as integral parts of the nation.

A serious danger threatened the present Albanian leaders on the occasion of the first conflict between Moscow and Belgrade in 1948. The ruling class of Tirana was sharply divided over the question, whether to follow Stalin or Tito. The Stalinist group, however, led by Party Secretary Enver Hoxha, who was at that time overshadowed by Belgrade's chief agent, Koci Xoxe, used this opportunity to accuse Xoxe of treason both to the Party and to the nation. He and many of his followers were arrested, tried, and executed. Yugoslavia strongly denounced these hostile acts of Tirana, but it could do nothing to prevent them, since Tirana had the full backing of the Kremlin.

In February, 1951, the regime survived another revolt from within the Party ranks. The revolt culminated in bomb explosions in the Soviet legation at Tirana, where an important joint conference of Soviet diplomats and Albanian leaders had been called. . . .

In 1956, during the Hungarian revolution, strong signs indicated that the Albanians would join the Hungarians in their struggle for freedom. But the bloody suppression of the uprising by Soviet tanks and the nonintervention of the Free World prevented a similar revolution in Albania. During the Party meetings in the Tirana district in the summer of the same year, Party leaders were violently criticized by rank-and-file delegates for their exploitation of the working class to the point of starvation, while they lived in abundance and luxury. The rebels were promptly silenced through a sweeping purge, which struck hard at the Party's roots.

Through all these years, the Party chief, Enver Hoxha, and the premier, Mehmet Shehu, having divided power between themselves, managed to keep the Party and the country under their strict control. . . .

THE COMMUNIZATION OF ALBANIA

Once the communist regime had consolidated its control over the country, the process of transforming Albania into a communist state was intensified. Yugoslav advisers and experts increased in number and all who resented their growing power were ruthlessly eliminated.

After the break between Stalin and Tito in 1948, the direction of the communization of Albania passed from Yugoslavia to the Soviet Union. Albania became a satellite of Moscow, and its leaders' policy became one of complete conformity to that of the Kremlin. While no troops were sent to Albania, a great influx of Soviet technicians and experts did take place. Their presence amounted, in fact, to a Soviet occupation of the country. Under Stalin's influence, Albania was finally included, in 1953, in the Warsaw Pact, along with the other European Communist countries. After a so-called "package deal" with the Western powers, Moscow managed to have Albania admitted to the United Nations in 1955.

The first stage in the transformation of Albania into a communist society was the nationalization of all banks, mines, petroleum industries, large farms, and other industrial and agricultural enterprises, without any compensation to the owners. This was followed by the confiscation of all private property.[2] Private land, industrial plants, factories, warehouses, shops of every kind, hotels, restaurants, and houses belonging to so-called "reactionaries" were seized by the government without compensation. Business people had to surrender the entire assets in gold, bank notes, or foreign currencies that they had deposited in banks or hoarded in their homes. . . .

THE CULTURAL LIFE

In the cultural life, notable changes took place. Where illiteracy was once at an extremely high level, in 1963-1964 some 400,000 students attended all kinds of state schools. Illiteracy has declined considerably and could well

---

[2] This does not refer to the private ownership of most consumer goods such as clothing or furniture, but to the private ownership of means of production. [EDITOR'S NOTE]

disappear within a few years. The state has increased the number of schools, especially elementary schools, where the introduction to communist propaganda and dogma begins. The school system is also being reorganized in order eventually to provide technicians and skilled workers for industries, agriculture, and various trades. The Tirana State University created in 1957 by combining several former institutes specializing in various fields, ranks among the main accomplishments of the regime. Special care is given to the development of music, dramatic and operatic theaters, ballet, and the other arts, all useful as instruments of Party propaganda. . . .

From the start, the regime imposed the Party line on the literary, as on the rest of the country's cultural life. In order to further communist aims, the Albanian Writers and Artists Union was created, which included most of Albania's intellectuals, of whom only a few were communists. As any cultural activity outside the Union is impossible, the Party has by this means achieved complete control of the country's cultural life. . . .

Even after Khrushchev's denunciation of Stalin, the Albanian communist leadership has remained utterly fanatical in matters of literature and the arts. Thus the entire literary production has served as a means of Party propaganda, and its value as art is most insignificant indeed.

RELIGIOUS PERSECUTION

In order to destroy all religious life in Albania, the communists have tried for years to reduce the entire religious structure of the country to spiritual and functional ineffectuality, while simultaneously exploiting whatever formal power the churches may possess in support of the aims of militant communism. . . .

Three trends are to be seen in the regime's policy toward religion in Albania: weakening of the power of Roman Catholicism, which had a solid organization and strong ties with the West; control of Islam, which is tolerated because of its propaganda value in the Moslem countries of Asia and Africa; and recognition of the value of Eastern Orthodoxy as an instrument for mobilizing the Orthodox population behind the regime's policy. (Catholicism claims about 10 percent, Islam 70 percent, and Orthodoxy 20 percent of the country's population.)

Methods of depriving the churches of their income, curbing their influence, and outlawing religious instructions were invoked in the early days of communist rule by the confiscation of monasteries, schools, seminaries, libraries, and large properties. According to new laws and especially promulgated orders, the election and appointment of personnel of all churches must be approved by the regime, and all religious communities are obliged to send immediately to the council of ministers all pastoral letters, messages, speeches, and memoranda which are to be printed or made public. Further, the law requires that the education of youth is to be conducted by the state, and religious institutions are to have nothing to do with it. It also forbids religious communities to operate hospitals, orphanages, institutions of welfare, or to own real estate. . . .

THE ECONOMIC SITUATION

In the economic field, where hardships are felt by all, the regime boasts of being the champion of outstanding progress and of transforming Albania from a backward agricultural country to an advanced agrarian-industrial state. The communists take credit for all this progress. The fact is, however, that all that was accomplished in the precommunist era has been of vital importance to its present development. . . .

When we analyze the communist regime's industrialization policy, we must recognize that it is based on an overweening presumption entirely at odds with Albania's nature, circumstances, and tradition, which should give first priority to agriculture.

In order to proceed with the usual communist five-year program, the regime continued to build more and more factories and plants when there was no demand for them, and when they had no usefulness to the population. On the other hand, progress has been made by increasing the production of mineral mines, particularly those of chrome ore, nickel ore, copper, coal, asphalt, and oil, and by creating artificial lakes for electric power and for other purposes.

These gains in the field of raw material production, however, have been constantly upset by serious failures and shortages. The annual percentage figures in production show for the most part, as is usual with communist reporting, the positive side of the matter, a fact which can easily lead one to distorted conclusions. It is therefore advisable to take such statistics with great care and some skepticism. Communist Albania, which started its economic program with a two-year plan (1949-1950), followed by three five-year plans in 1951-1955, 1956-1960, and 1961-1965, has been continually plagued by economic instability. The plans have repeatedly been upset by innovations based on the latest "Soviet experience," as well as by an endless series of changes designed to adjust them to Moscow's economic interests. The third five-year plan was faced with great difficulties because of the economic blockade set up by the Soviet Union and the other European communist countries as a consequence of the Albanian communist leadership challenge to Moscow.

This state of affairs has been aggravated by the lack of technicians, skilled workers, and administrative personnel, as well as of means of transport, which has caused shortages in output. Thus the production costs of many industries exceed by far the import cost of the items involved, a fact which underscores the futility of efforts to industrialize at all costs, especially in such an agriculturally-oriented country as Albania.

A similar and even greater instability has plagued the regime's policy in agriculture itself. In order to win the support of the peasant population, which represents the majority of the Albanian people, the communists at first introduced a so-called agrarian reform. Since only some 10 percent of the population engaged in agriculture did not own land, the agrarian reform had little economic significance. Nevertheless, the reform was used as an instrument of political propaganda in the initial phase of the agrarian program.

Soon after they had become "owners" of the land, the peasants were gradually forced to join collective farms. This program was met with strong opposition by the rural population. As in the Soviet Union, those farmers who resisted collectivization were labelled "kulaks." A series of new laws on taxation and compulsory deliveries favoring collective farmers were enacted, which discriminated against independent farmers. . . . Farmers reluctant to join collectives were constantly faced with night visits by police, threats of forced labor, discrimination against their children in schools, difficulties in obtaining seeds, fertilizers, working machines, and other essential facilities.

At first the peasants expressed their resistance by the steadily decreasing yield of their farms. In 1951, however, passive resistance broke into open rebellion, and the regime was forced to abandon such measures; it declared that future collectives were to be formed voluntarily. At this time there were only 90 collectives, with a membership, of 4,500 peasant families, covering less than 3 percent of Albania's cultivated area.

In 1955, after the regime had consolidated its position in the country and under renewed pressure from Moscow, the policy of forceful collectivization of the peasantry was resumed, and collectivization in the agricultural sector increased to 86 percent of the arable land, with some 1,484 collectives and a membership of 115,277 peasant families. . . .

THE ECONOMIC SITUATION OF THE WORKERS

The Albanian communists emphasize the rights that labor has won under their regime. But there is little evidence to support these claims. It is true that the labor code guarantees certain rights and privileges to the workers—among them an eight-hour working day for six days a week, prohibition to employ children under fourteen years of age, classification of workers according to skill, provisions for social benefits, and the like. However, most of these are merely paper guarantees. . . .

After nearly twenty years of the hardest work, the material situation of the Albanian working class under communism stands as follows: The average monthly wage of a skilled worker ranges between 3,000-5,000 leks,[3] equivalent to some $24-$40 monthly. And here are the prices *per pound* of some important commodities: bread, 10 leks; sugar, 60 leks; coffee, 450 leks; olive oil, 100 leks; butter, 200 leks; cheese, 110 leks; meat, which is considered a luxury for ordinary workers, costs 100 leks, and whole milk, also a luxury, costs 25 leks a quart. One pair of shoes costs some 1,800 to 2,200 leks, and a moderate suit around 7,000 to 10,000 leks.

The trade unions, which allegedly protect the vital interests of the working class, are considered the most important official agency of the Party and state in "building socialism." The trade unions fully support and promote the economic plans of the regime, however these may affect the welfare of the workers. They help to boost production, prevent strikes, conclude collective agreements, determine wages; and they are instrumental in the rapid expansion of industry by relentlessly pushing the workers to surpass the quotas. The president of the Labor Council of the Albanian Trade Unions, Gogo Nushi, is a politburo man of the Party's Central Committee.

It is, therefore, small wonder that a Western newsman who visited Albania during the summer of 1962 described the situation of the country as "mired in misery, poverty, and stagnation."

FOREIGN RELATIONS

For nearly two decades, now, the Tirana regime has hermetically isolated Albania and its people from the outside world. Except for carefully screened Party and government members and delegations, no ordinary citizen is permitted to leave the country, not even to visit the communist-ruled states. . . . Albania has been cut off politically, economically, and culturally from her neighbors, and artificially linked with an alien world thousands of miles away, at first with the Soviet Russian people, and more recently, with Far Eastern nations. . . .

Until 1961 the major partners in Albanian foreign trade were the Soviet Union and the countries of the Soviet Bloc. After the break with Moscow, it was thought that this rift might have grave effects on its trade with them. These fears, however, did not materialize, for Albania has renewed trade agreements with all the European communist states except Soviet Russia. The main reason for this, it seems, is that Albania is the main and the cheapest supplier of chrome ore to these countries. Albania produces some 300,000 tons of chrome ore a year, of which 90 percent is exported to those countries. . . .

[3] Since this was written, the lek has been reformed; 10 former leks equal 1 present lek [footnote added by co-author, Dr. Krasniqi].

In 1962, trade with the socialist countries made up 90.3 percent of Albania's total foreign trade, of which Communist China accounted for 59.1 percent, Czechoslovakia 17.4 percent, and the other communist states 13.8 percent. These figures show clearly how poor are the trade relations between Albania and the West. Apart from trade accords with Italy, Yugoslavia, Ghana, the United Arab Republic, Iraq, Austria, and Cuba, Tirana has various types of trade arrangements with some West European firms. The volume of exchange with all these countries amounts to something less than 10 percent of Albania's total foreign trade.

In the total volume of Albanian exports, minerals hold first place with 51 percent, followed by industrial goods (33.5 percent), and by agricultural produce (14.5 percent). The main items of export are chrome ore, ferrous ores, petroleum, coal, asphalt, tobacco, cigarettes, cotton, and fruits.

THE BREAK BETWEEN MOSCOW AND TIRANA

The first sign of disagreement between Moscow and Tirana appeared as early as 1955. When, after Stalin's death, the Soviet leaders Bulganin and Khrushchev tried to settled their differences with Tito's Yugoslavia, the two Albanian leaders, Party Chief Enver Hoxha and Premier Memet Shehu, were told to follow the same policy. They therefore softened their extremely aggressive attitude toward Belgrade, but did not rehabilitate Koci Xoxe, who had been executed as a Titoist in 1949. They assumed, rightly, that to vindicate Xoxe would be to justify and restrengthen Yugoslavia's position in Albania, which meant jeopardizing their own status and security. Their reluctance to go along completely with the new Kremlin policy was demonstrated over and over by their deep devotion to Stalin. In venerating Stalin, they sought to disarm any accusation that they were disloyal to the Soviet Union.

When Khrushchev began his policy of de-Stalinization in 1956, he caused a great upheaval within the communist world, particularly in Poland and Hungary. The Albanian Communist leaders, who also reacted negatively to this action, never carried out Khrushchev's order to de-Stalinize Albania. . . .

Fully aware of the dispute between the two communist giants (Communist China and the Soviet Union), the Albanian Party chiefs sided with Peking in the latter's "ideological warfare" with Moscow, in answer to Khrushchev's continued wooing of Tito, whom they rightly regard as their principal enemy and the greatest threat to Albania. Red China's might, its Stalinist ruthlessness, and, most of all, its uncompromisingly rigid attitude toward "revisionist Yugoslavia" were other factors that impelled Hoxha and Shehu to choose the "Party line" of Peking. . . .

Khrushchev tried in many ways to bring the Tirana chiefs to "reason."

At first he tried to intimidate them through various moves in the diplomatic field. For that purpose, he held talks with Belgrade, and even Athens, both of which are considered as Albania's national enemies. This action gave the Tirana leaders a welcome opportunity to denounce Khrushchev for plotting with "revisionists, capitalists, and bourgeois elements" against a communist state. . . .

For some time the bitter Moscow-Tirana struggle went on behind the scenes. But in the course of the 22nd Congress of the Soviet Communist Party in Moscow in November, 1961, Khrushchev publicly denounced the Albanian leaders, accusing them of hostility toward the Soviet Party and people, and of persisting in following the Stalinist cult. He demanded their exclusion from the "socialist" camp. This move was adroitly frustrated by Chou En-lai, chairman of the Peking delegation, who backed the Albanian chiefs. For the first time, the existing deep rift between the two communist giants became known to the public. A month later the Soviet Union broke diplomatic relations with Albania, an unprecedented action within the communist orbit. Immediately thereafter, all East European communist states formally followed this move. . . .

Moscow adopted other drastic measures against Tirana. Trade and cultural relations were broken off, all credits granted for the third Five-Year Plan were cut off, and all Soviet technicians and specialists were withdrawn from Albania. With them, except for some Czechoslovak technicians, all East European aides received strict orders to return to their countries. From that time on, although Albania was formally a member of the Warsaw Pact (the Communist Bloc military alliance), and of Comecon (the Soviet-organized "Council for Mutual Economic Assistance"), it was excluded *de facto* from both organizations.

The moral, political, and economic support that the Albanian Stalinists have received from Communist China, however, has considerably weakened the Kremlin's moves to resolve the sharp issues raised by Albania. Enver Hoxha's regime remains as inimical as ever to the "modern revisionists". . . .

FURTHER READING SUGGESTIONS

Assembly of Captive European Nations: A Survey of Recent Developments in Nine Captive Countries. Reports published bi-annually since 1956.

Griffith, William E., *Albania and the Sino-Soviet Rift.* Boston, Mass.: MIT Press, 1962.

Hamm, Harry, *Albania, China's Beachhead in Europe.* New York: Praeger, 1963.

Prybyla, Jan S., "Albania's Economic Vassalage," *East Europe* (January, 1967), pp. 9-14.

Skendi, Stavro, *Albania*. New York: Praeger, 1957. A Volume in the Mid-European Studies Center Series.

————, "Albania and the Sino-Soviet Conflict," *Foreign Affairs* (April, 1962), pp. 471-478.

12

The People's Republic
of Albania: An Albanian
Marxist View

HARILLA PAPAJORGJI

ALBANIAN ECONOMIST

PETI SHAMBELI

FORMER ALBANIAN MINISTER
OF AGRICULTURE

PIPI MITROJORGJI

ALBANIAN DEPUTY MINISTER
OF EDUCATION AND CULTURE

BILBIL KLOSI

FORMER MINISTER OF JUSTICE

DR. FEJZI HOXHA

CHIEF OF ALBANIA'S HOSPITAL CLINICS

AND OTHERS *

INTRODUCTION

The Albanian people have traversed a long and glorious historic path. They have fought for centuries in succession against foreign invaders, much bigger and stronger than they, as well as against feudal rulers and the local bourgeoisie to achieve freedom, national independence, and better living

---

* Parts I-IV, VI, and X have been condensed from Harilla Papajorgi, *The Development of Socialist Industry and Its Prospects in the People's Republic of Albania* (Tirana, 1964). While every possible effort was made not to alter in the slightest the meaning of any passage and even to preserve as much as possible the flavor of the style, it was nonetheless necessary to correct the original for grammar, sentence structure, and occasionally for style (especially to improve upon unconventional usage of some words or terms).

The other parts of the article have been taken from a variety of sources. Footnote credit throughout will be given in each case so that each part can be readily identified as to author and original source of publication. In a few instances it was again necessary to make changes in order to improve on grammar, sentence structure, or vocabulary usage.

conditions. By their valiant struggle the Albanians preserved their existence as a people and nation: but not until the *People's Republic of Albania* was born had they ever been able to secure real freedom and independence. It was only under the leadership of the Communist Party that the Albanian people, after three years of a bitter National-Liberation Struggle against the fascist Italian and German invaders and traitors within their own country, scored the greatest victory in their entire history. On November 29, 1944, Albania won her complete national independence, the working masses took power in their hands and ensured real political and social liberation. Our country detached itself forever from the capitalist chain and finally set out on the road of building socialism.

The brilliant results achieved from that time onward in all fields of life are the fruits of the hard and selfless work of the labouring masses who, with a view towards socialist construction, have consistently implemented the Party's programme. This programme envisaged from the very outset that alongside the radical social changes, the construction of the material and technical basis of socialism should be carried out in Albania. The implementation of such a programme, however, was exceptionally difficult, in part because the new Albania had inherited from the past a marked and general technological and economic backwardness: industry, in the true meaning of the word, was almost nonexistent, agriculture was primitive, and educational and cultural backwardness was pronounced.

All this testifies to the fact that before liberation the landlords and bourgeoisie, and subsequently the foreign invaders, holding power in their hands, did not allow Albania to start a large-scale industrial development which would have been a decisive factor in leading the country out of its great age-old technical and economic backwardness, thus enabling it to take its place among the developed nations of the world.

ECONOMIC CONDITIONS PRIOR TO THE COUNTRY'S LIBERATION

As regards the level of economic and cultural development before liberation, Albania was the most backward country in Europe. At the time of the victory of the people's revolution, she was between two economic epochs—the epoch of feudalism and the epoch of capitalism. The capitalist form of economy had not succeeded in becoming the dominating feature in the country. . . .

The national economy had the features of a semi-feudal and semi-colonial economy. Until 1938 Albania had a total of only 150 industrial units. Excluding mineral enterprises, about 50 percent of them employed fewer than 10 workers each. Their equipment and machinery, in most cases, were obsolete. Such a situation existed also in the mines, where techniques were very primitive.

This extremely low technological level, the very small productive capacities of factories and plants, and bad organisation, were partially responsible for the rather low level of labour productivity in industry. But, apart from these factors, one of the main reasons for low labour productivity was the very miserable material situation of the workers. The workers were exploited by inhuman methods. The working day was 12 to 14 hours. Safety provisions were very inadequate. And the taxes and imposts levied by the state worsened further the workers' living standards. . . .

Only 15.4 percent of the population in 1938 were town dwellers; 84.6 percent were peasants. Industry contributed but 4.4 percent to the national income. Imports were growing from year to year, whereas exports were declining, causing a constant increase in the foreign trade deficit.

Backwardness was characteristic not only of industry, but also of agriculture and of all other sectors of the economy. Only 9.6 percent of the land area of Albania was cultivated; the major part which could have been cultivated was covered by swamps, bushes, shrubs and low-quality forests. Feudal relations were predominant. Forty percent of the land was in the hands of a few big landlords, and 21,500 peasant families were completely landless. . . .

The fascist occupation made our economic situation still worse. The war killed 7.3 percent of the population. During the war 22 percent of the homes in towns and villages were demolished, all the bridges, big and small, were blown up, the mines were destroyed, . . . the power-stations were in ruins. Even those factories that were saved from the war were not operating due to lack of raw materials. Unemployment was high everywhere. And nearly one-third of the cattle and especially the draft-animals were annihilated.

TOWARD THE SOCIALIST INDUSTRIALIZATION OF ALBANIA

The National-Liberation Struggle against the fascist Italian and German invaders and the traitors to the country was crowned with the complete liberation of the country on November 29th, 1944. State power passed from the hands of the exploiters, reactionaries, and oppressors, to those of the people. Thus, the old state with all its apparatus was destroyed and a new type of state, striving for the interests and the well-being of the working people, was set up. The radical political changes in Albania brought in their wake also deep changes in other fields of social activity, and especially in economic life.

The nationalisation of the principal means of production and trade was carried out in general during the years 1945-1946. In 1945 nationalisation included mainly all the industrial, commercial and transport enterprises, the joint-stock companies and the banks which were the property of foreign capital. . . . During 1946 the enterprises and joint-stock companies owned by the local bourgeoisie were nationalised and so was domestic and foreign trade. Now the factory is no longer a place of enslavement and exploitation for the worker; it has become a place where the worker works for himself and for society, a place where he learns to operate the machines more efficiently and to increase productive output.

Socialisation of the principal means of production and trade was completed within a very brief period of time. Early in 1947, industry, with the exception of some insignificant workshops, had been completely turned into state property. But it was not the same with regard to private craftsmen who were not exploiting other people's toil, but were working with their own hands. They were not affected, but on a voluntary basis they created handicraft cooperatives, where both the tools of work and the products turned out belong to them, collectively. It must be said that not all private craftsmen entered cooperatives right from the outset. But, seeing for themselves the superiority of collective work in cooperatives and the rapid rise of the material standards of the members, they applied to be admitted to the cooperatives, which therefore increased their membership with every passing day. . . .

Along with these measures of a socialist nature, another reform of great economic and social importance was introduced—a land reform based on the full implementation of the principle that land belongs to the one who cultivates it. Thanks to the direct support of the poor and toiling peasants the land reform was successfully carried out within a very short period of time. By November 17th, 1947, it had been completed everywhere. The peasants received the deeds and became masters of the land. Thus, under the people's regime, their age-old dream was realised. . . .

Implementation of the land reform ended the exploitation of man by man in the countryside; it contributed to raising the material standards of the peasantry; it created the conditions for the socialist transformation of the countryside; and for the peasants it paved a road of prosperity and of a new and happy life. . . .

The exploiting classes adopted a hostile attitude towards all socialist transformation. They sought by all means at their disposal to hamper the implementation of these important economic measures. This is why nationalisation was accompanied by a fierce class struggle. The imperialists gave extensive aid and support to the domestic reactionaries in their fight against the people's regime and against socialist transformation. Under these conditions, People's Power had to resort to confiscation without compensation of capitalist property. (It should be pointed out that efforts by our State to use state capitalism as an intermediate form for the gradual transformation of capitalist ownership into social ownership were rejected by the bourgeoisie. Thus, for instance, a plan for joint private-state co-ownership of productive enterprises was rejected by the bourgeoisie.)

Once the Socialist ownership of the means of production and trade in the People's Republic of Albania was accomplished, the economic exploitation of man by man disappeared and in its stead there came into being new socialist relations in production, relations based on mutual aid and cooperation.

Beginning in 1947 the national economy of Albania embarked on the road of planned development. At the beginning annual plans were worked out. These plans for the years 1947-1948 were aimed principally at quickly restoring the war-ravaged national economy and at reaching and exceeding the preliberation production levels in industry and agriculture. . . .

ACHIEVEMENTS AND PROSPECTS OF INDUSTRIAL DEVELOPMENT

The programme of Albania's industrialisation found its full expression in the plans for the development of the national economy, such as the two-year plan (1949-1950), and the three five-year plans (1951-55, 1956-60, and 1961-65).

Each of the above plans represents an important stage in our country's socialist industrialisation. Their successful implementation and the unheard-of mobilisation of the Albanian people have given great impetus to the development of the national economy, and have led to an unprecedented rise in the material and cultural standards of the whole population. In carrying out these plans, the People's Republic of Albania has been transformed into a big construction site, where factories and high tension lines are going up daily, where mineral resources are discovered and virgin lands cultivated, where schools, dwelling flats for workers and other facilities are being constructed. Table 12-1 shows the level of output of some principal industrial products as compared with the prewar period and with the year 1960 (which was the last year of the second five-year plan).

In 1962, Albanian industry turned out every 13 days an output equal to the country's total industrial output for the year 1938; the power industry produced its 1938 equivalent in about 8 days; the coal industry in about 4 days; the wood processing industry in about 5.5 days; the textile industry and the ready-made garments industry in 3 days; the food industry in about 15 days; etc. And many new industrial articles which previously were imported from abroad are now produced at home. . . .

This rapid development of industry has been achieved by applying the principle of socialist industrialisation, according to which priority must be given to heavy industry, to the production of means of production, as compared with light industry, the production of means of consumption. . . .

Table 12-1. Annual Output of Selected Industrial Commodities, 1938, 1960, and 1962

No.	Kind of Product	Measure Unit	1938	1960	1962
1.	Electric power	thous.	9,315	194,348	242,225
2.	Crude oil	ton	108,116	727,519	785,208
3.	Coal	ton	3,686	290,596	300,994
4.	Chromium ore	ton	7,000	289,075	251,297
5.	Sawn wood	m³	3,165	170,111	167,279
6.	Bricks	pieces	3,385	130,325	107,882
7.	Cement	ton	9,000	72,879	119,243
8.	Cotton textiles	thous. lms.	358	25,239	27,137
9.	Macaroni	ton	454	8,358	9,311
10.	Cigarettes	ton	132	3,436	3,197

Table 12-2 indicates that during the first five-year plan period the production of the means of consumption grew more rapidly than that of the means of production. But, this was a temporary phenomenon, made neces-

Table 12-2. Industrial Output in Selected Years, 1938-1963 (1938 = 100)

Kind of Production	1938	1946	1950	1955	1960	1963
Total industrial production	100	152	415	1146	2500	3700
Of which:						
Production of means of production	100	165	430	1066	2439	——
Production of means of consumption	100	143	402	1209	2547	——

sary by the great backwardness of light industry, and not a general line of development of our industry for the entire industrialisation period, as shown in Table 12-3.

Table 12-3. Output of Industrial Producers' and Consumers' Goods in Selected Years, 1938-1965 (In percent of total industrial output)

Kind of Production	1938	1950	1955	1960	1965
Production of means of production	43.8	45.4	40.7	42.7	50.4
Production of consumption goods	56.2	54.6	59.3	57.3	49.6

The high rates of industrial growth which have been achieved in the People's Republic of Albania after liberation, have been characterised by and based on high growth rates of labour productivity. The rise of the technological level of industry, its mastery on the part of the workers, the radical changes in the attitude towards work, the improvement of the material and cultural standards of the working people—such are the main factors that have led to the rise of labour productivity. During the 18 postliberation years, that is from 1944 to 1962, the average labour productivity per worker in industry has grown by 650 percent.

The high growth rates of labour productivity in Albanian industry testify to the indisputable superiority of the socialist economic system; they once more show the broad field opened by the socialist system for the quick development of productive forces. They considerably surpass the rates of growth of labour productivity in many other countries of Europe and in neighboring countries such as Greece, Yugoslavia, Italy, and Turkey.

One of the primary reasons for the growth of labour productivity and for the industrial development of Albania is the rise in the level of mechanization and electrification of production in all industrial branches, and the introduction of new modern techniques. With increasing technology, comes the need for qualified workers, for cadres directing the more complicated productive processes. Therefore, the People's Power has been paying, and continues to pay, special attention to the training of cadres and to continuous improvement in their qualifications and technical and professional capacities. Today 62 percent of all workers are skilled workers, such as mechanics, oil workers, metallurgists, and electricians.

Note should be taken of the great achievements of the Party and the People's Power in respect to the participation of women in production. Women now enjoy equal rights with men both at work and in life in general. The number of women employed in various sectors surpasses almost the entire number of workers Albania had in 1938; and in industry women account for more than 27 percent of the total number employed. . . .

In regard to the participation of women in production, the view has prevailed and continues to prevail in our country that women are entitled to certain special privileges (such as paid three-month leave for childbirth and a six-hour workday, with eight-hour pay, for nine months thereafter), and that they should work in the easier sectors and in those places where a man's work can be readily accomplished by a woman. Therefore, in some sectors in our country the work participation rate of women is relatively high. In the textile industry, for instance, over 60 percent of the workers are women. In the Public Health sector women account for more than 67 percent of the personnel, in trade for more than 46 percent, in Public Education and Culture for more than 43 percent, etc.

For the training of all these technicians and qualified workers in

Albania a broad educational network and other forms of training have been set up, and are free to everybody without exception. In addition, state scholarships are available for some.

The rapid development of industry in the People's Republic of Albania has been accompanied by the development of agriculture so that the national economy can stand on both feet, that is on industry and agriculture, giving priority always to industry. . . .

ACHIEVEMENTS AND PROSPECTS OF AGRICULTURE [1]

The socialist transformation of the agricultural sector, the setting up of large farms as agricultural cooperatives and state agricultural enterprises, has made possible the application of up-to-date techniques in production, the extension of arable land through reclaiming new areas, its better utilization, and the large scale planting of industrial crops like cotton, tobacco, sugar beets, and others. It has also enabled us to grow more fruit trees, olive trees, and grapes, to multiply and improve livestock, and to make full use of the achievements of science and of the experience of the more advanced workers. On the other hand the rapid progress made in the food processing industry, and in the tobacco, textile, leather, and other light industries has given further impetus to agricultural production.

Great progress has also been made in reclamation and irrigation in which, up to the end of 1961, the sum of 6 billion 300 million leks was invested. Drainage of marshes and swamps has yielded an improved area of land equal to about 33 percent of the whole land under cultivation, whereas irrigation schemes set up prior to the end of 1962 increased the area under irrigation sixfold in comparison with the preliberation period. Our agricultural processes are being continuously mechanized not only as far as ploughing and sowing are concerned but also in regard to cultivation, reaping and threshing, irrigating, transportation, and so on, as well as in many dairy processes. The number of 15HP tractors in use on our fields increased from 30 in 1938 to 6,027 in 1962. The number of 15HP tractors for every 1,000 hectares of land in the People's Republic of Albania today (1963) is 12.4 and this number has been increasing very rapidly. The 1963 figure is 118 percent above that of 1960, and similar advances have been made in the case of other agricultural machinery and equipment.

[1] Condensed from Peti Shamblli (former Albanian Minister of Agriculture) "Intensive Farming in the People's Republic of Albania" (answers given during an interview), *New Albania* (1963), No. 3, pp. 2-4. Supplemented by a few paragraphs from "The New Features of the Albanian Countryside," *New Albania* (1964), No. 1, pp. 8-9.

The State has placed at the disposal of the agricultural sector large sums of money in the form of agricultural credits every year and has distributed quantities of selected seeds, various seedlings of fruit trees, improved breeds of livestock, large quantities of selected seeds, various seedlings of fruit trees, improved breeds of livestock, large quantities of chemical fertilizers, and so on. A whole network of schools, primary, seventh grade, middle and upper agricultural institutes, have been set up throughout the country.

The goal which we aim to attain is to raise the average yield per hectare of wheat to over 25 quintals,[2] of maize to over 27, of rice to over 35, of sugar beets to above 200, of cotton to above 20, and of vegetables to over 200 quintals. In animal husbandry an average of 2,000 kg. of milk a year from every cow is anticipated, and for every 100 hectares of land under cultivation (including meadows and pasture grounds) the goal is to obtain an average of 400 to 480 kg. of milk and 75 to 90 kg. liveweight of meat. The State Agricultural Enterprises have set themselves much higher targets: an average of not less than 30 quintals of wheat and maize, 20 to 22 of cotton, and 380 quintals of sugar beet per hectare; and 3,300 kg. of milk for every cow, 9 quintals of meat (liveweight) from every sow, 4 kg. of wool from every sheep, and so on.

Intensive farming in Albania aims at increasing farm and livestock production to the extent of securing a per capita total of 350-400 kg. of cereals, 18-20 kg. of cotton, 140-160 kg. of vegetables and potatoes, 25-30 kg. of olives, 70-80 kg. of grapes, 100-100 kg. of other fruits, 40-45 kg. of meat (liveweight), 200-220 kg. of milk, and so on.

The good results attained so far by many agricultural enterprises are proof that possibilities of attaining these objectives are at hand. To get a better picture of the advance in living standards of the Albanian peasant, it should also be pointed out that 55,500 new houses have been built, 300 villages have been provided with electric current, and hundreds of kilometers of new roads have been built within the relatively short period of time from 1951 to 1961; that illiteracy has been totally wiped out among the youth and the great majority of the older people in the countryside; that the Albanian countryside boasts now of about 1,300 cultural homes and hearths and of 5,500 groups of amateur artists with 53,000 participants; that the turnover of retail sales of consumers' goods in the countryside has increased from 4 billion leks in 1955 to 7 billion 200 million leks in 1961; and that in 1961 the prices of consumption goods were 31 percent lower than they were in 1956.

---

[2] One quintal, or one centner, equals 100 kilograms or 220.46 pounds. One hectare equals 10,000 square meters or 2.471 acres. In the case of wheat, one quintal per hectare is the equivalent of 1.49 bushels per acre. [EDITOR'S NOTE]

MAIN ECONOMIC AND SOCIAL RESULTS OF SOCIALIST INDUSTRIALIZATION

The industrial development of the People's Republic of Albania, which has led to a great increase in industrial output, was achieved under an almost entirely socialist economic system. In industry, the capitalist elements were eliminated long ago, and 99 percent of total production is now attributable to the socialist sector. This means that the country's industrial output belongs to the whole society and is distributed among its members on the basis of the quantity and quality of work performed. The worker no longer works for a capitalist, but for himself and for society. . . . Under our socialist system, within a record period, we healed the grave wounds caused by the war, we restored our economy and set up a new and big industrial base, including the latest techniques. Albania has now been transformed from a backward agrarian country into an advanced agrarian-industrial country. And Albania is taking important steps forward in the construction of the material and technical basis of socialism, advancing more rapidly on the road of her transformation from an advanced agrarian-industrial country to an industrial-agrarian country with the prospect of becoming later an advanced industrial country. . . .

The change in the structure of social production is shown in Table 12-4.

Table 12-4. Classification of National Income by Sectors of Origin
in Selected Years, 1938-1960
(In percent of total national income; for computation and comparison,
each year's national income was converted into 1956 prices.)

Branches of Material Production	1938	1955	1958	1960
1. Industry	4.4	27.6	38.1	44.2
2. Agriculture and forestry	92.4	56.5	43.1	43.6
3. Construction	—	6.4	8.2	10.0
4. Transportation of commodities	—	1.8	2.3	3.2
5. Social food trade and stock-piling	3.2	7.0	7.3	6.8
6. Other branches	—	0.7	1.1	1.2

Socialist industrialisation in our country has been coupled with incomparable advances in the educational, technical, professional, and cultural level of the workers. . . .

The industrial development of the People's Republic of Albania has brought about deep changes also in the structure of the country's foreign trade. Thus, while before the liberation of the country more than 70 percent of our exports consisted of agricultural raw materials and food products, finished and semi-finished products account now for almost one half of our total exports, and mineral raw materials for over 30 percent. The structure of imports has changed, too. While before liberation over 95 percent of total imports consisted of consumer goods and grains, the main import items nowadays include machinery, industrial equipments semi-finished manufactures, spare parts which cannot be produced at home, etc. . . . .

The development of industry and of the other branches of the national economy has always aimed and continues to aim at meeting in the best possible manner the material and cultural needs of the working people. So far, (by 1964) this has been acomplished by a rise of nearly 500 percent in our national income in comparison with the year 1938. However, not only the growth of national income, but also the way it is distributed is important: it now belongs to the broad labouring masses. Some three-fourths of it is distributed as consumption funds for the material and cultural needs of the peasant and town working people, while one-fourth is accumulated and used for the further development of the national economy and culture. Thus, it is evident that our working people are living today several times better than in the preliberation period, when hunger, poverty, unemployment, and disease had been their lot. . . .

THE EDUCATIONAL AND CULTURAL REVOLUTION [3]

The People's Republic of Albania changed from a country where illiteracy prevailed, where only one out of eighteen persons attended school, to one of a high percentage of school attendance, where one in every four persons attends school; illiteracy among persons below forty was wiped out as early as 1955.

During the 1938-39 school year there were only 643 elementary schools with 52,024 pupils and 1,349 teachers. In 1945, the first year after liberation, the number of schools was almost doubled and so was the number of students and teachers. Twenty years have gone by and the number of schools and students is nearly five times as large while the teaching staff has increased tenfold.

Before liberation there were cases when ten villages were obliged to send their children to one and the same school. This was in part due to a lack of buildings, teachers, and equipment, but, first and foremost, to the

[3] Condensed from Pipi Mitrojorgji (Deputy Minister of Education in Albania), "The Cultural Revolution in the People's Republic of Albania" (answers given during an interview), New Albania (1964), No. 5, pp. 22-23.

scandalous unconcern of the antipopular regimes for education. Today there is a primary school in every village of Albania. . . .

Compulsory elementary education for our children was only a dream before liberation. Not until 1946, when the school reform went into effect, were the doors of schools flung open for the sons and daughters of workers and peasants. . . . Compulsory seventh grade education was introduced in the country in 1952; at present compulsory eighth grade education is the law in the People's Republic of Albania.

While thus broadening our primary education, visible progress has also been made in the People's Republic of Albania in regard to the other and higher links of our People's educational system. By 1962-63 the number of high schools of general education had increased tenfold in comparison with that before liberation. The number of students and teachers had also increased from three to six times. High school level technical and vocational schools have scored similar progress. During the 1938-39 school year there were only five such schools in operation attended by 879 students with a staff of thirty-four teachers. Now we have twenty different technicums and eleven teacher training schools, attended by 14,499 students where 685 cadres teach. There is also a wide network of lower vocational schools, of schools for labor reserves, which train qualified workers for the various branches of the economy and for certain social sectors.

There were no schools of higher education in Albania before liberation. Under the former feudal regime of King Zog, there were only 380 Albanians with a higher education, and all of them had received their training abroad. It goes without saying that they were sons of landowners and rich merchants, sons of the ruling class.

The cornerstone of our higher education was laid in December 1946, when a two-year teachers' college was opened in Tirana. In 1951-52, five four-year schools of higher learning were opened in the country. On September 16, 1957, the State University of Tirana was founded with seven departments training students in more than twenty-five specialties. The State University of Tirana fulfills the age-long aspirations of the patriots, the scholars and the people of Albania who thirst for education. There are now in our country seven additional institutes of higher learning, namely, the Higher State Institute of Agriculture, the Higher Institute of Fine Arts, the "Alexander Moisi" Higher School for dramatic art, the State Conservatory of Tirana, the "Vojo Kushi" Institute for Physical Culture, and two Higher Teacher Tranining Schools in Tirana and Shkodra. Attendance in all these institutes of higher learning totals 6,300 students; their teaching staffs are made up of 582 pedagogues, professors, doctors, lecturers, candidates of science, assistants, and others.

One major result of our cultural revolution is the creation of the people's new intelligentsia. Over 4,000 specialists have been trained during these twenty years in our institutes of higher learning whereas in 1938 there had been oly 380, all trained abroad. In addition we have tens of thousands of cadres with high school training. In the "Stalin" Textile Mills in Tirana alone there are today as many engineers at work as there were in the entire country during the period from 1912 to 1938.

A system of adult education for people who want to study in their spare time was inaugurated in our country, offering courses ranging from elementary to higher grades. This category of schools is being attended this year (1964) by over 30,000 students, which, it must be stressed, amounts to more than half of *all* students and pupils in Albania in 1938.

Our revolution in education has been matched by a cultural revolution that has witnessed the growth of a wide range of cultural institutions, built for the masses. Before liberation these were limited in number: 2 museums, 5 public libraries, 17 motion picture theaters; the number of new books published during a year was 61, that of newspapers 6, and that of periodicals 15. Measures were taken right after liberation to remedy this situation. Many institutions were set up, like public libraries, museums, reading rooms, and clubs. Today we boast of 23 state lending libraries in regional centers, and every educational and cultural institution and center of work has its own smaller library. The National Library alone has about half a million volumes. Eighteen museums and sixteen museum homes have been set up, the latter to immortalize distinguished figures of our country. About 515 new books, 11 newspapers and 36 periodicals are published every year in our country. The "Zeri i Popullit" daily alone has a circulation of over 60,000. Regular performances are given in 8 theaters and 15 variety theaters in the principal cities of the country. Plays by the best Albanian and the most famous foreign playwrights are put on the stage in our theaters.

There are also two and one-half times as many motion picture theaters in Albania as there were before liberation, and a number of mobile motion picture theaters circulate throughout the country regularly. . . .

These are some highlights of our cultural activities during these twenty years of free life.

MEDICAL AND SOCIAL INSURANCE [4]

In Albania all the workers and employees without exception are insured by the state and enjoy a series of rights in cases of misfortune.

[4] This part has been put together from condensed versions of the following three articles: "What Are the Benefits that the Working People in the P.R. of Albania Enjoy from the Social Insurances?" (Editor's answer to readers' questions), *New Albania* (1963), No. 1, p. 28; Bilbil Klosi (Albania's Minister of Justice), "Medical Service Is Given Free of Charge for all the Albanian People," *New Albania* (1964), No. 1, pp. 6-7; and Dr. Fejzi Hoxha (Chief of Albania's hospital clinics), "Everything Free of Charge for the Health of the People," *New Albania* (1964), No. 5, p. 12.

Note that references to medical insurance for working people and their families were taken from the 1963 article; references to more universal coverage were taken from the two 1964 articles, when coverage was being extended as explained in the text.

The system of state insurances in Albania gives the insured the right to free medical assistance, including medical examination and treatment for himself and his dependents, and their accommodation and treatment in the various medical facilities, in the sanatoria, and in all other health and rehabilitation-for-work institutions. The measures aimed at health protection include also the food in the dietetical canteens as well as the stay of the working people and of their children in the rest and recreation homes in the health resorts of the country.

The workers who get sick or for some other cause become invalid, besides medical aid, receive also a cash allowance which is paid until the day of their recovery. They are paid in quarantine cases also, when the child or any other member of the family gets sick.

The law on social insurance gives women workers and employees the benefit of paid pregnancy and delivery leave, which ranges from 12 to 13 weeks. When a child is born, the working parent receives also an allowance for the outfit and for nursing care of the child.

The insured enjoys also the right to old-age, length of service, invalid, and service merits pensions. According to the labour category, male workers may retire and receive a pension even at the age of 50—women even at the age of 45.

Under a recently enacted law, medical services are now given free to peasants also and to all persons not employed by the state or by the socialist organizations. As a consequence of the adoption of this law *all* the inhabitants of the People's Republic of Albania are entitled to receive medical service free of charge. . . . It is further stipulated in this law that foreigners married to Albanian citizens as well as foreigners employed by our institutions, enterprises, or social organizations are entitled to free state medical service provided no special agreements are concluded by the corresponding states in this respect.

Twenty years ago, Albania could boast of only 110 physicians and a few hospitals with 820 beds all told. The bulk of the population who did not have the means to meet medical expenses received no medical treatment whatsoever. By now, the network of health institutions has been greatly extended as compared with the past. Today (1964), our hospitals have 10,759 beds while our maternity homes have an additional 1,458 beds. No pediatric hospital existed in the country before, whereas now every locality has its own, and the Tirana pediatric hospital alone has a capacity of 450 beds. Specialized services have been set up in various regions of the country. There are today nearly 700 physicians in addition to hundreds upon hundreds of other medical personnel. And 100 new doctors receive their degree every year from the Medical College of the State University of Tirana.

To cover the great social insurance expenditures, the state earmarks considerable funds—and they increase with every passing year. . . .

Social insurance in our country, which in the past was unknown altogether, has developed during the years of the People's power into a whole system of measures and a most powerful means of raising the material and the cultural well-being of the working people.

THE RIGHTS AND DUTIES OF CITIZENS [5]

Article 14. All citizens are equal before the law. It is their duty to comply with the Constitution and the laws.

No privileges are recognized for reasons of origin, position, wealth or cultural standard.

Article 15. All citizens are equal with no differences of nationality, race or religion. Any act which brings about privileges in favor of citizens or limits their rights on account of differences of nationality, race or religion is contrary to the Constitution and incurs punishment provided by law. Any attempt to sow hatred and cause dissension among nationalities, races and religions is contrary to the Constitution and liable to punishment according to law.

Article 16. All citizens, without distinction of sex, nationality, belief, cultural standard or residence, who have reached the age of 18 years, have the right to vote and stand for election to all the organs of state power.

These rights are enjoyed also by citizens serving in the army.

The right of the ballot is universal, equal, direct and secret.

The right of the ballot is refused to persons who are excluded by law.

Article 17. Women enjoy equal rights with men in all spheres of private, political and social life.

Women enjoy the rights of equal pay with men for the same work. They enjoy the same right to social insurance. . . .

Article 18. All citizens are guaranteed freedom of conscience and of faith.

The church is separated from the State.

The religious communities are free in matters of their belief as well as in their outer exercise and practice.

It is prohibited to use the church and religion for political purposes. Political organizations on a religious basis are likewise prohibited.

The State may give material aid to religious communities.

Article 19. Marriage and the family are under the protection of the State. . . .

Lawful marriage can be contracted only before the competent organs

[5] Excerpts reprinted from Chapter III of the *Constitution of the People's Republic of Albania,* published by the Albanian Committee for Cultural Relations and Friendship with Foreign Countries (Tirana, 1964), pp. 8-15.

of the State. After the celebration of lawful marriage the citizens may also celebrate religious marriage according to the rules of their religion. . . .

Children born outside marriage enjoy the same rights as children born within marriage.

Article 20. All citizens are guaranteed freedom of speech, of the press, of organization, of meetings, of assembly and of public manifestations.

Article 22. All citizens are guaranteed inviolability of the person. No one can be detained under arrest more than three days without a decision of the court or without the approval of the public attorney.

Nobody can be condemned for a crime without a sentence of the court having jurisdiction according to the law which fixes the jurisdiction and specifies the crime.

No sentences can be passed except on the basis of law.

Nobody can be convicted without being heard and without being called to defend himself according to the provisions of law, except when his absence is legally verified. . . .

Article 23. Dwellings cannot be violated.

Nobody can enter and search any domicile without the consent of the head of the household, except when he is in possession of a search warrant.

Searches cannot be made except in the presence of two witnesses. The head of the household also has the right to be present.

Article 24. The secrecy of correspondence and other means of communication cannot be violated, except in cases of inquiries on crimes, of mobilization and of a state of war.

Article 25. The State guarantees citizens the right of work for a remuneration according to the amount and quality of the work.

The State guarantees citizens the right to rest through a shortening of the hours of work, through granting an annual paid vacation, and through setting up sanatoria, rest homes, clubs, etc.

Through social insurance the State guarantees to citizens the material means of subsistence in old age and in case of illness and disability.

Article 26. Under conditions specified by law, all citizens have equal rights to be admitted to state posts. . . .

Article 35. Every citizen is duty-bound to safeguard and consolidate social property (state and cooperative property), the sacred and inviolable basis of the people's democracy, the source of power of the Fatherland, of the welfare and culture of all the working people.

Those who lay hands on social property are enemies of the people.

Article 38. Citizens are not entitled to use the rights granted to them by this Constitution, in order to change the constitutional order of the People's Republic of Albania for anti-democratic purposes.

Every act in this direction is considered contrary to law and incurs punishments provided by law.

Article 40. The People's Republic of Albania grants the right to asylum in its territory to foreign citizens persecuted on account of their activity in favor of democracy, of the struggle for national liberation, of the rights of working people or in favor of freedom in scientific and cultural work.

MARXISM-LENINISM FOREVER!

The road traversed by the People's Republic of Albania testifies to the correctness of the Marxist-Leninist line followed by our Party of Labour. Solidly based on the material foundation which we have created and on the inexhaustible mineral wealth of our country, the continuous implementation of this line is assured by the Marxist-Leninist leadership of the Party Central Committee, headed by Comrade Enver Hoxha, and by the great socialist patriotism of our heroic people.

FURTHER READING SUGGESTIONS

Bihiku, Koco, *An Outline of Albanian Literature.* Tirana: The "Naim Frasheri" State Publishing House, 1964.

Constitution of the People's Republic of Albania. Tirana: Albanian Committee for Cultural Relations and Friendship with Foreign Countries, 1964.

The Development of Agriculture in the People's Republic of Albania. Tirana: The "Naim Frasheri" State Publishing House, 1962.

Frasheri, Kristo, *The History of Albania, A Brief Survey.* Tirana: (no publisher given), 1964.

Papajorgji, Harilla, *The Development of Socialist Industry and Its Prospects in the People's Republic of Albania.* Tirana: (no publisher given), 1964.

Twenty Years of Socialism in Albania. Tirana: The "Naim Frasheri" State Publishing House, 1964.

VII

The Mongolian People's Republic: The Asian Member of the Soviet Commonwealth of Nations

SOVIET UNION

MONGOLIA

o Ulan Bator

CHINA

Area
(in square miles)
592,667

Population
(mid-1967 estimate)
1,144,000

Mongolia was the first country in the world to set out on the road of building a socialist society, bypassing the capitalist stage of development.

LEONID BREZHNEV
GENERAL SECRETARY, CENTRAL COMMITTEE
COMMUNIST PARTY OF THE SOVIET UNION

Under the leadership of its tested vanguard, the Mongolian People's Revolutionary Party, the Mongolian people will achieve the complete building of socialism and create conditions for the gradual transition later on toward building of a Communist society—our great final goal.

(NEW, 1966) PROGRAM OF THE MONGOLIAN
PEOPLE'S REVOLUTIONARY PARTY

The knowledge that our positive experience can benefit other peoples and thereby make some contribution, however modest, to facilitating their social development is the true source of the national pride of our people.

YUMZHAGIN TSEDENBAL
PRESIDENT, COUNCIL OF MINISTERS
MONGOLIAN PEOPLE'S REPUBLIC
FIRST SECRETARY, CENTRAL COMMITTEE
MONGOLIAN PEOPLE'S REVOLUTIONARY PARTY

INTRODUCTION

WITH A LAND AREA EQUAL TO THAT OF ENGLAND, FRANCE, GERMANY, Italy, and Portugal combined, and with a mid-1960's population of barely a million, Mongolia was the only country apart from the Soviet Union to embrace communism in the pre-World War II era. Centuries ago the Mongols had ruled over an empire that stretched from Peking to the Danube and from Lake Baikal in Siberia to the Persian Gulf. In those days, the very thought of Mongol hordes brought fear into the hearts of Europeans; and the Chinese found that not even their Great Wall protected them from the conquerors of the land of Genghis Khan.

Great as their fame and power half a millennium ago may have been, the Mongols eventually fell under the sway of the neighboring Manchurians and made little progress between then and the second quarter of the twentieth century. At the time of the Revolutionary birth of New Mongolia in 1921, the population was still predominantly nomad, agriculture was hardly known outside of the monasteries, and industry was nonexistent. Thus, Mongolia became the first country to venture unto the path of

Marxist-Leninist construction without having been touched by anything even remotely approaching a capitalist stage of development.

In the Sino-Soviet split, the Mongols have loyally remained on the side of the Soviets, their benefactors for over four decades. In the spring of 1965 a new Soviet agreement with the Mongolian People's Republic was signed under which the Soviet Union is contributing some 660 million rubles to Mongolia's economic development over a period of five years— *the approximate equivalent of $140 annually for every citizen of Mongolia.* A new Soviet-Mongolian Treaty of Friendship, Cooperation, and Mutual Assistance was signed in January, 1966, in the face of potential Chinese territorial claims. This treaty, Albania charges, "transforms sister Mongolia into a colonial base of supply for the Soviet revisionists against the sister Chinese People's Republic."[1] In spite of Mongolian loyalty to the Soviet Union, the charge of "Soviet colony" would be difficult to prove since there are no troops of the Red Army anywhere in Mongolia, and since the Mongols themselves have been taking over administrative and other duties everywhere, even in places where not so long ago, their lack of trained manpower made them grateful for whatever expert personnel the Soviets originally supplied.

The non-Marxist view on Mongolia has been contributed by Harrison E. Salisbury. A graduate of the University of Minnesota, Salisbury joined the staff of *The New York Times* in 1949. For the next five years, Mr. Salisbury served as the paper's Moscow correspondent. In 1955, after his return to the paper's New York staff, he was awarded a Pulitzer Prize for his distinguished reporting from the Soviet Union. In 1959 and again in 1961, he revisited the Soviet Union and made extensive tours of the country. He also toured Siberia and Central Asia, and visited areas usually sealed off from the outside world. In September, 1964, Mr. Salisbury was appointed to his present executive position as assistant managing editor of *The New York Times.*

Mr. Salisbury has written several books on the Soviet Union and a novel, *The Northern Palmyra Affair,* which is set in the Soviet Union. His latest book, *Behind the Lines—Hanoi*—a result of his much-publicized visit to North Vietnam—was published in April, 1967. In recent years, Mongolia has become one of Mr. Salisbury's special areas of interest. He has visited the country three times, the last time in 1966; has published numerous articles on it; and he refers to his extensive study of it as his "hobby."

The Marxist view on Mongolia comes from the pen of Yumzhagin Tsedenbal, with a supplement by Ivor Montagu. Born in Mongolia in 1916,

[1] Albanian Telegraph Agency (February 12, 1966).

and with higher education and experience as an instructor in the field of economics, Tsedenbal has held such high positions in Mongolia as Minister of Finance, Deputy Commander in Chief, Chief of the Political Directorate, Chairman of the State Planning Commission, and Deputy Minister of the Mongolian People's Republic. In May, 1952, Tsedenbal became President of the Council of Ministers of the Mongolian People's Republic and in November, 1958, he was elected First Secretary of the Central Committee of the Mongolian People's Revolutionary Party (a position he had held once before for several years). In the mid-1960's Premier Tsedenbal still occupies these top positions in the Mongolian government and Party.

British Marxist Ivor Montagu, originally trained as a zoologist, has also been a film producer, journalist, and author. Recipient of the Lenin Peace Prize of 1960, Montagu has travelled in Mongolia several times and is known as one of the experts on that country in the Western World. His numerous publications include a book on Mongolia.[2]

[2] Ivor Montagu, *Land of the Blue Sky* (London, D. Dobson, 1956).

13

The Asian Heartland:
A Non-Marxist View on the
Mongolian People's Republic

HARRISON E. SALISBURY *

ASSISTANT MANAGING EDITOR, *The New York Times*

Well over a half century ago Sir Halpert MacKinder, the father of modern geopolitics, coined an aphorism: he who rules the heartland rules Asia; he who rules Asia rules the world.

With the imprecision which provides redundancy to such phraseology MacKinder was careful not to define the boundaries of his "heartland." But a look at the map reveals that Mongolia, an enclave—1600 miles long and 800 miles wide—landlocked in the high Asian escarpment, might well fit the needs of his concept.

True, history would not—with one remarkable exception—bear out his premise. Mongolia does not today control either the Asian continent nor the wider world. Indeed, she has for two or three centuries been hard-pressed to control her own high plateau, the "land of the blue skies," the historic subject of her legends and chronicles. Nor have the recent contenders for dominant influence in that remote land possessed either continental or global mastery.

But there was a time—some 800 years in the past—when the men who ruled the high plateau did, indeed, rule Asia and with Asia most of the known world.

This was in the era of Genghis Khan and of his proud and able heirs, the amalgamation of nomadic tribesmen which set out upon sturdy Asian ponies to overwhelm the kings, emperors, and satraps of the known world. And they succeeded so well that when their power was at its height in the

* This contribution was written especially for this book.

thirteenth and fourteenth centuries Mongol princes ruled over China, India, the dazzling principalities of Central Asia, much of the Middle East, the wild vastness of Siberia, Russia, the Caucasus, and Europe's eastern frontiers.

Genghis Khan lies 800 years in the past but his aura still lies like a haze over the Mongol people, coloring their traditions, giving romance and mystery to their name in the western (and eastern) world, and even in this day of harsh and quasi-objective ideology playing a dramatic role in the political struggles of contemporary Mongolia.

Without Genghis Khan and the heritage of the great Mongol Empire this would be but a remote and obscure country, hardly known, seldom visited with (quite possibly) but a rudimentary sense of nationality and tradition. History cannot change geography. Mongolia remains one of the most remote of regions. She is seldom visited, and in the West the details of her life and status are obscure to most. But her name is known to all and there are areas of Asia where the word Mongol inspires dread and stirs nightmares surviving from centuries past.

There are today in Mongolia about one million people. Another 400,000 Mongols live across the border in the Soviet Union, mostly in Buryatia— formerly known as Buryat-Mongolia. Another estimated 1,500,000 Mongols live in China, most of them in Inner Mongolia which once was an integral part of so-called Outer Mongolia, now known as the Mongolian People's Republic.

Mongolia occupies about 600,000 square miles—an area more than twice the size of Texas and five times larger than Italy. Most of Mongolia lies at an elevation of nearly one mile with mountain peaks up to 10,000 feet. Mongolia has but two neighbors—China with whom she shares a frontier of 4270 kilometers and the Soviet Union with a common boundary of 2730 kilometers.

Today as in the time of Genghis Khan the chief occupation of the Mongols is herding livestock—horses, cattle, sheep, camels, and goats. The total livestock population of Mongolia in recent years has been in the range of 22,000,000 to 23,000,000 of which sheep accounted for about one-half, horses about 2,400,000, cattle just under 2,000,000, goats about 5,500,000 and camels 860,000.

Today as in the time of Genghis Khan the horse is traditionally the center of Mongol life, large herds being maintained even by industrial and mining establishments to provide horse milk and its derivative milk products to workers and their families. And while there has in recent years been a steady increase in sedentary occupations and permanent housing (particularly in the capital, Ulan Bator, where about one-fifth of the country's population now resides) the *yurt*, the traditional Mongol conical felt tent, collapsible and easily transported and re-erected from one herding ground to another, remains as much the national trademark as the windmill does in Holland.

The communist regime in Mongolia was established in a revolution carried out in July of 1921 in which Khalka Mongols (the principal Mongol group), Buryat Mongols and Russians all had a hand. The revolution was at least in part the by-product of several years of civil war and anarchy in eastern Siberia and adjacent parts of Asia in which White Russians, communist forces, Chinese warlords, Japanese forces, and ravaging bandit hordes played a role.

Imperial Russia had achieved a dominant position in Mongolia concurrent with the Mongol Revolution of 1911 in which the Mongolians overthrew their long vassalage to Imperial China. Now, under Soviet Russia, the Mongol-Russian ties were recemented and strengthened.

The People's Revolutionary Government of Mongolia was established in Urga (now Ulan Bator) on July 11, 1921, and it is from this date that the founding of the contemporary Mongol state is traced. The principal figures among the Mongol revolutionaries were Sukhe Bator and Choibalsan. Sukhe Bator died in 1923 in suspicious circumstances, possibly being poisoned. Choibalsan lived on to become the chief architect of Communist Mongolia. He died in Moscow on January 28, 1952, of cancer, having achieved an eminence and authority in his country, roughly similar to that of Stalin in the Soviet Union. Like Stalin, Choibalsan has in recent years been subjected to de-Choibalsan-ization; in other words, an attempt has been made by the Mongols to assess the pros and cons of his rule realistically.

One of the most striking characteristics of Mongolia's new revolutionary regime was the fact that, technically, Jebtsun Damba Khutukhtu, the "Living Buddha" and chief of the theocratic state which had been established in 1911 was retained although most of his real powers were transferred to a Council of Ministers. This odd situation in which a Buddhist Lama headed up a communist state continued for three years, until the death of the Living Buddha, May 20, 1924, after which a People's Republic was proclaimed.

The ability of the Mongol communists to blend national and traditionalist elements into their regime is symbolized by their treatment of the Living Buddha. For many years, despite Mongolia's technical state of communism, there was little actual change in the Mongol way of life. The power of the Buddhist priesthood was broken and, concurrently with the collectivization and purges in the Soviet Union, terrible internal campaigns were waged in Mongolia.

The Buddhist Church (concentrated in a series of huge monastic establishments) had owned nearly half the property in Mongolia, including at least a quarter of the livestock. More than 200,000 persons either belonged to monasteries or worked for them. About 30 percent of the male population was in the priesthood.

These struggles occupied the Mongol Communist leadership through the 1920's and 1930's.

Externally, the chief threat was Japan which, expanding in north

China, was colliding with Russia. The Soviet Union guaranteed Mongolia's defense in a 1936 treaty, and in 1939 a sizable war was fought on the Mongol frontier near Khalkin-gal in which several hundred thousand troops including thousands of Mongol troops under Soviet command were involved. The Japanese were sharply defeated by the combined Soviet-Mongol force, commanded by Marshal Georgi K. Zhukov, later to become the top Soviet World War II commander.

From the economic and social viewpoint the Mongol way of life did not materially change under communism up to the end of World War II. After terrible experiences in 1931-32, Mongolian agriculture—that is, livestock herding—was decollectivized and went back to its traditional nomadic feudal pattern. Industry (except for a few small meat and leather processing plants, established largely to provide a source of commissary supplies for the Soviet and Mongol armed forces) was virtually nonexistent. A census of Mongol workers showed 10,100 to be engaged in industry in 1940—mostly in small artisan shops. Literacy rose only from 6 percent in 1933 to 9.6 percent in 1940. An estimated 21,700 children attended school that year out of an estimated 85,000 children of school-going age.

The most important single influence in contemporary Mongolia is the fact of Soviet-Chinese rivalry. Post-war Mongolia showed little signs of change until the deaths, in successive years, of the Mongol dictator, Choibalsan, and the Soviet dictator, Josef Stalin.

Nationalist China, under wartime pressure, had reluctantly recognized the independence and territorial integrity of Mongolia in 1945. Now, however, with the emergence of a Communist regime in Peking, China moved vigorously and imaginatively to re-establish her traditional stewardship in Mongolia.

The period of slightly more than a decade since Stalin's death, March 5, 1953, has marked the most striking period of Mongol development in modern times.

The principal achievements have been the following:

A marked increase in Mongolian independence and freedom of action, stemming from relaxation of external controls by the Soviets; skilled maneuvering by Mongol rulers within the focus of Soviet-Chinese rivalry; and rapid extension of Mongolia's contacts and connections with other nations, both Communist and non-Communist.

A striking rise in industrialization and urbanization, marked by the growth of the population of Ulan Bator, the capital, to 175,000 and by an increase in the net weight of industrial production to the point at which it almost equals agricultural production.

Rapid development of educational and scientific facilities, increase in literacy, and progress in solution of public health problems. Literacy has now risen to better than 75 percent. Close to 95 percent of the children of school age now attend school, including about 125,000 in public and trade schools and more than 7,000 in colleges and higher educational institutions.

Two changes have occurred in the field of agriculture. The livestock industry has been almost entirely collectivized—at least on paper. The tribal herding groups have been turned into cooperatives or collectives. Thus far, there has been little interference with traditional grazing patterns. But the technical basis for change has been laid.

A more radical change has been the introduction of crop cultivation. Mongols traditionally have been herdsmen. Their diet has been almost exclusively meat and milk products (principally cheeses and fermentations derived from horse milk). Now, under Soviet inspiration a major effort to introduce grain farming is under way. Sown areas have expanded from about 26,000 hectares in 1941 to more than 265,000 in 1960, the bulk of which is sown to grain, much of it under irrigation. Mongolian wheat production in 1960 was 215,500 tons, more than double the previous year and seven times as high as 1958.

The Mongolian government is a typical communist establishment. The Communist Party is the only political organization which is permitted. Since the death of Choibalsan in 1952 the Premier and principal figure in the Party has been Y. Tsedenbal whose education was largely obtained in the Soviet Union. Mr. Tsedenbal is one of the few Mongols to have visited the United States, prior to Mongolia's admission to the United Nations in 1961. He came to New York to represent Mongolia during her unsuccessful 1946 bid for U.N. membership.

Political changes within the Mongolian Communist Party structure in recent years have seemed to revolve largely around issues of Mongol nationalism and/or support or opposition to various maneuvers on the part of competing Moscow and Peking.

China's move to reassert influence in Mongolia began almost immediately after Stalin's death and increased in momentum with the completion of the trans-Mongolian railroad January 1, 1956, which provided direct connections between Ulan Bator and Peking. That same year the first 10,000 Chinese laborers appeared in Mongolia to work on construction projects and in August, 1956, China provided Mongolia with a 160,000,000 ruble grant-in-aid. Contact between Mongolia and China's Inner Mongolia was encouraged and the Chinese began tentatively to create a Genghis Khan cult, centered around construction of an elaborate mausoleum at Ejen Khoro in Inner Mongolia to house the supposed sarcophagus of the great Khan.

The Chinese followed up with 300,000,000 rubles more in aid in succeeding years. Apparently stimulated by the Chinese activity the Soviets pumped in nearly 1,000,000,000 rubles in direct grants and loans. They also deferred payment on another 245,000,000 rubles of past debts.

It is this heavy infusion of outside capital which has enabled Mongolia to expand so rapidly in industry, housing, irrigation, water control and agriculture in recent years.

Outside aid was not limited to the two major powers. Following Moscow's lead the eastern European Communist countries have sent substantial delegations of specialists to Mongolia and have made efforts to develop trade. The Soviets remain, however, Mongolia's principal trading partner, importing up to 15 percent of Mongolia's sheep and 5 to 10 percent of her cattle. China's imports are largely horses, running up to 40,000 a year.

Since 1962 the Soviet Union has steadily pushed Chinese influence in Mongolia onto the defensive. The building programs on which the Chinese were engaged have been completed. The Chinese labor force which had reached a peak variously estimated at from 20 to 40 thousand has been withdrawn almost in entirety. Meanwhile, about 1,000 Russian and East European technicians have been sent in and considerable numbers of Mongols have been sent to the U.S.S.R. for training.

At the same time the Mongolian diplomatic line has taken a consistently anti-Chinese tone. Whereas, during the late 1950's Mongolia expended much effort in emphasizing her friendship with both Moscow and Peking, she now sides firmly with the Soviet Union in the Sino-Soviet dispute. Mongol observers have participated in Comecon conferences. Mongol representatives have participated in all of Moscow's Communist meetings at which China's position has been denounced. A succession of distinguished Soviet delegations has visited Mongolia, including one headed by Party Secretary Leonid I. Brezhnev.

Soviet concern over the security of the long Mongolian frontier with China has been manifest. In 1965 a Soviet group headed by Alexander Shelepin, Presidium member, Central Committee Secretary, and security specialist, visited Mongolia and toured areas close to the Mongol-Chinese border. The delegation included a number of Soviet high-ranking military specialists.

There have been two major shakeups in high Mongol circles which some observers have linked with Soviet-Chinese tensions. The first occurred in 1962, apparently as an outgrowth of a Chinese propaganda move, connected with the 800th anniversary of the birth of Genghis Khan. The event was extensively celebrated in China's Inner Mongolia and, to a lesser extent, in Mongolia. Suddenly, however, the Soviets criticized Genghis as a cruel and tyrannical despot (he had, of course, launched the Mongols on the Western drive which fastened a Mongol despotism on Russian backs for nearly 300 years).

Mongolia bowed to Moscow's line by removing a leading member of the Mongol Politburo, attacking him as a partisan of Mongol nationalism which he was accused of furthering through excessive praise of Genghis Khan. There was a concurrent shakeup in the high command of the Mongol Army.

There has been speculation that the shakeup was designed to eliminate individuals suspected of leaning to the Chinese side. China was known to have been sedulously encouraging Mongol nationalism, suggesting that Russia was Mongolia's enemy and China its friend.

A little more than a year later another shakeup occurred in the top echelon. Luvsantserengiin Tsende, the right-hand man of Premier Tsedenbal, second secretary of the Mongol Communist Party and the man who acted as Premier when Tsedenbal was out of the country, was suddenly denounced and removed from office. He was also charged with being a backer of "nationalist" ideas.

The frequency with which charges of "nationalism" have been advanced in purging Mongol officials tends to bulwark the theory that a consistent theme of Mongol politics is a desire for increased national independence. Substantial advances in this direction have been made in the last decade. But the intensity of the Sino-Soviet dispute causes Moscow to view nationalist aspirations with continuing suspicion.

Mongolia is certain to continue its aggressive drive to broaden its relations with the world. In Mongol terms the great event of the 1960's was entry into the United Nations in 1961. Mongolia is almost equally desirous of establishing diplomatic relations with the United States and has frankly stated its desire for broad diplomatic, economic and cultural contacts with America.

The United States actively explored the possibility of establishing relations in 1961 but was deterred by the vigorous opposition of Nationalist China which threatened reprisals in the United Nations if U.S. action was taken.

However, UN membership has produced a substantial broadening of Mongol diplomatic contacts, including the exchange of missions with the United Kingdom in 1963. Mongolia now has diplomatic relations with about forty nations of which fifteen or sixteen maintain permanent missions in Ulan Bator.

The long-range ambition of many Mongols is the creation of a Greater Mongolia in which the 400,000 Mongols in the U.S.S.R. and the 1,500,000 in China would be reunited with their kinsmen. However, Mongol political leaders are too realistic to presume that such a radical development is likely at any time in the near future.

The general goal of the country may be stated as utilizing the present period of rivalry within the communist sphere to achieve as rapid development as possible, meanwhile increasing Mongolia's freedom of action and opportunity for maneuver by broadening contacts both in the West and in Asia.

Within another decade industrialization, the rise in the educational level, and the spread of crop cultivation can be expected to create a radical change in the overall aspect of Mongolia. The traditional life of the nomad, of the *yurt,* the glorification of the horse is not likely to survive the on-rushing era of rapid technological and cultural change. Whether Russia's superior economic and technical resources will succeed in overbalancing geographical propinquity in the continuing Sino-Soviet struggle for Mongolian allegiance remains to be seen. The more likely outcome, perhaps, may be a growing Mongol indifference to partisanship with either of the two contenders.

FURTHER READING SUGGESTIONS

Bisch, Jorgen, *Mongolia, Unknown Land.* London: G. Allen, 1963.
Douglas, William O., "Journey to Outer Mongolia," *National Geographical* (March 1962), 121:289-345.
Friters, Gerard, *Outer Mongolia.* Baltimore: Johns Hopkins Press, 1949.
Lamb, Harold, *Ghengis Khan, the Emperor of All Men.* Garden City, New York: Doubleday, 1952.
———, *Ghengis Khan and the Mongol Horde.* New York: Random House, 1954.
Lattimore, Owen, *Nomads and Commissars.* New York: Oxford University Press, 1962.
———, *Studies in Frontier History.* London, New York: Oxford University Press, 1962.
Montagu, Ivor, *Land of Blue Sky.* London: D. Dobson, 1956.
Prawdin, Michael, *The Mongol Empire.* London: G. Allen, 1952.
Rupen, R. A., *The Mongolian People's Republic.* Stanford, Calif.: Stanford University Press, 1966.
Salisbury, Harrison E., *A New Russia?* New York: Harper & Row, 1962.
———, *To Moscow—and Beyond.* New York: Harper & Row, 1962.
Waley, Arthur, *The Secret History of the Mongols.* New York: Barnes & Noble, 1964.

14

From Feudalism to Socialism:
A Mongolian Marxist View on
the Mongolian People's Republic

Yumzhagin Tsedenbal *

PRESIDENT, COUNCIL OF MINISTERS,
MONGOLIAN PEOPLE'S REPUBLIC, AND
FIRST SECRETARY, CENTRAL COMMITTEE,
MONGOLIAN PEOPLE'S REVOLUTIONARY PARTY

WITH A SUPPLEMENT BY

Ivor Montagu †

BRITISH JOURNALIST, AUTHOR, AND EXPERT ON MONGOLIA

Now that the system of colonial slavery is crashing under the impact of the national-liberation movement, the question facing the new sovereign states is what path of development should they choose. Should they go along the old capitalist way with its accompanying crises, unemployment and fear of the morrow, with its unequal distribution of the good things of this world among the members of society, and its political inequality? Or should it be the new path, the path which will enable them to bypass the "blood and dirt, misery and degradation?" (Karl Marx).

Seen in this light the experience of Mongolia acquires a special significance. In its transition from feudalism to socialism Mongolia has bypassed the capitalist stage. It was not so very long ago that serfdom prevailed

* Tsedenbal's article has been condensed from the *World Marxist Review* (March, 1961), pp. 11-18 and is reprinted by permission of the publisher.

† Montague's contribution, especially written for this book, brings Premier Tsedenbal's article up to date. It starts on p. 420 under the subheading "Mongolia in the Mid-1960's: A Supplement."

in the country; the life of the Mongolian herdsman was wholly in the hands of his feudal lord. Only in 1921, after the people's revolution, did the emancipation of the serfs and the general economic and cultural advance of our people begin.

In the space of forty years Mongolia has traversed the distance from feudalism to the complete victory of socialist production relations in all spheres of the economy; other countries needed centuries for this. How did the Mongolian people do this?

NONCAPITALIST PATH OF DEVELOPMENT IS A REALITY

That a country which had not gone through the crucible of capitalism and which until recently was one of the most backward in Asia could switch to building socialism is regarded by some bourgeois sociologists as being inconsistent with the Marxist teaching on the succession of socio-economic formations. How do things stand in reality? History knows not a few cases of countries and nations having bypassed the usual stage of development in their advance to a new and more progressive social system. Many of the nomad peoples in Asia and Africa, for example, did not experience the system of slavery; North America and Canada bypassed feudalism, etc. And certainly the founders of scientific communism did not regard this as a denial of the law of social development. What is more, their view was that the underdeveloped countries could take the "short cut" to socialism by skipping capitalism and they discovered the general law of the noncapitalist way of development for the backward countries.

The socialist revolution in Russia, one of the biggest countries in the world, bordering on underdeveloped colonial countries in the East, enabled the oppressed people of these countries, including the Mongolian people, to win national independence and to step out along the road of non-capitalist development.

The Marxist-Leninist teaching on non-capitalist development of backward countries became the guide to action for the Communist and revolutionary parties in a number of countries of the East, including our People's Revolutionary Party (MPRP). The contact between the working people of Russia and Mongolia which steadily became wider and stronger after the October Revolution, was of decisive help in this respect. *This was, in fact, a class alliance between the victorious working class of Russia and the Mongolian arats* (peasants), which ensured the victory of our revolution, and thanks to which we were able to step out successfully along the road to socialism without going through the capitalist stage.

A big impression was made in Mongolia by the fact that immediately after the October Revolution the government of Soviet Russia declared its readiness to base its relations with Mongolia on full equality. Our people knew that the first socialist country in the world would be a sincere friend in their struggle for freedom and national independence.

Nor were they disappointed. At the request of the Provisional People's Government of Mongolia, the Soviet Government helped us to smash the Whiteguard gangs of Baron Ungern who were committing outrages on Mongolian soil. The common enemy of the two neighboring countries was destroyed by the joint action of the Soviet and Mongolian armed forces.

The people's revolution in Mongolia, a backward stock-breeding country in which there was no working class, was headed by the People's Revolutionary Party. From the outset, this party, exclusively a peasant party fighting for national liberation and democratic aims, developed in close co-operation with the international Communist movement and assimilated Marxism-Leninism, the revolutionary teaching of the working class.

The founding of the MPRP[1] signified a new stage in the liberation struggle of the Mongolian people; for the first time the struggle was headed by a militant political organization upholding the fundamental class interests of the working people. In a conversation with a Mongolian delegation which visited him in 1921, Lenin, when asked by a member of the delegation whether the MPRP should be *turned* into a Communist Party, expressed the view that the revolutionaries still had much to do in the matter of building their state and developing their economy and culture before a proletarian mass could be created from among the herdsmen, a mass which in due course would help to "turn" the People's Revolutionary Party into a Communist Party. The subsequent years and developments in the People's Revolutionary Party have confirmed the soundness of these words.

Repeated attacks were made on the Party's general line by Right-wing opportunist groupings opposed to the noncapitalist path of development. Dogmatism and sectarianism, expressed in petty-bourgeois "ultra-leftism" and in ignoring the national features, were also a grave danger. Under pressure of the "Left" elements the Eighth Party Congress (1930) erroneously proclaimed that the Mongolian revolution had entered the socialist stage, and called for wholesale collectivization of the arat households. This error, resulting in Left deviations, gravely discredited the idea of collectivization and slowed down the development of the co-operative movement.

The MPRP, however, withstood all the attempts to divert it from the correct path, thanks to its fidelity to Marxism-Leninism, and its close contact with the people whose interests it cherishes and whose support it enjoys.

Our experience has shown that a political party of the working people guided by Marxist-Leninist teaching, can, in certain conditions, successfully lead the struggle in an underdeveloped country where the working class has not yet emerged or where, if it has, it is still numerically small.

---

[1] The organizational structure of this Party was defined at its First Congress in March, 1921.

TWO STAGES OF THE MONGOLIAN REVOLUTION

The people's revolution in Mongolia, more so than anywhere else, was not a "pure" social revolution. In the early phase of the revolution, some of the feudal elements, the monks and the old officials, disgruntled by the occupation of the country first by the Chinese militarists and then by Ungern's Whiteguard gangs, aligned themselves alongside the arats—the driving force of the revolution—and the People's Revolutionary Party which, basing itself on the teaching of Marxism-Leninism, headed the revolution.

Our Party drew representatives of these sections into the liberation struggle and isolated the leaders of the reactionary feudal-theocratic elements. However, the platform adopted at the Party's First Congress in March 1921 stated clearly that "in the event of other political parties appearing in Mongolia and accepting our basic aims, the People's Revolutionary Party will enter into an interim agreement with them," [2] but any attempt on their part to hamper the Party in its fight would not be tolerated.

At that time the revolution was spearheaded against imperialism. The Party took into account that the majority of the feudal elements were opposed to foreign imperialism and that the masses of religious arats and particularly the lamas [3] believed in the "sacredness" of Bogdo-Hehen, the monarch and head of the Lamaist Church. For this reason, after the victory of the revolution, the Party considered it expedient to establish a constitutional monarchy. To have proclaimed a republic in those conditions would have meant running ahead, and this could have instilled a fear of the revolution in some sections of the population. For the same reason the feudalists were allowed to participate in state affairs. It should be emphasized, however, that the activities of the monarch-theocrat and the feudal officials were under the control of the People's Government. Real power was exercised by the people's state which carried out the functions of the revolutionary-democratic dictatorship of the people.

That was how the *first stage* of the revolution, which lasted from 1921 to the 'forties, began in Mongolia. During this time the anti-feudal revolution was completed and the way was cleared for noncapitalist development. From the outset, in the complex situation then prevailing, the People's Revolutionary Party set about paving the way for a fundamental reconstruction of the country along democratic lines, and laying the foundations of a new economy and a new culture. Suhe-Baatar and Choybalsan, the founders of the Party, wrote in 1921: "The growth of national awareness among the arats will enable us in a year or two to advance the revolution in order to abolish the rights of the princes once and for all."

[2] H. Choybalsan, *Short History of the Mongolian People's Revolution.*
[3] Before and for a number of years after the revolution the lamas comprised 45 percent of the adult male population of Mongolia.

The Party, in the immediate post-revolutionary years (1921-24), did not set itself the task of confiscating the feudal estates and the land owned by the monasteries. The task at this time was to destroy the *political* base of feudalism and feudal-serf relations, to consolidate the rule of the people and its local agencies and develop the arat economy. By the end of 1924 serfdom had been abolished, the privileges of the feudal class had been annulled and equal rights established for all citizens. The feudal administration in the localities was replaced by democratic bodies—the people's *khurals*. The state annulled the extortionate debts owed by the arats to the foreign merchants and usurers, and introduced customs tariffs, taxes and other levers designed to oust the capital of the foreign merchants and money-lenders.

Land nationalization in 1921 and the setting up of consumer co-operatives marked the beginning of the state-cooperative sector. The importance of the nascent co-operatives for the noncapitalist development of the country was emphasized by Lenin. From the islets of the new economic formation, Lenin said, a new noncapitalist system would develop.

The consistent revolutionary policy pursued by the Party and the People's Government encountered bitter opposition from the overthrown exploiter classes who, although removed from political power, had not yet abandoned the class struggle.

Headed by the former Prime Minister Bodo, the counter-revolutionary group, who upheld the feudal interests, plotted to overthrow the People's Government and to re-establish the absolute rule of King Bogdo-Hehen. At the same time the representatives of the incipient bourgeoisie, closely associated with foreign capital, aimed at diverting the country onto the path of capitalist development.

External enemies, first and foremost the Japanese and the Chinese warlords, frequently encroached on the independence of the young democratic state and they repeatedly perpetrated acts of direct aggression against us. Since we had a border of more than 4,000 kilometers with the enemy countries, our people had to be constantly on the alert, which could not but divert them from their peaceful labors.

But despite the difficulties, the revolution went ahead and by mid-1924 the Third Congress proclaimed the Leninist teaching on the possibility of non-capitalist development of underdeveloped countries as the general line of the Party, and *declared the noncapitalist way as the only way which would take Mongolia to socialism*. The abolition of the monarchy and the proclamation of the People's Republic in 1924 were landmarks on this road.

One of the most difficult problems of non-capitalist development was that of building the new economy. Important measures such as the establishment of the State Bank, the issue of a national currency and the introduction of a state monopoly of foreign trade, were carried out between 1924 and the 'thirties; we began, too, to build industry and install transport facilities—all state-owned. The main economic levers were, therefore, in the hands of the people's democratic state.

Relying on the consolidated state-cooperative sector and the growing revolutionary enthusiasm of the working people, the Republic, between 1929 and 1932, expropriated the big feudal property and elbowed out most of the foreign merchant and usurers' capital. This was of the utmost importance for the noncapitalist development of the country.

The solution of the lama problem was another difficult and specific task of the antifeudal revolution. Lamaism, with its hundreds of monasteries, vast estates, and masses of parasitic lamas, was a grave obstacle in the way of the socio-economic reconstruction of the country.

In this matter the Party pursued a policy of differentiation, isolating the upper clergy from the ordinary lamas. Political and educational work was conducted among the latter, and they were encouraged in every way to go over to the life of laymen. Those who did so were given help in building their own homes, in joining co-operative handicrafts, etc. As a result many of the lamas voluntarily left the monasteries, broke with celibacy, became family men, and began to take part in socially useful labor.

On the whole, the antifeudal stage of the revolution had been completed by 1940. Its main feature was *the abolition of feudal production relations and the expulsion of foreign merchant and usurers' capital, on the one hand, and the birth of a socialist sector in the economy and the creation of a firm base for non-capitalist development, on the other.* By the end of the 'thirties industry had become an independent branch of the national economy, accounting for nearly 20 percent of the country's overall output.

The industrialization was accompanied by the birth of a working class. This was an industrial working class formed not under capitalism but under an emerging economic and social order in which socialist production relations reigned supreme.

Important changes also took place in agriculture, where the socialist sector emerged in the shape of state farms, mowing-machine depots and simple forms of arat co-operation.

As the organizational, economic, cultural and educational functions of our democratic state broadened, as the socialist sector grew stronger, and as the political consciousness of the working people deepened, the *democratic revolution gradually evolved into a socialist revolution.*

Mongolia had entered a new stage—the socialist stage of its development.

MONGOLIA AN AGRARIAN AND INDUSTRIAL COUNTRY

The experience of Mongolia confirms the Marxist-Leninist teaching to the effect that, *in essentials, the road to socialism is the same* for all countries, despite the diversity of forms and methods conditioned by the national, historical and economic features of the particular country. It is important to stress this in view of the fact that our country took the socialist road without having previously passed through capitalism.

The extreme economic and technical backwardness and the low level of the productive forces *were not an insurmountable obstacle to building socialism*. The fraternal help accorded by Soviet Russia, where the socialist revolution had already triumphed, was of decisive importance.

Soviet aid enabled Mongolia to become economically independent of enslaving foreign capital and to develop the national economy. It was with Soviet help that the first schools and medical and scientific establishments were built and an intelligentsia trained. Also with Soviet aid our people tackled the job of industrialization—a vital prerequisite for the noncapitalist way. A number of enterprises were commissioned in the early 'thirties; they included a big industrial complex of several factories in Ulan-Bator, a machine-repair works and a power station; motor and rail transport was initiated—the latter just before the outbreak of the Second World War.

To a degree the war delayed the realization of a far-reaching economic and cultural program. But the growth of the productive forces, the development and consolidation of the socialist sector in agriculture, the rise in the living standards and the cultural level of the people proceeded rapidly after the war. In addition to increasing Soviet aid, an important factor making for our accelerated tempo of socialist construction was the rise of new socialist countries in Europe and in the East, and the formation of the socialist world system. As the Statement of the Meeting of Representatives of Communist and Workers' Parties points out: "The people's revolution in China delivered a crushing blow to imperialism in Asia and in great measure contributed to the balance of world forces changing in favor of socialism." This development radically improved the international position of Mongolia, enabling it to release a considerable labor force and substantial funds for the needs of the economy by reducing defense costs.

*   *   *

Compared with the feudal system, capitalism was, in its time, progressive. But its progress was achieved at the cost of incalculable suffering. That is precisely why the non-capitalist road accords with the interests of the people in the underdeveloped countries.

The whole history of the national rebirth of Mongolia, of its building a socialist republic, shows that, given the guidance of a Marxist-Leninist Party and the support of the international working-class movement, even the most economically backward countries can win and consolidate national independence and confidently take the noncapitalist road, the road leading to democracy and socialism.

MONGOLIA IN THE MID-1960'S: *A SUPPLEMENT* [4]

It has been asserted that the standard of living in Mongolia is the highest on the Asian mainland. Such an assertion would be difficult to prove. There is however little doubt that in all Asian countries other than Mongolia poverty and a tragically low subsistence level are the lot of a considerable part of the population.

To understand Mongolia's transformation during the forty-five years since July 11, 1921 [5]—the day new Mongolia was born—it is necessary to take a look at the picture of old Mongolia as it has been painted by explorers, missionaries, and other western travellers before and since that fateful summer day in 1921: population, then, stood at about 650,000; there were no doctors; [6] less than one percent of the population knew how to read or write; schooling was scarce and reserved for the wealthy few; 40 percent of all adult males lived in monasteries; up to 90 percent in many areas were afflicted by venereal disease; one third of all babies were stillborn, and 40 percent of the rest died before the age of three; there was no industry whatsoever; agriculture was practiced only in a few temple corners and in villages of Chinese settlers; and those engaged in raising livestock—the country's basic, and only major economic occupation—were bled white by foreign (mainly Chinese) merchants. (One single firm took out more than half a million sheep over a twenty-year period; herds were mortgaged years ahead; and not only herdsmen but even feudal princes were fantastically in debt.) An English traveller, a certain Mrs. Bulstrode, blamed it all on the Mongolian character: "His utter laziness and lack of gumption," she wrote in 1923, "make him useless in an emergency . . . stupid and shiftless in the extreme. . . . The Mongols never have worked and it is highly improbable they ever will." And the great American paleontologist Chapman Andrews passed the following, somewhat premature, judgement upon new Mongolia in 1932: "The establishment of the Bolshevik regime is, I believe, the last act in the tragedy of Mongolia. The doom of the Mongols, as a race, is sealed."

The fundamental change in Mongolia's economy during the past four and a half decades has been a continuous decline in the relative importance of animal husbandry. Depicted on the country's old emblem in the form of five animals—the horse, the cow (which includes the yak), the camel, the

---

[4] By Ivor Montagu. (*See* footnote, p. 413.)

[5] It was in the summer of 1921 that Mongolian revolutionary forces with the aid of Soviet troops, took over the reins of government. [EDITOR'S NOTE]

[6] In terms of Western medicine, that is. Chinese pharmacopoeias were resorted to. (This is the stock of medicines traditional to Chinese science and taught in the lamaseries. [Lamaseries are monasteries of lamas, i.e., of Buddhist priests or monks. EDITOR'S NOTE])

goat, and the sheep—livestock raising in presocialist Mongolia was the whole of life, and animal products the almost exclusive source of food supplies. Today, agriculture and industry play equally important roles.

Animal husbandry has been almost completely collectivized since 1959; nomadism (the seasonal movement of herds and their attendants) has been reduced even where it had been most prevalent—in the arid south—to no more than a fairly regular neighboring-pasture change; and life in the countryside nowadays typically centers around the cooperative, complete with shops, medical and veterinary clinics, school, cinema, club room, and sporting grounds. This new way of life has been made possible by the large-scale development of irrigation, the digging of wells, the introduction of hay for fodder, and the erection of winter shelters for livestock. The average cooperative today owns about 50,000 head of livestock and has about 500 acres under crops.

The Western image of Mongolia is often that of a desert. But Mongolia is by no means a wasteland, and even the word Gobi means "plain" rather than desert. The northern parts are fertile and forested mountain; the center and the south consist of the great grassland plains, with sandy and rocky wilderness only along the southern border, extending along the frontier with China. There are ample water supplies to be tapped—in lakes, in rivers, and beneath the ground. In the year 1965 alone, according to official figures, 1942 wells were dug, shelters for 200,000 head of livestock were built, and 12 million acres of pasture were supplied with water in the southern near-desert provinces of South, Middle and East Gobi, Ubur Khangai, and Bayan Khangor.

In 1965, 32 state farms and 337 large agricultural cooperatives were in operation; of the latter, 86 percent were serviced by 40 so-called machine and livestock improvement stations. Following the example of the large state farms, grain and vegetable growing and pig and poultry raising have been widely introduced. The sown area totalled 1,200,000 acres in 1965, two-thirds of which was in wheat. Mongolia is now in a position to export grain, since her grain production exceeds her domestic needs.

Coal and other mineral resources are now mined in Mongolia; oil is produced at Sain-Shand, in north central Gobi; and thermal power electrifies the coal mines and the capital. (Coal production is reported to have increased fourfold, and electrical power output tenfold, in the twenty-year period from 1940 to 1960.) The transportation system includes the trans-Mongolian section of the Moscow-Peking railway (completed in 1949), internal airlines, and steamships which carry cargo and passengers on the northern frontier lakes. Side by side with the ubiquitous pony rider and the horse and camel caravans, motor transport now accounts for 50 percent of all passenger, and 80 percent of all freight traffic.

Urbanization and urban building have made considerable progress. Of the more than one million inhabitants of the land, over 200,000 now live in the capital, Ulan Bator. In Ulan Bator, one finds wide streets, numerous stores, entire city blocks of administration buildings, hotels, hospitals, a university, an Academy of Sciences, an opera, a theater, and a music conservatory; but within the city limits, side by side with huge blocks of modern apartment houses, one also finds neat rows of *yurts* (the traditional rounded tent)—each with electric light, stove vent, and radio—as well as remnants of the old one-story wooden shacks that were the capital city's only dwelling places when it was still called Urga, two-score years ago. There are other cities such as Darkhan, to the north near the Soviet frontier. Founded as recently as 1961, Darkhan already has a 50,000 kilowatt power plant and a grain elevator with a 32,000 ton capacity. With thirty factories either completed or planned, the city's population is expected to reach 60,000 by 1980. The population in the typical provincial centers, on the other hand, varies from five or six thousand in winter to two or three thousand in summer when more herdsmen are out on the plains.

In its growing industrial sector, Mongolia has wisely concentrated on goods that would meet the country's special needs and for the production of which it is particularly well adapted by its resource endowment. Hence, Mongolia's industrial sector consists primarily of milk and meat producing plants, bakeries turning out cakes and biscuits, distilleries, chemical plants specializing in the production of fertilizer, machine (including motor transport) repair stations, wool processing plants, and factories turning out woolen textiles and fine cloths, leather goods, and cement and other building materials. The output of textiles and clothing, of hides, and of boots and shoes is reported to have increased about sixfold from 1940 to 1960 and that of bricks nearly fortyfold. According to official figures, the number of workers and employees engaged in industry has increased during the same period from 33,000 to 136,000. And foreign trade is growing.

Now, in the mid-1960's, industrial output amounts to more than two-fifths of Mongolia's total national product, and it is expected to rise to more than half by 1970. In the summer of 1965, Premier Tsedenbal forecast an annual increase in production of 12 to 15 percent for the 1966-1970 period. So far, prices of some consumer goods have been kept stable while those of others have been periodically reduced. Hence, such statistical figures as those which show that money incomes of collective farmers have risen by 69 percent from 1960 to 1965 indicate an equivalent of greater increase in real income and living standards. And whereas, in conformity with the usual pattern of developmental expenditures in socialist countries, only 24 percent of industrial investment under the third five-year plan (1960-1965) had been allocated for light and food industries, it is planned that that share be increased to 43 percent under the fourth five-year plan (1966-1970).

Illiteracy, official reports have it, has been completely wiped out. In 1964, there were 440 primary and secondary schools with some 147,000 pupils in attendance. Education is free, and schooling is compulsory for seven years in urban and four years in rural areas. The current five-year plan calls for universal seven year schooling, a goal which is to be accomplished by doubling the number of secondary schools and by providing boarding schools for 70 percent of all rural school children by 1970. At present, there are also five institutions of higher learning in Mongolia and fifteen specialized colleges with an enrollment of 20,600.

Medical service is also free. The number of doctors is expected to reach 20 per 10,000 population by 1970. The present five-year plan envisages an increase of one-fourth in the number of children's hospitals, and of one-third in the number of maternity homes, which would bring the overall hospital accommodations to 99 beds per 10,000 population.[7]

The Academy of Sciences runs a big observatory; conducts field research in paleontology and archaeology; maintains the palaces and some lamaseries as museums; and has history and economics departments, animal and plant breeding institutes, experimental fisheries, and sections devoted to the application of chemistry to agriculture. One can see Shakespeare plays and hear Bach in the provinces; in the capital, one can watch Moliére, Goldoni, and Chekhov, listen to Beethoven and Tchaikovsky, see Mongolian plays, opera, and ballets, hear choruses, and enjoy music played on the morin hur, the traditional Mongolian stringed instruments, ornamented with a carved horse's head.

Mongolia boasts of 40 newspapers and 20 other periodicals, produced in 20 printing works. Daily papers have a circulation of 180,000. Printed books increased in number from 19.2 million in 1940 to 111.7 million in 1960. And near Ulan Bator is the tallest radio mast in all of Asia.

The political structure includes an executive branch (the Little Hural) responsible to a parliament (the Grand Hural) elected by universal suffrage. Women play a big part in public life (they never have been degraded or *purdahed*[8] in Mongolia). Women constitute one-third of Mongolia's cultural workers, a high percentage of doctors, Hural deputies, etc., and they can be found in positions of responsibility in all fields.

Mongolia is a socialist country. Land and resources are public property, most of the economy is either state owned and operated or collectivized, and there is a one party system. The single party—the Mongolian People's Revolutionary Party—is, it should be noted, *not* a Communist Party in the strict, Marxist sense of the word. It has been working towards the construc-

---

[7] To compare: According to United States' sources, there were 14.7 doctors and 88 hospital beds per 10,000 population in the United States in 1964, while the equivalent figures for the Soviet Union were 20.5 doctors and 94 hospital beds. (*New Directions in the Soviet Economy*, Studies prepared for the Subcommittee on Foreign Economic Policy, Joint Economic Committee, Congress of the United States [Washington, U.S. Government Printing Office], Part II B, p. 503.) The Soviet Union claims 23 doctors per 10,000 population in 1966, and plans for 109 hospital beds per 10,000 population by 1970 (*Soviet News* [July 21, 1966]). [EDITOR'S NOTE]

[8] Derived from the Hindustani and Persian *purdah* (veil), *purdah* refers to the Hindu system of secluding women. [EDITOR'S NOTE]

tion of a socialist society and, in general as well as in specific details, it has supported the foreign policy position of the Soviet Union. All these are characteristics which make the Party appear to be a Communist Party in the eyes of Western, non-Marxist publicists; but to the Marxist a Communist Party is a revolutionary party whose primary function is to lead industrial workers in a developed industrial nation. Suitable conditions for such a party do not exist in Mongolia; indeed, in the sense of predominantly representing social interests separate from those of the herdsmen and farmers, such a party may never come into existence there.

This brief survey, appended to Premier Tsedenbal's article on Mongolia, is in no way intended to present the country as some kind of Utopia. The reader from a land with an already developed industrial civilization, high living standards, and wide cultural opportunities has little reason to be astounded at and perhaps none to be envious of the level of well-being attained by the Mongolians. Nonetheless, Mongolia's achievement has great significance for mankind when it is compared—as all such achievements must be for proper evaluation—with the country's own past.

Mongolia's progress has not been easy. Mongolia has experienced intense internal strains and conflicts, has made costly errors of "leftism" and "rightism," and has been subjected to pressures, backed by military force, from some of its neighbors. On the other hand, it has enjoyed the benefits of generous aid from countries in the Socialist camp: liberal trading terms, loans (and subsequent remission of loans) from the U.S.S.R.; badly needed labor from the People's Republic of China provided in part in the form of generously donated hand labor and work of craftsmen, and in part in the form of the services of road and building workers recruited from among China's Japanese prisoners of war;[9] and teachers, training facilities abroad, and scientific experts from many of the socialist countries.

Other countries have received assistance from abroad, but often with much less happy results. Perhaps Mongolia's more favorable experience can be attributed to the fact that its aid has come from no single, dominant source. For example, at this moment (early 1966) Soviet experts are helping with the construction of power stations and the automation of coal mines, East Germans and Bulgarians with meat packing plants, Czechoslovaks with leather and cement factories, Poles with a silicate bricks factory, and Hungarians with drilling wells. And the visitor to Ulan Bator can also see a splendid factory equipped with the most modern automated British textile machinery, imported from and donated by China who also trained the Mongolian managers, research chemists, and operators—all sons and daughters of herdsmen—who are now operating it entirely on their own.

[9] In a recent study on Mongolia (Robert A. Rupen "The Mongolian People's Republic: The Slow Evolution," *Asian Survey*, January, 1967, p. 19) the author states that "All signs indicate the phasing out of all Chinese projects and the gradual return home of the 4,000 or so Chinese still in the MPR." [EDITOR'S NOTE]

Whenever these foreign experts have come in, they have worked for short periods of time side by side with Mongolians, and then turned the jobs over to Mongolians. The writer and his wife, entering a hospital in Ulan Bator as patients twelve years ago, were received by *two* smiling female physicians, the Mongolian examining, diagnosing, and prescribing under the silent supervision and encouragement of her Russian colleague.

Perhaps even more than most peoples, the Mongolians have intense feelings of national identity and pride. Their centuries of Manchu rule and the period of lamaistic degeneration [10] left them shy and humiliated. But they are a cheerful, friendly people, delighted to be recognized and "with it" in the family of nations as an accepted member of the United Nations, elected, even, as the host country for the summer-1965 UN Seminar on Women's Participation in Social Life. They take great pride in their widely respected female astronomers, their internationally renowned male chess players and wrestlers, and their increasing number of technicians capable of handling the most refined machinery. And, above all, they take pride in being capable of running, by themselves, a modern country, or at least one well on its way towards becoming modern.

To what extent Mongolia's progress has been due to outside aid, to what extent to her freedom from the common Asian curse of overpopulation, to her resolve to achieve national regeneration, and to what socialists consider the primary reason for the country's accomplishments—the socialist basis on which it operates—all this may be a matter of controversy. But whatever the diagnosis may be, it is hardly possible to gainsay that Mongolia's successful renaissance contains pregnant lessons for our time.

FURTHER READING SUGGESTIONS

Andrews, R. C., *The New Conquest of Central Asia*. New York: The American Museum of Natural History, 1932.

Bisch, J., *Mongolia, Unknown Land,* trans. from Danish. London: G. Allen, 1962.

Central Statistical Board of the Council of Ministers of the M. P. R., *National Economy of the Mongolian People's Republic for 40 Years, Collection of Statistics,* in English and Russian. Ulan Bator: 1961.

[10] The Manchu Dynasty ruled China from 1644 to 1912. Outer Mongolia, today renamed the Mongolian People's Republic, was occupied by China from the late 17th century to 1911 (and again from 1919 to 1921). The rise of Lamaist Buddhism was of great assistance to the Chinese in keeping the Mongols suppressed. Inner Mongolia, by the way, was occupied by China towards the end of the 16th century, was incorporated into China, and has remained part of China ever since. [EDITOR'S NOTE]

Douglas, Wm. O., and D. Conger, "Journey to Outer Mongolia," *National Geographic Magazine* (March, 1962).

Friters, G. M., *Outer Mongolia and Its International Position*. London: G. Allen, 1951.

Lattimore, O., *Nationalism and Revolution in Mongolia*. New York: Oxford University Press, 1955.

————, *Nomads and Commissars*. New York: Oxford University Press, 1962.

Ma Ho-tien, *Chinese Agent in Mongolia,* trans. by John De Francis. Baltimore: Johns Hopkins Press, 1949.

Maisky, I. M., *Mongolia at the Dawn of the Revolution,* published for the USSR Academy of Sciences' Institute of Eastern Studies by the Institute of Eastern Literature. Moscow: 1959.

Mongolia Today, bimonthly magazine in English issued by the Information and Broadcasting Department of the M. P. R. (Mongolian Embassy, New Delhi).

Montagu, Ivor, *Land of Blue Sky, A Portrait of Modern Mongolia*. London: D. Dobson, 1956.

Salisbury, H. E., Series of articles on a Mongolian visit, *New York Times* (August, 1959).

VIII

The Korean People's
Democratic Republic and
the Democratic Republic
of Vietnam: Between
Moscow and Peking?

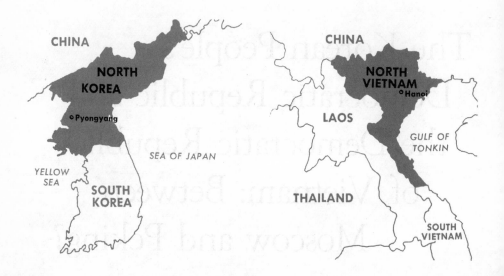

	Area (in square miles)	Population (mid-1967 estimate)
The Korean P.D.Rep.	6,540	12,894,000
The D.Rep. of Vietnam	61,294	20,341,000

> The Soviet Union and the Chinese People's Republic
> are not only our great brother countries but our closest
> neighbors. Firm unity with the peoples of the two coun-
> tries is an important guarantee for all victories of our
> people.
>
> KIM IL SUNG
> CHAIRMAN, CENTRAL COMMITTEE
> KOREAN WORKERS' PARTY

> Our people are very grateful for and highly value the
> fraternal solidarity and devoted assistance of the socialist
> countries, especially the Soviet Union and China. . . .
>
> HO CHI MINH
> CHAIRMAN, VIETNAMESE WORKERS' PARTY
> PRESIDENT, DEMOCRATIC REPUBLIC OF VIETNAM

> The Korean people are one; Korea belongs to the Ko-
> reans. . . . The desire and will of the Korean people
> to unify the fatherland can never be frustrated by any
> aggressive force.
>
> KIM IL SUNG

> Our compatriots in South Vietnam are people of the
> Vietnamese nation. Rivers can dry up, mountains can
> be leveled, but this truth will never change. . . . We
> will certainly be victorious . . . in the implementation
> of national re-unification, and completion of independ-
> ence and democracy throughout our beloved land. . . .
>
> HO CHI MINH

INTRODUCTION

THERE ARE GREAT SIMILARITIES BETWEEN THE KOREAN PEOPLE'S DEMO-
cratic Republic (KPDR, North Korea) and the Democratic Republic
of Vietnam (DRV, North Vietnam) in regard to their geographic
location, political situation, economic structure, military experience, ideological orientation, and so forth. Both are located on peninsulas in East Asia,
protruding in a southeastern direction from the Chinese mainland—the
KPDR at the northeastern, and the DRV at the southeastern border of
China. Both languished under foreign domination for many generations,
gained independence in the post-World War II era, and each thereupon embarked on a course of constructing a society along Marxist-Leninist lines.
Separated from fellow countrymen to the South by an artificial demarcation
line, each has made considerable advances on its road towards industrializa-

tion while the southern half of the country has more or less continued its age-old concentration on agriculture. Each has shown its willingness to fight for the unification of the country under the banner of Marxism-Leninism: the KPDR was engaged—and the DRV (at the time this is being written) is still engaged—in a costly war, with the United States as the major opponent.

Each has pledged never to give up its efforts to reunite the country. And, in the Sino-Soviet split, both are at present trying to steer a neutral course between the two giants in the Communist World, sparing no efforts to befriend both and antagonize neither. In this last respect North Vietnam must be particularly careful at this point in its history, since it desperately needs all the military and technical aid it can get in its fight against the greatest military power on earth. North Korea, on the other hand, while obviously desiring to retain the friendship of China and the Soviet Union, issued a policy statement in the late summer of 1966 that was widely hailed in the Western World as North Korea's Declaration of Independence. Calling on all Communist Parties to stop worshipping "everything concerning the great powers," the statement declares unequivocally that "Communists cannot live ideologically shackled to anyone." [1]

The non-Marxist view on both North Korea and North Vietnam has been contributed by Klaus H. Pringsheim. Pringsheim holds a diploma from the School for Japanese Language and Culture at Tokyo, an undergraduate degree from UCLA, an M.A. from Columbia University, and at the time this book goes to press, his Ph.D. degree from Columbia is pending, subject to completion of his Ph.D. dissertation. Pringsheim has taught at many institutions of higher learning in the United States, including the University of Missouri, the University of Kansas, City College of the City of New York, and California State College at Hayward, and he has given public lectures at many more. He held a Ford Foundation Fellowship for five consecutive years. He gave lectures and a lecture series over five different radio stations in New York, California, and Kansas. Included in his publications are two book-length monographs and numerous articles in professional journals. At present, he is Associate Professor of Political Science at McMaster University, Hamilton, Ontario, Canada. "Further Reading Suggestions" have been omitted from the Marxist sections of this chapter since Professor Pringsheim's reading suggestions at the end of his non-Marxist Views on North Korea and North Veitnam include both Marxist and non-Marxist materials.

The Marxist views in this chapter have been compiled from eight

[1] The statement, issued by the (North) Korean Workers' Party, was published by the Party paper *Nodong Sinmun* (August 12, 1966).

North Korean and seven North Vietnamese publications respectively, all official and recent, thus representing these countries' Marxist-Leninist positions. Among the North Korean authors from whose writings extensive passages have been reproduced are a Director of the Ministry of Common Education, a Vice-Chairman of a County People's Committee, and an assistant manager of a silk mill in the nation's capital. The Marxist viewpoint is represented by selections from the speeches and writings of Ho Chi Minh, North Vietnam's President and Party leader; Pham Van Dong, the country's Premier; and Nguyen Con, Chairman of the country's State Planning Commission.

15

North Korea Under the
Hammer and Sickle:
A Non-Marxist View

KLAUS H. PRINGSHEIM *

ASSOCIATE PROFESSOR OF POLITICAL SCIENCE
MC MASTER UNIVERSITY

The territory of the Democratic People's Republic of Korea (DPRK) encompasses approximately 60 percent of the Korean peninsula, is similar in size to the State of Mississippi,[1] and is situated almost entirely north of the 38th parallel. However, only roughly a third of the total population of Korea lives in the DPRK, present estimates putting the figure at 11 million people.

For reasons both of terrain and climate, North Korea is less suitable for agriculture than South Korea, but industrially and in terms of natural resources the DPRK has by far the advantage over South Korea. Coal, iron ore, power generating dams, steel mills, fertilizer plants, cement factories, and chemical factories are found almost exclusively in the north. Therefore, the DPRK has greater economic viability than South Korea.

As a political entity, the DPRK has officially existed since September 9, 1948, the day on which the Supreme People's Assembly proclaimed the new state. The necessary preparations for the establishment of the DPRK had commenced when the Soviet Army of Occupation first entered Korea three years earlier on August 15, 1945. The first important step was the creation (in close collaboration with the Soviet Army) of local "People's Committees" and units of a "People's Militia." The people's committees functioned at the provincial, municipal, county, district, and village levels, their members being selected by a variety of procedures including direct

---

* This contribution has been written especially for this book.
1 DPRK, 46,539 square miles; Mississippi, 47,716 square miles.

433

and indirect elections. The fact that these committees, among other functions, supervised the distribution of food rations enhanced their ability to control the local population.[2]

Leadership and party politics in North Korea in the immediate post-1945 period were exceedingly complex, but can be interpreted essentially as the story of how one man, Kim Il Sung,[3] came, saw, and conquered all competitors. He became the supreme Party leader, folk hero, ideologue, and the object of a personality-cult which rivals the idolization accorded to Stalin (during his lifetime) and to Mao Tse-tung.

According to the *Great Soviet Encyclopaedia,* Kim Il Sung was born in Korea in 1912 and emigrated to Manchuria with his family in 1925. It appears that his original name was Kim Song Ju, and that at some point he simply adopted the name of Kim Il Sung, a man who had been a nationally known anti-Japanese guerilla fighter before Kim Song Ju (the reincarnated Kim Il Sung) was even born.[4] In 1948 Kim Il Sung told Anna Louise Strong[5] that already his father before him had been a revolutionary and had been arrested by the Japanese during an uprising in 1919. As a fifteen-year-old student in Kirin Province, Manchuria, Kim Il Sung became Secretary of a Komsomol[6] organization, and later allegedly spent a year in prison (1927-28) for his revolutionary activities. In 1931, when the Japanese occupied Manchuria, Kim's father was dead and the boy just 19 years old. He then joined the Communist Party and commenced activities as leader of an anti-Japanese partisan guerilla group. In the spring of 1935 he organized and led a "Fatherland Restoration Association"[7] with branches in several Southern Manchurian and Northeastern Korean population centers. From 1937 on he commanded a part of the North Korean "People's Revolutionary Army" in anti-Japanese guerilla activities in the Manchurian-Korean border area in the upper reaches of the Yalu (Kaplock) river around Kapsan.[8] (Kim and those associated with him in these early communist revolutionary activities hence came to be known as the "Kapsan Faction.") While North Korean official sources in recent years convey the impression that Kim Il Sung and his Kapsan faction were the mainstream of the Korean

[2] Philip Rudolph, *North Korea's Political and Economic Structure* (New York, Institute of Pacific Relations, 1959), pp. 9-10.

[3] Some western writers spell his name Kim Il-song. All Korean names will be given in the version used by the Foreign Languages Publishing House in Pyongyang. Alternate versions will be given in footnotes. Pyongyang is the capital of the DPRK. [EDITOR'S NOTE]

[4] *Report of the United Nations Commission for the Unification and Rehabilitation of Korea,* General Assembly, Official Records, 6th Session, Supplement No. 12 (A/1881) (New York, 1951), p. 26.

[5] A. L. Strong, *Inside North Korea* (Montrose, Calif., 1950), p. 18. (Anna Louise Strong is a pro-Chinese Marxist American writer who has been living in mainland China for several years. [EDITOR'S NOTE]

[6] Communist youth organization. [EDITOR'S NOTE]

[7] Rudolph, *op. cit.,* pp. 25-26, calls it the "Society for the Rebirth of the Fatherland."

[8] Gaimusho Ajiyakyoku, *Gendai Chosen Jinmei Jiten* (Tokyo, 1960), p. 199.

Communist Revolutionary Movement, this view is regarded as an historical distortion by Professor Chong-sik Lee of the University of Pennsylvania, who attributes the rise and triumph of Kim Il Sung after 1945 to political intrigues and the support of the Soviet authorities. The guerilla activities of the Kapsan group (1937-45) may indeed have been little more than nuisance raids against the Japanese and the other groups of Korean communists (the Yenan faction headed by Kim Tu-bong and the domestic faction headed by Pak Hun-yung) may have been the legitimate "mainstream" of Korean communism during the 30's and 40's.

Kim Il Sung, wearing the uniform of a Russian Major, arrived in Korea with the Soviet forces[9] early in September, 1945, but did not immediately show himself to the general public in Pyongyang. Anna Louise Strong reports that Kim traveled through the countryside incognito and for a month participated in the establishment of local people's committees, thus refamiliarizing himself with the Korean domestic scene after his prolonged absence.[10] On October 3, 1945, Kim was finally introduced to the public as a national hero at a rally in Pyongyang by Cho Man-sik. The Soviet authorities had initially appointed Cho Man-sik, a Christian teacher and newspaper editor, as Chief of a *Provisional Political Committee*. A veteran communist named Hyon Chun Hyok was a vice-chairman of the same committee. When Cho Man-sik showed signs of excessive independence of viewpoint (he violently opposed the idea of placing Korea under a five-year United Nations Trusteeship, as decided by the December, 1945, foreign ministers conference in Moscow) the Russians interned him in January, 1946. Cho had founded a Korean Democratic Party (Choson Minjudang) in November, 1945, which might have become a significant political force had Cho not been removed from the political scene. Hyon Chun-Hyok, also a potential rival of Kim Il Sung, was removed even earlier, on September 28, 1945, by assassination. Hyon had been to a conference with the Soviet Commandant and other communists. His assassin was never found, but Hyon was given a fine funeral. Less than two weeks later Kim Il Sung was elected First Secretary of the North Korean Central Bureau of the Korean Communist Party, which was to be the launching pad for his rise to the highest leadership position. He commenced operations by using members of his own Soviet-sponsored Kapsan faction to control the party throughout North Korea.[11]

On February 8, 1946, shortly after the removal of Cho Man-sik, Kim Il Sung became Chairman of the North Korean Provisional People's Committee, the Vice-Chairmanship going to Kim Tu-bong, who headed the

[9] It appears that Kim Il Sung (and his partisans) had retreated from Manchuria into Soviet territory in 1942 and served in the Soviet Army. Kim was supposedly at the Battle of Stalingrad before returning to Korea in 1945.

[10] A. L. Strong, *op. cit.,* p. 19.

[11] See Table I for factions and leadership positions as of summer, 1966.

Table 15-1.   Korean Communist Party Factions, Their Leaders,
and Purge Data

Names of Leaders	Position Held	Purge Date	Ultimate Fate
THE KAPSAN FACTION (ACTIVE IN GUERRILLA WARFARE IN MANCHURIA AND NORTH KOREA)			
Kim Il Sung	Premier, Chmn. KWP		
Ch'oi Yong Kun	President, SPA		
Kim Il	Vice Premier		
Pak Kum-chol	Vice Pres., SPA		
Kim Kwang Hyop	Vice Premier		
SOVIET KOREAN FACTION (KOREAN COMMUNISTS BORN AND/OR TRAINED IN S.U.)			
Ho Ka Ui (Ho Kai)*	Vice Chmn. KWP	1951	Suicide
Pak Chang Ok	Vice Premier	Aug. 1956	Expulsion KWP, arrest
Pak Ui Wan	Vice Premier	Aug. 1956	Expulsion KWP
YENAN KOREAN FACTION (KOREAN COMMUNISTS LINKED WITH THE CHINESE COMMUNISTS IN THE YENAN DAYS)			
Kim Tu-bong	Chmn., SPA	Aug. 1956	Expulsion KWP, house arrest
Ch'oe Chang Ik	Vice Premier	Aug. 1956	Expulsion CC, KWP; arrest
Yun Kong Hum	Minister of Commerce, CC Me.	Aug. 1956	Expulsion KWP Escape to China
Mu Chong	Army General	1950	Penal servitude, exile to China where he died
NORTH KOREAN DOMESTIC FACTION (ACTIVE IN NO. KOREA UNDER JAPANESE RULE)			
Hyon Chun Hyok	Vice Chmn., Prov. Political Comm.	Sept. 1945	Assassination
O Ki Sop	Me., CC, KWP	Aug. 1956	Expulsion KWP 1958
SOUTH KOREAN DOMESTIC FACTION (ACTIVE IN SO. KOREA UNTIL 1948)			
Pak Hon Yong	Vice Premier Foreign Minister	Aug. 1953	Executed (Dec. 1955)
Li Sung Yop (Yi Sung Yop)*	Minister of Justice Sec. CC, KWP	Aug. 1953	Executed

* Alternate spelling.

Note: The extensive purge of 1956 caused such agitation in Peking and Moscow that they sent respectively Marshal Peng Teh-huai (then the Chinese Defense Minister and former Commander of the Chinese Volunteers in Korea) and First Deputy Premier Anastas Mikoyan to Pyongyang for an investigation. Upon reviewing the evidence, Peng and Mikoyan recommended that the party memberships of the accused be restored. This was done in the cases of Pak Chang Ok, Ch'oe Chang Ik, and Yun Kong Hum, but they were not restored to their prominent positions and have lost all influence, as have their friends.

Abbreviations:

KWP = Korean Worker's Party	SU = Soviet Union	Me. = Member
SPA = Supreme People's Assembly	Chmn. = Chairman	Sec. = Secretary
	Exp. = Expulsion (from)	Comm. = Committee
	CC = Central Committee	

Yenan faction of the Korean communists. Kim Tu-bong's group had been
known as the League for Independence (1942-46) and appealed to the
intellectuals and petty bourgeois elements rather than the proletariat and
the poor peasants. In March, 1946, the League for Independence was renamed the New People's Party (Shinmindang). At this point Kim Il Sung
and Kim Tu-bong seem to have agreed that it was advantageous to merge
their forces, and in July, 1946, they coalesced into the North Korean Worker's
Party (NKWP). Kim Il Sung, with rare modesty, accepted the Vice-
Chairmanship of the newly formed NKWP, while Kim Tu-bong (twenty-
three years Kim Il Sung's senior) was elected Chairman.[12] It is possible
that Kim Il Sung allied himself with Kim Tu-bong to strengthen his own
position for future moves against the leading personalities of other communist factions. Meanwhile, the North Korean Provisional People's Committee, headed by Kim Il-sung, was acting as the central government of
North Korea, supervising the Local People's Committees and largely depriving them of their autonomy. (A comparison of these local committees
with the local Soviets in Russia seems entirely appropriate.)

Land reform was carried out in March and April of 1946, by first confiscating some 2 and a half million acres of land, and then distributing some
98 percent of this acreage as private property to individual peasant households. It cannot be doubted that this measure, completed in about one
month, brought much of the indigent peasantry to the side of the regime.[13]
As to industry, by August, 1946, some 90 percent of the major industry of
the country had been nationalized. The presence of the Soviet Army in
North Korea, while these basic measures were being carried out, no doubt
guaranteed their implementation. Mr. Robert T. Oliver asserts that between
1905 and 1945 300,000 Koreans fled from Korea to Siberia, and were there
converted to communism by the Russians. Another 2 million Koreans are
alleged to have fled to Manchuria and North China. If it is assumed that the
majority of these Korean exiles returned to North Korea in the wake of
the Soviet Army of occupation, they must have supplied an ample reservoir
of communist cadres for the communization of North Korea.[14] By No-

[12] It is likely that Major General Romanenko, the Soviet political officer during the
Russian occupation of North Korea, participated in the decisions affecting party politics.
According to Kim Chang-sun, who attended the merger conference, Kim Il Sung was
first nominated and eulogized, causing some suspicion and misgivings among New
People's Party delegates that they were being used by Kim Il Sung's Kapsan faction. A
Soviet's officer, acting as an observer at the meeting, then called for a recess, Kim Il Sung
himself nominated Kim Tu-bong for the chairmanship thus effecting enthusiasm and
mutual confidence in the ranks of the newly formed NKWP.

[13] Collectivization, which might have aroused opposition if pressed at this point, was
not initiated until seven years later.

[14] Robert T. Oliver, *Why War Came in Korea* (New York, Fordham University
Press, 1950), p. 5. Oliver also mentions that the so-called People's Militia of more than
200,000 men was drawn from this group and equipped with tanks, artillery and planes.
More than half of the militiamen were seasoned veterans of the guerilla war against the
Chinese Nationalist troops.

vember, 1946, elections for the local people's committees were held. The deputies chosen in these elections in February, 1947, formed the North Korean People's Assembly (NKPA), chaired by Kim Tu-bong. Candidates in these elections were endorsed by a united-front organization called the United Democratic National Front formed shortly before the merger of the New People's Party and the North Korean Communist Party into the NKWP. Two other parties participating in the elections were the Democratic Party of North Korea (originally led by Cho Man-sik) said to have had a membership of some 30,000, and the Chundogyo Chungwoo Party (the Party of Young Friends of Chundogyo, a religious group) with some 200,000 members, led by Kim Tal Hyon. Both of these parties had been deprived of their original leadership by the communists and did not really have meaningful influence in the political process, though they were represented in the Assembly and the government. The United Democratic National Front (UDNF) which endorsed candidates for election, on the other hand, embraced all political parties and organizations in North Korea (with a collective membership of five million in 1946) but was controlled by the NKWP. The mass organizations represented in the UDNF included: The General Federation of Trade Unions of Korea, the Democratic Youth League, the Women's Democratic Union, their counterparts in South Korea, and many smaller social organizations. In the elections, the candidates endorsed by the UDNF (renamed the United Democratic Fatherland Front in June, 1949) are almost always elected.[15]

On February 21, 1947, the North Korean People's Assembly (NKPA) elected a North Korean People's Committee, and its Chairman Kim Il Sung. This Committee proceeded to implement the blueprint for making North Korea a socialist state. The measures undertaken were labeled "the creation and consolidation of the revolutionary democratic base in the North," and in addition to the aforementioned land reform and nationalization of industry included such measures as currency reform, introduction of social insurance, the proclamation of the equality of the sexes, abolition of child labor, and the nationalization of transportation, communication and banking. A national economic plan for 1947 was also adopted.[16]

In November, 1947, a committee headed by Kim Tu-bong was entrusted with the task of drafting a constitution.[17] As had happened in the

[15] Similar to voting in other People's Democracies," 99.85 percent of the eligible voters voted; 86 percent voted for UDNF candidates. The NKPA had 237 members of whom 88 were NKWP members, 30 each belonged to the Democratic and Chundogyo Parties, and 89 were non-Party members.

[16] The question might arise as to just how popular the Kim regime was during the pre-Korean War years. One answer is that between October, 1945, and April, 1948, 800,000 Koreans fled to South Korea, so that almost 16.5 percent of the North Korean electorate voted with their feet against the Kim regime. While no precise statistics are available, as many as 250,000 of this refugee group could conceivably have been Christians.

[17] By the Third Session of the NKPA, held on November 18, 1947.

Soviet Union twelve years earlier the completed draft was circulated among the people and "widely discussed." [18] In April, 1948, the revised draft was approved by the NKPA with the proviso that it be subsequently endorsed by the nascent Supreme People's Assembly (SPA). The new constitution and flag were publicly announced in North Korea on May 1, 1948, and it was then disclosed that elections were to be held on August 25, for the new SPA in both North and South Korea. It is not entirely clear whether these elections, which were against the law in South Korea and thus had to be conducted in secret, were ever actually held. The North Korean government claims that they were indeed held "indirectly," and that 77.8 percent of the South Korean electorate had endorsed candidates. (A total of 8.68 million people are said to have voted. In the elections sponsored and "encouraged" by the South Korean government three months earlier, only about 8 million people had voted.) From August 22 to August 24, 1948, 1002 delegates met in Haeju, North Korea, and selected 360 deputies to represent South Korea in the SPA. With the addition of 212 deputies from North Korea the SPA reached a total membership of 572 deputies.[19] At its first session (on September 8, 1948) the SPA unanimously adopted the constitution. On the next day, September 9, the Democratic People's Republic of Korea (DPRK) was officially proclaimed. To no one's surprise, Kim Il Sung became Prime Minister and thus head of the government, a position he has retained ever since. Kim Tu-bong became chairman of the Standing Committee of the SPA. The first country to recognize the DPRK was the Soviet Union, which did so on October 13, 1948. The remaining communist countries soon followed suit—China in October, 1949, shortly after the establishment of the Chinese People's Republic. The DPRK has since then and as of mid-1966 also established embassies in Algeria, Cuba, Guinea, Mali, Yemen, Uganda, UAR, Indonesia, Cambodia, Mauretania, Congo (B), Ghana, and Tanzania and maintains consulates in Rangoon, Colombo, and New Delhi. While in the area of official diplomatic contacts the DPRK thus remains relatively isolated, she has cultivated contacts with some seventy countries by other means, such as the exchange of visiting delegations, trade relations, her membership in various communist-fronting international organizations and her attendance at international conferences. Professor Scalapino points out that the DPRK apparently values her relations with the U.S.S.R., China, East Germany, North Vietnam, and Albania most highly since her ambassadors in these countries are all members of the Central Committee of the KWP.[20]

Since the Korean People's Army, which had been inaugurated on

18 58,000 resolutions of approval, and 2,238 suggestions for revision or supplementation were received by the Committee.

19 George M. McCune, *Korea Today* (Cambridge, Mass., Harvard University Press, 1950), pp. 246-247.

20 R. A. Scalapino, "The Foreign Policy of North Korea," *China Quarterly*, No. 14 (Spring, 1963), p. 33.

February 8, 1948, was an apparently adequate military force for the purposes of the regime, the Soviet troops could now be withdrawn, the last units departing at the end of December, 1948.[21] On March 17, 1949, the DPRK signed a ten-year agreement on economic and cultural cooperation with the Soviet Union. The agreement spoke of an "exchange of experience" in the fields of industry and agricultural production, and of "the dispatch of specialists, the rendering of technical assistance, and other methods." Certainly, the principal beneficiary in these exchanges was the DPRK. Soviet aid to the DPRK between July, 1949, and July, 1952, is said to have been in the neighborhood of 212 million rubles.[22] The most important North Korean political event of 1949 was the final consolidation of communist groups in the country by the merger of the NKWP and the South Korean Worker's Party led by Pak Hon Yong. The merger was accomplished in June, 1949, the new party being named The Korean Worker's Party (KWP), with Kim Il Sung as Chairman. Pak Hon Yong, who at an earlier stage had had hopes of becoming leader of the Korean communist movement, had to flee from South Korea to North Korea in 1948. By summer of 1949, however, Pak was forced to subordinate himself to the master-schemer Kim Il Sung. Pak thus accepted the posts of Vice Premier, Foreign Minister, and Vice-Chairman of the KWP. Less than six years later, Kim had him executed. Another of the new Vice-Chairmen, Ho Kai of the Soviet Faction, wound up committing suicide within two years. Finally Kim Tu-bong, who had been chairman of the NKWP, achieved no prominent position in the new KWP, though he became chairman of the Presidium of the SPA. By 1956, he too was to disappear totally from the North Korean political scene. (See Table I.)

Kim Il Sung had indeed been a busy man in the four years following the arrival of the Russian troops. He had succeeded in bringing all communist factions under one organizational roof, the KWP, in making himself the head of that party, and in organizing local communities into an electorate which approved the constitution, established the legislature, and made him the head of a newly founded state. Kim was now in control of the party, the government, and the armed forces and was well prepared to defeat subsequent attempts to remove him from his position of absolute power. His position has thus in most respects been similar to that of Joseph Stalin, who had held the corresponding positions in the Soviet Union during his lifetime.

The new constitution of the DPRK, adopted in September, 1948, is in its broad outlines similar to the Soviet constitution. It calls the republic "a state of People's democratic dictatorship" based on the worker-peasant alliance, under the leadership of the working class, with the SPA and the

---

[21] The DPRK was founded twenty-four days after the Republic of Korea (ROK; South Korea) which was recognized by the U.N. General Assembly as the only legal government of Korea on December 12, 1948. American recognition of the ROK came in January, 1949, and U.S. occupation forces were withdrawn in June, 1949.

[22] John N. Washburn, "Soviet Russia and the Korean Communist Party," in *Pacific Affairs*, Vol. XXIII, No. 1 (March, 1950), p. 64.

local people's assemblies exercising state power. Democratic centralism is the guiding organizational principle. There is universal, equal, and direct suffrage by secret ballot for all citizens who have reached the age of eighteen. The KWP, led by Comrade Kim Il Sung, is seen as the leading and guiding force of the society, constituting the vanguard of the working masses. The SPA is officially the highest organ of state power, in that it legislates, approves the budget, elects its own presidium, forms the cabinet, elects the Supreme Court, and has a supreme supervisory function. When the SPA is not in session its broad powers are exercised by the presidium. The cabinet, being the chief executive organ, consists of a premier, vice-premiers, ministers, and the chairmen of committees, its decisions being reached by a majority vote. An inner cabinet consists of the premier and vice-premiers.[23]

In 1949 the DPRK began an energetic political offensive for the re-unification of Korea. A declaration issued at the founding of the United Democratic Fatherland Front (UDFF) in June, 1949, demanded: the peaceful reunification of Korea, the withdrawal of the U.S. Army of occupation from South Korea, and the formation of a government of national unity by a nationwide general election. The "traitor clique" of Synghman Rhee was to be excluded from this process. The UDFF continued its efforts to topple the Rhee regime by conspiring with Rhee's enemies in South Korea until the weeks just preceding the outbreak of the Korean war. An embarrassing incident for the DPRK occurred when two representatives of the UDFF traveled to Seoul on June 11, 1950, to establish contact with South Korean politicians, but were immediately arrested and then publicly declared their defection to the Rhee regime. On June 20th the DPRK government once again proposed reunification, insisting, however, that President Rhee and his group be arrested. Five days later the Korean war broke out. While both sides maintained that "the other side" had planned and begun the attack, the course of the war clearly indicated that the DPRK was far more adequately prepared for the conduct of a military campaign. Without further reference to the course of the war, it should be noted only that the hostilities ended with a cease-fire three years later, on July 27, 1953. An attempt made at the Geneva conference (Spring, 1954) to solve the reunification problem peacefully failed, as have all efforts since that time, principally because the DPRK has refused to recognize the competence of the U.N. to supervise elections and other political processes in Korea.

In a study of the Korean war published in 1960, Dr. Allen S. Whiting[24]

---

[23] *The Democratic People's Republic of Korea* (Pyongyang, Foreign Languages Publishing House, 1958), pp. 141-159.

[24] At the time the study was made, Whiting was a senior researcher at the Rand Corporation investigating the Chinese involvement in the Korean war. (From 1961 to 1966 Whiting was director of the Office of Intelligence and Research, Far East, U.S. Department of State.) His research, eventually published as Allen S. Whiting, *China Crosses the Yalu* (New York, Macmillan, 1960), *see esp.* pp. 37-46, was the first evidence anywhere that the general assumption of China's responsibility for the Korean war was subject to challenge. Most responsible scholars in the field today accept Whiting's general thesis of the involvement of Stalin's Russia.

contends that in 1948 the DPRK was a Soviet satellite in the full sense of the expression. The influence of Stalin's Russia supposedly increased steadily between 1945 and 1949 to the detriment of the Korean groups oriented toward Peking. Whiting maintains that the Soviet Union planned the Korean war on the mistaken assumption (for which there was, however, positive evidence at the time) that the U.S. would not intervene. Yet, in spite of the Soviet influence, the DPRK remained within the sphere of interest of Communist China. Whiting points out that the leading personalities in the DPRK government were Soviet citizens of Korean origin, that there were Soviet advisers in all branches of Korea's government, and that vital sectors of the economy of the DPRK were under direct Soviet control through Soviet-Korean joint stock companies. Whiting further suspects that simultaneously with the economic agreements of March 17, 1949, a secret military aid agreement was concluded. The DPRK army was completely trained and equipped by the Soviet Union—the invasion of South Korea occurring two months after significant deliveries of Soviet tanks, trucks, and artillery pieces. By contrast, the initial relations between the DPRK and the CPR [25] were not nearly so close and, because of some minor disputes, not always harmonious. Though the CPR recognized the DPRK in October, 1949, it was August, 1950, before a Chinese Ambassador was posted in Pyongyang. He disappeared again after a few months, and the CPR was then represented by a chargé d'affaires until 1955. Whiting notes that between 1949 and 1950, 12,000 Korean soldiers (the so-called 164th Division of the People's Liberation Army) were transferred from Manchuria to Korea, but does not feel that this proves Chinese participation in the planning of the Korean war. However, since Mao Tse-tung was on an extended visit to Moscow (from December, 1949 to March, 1950) it is likely that Stalin told him of Russian plans for the "liberation" of South Korea. The fact that General Lin Piao's Fourth Field Army was transferred from South China to Manchuria between May and June of 1950 underlines this possibility.

That a North Korean victory would have been a boon to China cannot be doubted, even if China herself was too much preoccupied with other problems in the summer of 1950 to have originated this particular adventure. Actual Chinese intervention did not occur until mid-October, 1950, after U.S. forces had crossed the 38th parallel and deeply penetrated into North Korea, in spite of Chou En-lai's warning that China would intervene in that event. The intervention of the Chinese People's Volunteers (CPV) marked the beginning of a significant increase in Chinese influence in the DPRK. In the official Pyongyang chronicle of these events it says:

It will eternally be remembered, that in the most difficult times for our country, the Chinese people sent the People's Volunteers, composed of the sons and daughters of China, to help our people with their own blood. When the

25 Chinese People's Republic. [EDITOR'S NOTE]

Chinese People's Volunteers on October 25, 1950, arrived at the Korean front under the banner of: "Resist the USA, Aid Korea, Protect your homes, and Defend the fatherland," this caused a basic change of the power relations between the enemy and ourselves, and reversed the situation in our favor.[26]

Between October and November, 1950, more than 300,000 CPV crossed the Yalu river, saved the DPRK from military collapse, and gradually drove the U.N. forces back to the vicinity of the 38th parallel.

A former Polish military Attaché in the DPRK, Colonel Pawel Monat, who defected to the U.S. in 1959, has given an interesting and believable account of the war years in the DPRK. Monat reports that the Chinese officers in the DPRK trusted no one, including the Soviet Russians who controlled the DPRK army. Most Soviet soldiers and advisors in the DPRK were wearing the uniform of the CPV. The Soviet Ambassador to the DPRK, Lt. General Vladimir N. Razuvayev, was supposedly the real boss in the DPRK rather than the obese and lethargic Kim Il Sung who was merely a front man for the Russians. All military orders were drafted in Russian and had to be signed by a Soviet officer before they went into effect. Nevertheless, the pretense of DPRK independence was carefully maintained, and no Soviet officer ever publicly gave an order. The fairy tale that the South Korean forces had attacked first was also officially maintained by telling the troops in each sector that the South Koreans had begun their attack in another sector. Soviet Staff Officers told Colonel Monat that Marshal Stalin had personally given the order for the attack. The two highest General Staff Officers of the DPRK, Chief of Staff General Nam Il and his deputy, Lt. General Kim Kwang Hyop had both been Soviet citizens and spent most of their life in the Soviet Union. Dr. Whiting's hypotheses and Colonel Monat's report are in agreement almost word for word on the events leading to the Chinese intervention. Monat estimates the Chinese troops in Korea at almost one million men who took over 130 miles of a 155-mile front. A joint General Staff of the Chinese and Korean forces was effective only because when differences arose the North Koreans usually gave in to the Chinese. When Soviet officers tried to visit the Chinese sectors or to "advise" Chinese commanders they were politely but unmistakably rebuffed. The fiction that the Chinese troops were "volunteers" was maintained by asking them in Manchuria to volunteer for duty in Korea, and then exchanging the PLA insignia for new "Chinese People's Volunteer" insignia. Colonel Monat reports that the Chinese troops were more popular among the Koreans than the Russian troops had been (1945-48) and at times even than the North Korean troops, because they were considerate in their treatment of the people, brought their own food supplies, and upon occasion helped the peasants with the harvest and shared their rations with the starving population. Russian and North Korean troops on the contrary had been

[26] *The Democratic People's Republic of Korea, op. cit.,* p. 100.

known for carrying off everything that was edible or valuable and for violating the women and girls.[27] Thus while the Chinese troops were establishing good relations with the Korean people, the relations between the Chinese generals and the Soviet-dominated North Korean leaders were less cordial. The revival of Chinese influence in the DPRK may thus be said to have begun among the general population rather than within the pro-Soviet leadership group.

The Korean cease-fire negotiations began in June, 1951, and dragged on in endless argumentation about the prisoner exchange and the interzonal boundary until July 27, 1953, when the armistice was signed. North Korean propaganda now proclaimed:

The just war for the liberation of the fatherland thus ended with a historic victory for the Korean people after the bloodshed had lasted three years and one month. The correct policy and wise leadership of the CC [28] of the KWP, led by Kim Il Sung, was a decisive factor enabling the people to accomplish miracles. The power of the people united around the Party, the organizer and originator of all victories, and defeated the armed American aggressors. After the war the Korean people confidently embarked upon the road of a great struggle for the peaceful reunification of Korea with the same determined spirit which had repulsed the enemy and won the war.[29]

The fact that the DPRK had failed in its attempt to absorb the Republic of Korea and had been devastated and decimated in the process, was not mentioned.

THE POSTWAR RECONSTRUCTION OF THE DPRK

The war, and particularly the constant U.S. air attacks had reduced the cities and the industry of the DPRK to ruins and ashes. Since the U.S.A. and the UN could be expected to make efforts for the economic reconstruction of South Korea, a great material and technical effort was now indicated to make the DPRK a successful economic and political competitor with South Korea. This became an objective of great political importance for the entire Soviet bloc.

On September 1, 1953, Marshal Kim Il Sung led a mission to Moscow. It was later announced that the Soviet Union was granting the DPRK one billion rubles' worth of outright financial aid. On November 10, 1953, Kim

---

[27] Colonel Pawel Monat and John Kille, "Russians in Korea, the Hidden Bosses," *Life,* Vol. 48, No. 25 (June 27, 1960), pp. 76-102.

[28] Central Committee. [EDITOR'S NOTE]

[29] *The Democratic People's Republic of Korea, op. cit.,* pp. 107-08; and Pak Yun Baik, *The Struggle of Korean People for Peaceful Unification of the Country* (Pyongyang, Foreign Languages Publishing House, 1959), p. 43.

proceeded to Peking and there obtained a promise of 800 million yuan[30] of outright aid. Thus the war continued after the cease-fire, in the sphere of economic competition.

The DPRK proclaimed the years 1954-56 to be a three-year period for the rehabilitation and development of the economy. The following official figures may give some idea of the degree of damage suffered by the DPRK during the war years:

8700 factories destroyed
Industrial production down to 64 percent of 1949
Electric power generation down to 26 percent
Fuel production down to 11 percent
Metal production down to 10 percent
Chemical products down to 22 percent

The production facilities for iron ore, pig iron, lead, motors, transformers, cement, soda, carbide, coking coal, chemical fertilizer, and copper were totally destroyed. In agriculture 250,000 cattle and 380,000 swine were lost. The transportation system was almost totally destroyed and 28 million square meters of dwellings were leveled (75 percent of state owned flats, 5000 schools, 1000 hospitals and clinics, 260 theatres, etc.). Total damage was estimated at 420 billion won.[31]

Reconstruction was to be accomplished in three stages. Six months to a year would be required for cleanup, removal of the rubble, and the creation of the initial prerequisites for reconstruction. The three-year plan 1954-56 was to restore the economy to the prewar level of 1949. A subsequent five-year plan (1957-61) was to create the preconditions for the socialist industrialization of the DPRK. Priority was given to heavy industry and particularly the machine-building industry. Light industry and agriculture came second and third respectively.[32] In April, 1956, at the Third Congress of the KWP, Kim Il Sung announced that the goals of the three-year plan were already being achieved and that most industrial targets would be reached by mid-1956. The countries of the Soviet bloc were major contributors in the reconstruction of the DPRK. The Soviet Union and the CPR led the way in factory construction and the rehabilitation of transportation facilities such as bridges and rolling stock, and East Germany undertook the rebuilding of the totally destroyed city of Hamhung. The other Soviet satellites in East Europe and the Mongolian People's Republic also made similar contributions. See Table 15-2.

[30] At the exchange rate officially decreed in Peking, one U.S. dollar will bring 2.367 (Communist) Chinese yuans (*1966 Shin-Chugoku Nen-Kan,* Chugoku, Kenkyujo, Tokyo, 1966). The purchasing power of the yuan in China is probably considerably higher than indicated by this exchange rate.

[31] One yuan (*see* footnote 30 above) equals 1.05 won.

[32] *Postwar Reconstruction and Development of the National Economy of the Democratic People's Republic of Korea* (Pyongyang, Foreign Languages Publishing House, 1957), pp. 8-9.

Table 15-2. Soviet Bloc Grants-in-Aid to the DPRK (Nonrepayable) (After end of Korean War—in millions of rubles,[33] unless otherwise stated)

U.S.S.R.	1,300	Bulgaria	13
CPR	820	Czechoslovakia	11
Poland	45	Rumania	11
East Germany	17	Outer Mongolia	23,000 sheep
Hungary	15	Albania	2,800 tons of fish [a]

[a] Kiesewetter, *Der Ostblock—Aussenhandel,* p. 302.

Agricultural production did not suffer as much from the war as industry, and since then it has increased slowly but steadily. The DPRK government now claims that the food problem has been "solved" and it has even been offering to export food grains to South Korea as "aid." Agriculture in the DPRK is now completely "socialized," that is, organized in what they call "co-operatives." These co-operatives are actually somewhat like the Soviet collectives, in that the collective farmers are permitted to retain small private plots, fruit trees, and some cattle for their own use. The word "commune" is not used in the DPRK, but Professor Chong-sik Lee holds the view that the DPRK co-operatives are not operated very differently from the Chinese communes.[34] The agricultural cooperation movement started in 1953 and quickly proceeded through three stages (1) mutual aid teams (2) semi-socialist co-operatives (3) socialist co-operatives (collectives). By August, 1958, *all* farms in the DPRK had advanced to the third (collective) stage and what had been as many as 16,000 co-operatives was consolidated into only 3,843 co-operatives. In these co-operatives, the farmers receive salaries based solely on the work they perform. Partly due to the large-scale defections to South Korea, there is a continuing shortage of both industrial and farm labor in the DPRK. Along with "co-operativization" the DPRK government initiated the construction of "agro-cities" designed to organize the rural population residentially and socially like industrial workers. This is supposed to advance the march toward communism by eliminating the differences between the cities and the countryside and speeding the arrival of a one-class society. It should be noted here that as of 1960 only 44 percent of the DPRK population was classified as "farmers," while 52 percent were workers and office employees.[35] There is no doubt that in these and other economic and political measures and policies the DPRK is largely following the example of the CPR, though Kim Il Sung has carefully avoided the use of such

[33] These are old rubles. The "new ruble" introduced in January, 1961, is exchanged in the Soviet Union at the official exchange rate of 1 ruble equal to $1.11. The old ruble, at the official exchange rate was worth 25¢, but the tourist rate of 10¢ per ruble was probably more realistic in terms of purchasing power comparisons. [EDITOR'S NOTE]

[34] Chong-sik Lee, "The Socialist Revolution in the North Korean Countryside," in *Asian Survey,* Vol. II, No. 8 (October, 1962), pp. 9-22.

[35] *Ibid.,* p. 12.

words as "communes," and has not imitated those measures which have failed in China. China's so-called "Great Leap Forward"[36] can be cited as an example. This term was first used in the CPR in February, 1958. In June, 1958, Kim Il Sung spoke of "a giant step forward" and added that in the DPRK "all workers strode forward toward socialism on a flying horse (Chullima, the Pegasus of Korea)." Thus, in terms of propaganda slogans the DPRK frequently follows the lead of the CPR. The "Chullima" concept became the symbol of dramatic production increases with model workers forming "Chullima Production Teams" in the tradition of the Soviet Stakhanovites.[37] Yet, most of the mistakes of China's "Great Leap Forward" (such as the disastrous backyard furnace movement) were avoided by Pyongyang. The DPRK was more successful in the industrial sector and was spared most of the disasters in the agricultural sector by luck, perhaps, as well as by planning. After years of emphasis on heavy industry alone, Kim Il Sung, at the outset of the present seven-year plan (1961-67), shifted emphasis in an attempt to balance investments in heavy industry, light industry, consumer goods, public facilities, and agriculture, thus correcting the shortcomings of the economy created by the previous imbalances. It is thus a mistake to conclude from certain superficial evidences that Pyongyang is a slavish satellite of the Peking regime in economics or politics.

Pyongyang is emphatically independent, autonomous, and increasingly keeping her own counsel no matter what Peking or Moscow says. She is helped in this by her insistence upon economic self-sufficiency for the DPRK. Kim Il Sung stressed the importance of remaining free from dependence upon either Soviet or Chinese technical, material, or financial aid. This was done in clear defiance of Khrushchev's desire to encourage economic specialization and a "division of labor" in the socialist camp. In the early 60's U.S.S.R.-DPRK trade has actually been almost precisely in balance, amounting to an average of approximately 80 million dollars per annum each way. Outside of the bloc, the DPRK's most significant trading partner is Japan (doing 9, 16, and 30 million dollars' worth of business with the DPRK in 1962, 1963, and 1964 respectively), though Japan has not recognized the DPRK regime and is unlikely to do so at this stage. The DPRK has apparently been able to keep her food problem under control both by increasing domestic production and importing the remainder of what she needs, thereby maintaining a tolerable if not generous standard of living. It is nevertheless suspected that the officially claimed grain output figures (5 million tons) are inflated by more than a million tons in excess of actual production. Many of the official goals of the seven-year plan (e.g., 6.6 million tons of grain, 4.5 million tons of cement, 2.3 million tons of steel, etc., by 1967) may be totally unrealistic and impossible of achievement, yet it

---

[36] *See* pp. 173-176 above. [EDITOR'S NOTE]

[37] The title "Stakhanovite worker" is no longer bestowed in the Soviet Union; it has been replaced by the title "Hero of Labor." [EDITOR'S NOTE]

cannot be denied that continuing steady progress is being made. Eventual expansion of trade with the West may provide the DPRK's chance to improve her general economic condition.[38]

In the political sphere there is unmistakably a continuing struggle between Moscow and Peking for predominant influence in Pyongyang. On the surface Peking appears to be dominant, but during 1965 there were increasing signs of the reestablishment of a balance, with a high-ranking Soviet delegation headed by Alexander Shelepin arriving in Pyongyang in August to celebrate the 20th anniversary of Korea's liberation from Japan by Soviet troops. Kosygin has since then also made appearances in Pyongyang and neither Kosygin nor Brezhnev have been singled out by the DPRK press for the kind of critical comments made in reference to Khrushchev during the last years of his rule. The signing by Kim Il Sung within one week (on July 6th and 11th of 1961) of identical mutual military assistance treaties with both the Soviet Union and the CPR indicated, even then, Kim Il Sung's tendency to hedge on the matter of alignment in the dispute.

Pyongyang's desire to be dissociated from alignment with Peking was clearly indicated in the summer of 1966 when the DPRK regime published an editorial in its official newspaper Rodong Shinmoon stating that it did not wish to follow the line of any other communist party and would not tolerate interference in the internal affairs of the DPRK by any other communist party. While neither China nor the Soviet Union was specifically mentioned, it was clear that the editorial was a declaration of independence from Chinese political interference.

The 1961 treaties with the Soviet Union and the CPR assured the DPRK that an attack on either signatory was an attack on both and that the signatories would strive for the unification of Korea along peaceful and democratic lines. The DPRK has indeed attempted, in recent years, to broach the matter of reunification in propaganda campaigns beamed across the 38th parallel. The DPRK proposals ranged from exchanges of newspapermen and other delegations, the lifting of the North-South travel ban, and the institution of a North-South postal service, to preparatory discussions on federation and eventual reunification. The first precondition in these approaches has always been the withdrawal of U.S. troops from South Korea, and the abrogation of South Korea's treaty with the U.S. Eventually nationwide elections are suggested which would presumably reunify Korea under the leadership of Kim Il Sung. Most recently, the signing of the South Korean-Japanese normalization treaty and the dispatch of South Korean troops to Vietnam have been most violently condemned in the DPRK press. Because of the continuing confused conditions in South Korea both in the economic and political realms, the efficacy of such DPRK propa-

[38] J. A. Kim, "The 'Peak of Socialism' in North Korea: The Five- and Seven-Year Plans," in *Asian Survey*, Vol. V, No. 5 (May, 1965), pp. 255-269.

ganda appeals to some South Koreans should not be underestimated. An illustration of the DPRK's appeal to the 600,000 Koreans still living in Japan
is rendered by the fact that by 1965 83,000 Korean residents in Japan had
voluntarily chosen to be repatriated to the DPRK (and had indeed gone to
North Korea) despite the fact (says Pyongyang), that 94 percent of the
voluntary repatriates were originally from South Korea. Few, if any of the
Korean residents in Japan (and in the United States for that matter) wish
to go to South Korea. Whether Pyongyang can ever succeed in her scheme
to reunify Korea under the hammer and sickle may largely depend upon
the degree of success achieved by the U.S. supported South Korean governments in meeting the economic and nationalistic aspirations of the majority
of South Korea's population.[39] As Kim Il Sung likes to say: "South Korea belongs to the Americans, but North Korea belongs to the Koreans." The appeal of such ideas is relevant both to Vietnam and Korea and makes for
frighteningly similar American dilemmas in the two divided Asian nations.

FURTHER READING SUGGESTIONS

PERIODICALS: *
*Korea, Korea Today, Asian Survey, Pacific Affairs, Far Eastern Survey,
The China Quarterly, Peking Review, Far Eastern Economic Review,
Journal of Asian Studies.*

BOOKS:
Barnett, A. Doak, ed., *Communist Strategies in Asia.* New York: Praeger,
1963.
Bromke, Adam, ed., *The Communist States at the Crossroads.* New York:
Praeger, 1965.
Chung, Kyung Cho, *Korea Tomorrow.* New York: Macmillan, 1956.
Democratic People's Republic of Korea. Pyongyang: FLPH, 1958.

[39] The first Seven-Year Plan (1961-67) was extended in 1966 to run for another
three years, possibly indicating that the rate of economic development in the DPRK
was slowing down. In the political sphere, Kim Il Sung and his Kapsan faction firmly
established their complete political dominance in the DPRK in October, 1966, with
the establishment of a six-man "Presidium of the Politburo" of the KWP. (Glenn
D. Paige, "1966: Korea Creates the Future," *Asian Survey,* Vol. VII, No. 1, p. 29.)
The new Presidium excluded members of other factions, such as Vice Premier and
ex-Foreign minister Nam Il (Soviet faction) and the Vice Chairman of the Central
Committee and ex-1st Vice Premier Yi Chong Ok, both of whom had belonged to the
eleven-member Political Committee which was previously the center of power.
  * Periodical articles are cited in footnotes.

Department of State, *North Korea: A Case Study in the Techniques of Takeover*. Washington, D.C.: 1961.

Joy, C. Turner, *How Communists Negotiate*. New York: Macmillan, 1955.

McCune, George M., *Korea Today*. Cambridge, Mass.: Harvard University Press, 1950.

Paige, Glenn D., *The Korean People's Democratic Republic*. Stanford, Calif.: The Hoover Institution, 1967.

Rudolph, Philip, *North Korea's Political and Economic Structure*. New York: I.P.R., 1959.

Scalapino, R. A., *North Korea Today*. New York: Praeger, 1963.

————, ed., *The Communist Revolution in Asia*. Englewood Cliffs, N.J.: Prentice-Hall, 1965.

Whiting, Allen S., *China Crosses the Yalu*. New York: Macmillan, 1960.

16

Socialist Korea:

A Korean Marxist View

JANG WOO TAI

A DIRECTOR OF THE KDR'S MINISTRY
OF COMMON EDUCATION

KIM SUK DOO

ASSISTANT MANAGER,
PYONGYANG SILK MILL

PAK YUNG RYONG

VICE CHAIRMAN,
KANGSU COUNTY PEOPLE'S COMMITTEE,
SOUTH PYUNGAN PROVINCE

AND OTHERS *

Twenty years have passed since the country's liberation from the half-century long Japanese colonial rule.

Of course, twenty years is not a long time seen against the background of human history. During this period, however, much happened in Korea. The three-year long war which the U.S. imperialists unleashed, played havoc with the country. When hostilities ended in Korea, the whole country lay in waste. . . .

Half of our country has been reduced to an American colony, and we are confronted with a situation in which we foresee a prolonged and arduous struggle against the U.S. imperialists.

Under the circmustances, we had to lay a firm economic foundation in the shortest time possible so as to put an end to the economic onesidedness

* The introductory paragraphs and the first four sections have been put together from sections of three articles, i.e., "Self Reliance" (no author given), *Korea Today* (August, 1965), pp. 4-9; Jung Ha Chul, "Independent National Economy and National Identity," *Korea Today* (November, 1965), pp. 2-5; and Hong Choon Keun, "Fruition of Self Reliance," *Democratic People's Republic of Korea* (May, 1966), pp. 10-15. Parts of another article, "More Machines in the Countryside" (no author given), *Korea Today* (November, 1965), pp. 12-13 have been incorporated in section 3. In sections 5 to 9, separate footnote references are given to enable the reader to identify the authors and the original source of publication of each section.

and backwardness inherited from the old society, stabilize and enhance the people's living deteriorated by the war, and build an independent, united country, prosperous and strong.

An independent national economy presented itself as a life-and-death question for the country. The destiny of the country and the rise or fall of the Korean revolution hinged on it. . . .

Our country was economically backward and was short of trained personnel in the past. On top of it, we had little experience in building an economy. Under the circumstances, it was by no means easy for the country to build an independent national economy.

However, the Korean people have devotedly worked to this end. They wanted no repetition of the bitter past—the humiliating past when they were suppressed by foreign aggressors because they were backward and weak. They wanted to become a civilized nation independent and powerful. They wanted to become a nation that can stand proudly on the same footing with all nations of the world.

The building of an independent national economy began in real earnest, when hostilities ended, when the subjective and objective conditions matured.

HEAVY INDUSTRY, THE BASIS OF AN INDEPENDENT ECONOMY

Priority development of heavy industry and simultaneous growth of light industry and agriculture was taken as the basic line of the country's economic construction. It was a correct line most suitable to the situation. . . .

Heavy industry plays a leading role in the building of any independent national economy and machine-building industry is the core of heavy industry. Our heavy industry was in a backward state, especially so the machine-building industry.

Before liberation, there was not a single machine-building plant worth mentioning. Few insignificant machine-repair shops were all there was. . . . But by 1964 the country supplied 94.3 percent of all the machines it needed. Moreover, quite a few of our machines and equipment are now going abroad.

Today, Korea's heavy industry, with the machine-building industry as its core, has become a reliable foundation of the independent national economy.

LIGHT INDUSTRY

Thanks to the powerful heavy industry there have also been radical changes in light industry. . . .

Light industry has laid its own solid material and technical foundations; more machines for light industry were turned out and solid raw material bases were built.

Today, our textile mills are equipped with Korea-made "Chullima" looms. Moreover, cotton gins, spinning machines, and thread-making machines are turned out at the Pyongyang, Sinuijoo, and Sariwon textile-machine factories. The country counts more than 100 modern cotton, woolen, and silk mills in the northern part of the country, which had only one textile mill in Pyongyang with 4,000 spindles before the country's liberation.

Now our country produces 195 times as many textile goods as in the pre-liberation year 1944. The figure means that it produces in two days as much fabrics as were turned out in a whole year before the liberation.

Mention must be made here of improving the quality of products. More woolen goods and silks are produced, and thread-twisted materials make up a big portion of our cotton goods. The textile industry, which was most conspicuous in its colonial one-sidedness, has completely got rid of its backwardness.

With the backing of the heavy industry, foodstuffs and daily necessities industries were expanded greatly. Meat-packing plants, fish canneries, corn starch factories, soy and bean paste factories and other foodstuffs factories were newly built or expanded.

But, the centrally controlled light industry factories alone cannot meet fully the daily growing demands of the people. Hence bold steps were taken to build locally run factories also. . . . The June 1958 Plenum of the Central Committee of the Workers' Party of Korea called for every city and county to erect and run local factories, and thus opened a new phase in the advancement of light industry.

In a short space of time a large number of local factories were erected without state investments. Now, local factories account for more than one-half of the total output of daily necessaries. . . .

Thanks to the ever expanding light industry all the department stores and shops in the country are stocked with goods produced in the country, and they are meeting the people's demands for daily necessities.

AGRICULTURE

After liberation, the most important problem in Korea, formerly a colonial, agricultural country with the peasantry making up the overwhelming majority of the population, was to put an end to the feudal land ownership. To this end, the land reform was enforced, under which only tillers were authorized to possess land. All land formerly owned by the Japanese imperialists and landlords was confiscated without compensation and distributed free of charge to the peasants.

It was no easy task to root out the centuries-long backwardness so firmly settled in the rural areas, build a large-scale, advanced rural economy, and turn the countryside into a food and industrial raw material supply centre. In particular, difficulties were added by the severe destruction of the countryside in the Korean war.

After the war, the state appropriated large sums for giant nature-remaking irrigation projects. Now the 800 kilometer-long canals of the Pyungnam Irrigation System water the Yuldoosamchunri Plain on the west coast, where once drought and flood were the annual events. Then water is pumped up 200 metres from the Ryesung River to the Miroo Plain in Sinkye—the place once termed as "unsuitable for human inhabitation."

The Korean peasants who had toiled and moiled with primitive farming tools for thousands of years, have been emancipated from labour-consuming work. Now modern farm machines work for them.

Today in the countryside are over 20,000 tractors (in terms of 15 h.p.) and some 25,000 electric motors. There is one tractor (in terms of 15 h.p.) for every 100 *jungbo* [1] of farm land on the average. Machines do everything —ploughing, land leveling, transport.

"Chullima" tractors which are mass produced in the country, do the ploughing and harrowing. They also level the fields.

In 1964 the total area ploughed by tractors had increased 18 times over 1956.

Now the co-op farm members use seeders, weeders, harvesters and other modern farm machines. And threshing is mostly done by machines. Mechanization has been introduced in stock farming, too. Hatching, fodder preparing, and transport are mechanized. The level of mechanization of transport is very high. Lorries, tractors, trailers and other machines are used in an extensive way. . . .

To supply more tractors, lorries, and other large-sized modern farm machines to the countryside the state newly built and expanded large-scale, up-to-date factories and plants. In addition to them, in every city and county medium- and small-sized farm implements plants are opened to turn out and repair medium and small farm machines and tools.

Today the country boasts of a dozen or so big-scale, Centre-controlled farm machine plants and some 200 locally run, medium- and small-sized farm implements plants. . . .

Chemical industry turns out every year hundreds of thousands of tons of fertilizer for the countryside, and various kinds of agricultural chemicals —insecticide, weedkillers, etc.

Electricity has driven the darkness of the preliberation days out of 95.5 percent of the villages and 81 percent of the peasant households. . . .

A large army of technicians have been trained and dispatched to the countryside for the all-round mechanization of farming.

The completion of agricultural co-operation and promotion of the

[1] One *jungbo* equals 2.45 acres. [EDITOR'S NOTE]

technical revolution have turned our agriculture, once feeble, backward, and leaning heavily on grain production, into a diversified one. It gives the nation ample food and industrial raw materials. And it keeps advancing. . . .

ECONOMIC GROWTH

Compared with the preliberation year of 1944 the gross value of industrial output in 1964 increased thirteen-fold, and the grain harvest doubled.

Between 1954 and 1963, after the war, industrial production grew annually at the rate of 34.8 percent. In the total value of industrial and agricultural output, industry accounted for 28 percent in 1946, but the figure stood at 75 percent last year (1964). . . .

During the past twenty years the Korean people have converted their country, a backward, colonial agricultural country, into an advanced industrial-agricultural one.

Now all our government offices, and economic and cultural activities are run by our own people, and the country turns out almost all the industrial goods and agricultural produce it needs. Thus, with the building of an independent economy, Korea has jealously guarded its sovereignty. It has established relations with a number of countries under the principles of equality and mutual benefit, supplementing each other's needs.

During the twenty years since liberation, the country has gone a long way towards satisfying the requirements of the working people for daily necessities with domestic products.

At present the country is in the midst of the Seven-Year Plan (1961-1967), the main tasks of which are an all-round technical reconstruction, a cultural revolution, and a radical betterment in the people's living standards.

When the plan is fulfilled, the country will become a socialist industrial state with a diversified, advanced independent national economy. Then the question of food, clothing, and housing will be solved yet more satisfactorily for the people.

THE FIGHT AGAINST ILLITERACY [1]

During the Japanese occupation of Korea, every obstacle was laid to setting up schools for Korean children. It was hard for the children of the ordinary people to have any kind of schooling. In the few schools that existed an out-and-out colonial enslavement education was enforced—even the use of the Korean language was barred.

[1] Condensed from Jang Woo Tai, A Director of the Ministry of Common Education, "The Fight Against Illiteracy" (answers given to readers' questions), *Korea Today* (December, 1965), pp. 14-15.

When the country was liberated in August 1945, 76 percent of the population in the age group between 12 and 50—2,300,000 people in all—were illiterate. This equalled 25 percent of the total population of North Korea. The percentage was particularly high among the workers and peasants, and almost the entire female population could neither read nor write.

It was under such circumstances that the Korean people embarked upon the road of building a new country. And this big undertaking demanded knowledge. Consequently, it was urgent, first of all, for the workers and peasants, the basic masses for building a new country, to cast aside illiteracy and acquire learning. Otherwise, we could make no advance. . . .

The fight against illiteracy and for setting up adult education was a very serious problem for the state, which called for a nation-wide movement.

In all parts of the country, from the capital down to villages, committees were set up to guide the fight against illiteracy. All the political parties and social organizations came out to aid actively this work.

In the first twelve months after liberation in August 1945 "teams to fight illiteracy" were set up in all factories, mines, and rural villages throughout the country. Korean-language schools were opened where people were taught to read and write, and able to study politics and democratic ideology. About 400,000 were taught at these schools, and over 320,000 cast aside illiteracy. To this end, thousands upon thousands of intellectuals, school teachers and especially students were mobilized.

Textbooks and school supplies were given by the state free of charge. All school equipment and furnishings were provided by the state or acquired through nation-wide campaigns.

The work of wiping out illiteracy kept on every year. Particularly in winter, about four months were specially designated for this purpose. In this way by the end of March 1949, illiteracy was practically wiped out in North Korea. However, the three-year long Korean war unleashed by U.S. imperialism in June, 1950, made it impossible for the country to continue the education program on a regular basis. As a result some people became illiterate again. Besides, illiteracy was quite rampant in those liberated areas, which had been under U.S. occupation and came to belong to North Korea after the war. The Government set up two-year-course adult schools for those people, and solved the problem.

EDUCATIONAL FACILITIES [2]

When liberated, the country felt keenly the shortage of trained personnel. Right after liberation the technicians in North Korea accounted for only 0.2 percent of the total number of employees!

[2] Condensed from "Self Reliance," *Korea Today* (August, 1965), p. 9.

Under the circumstances, the problem of national cadres was a most urgent and important one in building an independent national economy. To this end, measures were taken for making the existing intellectuals join actively in building a new society while sparing no effort for training new cadres. The state set up many institutes of higher learning and expanded various school networks. Now seven-year compulsory secondary schooling is in effect. In a few years the state will put into practice nine-year compulsory technical education. Today one-fourth of the population are studying at over 9,000 schools at all levels. The younger generation is equipped with theory and practice through the close combination of general and technical education and of education with productive labour. Besides, many working people study without leaving their jobs. Correspondence courses, factory colleges, communist institutes and other spare-time schools are run for the workers. Now, working people, who were denied education in the pre-liberation days, receive secondary and higher education while working.

As of the end of October of last year (1964) the number of technicians and experts in North Korea surpassed the mark of 290,000.

This great army of trained personnel of Korea ably runs all factories, mines, and offices.

LAND REFORM: COMRADE PAK YUNG RYONG'S PERSONAL RECOLLECTIONS [3]

When every spring comes around, I come to think of the days when land reform was carried out. It was twenty years ago, in March 1946 that the law on land reform was issued to materialize the centuries-old aspiration of the peasants of our country. What a joyful event it was for the country's peasants who knew so well what it meant not to have land.

In preliberation days, our peasants had suffered from cruel exploitation by the Japanese imperialists and landlords. In Borim Sub-county, Kangsu County, South Pyungan Province, my native place, too, the landowners had more than 90 percent of the total land and collected 70 to 80 percent of the harvests from the tenants. On top of it, the Japanese colonialists levied various kinds of taxes on the peasants. Though the peasants had toiled and moiled, the largest part of their harvests found its way into the barns of the landlords. Every year they were up to their ears in debt. . . .

For generations the farmers had wished to farm on their own land. Now at last their dreams came true, in March, 1946, the first year after liberation, when the land reform was carried out. . . .

[3] Condensed from Pak Yung Ryong, Vice-Chairman of the Kangsu County People's Committee, South Pyungan Province, "Recalling Land Reform," *Korea Today* (March, 1966), pp. 12 and 13.

Highlights of the law were as follows. All land of the Japanese and traitors will be taken away, land holdings of landlords in excess of 5 jungbo shall be confiscated. Land so confiscated shall be distributed to the peasants who had little or no land, and to hired hands. All confiscation and distribution shall be made without compensation, and the tenant system be abolished once and for all. Moreover, the law nullified all debts that the peasants owed to landlords and ordered confiscation of agricultural facilities that belonged to the Japanese, traitors, and landlords and distributed them to the farmers without compensation.

When the law on land reform was made public the whole village was seething with excitement and joy. In our sub-county a mass rally was held in support of the law, where a letter of thanks addressed to Marshal Kim Il Sung, the beloved leader of our people, was adopted on behalf of the entire people of the sub-county. . . .

When the farmers were given deeds to land, they were so overwhelmed that they were speechless, with tears in their eyes. Kim Ki Taik, one of my neighbours, who had been poverty-stricken all his life, was given about 11,600 square metres of paddy field and nearly 10,000 square metres of dry field. Still ringing in my ears are his words: "Our land has come back to us at long last!" He planted a new marker which bore his name. . . .

Bringing to an end the feudal land ownership and depriving the land-lords and reactionaries of their foothold in the countryside, the land reform brought about radical changes in the life of the peasants in our village. With boundless joy of being the masters of land they enthusiastically worked to increase agricultural production under a slogan: "Don't leave even an inch of land idle."

The production zeal of the peasants rose markedly. The per-unit yield of crops was 2.5 tons under the feudal landownership during the Japanese rule, but the figure went up 3 to 3.5 tons in autumn 1946.

With a steady upsurge in agricultural production the life of peasants improved day by day. The peasants could dispose of all the products after paying a low rate of agricultural tax in kind. (The tax system will be abolished this year, 1966, for good.)

Kim Rak Sung built a new house and bought an ox and a radio by selling extra grain.

The agricultural output showed an increase of 35 percent in our sub-county in two to three years after the land reform. Tile-roofed houses for 500 households were built and the number of cattle, farm machines and furniture also increased.

Twenty years have passed since the land reform. During this period our peasants have completed socialist collectivization of agriculture. By doing so, our peasants completely liquidated the source of poverty and exploitation and increased agricultural production by consolidating the successes they have achieved in the land reform. The agricultural output in our country is on the increase since the land reform. . . .

WORKERS' LIFE, NOW AND THEN: COMRADE KIM SUK DOO'S PERSONAL OBSERVATIONS AND COMMENTS [4]

Our silk mill, a modern mill, stands by the Daidong River that runs through the capital. Fruit trees and lovely gardens are everywhere in its wide compound.

Most of the workers and staff are women. Before liberation the plant was run by a Japanese capitalist. Those were dark days for the workers; numerous Korean girls and women suffered here, and they were humiliated. No worker was allowed to step outside the compound of the mill, which was fenced with electric-charged high walls!

No wonder people called the mill "Pyongyang Prison No. 2."

But with the country's liberation (August 15, 1945), the lot of the workers was radically changed. The state put the progressive labour law into effect guaranteeing them every democratic right—employment, education, recreation, and social insurance.

RIGHT TO LEARNING

In the days of Japanese rule our workers could not have schooling. Then most of the workers of our mill had little schooling. But, today the educational level of our employees is that of middle school graduates or above. Every condition is provided for the workers to study without leaving their jobs. The silk mill, like other factories, has schools. We have a textile school and a higher textile school, where the students are given a general education and are taught textile skills. And many spinners take the evening and correspondence courses of higher learning institutes.

The management sees to it that these "students" are given every opportunity for their studies. When those who take correspondence courses have to be away to attend the classes, they receive full wages; the factory even pays their traveling expenses.

Thanks to the solicitude of the state and to their high zeal, the level of the workers has swiftly risen. The number of the graduates of the specialized schools and colleges is increasingly rapidly. In 1960, 3.3 percent of the total employees were college or specialized school graduates, but the figure went

[4] Condensed from Kim Suk Doo, Assistant Manager of the Pyongyang Silk Mill, "Work and Life," *Korea Today* (June, 1966), pp. 2-5.

up 12.8 percent in 1965. . . . Twenty-three percent of them are those who finished the evening and correspondence courses and passed the state qualifications examination.

The silk mill maintains a library, a movie hall, and a club-house. Hundreds of musical instruments are at the disposal of the workers. The library is always crowded; art performances are often given at the club-house.

THE RIGHT TO REST

Before liberation, our workers were forced to work fourteen to sixteen hours a day. But now an eight-hour day is in effect. Everyone enjoys a regular, paid vacation every year. Those who are engaged in hazardous work are granted an additional leave of two weeks. Workers spend a pleasant time at rest homes at the state expense. The state, also, pays traveling expenses for them. In the country there are special holiday homes for those who want to spend their vacations with their families. Mothers with infants are entitled to a vacation specially designed for them.

A great number of our workers spend their vacations at the state-run holiday homes and sanatoria or at the sanatorium of the mill.

LIVING STANDARD IMPROVING

Like other workers, our spinners had led a miserable life under Japanese imperialist rule in the past. Hunger and poverty was their lot, and they were humiliated and exploited. They lived in crumbling huts. Then the dormitory of the mill was little different from prison. But the picture is quite different now. Our workers do not worry about food, clothing, and housing.

In the past, under the Japanese, women workers were paid less than half what the men got. Today, everyone receives wages according to the quality and quantity of his work.

The state has built modern houses for workers and special apartments even for unmarried ones. In the past, workers had to pay 30 to 50 percent of their wages for rent, but now they pay only 3 percent of their incomes for fine modern apartments, including electricity and water.

Rice, the staple food in Korea, is supplied by the state at a price next to nothing, and fuel is also provided by the state at a reasonable price.

Our factory has a day nursery and a kindergarten accommodating 800 and 350 children respectively. There are also a pediatrics ward with 30 beds and a week-nursery. Altogether 74 nurses, 13 kindergarten teachers, and 5 doctors are connected with these. Meals and snacks are supplied to children at the expense of the state.

SAFETY MEASURES

The state appropriated large sums to provide every safety measure for the workers. Particular emphasis was put on this matter when our mill was rebuilt after the war ended. Our plant is equipped with a modern ventilation system to prevent dampness and heat. It is designed in such a way that it gets enough sun, but not the direct sun.

Before liberation, the Japanese proprietor hardly did anything to improve working conditions. Workers worked in a temperature of 35 degrees Centigrade (95 degrees Fahrenheit) and humidity of 85 percent. Therefore, 80 percent of the workers suffered from arthritis; most of them had eczema and athlete's foot. Now the manager of the mill pays much attention to installing safety measures and sanitation devices and preventing accidents. Besides, there is a section in charge of safety measures, the staff of which tell the workers about safety and check if every work shop is amply equipped with all necessary safety measures. All new-comers and those who come from other trades, take special courses in safety measures before starting to work. The state supplies the workers with uniforms. . . . Those who work at the hazardous sections—boilers and transport—are supplied with a variety of nutritive foodstuffs at the state expense.

SOCIAL INSURANCE

In our country a subsidy is given to those factory and office workers who are incapacitated temporarily due to sickness, or injury, or who have to attend the sick in the family. The subsidy varies according to the length of the service but it is about 70 percent of one's wages. Women are entitled to take a seventy-seven-day maternity leave with pay. When a worker dies, the family is given a subsidy. Those workers who reach the age of sixty (women, fifty-five years) retire on pension. If one wishes to continue working one is paid wages plus the pension. In 1965, the total amount of pension and subsidy our mill paid out to the workers was tantamount to the total yearly wages of 120 workers. Free medical service has been in effect for some years in our country. Our factory has a clinic with five doctors and a maternity nurse to serve the employees of our mill.

KOREA SHALL BE REUNITED! [5]

At the end of the Second World War, Korea was split into two parts. . . . The territorial division has brought untold hardship and misfortune to the

[5] Condensed from Kim Suk Hyung, Academician, "Korea Has Been Always One," *Korea Today* (August, 1966), pp. 2-3.

Korean people. They demand an end to this abnormal state. They want to see their country reunited again as the Korean nation is a homogeneous nation. . . .

In the Middle Ages, in any country, rivalry of powerful lords manifested itself. However, in our country such phenomena were very weak because the people had waged together frequent battles against strong foreign aggressors, and because there was a spirit of strong cohesiveness. In modern times, since the latter part of the 19th century, the development of capitalist industries accelerated the growth of transportation and communications, which served to further strengthen the uniformity of the Korean people's economic life.

The entire Korean people, united as one, fought against the American imperialists who crept into the Daidong River in 1866 and invaded Kanghwa Island in 1871. Then they organized the Volunteers Army to struggle against the Japanese aggressors in the latter part of the 19th century and the early 20th century.

Particularly, the anti-Japanese partisans organized and led by Comrade Kim Il Sung in the 1930's, having set forth the national independence of the country as the first and foremost task, waged an armed struggle against Japan for more than fifteen years.

Even when the country faced the darkest days under Japanese rule, all sections of the Korean people could look forward to a bright future. But the nation has been separated into north and south due to the artificial barrier created by the U.S. army which landed in South Korea on the pretext of disarming the Japanese army. And the U.S. imperialists have turned South Korea into a colony and a base for their aggression in the Far East. They went so far as to launch a war of aggression in 1950 in an attempt to conquer the whole of Korea. But they sustained an ignominious defeat in the war and had to sign the Armistice Agreement in 1953. Ever since the conclusion of the truce, they have remained in South Korea and they are working like mad to perpetuate the division of Korea.

Today, Korea has been divided into the two diametrically different parts by the Military Demarcation Line. The United States and its puppet clique have turned down all reasonable proposals of the Government of the Democratic People's Republic of Korea for the peaceful unification of Korea based on independence and democracy. They are dead set against any North-South travel and economic exchange. They are preventing parents and children, husbands and wives, brothers and sisters, relatives and friends, who have been separated, from writing to each other. However, never can they perpetuate the division of the Korean people, a homogeneous nation, who have lived on one and the same territory from olden times and who have a strong national consciousness.

The ardent aspiration of the entire people of north and south for unification is manifested in the twenty-year-long struggle after liberation—the struggle for socialist construction in North Korea and the struggle against the U.S.-Pak Jung Hi clique in South Korea. U.S. imperialism must be made to withdraw from South Korea, and Korea must be unified according to the wish of the Korean people without any outside interference.

The struggle of the Korean people for the country's unification will surely be crowned with a final victory!

17

Ho Chi Minh's Democratic Republic of Vietnam: A Non-Marxist View

KLAUS H. PRINGSHEIM *

ASSOCIATE PROFESSOR OF POLITICAL SCIENCE
MC MASTER UNIVERSITY

The Democratic Republic of Vietnam (DRV), generally referred to as "North Vietnam" in the West, was formally proclaimed into existence and independence on September 2, 1945, at Ba Dinh Square in Hanoi by Dr. Ho Chi Minh, a lifelong communist and President of the Provisional Government of the DRV. But in September, 1945, the effective power of Ho Chi Minh's movement extended only over a small part of Tonkin,[1] and it lacked an administrative apparatus as well as most other attributes of statehood. President Ho boldly stepped into a vacuum created by the sudden defeat of Japan and the confusion among the victorious allies. During the ten years that followed, President Ho and the DRV overcame these original shortcomings through clever political intrigue, circumstance, good luck, and tenacious struggle against seemingly impossible odds.

By 1954 Ho had defeated the French in a bitterly fought guerilla war and had established political and military control in much of the entire territory of Vietnam both North and South. The Geneva Cease-Fire Agreement with France called for the withdrawal of Ho's Vietminh[2] forces from the territory south of the military demarcation line at the 17th parallel thus forcing Ho to give up temporarily the control he had previously exercised over substantial portions of South Vietnam. But while the government of

* This contribution has been written especially for this book.
[1] Formerly a state of French Indo-China, Tonkin now constitutes the major part of North Vietnam.
[2] The Vietminh was the League for the Independence of Vietnam, formed in May, 1941, as a front organization for the Vietnamese communists.

the DRV accepted the temporary partition of Vietnam at the 17th parallel, it did so, hoping that the country would be united under a government headed by Ho Chi Minh by the elections scheduled for July 20, 1956. Ho Chi Minh's government did not in 1954, nor does it now, accept the idea of a permanent partition of Vietnam into two separate states. Both the original constitution of the DRV (November 9, 1946) and the revised Constitution of January, 1960, clearly establish the claim of the DRV to sovereignty over North, Central, and South Vietnam. It is therefore to be expected that the government of the DRV, as long as it exists and has the power to do so, will continue its attempts to unite all of Vietnam under the aegis of the communist government of North Vietnam.

The Geneva Cease-Fire Agreement of 1954 states that "the military demarcation line is provisional and should not in any way be interpreted as constituting a political or territorial boundary.[3] Yet that is precisely what it has become since 1955, when it became clear that the elections provided for by the Cease-Fire Agreement would not take place as scheduled. It is thus that a state of North Vietnam (DRV) has actually existed since 1954.

The territory of the DRV stretches from the Chinese border to the 17th parallel, comprises roughly 62,000 square miles and is thus slightly smaller than the State of Missouri (69,000 square miles). The population of the DRV is now estimated at approximately 19 million people, of whom about one million live in the two principal cities, Hanoi, the capital, and Haiphong, the DRV's largest port. (This compares with 66,000 square miles and a population of more than 15 million people for South Vietnam.) The territory of the DRV, like its southern counterpart, falls within the sphere of historical Chinese influence, the evidences of which are abundant in all aspects of Vietnamese culture and society. Whether the Vietnamese like it or not, the influence exerted by their Chinese neighbor to the north seems certain to continue as a dominant factor in the history and development of all of Vietnam.

Vietnam was first conquered by the Chinese in 111 B.C. It was not until more than a thousand years later—in 939 A.D. that the Vietnamese fully regained their independence. In 1406 A.D. the Vietnamese were invaded by the Chinese of the Ming Dynasty who stayed for another twenty years. In 1858 the French came to Tourane (now known as Danang) and stayed for ninety-six years until 1954, being interrupted only by the Japanese invasion from 1940-45 and another Chinese sojourn (soldiers of the Kuomintang [KMT])[4] from 1945-46.

[3] Article 6, "Final Declaration of the Geneva Conference" (July 21, 1954) as cited in: Allan B. Cole, ed., *Conflict in Indo-China and International Repercussions* (Ithaca, Cornell University Press, 1956), p. 162.

[4] The Kuomintang is the Nationalist Party of Sun Yat-sen (1866-1925) and Chiang Kai-shek (1886-19??) which controlled large portions of China from 1928 until 1949, and which now controls Taiwan (Formosa), the Pescadores, and the offshore islands Quemoi and Matsu.

These historical facts create the background for the extraordinary nationalist fervor of the Vietnamese people and the peculiar ambiguities of Vietnam's relationship to China. The Vietnamese have adopted Chinese culture *in toto* and made it their own, but their fear and hatred of domination by the Chinese state (no matter who governs there) is a concern which goes beyond similar adverse feelings towards the French. The French were unwelcome, but are now gone and seem unlikely ever to return. The Chinese, on the other hand, first came more than 2000 years ago and are likely to loom powerfully just across the Northern Frontier of any Vietnamese state.

While Ho Chi Minh is indubitably devoted to the idea of a world communist movement, he could not function outside of the context of the Vietnamese independence movement. His success as a nationalist leader can be measured in terms of the degree to which he became recognized throughout Vietnam as a leader not only of the Vietnamese communists but of all anticolonial patriotic elements. He was extremely well aware of his need for broad support from other than communist elements. In his pursuit of the leadership of the Vietnamese independence movement, Ho Chi Minh, during the 1940's at one time or another sought and obtained the support of almost every party involved in the confused struggle, the Chinese Nationalists, the American OSS,[5] the French, and anyone else who was willing or able to further his aims. He went by several different names (Nguyen Ai-Quoc, Tong Van So) and it is even claimed that the OSS was responsible for his release from imprisonment by the Chinese. In 1945, when he was leading the Vietminh, Ho Chi Minh dissolved the Indochinese Communist Party to placate the Kuomintang generals and to gain broader support for his Vietminh. When the Vietnamese Communist Party was officially reestablished on March 3, 1951, it was done under the name of "Vietnamese Worker's Party" (VWP; Dang Lao-Dong in Vietnamese) and the Vietminh went out of existence on the same day. A united front organization continued to co-exist with the Dang Lao-Dong under the name of "Vietnamese United Front" (Mat-tran Lien-Viet). By the clever manipulation of the Mat-tran Lien-Viet and the appointment of a number of noncommunists to important positions Ho continued to conceal the true state of affairs. Documents captured in Vietnam show that an effort was made even to conceal the completely communist nature and leadership of the Dang Lao-Dong (and later of the People's Revloutionary Party in South Vietnam) so as to enable the "Workers Party" to assume leadership of all nationalist elements without letting noncommunists become aware that the communists were in complete control and would be in a position to establish a communist dictatorship once victory had been won. There is also evidence that the Vietnamese com-

---

[5] Office of Strategic Services, the American Military Intelligence Organization, operating in overseas areas during World War II. The collaboration between Ho Chi Minh and the OSS has recently been documented by U.S. Army Intelligence Officer Rene Defourneaux in *Look* Magazine (August 9, 1966), pp. 32-33.

munists were involved in the disappearance or murder of a number of non-communist Vietnamese nationalist leaders. Ho Chi Minh's path to the presidency of the DRV and thus to the establishment of a communist dictatorship in North Vietnam was made possible by this amazing odyssey of relentless patriotic struggle, deception, treason, clever political intrigue, cold-blooded murder, patient plotting, and ruthless pursuit of power for the communists. After 1949, Chinese communist military aid was also undoubtedly a decisive factor.

THE ECONOMY

Large areas of North Vietnam adjacent to the Chinese Peoples Republic (CPR) and Laos are mountainous and hence agriculturally relatively unproductive. These regions are predominantly inhabited by North Vietnam's minority peoples: the Thai, Meo, Tho, Nung, Man, and Muong. (Montagnards) The majority of Viets live mostly in the coastal plains where the agricultural crops are grown and where the cities, harbors, and traffic centers are located. The fertile Red River delta is the most heavily populated area. But because of the high population density and the prevailing limitations on agricultural productivity in the DRV the partition at the 17th parallel has been particularly painful to the Hanoi regime, since their area had previously relied on the import of surplus rice from South Vietnam. This supply was automatically cut off in 1954, once the border between the two zones was closed. The result has been an almost uninterrupted series of food shortages in the DRV since Geneva, 1954. The initial attempts at forced collectivization (1954-56) had an adverse effect on agricultural productivity though the acreage under cultivation had been substantially increased. The general economic plan of the DRV called for rapid industrialization along Leninist lines, and for the subsequent importation of food in exchange for exported manufactured goods. As yet it has not been possible to establish such a pattern, since industrialization did not progress as rapidly as expected, and since the goods produced were largely of so inferior a quality as to be unsuitable for export. Communist China was most helpful to the DRV in the initial period of reconstruction, when only general guidance, planning, and elementary level technical help were needed. But the Chinese were not able to follow up at the later stages, having no surplus of either the sophisticated industrial equipment or the advanced technicians needed by the DRV. China was also unable to help with the food situation after 1959 because of her own serious food shortages. This forced the DRV to rely mostly on the Soviet Union and the East European countries for the machinery and technicians needed to implement the planned industrialization. Meanwhile, the food shortages persisted, and they have undoubtedly played a decisive role in predisposing the Hanoi regime to increase its efforts to absorb South Vietnam by force, in the hope that South Vietnam's rice crops would restore the economic viability of the DRV. The ironic fact is, that due to the intensification of the war, even South Vietnam, formerly a rice exporter, is now suffering food shortages and importing rice from the United States.

The agrarian reform program adopted in the DRV after 1954 at the urging of Truong Chinh, then Secretary General of the Dang Lao-Dong, closely followed the Chinese communist model. Rapid and relentless collectivization was enforced so strictly that violent reactions on the part of the rural population resulted—including a peasant rebellion in Ho Chi Minh's own native province, which had to be put down by the DRV Army. Truong Chinh, who had been head of the Central Land Reform Committee, was subsequently dismissed as Party Secretary General (the post being assumed by President Ho Chi Minh himself) and publicly confessed his "errors" in connection with the land reform. His eclipse was temporary, however, and he was named Vice-Premier in 1958. Truong Chinh's declining influence after 1956 spared the DRV an imitation of both the Chinese Commune system and the so-called "Great Leap Forward." Yet, some 95 percent of the lowland farming area is now organized into cooperatives (*kolkhozi*) and there are also fifty-nine State farms operated largely by the DRV Army. Crops continue to be unsatisfactory, however,[6] food shortages persist, and rationing is still in effect. At the same time the population of the DRV, now close to 19 million, is increasing at the alarming rate of 3.2 percent per annum, thus adding another half million to the population each year. Meanwhile, the large scale bombardments of North Vietnam by the U.S. Armed Forces since February, 1965, are certain to bring about further declines in the DRV's agricultural production. The economic outlook for the rapidly increasing population of the DRV at the present juncture is thus rather poor, since neither the CPR nor the Soviet Union, both of whom have their own agricultural problems, have as yet taken major steps to remedy this situation.

Industrial development, begun with a three-year plan (1958-60), was continued under a faltering five-year plan (1960-65) and has been increasingly jeopardized if not halted by continuing bombings of the major industrial installations in the DRV. In 1963 industrial output is said to have increased 6.5 percent which was 50 percent short of the original goal of a 13 percent increase. In spite of difficulties in the implementation of excessively optimistic plans, it cannot be denied that the DRV has made certain strides towards industrialization with the help of the Soviet Union, Eastern Europe, and Communist China, each playing an important role. There is now a steel mill

[6] A production of 4.3 million tons of rice was claimed for 1964, an increase of only 100,000 tons over the previous year, leaving the DRV 5 percent short of the planned level. The fact that as late as January, 1962, a yield of 7 million tons was being forecast for 1965, gives some indication of the extent of the failure to develop as expected.

at Thai Nguyen (1964 production claim: 50,000 tons), a super phosphate plant at Thu To (1963) production claim: 163,000 tons), a machine tool plant in Hanoi, and there are many other factories producing the sinews of modern industry, all within 100 miles or less of the capital of Hanoi. Most of these factories and other industrial enterprises have so far [mid-1966] escaped bombardment by the U.S. armed forces because of American hope that restraint will produce similar restraint and reluctance to escalate by Communist China and the Soviet Union in their respective intervention in the Vietnamese conflict.

It is estimated that between 1955 and 1963 the DRV received over one billion dollars' worth of aid from communist countries.[7] Most of this aid has come from Communist China, approximately one-third from the Soviet Union, and less than 3 percent from Eastern Europe.[8] While Soviet-bloc aid was originally in the form of grants, more recently it has been in the form of loans (long-term, low interest) or commercial credit, thus creating an increasing trade deficit burden for the DRV.

GOVERNMENT

In the extent to which it fails to express political realities, and often in its very wording, the 1960 Constitution of the DRV is reminiscent of both the Soviet Constitution and the Constitution of the Chinese People's Republic.

Thus the supposedly "highest organ of state authority" and "the only legislative authority" in the DRV is: The "National Assembly," which serves for "four years" but can "prolong its term of office" in the event of "war or other exceptional circumstances."[9] Like the Supreme Soviet and the National People's Congress of China, the DRV's National Assembly has mainly symbolic and ceremonial value and normally functions with "full unanimity and standing ovations."[10]

There are however some distinctive features of the DRV government, beginning with the position of the President, to whom an entire chapter of the constitution is devoted (Chapter V, Articles 61-70). The President (and that means Ho Chin Minh, whose "clearsighted leadership" is celebrated in the long and propagandistic preamble to the constitution) represents the people in internal affairs as well as in foreign relations. He is elected by the National Assembly for the duration of its term of office. He

[7] John C. Donnell, "North Vietnam," in R. A. Scalapino, ed., *The Communist Revolution in Asia* (Englewood Cliffs, N.J., Prentice-Hall, 1965), p. 147.

[8] Bernard B. Fall, "North Vietnam: A Profile," in *Problems of Communism*, Vol. XIV, No. 4 (July-August, 1965), p. 22.

[9] Quoted from the *Constitution of the DRV* (Hanoi, Foreign Languages Publishing House, 1960).

[10] Bernard B. Fall, *The Two Vietnams* (New York, Praeger, 1964), p. 142.

appoints[11] or removes the Prime Minister and other ministers, appoints or removes the Vice President, and the members of the National Defense Council. He grants pardons, awards medals, is the Supreme Commander of the Armed Forces and can also preside at the meetings of the Council of Ministers. He can further convene and preside over the Special Political Conference[12] which appears to function somewhat like an inner cabinet. Bernard Fall suggests that the powers of the DRV presidency curiously resemble those of General DeGaulle in the Fifth Republic, which may indeed have served as an inspiration. It is a curious fact that the Vice President, Ton Duc Thang, is a man in his eighties, a long-time associate of Ho's and evidently not destined to become his successor. The fact that the Premier (and presumably his five Vice-Premiers) wields little power is illustrated by the constitutional provision (Article 66) enabling the President to attend and preside over meetings of the Council of Ministers. Every indication is therefore that President Ho Chi Minh can, if he wishes, make or affect all decisions.

Ho was born in 1890 and, at the time this is being written, he is thus 76. It appears that he is in fairly good health and still fulfills most of his major political functions.[13] The great importance of his personal position is underlined by the existence of pro-Chinese and pro-Russian factions in the VWP, which have so far been carefully manipulated by Ho so that neither has won complete control. Apart from the personal leadership of Ho Chi Minh, the most important decisions are apparently reached in the Politburo,[14] the Central Committee of the VWP,[15] and the Special Political conference.

THE DRV'S POSITION IN THE SINO-SOVIET SPLIT

President Ho seems to have used his influence in the high councils of the VWP to bridge the factional differences and to neutralize power struggles

11 " . . . in pursuance of decisions of the National Assembly or its Standing Committee . . ." (Article 63).

12 Sometimes referred to as the Supreme Political Conference, it is composed of the President, Vice-President, Prime Minister, Chairman of the National Assembly Standing Committee, and "other persons concerned."

13 James Cameron and Felix Greene, both of whom visited Hanoi in November-December, 1965, and interviewed Ho, agree on President Ho's relative health and vigor. Greene calls him "neither senile nor ill" and asserts that Ho "is still the leader in function as well as in name." Cameron adds that Ho seems to delegate certain functions to Pham Van Dong and might be grooming him for the succession.

14 The eleven members of the Politburo of the VWP are indubitably the most important men in DRV politics. As of mid-1966, four of them appear to be pro-Soviet, four pro-Chinese, and three (including Ho) are not clearly aligned. It should be understood that such alignments are not necessarily static and thus are subject to realignment.

15 The Central Committee has forty-three full members and twenty-eight alternate members according to a 1960 list.

among Politburo members. The DRV eminently cannot afford to align herself completely with either Peking or Moscow. She needs economic help and military aid from both. She cannot affront her powerful neighbor Communist China by identifying with the Soviet Union, without risking political and economic retaliation and possibly even military intervention in Laos, Cambodia, South Vietnam, and conceivably even in North Vietnam, by the Chinese communists. There is little doubt that the DRV could be forcibly occupied by CPR troops ("Volunteers"). The various evidences seen in recent years of the DRV's supposed alignment with Peking (failure to sign the Test Ban Treaty, praise for Albania, condemnation of "Modern Revisionism," support for wars of national liberation, and the like) can be interpreted in terms both of DRV national interest and of the necessity to pay lip-service to solidarity with China, without concluding that the DRV has voluntarily and irrevocably committed herself to the Peking line. Complete commitment to Peking would result in abandonment by the Soviet Union and subsequent satellization by China. In either case the hated Chinese would once again assume control, and President Ho Chi Minh's dream of a Southeast Asian empire governed from Hanoi would collapse. Hence if the DRV is to retain any semblance of independence (and this is after all what President Ho and his comrades say they have been fighting for, ever since the 1920's), there is only one choice open to them—to continue to balance Soviet influence against Chinese influence and to work incessantly and earnestly for the prevention of a complete break between Peking and Moscow. Should such a break occur, the DRV would be forced to choose between the contenders and would thus be condemned to the status of a Peking satellite. It is considerations like the above, which have made American policy decisions in regard to Vietnam so difficult, since the American government has no desire to promote the satellization of the DRV by Peking. There are however a number of contingencies which may force the issue, such as the following:

1. The death or retirement of President Ho Chi Minh
2. A formal and irrevocable split between Peking and Moscow
3. An American land invasion of North Vietnamese territory
4. Prolonged and totally destructive bombardment of industrial, transportation, and population centers in North Vietnam's so-called "Red Envelope" (including Hanoi and Haiphong) which might well bring about the total collapse of the DRV economy

It is the opinion of this writer that if contingencies 2, 3, or 4 were to occur, the result would be large-scale Chinese intervention and the satellization of the DRV by Peking.

The departure of President Ho Chi Minh from the scene, however, would not necessarily be similarly disastrous. A power struggle between

General Giap[16] and Truong Chinh[17] might not occur. In the absence of conditions described by contingencies 2, 3, and 4 above, it seems likely that Pham Van Dong[18] could take over and continue to maintain a balance designed to preserve the independence of the DRV from Chinese domination. Meanwhile, as long as President Ho is alive and able, it will undoubtedly be his endeavor to maintain the delicate balance.

THE WAR

Another factor affecting political decisions in the DRV is the strong desire for reunification with South Vietnam. Failure to reunify means disaster for the economy, detracts from the prestige of the DRV government, and makes the DRV more dependent upon China, and hence more vulnerable to satellization by China. If the DRV wishes to maintain her independence from Peking she must reunify or at least maintain the impression that she is continuing to make efforts toward reunification.[19] It is not, as Secretary of State Dean Rusk so often states, merely a matter of "not leaving your neighbors alone." For the DRV reunification is a matter of life or death, and that is why any DRV government will continue the attempts (futile and suicidal as they may appear to us) to seize South Vietnam, however overwhelming the odds may seem to be against success. Men like Mao Tse-tung and Ho Chi Minh seem to thrive on impossible odds. At the same time the aim of reunification has served to moderate governmental policies within the DRV, in the hope that such moderation might keep alive a flame of sympathy for reunification under DRV auspices in South Vietnam as well. Notable evidence of this policy has been the appointment of a number of well-known noncommunists from South and North Vietnam to governmental positions in the DRV so that the "united front" (of all Vietnamese) concept might be kept alive among sympathizers in South Vietnam.[20] The various factors cited above have created a political and diplomatic pattern of great complexity involving a number of subtle nuances which raise some doubts as to whether this pattern is necessarily susceptible to simple military coercion. I would say that it is not.

While there are only 570,000 members[21] in the Vietnamese Workers

[16] Vice Premier, Minister of Defense, Commander of Peoples Army, and Hero of Dien Bien Phu, General Giap appears to belong to the pro-Soviet faction of the VWP.

[17] Vice Premier, Chairman of the Standing Committee of the National Assembly, and Chairman of the Party Cadre Training School, Truong Chinh appears to belong to the pro-Chinese faction of the VWP.

[18] Premier, himself probably on the Soviet side in the Sino-Soviet dispute.

[19] A comparison with the position of the Nationalist Government in Taiwan may not be totally inappropriate here.

[20] Needless to say the non-communists are only window dressing and exercise no power.

[21] This is the figure given for 1963 and constitutes some 3 percent of the population.

Party, the VWP leadership indubitably is the effective government of the country controlling and supervising all executive and administrative functions. The people of North Vietnam are probably no more enthusiastic about communist dictatorship and agricultural collectivization than the people of East Germany, Hungary, or Poland, but it is unlikely that increased military pressure by the United States on the DRV, in the form of aerial bombardment, for instance, will change the objective power relationships between the ruling VWP elite and the masses of the DRV population. A more likely result would be increased national unity in the name of defense against foreign imperialist aggression and eventually the absorption of the DRV into China's protective embrace. Such a result will please neither Washington, nor Moscow, nor the 19 million citizens of the DRV, but only the ambitious Emperor Mao Tse-tung in Peking, who may proceed from there to subsequent similar operations in Laos and Thailand.

The veteran British journalist James Cameron spent a month in the DRV (October-November 1965) and described it as an "unhappy and furious" country. He speaks of total drabness, barrenness, austerity, of man, beast, and machine all going about covered by foliage-like camouflage, appearing theatrical and overdone. However, the most important insight gained by Cameron, in my view, was the following short paragraph:

. . . what is quite clear in this lunar landscape of North Vietnam is that the people have a totally unshakable determination to win the war on their terms. Not to make an end of it or to find a way out of it, or "conclude an agreement" about it. They have the extraordinary and rather impressive nerve to insist upon winning it. Victory, however, has a strict definition which is the implementation of the Geneva agreement of 1954 which requires a Vietnam united under popular elections and the elimination of all foreign troops from both the South and the North.

Mr. Cameron adds that Hanoi wants even more than that: ". . . it wants to see the U.S. chastised for its behavior in the way especially punitive in Oriental eyes: By shame, by loss of face." [22]

Given these conditions, these attitudes, the bitterness and hatred which would be generated by continued escalation, and the continuing murderous cruelty on both sides, it is hard to see how more bombs and more soldiers can be expected to lead to the conference table. As fall of 1966 arrived, it looked like a long and increasingly embittered war.

While the American effort in Vietnam should guarantee the survival of some noncommunist (or non-Viet Cong) population centers in South Vietnam, it is equally probable—in spite of Sino-Soviet bickering and mutual denunciations—that Chinese communist and/or Soviet Russian counter-escalation will continue, somehow, to guarantee the survival (if little beyond

---

[22] James Cameron is one of the world's most distinguished and astute reporters whose experience goes back to the 1930's.

that) of the communist regime of the DRV. The often quoted truism that the U.S. cannot simply abandon its friends without a disastrous loss of face, has equal applicability in the communist world. This is a lesson we could have learned in 1950 in Pyongyang, and again in 1956 in Budapest, and yet again in 1962 in Havana. The course is likely to be offered once again in the latter half of the 1960's in Hanoi.

In a major speech delivered in Hanoi on March 20, 1966 Vice-Premier Truong Chinh denounced the American "peace overtures" of the winter of 1965-66 as a screen for American intensification of the war. He encouraged the people of North Vietnam to carry on their "defensive" war, to continue socialist construction, and to support actively the liberation war of the South Vietnamese people. For the future he forecast a "protracted war" and reliance mainly upon "our own forces." There is no evidence so far that Truong Chinh's words are not an accurate reflection of official DRV attitudes. They are also consistent with General Lin Piao's [23] September, 1965, thesis "Long Live the Victory of People's War" [24] and other subsequent Peking pronouncements on the Vietnamese war. The belated realization that an easy victory is not forthcoming is nevertheless unlikely to lead to the surrender or collapse of either the National Liberation Front (NLF) in South Vietnam or the DRV Regime in Hanoi and its aid to the NLF. The Vietnamese communists and their allies remain convinced that the U.S. will tire of the struggle eventually and that a political solution to their advantage will then occur. In the meantime they strike when they can and suffer or hide when they must, taking considerable comfort both from the continuing political fiascoes in South Vietnam and from domestic American disunity and frustration with the eternally inconclusive American efforts. There are conditions which could change this (from the U.S. viewpoint) bleak outlook. A collapse of the Peking regime coupled with withdrawal of Soviet support from Hanoi, or, alternatively, a convincing U.S. military victory over the NLF along with the emergence of genuine popular support for a non-NLF government of South Vietnam would indeed change the outlook entirely. As of fall 1966 it appears that such expectations are pipe-dreams and less realistic than the calculated long-range gamble of President Ho Chi Minh's Democratic Republic of Vietnam.

[23] Communist China's Minister of Defense, who in summer of 1966 appeared to gain stature as a possible successor to Mao Tse-tung in preference to Chairman Liu Shao-chi.

[24] See *Peking Review,* Vol. 8, No. 36 (September 3, 1965), pp. 9-30.

FURTHER READING SUGGESTIONS

For current bibliography, the reader is referred to the annual bibliography volume, published each September by the *Journal of Asian Studies* and its predecessor the *Far Eastern Quarterly.* For quick reference the Department of State, External Research Staff, has published External Research Paper 142, *The Democratic Republic of Vietnam (North Vietnam): A Bibliography* (August, 1953).

The two best noncommunist writers on the DRV are Bernard B. Fall and P. J. Honey, whose voluminous publications on the DRV have been the principal sources for this study. [Bernard Fall was killed in Vietnam, early in 1967. EDITOR'S NOTE.] The following is a short list of recent studies recommended to the nonspecialist:

Bernard B. Fall, *The Two Vietnams,* rev. ed. New York: Praeger, 1964.

————, *Street Without Joy,* 3rd rev. ed. Harrisburg, Pa.: The Stackpole Co., 1963.

————, "North Vietnam: A Profile," in *Problems of Communism,* Volume XIV, No. 4 (July-August, 1965), pp. 13-25.

————, "A Straight Zig-Zag: The Road to Socialism in North Vietnam," in A. Doak Barnett, ed., *Communist Strategies in Asia.* New York: Praeger, 1963.

————, "Power and Pressure Groups in North Vietnam," in the *China Quarterly,* No. 9 (January-March, 1962), pp. 37-46.

P. J. Honey, ed., *North Vietnam Today, Profile of a Communist Satellite.* New York: Praeger, 1962.

————, *Communism in North Vietnam: Its Role in the Sino-Soviet Dispute.* Cambridge, Mass.: M.I.T. Press, 1963.

John C. Donnell, "North Vietnam: A Qualified Pro-Chinese Position," in R. A. Scalapino, ed., *The Communist Revolution in Asia.* Englewood Cliffs, N. J.: Prentice-Hall, 1965, pp. 140-172.

Paul F. Langer, "North Vietnam," in Adam Bromke, ed., *The Communist States at the Crossroads between Moscow and Peking.* New York: Praeger, 1965, pp. 155-162.

For a detailed examination of local government and administration in the DRV based primarily on Russian sources, *see* three articles by George Ginsburgs in issues No. 10, 12, and 14 of the *China Quarterly,* pp. 174-204, 211-230, and 195-211 respectively.

As primary documentary sources from the DRV, the following six titles, all published in 1960 by the Foreign Languages Publishing House in Hanoi, are useful for basic reference and background:

1. *Constitution of the Democratic Republic of Vietnam*
2. *President Ho Chin Minh* (biography, Part I by Premier Pham Van Dong)
3. *Ho Chi Minh, Selected Works I*
4. *The Democratic Republic of Vietnam*
5. *Thirty Years of Struggle of the Party (VWP)*
6. *XVth Anniversary of the Democratic Republic of Vietnam, 1945 to 1960*

Also, an English language weekly, *Vietnam Courier,* is published by the DRV government in Hanoi (since 1964).

The American contention that the DRV is responsible for the Vietcong insurgency in South Vietnam is presented in:

Department of State, *Aggression from the North,* DOS Publication 7839, Far Eastern Series 130 (February, 1965). 64 pp.

While it is my view that the Vietnamese Communists have made little if any contribution to the development of either Marxist-Leninist-Maoist ideology or to the literature of Modern Revisionism, there are two works produced by Vietnamese Communists which are worth looking at:

1. Truong Chinh, *Primer for Revolt* (with an Introduction by Bernard B. Fall). New York: Praeger, 1963.
2. Vo Nguyen Giap, *People's War, People's Army.* New York: Praeger, 1962.

18

Heroic Vietnam:
A Vietnamese Marxist View

HO CHI MINH

PRESIDENT, DEMOCRATIC REPUBLIC
OF VIETNAM, AND CHAIRMAN, VIETNAMESE
WORKERS' (LAO DONG) PARTY

PHAM VAN DONG

PREMIER, NORTH VIETNAM

NGUYEN CON

CHAIRMAN, STATE PLANNING
COMMISSION

AND OTHERS *

I. AN INDEPENDENT AND DEMOCRATIC VIETNAM: (AN INTRODUCTION TO VIETNAM'S HISTORY) [1]

Vietnam is a single entity from Lang-son to Camau.[2]

The Vietnamese people, throughout their thousands of years of history, have been an industrious working people who have struggled unremittingly and heroically to build their country and to defend the independence of their Fatherland.

Throughout more than eighty years of French colonial rule and five years of occupation by the Japanese fascists, the Vietnamese people consistently united and struggled against domination by the foreign aggressors in order to liberate their country.

* Separate footnote references are given to enable the reader to identify the authors and the original source of publication of each section.

[1] The first four, and the eighth, ninth, and tenth paragraphs of this section have been taken from the "Preamble" to the *Constitution of the Democratic Republic of Vietnam* (Hanoi, Foreign Languages Publishing House, 1960), pp. 7-9. (This is the DRV's second Constitution, promulgated on January, 1960.) The rest of this section comes from "20 Years" (No author given), *Vietnam* (September, 1965), p. 15.

[2] Lang-son is on the Chinese border; Camau at the Southern tip of the peninsula. [EDITOR'S NOTE]

From 1930 onwards, under the leadership of the Indochinese Communist Party—now the Vietnam Lao dong Party—the Vietnamese revolution advanced into a new stage. The persistent struggle, full of hardship and heroic sacrifice, of our people against imperialist and feudal domination won great success: the August Revolution was victorious, the Democratic Republic of Vietnam was founded. . . .

September 2, 1945. On the solemn rostrum set up at the Ba Dinh Public Square stood a man whose name has gone down in the history of the Vietnamese revolution and is known in many countries: Ho Chi Minh. To the world he solemnly proclaimed the birth of the Democratic Republic of Vietnam. Before him stood the small units of the liberation army, predecessor of the present powerful and heroic Vietnam People's Army, the twenty-year-old generation of the newly independent country, and all those who had freshly emerged from the darkness of slavery the day before. To them, President Ho Chi Minh said:

"Vietnam has the right to be a free and independent country—and in fact is so already. The entire Vietnamese people are determined to mobilize all their physical and mental strength, to sacrifice their lives and property in order to safeguard their independence and liberty."

And when he asked, "Do you hear me distinctly, fellow countrymen?" the young generation before him, the shock force of the August Revolution, shouted in unison their firm answer: "Yes!" They heard him distinctly and acted upon his words, he whom they always call affectionately "Uncle Ho," he who represents all Vietnamese patriots, many of whom have laid down their lives under the guillotines or in the prisons of the French imperialists. . . .

However, the French imperialists, assisted by the U.S. imperialists, again provoked an aggressive war in an attempt to seize our country and once more enslave our people. Under the leadership of the Vietnamese working class Party and the Government of the Democratic Republic of Vietnam, our entire people, united as one, rose to fight the aggressors and save their country. At the same time, our people carried out land rent reduction and land reform with the aim of overthrowing the landlord class, and restoring the land to those who till it. The long, hard and extremely heroic war of resistance of the Vietnamese people, which enjoyed the sympathy and support of the socialist countries, of the oppressed peoples and of friends of peace throughout the world, won glorious victory. With the Dien-bien-phu victory, the Vietnamese people defeated the French imperialists and the U.S. interventionists. The 1954 Geneva Agreements were concluded: peace was restored in Indochina on the basis of recognition of the independence, sovereignty, unity, and territorial integrity of our country. . . .

Since the restoration of peace in completely liberated North Vietnam, our people have carried through the national people's democratic revolution. But the South is still under the rule of the imperialists and feudalists; our country is still temporarily divided into two zones.

The Vietnamese revolution has moved into a new position. Our people must endeavour to consolidate the North, taking it towards socialism; and to carry on the struggle for peaceful reunification of the country and completion of the tasks of the national people's democratic revolution throughout the country. . . .

The historic proclamation at the Ba Dinh Square on September 2, 1945 was not only a message for one generation but also for the future. That is why, those who were not present at Ba Dinh in 1945 simply because they were then too young to attend, also replied "Yes!" to President Ho Chi Minh's appeal when the U.S. imperialists started invading the country. They understand very well Uncle Ho's words uttered when he addressed not them but their elder generations, their fathers and uncles: "The Vietnamese people never suffer to live in slavery . . ."

The new regime has grown up. Of the past twenty years of its existence, nine years were devoted to the life-and-death struggle to defeat the French colonialists. The remaining eleven years saw enormous efforts of the North Vietnamese people to rebuild the war-torn country and build socialism. Today, a new land-grabber, after behind-the-scene manœuvres, brazenly breaks into our house to destroy and pillage what we have built up. The fruits gained with our sweat and blood are being menaced. The whole country has risen up as in the past, united as one man, resolved to defeat the U.S. imperialist aggressors. And the enemy will surely be defeated. That is the firm conviction of our entire nation.

II. ECONOMIC AND SOCIAL SYSTEM AND SOME OF THE FUNDAMENTAL RIGHTS OF CITIZENS AS PROVIDED FOR IN THE CONSTITUTION OF THE DRV [3]

Article 9. The Democratic Republic of Vietnam is advancing step by step from people's democracy to socialism by developing and transforming the national economy along socialist lines, transforming its backward economy into a socialist economy with modern industry and agriculture, and an advanced science and technology. . . .

Article 10. The State leads all economic activities according to a unified plan.

[3] From Chapters II and III of the *Constitution of the Democratic Republic of Viet Nam, op. cit.,* pp. 19-22 and 26.

The State relies on the organs of State, trade union organizations, co-operatives and other organizations of the working people, to elaborate and carry out its economic plans.

Article 11. In the Democratic Republic of Vietnam, during the present period of transition to socialism, the main forms of ownership of means of production are: state ownership, that is, ownership by the whole people; co-operative ownership, that is, collective ownership by the working masses; ownership by individual working people; and ownership by the national capitalists.

Article 12. The State sector of the economy, which is a form of owner-ship by the whole people, plays the leading role in the national economy. The State ensures priority for its development.

All mineral resources and waters, and all forests, undeveloped land, and other resources defined by law as belonging to the State, are the property of the whole people.

Article 13. The co-operative sector of the economy is a form of col-lective ownership by the working masses.

The State especially encourages, guides and helps the development of the co-operative sector of the economy.

Article 14. The State by law protects the right of peasants to own land and other means of production.

The State actively guides and helps the peasants to improve farming methods and increase production, and encourages them to organize producers', supply and marketing, and credit co-operatives, in accordance with the prin-ciple of voluntariness.

Article 15. The State by law protects the right of handicraftsmen and other individual working people to own means of production.

The State actively guides and helps handicraftsmen and other individual working people to improve their enterprises, and encourages them to or-ganize producers' and supply and marketing co-operatives in accordance with the principle of voluntariness.

Article 16. The State by law protects the right of national capitalists to own means of production and other capital.

The State actively guides the national capitalists in carrying out activi-ties beneficial to national welfare and the people's livelihood, contributing to the development of the national economy, in accordance with the eco-nomic plan of the State. The State encourages and guides the national capitalists in following the path of socialist transformation through the form of joint State-private enterprises, and other forms of transformation.

Article 17. The State strictly prohibits the use of private property to disrupt the economic life of society, or to undermine the economic plan of the State.

Article 18. The State protects the right of citizens to possess lawfully-earned incomes, savings, houses, and other private means of life.

Article 19. The State by law protects the right of citizens to inherit private property.

Article 20. Only when such action is necessary in the public interest, does the State repurchase, requisition or nationalize with appropriate compensation means of production in city or countryside, within the limits and in the conditions defined by law.

Article 21. Labour is the basis on which the people develop the national economy and raise their material and cultural standards.

Labour is a duty and a matter of honour for every citizen.

The State encourages the creativeness and the enthusiasm in labour of workers by hand and brain.

Article 23. Citizens of the Democratic Republic of Vietnam who have reached the age of eighteen have the right to vote, and those who have reached the age of twenty-one have the right to stand for election, whatever their nationality, race, sex, social origin, religion, belief, property status, education, occupation, or length of residence, except insane persons and persons deprived by a court or by law of the right to vote and stand for election. . . .

Article 25. Citizens of the Democratic Republic of Vietnam enjoy freedom of speech, freedom of the press, freedom of assembly, freedom of association and freedom of demonstration. The State guarantees all necessary material conditions for citizens to enjoy these freedoms.

Article 26. Citizens of the Democratic Republic of Vietnam enjoy freedom of religious belief; they may practise or not practise a religion.

Article 27. Freedom of the person of citizens of the Democratic Republic of Vietnam is guaranteed. No citizen may be arrested except by decision of a people's court or with the sanction of a People's Organ of Control.

Article 28. The law guarantees the inviolability of the homes of the citizens of the Democratic Republic of Vietnam and inviolability of mail.

Citizens of the Democratic Republic of Vietnam enjoy freedom of residence and movement.

Article 29. Citizens of the Democratic Republic of Vietnam have the right to complain of and denounce to any organ of State any servant of the State for transgression of law. These complaints and denunciations must be investigated and dealt with rapidly. People suffering loss owing to infringement by servants of the State of their rights as citizens are entitled to compensation.

III. AGAINST WIND AND TIDE, THE DRV KEEPS ON FORGING AHEAD [4]

We are conscious that war is not only a severe trial of strength between armed forces but also a great test of the soundness of the social regime and economy of the countries concerned. The socialist regime and the socialist economy of the DRV are facing this challenge. Two years have elapsed since the U.S. imperialist aggressors started their war of destruction which is growing in size and intensity. But there is no sign of weakening. Instead, the DRV is showing ever greater resolve to fight until final victory, and its economic and defence potentials have not ceased to grow while ever more important victories have been won on both the production front and the battlefield.

QUALITATIVE CHANGES

At its founding twenty-one years ago, the DRV possessed a very poor and crippled economy. That was the inevitable outcome of eighty years of colonialist domination and thousands of years of feudal oppression.

Then the country went through its infancy in the flames of eight to nine years' fierce fighting against the French colonialists. The Dien Bien Phu victory which led to the 1954 Geneva Conference on Indo-China only freed one half of the country. The U.S. imperialists occupied the other half and obstructed reunification. Due to this, tremendous losses have been caused to the Vietnamese people, in the political as well as in the economic, cultural and social fields.

However, the socialist revolution and the socialist construction, carried out right after one half of the country had been liberated, have established here widespread socialist relations of production and brought about a his-

[4] The major part of this section has been reprinted from "Against Wind and Tide the D.R.V. Keeps on Forging Ahead, *Vietnam Courier* (August 22, 1966), pp. 1 and 6. The subsections on "Communications and Transport" and on "Cultural and Social Activities" have been taken from Premier Pham Van Dong's 1966 report to the Third National Assembly of the D.R.V., published in *Vietnam Courier* (April 28, 1966), p. 6, under the title "More Glorious Victories Ahead for Us, the Victors." The subsection "The War Doesn't Stop Us" has been excerpted from the report of Nguyen Con, Chairman of the State Planning Commission, to the above mentioned assembly, published in *Vietnam Courier* of May 5, p. 3, and May 12, 1966, p. 3, under the title "Fighting the U.S. Aggressions While Building Socialism," Part I and Part II respectively. Part I bears the subtitle "Achievements of the First Five-Year Plan," Part II, "The Two-Year Plan (1966-67)."

torically significant change in the social structure of the economy. A new kind of relationship has taken shape in society, viz. the relation of co-operation and mutual assistance among the working people which firmly consolidates the worker-peasant alliance on a new economic basis, the steady foundation of socialist power.

The socialist regime and the socialist economy built and constantly developed on the basis of an agriculture already co-operativized and an industry owned by the entire people have been established with priority development of heavy industry as the guiding principle, aimed at equipping various branches of the national economy with modern techniques. The superiority of the social regime and the correctness of the line concerning economic development have resulted in the transformation, in a short time, of a very poor and backward agricultural economy and an undeveloped industry, incapable of ensuring even a minimum food ration for everybody, while everything, from a needle to an anchor, had to be imported from abroad, into a relatively comprehensive economy. In agriculture small-scale, individual and feeble production has been replaced by large-scale, collective production with the positive assistance of the socialist State and the ever more effective support of industry. Industry, from serving extractive and repair purposes, is developing towards a relatively comprehensive industry capable of equipping, step by step, various production branches with modern techniques and meeting the bulk of the needs for industrial consumer goods.

FROM INDIVIDUAL FARMING TO A CO-OPERATIVIZED AGRICULTURE

Over the past years, the co-operative agriculture has been recording brilliant achievements. Whereas in 1939, the average rice yield per hectare for a single crop was only 1.3 tons, in 1959, the figure was 2.07 tons for the Summer crop and 2.41 tons for the Autumn crop.[5] In 1955 rice output was around 3.5 million tons. In 1959 it already reached the 5.19 million mark. Even in war-time conditions, agricultural output in 1965 was still much higher than in 1964 and at present, firmly confident of their capabilities, various agricultural co-ops are striving to obtain 5 tons of paddy per hectare annually on a vast acreage. This effort has been crowned with success in many localities. By 1965, up to 680 co-ops had achieved such high yield, among which 20 had brought in from 6 to 6.75 tons.

The might of co-operative agriculture has shattered the theory advanced formerly by colonialist economists who affirmed that the agriculture of the D.R.V. was unable to produce enough food to support its population. Moreover, our agriculture has brought about an important change in

---

[5] Ricefields in Vietnam can yield two crops annually, provided that irrigation and drainage work is appropriately seen to.

the production structure by extending the acreage under industrial crops and fruit trees and realizing the balance between cultivation and animal husbandry. As a result, since 1960 the per capita food and foodstuffs consumption has increased: rice from 115 kilos to 172 kilos, meat from 3.4 kilos to 7.4 kilos, molasses from 0.3 kilo to 1.3 kilos . . .

Successes in agriculture have also created conditions for the stepping up of redistribution of social labour to the advantage of the economy. To date, about 650,000 labourers from the countryside have been supplied to various branches of industry, building, communications and transport. . . .

Along with the successes obtained on the production front, the co-ops have been consolidated and have been developing constantly and vigorously. From low level, small-scale co-ops embracing an average of 24 households in 1958 and 44 households in 1960, today their merging into large-scale, high-level ones, comprising from 200 to 300 households and owning from 150 to 200 hectares of land, has been achieved. Each co-op of this category has in fact become a bulwark of socialism in the countryside, fully capable of grappling with natural calamities and enemy destruction, a bulwark for continued, increased production to supply ever more food and foodstuffs to the army and the population, materials to industry, and farm products for export, and ever-increasing manpower to the fighting and to other branches of production.

In the present war conditions, the building of the material and technical foundations in agriculture, far from being discontinued, is forging ahead. The plan for equipping the agricultural co-ops with small engineering facilities is being pushed ahead and more hydraulic networks and pumping stations are under construction. In various localities, the laying-out of ricefields has begun in conformity with economic and modern technical standards in order to realize hydraulic planning along modern lines and prepare the ground for large-scale mechanization of agriculture.

BIRTH OF A MODERN INDUSTRY

Important achievements have also been registered in industrial construction and development. In 1957, total output value of industry and handicrafts was twice as much as in 1955. By the end of 1960, many medium and major State-run enterprises had been put back to operation or built. Regional industries have also seen rapid development.

Such development made it possible to increase the total output value of industry and handicrafts in 1960 by more than 420 percent over 1955, an average annual increase of 39.1 percent, the increase in group A being 43.9 percent and that in group B 37.1 percent.[6] By 1960, electricity out-

---

[6] Group A are producers' goods (goods used in the production of other goods such as machinery or tools); group B are consumers' goods. [EDITOR'S NOTE]

put had more than doubled compared with 1939, coal output had increased by 2.8 times and cement by 3.5 times compared with 1955, apatite 19.11 times and chromium 12.5 times compared with 1956.

In this period, a series of home-made machine-tools, machines for light industry, motor boats, tug boats, new-type farm implements and fertilizers came off the production line. Fairly satisfactory advance was also reported in various branches of light industry which could already meet about 90 percent of the needs for essential consumer goods. Cloth and silk output rose to 82 million metres in 1960, bringing up the average per capita share to 5.4 metres. Molasses output increased by 3 times and knit-wear, plastic goods, enamelled ware, office equipment, soap, tea, cigarettes, bicycles, car tires and tubes, etc. . . . were all produced by newly built factories.

During the First Five-Year Plan period (1961-1965) more than 40 percent of the total capital investments for economic and cultural building were appropriated for industrial construction annually; of these three-quarters went to the branches of industry producing means of production. This enabled industrial production to record an average annual increase of over 13 percent. The basic branches of heavy industry such as power, metal, chemical, building material, coal mining, timber development and processing also developed at a rapid tempo.

Major thermo-electric and hydro-electric centres were built along with the unified network of transmission lines with the result that the power generated in 1965 increased by more than 11 times compared with 1955. Electric power was not reserved for industrial production only, an important part of it being supplied to the countryside to help agricultural production.

In the same period, work was in the main completed on the construction of the Thai Nguyen Iron and Steel Complex, part of which went into operation, and alongside, the building of series of medium- and small-size factories producing chemicals and building material, major and modern factories producing nitrogenous fertilizer, superphosphate, basic chemicals, P.V.C., pre-cast concrete, glass, etc. . . . mushroomed. Cement works and wood processing factories were equipped with additional modern machines to enlarge production.

The engineering industry developed at a fairly rapid tempo, supplying a wide range of machinery and equipment for various production branches. It delivered to agriculture thousands of Diesel motors and mechanical pumps, tractor-drawn farm machinery, various types of processing machines and thousands of tons of farm implements. In the concluding years of the plan, agricultural engineering introduced the first two types of tractors. Important development was also seen in transport engineering. Following the successful production of rail carriages and motor car spare parts and mass production of bicycles and ball-bearing carts, this branch of engineering has successfully produced locomotives, river and sea tug boats, and at present the building of the first sea-going vessel of great displacement is nearing completion. The equipment of various production branches with modern technique by the engineering industry was also achieved in other fields. Most of the machines and equipment in use in regional industries, from machine-tools and small-size electric motors and power generators to whole sets of equipment used in the production of sugar, paper, building material, farm implements, etc. . . . have been produced locally. Sea fishery has been supplied with motor junks and the wood processing industry with various types of home-made machines.

In the First Five-Year Plan period too, light industry was shaping a structure comprising the most important branches such as food processing, weaving, leather making, tailoring, maize processing, paper making, earthen and glass ware, plastic and rubber goods, metal wares and electric appliances. Hundreds of factories were newly built including big and modern ones, paper making factories with a capacity of 10,000 odd tons, sugar mills capable of handling 1,000 tons of cane daily, factories producing chinaware, electric bulbs and thermos-flasks, the textile combinat, etc. . . . New items of elegant and good-quality goods appeared on the market and what is remarkable is that most of them are made of local material.

A young industry has not only been playing a leading role in the national economy but has also been effectively helping the strengthening of national defence. In accordance with the present wartime conditions and in preparation for future economic development, regional industries are being developed at a particularly high tempo. The building of a series of factories, on not too big a scale, will link still more closely industry with its basis—agriculture—and bring the factories nearer to the sources of raw materials and the markets, rapidly providing various localities with their own industrial bases to satisfy to the utmost their own needs in means of production for agriculture, communications and transport, and the requirements of the fighting and of everyday life. In a short time, the provinces have succeeded in enlarging existing engineering works, building a series of new medium- and small-size thermo-electric and hydroelectric stations and opening new coal mines. Many provinces have been producing themselves chemical fertilizers, cement and such consumer goods as cloth, paper, matches, soap, and cigarettes. While stepping up both production and the fighting, the State continues to invest much money in survey and prospecting work, scientific research work, designing work and the training of workers and technicians, on a large scale, in preparation for major construction plans to be carried out when victory is won.

COMMUNICATIONS AND TRANSPORT

To ensure communications and transport is an urgent central task of the North Vietnamese people in this war. U.S. air raids caused us certain difficulties in the first days. However, thanks to our high patriotism and the diverse experiences we had accumulated during the process of struggle, we rapidly regained the initiative and successfully coped with all enemy tactics.

With regard to the task of keeping communications open under the watchword *"if the enemy destroy our roads and bridges we rebuild them, if they destroy them again we again rebuild them,"* the cadres, workers, and people have displayed high devotion, day and night having remained at their posts, braving sacrifices and U.S. frenzied attacks, to repair roads and build ferries to ensure uninterrupted traffic in order to meet in time the imperative transport needs. In many localities the people introduced many innovations of economic and technical value to solve the difficulties which we had never foreseen, making it impossible for the enemy to seal off our roads, hamper our waterways or disrupt our communication and transport lines.

Deeply imbued with the people's war line of the Party, a powerful mass movement has been launched in all localities to keep communications clear. The population of the provinces along important communication lines have contributed millions of workdays to their restoration, to the building of new roads, the dredging of canals and rivers, the building of ferries, ferry boats and bridges of various types. . . . They also have taken an active part in the transportation by primitive means to assist the State transport service. The army has valiantly defended the bridges and roads and with the communication service has participated directly in ensuring traffic on the important lines. All branches concerned have actively helped, or worked in close co-ordination with, the communication service, supplying it with man-power, material and equipment and together with it have ensured the transportation of various kinds of goods in a more and more rational and faster and faster manner.

As regards the ensuring of transport, the cadres and workers in the transport units have been struggling under the slogan "to bring one kilogram of goods to its destination is to score a hit at the U.S. aggressors and contribute one more brick to the building of socialism." They have been working very diligently but with constant calmness, courage, perseverance, and staunchness, grasping firmly their steering wheels and never abandoning their oars, determined to hold their ground, showing much resourcefulness in dealing with enemy aircraft and fulfilling satisfactorily their transport missions in most difficult circumstances.

Due to the requirements of an arduous, fierce, and protracted struggle between us and the enemy, the contingent of cadres and workers in communications and transport has grown at a tremendous pace. In the period of only one year, generally speaking, it doubled compared with the previous period. That is a valuable capital of ours. We must see to it that it is used in the most satisfactory way.

For many months now, the average volume of goods transported per month has exceeded the level of late 1964. This is actually a brilliant victory of the people's war, of our people's national defence.

CULTURAL AND SOCIAL ACTIVITIES

The war of resistance against U.S. aggression for national salvation has blown a fresh wind into the cultural and social activities in North Vietnam, given rise to urgent requirements and opened up broad vistas for educational, cultural, medical, and sport activities.

The training of cadres has been promoted more vigorously than ever. The 1965-1966 student body increased considerably over any of the previous years. General education and adult complementary education was

Table 18-1. School Attendance in the DRV
(in numbers of total pupils or students enrolled)

School Year	Infant Classes	Nursery Classes	General Schools	Inter-mediate Professional Schools	Comple-mentary Education Classes [a]	University
1939-40[b]	82,000	(N.G.)[c]	567,300	400	(N.G.)	582
1955-56	522,000	800	716,100	2,800	458,343	1,200
1960-61	795,000	30,000	1,899,600	30,700	(N.G.)	13,000
1963-64	778,800	149,300	2,599,700	57,800	1,068,797	26,500

[a] Primarily adult education.

[b] The figures for the 1939-40 academic year include pupils and students for the whole of former French-occupied Indo-China, comprising Vietnam, Laos, and Cambodia.

[c] Figures not given.

SOURCE: *Vietnam,* November, 1964, pp. 4-5.

maintained and even developed. Nearly three million children are continuing their schooling in general education schools and more than one million labouring people are regularly attending cultural and technical classes in all co-operatives, factories, construction sites, public offices or town districts. A new orientation has been given to the school's curricula with a view to serving better production and the fighting and the education service has made many efforts to continue expanding and improving the training of cadres in the new conditions. The graduated students and pupils have zealously accepted any jobs assigned to them at any places and have been displaying great courage in the fight against the U.S. aggressors for national salvation.

For more than one year now, the cultural life of the people and the activities of the cultural, literary and art branches have given birth to works more stirring and beautiful in form and richer in content. Writers and artists have enthusiastically been immersed in the realities of the anti-

U.S. resistance for national salvation, and have been drawing the profound and noble inspiration for new creations—noted for their ideological and artistic value—which contribute to the enhancing of the revolutionary heroism of the various sections of the people. The mass movement for cultural and artistic activities, reading books and newspapers, and listening to the radio, has been spreading to all localities. The life in production and the fighting though strenuous and full of hardships is nonetheless filled with merriness, optimism, determination to fight and to win, and boundless confidence in the final victory.

The medical department continues to score outstanding achievements. In spite of the strain of production and fighting, the health of the armymen and the people remain fair and the fight against frequently met diseases continues unabated. The protection of mothers and children continues to develop in the right direction and initial good results have been achieved in many respects. The patriotic movement of physical training and hygiene combined with the prevention and combat against the chemical and biological warfare has also become widespread. A broad network of first-aid stations for victims of air raids has been set up from the co-operative upwards and has proved very effective in limiting to a large extent the losses caused by enemy raids. The movement of physical training and national defence sports to get ready to fight against the enemy to save the country has been forging ahead in many sections of the people, especially among the young men and women.

THE WAR DOESN'T STOP US

In 1965, the U.S. imperialists brought the war of destruction to the North.

In the same year, the First Five-Year Plan of the DRV ended successfully with outstanding achievements in the development of production and fighting. . . .

If 1965 witnessed the U.S. imperialists' launching their war of destruction with continued raids on hydraulic works, fertilizer factories and state farms, and even with savage bombings and strafings of villages and hamlets as well as peasants working in the fields, it also witnessed the annual food output reaching the level of the peak years in the plan period. In a situation in which production and fighting should be carried out simultaneously, paddy output in most heavily hit provinces (in the former 4th interzone) increased by up to 14.2 percent. In particular, Autumn rice output increased by 26.5 percent compared with 1964. . . .[7]

The successful fulfilment of the main economic norms of the Five-Year Plan brought about a marked improvement of the people's living

[7] Many of the detailed figures of production and production increases had to be omitted for reasons of space limitations. Such figures can be found, for instance, in *Vietnam Courier* (May 5, May 12, and August 22, 1966). [EDITOR'S NOTE]

standards. In 1965 the peasants' income showed an increase of about 24 percent over 1960. Whereas in the past only a few families could afford blankets, mosquito nets, various items of furniture and other household utensils, nowadays these are very common in the countryside. Many peasants were able to build brick houses. Most of their children have been receiving schooling and most of the country youth have completed the 4th or 5th grade. In the cities, every able-bodied person has been given employment. The state ensured the supply of food, and other necessities to everybody according to his rations and at stable prices. At the same time, more housing, more public eating places, more nurseries and more other social welfare amenities were provided to the people.

The tasks laid down in the First Five-Year Plan, starting in 1961, were to take an initial step in socialist industrialization, to build the first material and technical foundations of socialism and at the same time to continue to carry through socialist transformation.

At present, the Vietnamese people in the North have begun to carry out the revolutionary task set before them by the new Plan for economic construction and development, the task of simultaneously defeating the U.S. imperialists' aggressive war at whatever level it may be, and of going on with socialist building in the North.

War-time conditions call for a necessary changeover in the economy. The DRV has worked out a two-year plan providing for the continued socialist industrialisation and building of the material and technical foundations of socialism and the firm consolidation of the new relations of production. While paying attention to meeting the immediate war requirements, all-out efforts should be made to step up preparatory measures for future economic building and development.

THE DRV FORGES AHEAD

The socialist State belongs to the working people. Therefore, parallel with economic development, it always takes steps to increase social welfare and improve the people's living conditions.

The socialist regime and the socialist economy in the DRV have gone through two trying years in war, beginning right at the age of twenty full of vitality. The generation which carried aloft the banner of the August Revolution, which experienced nearly nine years of armed resistance against French colonialism and ten years of socialist revolution, and which has been building socialism successfully, is not yet gone. Nowadays, with the abundant experiences of twenty years of revolutionary struggle, this generation is being engaged in a new battle, the anti-U.S. war of resistance for national salvation, jointly with the new younger generation born and grown up with the Republic. Two generations are fighting shoulder to shoulder to defend the freedom and happiness won at the cost of their own blood and sweat. As a matter of course, it is no wonder that millions of co-operative farmers and factory workers, as collective masters of their co-operatives and factories are so deeply attached to socialism. How heroic they are in the fighting and in production! What splendid gallantry officers and men of the People's Army, sons of the workers and the peasants, have been displaying in combat action to defend their socialist Fatherland, their native villages and cities and the lives and property of their dear ones! . . .

IV. THE VIETNAMESE PEOPLE WILL SURELY DEFEAT THE AGGRESSORS! (A MESSAGE BY HO CHI MINH TO HIS PEOPLE) [8]

Compatriots and fighters throughout the country, the barbarous U.S. imperialists have unleashed a war of aggression in an attempt to conquer our country, but they have been sustaining heavy defeats.

They have rushed an expeditionary force of about 300,000 men into the Southern part of our country. They have used a puppet administration and a mercenary army created by them as instruments of their aggressive policy. They have been resorting to extremely savage means of warfare: toxic chemicals, napalm bombs, etc. They have been applying the "burn all, kill all, and destroy all" policy. With such crimes, they hope to subdue our southern compatriots.

But under the firm and wise leadership of the National Front for Liberation, the South Vietnam army and people, closely united and fighting heroically, have scored very glorious victories, and are determined to struggle until complete victory in order to liberate the South, defend the North, and achieve eventual national reunification.

The U.S. aggressors have been brazenly lanching air attacks on North Vietnam in an attempt to get out of the quagmire in the South and to impose on us "negotiations" on their terms.

But North Vietnam will not falter. Our army and people have shown redoubled eagerness in the emulation to produce and fight heroically. So far, we have blasted out of the skies over 1,200 enemy aircraft. We are determined to defeat the enemy's war of destruction and at the same time to extend all-out support to our dear compatriots in the South.

Of late, the U.S. aggressors hysterically took a very serious step further in the escalation of the war: they launched air attacks on the suburbs of Hanoi and Haiphong. That was an act of desperation comparable to the death throes of a grievously wounded wild beast.

[8] From "President Ho Chi Minh's Appeal," *Vietnam Courier* (July 21, 1966), p. 2. Complete text.

Johnson and his clique should realize this: They may bring in 500,000 troops, one million or even more to step up the war of aggression in South Vietnam. They may use thousands of aircraft for intensified attacks against North Vietnam. But never will they be able to break the iron will of the heroic Vietnamese people to fight against U.S. aggression, for national salvation. The more savage they are, the graver their crime. The war may last another five, ten, twenty years or longer. Hanoi, Haiphong and other cities, and enterprises may be destroyed, but the Vietnamese people will not be intimidated! Nothing is more precious than independence and freedom. Once victory is won, our people will rebuild our country and endow it with bigger and more beautiful constructions.

It is common knowledge that each time they are about to step up their criminal war, the U.S. aggressors always resort to their "peace talks" swindle in an attempt to fool world opinion and blame Vietnam for unwillingness to negotiate!

President Johnson, reply publicly to the American people and the peoples of the world: *Who has sabotaged the Geneva Agreements which guarantee the sovereignty, independence, unity and territorial integrity of Vietnam? Have Vietnamese troops invaded the United States and massacred Americans? Is it not the U.S. Government which has sent U.S. troops to invade Vietnam and massacre Vietnamese?*

Let the United States end its war of aggression in Vietnam, withdraw all U.S. and satellite troops from this country, and peace will return here at once. Vietnam's stand is clear: it is the four points of the Government of the Democratic Republic of Vietnam and the five points of the South Vietnam National Front for Liberation. There is no other alternative!

The Vietnamese people cherish peace, a genuine peace, a peace in independence and freedom, not a sham peace, not an "American peace."

For the defence of the independence of the Fatherland, and for the fulfillment of our obligation to the peoples struggling against U.S. imperialism, our people and army, united as one man, will resolutely fight till complete victory whatever the sacrifices and hardships may be. In the past, we defeated the Japanese fascists and the French colonialists in much more difficult circumstances. Today the conditions at home and abroad are more favourable, our people's struggle against U.S. aggression, for national salvation is sure to win a total victory.

Dear compatriots and fighters, we are strong because of the justice of our cause, the unity of our entire people from North to South, our traditions of undaunted struggle, and the broad sympathy and support of the fraternal socialist countries and progressive people throughout the world. We shall win!

At this new juncture, we are as one in our determination to undergo any hardships and sacrifices, and resolutely fulfill the glorious historic task of our people: to defeat the U.S. aggressors!

On behalf of the Vietnamese people, I take this opportunity to express heartfelt thanks to the peoples of the socialist countries and progressive people in the world, including the American people, for their devoted support and assistance. In face of the new criminal schemes of the U.S. imperialists, I am firmly confident that the peoples and governments of the fraternal socialist countries, and the peace- and justice-loving countries in the world will still more vigorously support and help the Vietnamese people until total victory in their struggle against U.S. aggression, for national salvation.

The Vietnamese people will win!
The U.S. aggressors will inevitably be defeated!
Long live a peaceful, reunified, independent, democratic, and prosperous
    Vietnam!
Compatriots and fighters throughout the country, march valiantly forward!

IX

The Republic of Cuba: Communism's Beachhead in the Western Hemisphere

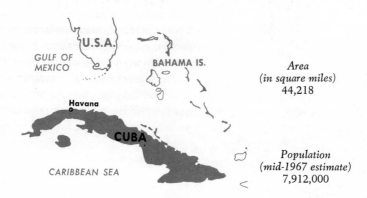

GULF OF
MEXICO

U.S.A.

BAHAMA IS.

Havana

CUBA

CARIBBEAN SEA

Area
(in square miles)
44,218

Population
(mid-1967 estimate)
7,912,000

We had to choose between remaining under the domina-
tion, under the exploitation and, moreover, under the
insolence of imperialism, continuing to put up with
Yankee ambassadors giving the orders here, keeping our
country in the state of poverty it was in, or making an
anti-imperialist revolution, a socialist revolution.

DR. FIDEL CASTRO RUIZ
PRIME MINISTER, REPUBLIC OF CUBA

After holding out in an unprecedented struggle against
the United States of America, the stronghold of world
imperialism and neocolonialism, little Cuba lighted a
fire of freedom in Latin America and like a lighthouse
shows the path to a new life to peoples who have suf-
fered long and much.

YURI GAGARIN
SOVIET ASTRONAUT AND PRESIDENT
OF THE SOVIET-CUBAN FRIENDSHIP SOCIETY

INTRODUCTION

WHAT WEST BERLIN IS TO EAST GERMANY, WHAT ALBANIA IS TO the Soviet Union, that Cuba is to the United States: a thorn in, or dangerously near, the flesh of the body politic, small in size and power but great in the pain it can cause.

The most serious danger that Cuba presents to the Western Hemisphere does not emanate from her military power and prowess, nor from her ability to train saboteurs and guerrillas for operations elsewhere. The most serious danger, rather, lies in the example she may set, the model she may provide for the poverty-stricken masses in other Latin American countries; for here on that little island, a band of men accomplished the well-nigh impossible: a mere handful,[1] without the benefit of aid, they succeeded in rallying sufficient support in their own country to overthrow a powerfully entrenched government that had the backing of the country's armed forces and of most of its wealthy classes. And, once in power, the revolutionaries proceeded to take over foreign property, to nationalize means of production, and, finally, to align themselves not with the governments of their neighboring countries in the Western Hemisphere but with those of the thirteen other countries of the Communist World. No wonder the United States has a direct interest in seeing that the experiment fails, while the Communist World has an equally great stake in making it succeed! Just as Washington was willing to pour

[1] Only eleven men out of Castro's invasion force of 82 in December, 1956, survived and reached the Sierra Maestra.

497

large sums of money into West Berlin to make this enclave a shining example of Western life within the frontiers of communism, so the Communist World wants to convert Cuba into a showplace within the Western
Hemisphere as an object lesson for all to observe, as proof that the short-
cut from underdevelopment to affluence leads along the path of revolutionary
Marxism-Leninism.

Few Western students of the Cuban Revolution deny that Cuba's
economic and political situation in the late 1950's was such as to provide
fertile ground for radical expressions of discontent. Here, within the very
shadow of fashionable southern Florida, was an island richly endowed with
fertile soil and with climatic conditions extremely favorable for the raising
not only of sugar cane but also of a wide variety of crops. Yet, here was also
an island in which the masses of the people, especially outside of Havana,
lived in extreme squalor and poverty, while a few enjoyed great wealth—a
fact which made even the relatively low "average" income rather meaningless
since that "average" was representative of neither extreme. But while the
Revolution may have appeared to many as a highly desirable and long over-
due event, welcomed indeed by the overwhelming majority of the Cuban
population, the question as to whether the new society had to be constructed
along Marxist-Leninist lines is a different question altogether.

In an interview granted to American journalists while he was still
fighting in the Sierra Maestra, Castro explained that he considered nationalization of private productive property troublesome and an interference with
industrialization, and that he would welcome foreign investments.[2] However,
on December 2, 1961, three years after his Revolutionary Government had
come to power, he asserted that his ideas at the outset of the Revolution
"were very similar to those I hold today," and that "I am a Marxist-Leninist
and shall be one until my last day on earth." Many Western scholars feel
that, whatever Castro's intentions may have been, actions of the United
States (trade embargo, refusal to purchase sugar, economic blockade, etc.),
even if they came in retaliation for some anti-U.S. steps by Castro, left the
Revolutionary Government no choice but to look for a benefactor to under-
write the Cuban Revolution, thus forcing Cuba to turn to the communist
countries and especially to the Soviet Union. In any case, the Cuban Revolution in many respects did not fit into the pattern of communist revolutions
elsewhere, since here was a revolution which was not led by the country's
Communist Party, a revolution in which the Party did not even participate,
a revolution which, when it turned "Marxist-Leninist," surprised and caught
off guard not only the United States but also the Soviet Union. Even today,
a Western scholar such as Alfred Meyer expresses uncertainty "whether
Cuba should be included" within the countries which comprise the "Communist World" (see p. 13 above) while another scholar, C. Ian Lumsden,

[2] See *Coronet* (February, 1958).

writes in the concluding paragraph of a recent article on Cuba that "Castro is committed principally to the Cuban revolution, and his involvement in the world Communist movement is incidental to this fact. . . . He became a Communist because it was the only way in which he could obtain the aid that he sought." [3]

Understandably, then, Cuba hesitated to become involved in the Sino-Soviet split, eager not to antagonize either side, and anxious to maintain cordial relations with both. During the era of its great revolutionary fervor and its hope of spreading "Fidelismo" in short order throughout much of Latin America, it was often reported that the hearts of the Cuban revolutionaries were with the Chinese, but their stomachs with the Soviets, who could more readily provide substantial and much needed economic support. But when the Chinese started sending quantities of anti-Soviet propaganda materials to Cuba to influence the Cuban Party members and government officials, and when, moreover, in the late summer of 1966 China reneged on a sugar-for-rice trade deal with Cuba, Cuba turned fairly strongly against China. Soviet aid to Cuba, in the meantime, is reported to continue at a rate of about one million dollars per day (and total aid from all communist countries may well total 500 million dollars annually). This Soviet aid, moreover, is expected to be sustained at the same rate until after 1970. By then Cuba may no longer be in need of such extensive economic assistance; by then she may have solved some of her most urgent problems, such as the training of the much needed professional, technical, and administrative personnel to take the place of the middle classes, whose ranks have been depleted by mass emigration.

As regards the U.S. attitude toward Cuba's revolutionary regime, it has, as of the time of this writing in November, 1966, not deviated from President Kennedy's position that "Communism in the Western Hemisphere is not negotiable." No more conciliatory is Cuba's position, exemplified by Fidel Castro's 1966 statement that "Cuba will be the last country ever to make peace with imperialism, because the United States imperialists have offended, injured, humiliated, exploited, molested, and threatened our country as they have no other."

Perhaps even more than is the case with most communist countries, there is a great divergence of opinion in the Western World regarding the Cuban Revolution and its leaders. Some comments are extremely critical: "Now your leaders are no longer Cuban leaders inspired by Cuban ideals," President Kennedy addressed the Cuban people during the missile crisis of

[3] C. Ian Lumsden, "Cuba," in Adam Bromke, ed., *The Communist States at the Crossroads Between Moscow and Peking* (New York, Praeger, 1965), p. 178.

October 1962. "They are," he continued, "puppets and agents of an international conspiracy which has turned Cuba against your friends and neighbors
in the Americas." A former Havana University economics professor and
dean, Dr. José R. Alvarez Díaz, referred to Castro as a "master of deceit," [4]
and Manuel Urrutia Lleó, Cuba's first President under the Castro regime,
writes that "The great Cuban democratic revolution was kidnapped by
communists, led by Castro." [5] But other Western scholars, although by no
means Marxists, nor uncritical of past events in Cuba, take a somewhat
more sympathetic view, trying to understand what happened in light of the
peculiar circumstances of the time. Dudley Seers, contributor of a non-
Marxist view on Cuba, would probably fall in the latter group.

Educated at Rugby and Pembroke College, Cambridge, Dudley Seers
has held numerous high positions in government and in academic life. He
was, for instance, Research Economist at the Prime Minister's Office of the
government of New Zealand, Research Economist and later Senior Lecturer
in Economic Statistics at Oxford, Research Economist at United Nations
Headquarters, Chief of the Special Studies Group of the U.N. Economic
Commission for Latin America, and Visiting Professor of Economics at Yale
University. He has worked with the governments of many countries including Burma, Ghana, Malta, Jamaica, Trinidad, and Guyana; he led the
1963-64 United Nations Economic Survey Mission to Zambia; he has
published numerous articles on economic topics; and he edited, and wrote the
first chapter of *Cuba: The Economic and Social Revolution.*[6] He has held
his present position as Director-General of the Economic Planning Staff of
England's Ministry of Overseas Development since 1964. Seers wrote this
article before he joined the British government; it was based on visits to
Cuba in 1962.

Since Seers' contribution does not deal with some of the questions that
have been of concern and interest to Americans, it was felt advisable to
include another, complementary, non-Marxist view on Cuba. The one
selected stresses the impact of Castro's "charismatic" personality on post-
Revolutionary Cuba. More critical of the Cuban regime than Seers, its
author, Ernst Halperin, is a Swiss citizen and holder of a Ph.D. degree in
history from the University of Zurich. His numerous writings include a
book on Titoism entitled *Triumphant Heretic* (London, Heinemann, 1958),
and another on *Nationalism and Communism in Chile* (Cambridge, M.I.T.
Press, 1965). In 1961 and 1963, Halperin spent several months in Cuba. At
the time he wrote the article included here, he was a Research Associate in
Communist Affairs at the Center for International Studies, Massachusetts

[4] Unpublished manuscript.
[5] Manuel Urrutia Lleó, *Fidel Castro and Company, Inc.* (New York, Praeger,
1964), p. vii.
[6] Dudley Seers, *Cuba: The Economic and Social Revolution* (Chapel Hill, N.C.,
University of North Carolina Press, 1964).

Institute of Technology. In 1967, Halperin became Professor of Political Science at the Miami University Institute of Inter-American Studies.

The Marxist view on Cuba has been contributed by Edward Boorstein. Recipient of an M.A. degree in economics from Columbia University, Boorstein has worked as an economist for several agencies of the United States government including the War Production Board, for the Economic Commission for Latin America of the United Nations, and as a private economic consultant. He worked for three-and-a-half years in the Cuban Ministry of Foreign Commerce under the revolutionary regime. He has written a book entitled *Cuba: The Political Economy of Socialist Revolution,* scheduled for publication in 1967 by Monthly Review Press.

19

Cuba: The Economic and

Social Revolution:

A Non-Marxist View

DUDLEY SEERS *

DIRECTOR-GENERAL, ECONOMIC PLANNING STAFF
MINISTRY OF OVERSEAS DEVELOPMENT,
HER MAJESTY'S GOVERNMENT

I

I should begin by stressing the fact that Cuba was not, on the eve of the
Revolution, by any means a developed country. Economically, socially, and
politically, it was in numerous ways different from the countries of North
America and Western Europe, even the small ones.

In the first place, it relied heavily on exports of a single product, sugar.
A sugar economy has certain well-known characteristics. Plantations are the
predominant form of agricultural organization, and sugar mills account for
the majority of industry.

To say that sugar output provided a fifth of Cuba's national product is
in a way an understatement, because a great deal of the rest of the product
was bought out of sugar incomes or out of taxes on imports financed by
sugar exports or out of incomes created by those incomes and taxes, and so
on. If exports of sugar rose, the national income rose, and investment became
profitable, sustaining the rise; when sugar markets fell, many forces combined to pull the whole economy downwards. This was true of seasonal
fluctuations, trade cycles, and long-term trends alike. . . .

Condensed from Dudley Seers' *Cuba: The Economic and Social Revolution*
(Chapel Hill, N.C., University of North Carolina Press), Chapter 1. Reprinted here by
permission of the author and the publisher.

Cuba must therefore be seen as one of many backward economies making attempts to break out of this impasse. Industrialization has become increasingly the order of the day. Yet this is not a simple business. . . .

Sooner or later, it becomes clear that what is needed is the reform of the social structure, especially land reform, to limit the demand for luxuries and to create mass markets, large middle classes, a dynamic farm economy, and an educated and flexible labor force. Such reform has been slow in coming in Latin America. . . .

Although economic statistics [on Cuba] are not firm enough to permit much confidence to be placed in them, especially for the years before 1947, the general impression they give is unmistakable. It is one of chronic stagnation from the 1920's onwards in real per-capita income. The upward trend in income barely kept pace with the rise in population, which averaged rather more than 2 percent a year between the censuses of 1919 and 1943. Very tentative estimates . . . indicate that the end-of-war boom of 1944-47 hardly brought average real incomes back to the levels of corresponding years for the previous war (1916-19) . . . and in 1958 per-capita real income was still only about the same as it had been in 1947. . . .

Slowing down of economic growth to a virtual standstill was matched by a similar halt in progress in social fields. Illiteracy, after falling to relatively low levels in the first quarter of the century, failed to decline further. In fact, the proportion of children of school age attending primary school in the 1950's was lower than in the 1920's.

Cuba in the 35 years from 1923 to 1958 showed little progress. The stagnation was more serious and lasted longer than in any other Latin American economy—excepting perhaps the economies of one or two very small and poor nations such as Bolivia and Haiti. . . .

Two institutional explanations for this chronic stagnation stand out. The first is that the great majority of the land was held in large estates. Twenty-two large sugar companies accounted for about one-fifth of the agricultural area, and some of this land was held in reserve against a boom in sugar prices. . . . Moreover, the sugar companies insisted on refining the bulk of their output overseas, inside the industrial countries, and Cuba did not therefore benefit much from the quite considerable income and employment generated in sugar processing.

The second reason is the trade treaties with the United States, especially the Reciprocal Trade Agreement of 1934, which was associated with the concessions on Cuban sugar and which remained in force (with some modifications) until the Revolution. Under this agreement, . . . doors were held open to imports from the United States, including foodstuffs. But the main effect was on Cuban manufactures. The industrialization to be found in other Latin American economies of a similar size was never attempted. Such factories as were established were mostly light consumer-goods industries which traditionally come at an early stage of industrializa-

tion (e.g., food and textile processing). Basic metal and engineering industries had already been firmly established in Chile, Colombia, and Mexico
by the middle of the 1950's, but not in Cuba. . . .

If further progress was almost impossible to achieve, the status quo in
1958 was intolerable, especially for a country so close to Florida and receiving
through many channels an imposing (perhaps exaggerated) picture of North
American levels of living. Income per capita per year averaged about $500
or one-fifth as much as the average in the United States (far lower even
than in any Southern state there). Yet by international standards this was
not so bad. Only Venezuela and Argentina, of the larger Latin American
countries, had a higher average income. What was intolerable was, first, a
level of unemployment some three times as high as in the United States.
In few families were all the male adults steadily employed. . . .

Second, in the countryside social conditions were very bad. About a
third of the nation existed in squalor, eating rice, beans, bananas, and root
vegetables (with hardly any meat, fish, eggs, or milk), living in huts, usually
without electricity or toilet facilities, suffering from parasitic diseases and
lacking access to health services, denied education (their children received
only a first grade education, if that). Particularly distressing was the lot of
the *precaristas,* those squatting in makeshift quarters on public land.

A substantial fraction of the town population was also very poor. Here,
too, there were squatters living in shacks, and of course there were slum
tenements. In 1953 no less than one-fifth of families lived in single rooms,
and the average size of these families was five, according to the census. . . .

II

So the revolutionary government took over an economy that was structurally
unsound. It depended excessively on exports of a single, not very promising
crop. . . . The country relied on imports for advanced engineering products
as well as for basic sources of energy. . . . Since most of the equipment
came from the United States, the economy depended on a flow of spare
parts from North American firms. The distributors in Cuba of both semi-
manufactures and consumer goods . . . knew only those sources of supply,
and customers were used to U.S. brands. The Cuban economy was so wedded
to the U.S. economy that the country was in many ways an appendage of it
—though without enjoying, as a poor state in the United States does, federal
social services or access to U.S. sources of employment. Such lack of independence would have hampered any policy of diversification, however
imaginative. . . .

The trade structure was reflected in an unbalanced structure of production and employment: . . . 42 percent of the labor force was engaged in agriculture and a further 37 percent in service industries of various kinds (a very high proportion). . . .

The educational structure of the labor force was another severe problem. Even in the cities, professional workers (other than lawyers and teachers) were few—especially engineers, who numbered less than 3,000 in 1953. There was, in fact, little incentive to educate oneself highly unless one wanted to work overseas; underemployment was not uncommon among lawyers, city doctors, architects, and engineers. . . . Skilled workers were not scarce for the needs of the time, but they were certainly far too few for rapid industrial advance.

The administrative system was inefficient and notoriously corrupt. . . .

In these various respects, Cuba was probably worse off even than other comparable Latin American countries, and these profound disabilities complicated the task of structural change which lay ahead. Yet the . . . Cuban Revolution started with advantages unknown to the other socialist regimes on taking power.

In the first place, it did not face the need to repair great physical (and psychological) devastation left by international and internal wars. . . . Second—in company with the Soviet Union, Yugoslavia, and China—it achieved its revolution without direct intervention by another socialist country; its success in this regard implied a firmer political base and moreover meant that nationalism could be more easily harnessed. . . . Third, because of the very structure of agriculture, a large fraction of the agricultural labor force was, like the sugar mill workers, accustomed to organized and disciplined paid employment. Fourth, the existence of a communications network, especially television, made it possible to convey new policies rapidly to the public (and later to organize extensive adult education). Fifth, a fairly high standard of living, by comparison with other new socialist nations (except Czechoslovakia) gave the government some room to maneuver. Declines in food consumption did not raise the specter of starvation, and it was not out of the question to think of devoting a high proportion of the national product to investment. Last, there were by 1959 other countries with a similar political system, especially the Soviet Union itself; these were economically strong enough to provide considerable quantities of equipment on credit, to supply petroleum, to make technical advisers and training facilities available, and to guarantee a market for the bulk of Cuban exports. . . .

Moreover, the relatively low level of economic activity in 1958 meant that there were idle resources which could be mobilized quite quickly. There was spare land; . . . much of the labor force was unemployed or underemployed; . . . in some sectors there was idle capital, or at least capital being used well below capacity, and quite high inventories. From another point of view, resources which were being used, but used to provide luxury goods or services (such as domestic service), could be diverted to more productive purposes. . . .

We must therefore judge Cuban performance since the Revolution against the relatively fast increase in output that was physically manageable. Nevertheless, there were some special disadvantages faced by the Cuban government, compared to the other socialist countries. The first was the close proximity to a country which had previously had a dominant position in the Cuban economy. . . . Conflicts of interest, which had to emerge as links were broken, were many and acute; . . . and relations deteriorated to a point not far short of war, with the United States government virtually ending trade with the island and endeavoring to induce its many allies to do likewise. . . .

The effort required to industrialize a country like Cuba is a tremendous one, whatever the specific external and local situation, particularly if the object is at the same time to raise local food consumption. A full-fledged industrial economy, whether socialist or capitalist, requires a technically trained labor force accustomed to factory or farm discipline, a large corps of professional people, and administrators accustomed to organized routine and capable of intelligent foresight. It needs some set of incentives which will induce people to study and to be willing to forgo immediate consumption for the sake of the future. It implies the creation of organizations in every sector and at every level, with channels of responsibility and the scope for decision clearly defined, and it involves finding people capable of filling top jobs satisfactorily and preparing them to do so. All this cannot be achieved in a few years, or painlessly, in an underdeveloped tropical country where such a small fraction of the adult labor force had received an education which was in any degree complete.

III

. . . Some account of the social change which had occurred is essential if other developments, especially in education, are to be understood and correctly assessed. To leave it out would be less "objective" than to attempt an accurate statement of its significance.

In the first place, there has been a general improvement in the economic lot of the country workers and many peasants. . . . The declared intention of the revolutionary regime is to integrate the population by eliminating the great differences between town and country. This policy has been put into effect partly by giving country districts a big share in new housing and roads, by constructing state shops (*tiendas del pueblo*) in these districts, by rapidly electrifying rural areas, and by expanding medical services in the countryside. The agrarian reform, which has given titles to squatters and tenants and eliminated rent obligations, was another means of achieving this end. So was decreeing a national minimum wage of 60 pesos a month in rural districts. Recruiting thousands of workers for the state farms (*granjas del pueblo*) and giving most rural workers year-round employment had the same effect.

Perhaps the biggest psychological impact has been that of the educational program. The campaign against illiteracy sent more than 100,000 people, mostly adolescents, into the countryside in 1961, the "Year of Education," with the declared aim of teaching all adults to read and write. The big expansion in primary education (now almost universal) has mainly benefited the children of country workers, because previously they were largely neglected. . . .

The urban worker has also benefited economically, but not to the same extent. His family's income probably has not risen as much, though here too the decline in unemployment has had significant economic effects. The reduction of rents in 1959 [1] and the assurance under the urban reform of 1960 that he would become the owner of the house he was living in particularly favored him.

There are some measures, apart from education, which benefit both town and country workers. One is that holiday facilities are now available cheaply to union members in hotels previously out of their reach—in some cases, they are free as prizes for high production. Private clubs, including all private beaches, have been thrown open to the public, and facilities for tourism and sports have been greatly extended. Much of the investment, especially in the first three years of the Revolution, was social rather than productive and in various ways raised living standards. [2]

Moves towards social equality have been matched by an egalitarian income policy. Very few new appointments are made at more than $300 a month, which can be compared with the $60-a-month minimum agricultural wage ($69 on a state farm) and the $85 minimum urban wage. The new wage structure . . . is matched by a proposed new pension plan with a minimum of $40 and a maximum of $250 in monthly benefits (rural workers would be brought into such a plan for the first time). The same social security bill establishes benefits for incapacitation, death (for burial), and widowhood. Since taxes are graduated (especially if one includes as taxes the profits made by nationalized industries on luxury products), the measure of equality in Cuba is very high.

The structural and social changes that have occurred have also meant

[1] Rents were reduced 50 percent if they were less than 100 pesos a month (40 percent if between 100 and 200 pesos, 30 percent if higher than 200), under the law of March 10, 1959.

[2] It seems that more than 20,000 dwellings were constructed in the first 4 years of the Revolution, of which 12,000 were in rural areas, according to data difficult to interpret in an article by Jose Carneado (*Cuba Socialista* [October, 1962]).

that there are almost countless vacancies in professional, supervisory, and technical jobs. Many of these are being filled by former workers. Large-scale vocational training courses of various types have been created; there are also numerous other programs of instruction of a less vocational nature available to workers. . . .

A point which must be stressed is the change that has come about in the quality of administrators, from a corrupt and self-seeking clique to a group which evidently cannot be influenced by bribery and which lives modestly and works extremely hard. This is not to say that there are no complaints. The restraint on wages, the scarcity of food (especially in the towns), the shortage of a wide variety of consumer goods, and price increases on some, offset, at least in part, economic gains in other directions. There are political reasons for objection, too, such as the absorption of religious education in the state system (July, 1961), the suppression of organized political opposition, the limitation of trade-union activity, the undoubted problems of dealing with bureaucrats (and such dealings are unavoidable), the lack of news media reflecting a critical point of view, the virtual impossibility of obtaining non-technical journals or newspapers from foreign countries, the use in the schools of a rather narrow form of Marxism. These are common grumbles. I would not attempt to judge whether the working class is in fact better off, for that would involve trying to weigh essentially incomparable changes.

The crucial question is whether wage-earners believe they are better off. . . .

A careful sample survey among factory workers carried out in 1962 by Dr. Maurice Zeitlin, of Princeton, . . . indicated that rather over two-thirds considered themselves in favor of the regime. Many have good reason to feel this way, particularly if one bears in mind the complete absence of grounds for hope before 1959, especially in the countryside. . . .

Groups other than wage-earners have more reason to oppose the Revolution. Certainly the former rich are in most ways worse off and feel strongly hostile. They suffer most from the political restraints and yet lose most by the economic changes. Luxury goods are hard to get; meals are difficult to vary; foreign travel is virtually impossible (except to the Soviet Union and Eastern Europe); the nationalization of property has reduced their incomes.[3] Moreover, social changes, such as the training of domestic servants for other jobs and the abolition of private schools and beaches, are directly against their interests.

The middle classes, too, have many possible grounds for discontent. The equalization of incomes is in part at their expense, and they may particularly resent conformist tendencies. The professional often cannot avoid

---

[3] Though in many cases they draw life pensions as compensations. One hundred and eighteen thousand who formerly owned houses for letting receive a total monthly pension of $6,000,000 (Carneado, *Cuba Socialista*).

taking a stand one way or another on political questions; many teachers, for example, object to the pressure put to them to adapt their instruction to current political requirements. . . .

In fact, support for the regime is evidently strongly correlated with former income, as it is also with skin color (though this may be largely a reflection of the income effect, since race was itself correlated with income), and with age.

Large numbers have been leaving Cuba as refugees. . . . The policy of the government in permitting emigration had obvious political consequences, since it gradually removed much of the opposition.[4] But it also has economic implications, for it meant a serious loss of professional and technical skill. Yet on the other hand, it provided the government with a supply of large houses and cars, since refugees who ran these had to give them up. . . .

IV

. . . Total wages rose by about 50 percent between 1958 and 1962 and, according to the Ministry of Labor, pensions had risen by more than 70 percent in the same period. . . .

However, there was a sharp decline in income from property, owing to expropriation, and deductions from employment incomes for all purposes (social security, income tax, etc.) rose from about 6 percent before the Revolution to nearly 12 percent in 1962 for incomes of less than 250 pesos a month; for higher incomes the increase in tax rates has been even larger (and evasion has been greatly reduced). All in all, it seems that disposable personal incomes must have risen by about a third in those four years.

We must now allow for price rises. According to the official index, there was at first a decline (due to the decreed reduction in rents and charges for services, such as transport and electricity, after nationalization), but in 1961 prices started to rise, so that by the middle of 1962 they were some 2.5 percent above their 1958 level. Although the index seemed . . . . soundly constructed and competently run, it understates the true increase for a number of reasons. One is that the goods available have changed beyond recognition in many cases (with Soviet products replacing those from the United States), and there is little doubt that quality has generally declined. Some attempt has been made to allow for this, but it is very hard

---

[4] It would be wrong to conclude, however, that all refugees (even all adult refugees) are strongly hostile to the regime. There is always a flow from poorer areas to richer ones when entrance requirements are lax, as they were for Cubans wanting to enter the United States. (The big migration of Puerto Ricans into the United States in the past two decades does not necessarily imply great political hostility, for instance.)

to estimate quantitatively what the deterioration of quality amounted to.[5] Second, one or two items which have become more costly are not included in the index—rum, for example, which has gone up in price from pesos 1.25 to 3.50 (standard grades). Third, the proportion for clothing looks low by international standards, and this would give the index a downward bias in the years following 1958. Fourth, the decline in rents would be less important to households outside Havana. Fifth, certain items are not readily available (e.g., a shirt in the size required), so people have to buy more expensive substitutes. . . . Broadly speaking, total real disposable income rose considerably in the country districts but perhaps hardly at all in Havana.

What happened to real consumption over the same period? Reliable data on consumption are very hard to find. One clue is the rations of food. . . .

It should not be concluded from the existence of rationing that food consumption standards are on the average lower than before the Revolution. In the first place, the scheme mainly applies to the one-fifth of the population living in Havana. . . . Food farmers may well be eating a good deal more; in country districts before the Revolution, the typical rural family hardly ever ate meat or eggs or drank milk. . . .

Second, there are several foodstuffs which are not rationed, even in Havana. The most important are wheat and sugar and their products. These are readily available at fairly reasonable prices. . . . The ration of eggs and milk in Havana is higher than national average consumption was in 1953. Food is also readily available in restaurants, bars, etc., though usually rather heavy in starch there (rice, spaghetti, etc.), and meals are provided at a considerable number of schools.

In the case of items rationed nationally, however, per-capita consumption has declined by one-half or more since before the Revolution. These used to provide much of the diet. . . . Still, what can be fairly confidently said is that there are far fewer people, especially children, seriously undernourished than before the Revolution. One must not forget that the departure of the rich and their partial impoverishment would in itself lower the average food consumption—or, to put this point another way, the average used to be unrepresentative of what the great majority of the people consumed. This would have been especially true of Havana.

Judging from shortages, although prices are much higher, private consumption of clothing and footwear has probably declined, especially of the latter, even ignoring quality deterioration. . . . In addition, a large range of consumer durables cannot be purchased (e.g., motor cars and refrigerators) or are now being imported in much smaller quantities than previously (e.g., motorcycles, electric irons); whisky and beer supplies have declined; and foreign travel is greatly reduced. On the other hand, the consumption of books and periodicals, inland travel (including restaurant services), entertain-

---

[5] Examples are wrappings left off foodstuffs, inferior finishing of clothing, and more standing on bus journeys.

ment, soft drinks, and cigarettes has probably increased greatly, and so has the use of dwelling space (through the building of large numbers of new homes and flats) and of electricity. All in all, it may well be that total real consumption has not fallen. . . . There may even have been some rise in real private consumption, but it was certainly less than 20 percent [between 1958 and 1962] and probably no greater than the rise in population (which amounted to about 8 percent in this period). If quality could be taken into account, a rise in private consumption would be more doubtful. On the other hand, the government is supplying a good deal of what would previously have been bought. Examples are meals for schoolchildren—especially for the tens of thousands of boarders (who also receive clothing)—militia uniforms and boots (which are worn off-duty), rural medical services, and new beach facilities. . . .

V

Institutional history since the Revolution falls into four distinct phases. The first, from January, 1959, to June, 1960, was a period in which there was little attempt at state control. Some properties were "intervened" (managed by an appointee of the state)—e.g., the telephone company.[6] Agrarian reform became law in June, 1959, and shortly afterwards expropriations of large holdings and the distribution of titles started, but the agricultural sector remained predominantly private. . . .

The next period, from June, 1960, to February, 1961, was one of rapid institutional change. First, the petroleum refineries were nationalized (after the companies refused to refine Soviet oil). In July (following the abolition of the Cuban sugar quota in the United States), U.S. sugar companies were expropriated and cooperatives formed. Shortly afterwards, the same happened to American-owned factories and the electric power and telephone systems; and in October, banks, as well as the bulk of urban housing, were taken over. In the same month, nationalization of businesses owned by Cubans began. Early in 1961, state-administered farms (and some non-sugar cooperatives) were consolidated into large *granjas del pueblo*.

After these expropriations, there at first was no very great change of economic substance. . . . The most noticeable change was a complete switch in the direction of the island's foreign trade. As relations with the United States deteriorated (culminating with the U.S. embargo on exports in October, 1960), trade negotiations with the Soviet Union were rapidly expanded. . . .

Although there was no real central direction of the economy in this period, a start was made. . . .

[6] A few were taken over; these were properties which associates of Batista were judged to have bought out of funds obtained illegally.

The third phase opened with the strengthening of the planning office, the so-called JUCEPLAN, in February, 1961. It was given the task of preparing an annual plan for 1962 and a four-year plan for the period 1962-65. The government modeled its planning techniques on those developed in the Soviet Union and Eastern Europe. . . .

This phase can be described as one of euphoric planning. Thus in August, 1961, at a conference on production, Regino Boti, the Minister of Economics and head of JUCEPLAN, stated that from 1962 to 1965 the total production of Cuba would grow annually by "not less than 10 percent and probably [!] not more than 15.5 percent." . . .

In March, 1962, the system of rationing was established, marking a recognition of the seriousness of the problems of supply and thus initiating the fourth phase, one of growing realism. . . .

The sugar crop of 1962 turned out to be only 4,800,000 tons, over 2,000,000 tons lower than in 1961 despite the mobilization of much voluntary labor. In August the new head of INRA,[7] Carlos Rafael Rodriguez, declared that the target for 1963 would simply be to repeat the 4,800,000 crop of 1962. . . . The final blow was that even the low target for the 1963 sugar crop was not nearly achieved.

One major cause of the difficulties was that equipment which had arrived from overseas was not being brought into production, often because the necessary management and labor had not been found. A good deal of machinery remained on the docks until it had to be removed (sometimes to lie in a field) in order to make way for other imports.

In retrospect, the mistakes of 1961 can be attributed to a number of serious miscalculations. The first was that, in the wave of the self-confidence generated by the successful sugar crop [8] and repulsion of the invasion attempt, the government did not notice the acuteness of certain problems. Equipment was running down, often owing to inadequate maintenance routines, and inventories were getting low. With imports from the United States declining fast, it was necessary to find new sources for materials, spare parts, and goods which were a customary part of the Cuban worker's standard of living. Buyers were not familiar with supply conditions in the Communist countries or even with the needs of the Cuban economy.

The magnitude of the task that Cuba was attempting does not seem to have been understood by the administration. To turn a country like Cuba in 1958 into an advanced industrial economy in a few years would be a most remarkable achievement, especially in view of the continuing departure (or dismissal) of managers and technicians. Everywhere else in the world that change took decades, if not centuries. It was not just a matter of establishing new factories and raising their output (though this is hard

[7] National Institute of Agrarian Reform. [EDITOR'S NOTE]
[8] This refers to the sugar crop of 1961 which totaled almost seven million tons, the second largest in Cuba's history. [EDITOR'S NOTE]

enough, especially since the increases in output of various products need to be synchronized). Such drastic industrial expansion meant that services such as transport and electricity had to be adapted to the needs of an industrial economy, rather than a sugar economy, and that the labor force had to be trained and reallocated, preferably without a big increase in the wage bill.

What has been thrown into sharp focus by the experience of Cuba, and this is of wider significance for all development policy, is that organization, rather than capital, is the clue to really rapid structural change.

. . . One big snag for Cuba was the shortage of statistics; and such statistics as did exist were of very doubtful reliability. . . . The consequences of this statistical weakness were aggravated by an overambitious attempt at detailed planning, owing to the uncritical adoption of planning methods being used in the Soviet Union and Czechoslovakia. . . .

VI

There is evidence that the administration is learning from its mistakes. In the course of 1962, attempts were made to cope with these weaknesses. More and more enterprises were brought under the discipline of accounting systems (including the compilation of estimates of the costs of production), and, as a by-product, statistics were gradually improving. Standard statistical questionnaires were drawn up for the monthly reporting of results, and efforts were made at the provincial level to collect returns from organizations that were not making them. Agriculture was given a much higher priority in the course of 1962, as it was realized that the failure which threatened here could be politically dangerous. . . .

A number of steps are being taken to tackle the problems of labor supply. A uniform salary scale has been drawn up, under which workers doing the same job in different industries will receive the same wage.[9] . . .

The problem of shortages of labor to harvest particular crops has been tackled in various ways. Plans were drafted for creating a mobile group of young workers who would pass from district to district, as migrant workers used to do on quite a big scale before the Revolution. Then, about 1,000 mechanical cane-cutters (assembled in Cuba) were used in the 1963 harvest. It was hoped that these machines would ease the most acute problem, but they had yet to prove their worth in long periods of heavy work, week after week, used by inexperienced operators, and in some cases far from spare parts or skilled mechanics.

[9] The policy is that nobody's wage will be reduced as long as he continues to hold the same job as he held in August, 1962, though new recruits are hired at the salary shown in the standard scale. The worker getting more than the standard rate receives two pay packets, one containing the standard wage for the job, the other a supplement to bring his pay up to the wage he received previously.

"Norms" were established for the output of individual workers or groups of workers so as to raise productivity, and "emulative" competitions are being increasingly used, with prizes (such as paid holidays at the beach) for those who are especially productive. The conversion of sugar co-operatives into state farms was partly designed to make it easier to require a full day's work from cane-cutters. Heavy propaganda was applied to discourage absenteeism, lateness, waste, etc.

As well, efforts are being intensified to provide education at primary, secondary, and university levels and also to lift rapidly the educational and technical standards of adults. . . .

VII

In view of the great international uncertainties, one must take into account the possibility that any assessment [of Cuba's prospective economic development] will be upset by a complete political change. It should be clear from what has already been said, however, that severe problems will have to be faced by anyone who proposes a completely different path, because the Revolution, like all social eruptions, is to a great degree irreversible. What has happened economically would be especially difficult to reverse, because new industries have been established and the pattern of employment has changed. Since by now a large part of the equipment comes from the socialist countries, and factories are becoming accustomed to materials from the same source, a switch back to other suppliers would cause almost as much difficulty as the former turn to Eastern sources. Similarly the identity of private units is becoming merged in new productive organs, and different networks of distribution are being established; another wholesale change in administration would create another organizational crisis. And if the people become accustomed to communal incentives, it may prove hard to return to a system based mainly on private gain. To turn the state farms back to *latifundia* or to foreign ownership would scarcely be practical politics, nor could differences in income be easily re-established. It is difficult to imagine the new social security system being dismantled, or former domestic servants returning to the kitchen. Educational advances, such as the newly acquired literacy, not merely could scarcely be taken away but have brought distinct changes in attitude. Each year tens of thousands of adolescents enter into adult life after a fairly heavy political education.

The expectations of fast industrialization, with an associated major expansion in higher education and the creation of large numbers of new executive and technical jobs, could not easily be extinguished. Nor could the belief that unemployment can be, and will be, eliminated. Any new regime would therefore be strongly impelled to adopt a program the economic content of which would not be very different (though the degree of popular co-operation, and thus the economic success, would also depend on the political form of the program). If awakened aspirations are a strong force anywhere in the world, they are certainly powerful now in Cuba. They could scarcely be held in check.

20

The Castro Regime in Cuba:
A Non-Marxist View

ERNST HALPERIN *

INSTITUTE OF INTER-AMERICAN STUDIES
MIAMI UNIVERSITY

Moving leftward from political reform to social upheaval, the Cuban revolution has followed the familiar pattern of the French and Russian revolutions. But whereas, in France and Russia, each phase had different leaders, in Cuba one man alone has dominated.

During his two-year guerrilla war against the dictatorship of Fulgencio Batista, Fidel Castro appeared to represent that democratic spirit which is generally (though not always correctly) attributed to the middle classes. Some months after coming to power he proclaimed the Agrarian Reform Law, and observers then saw him as the incarnation of the revolutionary spirit of the peasantry. The following year came the Urban Reform Law and the nationalization of industry: the revolutionary spirit of the urban proletariat seemed in some mysterious way to have taken possession of Castro.

Whom does he represent now as the head of a party whose leadership is largely composed of military men? Perhaps the interests of the rebel army that he himself had created? But this view of Fidel Castro as a puppet successively set in motion by the spirit or the interests of different social groups does not help us to understand the Cuban revolution.

Andres Suarez—to my knowledge the first Cuban to have undertaken a serious in-depth study of his country's revolution—points to what he terms "the administrative character of the Cuban Revolution." [1] He uses this term to indicate that all the sweeping social and political changes which have

* This contribution is reprinted from *Current History* (December, 1966), pp. 354-359, by permission of the author, the publisher, and the Center for International Studies of the Massachusetts Institute of Technology.
[1] In a study soon to be published by The M.I.T. Press.

hitherto taken place in the course of the revolution were decreed by Castro himself without previous signs of popular pressure, and usually with a minimum of propagandistic preparation. Castro's supporters applauded each revolutionary measure, but they did so as loyal followers, not as active revolutionaries with urgent demands. Any spontaneous demonstrations were "counter-revolutionary"; that is, they were directed against government measures and their negative effects.

Thus, it was not pressure from below that pushed Castro to the communization of Cuba, to transform a market economy to a command economy of the Soviet type. What, then, was the motivation behind his decisions?

Castro's first and fundamental decision—namely to carry the revolution further, instead of implementing his promise to hold elections and restore the democratic constitution set aside by Batista—seemed inexplicable at the time it was announced. Today, with what we know of Castro's character by analyzing his actions in the last seven years, it is no longer a mystery. Love of absolute power is his controlling passion. He will not share power or permanently delegate it even to close companions. In 1959, he could easily have had himself elected president of a democratic Cuban republic. But he would inevitably have had to share and delegate power, and he would have been restricted by constitutional provisions and legislative and judiciary institutions. By continuing the revolution he prevented the establishment of institutional controls.

The way in which the agrarian reform was implemented and Castro's various attempts to spread his revolution to other countries of the area [2] brought about a serious deterioration of Cuban relations with the United States. Then, toward the end of 1959, the first contacts with the Soviet Union were established. In February, 1960, Soviet Vice-Premier Anastas Mikoyan visited Havana and, in June of that year, the first arms shipments from the Soviet bloc arrived in Cuba. From that moment onward, foreign policy dictated the course of the Cuban revolution.

One must keep in mind that in 1960, the balance of power between the Soviet Union and the United States appeared a very different one from that of today. In 1960, the alleged missile gap was an important issue in the United States presidential election. The Soviet government was pressing for an Allied withdrawal from Berlin and seemed to be successfully challenging the West in Africa and southern Asia. Its military and economic aid to Cuba extended the challenge to the very doorstep of the United States.

In this situation, it was easy for a man like Castro to conclude that military supremacy had passed from the United States to Russia. Protected by what appeared to be the world's strongest military power, he would be able to carry out his plans to spread the revolution to all of Latin America, with the Soviet nuclear umbrella extended to cover each successive country as it

---

[2] The most important of these early attempts was the unsuccessful landing of a Cuban-led group of Dominican exiles in Santo Domingo on June 14, 1959.

fell under the sway of Castroite revolutionaries. But he could rely on Soviet protection only if he led his country squarely into the "socialist camp," for then the mystique of the irreversible trend to socialism would work in his favor; the Soviets would have to defend him to prove that no communist country ever reverts to capitalism.

COMMUNIZATION

The sequence of events from the summer of 1960 to 1962 shows that this is exactly what Castro had in mind. And it also shows that the Russians were not very eager to accept Cuba in the communist community. This was understandable; it was far more convenient for them to maintain him as an expendable ally. Castro thus literally had to crash his way into the socialist camp.

On July 9, 1960, Soviet Premier Nikita Khrushchev declared that "figuratively speaking, the Soviet artillerymen could, if it became necessary, back up the Cuban people with rocket-fire." [3] This was a statement clearly worded to give the impression that Cuba enjoyed nuclear protection, without actually committing Moscow to such protection. Castro is far too intelligent to have overlooked this. Nevertheless he chose to ignore Khrushchev's cautious wording. He effusively thanked the Russians without mentioning that their offer of nuclear protection was only "figurative." [4]

Two weeks later, Castro issued his first call for an "anti-imperialist" revolution in all of Latin America. In his speech on July 26, 1960, he declared that the Cuban example would "convert the Andes mountain range into the Sierra Maestra of all the Americas." [5]

Immediately thereafter, a series of measures designed to transform Cuba's market economy into a state-operated, centralized command economy of the Soviet type was undertaken. On August 6, 1960, the American-owned sugar mills, the oil refineries and the electric power and telephone companies were nationalized. In September, the Cuban tobacco factories were confiscated. In October, confiscation was extended to 380 of the most important Cuban-owned and to the remaining American-owned business enterprises. That same month, the Urban Reform Law confiscated all housing not inhabited by its owners. By the beginning of 1961, the Cuban economy was well on its way to socialism, since most of the smaller business enterprises, such as shops and restaurants, were also rapidly falling into the hands of the state as their owners emigrated.

The next step was Castro's announcement, on April 16, 1961, that the

[3] See the *Tass* agency report, as reproduced in *Revolution* (Havana, July 11, 1960).

[4] See the report on Castro's television appearance on July 10, in *Hoy* (Havana, July 12, 1960).

[5] See the text of this speech in *Revolution* (Havana, July 27, 1960).

Cuban revolution was a "socialist" one. It is, of course, no accident that the announcement was made one day before the Bay of Pigs landing. Castro had been alerted to the coming invasion by the bombing of his airfields. His declaration was evidently made in the hope that by proclaiming the socialist character of his revolution he would force the Soviet Union to intervene on his behalf.

Castro's victory at the Bay of Pigs was widely celebrated throughout the socialist camp. But the socialist nature of the Cuban regime was not recognized by the Russians, nor, for that matter, by the Chinese. Quite apart from practical considerations, there was an impelling doctrinal reason for this. All the member countries of the socialist camp—which at that time was not yet clearly split into two, although the Sino-Soviet conflict was moving toward a climax—were dictatorships of the Communist Party, with state leadership factually, though not formally, in the hands of the party leadership. Cuba, on the other hand, was the dictatorship of a single individual, a *caudillo* of the Latin American type. The Communist Party, or P.S.P. (*Partido Socialista Popular*), as it called itself in Cuba, was on good terms with the Cuban dictator, but he was not its leader, nor even a party member; and, although he had allowed the party to infiltrate the administrative machine, it was not represented in his government by a single person of cabinet rank.

This precluded the acceptance of Castro in the socialist camp. To receive Cuba as a member would have been a violation of the most fundamental law of Leninism; namely, that the leadership of the socialist revolution belongs to the party of the proletariat. Subsequently, Castro took steps to overcome this obstacle. In his speech of July 26, 1961,[6] he announced the merger of the P.S.P. with the two Castroite groups—"Movement of the 26th of July" and "Student Revolutionary Directorate"—which had been his mainstay during the two-year guerrilla war, but had since lapsed into inactivity. The new combined organization was to be called O.R.I. (*Organizaciones Revolucionarias Integradas*), and was to be regarded as the preparatory stage for the formation of a United Party of the Socialist Revolution.

One of the leaders of the P.S.P., Anibal Escalante, was entrusted with the task of organizing O.R.I. He saw to it that O.R.I. was formed around the P.S.P. nuclei which existed in every part of the island, with the P.S.P. members deciding who was worthy of admission to the organization. It thus seemed that Castro had capitulated to the P.S.P., handing over virtual control of the revolution to the Moscow-oriented Communist Party leadership. This impression was strengthened by Castro's speech of December 1, 1961, in which he abjectly apologized for having been prejudiced against the P.S.P. both before and after his advent to power.[7] This is the speech which Cuban refugee propaganda falsely represents as an admission

[6] *Ibid.* (July 26, 1961).
[7] See *Hoy* (December 2, 1961).

that, from the beginning, the revolution had been a conspiracy mounted by the communists. What Castro actually said does not warrant such an interpretation. He merely admitted that, like many others, he had become acquainted with Marxist literature and had been favorably impressed by it even in his student days.

It soon became clear, however, that Castro had merely been using the old guard of the P.S.P. In March, 1962, he suddenly turned against Escalante, accusing him of having favored the former P.S.P. members at the expense of the men who had actually initiated the revolution.[8] Escalante was exiled in disgrace. The old-guard communists lost control of O.R.I., and this body then underwent a complicated process of reorganization. In February, 1963, when it assumed the name of P.U.R.S. (*Partido Unificado de la Revolucion Socialista*),[9] it was not yet functioning as an effective ruling party.

By mid-1962, Castro had not obtained his objective of membership in the socialist camp. At this point, he was offered an alternative which may have seemed even better: the stationing of Soviet missiles on Cuban soil. This not only appeared to offer adequate insurance against a United States attack on his own country, it also opened the perspective of nuclear protection for Castroite revolutionary regimes in other Latin American countries. The greater part of the region was within range of missiles stationed in Cuba, and the threat of nuclear retaliation would thus be plausible enough to deter the neighboring countries from intervening directly or lending their territory as a base for United States military intervention.

Of course, all this presupposed that the United States would tamely submit to the installation of the missiles and to nuclear blackmail. The assumption may appear fantastic to Americans, but to foreigners unfamiliar with the temper of the country certain aspects of United States policy in the preceding year—the unfortunate Bay of Pigs affair, the failure to retaliate against the building of the Berlin Wall—indeed appeared to indicate that despite American military power, the people and the government of the United States were morally too weak to face the prospect of nuclear war.

The missile crisis of October, 1962, was a turning-point in the history of the postwar world, exposing the fact that the Soviet policy of nuclear blackmail had been based on bluff. To the peoples of Latin America, it revealed that the Soviet presence in Cuba was the result not of Soviet strength, but of American tolerance. From the military point of view, Cuba was shown to be worthless to the Soviets, for what use is a military base if one's enemy is in a position to dictate what arms may be kept there?

Castro managed to save face by refusing to submit to ground inspection of the missile sites. Nevertheless, it was evident that his entire foreign policy had been based on a miscalculation: the Soviet Union was not strong enough to confront the United States in the western hemisphere.

[8] See his speech of March 26, 1962, in *Revolution* (March 27, 1962).
[9] See Castro's speech of February 22, 1963, in *Hoy* (February 23, 1963).

As compensation for the withdrawal of the missiles Cuba was later officially accepted as a member of the socialist camp; in their slogans for the May Day celebrations of 1963, the Russians for the first time listed Cuba among the countries of the camp, and acknowledged that the Cuban people were actually "building socialism." But this could no longer satisfy Castro, since the missile crisis had cast serious doubt on the value of that membership.

Subsequent events revealed even more clearly how dubious is the protection of membership in the socialist camp. On February 7, 1965, American bombing raids on North Vietnam began and, with brief interruptions, have continued to this writing. Castro's reaction to the bombardment of a fellow member of the socialist camp is highly significant. Time and again, he has demanded drastic action to stop the American raids on North Vietnam. Thus, in his government statement of February 6, 1966 he declared:

We speak on behalf of a people who did not hesitate for the sake of strengthening the revolutionary movement, for the sake of strengthening the Socialist Camp, for the sake of firmness and determination, in defense of the revolution against the imperialists, to risk the dangers of thermonuclear war, of nuclear attack against us. . . .

Our position is this: We favor that Vietnam should be given all the help necessary! We favor that help should be given in weapons and men! We favor that the Socialist Camp should run the necessary risks for Vietnam! [10]

These cries of anguish are understandable. For the failure of the Soviet Union to take adequate measures against the bombardment of North Vietnam demonstrates the fundamental weakness of the socialist camp, and thus the bankruptcy of Castro's foreign policy, which had led Cuba into that camp.

ECONOMIC POLICY

Bankruptcy is also the appropriate term for the results of Castro's economic policy, which from the beginning was dictated by purely political considerations. It is a mistake to assume that Castro ever seriously tried to raise the general level of well-being to make Cuba a showcase for socialism. To consolidate his power by weakening the social groups most likely to conduct effective opposition against his dictatorship, he encouraged the mass emigration of the country's technological and administrative cadres, although he must have known that the economic effects of this exodus would be disastrous. As we have seen, the sweeping confiscation and nationalization

[10] See *Granma* (Havana, February 6, 1966). For further Cuban statements in the same vein, see for example, the speech of the Cuban guest delegate, Armando Hart, at the 23d Congress of the Soviet Communist Party in Moscow, reported in *Granma* (Havana, May 1, 1966); and Castro's speech on July 26, 1966, in *Granma* (Havana, July 27, 1966).

measures, and the establishment of a centralized command economy, were undertaken for reasons of foreign policy, with a complete disregard for economic commonsense, for the individualistic traditions of the Cuban people, and indeed for Soviet admonitions to proceed slowly and cautiously.[11] To date, the results of Castro's economic policy have been the failure of his ambitious industrialization plans and a decline in sugar production—the latter in spite of the fact that the area of sugar cultivation has been expanded at the expense of other crops, thus reinforcing the monocultural structure of the Cuban economy.

POWER AND CHARISMA

In view of these signal failures, the absence of any visible internal threat to the Castro regime must be attributed to his extraordinary skill in the manipulation of power. The Castro regime is indisputably a totalitarian dictatorship. As in most such regimes, there is much private grumbling and circulation of rumors and anti-regime jokes. But the dictator's decisions are never publicly challenged or even mildly criticized and all attempts at organized opposition are immediately suppressed.

There is, however, one puzzling circumstance. The National Socialist regime in Germany and the communist regimes in Russia and other countries have been minutely analyzed. The general consensus emerging from these studies would appear to be that totalitarianism is the result of an unusually thoroughgoing, rigidly disciplined organization of society. Yet Castro has what Andres Suarez in his aforementioned study aptly terms a very pronounced "allergy to organization." Within the seven years of his regime, its organizational base appears to have shifted first from the rebel army to the militia and the committees for the defense of the revolution, then from these to the O.R.I., dominated by the cadres of the former P.S.P., then to an O.R.I. no longer dominated by the P.S.P. O.R.I. was renamed P.U.R.S. and the P.U.R.S. was renamed the Communist Party of Cuba,[12] and each change of nomenclature was accompanied by sweeping changes in the composition of the leadership. Today, six of the eight members of the Politbureau of the Cuban Communist Party, and nearly 70 percent of the members of its central committee, are active officers of the armed forces. Thus the rebel army appears to have reestablished its ascendancy.

These frequent changes are certainly intentional. They constitute a deliberate policy of preventing the institutionalization of the revolution,

---

[11] As long as it was in a position to do so, the P.S.P., which was in close contact with the Soviet embassy, counselled a conciliation of the "national bourgeoisie" and the middle classes.

[12] This latest change occurred in October, 1965.

which in turn can only be ascribed to Castro's inordinate love of personal power. Institutionalization inevitably means the delegation of power to the leading personnel of the various institutions, and this, as we have already pointed out, Castro abhors.

The only institutions of Castro's regime which show any permanence are the two that are absolutely indispensable for the maintenance of power: the army and the political police. In the army, Castro does his best to prevent the formation of personal loyalties within the military hierarchy by constantly shifting the commanding officers from one post or function to another. And as for the political police, there are signs that some of its responsibilities have lately been transferred to other organs.

The one constant factor in the Cuban regime is the dictator's charisma, his ability to win unconditional devotion without giving anything in return. It is true that the range of his hypnotic powers has diminished. At first, the vast majority of his countrymen were under his spell. Yet even if, as some maintain, his supporters today constitute no more than five to ten percent of the active population, that would still be far more than one hundred thousand fanatics—more than enough to control a country of seven million in which there are no elections and any organized opposition or even public dissent is punished as a crime.

In this respect, it is interesting to compare Castro's methods with those of Joseph Stalin in the Soviet Union. The latter began his ascent to absolute power as an unobtrusive bureaucrat, lacking all charisma and not taken seriously by the brilliant intellectuals of the party leadership. Organization was the weapon which he used to beat his opponents. But even this organization man par excellence saw institutionalization as a danger to his dictatorial rule. In fighting it, he left the organizational structure of the regime intact, but wiped out its personnel in the great purge of the 1930's, replacing it by younger, more devoted men. From then on he ruled by carefully balancing the various organizations—party, state apparatus, army, police—against one another, never allowing one to become absolutely dominant. But apparently this did not suffice. In 1949, he instituted a second purge, and a third purge of all-encompassing dimensions appeared to be imminent when he conveniently died.

It thus appears that institutionalization, which is so often regarded as a prerequisite to totalitarian dictatorship, is actually a long-term threat to its existence. It may well be this which has impelled Chairman Mao Tse-tung to the present purge in China.

Castro is an innovator in the art of totalitarian control. His charisma enables him to rule by not allowing organizations and institutions to take a definite shape. One might call this the principle of permanent revolution through incessant disorganization. To phrase it thus at least shows up the innate instability of the system: as long as there is no institutionalization, the fate of the regime hangs on one thread—the life of the charismatic dictator.

FURTHER READING SUGGESTIONS

Bayard, James, *The Real Story of Cuba.* Connecticut: Monarch Books, Inc., 1963.

Burks, David D., "Cuba Seven Years After," *Current History* (January, 1966), pp. 38-44.

Draper, Theodore, *Castro's Revolution, Myths and Realities.* New York: Praeger, 1962.

———, *Castroism, Theory and Practice.* New York: Praeger, 1965.

Lumsden, C. Ian, "Cuba," in Bromke, ed., *The Communist States at the Crossroads Between Moscow and Peking.* New York: Praeger, 1965, pp. 164-178.

Matthews, Herbert L., *Cuba.* New York: Macmillan, 1964.

Morton, Ward, *Castro as a Charismatic Hero.* Lawrence, Kan.: Center of Latin American Studies, The University of Kansas, 1965.

Phillips, Ruby Hart, *The Cuban Dilemma.* New York: Ivan Obolensky, Inc., and Astor Books, 1963.

A Study on Cuba: Colony, Republic and Socialist Experiment. Miami, Fla.: University of Miami Press, 1965.

Tannenbaum, Frank, *Ten Keys to Latin America.* New York: Knopf, 1962.

21

The Cuban Revolution:
An American Marxist View

EDWARD BOORSTEIN *

ECONOMIST, AUTHOR

To appreciate the Cuban Revolution you do not have to be a Marxist or even a radical. All you need is intellectual honesty and courage—a willingness to face the facts, to follow them wherever they lead. If you face and follow the facts, you will arrive at a Marxist view of the Cuban Revolution.

What are some of the key questions about the Cuban Revolution? Why did it break out? Why was it so radical? Why did it move so quickly to socialism? What is the significance of the problems it has been facing?

THE BACKGROUND OF THE REVOLUTION

The answers to these questions begin with prerevolutionary Cuba. Cuba was poor. Its economy was deformed and stagnant. It was an economic colony of the United States which dominated everything.

Before the Revolution, the facts about Cuban poverty were largely ignored in the United States. Since the Revolution, they have appeared in so many articles and books that only two or three need be given here. "Per capita income (in Cuba) in 1950-54 averaged only 312 pesos per year, or slightly less than one-third that of the southeastern States of the United States. Cuba's highest per capita income during that period was 345 pesos . . . contrasted with $638 for the worst year reported by the State of Mississippi.[1] The average of 312 pesos was higher than the income of most of the population because it included the incomes of the rich and well-to-do which

---

* This contribution was written especially for this book.

[1] *Investment in Cuba* (U.S. Department of Commerce, 1956), p. 184. The Cuban peso was equal in value to the U.S. dollar. [EDITOR'S NOTE]

were many times higher than the average. A survey carried out by the Catholic University of Cuba in 1956 showed that average per capita income in the countryside, including home-grown food supplies, was less than $100 per year.

This same survey also showed that less than 12 percent of Cuba's rural families drank milk as part of their usual diet; only 4 percent ate meat; 2 percent eggs; and 1 percent fresh fish.[2] Only 28 percent of all dwelling units in Cuba had an inside toilet and 23 percent did not have any toilet, inside or outside; 55 percent did not have any bathtub or shower; 75 percent did not have any refrigeration, mechanical or ice.[3]

It is also now a commonplace that the Cuban economy was a one-crop economy, geared to the production and exportation of sugar. Together with its by-products, sugar accounted for about 80 percent of total exports; the sugar industry employed 25 percent of the labor force; the sugar companies controlled 70-75 percent of the arable land; the sugar mills owned two-thirds of the railroad trackage. The export of sugar and its by-products constituted about 20-30 percent of the gross national product. But this last percentage does not reflect the true importance of sugar since most of the rest of Cuba's gross national product depended on sugar.

The sugar industry was seasonal, unstable, and stagnant, and it imparted these characteristics to the whole economy. It employed about four to five hundred thousand workers to cut, load, and transport the cane during the three to four months harvest season and then left them to starve during the rest of the year. The price and demand for sugar went up and down with war and peace and business cycles, taking the whole Cuban economy with them. The export outlets for Cuban sugar were growing only slowly, so that the entire Cuban economy stagnated. "The Cuban gross national product in 1948-1954 grew sufficiently to permit the maintenance of the 1947 standard of living in only five of the seven years included in that period and was sufficient in only two years (1951 and 1952) to permit a 2 percent annual increase over the 1947 standard of living. . . ."[4]

But for all its importance, the dependence of the Cuban economy upon sugar was only part of a more basic phenomenon: the domination of Cuba by American imperialism. Not only was the sugar complex—plantations, mills, railroads, ports, and boats—an appendage of the American economy, but so were the Cuban import houses and many of the retail stores. The United States supplied 80 percent of Cuba's imports. American goods dominated the internal market. The competition from the giant monopolies of the North suffocated Cuban industry. The import of goods which in a country as poor as Cuba can only be classified as luxuries—automobiles,

[2] Maurice Zeitlin and Robert Scheer, *Cuba: Tragedy in Our Hemisphere* (New York, Grove Press, 1963), p. 17.
[3] *Investment in Cuba*, p. 187.
[4] *Investment in Cuba*, p. 7.

record players, alcoholic beverages, and fancy foods—drained Cuba of tens of millions of dollars in foreign exchange which could better have been used to feed the poor or develop the economy.

Most of the local factories owned by foreign corporations were little more than disguised import agencies. They operated with imported machinery and materials and created little local employment and income.

American corporations controlled everything worth controlling in Cuba: the resources, the key industries, the foreign trade, the internal market. U.S. direct investment in Cuba was over $900 million. U.S. corporations owned plantations and sugar mills, the telephone and electric industries, factories, railroads, hotels, and oil refineries. They did not own all the large enterprises, but this means little. All significant enterprises, even when owned by Cubans, were intertwined with the American economy; the only enterprises integrated in the Cuban economy were small and unimportant.

Behind the whole structure was U.S. power. The Cuban people were allowed to select their own government and officials—so long as they were acceptable to the United States. The U.S. did not constantly rely on open force to control Cuba—it did not have to. Most of the time, the financial power of the large corporations or the understanding that Cuba depended on the sale of sugar in the United States were enough. But whenever force was necessary, it was used. American troops landed in Cuba in 1906, 1912, and 1917. When the Cuban people showed signs of revolting against Machado, the Butcher, in 1933, President Roosevelt sent Sumner Welles as Special Ambassador to make sure that no government that would threaten U.S. interests would be installed. When a reformist government came to power after Machado fell, the United States refused to recognize it and maneuvered to bring it down. American warships were sent to Cuban waters to help Ambassador Welles. And in a few months Fulgencio Batista was installed in power.[5]

Under these circumstances, there was little the Cuban people could do to relieve their poverty or develop the Cuban economy. They were separated from the resources of their own country by the foreign monopolies with their local associates. There were five hundred thousand rural laborers and their families who were starving most of the time and there was idle and underutilized land. But the land belonged to the sprawling sugar plantations and cattle ranches and the laborers could not use it. Cuba could not control its foreign trade and domestic market to promote domestic industry: American-imposed reciprocal trade treaties and foreign exchange policies prevented the erection of any barriers to the inflow of American goods. Cuba could not

[5] Batista was in power twice; the first time from 1934-44; the second from 1952 until he fled from the Revolution on January 1, 1959. He took over in 1934 through a *coup d'etat,* setting up a puppet president and exercising power as Chief of Staff of the Army until 1940; then he was president from 1940-1944. His accession to power in 1952 was again through a *coup d'etat.*

make any serious attempt to broaden foreign markets for its sugar and other products; it was under U.S. pressure not to trade with the socialist countries and followed a U.S. policy of exporting only for dollars. To solve their problems the Cuban people needed sovereignty and independence—the control of their own country, the freedom to choose the kind of government and economic structure that best suited their needs. But sovereignty and independence was precisely what they did not have.

WHY WAS THE REVOLUTION SO RADICAL?

The question as to why the Revolution broke out needs almost no answer. What else could be expected? But why was the Revolution so radical? Why did it come into such sharp conflict with the United States? To get quickly to the core of the answers to these questions, one must ask: How much progress could have been made in solving Cuba's problems without radical measures? Could the Cuban revolutionaries have done anything without colliding with some American interest?

The margin for reform in Cuba was razor-thin. What reforms could have made a dent on the problems of the 450,000 sugar workers who were unemployed eight to nine months a year? With unemployment reaching 20 to 25 percent or more during the eight months of the dead season for sugar, would it have been possible to set up a system of unemployment insurance? Would a few additional schools and hospitals for the poor—assuming they could have been gotten—have changed anything basic? What reforms could have produced significant progress toward industrialization?

The Cuban Revolution was radical because only radical measures could have opened the road to solving the problems. The revolution could have avoided radical measures; but this would have meant not tackling the real problems; it would have meant doing practically nothing.

No serious attack on Cuba's problems could have avoided land reform. Without land reform, the enormous waste of land and labor in the countryside would have gone on indefinitely. The land had to be taken away from those who were monopolizing it—who were wasting it because they did not have to pay the cost of the waste—and be made available to the people.

Cuba had to try to broaden its foreign markets, to adopt a policy of trading with everyone, including the socialist countries. It was either this or resigning itself to economic stagnation and remaining a dependency of the United States. And awareness of the need to avoid economic dependence was not new in Cuba. José Martí, the leader of the movement for independence from Spain, had said: "A country that wants to be free has to be free in its trade."

Cuban industrialization could not have been carried out merely by providing the proper "climate" for investment and then waiting for private capital, foreign and domestic, to do the job. The Cuban investment climate could hardly have been improved. But for domestic industry to grow it was necessary to provide protection against foreign imports and to broaden the national market by raising the rural standard of living. It was necessary for the state to mobilize resources—far more than private capital would provide—and then use them to carry through a planned industrialization program.

But which of these steps could Cuba have taken without coming into conflict with American imperialism? None. It could not have touched the land, it could not have traded with the socialist countries, it could not have restricted the inflow of American goods, without bumping into American interests. It could not even have carried through reform measures, such as lowering electric power and telephone rates, without opposition from the United States.

This leads us to two important points which apply not only to Cuba but to many other countries in Latin America and elsewhere, and which we Americans must begin to face squarely. First, there was a fundamental conflict between American interests in Cuba—American imperialism—and the Cuban people. The struggle between the Cuban Revolution and the United States did not arise because of the personalities of the Cuban leaders or the policies of the United States; there was an inherent clash of interest. And, secondly, the central condition for the solution of Cuba's problems was the winning of sovereignty and of independence, the elimination of American domination. Economic development is at best a difficult job. It could not even begin to be carried out under foreign economic and political domination.

When Fidel Castro thundered that Cuba belonged to the Cubans and that they would decide what to do in their own land, he was not only insisting on simple justice: he was doing what had to be done to enable the Cubans to attack their problems.

Radical action was also necessary for political reasons. The chief bulwark of the Revolution is the unflinching support of the overwhelming majority of the Cuban people—a support they express in a willingness to fight for it. But this support arose because the people saw that the Revolution meant business, that it was attacking their problems. This popular support could not be maintained by empty verbiage. A disillusioned people would not be willing to fight for the Revolution; and if the support of the people had faltered, the United States would have made the Revolution toe the mark or would have snuffed it out.

All this goes a long way toward explaining why the Revolution moved so quickly to socialism. The Revolution had to take radical measures and this was bound to bring it into collision with American interests. How could the United States government be expected to react to such a collision? How does American imperialism everywhere react to a threat to its interests? The United States government fought the Revolution from the time it came to power, and the struggle culminated in the nationalization of American properties in Cuba and socialism.

The United States government was so accustomed to dominating Cuba that American officials found it hard even to conceive of a Cuban government that would try to be independent, that would stand up against it. True independence for Cuba was a dream that could only be indulged in by the immature. Any mature Cuban leader would surely understand the facts of life, the dependence of Cuba on the United States. And if the leaders of the Cuban Revolution did not arrive at such understanding quickly, there were ways to help them get it—or to deal with them if they persisted in being stubborn.

American officials and the United States government started complaining about the actions of the Revolution at the beginning. They complained about the trials of those who had committed crimes under the Batista regime, giving paternal advice about how civilized peoples and governments should act. They complained about the lowering of telephone and electric power rates and rents on housing. And when a land reform law was passed and Cuba made a couple of sales of sugar to the Soviet Union, things began to get rough. Planes from Florida flew in to drop incendiary bombs on the cane fields and sugar mills and the Cuban government began to find it difficult to buy arms—the United States was exerting pressure on other governments not to sell them to Cuba.

One thing led to another. As the land reform law began to be put into practice with the taking over of cattle ranches in the fall of 1959, hostility in the United States grew. The United States began to engage in economic warfare against Cuba. Tourism was discouraged, and dwindled; Cuban importers found they could no longer get normal credit; Cuban exports which had never met with difficulties before now began to be rejected at U.S. ports of entry for technical reasons. The United States brandished the quota for the sale of Cuban sugar in the United States more and more openly in an attempt to bring the Revolution into line. The specter of armed intervention began to take shape and the Revolutionary government took steps to set up a People's Militia. In February 1960, the Revolutionary government signed trade, payments and credit agreements with the Soviet Union. This action flowed from the policy of trading with the whole world; but in part it was also a defensive action against possible cancellation of the sugar quota by the United States. During the next several months, Cuba also signed agreements with other socialist countries. One of the commodities imported under the trade agreement with the Soviet Union was oil. When the Soviet oil arrived, the three large oil refineries—two American, one British—refused to accept it. The Cuban government "intervened," i.e., took over the refineries. The United States cancelled the Cuban sugar quota. Cuba had warned that if the sugar quota were cancelled it would nationalize American property in Cuba. In August, 1960, most of the large American properties—sugar mills and their lands, electric and telephone companies, oil refineries, etc.—were nationalized. In September and October, the nationalization was extended to the remaining large properties, American and Cuban. And in November the United States imposed an embargo on all exports to Cuba, except for foodstuffs and medicines. The exception was in good part theoretical, and in practice even the importation of food and medicines from the United States dwindled. Ferry and boat lines to Cuba stopped running. Cuban exports of tobacco to the United States continued until early 1962 when they were also embargoed.

By the end of October, 1960, the Cuban economy had become socialist. About 80 percent of industry and a large and important sector of agriculture had been nationalized. Trade with the socialist countries was climbing rapidly to replace that with the United States.

The key reason for the rapidity of Cuba's march toward socialism lay in the very extent of the American stranglehold on the Cuban economy. When American-owned and American-dominated properties were nationalized, what was left? When the United States cut off the market for Cuban sugar, where, besides the socialist countries, could a substitute be found?

In Cuba, all economic and political problems were intertwined. The land problem, the problem of industrialization, the problem of sovereignty and independence were different parts of one problem, the solution of which required socialism.

SOME ECONOMIC PROBLEMS AND THEIR SIGNIFICANCE

How should one look at Cuba's economic difficulties? An American reporter in Cuba sees that Cuba's automobiles are not in as good shape as before the Revolution: they may be missing lights or mufflers or look generally dilapidated. Or he may sometimes see people hauling pails of water to their houses because some part of the regular water system has broken down. So he writes sneeringly of the run-down Cuban economy. He is not telling lies about what he has seen, and yet his report is based on a kind of willful blindness, an unwillingness to try to understand what he sees.

Not that distortions and lies do not enter into reports from Cuba—on the contrary. The United States government is waging economic warfare against Cuba. It is trying to discredit the Revolution, to limit its influence on the rest of Latin America and other countries, to keep Britain and other capitalist countries from trading with Cuba. And the United States has not given up hope that economic difficulties will create a possibility for somehow overthrowing the Revolution. So it spreads stories about terrible conditions in Cuba, about disorderly finances which make Cuba a poor credit risk, and the like. Sometimes when I read these stories, I am reminded of the dispatches by the American news services that my family and I heard and read in Havana at the time of the Bay of Pigs invasion. We heard one dispatch over the radio announcing that the Havana Libre Hotel had been set afire by saboteurs and had burned to the ground; and as we were listening to this story we looked through the window of our apartment and there was the big, blue-colored hotel—standing as always.

Cuba's economic problems are not hard to understand for anyone who has a desire to understand, and is willing to apply a little common sense. Since the Revolution came to power, it has had to struggle with countless economic problems and difficulties. How could it be otherwise? No one has ever said that a revolution is a banquet. A revolution is a gigantic undertaking. It is a fight. It is an attempt to construct a whole new society. How could it fail to have problems and difficulties? One can't understand revolutions by looking at them through the eyes of a bank teller who has to count all his small change and balance every little account every night.

With the Revolution, the Cuban people took over the operation of their economy—the farms, the factories, the foreign commerce. They had to manage with whoever was available. But the technical knowledge and skill of most Cuban *campesinos* [6] was limited. The rural workers knew how to cut cane and pick coffee, but they did not know much about raising crops, caring for livestock, handling machinery, treating plant and animal diseases. How could they have learned these things?

The American technicians and a good part of the Cuban technicians who had run the factories left. So the factories had to be run by bearded young revolutionaries, by workers, by the harassed and overworked technicians who had remained.

The break in commerce with the United States brought innumerable difficulties. Everything in Cuba, from industrial machinery to electric sockets, had been geared to American specifications and standards, to American materials and spare parts. Without the American formula, Coca Cola began to taste—as Che Guevara put it—like cough syrup. A delay in finding a new source for the raw materials for toothpaste resulted in its temporary disappearance from the market. The lack of American spare parts caused difficulties in Havana's water supply system, in many factories, and keeping the buses running.

In the summer of 1961 sporadic food shortages began to appear, and in the spring of 1962 it became necessary to institute rationing. The Revolution had brought about a large rise in income, especially in the countryside, and as a result food consumption had gone up sharply. Milk supplies, for example, were inadequate to meet demand, even though production was much greater than before the Revolution. The consumption of meat had gone up so rapidly

[6] Peasants. [EDITOR'S NOTE]

that cattle were being slaughtered at a rate which was reducing the cattle population: the rate of slaughter had to be controlled. The importation of certain foods, like lard, formerly obtained in large quantities from the United States, had declined. There was also disorganization in the distribution of vegetables and other food products.

For the middle and upper classes, who in Cuba have always constituted a far smaller part of the population than in the United States, rationing has been a discomfort. But, even during the worst months of rationing, there was simply no comparison between the diet of the Cuban agricultural worker before and after the Revolution. A large number of city dwellers have also been eating better, though not by as wide a margin. Now everyone can have milk, even though adults must do with canned instead of fresh milk. Many who almost never ate eggs or meat before now get their regular ration. And the middle and upper classes can mitigate their discomfort—they can supplement their supplies by going to restaurants.

The Revolutionary Government has also made mistakes. The most serious was pressing agricultural diversification at the expense of sugar. Sugar was deprecated as the symbol of a one-crop economy and in 1961 it was decided to reduce the area devoted to cane. This reduction, along with droughts and the 1963 hurricane caused a sharp reduction in the sugar harvests for 1962, 1963, and 1964. But it is one thing to develop agricultural diversification using idle land and labor; it is another when it cuts into the output of sugar. Then it becomes necessary to weigh the alternatives carefully. Sugar production in Cuba yields more income than most other crops, and this income can be used to buy all sorts of goods, including many more important ones than the tomatoes and cucumbers whose production takes land and labor away from sugar.

But along with the problems and errors came great accomplishments. The Revolution got rid of racist restrictions on beaches, in hotels, in factories —everywhere. It turned barracks into schools and hospitals and started the construction of thousands of additional ones. It built thousands of new houses for the peasants and the inhabitants of the slums in the cities. And in 1961, in a campaign in which the whole literate youth of the country was mobilized as teachers, it eliminated illiteracy.

One of the least known but most important measures of the Revolution was the rationalization of Cuban imports. The import of luxuries was stopped. The millions formerly spent on the importation of automobiles and parts, the tens of millions wasted on fancy goods for a small part of the population, are now used to help feed and clothe the people and to buy trucks, tractors, and machinery.

The Revolution has changed the face of the countryside. Everywhere new installations for raising chickens, pigs, and cattle have been sprouting. Eventually, the Cuban people will receive increasing quantities of meat, eggs, milk, and other dairy products, and the cattle will provide export earnings.

The sugar workers who counted for nothing before the Revolution are now human beings, respected for the hard and important work they do. Rural unemployment has been eliminated—instead there is now a shortage of labor for the sugar harvest. Before the Revolution, mechanization would only have added further to the misery of the rural population. Now it can release laborers from sugar production for other work. With the aid of the Soviet Union, machines for cutting and loading cane are being developed. The loading machines have already proved successful and are being used on a wide scale. There are still technical problems with the cutters, but the Cuban leaders expect them to be eliminated in another year or two.

The downgrading of sugar was recognized toward the end of 1962 to have been an error and steps have since been taken to correct it. An output goal of 10 million tons—about 3 million tons more than Cuba has ever produced—has been set for 1970. The area devoted to cane is being increased. Irrigation, which multiplies yields, is being extended. More fertilizer is being used. This program has already begun to show results. The harvest was 3.9 million metric tons in 1963 and 4.4 million in 1964. In 1965 it jumped to 6.1 million metric tons—more than Cuba has ever produced except during the record years 1952 and 1961. There is no doubt that Cuba will meet the goal of 10 million tons she has set herself for 1970.

Other agricultural programs are also beginning to pay off. Egg consumption jumped from 13.7 million in January, 1964 to 60 million in January, 1965. An increase in the output of beef has been making itself felt in the countryside.

As sugar production develops and is mechanized it will both provide increased earnings of foreign exchange and release workers to other areas of agriculture and to industry. As the rest of agriculture develops it will enable the Cubans to eat better, and after a while it will provide foreign exchange. The foreign exchange can be used both to raise the standard of living and develop the economy. Using credits and its own funds, Cuba has already begun to develop industry. As one travels around Cuba, one can see the new construction, such as the plant for producing refrigerators and other household appliances in Santa Clara or the large power station near Mariel. If one visits factories, one can see the many new machines brought in from the socialist countries. But industrialization will really get under way as the earnings from sugar and cattle begin to flow in.

There will still be many problems. A bridge can't be built without problems, much less a new society. But those who are worried about the "poor Cubans" would do much better to concern themselves with the shoeless peasants of Northeast Brazil, the inhabitants of the slums of Mexico City or Santiago, Chile, or with the bloody dictatorships that hold power in all but two or three countries of Latin America. Apart from possible aggression by the United States, Cuba's future is assured.

FURTHER READING SUGGESTIONS

Dumont, Rene, *Cuba, Socialisme et Developpement.* Paris: Editions de Seuil, 1964.

Gerassi, John, *The Great Fear In Latin America.* New York: Collier Books, 1965.

Huberman, Leo, and Paul Sweezy, *Cuba: Anatomy of a Revolution.* New York: Monthly Review Press, 1961.

Mills, C. Wright, *Listen, Yankee.* New York: McGraw-Hill, 1960.

Morray, J. P., *The Second Revolution in Cuba.* New York: Monthly Review Press, 1962.

Seers, Dudley, ed., *Cuba, The Economic and Social Revolution.* Chapel Hill, N.C.: University of North Carolina Press, 1964.

U.S. Department of Commerce, *Investment in Cuba.* 1956.

Zeitlin, Maurice, and Robert Scheer, *Cuba, Tragedy in Our Hemisphere.* New York: Grove Press, 1963.

APPENDIX:
Index of Selected Periodicals on Communism and the Communist World*

Articles on Communism, on the Communist World, or on one or another of the Communist countries can be found in countless periodicals, popular as well as scientific. The list below includes only those which concentrate exclusively, primarily, or very frequently on subject matters of concern to students of Communism whose interest lies in the social sciences, the humanities, or in related fields. Omitted, then, are most periodic publications which are not primarily devoted to Communist studies, such as *The New York Times, Fortune, Harper's,* the *Harvard Business Review,* the *American Economic Review,* the *American Political Science Review.* Also omitted are periodicals which deal with technical subjects of interest only to specialists in fields other than the social sciences and humanities, such as the *Review of Soviet Medical Sciences* or *Soviet Radio Chemistry.* Finally, space limitations preclude the inclusion of those periodic publications which, while concerned with communism, deal primarily with one, noncommunist country (such as the U.S. pro-communist *Worker* or the anticommunist *American Opinion*).

Many American and British embassies in communist countries publish abstracts or summaries of some of these countries' newspaper and magazine articles in English translation; some publish analyses of news events. For China, the U.S. Consulate General in Hong Kong publishes *Survey of China Mainland*

* The editor wishes to express his sincere gratitude to the many scholars who checked his original index of selected periodicals and made valuable suggestions for additions, deletions, corrections, and alterations: George W. Beckman, Stanly Humenuk, George Jerkovich, Roger E. Kanet, Michael Klimenko, Jerzy B. Krzyzanowski, and Heinrich Stammler, all of the University of Kansas; Hans Apel (Prof. Emeritus, U. of Bridgeport); Robert W. Campbell (Indiana U.); R. P. Dutt (Labour Monthly); Holland Hunter (Haverford C.); Cvijeto Job (Yugoslav Embassy, Washington, D.C.); Rexhep Krasniqi (Free Albania Committee); Emanual Litvinoff (Contemporary Jewish Library, Ltd.); K. L. London (George Washington U.); Henry H. Noyes (China Books and Periodicals); Howard L. Parsons (U. of Bridgeport); Jan S. Prybyla (Pennsylvania State U.); Louis Sharpe (International Arts and Sciences Press); Anne Shworak (Progress Books); Marion Szigethy (Radio Free Europe/Munich); Lynn Turgeon (Hofstra U.); and Al Ungur (Rumanian Embassy, Washington, D.C.).

Press and *Extracts From China Mainland Magazines.* Many of these embassy and consulate publications are issued only in very limited mimeographed editions and are not available for private distribution. These publications are not included in this Index of Selected Periodicals.

The periodicals are subdivided into two groups, non-Marxist and Marxist. The latter group includes periodicals published in any of the fourteen communist countries, Western translations of materials published in the communist countries and periodic publications by individuals and groups outside the communist countries who consider themselves Marxists. No further subdivision (pro-China, pro-Soviet, Trotskyite, Western Marxist; scientific, semiscientific, and popular) has been attempted and the reader is warned not to expect homogeneity either in ideological orientation or in scientific value among the journals in either of the two major subdivisions. Conclusions as to ideological orientation can often be drawn either from the title, the place of publication, or from the description of the periodical. Such a description has been added whenever the periodical's title does not make explanatory comments superfluous. Some publications (for instance those which contain communist articles as well as noncommunist commentaries) are listed in both subgroups.

Articles, such as "a," "an," and "the" have been left out at the beginning of periodical titles. Subscription prices quoted are recent, but the reader should bear in mind that they change frequently. Where price, name of publisher, address of publisher, or other information is not included, the editor has been unable to obtain it.

NON-MARXIST PERIODIC PUBLICATIONS

ABN Correspondence (Anti-Bolshevik Block of Nations). Illustrated political analysis. Published bimonthly by Verlag ABN Korrespondenz Zeppelinstrasse 67, 8 Munich 8, Germany. $8.00 per year.

ACEN News. Reviews activities of the Assembly of Captive European Nations and contains articles primarily on East European communist countries and on Western, non-Russian parts of the Soviet Union incorporated into the Soviet Union at the end of World War II. Published bimonthly by the Press Bureau of ACEN, 29 West 57th Street, New York, N.Y., 10019. $3.00 per year.

American Bulletin. Commentaries on and analyses of political, economic, and social conditions in Czechoslovakia. Published monthly by the Czechoslovak National Council of America, 4125 West 26th St., Chicago, Illinois 60623. $2.00 per year.

Analysis of Current Developments in the Soviet Union. Published 40 times per year by the Institute for the Study of the U.S.S.R., Mannhardtstr. 6, Germany. $10.00 per year.

Anglo-Soviet Journal. Concentrates on Soviet cultural activities. Published quarterly by the Society for Cultural Relations with the U.S.S.R. (a non-political organization sympathetic to the Soviet Union), Kensington Square, London, W.8, England. $2.00 per year.

Arts and Sciences in China. Cultural and scientific achievements in Communist and Nationalist China. Published quarterly at 692 Holloway Road, London N.19, England.

Asian Almanac. Abstract of Asian affairs, primarily concerned with political issues. Published weekly at 2 J Clifford House, Collyer Kay, P.O. Box 2737, Singapore. $37.00 per year.

Asian Review of Art and Letters. Cultural review of all of Asia, communist and noncommunist. Published three times per year by "Asian Review," 2 Temple Chamber, Temple Avenue, London, England. $2.80 per year.

Asian Survey (Supersedes *Far Eastern Survey*). Deals primarily with "contemporary problems, the analysis of which contributes to the development of systematic social science theory." Published monthly by the Institute of International Studies, University of California, 2334 Piedmont Avenue, Berkeley, California. $6.00 per year.

ASTE Bulletin. Publishes or reprints papers in Soviet Slavic Area Studies presented at professional conferences, summaries of proceedings of such conferences, and excerpts from books in the field. Published by The Association for the Study of Soviet-Type Economies, University of Pennsylvania, Philadelphia, Pennsylvania. Free to members (membership fee is $3.00 per year).

Baltic Review. Review of literature and culture in the Baltic region. Published semiannually by the New York Board of Education, 29 West 57th Street, New York, N.Y. 10019. Free.

Byelorussian Review. Has been incorporated into *Studies on the Soviet Union.*

Bulletin. Short articles on various aspects of Soviet life. Published monthly by the Institute for the Study of the USSR, 8 Munich 22, Mannhardtstr. 6, Germany. $6.00 per year.

Canadian Slavic Studies (*Revue Canadienne d'Etudes Slaves*). Articles dealing with history, government, international relations, economics, geography, literature, philosophy, and other subjects, all relating to the Soviet Union and East Europe (including the Baltic countries, Greece, and East Germany). Some contributions from East Europe and the Soviet Union. Some articles in English, others in French. Published quarterly by the Department of History, Loyola College, Montreal 28, Canada. $6.00 per year.

Canadian Slavonic Papers. Articles on economics, politics, history, culture, and literature of the Soviet Union and Eastern Europe. Published quarterly by the Canadian Association of Slavists at Carleton University, Ottawa, Canada. $8.50 per year.

Central Asian Review. Analysis of Soviet writings on social, political and cultural developments in Soviet Central Asia and adjacent countries. Published quarterly by the Central Asian Research Centre, 66A Kings Road, London S.W.3, England. $7.70 per year.

Central Asiatic Journal. Concentrates principally on cultural aspects of communist life in central Asia. Published quarterly by Mouton and Co., The Hague, Netherlands. $9.45 per year.

China News Analysis. News items about Mainland China. Published 48 times per year. P.O. Box 13225, Hong Kong. For institutions, $30.00 for six months; individual subscriptions by arrangement.

China Quarterly. Articles on recent developments in Chinese economics, politics, literature, etc. Published quarterly by Information Bulletin Ltd., 133 Oxford Street, London W.1, England. $6.00 per year. ($4.00 per year for students.)

China Today. Articles on life and problems both in mainland and in nationalist China. Published monthly by United Publishing Center, 174, Section 2, Chung Shan North Road, Taipei, Taiwan, Republic of China. $4.00 per year.

China Trade Report. News reports and statistics from a wide range of published and other sources. Published monthly by the *Far Eastern Economic Review,* P.O. Box 160, Hong Kong. 17.2s6d ($47.95) per year.

Chinese Communist Affairs. Articles on political, social, and economic conditions and problems in Mainland China. Published bimonthly by the Institute of Political Research, P.O. Box 518, Taipei, Taiwan, Republic of China. $1.00 per year.

Communist Affairs. Research papers and analyses in the field of Communist affairs. Published bimonthly by the Research Institute on Communist Strategy and Propaganda, University of Southern California, Los Angeles, California. $5.00 per year.

Current History. Sometimes entire issues devoted to one or another of the Communist countries. Other issues deal with noncommunist countries and regions. Published monthly by Events Publishing Co., 1822 Ludlow St., Philadelphia 3, Pennsylvania. $7.50 per year.

East Europe. "A Review of East European Affairs," with special emphasis on the analysis of economic and political events in the communist countries of East Europe. Published monthly by Free Europe Inc., 2 Park Avenue, New York, N. Y. 10016. $5.00 per year.

East European Quarterly. An "international journal of the social sciences for scholars of all nations," focusing attention primarily on the "the many different aspects of peoples living in the Baltic, Adriatic, Aegean, and Black Sea areas." Articles by Marxist scholars from the Soviet Union and East Europe are accepted. Published quarterly by the University of Colorado, Boulder, Colorado. $6.00 per year.

East West. A Chinese-American news magazine which presents news, features and analysis on China. Printed in English and in Chinese. Its views are "those of the Chinese-American and neither pro-Red nor Nationalist China." Published at 863 Stockton Street, San Francisco, California 94108. $3.60 per year.

Economic Bulletin for Europe. See United Nations Periodicals.

Economics of Planning (Formerly *Ost-Okonomi*). Theory and practice of central economic planning; need for such planning and problems connected with it, both in communist and noncommunist countries. Articles by Marxist and non-Marxist authors. Published quarterly by the Norwegian Institute of International Affairs in cooperation with the Centre for Russian and East European Studies, University of Birmingham, P.O. Box 7030, Oslo, Norway. $6.00 per year.

Economic Survey of Europe. See United Nations Periodicals.

Etudes Slaves et East-Europeennes. See *Slavic and East European Studies.*

Far Eastern Economic Review. Articles on trade, industry, finance, transportation, and public affairs in South and East Asia. Published weekly by the Far Eastern Economic Review, Ltd., 401-406, Marina House, Hong Kong. $16.00 per year.

Far Eastern Quarterly. See *Journal of Asian Studies.*

Far East Reporter Publications. Articles, usually about China but also about other areas of the Far East, showing a sympathetic understanding of Communist countries in Asia. While some readers may be inclined to classify the journal as "Marxist" in content, the publisher, Miss Maud Russell, does not wish to have her views classified as "Marxist." Published irregularly by Maud Russell, P.O. Box 1536, New York, N.Y. 10017. $2.00 per year.

Free China and Asia. Illustrated magazine. Reports on struggle of anti-Communist Chinese against Communism. Published monthly by Asian Peoples Anti-Communist League, Republic of China, 1707 Chung Cheng Rd., Taipei, Taiwan, Republic of China. $1.20 per year.

Free China Weekly. News items, mostly economic and political in nature, covering both Chinas. Published weekly by China Publishing Company, P.O. Box 337, Taipei, Taiwan, Republic of China. $2.50 per year.

Global Digest. See Marxist section.

Jews in Eastern Europe. Survey of events affecting Jews in the Soviet Bloc. Published quarterly by European Jewish Publications Ltd., 31 Percy Street, London, W.1, England. $5.00 per year.

Journal of Asian Studies (Formerly *Far Eastern Quarterly*). Articles on Asian history and Asian economic, political, and social affairs. Published quarterly by The Association for Asian Studies, Inc., 48 Lane Hall, Ann Arbor, Michigan. Subscription includes annual bibliography on Asian studies. $15.00 per year.

Lituanus: Lithuanian Quarterly. Review of Lithuanian literature and politics. Published quarterly by Lituanus Foundation, Inc., Box 9318, Chicago, Illinois 60690. $3.00 per year.

Mizan. Deals with policies of the Soviet Union and China towards the developing countries. Published bimonthly by Central Asian Research Center, 66 A & B King's Road, London S.W. 3, England, in association with St. Anthony's College (Oxford) Soviet Affairs Group. $10.00 per year. Also available

Mizan Supplement A (Middle East and Africa, Soviet and Chinese Press Reports) and *Mizan Supplement B* (Southeast Asia, Soviet and Chinese Press Reports). Each published bimonthly. $5.00 per year to subscribers.

Ost-Okonomi. See *Economics of Planning.*

Polish Review. Articles, primarily on Polish history. Published quarterly by the Polish Institute of Arts and Sciences in America, 59 East 66 St., New York, N.Y. 10021. $5.00 per year.

Problems of Communism. Analyses and background information on various aspects of world Communism today. Published bimonthly by the United States Information Agency, 1777 Pennsylvania Avenue, N. W., Washington, D. C. Obtainable free of charge outside the United States by writing to the nearest office of the U.S. Information Service. For residents of the United States, obtainable from Superintendent of Documents, U.S. Government Printing Office, Washington, D. C. 20402 at $2.50 per year.

Quarterly Economic Reviews. There are 58 such reviews, each dealing with a country or region. Contents include statistical material and economic analyses covering, in all, more than one hundred countries. Four of these 58 reviews are classified as the "Communist Group," that is, "China, Hong Kong, North Korea," "Eastern Europe North: Czechoslovakia, East Germany," "Eastern Europe South: Albania, Bulgaria, Rumania, Hungary," and "U.S.S.R." There is a separate *Quarterly Economic Review* on Yugoslavia. Cuba is in a *Review* containing "Cuba, Dominican Republic, Haiti, Puerto Rico," which is part of the Latin America series. Published quarterly by the Economist Intelligence Unit, *The Economist,* Spencer House, 27 St., James Place, London, S.W.1, England. $28.00 per year for each of the 58 reviews. Duplicate copies, $12.00 per year. Subscription rate for all reviews that constitute the "Communist Group," $96.00 per year. Fifty percent discount on all prices to university subscribers.

Radio Free Europe Publications: Those listed below are published almost daily by Radio Free Europe, Munich, and are distributed in the United States by the parent organization, Free Europe, Inc., 2 Park Avenue, New York, N. Y. 10016. Mailed several times per month. $15.00 per year.

> *Research Departments of Radio Free Europe, Background Papers.* Research and evaluation papers dealing with Communist countries and with communism in non-Communist countries prepared by staff members of Radio Free Europe, Munich. A quarterly index of background papers is also published.

> *Situation Reports.* Prepared by staff members of Radio Free Europe, Munich; contain up-to-date news items on events in the five East European countries to which Radio Free Europe broadcasts, that is, Bulgaria, Czechoslovakia, Hungary, Poland, and Rumania.

> *Press Surveys.* Translations from the press of the five countries, listed above, to which Radio Free Europe broadcasts.

Radio Liberty Dispatch. Information on and brief analyses of recent occurrences in the U.S.S.R. Published several times per month by Radio Liberty Committee, 30 E. 42d St., New York, N. Y. 10017. Mailed on request, without charge, to libraries, institutions, and individuals engaged in research in the field.

Radio Liberty Research Paper. Analyses of recent developments in the U.S.S.R. Published several times per year by Radio Liberty Committee, 30 E. 42d St., New York, N. Y. 10017. Mailed on request, without charge, to libraries, institutions, and individuals engaged in research in the field.

Revue Canadienne d'Etudes Slaves. See *Canadian Slavic Studies.*

Russian Review. Articles on Russia past and present, dealing with politics, economics, social developments, culture, art, and literature. Published quarterly by Russian Review, Box 146, Hanover, New Hampshire 03755. $6.00 per year.

Selected International Indicators. "Economic trends in 63 countries." Published monthly by Selected Indicators, Inc., 11 W. 42nd St., New York 36, N. Y. $37.50 per year.

Slavic and East European Journal. Articles on Slavic and East European pedagogy, linguistics, and literature. Published quarterly for the American Association of Teachers of Slavic and East European Languages by the University of Wisconsin Press, Box 1379, Madison, Wisconsin. $10.00 per year.

* *Slavic and East European Studies.* Articles primarily on Slavic and East European history and literature. Some articles in English, others in French. Published quarterly for the Eastern Canada Association of Slavists and East-European Specialists by E.S. Slavic and East European Studies, Loyola College, 7270 Sherbrooke W., Montreal 28, Canada. $4.00 per year.

Slavic Review (Formerly American Slavic and East European Review). An "American Quarterly of Soviet and East European Studies," with special emphasis on history, literature, and culture. Published quarterly by the American Association for the Advancement of Slavic Studies. The American Association for the Advancement of Slavic Studies is an international organization of persons interested in the Slavic and East European field. Regular memberships are $12.00 per year, sustaining memberships $25.00 per year; and student memberships (without vote) $5.00 per year for full-time students with U.S. mailing addresses. (Nonvoting associate memberships, and joint memberships for married couples with only one copy of publications and one vote are available also.) All memberships receive quarterly the *Slavic Review;* the *American Bibliography of Russian and East European Studies* (regular price $3.50) published yearly by Indiana University; the Association's *Newsletter* (regular price $1.50 per year) published semiannually at the University of Illinois; and the *Directory* of the Association (sold to nonmembers at $5.00) in the years when it is published. For application blanks write to the American Association for the Advancement of Slavic

---

* As this book goes to press (in mid-1967), information has reached the editor that Loyola College is no longer publishing this journal. It is not known whether the Eastern Canada Association of Slavists and East-European Specialists will make other arrangements or whether the journal will be discontinued.

Studies, 1207 West Oregon Street, University of Illinois, Urbana, Illinois 61801.

Slavonic and East European Review. Articles on history and literature in the Slavic and East European countries. Published semiannually by the Athlone Press for the School of Slavonic and East European Studies, University of London, Malet Street, London W, C. 1. $6.00 per year.

Soviet Studies. A review of the social and economic institutions of the USSR. Published quarterly by the Department for Study of Social and Economic Institutions of the U.S.S.R., University of Glasgow, Glasgow, Scotland. $6.00 per year (See also *Soviet Information Supplement* in Marxist section).

Soviet Survey. See *Survey.*

Studies in Soviet Thought. Primarily devoted to the publication of research papers on contemporary Soviet philosophy. Published quarterly by the Institute of East-European Studies, Rue de l'Hopital, Fribourg, Switzerland. $11.20 per year.

Studies on the Soviet Union. Articles on all aspects of Soviet life. Published quarterly by the Institute for the Study of the U.S.S.R., 8 Munich 22, Mannhardtstr 6, Germany. $6.00 per year.

Survey. "A Journal of Soviet and East-European Studies." Published quarterly by Information Bulletin Ltd., 133 Oxford Street, on behalf of the Congress for Cultural Freedom. $4.00 per year.

Survey of Recent Developments in Nine Captive Countries. Covers current events in Albania, Bulgaria, Czechoslovakia, Estonia, Hungary, Latvia, Lithuania, Poland, and Rumania. Published annually by the Assembly of Captive European Nations, 29 West 57th Street, New York, N.Y. 10019. Free.

Ukrainian Bulletin. Articles on Ukrainian culture, history, and current events. Published semimonthly by the Ukrainian Congress Committee of America, 302 West 13th Street, New York, N.Y. 10014. $2.00 per year.

Ukrainian Quarterly. Political, social and economic problems of Eastern Europe, particularly the Ukraine. Published Quarterly by the Ukrainian Congress Committee of America, 302 W. 13 St., New York, 14, N. Y. $5.00 per year.

Ukrainian Review. Illustrated review of news, culture, and life in the Ukraine. Published quarterly by the Association of Ukrainians in Great Britain Ltd., 49 Linden Gardens, London W.2, England. $4.00 per year.

* *Ukrainian Review.* Has been incorporated into *Studies on the Soviet Union.*

United Nations Documents Index. See United Nations Periodicals.

United Nations Periodicals. Distributed through United Nations Sales Section, New York, N.Y. 10017. For more information on the ones listed below and others, write for Periodicals and Recurrent Publications, free upon request.

---

* This *Ukrainian Review,* originally published in Munich, Germany, is different from the journal by the same name, published in London, England, listed immediately above it.

Economic Bulletin for Europe. Current information and statistical data. Published quarterly. Price varies, recently between $0.75 and $1.50 per issue.

Economic Survey of Europe. Comprehensive economic and statistical information with a major part devoted to Eastern Europe and the Soviet Union. Published annually. Price varies, recently between $2.00 and $3.00 per year.

Monthly Bulletin of Statistics. Statistics from 170 countries on more than 60 subjects such as population, food, trade, production, finance, and national income. Published monthly. $10.00 per year.

Population and Vital Statistics Report. Latest census returns; statistics on birth, death, and infant mortality for all countries. Published quarterly. $1.00 per year.

United Nations Documents Index. Lists, describes, and indexes by subject all the unrestricted documents and publications of the UN and the International Court. Published monthly. $10.00 per year.

Yugoslav Observer. A review of Yugoslav and Balkan affairs. Published quarterly by Free Yugoslav Information Center, Lansing, Michigan.

MARXIST PERIODIC PUBLICATIONS AND PERIODIC TRANSLATIONS OF ARTICLES ORIGINALLY PUBLISHED IN COMMUNIST COUNTRIES *

Acta Oeconomica. Deals primarily with economic problems, challenges, and opportunities confronting Socialist countries. Most articles in English; the few that are not are in Russian or German and contain English-language summaries. Published by the Hungarian Academy of Sciences, Budapest, Hungary. $12.00 per year.

AIMS Newsletter. Information, announcements, and bibliographies, of interest primarily to students of Marxism. Published bimonthly by the American In-

---

* In the United States, orders for periodicals published in Communist China can be placed with China Publications, 95 Fifth Avenue, New York, N. Y. 10003 or with China Books and Periodicals, 2929 Twenty-fourth Street, San Francisco, California 94110. Orders for Soviet newspapers, journals, and magazines can be placed with Cross World Books and Periodicals, Inc., 333 S. Wacker Drive, Chicago, Illinois 60606, or with Four Continent Book Corporation, 156 Fifth Avenue, New York, N.Y., 10010. In Canada, orders for both Chinese and Soviet publications can be placed with Progress Books, 487 Adelaide Street W., Toronto 2 B, Ontario, Canada.

It appears that some periodicals published in Communist China (for example, *China's Foreign Trade, China's Sports,* and *Women of China*) may have discontinued publication under the impact of the "Cultural Revolution." Since it is not known whether cessation of publication is temporary or permanent, they are included in this list.

For an explanation of the criteria for inclusion of periodic publications in this section, see p. 538 above.

stitute for Marxist Studies, 20 E. 30th St., New York, N.Y. 10016. $2.00 per year.

Anglo-Soviet Journal. See non-Marxist section.

British-Soviet Friendship. Covers Anglo-Soviet relations and all aspects of life in the Soviet Union. Published monthly by British-Soviet Friendship Society, 36 Spencer Street, London E.C.1, England. $0.85 per copy.

British-Soviet News Letter. Emphasis on international relations. Published monthly by British-Soviet Friendship Society, 36 Spencer Street, London, E.C.1, England. $1.40 per year.

Broadsheet. China's views on peace and war, basic issues in the Sino-Soviet polemics, the atom bomb, and the national liberation movement. Published monthly by the China Policy Study Group, 62 Parliament Hall, London, N.W. 3, England. $1.70 per year.

Bulgaria News Release. News items from Bulgaria. Published by the Legation of the People's Republic of Bulgaria, 2100 16th St., N.W., Washington, D.C. Free.

Bulgarian Foreign Trade. Illustrated magazine. Published quarterly by the Bulgarian Chamber of Commerce, 11-a A 1. Stambolisky Blvd., Sofia, Bulgaria. $4.00 per year.

Bulgarian News (Formerly *News From Bulgaria*). News items primarily dealing with Bulgaria. Published monthly by the Legation of the People's Republic of Bulgaria, 12 Queens Gate Gardens, London, S. W. 7, England. Free.

Bulgarian Press Survey. See Radio Free Europe Publications in non-Marxist section.

Bulgaria Today. Pictorial magazine dealing with all aspects of life in Bulgaria. Published monthly at 1 Levski St., Sofia, Bulgaria.

Canadian Slavic Studies (*Revue Canadienne d'Etudes Slaves*). See non-Marxist section.

China's Foreign Trade. Illustrated magazine. Published bimonthly by the China Council for the promotion of International Trade. Peking, China. $2.50 per year.

China News Analysis. News items from Mainland China. Published 48 times per year, P. O. Box 13225, Hong Kong. For institutions, $30.00 for six months; individual subscriptions by arrangement.

China Pictorial. Picture magazine covering all aspects of life in Communist China. Published monthly by China Pictorial, Chegongzhuang Road, Peking 28, China. $2.50 per year.

China Reconstructs. Illustrated magazine dealing with current scientific and economic advances in China. Published monthly by the China Welfare Institute, P. O. Box 399, Peking, China. $3.00 per year.

China's Sports. Illustrated magazine. Published monthly by The China Sports Editorial Board, 8 Ti Kuan Road, Peking, China.

Chinese Economic Studies. See IASP Journals.

Chinese Education. See IASP Journals.

Chinese Law and Government. See IASP Journals.

Chinese Literature. Contemporary Chinese writings, folk and classical; art reproductions; China's policies concerning literature and art. Published monthly by Foreign Languages Press, Pai Wan Chuang, Peking 37, China. $3.00 per year.

Chinese Studies in History and Philosophy. See IASP Journals.

Chinese Studies in Sociology and Anthropology. See IASP Journals.

Cooperation in Romania. Published semiannually by the Central Union of Consumer Cooperatives of the Socialist Republic of Romania, Bucharest, Rumania. $2.00 per year.

CTK Daily Press Survey. A review of news, information, and commentaries from the daily press in condensed versions, as well as excerpts from Party and Government statements. Published monthly by Pragopress, Opletalova 5, Prague 1., Czechoslovakia. $4.50 per year.

Culture and Life. Illustrated magazine dealing with the participation of Soviet people in public life and in the national economy. Also features Soviet scientific and cultural news. Published monthly by the Union of Soviet Societies for Friendship and Cultural Relations with Foreign Countries, Moscow, U.S.S.R. $2.50 per year.

Current Digest of the Soviet Press. Translations from Soviet newspapers, journals, and magazines. Includes a weekly index to *Pravda* and *Izvestia,* and a quarterly index, separately bound, to the *Current Digest* and to some major English language Soviet publications. Published weekly by the Joint Committee on Slavic Studies (appointed by the American Council of Learned Societies and the Social Science Research Council), 2500 S. State Street, Ann Arbor, Michigan. First subscription $200.00 per year; each additional concurrent subscription for nonacademic subscribers, $150.00 per year; each additional subscription to college libraries, $40.00 per year; additional subscriptions for faculty, staff, and enrolled students of academic institutions which maintain a subscription, $25.00 per year.

Czechoslovak Digest. Background information concerning politics, economics, trade, sciences, education, culture, sports, and a chronology of important events in Czechoslovakia. Published weekly by Pragopress, Opletalova 5, Prague 1., Czechoslovakia.

Czechoslovak Economic Papers. Published semiannually by Academia, Publishing House of the Czechoslovak Academy of Science, Vodickova 40, Prague 1, Czechoslovakia. $2.80 per year.

Czechoslovak Foreign Trade. Illustrated magazine. Published monthly by the Czechoslovak Chamber of Commerce, Ulice 28, Rijna 13, Prague 1, Czechoslovakia. $5.00 per year.

Czechoslovak Trade Unions. Illustrated magazine. Published monthly by the Central Council of Trade Unions., 15 Wenceslas Square, Prague 1, Czechoslovakia. $1.50 per year.

Czechoslovak Life. Pictorial magazine dealing with all aspects of life in Czechoslovakia. Published monthly by the Oris Publishing House in Prague. Address all correspondence to *Czechoslovak Life,* Editorial Office, Kalininova 5, Prague 3, Czechoslovakia $3.00 per year.

Czechoslovak Press Survey. See Radio Free Europe Publications in non-Marxist section.

Czechoslovak Woman. Illustrated magazine. Published quarterly by the Czechoslovak Women's Committee. Editorial Office: Panska 7, Box 60, Prague 1, Czechoslovakia. $1.00 per year.

Daily News Release. (Hsinua News Agency). News items reported from a Communist Chinese point of view. Published daily by Asia News Service, 9-9 3 Chome Tsuiji Chuo-ku, Tokyo, Japan. $54.00 plus postage for three months.

Daily Report of Foreign Radio Broadcasts. Foreign broadcasts monitored and translated into English, with heavy emphasis on news items. Published daily by the Foreign Broadcast Information Service, 2430 E. Street, N.W., Washington 25, D.C. Free to press and radio correspondents in Washington, D.C. and to certain university and college libraries. Not available for private distribution.

Daily Report, Foreign Radio Broadcast Supplements. Summaries, excerpts, and full texts of foreign radio broadcasts, translated into English. Among the supplements there is one on the U.S.S.R., one on East Europe, and one on the Far East. Special attention is given to the communist countries. Published almost daily by the Foreign Broadcast Information Service, 2430 E. Street, N.W., Washington 25, D.C. Free to press and radio correspondents in Washington, D.C. and to certain university and college libraries. Not available for private distribution.

Daily Review of the Soviet Press. Translations from the Soviet press. Includes material from the newspapers *Pravda, Izvestia, Trud,* and *Komsomolskaya Pravda* on the day of publication; digest of articles from Soviet periodicals; texts of official documents; commentaries on foreign policy; articles on international cooperation, the communist and working class movement, the Soviet economy, science, culture, arts, medicine, sport, and on so. Published twice a day, except Sundays and national holidays, plus three weekly supplements, one of them reviewing the provincial press, by Novosti Press Agency, Moscow, U.S.S.R. and airmailed daily from Moscow. $156.00 per year.

Democratic German Report. Articles on various topics, especially politics and economics, as related to present day East Germany. Published semimonthly at Krausenstrasse 9, Berlin 108, East Germany. $1.25 per year.

Digest of the Soviet Ukrainian Press. Translations of current articles from the Soviet Ukrainian Press dealing with all phases of Soviet life. Published monthly by Prolog, 875 West End Avenue, New York, N.Y. 10025. $7.50 per year.

Documents, Articles and Information on Rumania. Articles on economic, political, and cultural topics. Frequent supplements usually contain speeches by important public or party officials. Published 36 times per year by the Rumanian News Agency Agerpress, Scinteia Square, Bucharest, Rumania. $8.00 per year.

East European Economics. See IASP Journals.

East European Quarterly. See non-Marxist section.

Eastern European Studies in History. See IASP Journals.

Eastern European Studies in Law and Government. See IASP Journals.

Eastern European Studies in Literature. See IASP Journals.

Eastern European Studies in Psychology. See IASP Journals.

Eastern European Studies in Sociology and Anthropology. See IASP Journals.

Eastern Horizon. Deals with Communist politics, culture, and art in China. Articles appear to be pro-Chinese but there is a statement in each issue that "signed articles express the views of the writers, not necessarily of the editors." Published monthly by Eastern Horizon Press, 18 Causeway Road, Hong Kong. $5.00 per year.

Economic Bulletin for Europe. See United Nations Periodicals, Non-Marxist section.

Economic Review. Published monthly by the Yugoslav economic daily, "Privredni pregled," Birjuzova br. 3, Belgrade, Yugoslavia. $10.00 per year.

Economic Survey of Europe. See United Nations Periodicals, Non-Marxist section.

Economics of Planning. See non-Marxist section.

Education in Eastern Europe. See IASP Journals.

Evergreen. A magazine of Chinese youth and students. Published monthly by the All-China Youth Federation and All-China Students' Federation, 3 Yu Ho Chiao, Peking, China. $1.00 per year.

Far East Reporter Publications. See non-Marxist section.

Foreign Trade. Deals with various aspects of the foreign trade of the Soviet Union. Published monthly in Moscow, U.S.S.R. $5.40 per year.

Fourth International. English language edition of the theoretical organ of the International Executive Committee of the Fourth International. Published quarterly at 64 rue de Richelieu, Paris, France. $1.25 per year.

G.D.R. Review. Illustrated magazine dealing with a variety of topics, but with special emphasis on art and culture in East Germany. Published monthly by the League of the G.D.R. (German Democratic Republic) for Friendship Among the Peoples, Thalmannplatz 8/9, 108 Berlin 8, East Germany. $2.50 per year.

German Foreign Policy. Articles concerning international questions. Published bimonthly by VEB Deutscher Verlag der Wissenschaften, Taubenstrasse 10, 108 Berlin, East Germany. $5.00 per year.

Global Digest. Translations and reprints from English language publications. Main emphasis on materials originally published in Communist China and North Vietnam; a substantial part of each issue is, however, devoted to materials published in the Marxist and the non-Marxist press of other countries, including that of Japan, England, and the United States. Published monthly by the Global Digest Press, 13 Leighton Road, 3rd floor, Happy Valley, Hong Kong. $3.00 per year.

Horizons (formerly *Marxist Quarterly*). Articles on philosophy and on economic and social problems, especially in the West, treated from a Marxist point of view. Published quarterly by Progress Books, 487 Adelaide Street W., Toronto 2 B, Ontario, Canada. $2.00 per year.

Hsinhua Selected News Items. News items from Mainland China. Published weekly by Hsinhua News Agency, Hong Kong Branch, 5 Sharp Street W., Hong Kong.

Hungarian Exporter. Covers economic, business, and foreign trade matters of primary interest to exporters and importers. Published monthly by the Hungarian Chamber of Commerce, u. 6. Budapest, Hungary. $3.00 per year.

Hungarian Foreign Trade. Illustrated magazine dealing with economics, travel, culture, science, Hungarian products, exports and imports, etc. Published quarterly. Editorial Office: P.O.B. 223, Budapest 62, Hungary. $3.60 per year.

Hungarian Press Survey. See Radio Free Europe Publications. See Non-Marxist section.

Hungarian Review. Pictorial magazine covering all aspects of life in Hungary. Published monthly at Lenin Körut, 9-11, Budapest, Hungary. $2.00 per year.

IASP Journals. Complete translations of scholarly articles from Soviet and East European Journals, published by the International Arts and Sciences Press (IASP), 108 Grand Street, White Plains, N. Y. 10601.

Monthly IASP Journals:

    Problems of Economics. $50.00 per year ($25.00) *

    Soviet Education. $70.00 per year ($25.00) *

Bimonthly IASP Journal:

    American Review of Soviet and Eastern European Foreign Trade. $35.00 per year. ($15.00) *

Quarterly IASP Journals: All quarterlies are $35.00 per year, except *The Soviet Review* which is $6.00 per year. ($15.00 except *The Soviet Review* which is $6.00) *

---

* Early in 1967, the publisher notified the subscribers that the *Global Digest* has been "temporarily suspended to carry out a replanning of the magazine."

* Prices in parentheses are annual subscription charges for all individuals associated with subscribing institutions. Bulk orders for class room use are available at substantially reduced rates.

Chinese Economic Studies.

Chinese Education.

Chinese Law and Government.

Chinese Studies in History and Philosophy.

Chinese Studies in Sociology and Anthropology.

Eastern European Economics.

Eastern European Studies in History.

Eastern European Studies in Law and Government.

Eastern European Studies in Literature.

Eastern European Studies in Philosophy.

Eastern European Studies in Sociology and Anthropology.

Education in Eastern Europe.

Management Science and Operations Research.

Mathematical Studies in Economics and Statistics in the U.S.S.R. and Eastern Europe.

Soviet Anthopology and Archeology.

Soviet Law and Government.

Soviet Psychiatry.

Soviet Psychology.

Soviet Sociology.

Soviet Statutes and Decisions.

Soviet Studies in History.

Soviet Studies in Literature.

Soviet Studies in Philosophy.

Soviet Studies in World Economics and Politics.

Information Bulletin of the World Marxist Review. Speeches, official statements, and other items of important Communists and of Communist parties. Published monthly by Progress Books, 478 Adelaide St. W., Toronto 2B, Ontario, Canada. Free to subscribers of *World Marxist Review,* $3.50 per year for nonsubscribers.

Information Bulletin of the Chamber of Commerce of the Socialist Republic of Rumania. Deals primarily with economic matters in or related to Rumania. Published monthly under the auspices of the Rumanian Chamber of Commerce, "Cartimex," 13 Decembrie Street, Bucharest 3, Rumania. $4.00 per year.

* *International Affairs.* "A Journal of Political Analysis." Published monthly by

---

* Not to be confused with a different journal by the same name published in London, England.

the All-Union Society "ZNANIYE," 14 Gorokhovsky Pereulok, Moscow, K-63, U.S.S.R. $3.50 per year.

Jews and the Jewish People; Collected Materials From the Soviet Daily and Periodical Press. A selection of news and articles concerning Jews within the Soviet Union, translated from the Soviet press. Published six times per year by Contemporary Jewish Library Ltd., 31 Percy Street, London W.1., England. $2.00 per copy.

JPRS Reports. Translations from newspapers, journals, and magazines of all the communist (and also of other) countries include unclassified foreign documents, scholarly works, technical articles in numerous fields, and research reports. Published continuously by the Joint Publications Research Service (JPRS) at the rate of several thousand pages per month. All current JPRS reports are listed in the *Monthly Catalog of U.S. Government Publications.* Subscription prices depend upon the number of series (arranged by region or country, as well as by topics) one wishes to subscribe to, the number of pages published in each series, and the type of publication (xeroxed, printed, or microfilmed). All JPRS reports may be ordered from the U.S. Department of Commerce, Clearinghouse for Federal Scientific and Technical Information, Joint Publications Research Service, Building Tempo E., Adams Drive, 4th and 6th Streets, S. W. Washington, D. C. 20043. Details on special subscription arrangements for any JPRS reports will be provided on request.

Journal of Yugoslav Foreign Trade. Journal dealing with imports and exports, industry, mining, agriculture, finance, tourist information, and similar items. Published quarterly by "Export Press," Francuska br. 27, Belgrade, Yugoslavia. $2.00 per year.

Korea Today. Pictorial magazine dealing primarily with subjects related to the cultural and industrial progress of North Korea. Published monthly by the Foreign Languages Publishing House, Pyongyang, North Korea. $2.00 per year.

Labour Monthly. Articles on international affairs and problems of our times. Published monthly by the Trinity Trust, 134 Ballards Lane, London, N-3, England. $4.50 per year.

Letter From China. Covers primarily U.S. Chinese relations, domestic developments in China, and economic problems. Published 10 times per year by American pro-Chinese Marxist Anna Louise Strong, Tai Chin Cheng, Peking, China.

Management Science and Operations Research in the USSR and Eastern Europe. See IASP Journals.

Marx Memorial Library Quarterly Bulletin. Primarily historical articles. Published quarterly by Marx Memorial Library, 37 a Clerkenwell Green, London, E.C.1, England. Free to members; 4 shillings (54¢) plus postage per year to nonmembers. The Marx Memorial Library is a subscription library, membership being open to all, irrespective of political affiliations or nonparty status.

Marxism Today. "Theoretical and Discussion Journal of the Communist Party" (of Great Britain). Published monthly by the Communist Party, 16 King Street, London, W.C. 2, England. Orders and subscriptions: Central Books Ltd., 37 Gray's Inn Road, London W.C. 1, England. $4.00 per year.

Marxist Quarterly. See *Horizons.*

Mathematical Studies in Economics and Statistics in the U.S.S.R. and Eastern Europe. See IASP Journals.

Mongolia Today. Political, economic, social, and cultural news, as well as short stories. Published monthly by B. Sandagsuren for the Information Section of the Mongolian Embassy in India, 21/48 Panch Sheel Marg, Chanakyapuri, New Delhi 11, India.

Monthly Bulletin of Statistics. See United Nations Periodicals, Non-Marxist section.

Monthly Review. "An independent Socialist magazine." Marxist analyses of events in communist and noncommunist countries. Published monthly (except combined issue for July and August) by Monthly Review, Inc., 333 Sixth Avenue, New York, N. Y. 10014. $6.00 per year.

Moscow News. News items on all aspects of life in the U.S.S.R. Published weekly by the Union of Soviet Societies of Friendship and Cultural Relations with Foreign Countries, 16/2 Gorky Street, Moscow, U.S.S.R. $2.00 per year.

New Albania. A pictorial magazine dealing with all aspects of life in Albania. Published bimonthly by the "Naim Frasheri," State Publishing House, Rruga, "Konference e Pezes," Tirana, Albania. $2.80 per year.

New Hungarian Quarterly. Articles on Hungarian culture, economics, literature, art and music. Published quarterly by Lapkiado Publishing House, Budapest. $4.00 per year.

New Hungary. Pictorial magazine dealing with all aspects of life in Hungary. Published monthly by the Hungarian News and Information Service, 167 Kensington High Street, London, W.8, England.

New Times. "A Journal of World Affairs." Published weekly by *Trud* at 1/2 Maly Putinkovsky, Pushkin Square, Moscow, K-6, U.S.S.R. $3.50 per year.

New Trends in Czechoslovak Economics. Articles dealing with economic developments and policies in Czechoslovakia. Published by Pragropress, Slavickova 5, Prague 6, Czechoslovakia.

New World Review. Marxist analyses of events in communist and noncommunist countries. Published monthly (except combined issue for August and September) by N.W.R. Publications, Inc., Suite 308, 156 Fifth Avenue, New York 10, N. Y. $3.50 per year.

News From Bulgaria. See *Bulgarian News.*

Peking Review. A magazine of Communist Chinese news and views. Contains documents, articles on development in Communist China, views on current international questions, and other similar items. All articles are translated from the two major Chinese newspapers, *People's Daily* and *Red Flag.* Published weekly by Pai Wan Chung, Peking 37, China. $4.00 per year.

Poland. Illustrated magazine covering all aspects of life in Poland. Published monthly by Polonia Publishing House, Koszykowa 60, Warsaw 1, Poland. $2.25 per year.

Polish Academy of Sciences, Quarterly Review of Scientific Publications. Series A: Social Sciences. Published quarterly by Foreign Trade Enterprise "Ars Polona," Krakowskie Przedmieście 7, Warsaw, Poland.

Polish Economic Survey. Articles on the Polish economy. Published bimonthly. Editorial Office: Al. Jerozolimskie 7, Warsaw, Poland. $7.50 per year.

Polish Foreign Trade. Illustrated magazine. Published quarterly by the Polish Chamber of Foreign Trade, Trembcka 4, Warsaw, Poland. $3.00 per year.

Polish Perspectives. Essays on Polish life and economic affairs. Published monthly at ul. Wilcza 46, Warsaw, Poland. $4.80 per year.

Polish Press Survey. See Radio Free Europe Publications in Non-Marxist section.

Polish Reports. Speeches by Polish officials and documents. Published monthly at Al. Jerozolimskie 7, Warsaw, Poland. $5.00 per year.

Polish Sociological Bulletin. Published semimonthly by the Polish Sociological Association, Krakowskie Przedmieście 3, Warsaw, Poland. $3.00 per year.

Polish Weekly. Current events in economics, politics, culture, sports; speeches by government and Party officials; survey of the Polish press. Published 50 times per year by the Polish Press Agency. Editorial Office: Al. Jerozolimskie 7, Warsaw, Poland.

Polish Western Affairs. Articles on present-day economic and social problems of Central Europe. Published semiannually by the Institute for Western Affairs (Instytut Zachodni), Stary Rynek 2, Poznan, Poland. $2.00 per year.

Political Affairs. "A theoretical and political magazine of scientific socialism." Published monthly by New Century Publishers, Inc., 832 Broadway, New York 3, N. Y. $4.00 per year.

Prague News Letter. Political, economic, and cultural news with emphasis on Czechoslovakia. Nakladatelstvi Orbis n.p. Prague 2, Czechoslovakia. Free.

Praxis. A philosophical journal, "mainly devoted to articles on some important theme or problem." Articles in French, English and German. Published quarterly by the Croatian Philosophical Society, Zagreb, Dure Salaja b.b. Yugoslavia. $5.00 per year.

Problems of Peace and Socialism. See *World Marxist Review.*

Pyongyang Times. Emphasis on current news items. Published weekly by Pyong Times, Pyongyang, North Korea.

Religion in Communist Dominated Areas. Consists mainly of translated excerpts from original communist sources. Published semimonthly by the International Affairs Commission of the National Council of Churches, 475 Riverside Drive, New York, N.Y. 10027. $10.00 per year.

Reprints From the Soviet Press. Current articles, speeches, documents, and reports, translated from the Soviet press. Published biweekly by Compass Publications, Inc., Box 47, Old Chelsea Station, New York, N. Y. 10011. $25.00 per year.

Review. Illustrated magazine containing articles on life, culture, and tourist attractions in Yugoslavia. Published monthly by Tourist Press, Terazije br. 31, Belgrade, Yugoslavia. $2.20 per year.

Review of International Affairs. Articles on international politics, economics, sociology, and law. Also a regular column on topics related to Yugoslav development. Published semimonthly by "Medjunardona Politika" 34, Menanjina–POB 413, Belgrade, Yugoslavia. $5.00 per year.

* *Romanian Bulletin.* Articles on Rumanian politics, education, literature and the Rumanian economy. Published monthly by the Embassy of the Socialist Republic of Romania, 1601 23rd St., N. W., Washington, D. C. 20008. Free.

Romanian Foreign Trade. "Advancements and Prospects." A quarterly review edited by the Rumanian Chamber of Commerce, "Cartimex," 13 Decembrie St., Bucharest, 3, Rumania. $4.00 per year.

Romanian Review. Reviews of Rumanian literature and fine arts. Published quarterly by "Cartimex," Bucharest, Rumania, P.O.B. 134-136. $6.00 per year.

Romanian Scientific Abstracts: Social Science. English-language abstracts of articles published in Rumanian journals. Fields covered are economics, philosophy, logic, sociology, psychology, history, archeology, ethnography, literature and arts, jurisprudence, linguistics, and philology. Published monthly by the Academy of the Socialist Republic of Romania, Scientific Documentation Service, str. Gutenberg, nr. 3 bis. Bucharest, Rumania. $10.00 per year.

Romania Today. Pictorial magazine dealing with all aspects of life in Rumania. Published monthly at str. Ion Ghica Nr. 5, Bucharest, Rumania. $4.00 per year.

Rumanian Press Survey. See Radio Free Europe Publications in Non-Marxist section.

Science and Society. "An Independent Journal of Marxism." Research articles on many topics, presented from a Marxist point of view. Published quarterly by Science and Society, Inc., 30 E. 20th St., New York 3, N. Y. $5.00 per year.

Socialist Thought and Practice. Marxist theory, and political and economic problems treated from a Marxist point of view. Published quarterly by the Socialist Alliance of the Working People of Yugoslavia, Trg Marksa i Engelsa br. 2/1v, Belgrade, Yugoslavia. $2.00 per year.

---

* Romania is frequently spelled "Roumania" or "Rumania." The last spelling is most widely used in Europe (and is used by this author); the Rumanians themselves prefer "Romania."

Soviet Anthropology and Archaeology. See IASP Journals.

Soviet Booklets. Booklets of varying length on all aspects of Soviet life. Published intermittently, about 30 each year, by Novosti Press Agency. Distributed by Soviet Booklets, 63 Rosary Gardens, London, S. W., 7, England. $1.50 per year.

Soviet Film. Illustrated features concerning Soviet films, actors, producers; reviews of motion pictures. Published monthly in Moscow, U.S.S.R. $3.50 per year.

Soviet Geography. Review and translations of current Soviet research in geography. Published monthly (Sept.-June) by the American Geographical Society, Broadway at 156th St., New York 32, N. Y. $10.00 per year.

Soviet Law and Goverment. See IASP Journals.

Soviet Life (Formerly USSR). Pictorial magazine covering all aspects of Soviet life. Published monthly by the Soviet Embassy, 1706 Eighteenth Street N. W., Washington, D.C. 20009. $1.90 per year.

Soviet Literature. Selected works of Soviet literature; literary and critical articles. Published monthly by the Union of Writers of the USSR. 9-11 Dobrolyubov St., Moscow, U.S.S.R. $2.50 per year.

Soviet Military Review. Illustrated military-political journal, featuring theory and practice of modern military science both in the U.S.S.R. and abroad. Published monthly by Soviet Military Review, 38 Kheroshevskoe, Shosse, Moscow, U.S.S.R. $6.00 per year.

Soviet News. News items, usually translated or summarized from the Soviet press. Published intermittently, several times each month, by Soviet News, 3 Rosary Gardens, London S. W., 7, England. Free.

Soviet Psychiatry. See IASP Journals.

Soviet Psychology. See IASP Journals.

The Soviet Review. See IASP Journals.

Soviet Sociology. See IAP Journals.

Soviet Statutes and Decisions. See IASP Journals.

Soviet Studies Information Supplement. Excerpts and brief summaries of current articles from the Soviet press. Published quarterly by the Institute of Soviet and East European Studies, University of Glasgow, Glasgow, Scotland. $1.20 per year. (See also *Soviet Studies* in Non-Marxist section.)

Soviet Studies in History. See IASP Journals.

Soviet Studies in Literature. See IASP Journals.

Soviet Studies in Philosophy. See IASP Journals.

Soviet Studies in World Economics and Politics. See IASP Journals.

Soviet Union. Illustrated magazine, dealing with all aspects of Soviet life. Published monthly at 8 Witza Moskvina, Moscow, K-31, U.S.S.R. $2.50 per year.

Soviet Weekly. Concentrates on current affairs. Published weekly by Soviet Weekly, 3 Rosary Gardens, London S.W., 7, England. $3.50 per year.

Soviet Woman. Illustrated magazine devoted to social and political problems, literature, art, and topics of special interest to women. Published by the Soviet Women's Committee and the Central Council of Trade Unions of the USSR., Kuznetsky Most 22, Moscow, U.S.S.R. $2.50 per year. $3.75 for two years.

Sports in the U.S.S.R. Illustrated magazine highlighting sports in the Soviet Union. Published monthly in Moscow, U.S.S.R. $5.40 per year.

Sputnik. Illustrated Digest. Condensation of articles from Soviet magazines and newspapers on topics of general interest. Articles in English and Russian. Published monthly by the Novosti Press Agency, 2 Pushkin Square, Moscow, U.S.S.R. $5.00 per year.

Studies. Monographs on economic, political, social, educational, ideological etc. aspects of Yugoslavia. Published irregularly, several times per year, by Medunarodna Politika, 34 Nemanjina–POB 413, Belgrade, Yugoslavia. $0.40 per issue.

Tanjug Features. Speeches by Yugoslav officials; other news items, especially of a political nature. Published by the Yugoslav News Agency "Tanjug," Prog Maja, Belgrade, 28, Yugoslavia.

Union Research Service. Translations of articles from the Chinese press and radio broadcasts monitored by the Union Research Institute, preceded by brief editor's notes. Also "biographical service" giving two-page biographical sketches of important Chinese personalities. Published bi-weekly by Union Research Institute Limited, 9 College Road, P.O. Box 5381, Kowloon, Hong Kong. $108.00 per year.

United Nations Documents Index. See United Nations Periodicals, Non-Marxist section.

United Nations Periodicals. See Non-Marxist section.

USSR. See *Soviet Life.*

* *Vietnam.* Illustrated magazine with articles on economic, political, and military affairs of North Vietnam. Published monthly at 79 Ly Thuong Kiet, Hanoi, North Vietnam. $2.50 per year.

Vietnam Courier. Main emphasis on news items, especially those related to the war in Vietnam. Published weekly at E. O. 46 Tran Hung Dao St., Hanoi, North Vietnam. $1.50 per year.

Vietnamese Studies. Two series. 1) "Facts and Events," which deals with current developments and 2) "Problems," which deals with economic, political, historical, literary and other questions. "Facts and Events" is published bimonthly; "Problems" is published irregularly, several times a year. Edi-

---

* No non-Marxist publications on North Vietnam have been found. Such periodicals as *Vietnam Perspectives* and *Vietnam Review* concentrate almost exclusively on South Vietnam and are, therefore, not included in this list.

torial Offices: 18 Ton Dan Street, Hanoi, North Vietnam. $45.00 per year.

Vietnam Youth. Illustrated magazine. Primary emphasis on problems and achievements of Vietnamese youth, especially in connection with the war in Vietnam. Published monthly. Editorial Offices: 64 Ba Trien Street, Hanoi, North Vietnam. $1.36 per year.

Women of China. Pictorial magazine of women's participation in the cultural, economic, and political life of China. Published bimonthly by National Women's Federation of the People's Republic of China, 82 Teng Shih K'ou, Peking, China. $1.00 per year.

World Marxist Review. Canadian edition of the Czechoslovak periodical Problems of Peace and Socialism. Marxist ideology, developments in Communist countries, analyses of events in non-communist countries. Published monthly by Progress Books, 487 Adelaide Street W., Toronto 2 B, Ontario, Canada. $3.50 per year.

Yugoslav Exports. Illustrated periodical. Articles on economics, trade, products, and other subjects of special interest to exporters and importers. Published monthly by Yugoslaviapublic, Publicity Office of the Federal Chamber of the Economy, Knez Mihajlova 10, Belgrade, Yugoslavia. $5.00 per year.

Yugoslav Facts and Views. Deals with current events in Yugoslavia. Published intermittently by the Yugoslav Information Center, 816 Fifth Avenue, New York, N. Y. 10021. Distributed without charge to institutions, libraries, and scholars engaged in research on Yugoslavia.

Yugoslav Life. Illustrated magazine covering economics, politics, culture, and sports in Yugoslavia. Published monthly by the Federation of Yugoslav Journalists, Nemanjina 34, P. O. Box 609, Belgrade, Yugoslavia. $2.00 per year.

Yugoslav News Bulletin. News items primarily those pertaining to Yugoslavia. Published irregularly. Distributed by the Yugoslav Information Center, 816 Fifth Avenue, New York, N. Y. 10021, on request to libraries, institutions, and scholars engaged in research on Yugoslavia.

Yugoslav Survey. Documents and articles on political, economic, social, and cultural developments in Yugoslavia. Published quarterly by the Federal Secretariat of Information, Terazije br. 41, Belgrade, Yugoslavia. $5.00 per year.

Yugoslav Trade Unions. Illustrated magazine. Published quarterly by the Central Council, Confederation of Trade Unions of Yugoslavia, Trg Marksa i Engels Br. 5, Post F H A 765, Belgrade, Yugoslavia. $0.10 per copy.